DATE DUE

APR 22 1998	

COMMUNIST AND MARXIST
PARTIES OF THE WORLD

COMMUNIST AND MARXIST

PARTIES OF THE WORLD

A KEESING'S REFERENCE PUBLICATION

Compiled and written by

CHARLES HOBDAY

ABC-CLIO

Santa Barbara, California

COMMUNIST AND MARXIST PARTIES OF THE WORLD

Published by Longman Group Limited, Longman House,
Burnt Mill, Harlow, Essex CM20 2JE, United Kingdom

Distributed exclusively in the United States and Canada
by ABC-Clio, Inc., 2040 Alameda Padre Serra, P.O. Box 4397, Santa Barbara,
California, CA 93103-4397, USA

ISBN 0-582-90264-9 (Longman)
ISBN 0-87436-476-0 (ABC-Clio)

British Library Cataloguing in Publication Data
Hobday, Charles
    Communist and Marxist parties of the
    world.—(A Keesing's reference publication)
    1. Communist parties—Directories
    2. Socialist parties—Directories
    I. Title   II. Series
    324.2'025   JF2051
    ISBN 0-582-90264-9

Printed in Great Britain by
The Eastern Press Ltd., London and Reading

CONTENTS

SECTION THREE
APPENDICES

INTRODUCTION

At the time of writing political parties claiming to be Marxist hold power in nearly thirty countries of Europe, Asia, Africa and Latin America, with a total population of about 1,700,000,000. In other countries, such as Italy, Marxists form the strongest opposition party. In India Marxist parties rule states with an aggregate population of over 50,000,000. In several Asian and Latin American countries Marxist guerrillas control large areas. Marxist parties, in fact, constitute one of the strongest forces in world politics, yet on few subjects of such importance is there so much confusion in the public mind. This book attempts to present the salient facts on the world's Marxist parties as objectively as is possible when dealing with a subject which arouses such intense emotional reactions among both supporters and opponents of Marxism.

To begin with, it is necessary to draw a distinction between Marxism and communism. All communists claim to be Marxists, but many Marxists would repudiate the name communist. Marxists accept the teachings of Karl Marx, communists accept Marx's teachings as interpreted by Lenin. Even this distinction needs to be qualified, however. Most Trotskyist parties do not use the name communist, although the Trotskyists claim to be Lenin's most faithful followers, and some communist parties have ceased to describe themselves as Leninist. This survey includes within its scope Marxist parties of all types, whether or not they describe themselves as communist or accept Lenin's interpretation of Marxism.

During the period between the two world wars it was comparatively easy to define a Marxist party. With a few exceptions, all the world's major Marxist parties described themselves as communist parties. They were affiliated to the Communist International and pursued policies laid down by it. They accepted the leadership of the Soviet Communist Party, and could be relied upon to defend every action taken by the Soviet government. They would have defined their ultimate aim as a proletarian revolution and the establishment of the dictatorship of the proletariat. Today this definition has long since ceased to be valid. Marxist parties, including many of those recognized by Moscow as communist parties, describe themselves as socialist, democratic, progressive, revolutionary, workers', labour or people's parties, or use a combination of these terms. Some have even abandoned the word party, and use such names as Communist League, Socialist League or Spartacus League, which are associated with Marx, William Morris or Rosa Luxemburg rather than with Stalin. The Communist International was dissolved in 1943, and the majority of Marxist parties do not regard the Soviet party as the leading or "vanguard" party. So far from being unquestioning champions of the Soviet Union, some even of the communist parties which it recognizes are critical of many of its policies, and others (pro-Chinese, pro-Albanian, Maoist or Trotskyist) are violently hostile to it. Although the Soviet party prides itself on being the party of Lenin, parties which attach "Marxist–Leninist" to their names are invariably hostile to the Soviet Union, which they regard as having betrayed Lenin's heritage. The Eurocommunist parties gave up thinking in terms of a proletarian revolution or the dictatorship of the proletariat many years ago. It has been suggested that the one factor uniting the world's

1

Marxist parties today is anti-Americanism, yet even this is open to question; the pro-Chinese parties tend to be less hostile to the United States than to the Soviet Union, which they regard as the more aggressive of the two superpowers.

Today, in fact, to describe a party as communist or Marxist tells one very little about it, and it is necessary to define what sort of a communist or Marxist party it is. Marxism is open to as many interpretations as Christianity, and two communist parties (the Italian Communist Party and the Albanian Party of Labour, for example, or the Swedish Left Party—Communists and the Party of Democratic Kampuchea) may have as little in common as the Roman Catholic Church and Jehovah's Witnesses. This book attempts to present the world's Marxist parties in all their multitudinous variety.

Some explanation of its arrangement may be called for. The opening section on the world communist movement attempts to put the sections on individual parties in an international perspective by providing a broad (and inevitably over-simplified) picture of the development of communism from Marx to the present day. Sections follow on the various ways in which Marxist parties from different countries have co-operated, whether through permanent organizations such as the four Internationals or through international conferences, and on the international communist front organizations now operating.

The main body of the book, dealing with individual parties, is arranged under states, with two exceptions. As British Marxist parties do not operate in Northern Ireland and Irish Marxist parties operate both in the Republic and in the North, there are entries for Great Britain and Ireland but not for the United Kingdom or the Republic of Ireland. As there are Palestinian Marxist organizations but no Palestinian state, a separate section has been devoted to Palestinian movements. Perhaps it is necessary to add that this arrangement has been adopted purely for the sake of convenience, and does not imply any particular attitude on the part of the author or publishers towards either the Irish or the Palestinian question.

Each section on a particular country begins with a brief introduction on the historical and constitutional background, intended to put the history of the parties dealt with in perspective. These introductions vary considerably in length and fullness. In some countries, such as France, where Marxist parties have long played a considerable part in political life, it has seemed necessary to summarize these countries' recent history at some length. On the other hand, it has been assumed that the reader is familiar with the recent history and the constitutions of Britain and the United States, countries in which Marxist parties are of only marginal significance in political life; hence the introductions to these sections deal solely with the origins and early history of Marxist movements in these countries.

In the selection of organizations for inclusion, the word "party" has been interpreted in a broad sense. Organizations which deny that they are political parties but in fact operate as such (e.g. the Militant Tendency in Britain) have been included, as have guerrilla and terrorist organizations claiming to be Marxist, whether or not they describe themselves as parties. Dissident Marxist activities in communist countries are also included, whether or not they have assumed an organized form. Trade unions and purely social or intellectual organizations which are under Marxist control do not generally receive entries, however, although they may be referred to under the political parties with which they are linked.

Although a comprehensive coverage has been attempted, some parties are bound to have been omitted. Marxist parties are founded, split, merge with other parties, change their names and their political orientation and dissolve themselves with dizzying rapidity. To draw up a full list of Trotskyist and Maoist parties in particular is as hopeless a task as to conduct a census in a rabbit warren. Some

2

parties, which will be deeply offended by their omission, have no doubt escaped notice by their insignificance. To them the author can only tender his apologies.

The amount of space devoted to each party and the amount of detail in which it is treated is intended to be roughly proportionate to its importance. The Soviet and Chinese parties, with a membership of many millions, completely control two of the largest and most powerful states in the world, and the decisions of their leadership may affect the lives of every one of us. The other ruling Marxist parties and those parties, such as the French and Italian Communist parties, which although in opposition are of major importance in national politics also demand extensive treatment. At the other extreme we have tiny sects, counting their membership in hundreds or even in tens, which warrant little more than a mention. However, as this book is intended primarily for English-speaking readers, the Marxist parties of Great Britain, Ireland, the English-speaking Dominions and the United States are dealt with in some detail, even though none of them has succeeded in establishing itself as a major political force.

The history of each party, with particular emphasis on the period since 1945, is summarized in greater or less detail in accordance with these criteria, and details are given of its leadership and organization. For the more important ruling parties full lists are given of the membership of the political bureau or corresponding body.

An attempt is then made to assess each party's political importance by answering three questions: How large is its membership? How many people vote for it? And how much influence does it exercise in the trade union movement? For each party the most recent membership figures available are given, although it must be borne in mind that political parties (and not only Marxist parties) are apt to exaggerate their importance by giving inflated estimates of their membership, just as their opponents are apt to underestimate it. Membership figures, of course, must be considered in relation to the size of the population; the Communist Party of San Marino, with a few hundred members, plays a far more important part in national life than the US Communist Party, with a claimed membership of 17,500. In answer to the second question, details are given of the share of the total vote won by each party in the most recent elections in the parliamentary democracies. A Marxist party, however, may have a dismal record of electoral failure and yet wield considerable influence inside the trade unions (the British Communist Party being a case in point); particulars are therefore given where information is available of each party's industrial influence, if any.

A party's political importance may vary drastically as political circumstances change. A seemingly insignificant party may develop into a major political force in a very short time, as the Italian Communist Party did in the 1940s. A rapid expansion in membership, such as several Western communist parties experienced in the mid-1940s, may be followed by a seemingly irreversible decline. A powerful party may be quickly crushed and reduced to impotence, as happened to the German Communist Party in 1933 and to the Indonesian Communist Party in 1965; or its electoral support may decline sharply, as the French Communist Party has found in recent years. A banned and apparently dead party may emerge from underground as lively as ever. The entries on individual parties therefore attempt to indicate whether the party in question is expanding, stagnating or in decline.

Under the heading "orientation" an indication is given of what type of party each one is. Most Marxist parties fall into seven main groups. Pro-Soviet parties accept and follow the Soviet party's leadership, while pro-Chinese and pro-Albanian parties adopt a similar attitude towards the Chinese and Albanian parties. Maoist parties accept Mao Zedong's interpretation of Marxism, but reject

3

the Chinese party's leadership. Eurocommunist parties do not accept the leadership of any foreign party, and attempt to adapt Marxism to the conditions of a highly developed country with a parliamentary system of government. Trotskyist parties accept Trotsky's interpretation of Marxism. Finally, a number of communist parties, including some of major importance (e.g. the Yugoslav, Romanian and North Korean), reject the leadership of any foreign party and have attempted to formulate a distinctive type of Marxism appropriate to the conditions of their particular country; these are classified as independent parties.

This classification is useful as a rough and ready guide to the nature of a party, provided that it is borne in mind that Marxist parties usually contain contending factions, and in the course of the struggle between them may move rapidly from one type to another or take up an intermediate position. Pro-Soviet minorities, for example, exist inside most of the Eurocommunist parties, including the French, which vacillates between a Eurocommunist and a pro-Soviet position, while the Australian Communist Party within a decade was successively pro-Soviet, pro-Chinese, pro-Soviet again and finally Eurocommunist.

All these types of party belong to the Leninist tradition, in that they were originally orthodox communist parties affiliated to the Communist International or are offshoots of such parties. There are other types of Marxist party, however, which may be described as pre-Leninist or post-Stalinist. Before 1914 most of the leading socialist parties of Europe claimed to be Marxist, and many of them continued to do so even after their more radical members had broken away to form communist parties. The German Social Democratic Party did not repudiate Marxism until 1959, and the decision of the Spanish Socialist Workers' Party in 1979 that Marxism should be viewed as "a critical but not dogmatic instrument for the analysis and transformation of social reality" left its position an equivocal one. Such parties, which belong to the social democratic rather than the Marxist tradition, are not dealt with, but a number of small parties founded before 1914, such as the Socialist Party of Great Britain and the Socialist Labor Party of America, which while rejecting Leninism continue to preach their own distinctive brands of Marxism, clearly qualify for admission. Since Khrushchev's denunciation of Stalin in 1956 many new Marxist parties have been formed which reject both Stalinism and Leninism, the most important being the Pan-Hellenic Socialist Movement in Greece; such parties may be described as independent, non-Leninist or New Left. Finally, movements such as Islamic Marxism have emerged in the Third World in recent years, which attempt to interpret Marxism in terms congenial with the national or regional culture. The distinctive orientation of such movements is indicated in the entries devoted to them.

The attempt to define the nature of each party covered is continued in a summary of its programme, where information is available, and details are given of its publications, with circulation figures, again where available, as another indication of the extent of its influence. In conclusion, the party's international affiliations, if any, are noted; no international Marxist organization corresponding to the Comintern now exists, apart from the various Trotskyist Internationals, but a party's representation on the editorial board or editorial council of *World Marxist Review* and its relations with other Marxist parties can throw light upon its political position. The appendix listing parties under the various trends within the international Marxist movement with which they are associated is intended to supplement this information.

The book concludes with a selection of documents. The literature of Marxism is enormous, and considerations of space have imposed severe restrictions. The documents given, inevitably in extracts or abridged versions, are confined to the political aspects of Marxism, as distinct from the philosophical and economic, and are intended primarily to illustrate Marxist attitudes to the state and the party. Some represent what may be described as the mainstream of the history of Marxism: the Communist League, the *Communist Manifesto*, the Paris Commune, Lenin's conception of the revolutionary party, the Russian Revolution, the Communist International, the Popular Front, the Khrushchev report. Marxism, however, owes its vitality to its stubborn refusal to be confined within the limits of an orthodoxy, and documents are also included to represent the major dissident trends associated with Bernstein, Rosa Luxemburg, Trotsky, Tito, Djilas, Mao Zedong, Castro and the Eurocommunists. Thus the selection of documents reinforces the book's emphasis on the heterogeneous nature of international Marxism.

The author wishes to extend his thanks to Alan Day, Ciarán Ó Maoláin and Len Wells for supplying information and documents; to the staff of the Chatham House and Canning House libraries; and to the editorial staff of *Keesing's Contemporary Archives,* who have placed its resources at his disposal and have patiently answered his frequent demands for information on specific points.

London, March 1986   C. H.

ABBREVIATIONS

The following abbreviations are used for the titles of party leaders:

cent.	= central		l.	= leader
ch.	= chairman		nat.	= national
C.-in-C.	= commander-in-chief		perm.	= permanent
g.s.	= general secretary		pres.	= president
hon.	= honorary		sec.	= secretary

SECTION ONE

HISTORICAL AND INTERNATIONAL PERSPECTIVES

1. The World Communist Movement

2. International Marxist Organizations and Conferences

3. International Communist Front Organizations

1. THE WORLD COMMUNIST MOVEMENT

Origins

The word "socialism" first came into use about 1827, "communism" about 1840. Although in the 1840s they were often used interchangeably, a clear distinction between them soon emerged. "Socialist" was used of the followers of the "Utopian socialists", such as Robert Owen in Britain and Claude Henri Saint-Simon and Charles Fourier in France, who sought to replace a society based on competition by one based on co-operation, and believed that such a society could be evolved peacefully with the assistance of the ruling classes. "Communist", on the other hand, was applied to those who maintained that such a fundamental transformation of society could be achieved only after the proletariat had forcibly seized control of the state.

The communist tradition, in this sense of the word, can be traced back to the Conspiracy of the Equals, led by François Noël Babeuf, who in 1796 planned to overthrow the French government and establish an egalitarian society based on common ownership. The conspiracy was easily crushed and Babeuf was guillotined, but in 1828 one of the surviving conspirators, Filippo Buonarroti, published a history of it, *La Conspiration pour l'Égalité, dite de Babeuf*, which profoundly influenced young revolutionaries throughout Western Europe. Among them was Auguste Blanqui, who believed that it was possible for a small body of disciplined revolutionaries to seize power, and from 1834 onwards organized a series of secret societies for this purpose. From Babeuf and Buonarroti he took over the belief that a transitional period of revolutionary dictatorship would be necessary between the seizure of power and the establishment of a democratic communist society—a concept to which he gave the name of the dictatorship of the proletariat.

In 1836 a number of German working men in Paris formed the League of the Just, a secret society which co-operated closely with Blanqui's organization. The League later moved its headquarters to London, where in 1847 it was joined by two young intellectuals, Karl Marx and Friedrich Engels, whose independent study of the nature of society had led them by 1844 to adopt a communist position. Under their influence it was renamed the Communist League, and changed its motto from "All men are brothers" to "Proletarians of all countries, unite". In November 1847 Marx and Engels were asked to draw up a statement of the League's aims. The result was the *Manifesto of the Communist Party* (usually known as *The Communist Manifesto*), published in February 1848—the first programmatic statement of communism and the fundamental document of Marxism (for extracts, see Appendix 2: Documents).

Marx and Engels at this time were in close contact with some of the leaders of the Chartist movement in Britain. Although it included many Owenite socialists, and some of the younger Chartist leaders, such as Ernest Jones, were deeply influenced by Marx, Chartism was essentially a radical democratic rather than a socialist or communist movement. Nevertheless, as the first mass political movement of the industrial working class, it convinced Marx that a communist revolution must be the work of such a movement and not, as Blanqui envisaged, of a conspiratorial élite. It was a Chartist paper, *The Red Republican*, which in 1850 published the first English translation of *The Communist Manifesto*.

The writing of the *Manifesto* immediately preceded the outbreak of revolution in France in February 1848 and in Germany in March. In Paris a brief period of co-operation between bourgeois republicans and socialists ended with the street battles of June, in which the red flag first appeared as the symbol of socialism, and which Marx saw as the first major confrontation between the bourgeoisie and the proletariat. Most of the members of the League, including Marx and Engels, had already left for Germany, where they played a minor part in the revolution in the Rhineland. By the end of 1849, however, reaction had triumphed all over Europe. Expelled first from Germany and then from France, Marx settled in London. The Communist League was dissolved in 1852.

During the 1850s socialism and communism seemed dead, and even the Chartist movement withered away. With no active role to play in politics, Marx was able to concentrate on study and writing. In *The Class Struggles in France* and *The 18th Brumaire of Louis Napoleon* he used the French revolution of 1848 as material for his analysis of the nature of the class struggle and the state. In *A Contribution to the Critique of Political Economy* he began his analysis of the nature of capitalism, although the first volume of his definitive study, *Capital*, did not appear until 1867, and the remaining two volumes were not published until after his death.

The First International and the Paris Commune

A number of factors, including the growth of trade unionism in Britain, France and Germany, the struggle for universal suffrage in Britain and Germany and for trade union rights in France, and popular support for the nationalist movements in Italy and Poland and the struggle against slavery in the United States, contributed to bring about a revival of independent working-class political activity after 1860. In 1864 the International Workingmen's Association, commonly known as the First International, was formed, with Marx as one of its leading members (see below under "International Marxist Organizations and Conferences").

The Paris Commune of 1871 was not organized by the International, as was widely believed at the time, although some members of the International were among its leaders. During the siege of Paris by the Prussians the Parisian workers, organized into the National Guard, had largely conducted its defence. An unsuccessful attempt by the conservative provisional government to disarm them left Paris in the control of the central committee of the National Guard, which organized elections to a municipal council, the Commune. After a two months' siege the Commune was suppressed and some 20,000 Communards massacred.

Despite its name, the Commune was not a communist body. Most of its members were neo-Jacobin left-wing republicans, Blanquists or Proudhonists, and only one might be described as a Marxist. This did not prevent Marx from hailing it as the first example in history of the dictatorship of the proletariat, although his description of its political institutions in *The Civil War in France* (decentralized government, abolition of the standing army, officials serving at workingmen's wages etc.—see Appendix 2: Documents) bore little resemblance to later systems of government which have laid claim to the name. In particular, he made no reference to a single-party system (the Commune was a multiparty

10

assembly) or to "elections" in which there would be only one candidate in each constituency.

The Rise of Marxist Parties

After the dissolution of the Communist League no Marxist party existed for nearly 20 years, but by the 1860s the conditions were ripening for the formation of such parties, among them the rapid expansion of industry, especially in Germany, the growth of large industrial centres and the spread of popular literacy. Manhood suffrage, already existing in France, was introduced in Germany in 1867, and in Britain the reform bills of 1867 and 1884 extended the suffrage to large sections of the working class. The first major socialist party, Ferdinand Lassalle's General Association of German Workers, founded in 1863 with a programme of universal suffrage and the formation of producers' co-operatives with state assistance, was non-Marxist. In 1869, however, Wilhelm Liebknecht and August Bebel, both of whom were in close contact with Marx, founded the Social Democratic Workers' Party, which affiliated to the International, and in 1875 the two parties merged in the Social Democratic Party of Germany (SPD). Despite Bismarck's attempts to suppress it by the Anti-Socialist Laws, introduced in 1878, SPD representation in the *Reichstag* increased from 12 in 1877 to 35 in 1890 (when the laws were allowed to lapse) and to 81 in 1903. In 1891 the SPD formally declared itself a Marxist party, and adopted a new programme drawn up by Karl Kautsky in collaboration with Engels.

Largely because of its electoral successes, the SPD was regarded throughout most of Europe as the model socialist party, and from about 1880 to 1917 the term "social democrat" became synonymous with Marxist. The Austrian Social Democratic Party, founded in 1874, adopted a Marxist programme drafted by Kautsky in 1889. Jules Guesde and Paul Lafargue, Marx's son-in-law, formed in 1880 the French Workers' Party, with a programme drafted with Marx's assistance. The first British Marxist party, the Social Democratic Federation, was founded in the following year by H. M. Hyndman. Between 1885 and 1894 social democratic parties on the German model were founded in Belgium, the Netherlands, Hungary, Poland, Bulgaria and Romania. The first Russian Marxist organization, the Emancipation of Labour Group, was formed in 1883 by Georgi Plekhanov, and in 1898 collaborated with a number of other small groups to found the Russian Social Democratic Labour Party.

Marx and Engels, who died in 1883 and 1895 respectively, were actively involved in the formation and development of the social democratic parties, to which they acted as advisers. During this period their views on the possibility of a peaceful transition to socialism changed considerably. Whereas in *The Communist Manifesto*, written when manhood suffrage did not exist in any European country, they had declared that the Communists' ends could be attained "only by the forcible overthrow of all existing social conditions", as early as 1852 Marx wrote that in Britain the inevitable result of universal suffrage would be "the political supremacy of the working class"; moreover, in 1863 he expressed the view that in certain countries, such as the United States and Britain, "the workers can achieve their aims by peaceful means". Engels welcomed the SPD's electoral successes (see Appendix 2: Documents), condemned those British Marxists who refused to take part in parliamentary elections, and supported the non-Marxist but broadly-based Independent Labour Party against the narrowly sectarian Social Democratic Federation. At the same time Marx and Engels continued to reaffirm their support for the concept of the dictatorship of the proletariat, on the model of the Commune, and their belief that in most European countries a violent revolution was inevitable.

In 1889 the existing socialist parties united to form the Second International (see below under "International Marxist Organizations and Conferences"). Ten years later two events brought to light the fundamental divisions between socialists, including professed Marxists. The German socialist Eduard Bernstein, a close collaborator of Engels, published in 1899 *Evolutionary Socialism*, in which he contended that Marx's theories needed revision in the light of changing circumstances, and in particular the theories that under capitalism working-class living standards were bound to fall, that wealth was becoming increasingly concentrated and that the collapse of capitalism and proletarian revolution were inevitable (see Appendix 2: Documents). Hence he advocated that the SPD should cease to pose as a revolutionary party and should "strive to appear as in fact what it now is, a democratic socialist party of reform". Although his views, condemned as "revisionism" by Kautsky, were rejected by both the SPD and the International, they continued to exercise a potent influence. Also in 1899, during the crisis caused by the Dreyfus case, the French socialist Alexandre Millerrand entered a cabinet which included General Gallifet, notorious for his share in the suppression of the Commune. His action was condemned by the International, but like the revisionism controversy it raised the question whether socialism was fundamentally a reformist or a revolutionary movement.

Leninism

Communism in its modern form may be said to have originated with the publication in 1902 of Lenin's pamphlet *What is to be done?*, in which he advocated the formation of a highly centralized party of professional revolutionaries (see Appendix 2: Documents). In the following year this concept split the Russian Social Democratic Labour Party at its second congress into a Leninist majority (the Bolsheviks) and their opponents (the Mensheviks or minority). In 1905 Lenin developed his views on party organization into the principle of democratic centralism, whereby all party bodies were to be elected democratically by the membership, decisions adopted by majority vote were to be accepted and implemented by the minority, and decisions made by higher bodies were to be binding on lower bodies and on the membership. Lenin's concept of the party, produced in a country with a despotic government and no tradition of parliamentary democracy, was widely compared to Blanqui's, and was condemned by almost all leading left-wing Marxists, including Kautsky, Rosa Luxemburg, Plekhanov and Trotsky. The last-named predicted that it would lead to a situation in which "the party organization substitutes itself for the party, the Central Committee substitutes itself for the organization, and finally a 'dictator' substitutes himself for the Central Committee".

In 1905 revolution broke out spontaneously in Russia, without being organized by any political party. Although the Tsar was forced to grant a constitution, by the end of 1906 the revolution had been crushed. It produced a new form of revolutionary organization, however, in the councils (in Russian soviets) of workers' deputies, the first being the St Petersburg soviet, in which Trotsky was the dominant figure. It also raised the question of the nature of revolution in an economically backward country such as Russia. Lenin believed that such a revolution must be the work of an alliance between the industrial proletariat (still comparatively small, but concentrated in large enterprises) and the peasant masses, but that it would be bourgeois-democratic in content and would facilitate capitalist development. Trotsky maintained that it would be possible to proceed directly from a bourgeois to a socialist revolution, but that the survival of the latter would be dependent on the success of the revolution in the advanced countries.

The First World War and the Russian Revolution

Despite the anti-war resolutions adopted by the Second International, when war broke out in 1914 almost all the socialist parties in the belligerent countries threw their support behind their governments. The SPD, regarding the war as one of national defence against tsarism (considered by Marx and Engels as the arch-enemy of socialism and democracy), voted for the war credits in the *Reichstag*. The French Socialist Party supported the war as one in defence of the republic against Prussian militarism, and the Marxist Guesde became War Minister. As the war progressed, however, anti-war groups emerged in many socialist parties, the most notable being the Spartacus League in Germany, led by Karl Liebknecht and Rosa Luxemburg.

The one major socialist party which consistently opposed the war was the Russian Bolsheviks, led by Lenin, who put forward the slogan "Turn the imperialist war into civil war". The collapse of the tsarist regime in March 1917 under pressure from popular demonstrations and army mutinies was followed by the proclamation of a republic, the formation of a provisional government and the re-emergence of soviets. The revolution led to a rapprochement between Lenin, who accepted Trotsky's view of the possibility of converting a bourgeois-democratic into a proletarian revolution, and Trotsky, who accepted Lenin's view of the necessity of a highly centralized party. The provisional government's attempt to continue the war alienated the soviets, which largely threw their support behind the Bolsheviks, and on Nov. 7 the Bolsheviks seized power with the slogan "All power to the soviets!"

The Bolshevik wing of the Russian Social Democratic Labour Party changed its name in 1918 to the Russian Communist Party (Bolsheviks). The word "communist" had since the 1870s been almost entirely replaced by "social democrat" as the normal term for a Marxist, and was applied mainly to the anarcho-communist followers of Peter Kropotkin. Lenin, however, believed that the name "social democrat" had been disgraced by the German Social Democratic leaders' support for the war, and reverted to the term originally used by Marx. "Communist" in consequence became identified with the Leninist interpretation of Marxism, while "social democrat" joined "revisionist" in the communist vocabulary of abuse.

The Bolsheviks' expectation that the Russian revolution would speedily be followed by revolutions in Central and Western Europe appeared likely to be fulfilled. The German and Austrian empires were overthrown in November 1918, and unrest was widespread in Italy, France and Britain. Although a Spartacist revolt in Berlin in January 1919 was crushed, soviet republics were established in Hungary in March and in Bavaria in April. Lenin's close collaborator Grigory Zinoviev prophesied in the same month that "in a year's time the whole of Europe will be communist", and that in Britain and America capitalism could not survive for more than two years longer. In fact, the soviet regimes were overthrown in Bavaria in May and in Hungary in August, and the Bolsheviks were left to fight alone against the White armies and foreign intervention forces. The Red Army repelled a Polish invasion in June 1920, but Lenin's hopes that its advance would precipitate revolution in Poland and possibly in Germany were frustrated by its defeat before Warsaw in August.

The civil war in Russia and the defeat of the revolution in Central Europe profoundly affected the nature of the Soviet regime. The Council of People's Commissars assumed dictatorial powers, and the role of the soviets diminished in importance. A secret police, the Cheka, was established to combat white terror with red terror. Although other socialist parties, such as the Mensheviks and the Left Socialist Revolutionaries, were tolerated during the civil war, by 1922 they had been eliminated and a single-party system established. The factional groups which existed inside the Communist Party were banned in 1921 and the concept of a monolithic party accepted. These developments, which were viewed with grave uneasiness by foreign Marxists such as Rosa Luxemburg (see Appendix 2: Documents) and Kautsky, created within Lenin's lifetime the preconditions for Stalin's dictatorship.

The Development of Communist Parties

The Russian revolution deepened the split in the socialist parties of the belligerent countries that had already been caused by the war. Between 1918 and 1922 communist parties looking to Russia for inspiration and guidance were founded in almost all the European countries, in the United States and the British dominions, in some Latin American countries and in a few Asian countries, including China and Japan. In some countries, such as Germany, France and Italy, they originated in a split in the major socialist party; in others, such as Great Britain, they were formed by the merger of several Marxist sects. With a few exceptions, notably the German and French parties, they were all small and weak bodies.

The Communist International, founded in 1919, attempted to impose the Bolshevik pattern on all communist parties. This involved a struggle on the one hand against "centrists" who were thought to retain a social democratic outlook and on the other against ultra-leftists (many of them former anarcho-syndicalists) who opposed participation in "reactionary" trade unions and "bourgeois" parliaments. It was against the latter tendency that Lenin in 1920 directed his pamphlet *"Left-wing" Communism: An Infantile Disorder* (see Appendix 2: Documents). After Lenin's death in 1924 the communist parties outside the Soviet Union became involved through the International in the struggle for power inside the Soviet party. As a result they suffered from periodic purges and frequent changes of leadership, until by 1930 almost all of them had been brought under the control of leaders such as Ernst Thälmann in Germany, Klement Gottwald in Czechoslovakia, Maurice Thorez in France and Harry Pollitt in Britain, who could be relied on to carry out Stalin's directives without question.

The period when revolution still seemed possible in Western Europe ended in March 1921, when an attempted communist uprising in Germany was easily suppressed and in Russia the Kronstadt garrison mutinied, demanding an end to the Communist Party's monopoly of power and its economic policy of "war communism". In consequence, war communism was replaced in Russia by the New Economic Policy, which provided for a mixed economy, and the Communist International approved the United Front policy of co-operation with other socialist parties. After a temporary reversion to revolutionary policies in 1923–24, when unsuccessful insurrections took place in Bulgaria, Germany and Estonia with the International's approval, the communist parties attempted to apply the United Front policy, although there was considerable confusion whether this implied a United Front from above (i.e. co-operation with the leadership of other socialist parties) or from below (i.e. co-operation with their rank and file against their leaders). The most spectacular example of a United Front from above, the alliance formed in 1923 between the Chinese Communist Party and the Kuomintang against the northern warlords, ended in disaster four years later, when Chiang Kai-shek massacred his Communist allies. Thereafter the Chinese party, under Mao Zedong's leadership, pursued its own policy of basing the revolution on peasant support, virtually ignoring the International.

After Stalin's victory over his rivals in the Soviet leadership, communist policy swung sharply to the left. In the Soviet Union industrialization was speeded up by the First Five-Year Plan, the land collectivized and the kulaks liquidated. The Communist International in 1928 abandoned the United Front policy in favour of one of "class against class", in accordance with which social democrats were no longer regarded as potential allies but denounced as "social fascists". As a result the communist parties found themselves politically isolated, and the membership of many parties slumped to unprecedentedly low levels. What was more serious, the mutual hostility of communists and social democrats facilitated Hitler's coming to power and the destruction of the German Communist Party, the largest in the world outside the Soviet Union.

The Popular Front

The Nazi victory in Germany and the emergence of fascist movements in many other European countries forced communists to reconsider their tactics. After fascist riots in Paris in 1934 the French Communist Party formed an alliance with the Socialist Party, and in the following year the Communist International approved the strategy of the Popular Front, whereby communist parties were encouraged to ally themselves not only with socialist parties but also with bourgeois anti-fascist parties in defence of democracy (see Appendix 2: Documents). In France the Popular Front was broadened to include the Radicals, and in Spain the Communists formed an alliance with the Socialists and Republicans. The same policy was applied outside Europe. The US Communist Party, which had previously denounced President Roosevelt's New Deal as "fascist", switched to supporting it; the Indian Communist Party allied itself with the Congress; and the Chinese Communist Party allied itself with the Kuomintang against the Japanese invaders.

For a time the new policy appeared brilliantly successful. General elections in France and Spain in the early months of 1936 resulted in victories for the Popular Front, and in many countries the communist parties' new moderation and their role as the most vigorous opponents of fascism attracted thousands of new members from both the working class and the middle class. The Popular Front victory in Spain, however, was followed by civil war, which ended in 1939 with the establishment of Franco's dictatorship. The Spanish civil war in turn contributed to bring about the disintegration of the Popular Front in France. Many of the communist parties' new recruits, whose enthusiasm had been aroused by the supposedly more democratic Soviet constitution of 1936, were appalled by the reign of terror which immediately followed it and in which many of Lenin's closest associates perished. Meanwhile the British and French governments rejected proposals for a military alliance with the Soviet Union, and by signing the Munich agreement in 1938 facilitated Hitler's subsequent occupation of Czechoslovakia.

The Second World War

In August 1939 Stalin, suspecting that the Western powers were encouraging Hitler's eastward expansion in the hope that it would involve him in war with the Soviet Union, signed a non-aggression pact with Germany. The German invasion of Poland and the declaration of war on Germany by Britain and France followed in September. On the International's instructions the British and French Communist parties, which had declared their support for the war as one against fascism, denounced it a month later as an imperialist war. The French party was promptly banned, and suffered a catastrophic loss of membership.

Communist parties throughout the world maintained this attitude of opposition to the war against Germany (though not to the Chinese war against Japan) until Germany invaded the Soviet Union in June 1941. The Soviet Union became the ally of Britain and, after the Japanese attack on Pearl Harbour in December, of the United States; accordingly, the communist parties of the allied countries called for national unity in support of the war effort. Throughout occupied Europe communists played a leading part in the resistance movements. Admiration for the Soviet struggle against the invaders and the communist contribution to the resistance brought thousands of recruits to the communist parties, many of which reached their maximum membership during or immediately after the war. In the name of allied unity they made extraordinary concessions. The Communist International was dissolved in 1943 (see Appendix 2: Documents); the US Communist Party converted itself in the following year into a purely propagandist organization, although it reversed this policy in 1945; and the British party appealed for the continuation of all-party government after the war. Even after the defeat of Japan Stalin advised the Chinese communists to continue their co-operation with the Kuomintang.

In 1944-45, as the Soviet army advanced beyond its borders, communist control was established over most of Eastern Europe. In Yugoslavia and Albania, where the communist parties had formed the backbone of the resistance and had defeated the Germans without Soviet assistance, communist governments took power, although in Greece an attempt by the communist resistance organization to seize control was crushed by the British army. In Poland, Romania, Bulgaria, Hungary, Czechoslovakia and the Soviet-occupied zone of Germany communist-dominated coalition governments of anti-fascist parties were set up in the wake of the advancing Soviet army. In Western Europe the communist parties entered coalition governments, although not as the dominant party, in France, Italy, San Marino, Belgium, Luxembourg and Denmark.

The Asian communist parties played a prominent part in the war against Japan. In China the communist armies bore the brunt of the fighting, and in occupied Vietnam, Malaya and the Philippines communist-led resistance movements formed the nucleus of post-war guerrilla revolts. In most of the allied countries communist parties profited by their appeal to patriotic feeling; in India, however, the Communist Party isolated itself from the Congress-led nationalist movement by its support for the British war effort.

The Post-War Period

Co-operation between the Soviet Union and the Western powers, which had already been under strain while the war was in progress, quickly broke down after 1945. In the East European countries the coalition governments had all been brought under communist control by 1949, and their social democratic parties were forced to merge with the communist parties. Soviet domination of the bloc was strengthened by the establishment of the Communist Information Bureau (Cominform) in 1947 (see Appendix 2: Documents). Yugoslavia, which under President Tito's leadership had insisted on asserting its independence of the Soviet Union, was expelled from the Cominform in the following year, and in Albania,

Hungary, Bulgaria, Czechoslovakia and Poland leading communists suspected of favouring greater independence were executed or imprisoned on charges of "Titoism". In Greece a communist revolt in 1946 led to civil war. In the West European countries, with the insignificant exception of San Marino, all the communist ministers who had entered coalition governments during or after the war were dropped by the end of 1947.

In Asia the anti-Japanese resistance movements organized by the communists made a number of successful or unsuccessful attempts to seize power after the war. The Chinese communists, ignoring Stalin's advice, defeated the Kuomintang in a civil war, and by 1949 had obtained control of the whole of China except Taiwan and a few offshore islands. In Vietnam the Communists, after a long war with the French, were left in control of the northern half of the country in 1954. A third communist regime was established in 1948 in the Soviet-occupied northern zone of Korea. Uprisings launched by communist guerrillas in the Philippines in 1946 and in Malaya, Burma and Indonesia in 1948 met with no success, however.

Eastern Europe after Stalin

The death of Stalin in March 1953 and the succession of Nikita Khrushchev to the general secretaryship of the Soviet Communist Party marked the end of an epoch. Relations with Yugoslavia were normalized in 1955 and the Cominform dissolved in the following year. At the 20th Communist Party congress in February 1956 Khrushchev rejected Lenin's theory that war was inevitable under capitalism, declared that the transition to socialism could take a number of forms, including a peaceful transition by parliamentary means, and condemned the personality cult of party leaders. In a secret report to the congress, the text of which soon found its way abroad, he vehemently denounced Stalin's terrorist methods, the cult surrounding him and the breach with Yugoslavia (see Appendix 2: Documents).

Khrushchev's speech produced profound repercussions in the East European countries, where a number of party and government leaders associated with the Stalinist regime were removed from office, many political prisoners were released and some of the executed "Titoists" were rehabilitated. In Poland serious riots in June 1956 were followed by a political crisis in October, when Stalinist elements were removed from the party leadership and the Soviet Union threatened to intervene by force. In Hungary a popular uprising in October led to the establishment of an all-party government, which announced its decision to end Hungary's military alliance with the Soviet Union and adopt a policy of neutrality. Soviet troops then crushed the uprising and imposed a communist government headed by Janos Kádár on the country.

After the Hungarian revolt the Soviet party temporarily retreated from the comparatively liberal position adopted at the 20th congress. The Moscow declarations of 1957 and 1960 (see below under "International Marxist Organizations and Conferences" and also Appendix 2: Documents) attacked revisionism rather than dogmatism or sectarianism as the main enemy, and relations with the Yugoslav League of Communists passed through two periods of strain in 1956–57 and 1958–61. The widening breach between the Soviet and the Chinese and Albanian parties, however, led to a new shift in policy, and at the 22nd congress in 1961 Khrushchev renewed the attack on Stalin and broke publicly with the Albanian party. His overthrow three years later and his replacement by Leonid Brezhnev were not followed by any fundamental policy changes.

In the East European countries it proved impossible to return to the pre-1953 position, when a rigid Stalinist pattern had been imposed on their communist parties. Yugoslavia continued to pursue and develop the policy of decentralization and workers' self-management which it had adopted after the breach with the Cominform. In Poland the collectivization of agriculture was abandoned. After an initial period of repression, the Kádár regime in Hungary adopted a policy of reconciliation and liberalization, summed up in the slogan "He who is not against us is with us", with the result that Hungary achieved greater prosperity and intellectual freedom than any other Soviet satellite. Albania, which aligned itself with China against the Soviet Union, made itself a model of Stalinist orthodoxy, and in some matters, such as its attempt to abolish religion, proved less liberal even than Stalin.

The Soviet regime showed that there were limits to its toleration of dissent when in 1968 the Czechoslovak party embarked on a sweeping programme of liberalization, under the slogan "Socialism with a human face". The Soviet army, supported by East German, Polish, Hungarian and Bulgarian units, thereupon invaded Czechoslovakia and installed a more orthodox government and party leadership. Brezhnev defended the Soviet intervention on the ground that "when internal and external forces try to turn the development of some socialist country towards the restoration of a capitalist regime" other socialist countries were justified in granting "military assistance".

One effect of the invasion of Czechoslovakia and the threat implied in the "Brezhnev doctrine" that such action might be repeated in other countries was to strengthen national feeling in Romania and Yugoslavia and to drive Yugoslavia to improve its relations with China, which in the past had consistently denounced the Yugoslav regime as the supreme example of revisionism. The imposition of martial law in Poland in 1981, probably under Soviet pressure, following a political crisis which had led to the removal of the party and government leadership and the formation of the independent trade union federation Solidarity, again exemplified Soviet determination to maintain Communist Party control of the East European countries, and produced new tensions in Soviet-Yugoslav relations.

The Sino-Soviet Schism

From 1956 onwards differences between the Soviet and Chinese parties on questions of theory and policy rapidly developed into an open split. The Chinese contested Khrushchev's view that Lenin's theory of the inevitability of war under capitalism was no longer valid; regarded his advocacy of peaceful coexistence with capitalist countries as involving an abandonment of the class struggle and a policy of peace at any price; and questioned the Soviet view that nuclear war would prove equally disastrous to all involved. The Soviet party was more cautious than the Chinese in supporting nationalist movements in colonial and under-developed countries, and was more willing to throw its support behind the national bourgeoisie in struggles for national independence. The Chinese party was sceptical about the possibility of communist parties' attaining power by parliamentary means. The Soviet party regarded Mao Zedong's plan for progressing from socialism to full communism by means of communes combining agriculture with industry as a foredoomed attempt to bypass certain historical stages. After 1959 the Soviet party laid increasing emphasis on the dangers of dogmatism and sectarianism, whereas the Chinese party continued to uphold the assertion of the 1957 Moscow declaration that revisionism was the main danger. Relations were further exacerbated by particular issues, such as the Soviet party's failure to consult other parties before condemning Stalin, the Soviet Union's neutral attitude during the Sino-Indian border dispute of 1959, its refusal to supply China with nuclear weapons and the withdrawal of Soviet economic aid to China in 1960.

The controversy, which came into the open at the Romanian Workers' Party congress in June 1960, was debated at the Moscow world conference of communist parties in November, at which a compromise statement was adopted (see Appendix 2: Documents). A series of developments in 1961–62, including the break between the Soviet Union and Albania, the rapprochement between the Soviet Union and Yugoslavia, the granting of Soviet military aid to India, the subsequent Chinese invasion of India and the Soviet Union's agreement under US pressure to withdraw its missiles from Cuba, widened the breach, however, and in 1963–64 an acrimonious exchange of correspondence took place between the two parties, in which they expounded their opposing theoretical viewpoints at length (see Appendix 2: Documents). The breaking point was reached with the Cultural Revolution in China in 1966, when the Chinese party severed relations with the Soviet party and those communist parties which supported it.

The controversy split the entire world communist movement. Although China received total or partial support in the early 1960s from several of the strongest Asian parties, by 1966 the North Vietnamese, North Korean and Japanese parties had adopted a neutral position, and the Indonesian party (then the largest communist party in any non-communist country) had been virtually wiped out after an abortive attempt to seize power. Henceforward China drew its main support in Asia from small parties engaged in never-ending guerrilla warfare, such as the Burmese, Thai and Malayan. The Indian party split into pro-Soviet, neutral and pro-Chinese parties, the last of which devoted itself to terrorism and disintegrated into a host of warring factions. In Europe China was supported only by the Albanian party and a number of tiny sects, none of which attained any influence. The controversy, however, encouraged the ruling parties in Romania, Yugoslavia, North Korea and North Vietnam to assert their independence and play off one side against the other, and other parties to take up an independent Eurocommunist position.

Although ostensibly ideological in its origins, the Sino–Soviet split rapidly assumed the character of a rivalry between two major powers. Border disputes led to clashes in 1969 which threatened to develop into open war. One of the causes of the split had been Khrushchev's attempt to pursue a policy of peaceful coexistence with the United States, yet after 1971 the Chinese government's hostility to the Soviet Union led it to adopt a policy of improving relations with the United States and other countries which were on unfriendly terms with the Soviet Union, including countries with extreme right-wing governments such as Chile. This policy was justified by the adoption in 1974 of the "three worlds theory", which divided the world into (i) the two superpowers, the United States and the Soviet Union, of which the latter was said to be the more aggressive, (ii) the other developed countries, which were striving to free themselves from the superpowers' control, and (iii) the developing countries of Asia, Africa and Latin America. On the basis of this theory, China advocated an alliance between the second and third worlds against the superpowers.

While claiming to be the champion of world revolution, in practice China confined its support to revolutionary movements, often enjoying little popular backing, which seemed likely to further its own foreign policy aims, including non-communist guerrillas such as the Christian Nagas in India. On the other hand, its hostility to the Soviet Union ensured that when revolutions based on genuine mass support occurred, as in Bangladesh in 1971 and in Iran in 1979, China was apt to be found on the side of the counter-revolutionaries.

The victory of the communist forces in the civil wars in Indo-China in 1975 resulted in the establishment of a pro-Chinese regime in Kampuchea and regimes pursuing a neutral policy towards China and the Soviet Union in Vietnam and Laos. When China attempted to establish its hegemony in this region by bringing pressure to bear on Vietnam, both directly and by encouraging Kampuchean attacks on the Vietnamese border, Vietnam was driven into an alliance with the Soviet Union, and in 1979 overthrew the Kampuchean government and installed one under its own control. After unsuccessfully invading Vietnam, China sought to strengthen its relations with the ASEAN countries by abandoning its support for the Thai and Malaysian communist guerrillas.

After the death of Mao Zedong in 1976 China's internal policies swung sharply to the right, the communes being gradually dismantled and foreign investment and small-scale private enterprise encouraged. The Communist Party admitted in 1980 that the theoretical positions adopted in 1963–64 had been incorrect, and in the following year condemned virtually all the policies pursued by Mao since 1957 (see Appendix 2: Documents). These developments in China's home and foreign policies greatly reduced its influence in the world communist movement. Albania broke with China in 1978, and the Pol Pot regime in Kampuchea, the only remaining pro-Chinese communist government, was overthrown in the following year. The Thai Communist Party split into pro-Chinese and pro-Vietnamese parties, and other pro-Chinese parties transferred their allegiance to Albania or, while continuing to proclaim themselves Maoist, denounced Mao's successors as revisionists.

Eurocommunism

The term "Eurocommunism", which came into use about 1967, is applied to a system of thought which attempts to adapt Marxism to the conditions obtaining in highly-developed capitalist countries with a system of parliamentary democracy. The name is not strictly accurate, for although Eurocommunism originated in Western Europe a number of communist parties in other continents, notably the Japanese, also advocate policies to which it can be applied. Many of its fundamental concepts were adumbrated before World War II in Antonio Gramsci's *Prison Notebooks*. The periods of co-operation with other anti-fascist parties in 1934–39 and 1941–47 compelled the Western communist parties to reformulate many of their ideas, and Khrushchev's revelation of the true nature of Stalin's regime encouraged them to carry this process much farther.

The Italian communist leader Palmiro Togliatti in 1956 called for a polycentric communist movement composed of autonomous parties; affirmed that for socialist countries "the Soviet model cannot and should not any longer be obligatory"; and declared his support for the attainment of power through parliamentary means and for a multiparty system. In his "testament", written shortly before his death in 1964, he opposed the creation of any new centralized international communist organization; advocated "liquidating old formulae which no longer correspond to present realities"; and criticized the slowness of the socialist countries in reversing Stalin's suppression of individual freedom. All these themes were to be developed by the Eurocommunist parties.

Although the West European parties supported the Soviet Union in its controversy with China, during the 1960s they increasingly asserted their independence. A number of them expressed dissatisfaction at the manner in which Khrushchev was removed from office and at the suppression of dissident opinions under his successors. They welcomed the reforms introduced in Czechoslovakia in 1968, and the majority of them condemned the subsequent

Soviet invasion. They repeated their criticisms at the 1969 world communist conference in Moscow, and secured the inclusion in the declaration adopted of the statement that "there is no leading centre of the international communist movement", in contrast to the declaration adopted at the 1960 world conference, which recognized the Soviet party as the "vanguard" of the movement.

Eurocommunism took shape as a separate ideology in the joint declaration issued in 1975 by Enrico Berlinguer and Georges Marchais, the general secretaries of the Italian and French parties, which stated that "the advance to socialism and the building of a socialist society . . . must take place within a framework of continued democratization of economic, social and political life" (see Appendix 2: Documents). Socialism would form "a higher stage of democracy and liberty", within which political, religious and intellectual freedom must be guaranteed and developed. The two parties declared themselves in favour of a multiparty system, the right of opposition parties to activity, the possibility of parties alternating democratically, the independence of the judiciary, the independence of the trade unions and industrial democracy. Shortly afterwards the French party dropped the reference to the dictatorship of the proletariat in its statutes, and its example was followed by the Japanese party, which also replaced the term "Marxism-Leninism" by "scientific socialism". The Spanish party ceased to describe itself as "Leninist" in 1978.

At the 1976 conference of European communist parties (since when, significantly, no further such international conference has been held) Berlinguer and Marchais upheld the principles laid down in their declaration, and were strongly supported by Santiago Carrillo, general secretary of the Spanish party, and by the British and Swedish spokesmen (see Appendix 2: Documents). In their affirmation of the principle of the complete independence of communist parties they found themselves in alliance with President Tito of Yugoslavia and President Ceausescu of Romania, even though these leaders did not share their views on political freedom; in his statements of the period President Ceausescu combined declarations of Romania's political and economic independence with insistence on the necessity of the dictatorship of the proletariat. The Soviet leadership retaliated by convening a conference of the Soviet-bloc parties, which reaffirmed their loyalty to Soviet leadership and the dictatorship of the proletariat and condemned Eurocommunism. The division between the pro-Soviet and the Eurocommunist parties was widened further by the Soviet intervention in Afghanistan in 1979 and the introduction of martial law in Poland in 1981, both of which were condemned by most of the Eurocommunist parties. Since 1980 several Eurocommunist parties have re-established relations with the Chinese party.

The Eurocommunist controversy led to splits in many parties. Pro-Soviet factions broke away from the Spanish, British, Swedish, Japanese and Australian parties, and Eurocommunist factions from the Greek, Danish and Norwegian parties. The Finnish party split into Eurocommunist and pro-Soviet factions, which in effect operated as separate parties.

The New Left

Like Eurocommunism, the New Left emerged after the Soviet brand of communism had been discredited by Khrushchev's exposure of Stalin's crimes and the suppression of the Hungarian uprising. In its most typical form the movement, which drew its support mainly from students and intellectuals in Western Europe and the United States, attempted to synthesize Marxism with elements of anarchist and syndicalist thought, although the term was sometimes extended to cover other forms of non-Stalinist communism such as Trotskyism, Maoism and Castroism. Its most influential theoretician was Herbert Marcuse, who held that the industrial working class had been absorbed into the capitalist system, and that in contemporary society the main revolutionary force was the "outsiders", such as radical intellectuals, the least privileged sections of capitalist society and the peoples of the Third World.

Originating in the late 1950s, the New Left reached its peak in 1968 with the student riots in Paris and other Western cities, after which it declined. One offshoot of the movement was the terrorist groups which became active after 1968, such as the Red Army Faction in West Germany, the Red Brigades in Italy and the Weathermen in the United States. Other former elements of the New Left threw their support behind ecologist organizations such as the Greens in West Germany or the movements against nuclear weapons and the use of nuclear energy.

The term "New Left" can also be applied to certain left-wing socialist parties formed since 1960 which describe themselves as Marxist but not Leninist, outstanding examples being the Unified Socialist Party in France and the Pan-Hellenic Socialist Movement in Greece. In their ideology and policies these parties have much in common with the Eurocommunists.

Trotskyism

Groups of supporters of Trotsky in his controversy with Stalin were formed from 1924 onwards in a number of communist parties, from which they were subsequently expelled. In 1938 they founded the Fourth International, which stood for a form of Leninist fundamentalism, accepting the rulings of the first four congresses of the Comintern while rejecting the "opportunist" vacillations of the Comintern in its later Stalinist period. Hence the Trotskyists opposed both the ultra-leftism of the "third period" and the Popular Front, which they condemned as a form of class collaboration, and during World War II advocated a policy of revolutionary defeatism, modelled on that of the Bolsheviks in 1914–17. Trotsky regarded the Soviet Union as a degenerated socialist state, in which power had passed from the working class to the bureaucracy, although some of his followers maintained that it had reverted to capitalism.

Khrushchev's denunciation of Stalin in 1956 gave a new impetus to the Trotskyist movement, which could claim to have anticipated all his criticisms, and in many countries Trotskyist parties expanded or new ones were formed. Almost all of them, however, remained mere sects; the only Trotskyist party to achieve strong popular support, the Sri Lanka Equal Society Party, was expelled from the Fourth International in 1964 when it entered a coalition government, and subsequently abandoned Trotskyism. Even more than other sections of the world communist movement, both the Fourth International and individual Trotskyist parties suffered from splits over questions of theory and tactics. At the international level the process began in 1953, when a section of the Fourth International broke away to form the International Committee. By 1981 some 10 international Trotskyist organizations existed, each claiming to be the true successor to Trotsky's Fourth International. Some Trotskyist parties, despairing of obtaining mass support as independent parties, have adopted the tactic of "entryism", whereby they seek to infiltrate and to gain control over socialist parties.

Marxism in Latin America

Before 1959 the history of the Latin American communist parties largely paralleled that of the European parties. Up to 1928 the young parties, which then numbered only eight, were struggling to find their feet. During the "third period" from 1928 to 1935, in obedience to the Comintern's instructions, they adopted an ultra-leftist policy, with disastrous results. The Mexican party was banned in 1929 after an abortive uprising, and a communist-led peasant revolt in El Salvador in 1932 was followed by the virtual extermination not only of the Salvadorean but also of the Guatemalan and Honduran parties. After another attempted revolt in Brazil in 1935 the use of force was replaced by a policy of forming broadly-based anti-fascist alliances, which achieved its greatest successes in Chile and Cuba, where Popular Front governments took power in 1938 and 1940 respectively.

During World War II the Latin American communist parties, now numbering 18, attained respectability by throwing their support behind all governments which aided the allied war effort, whatever their political complexion. As a result, by 1946 almost all of them had been legalized, and between 1943 and 1947 communist ministers held office in Cuba, Ecuador and Chile. Their total membership passed the 375,000 mark in 1947, and their vote and parliamentary representation had grown in proportion. Alarmed at this formidable rival, the Latin American governments welcomed the pretext to suppress it afforded by the onset of the Cold War. Between 1945 and 1950 communist parties were banned in 11 countries, and Cuba, Guatemala and Colombia followed suit between 1953 and 1956.

The fact that the suppression of the Guatemalan party followed a US-organized coup against a left-wing government serves as a reminder that the parallel between the European and Latin American communist parties is bound to be incomplete. Latin America has always been dominated politically, economically or both by foreign powers, and in the 20th century especially by the United States. In Central America and the Caribbean the United States has repeatedly intervened since 1898 in the internal affairs of such supposedly independent countries as Cuba, Panama and Nicaragua, and its political influence in South America, although exercised less openly, remains powerful.

As a reaction to this situation, what have been described as national revolutionary parties emerged in many Latin American countries in the second quarter of the 20th century—the Institutional Revolutionary Party in Mexico, the American Popular Revolutionary Alliance in Peru, the Revolutionary Nationalist Movement in Bolivia and Democratic Action in Venezuela being outstanding examples. Such parties, which although influenced by Marxism derived their inspiration from the Mexican revolution of 1910 rather than the Russian revolution, advocated political and economic independence, nationalization of foreign-owned enterprises, a mixed economy and agrarian, labour and social reform; similar programmes were adopted by a number of military regimes, such as Perón's in Argentina, Velasco's in Peru, Torres' in Bolivia and Torrijos' in Panama. The national revolutionary parties, with their combination of nationalism and radicalism, have often been divided between a right wing which sometimes came very close to fascism and a left wing which sometimes adopted Marxist views, and in consequence their relationship with the Marxist parties has been a complex one, ranging from close alliance to mutual hostility. On the one hand it has produced such political oddities as the Trotskyist-Peronist parties in Argentina, on the other such situations as that in Venezuela in 1962–69, where a Marxist-Leninist party which had broken away from a ruling national revolutionary party remained in armed rebellion against it even after the Communist Party had laid down its weapons.

The major turning-point in the history of the Latin American Marxist parties was the Cuban revolution of 1959. The revolution was the work of Fidel Castro's July 26 Movement, which was not a Marxist but a national revolutionary party, and received no support from the official Cuban communist party, the Popular Socialist Party (PSP), until its closing stages. Even after US hostility had driven Castro to adopt Marxism-Leninism in 1961 it was he who took over the PSP, not the PSP which took over Castro, and the brand of communism which he preached was very much his own. Castro and his close associate Ernesto "Che" Guevara believed that, as in Cuba so throughout Latin America, small bands of dedicated guerrillas could gain the support of the peasantry, wear down the armed forces through a protracted popular war and bring about a revolution (see Appendix 2: Documents). This theory owed much to the experience of the Chinese and Vietnamese as well as the Cuban revolution, but it diverged from the thought of Mao Zedong and Ho Chi Minh in that it rejected their insistence on the necessity for strict Communist Party control over the guerrilla forces. For Castro and Guevara, generalizing from the Cuban experience, the guerrilla movement came first, the party was secondary—an analysis given theoretical amplification by Régis Debray in his *Revolution in the Revolution?* (see Appendix 2: Documents).

Guerrilla warfare was attempted in many Latin American countries in the 1960s, often with Cuban encouragement and support, but every attempt to imitate the Cuban example ended in failure. With a few exceptions, as in Colombia and Venezuela, they were not supported by the official communist parties, which preferred, even where they were illegal, to operate constitutionally through front organizations and political alliances. In general the guerrilla revolts were the work of the Maoist parties which broke away from almost all the Latin American communist parties in the 1960s, existing Trotskyist parties or newly-formed "Castroist" parties, sometimes, as in Venezuela and Peru, offshoots of national revolutionary parties. The Soviet Communist Party viewed Castro's zeal for the export of revolution with deep distrust; not only did it bear a disturbing resemblance to Mao Zedong's current pose as the champion of Marxism-Leninism against Soviet revisionism, but it threatened to embarrass Soviet relations with Latin American governments and the United States. The failure of Guevara's bungled attempt in 1966–67 to establish a base in southern Bolivia whence guerrilla activity might spread to Argentina, Brazil and Peru, combined with economic problems which made Cuba increasingly dependent on Soviet aid, finally compelled Castro to abandon his messianic role.

The failure of rural guerrilla warfare to produce socialist revolution drove Latin American Marxists to seek for other methods. The pro-Soviet parties' insistence on strict constitutionalism seemed justified when in 1970 an alliance of Socialists, Communists and left-wing Radicals and Christian Democrats headed by Salvador Allende took office in Chile. National revolutionary military regimes already held power with Marxist support in Peru, where Gen. Juan Velasco Alvarado had taken control in 1968, and in Bolivia, where the reformist Gen. Alfredo Ovando Candia was succeeded in 1970 by the more radical Gen. Juan José Torres. In the following year, however, Torres in turn was supplanted by the right-wing Gen. Hugo Banzer Suárez; the Allende government was overthrown by the armed forces in 1973; and Velasco was compelled in 1976 to make way for the more conservative Gen. Francisco Morales Bermúdez. To many Latin American Marxists these events confirmed the truth of Marx's saying that the working class cannot merely take over the bourgeois state machinery and use it for its own purposes but must smash it, a dictum to which the long-established Latin

American tradition of military intervention in politics gave additional point. It is significant that in Latin America Eurocommunism is confined to Mexico, where the last military revolt was crushed in 1938, and Venezuela, which has been under civilian rule since 1958.

As an alternative to constitutionalism and rural guerrilla warfare, the National Liberation Alliance in Brazil, the Tupamaros in Uruguay and the Montoneros in Argentina practised urban guerrilla warfare. The Brazilian military government crushed the National Liberation Alliance with little difficulty, however, and the main achievement of the Tupamaros and Montoneros was to provide the pretext for military takeovers in Uruguay in 1973 and in Argentina in 1976. The Argentinian coup completed the process whereby all the South American republics except Colombia and Venezuela were subjected to military regimes, of which only that in Peru could make any claim to be revolutionary. The Marxist parties, driven underground, were faced with the choice between co-operation with the bourgeois parties in an agitation for the restoration of constitutional government or armed resistance to an opponent who had all the odds on his side, and most chose the former. Popular agitation, strikes, demonstrations, pressure from President Carter's administration in the United States and the catastrophic failure of many of the generals' political and economic policies finally produced their effect, and by 1985 civilian rule had been re-established throughout South America except in Chile and Paraguay.

A third period of guerrilla struggles had meanwhile begun with the Nicaraguan revolution. The Sandinista National Liberation Front, which took power in 1979 after 16 years of guerrilla warfare, had much in common with Castro's July 26 Movement; neither was an orthodox communist party, neither enjoyed the support of the official Communist Party in its struggle and both owed much of their popular support to the fact that their revolt was directed against a brutal and corrupt dictatorship. Politically, however, the Sandinista leaders were more sophisticated than Castro, and their strategy, which combined rural guerrilla offensives with the formation of broad political alliances, demonstrations, strikes and popular insurrections in the towns, provided a new model for future revolutions. The Nicaraguan revolt produced profound repercussions in El Salvador and Guatemala, where guerrilla opposition to repressive military regimes had developed rapidly in the 1970s. In both countries the communist parties after 1979 abandoned their policy of forming electoral alliances for one of armed struggle, and in El Salvador a political crisis led to civil war in 1981. The Salvadorean government, however, enjoyed the US political and military support which the Nicaraguan dictatorship had lacked in 1979, and after four years of war a stalemate seemed to have been reached.

The Middle East and the Arab World

Although communist parties were founded in the 1920s in several Middle Eastern and North African countries, either as independent parties or (in French North Africa) as sections of the French party, they achieved little success. After the war they suffered from the competition of Arab nationalist movements such as Nasserism and Baathism, of Islamic fundamentalism or (in Israel) of Zionism. They frequently attempted to attach themselves to such movements, but were either reduced to mere subsidiaries of the ruling party, as in Syria, or after a period of toleration were suppressed, as in Sudan in 1971, in Iraq in 1978 and in Iran in 1983. Another obstacle to the spread of communism in the Middle East was the strength of popular attachment to Islam; one result of this was the emergence of movements attempting to reconcile Marxism with Islam, of which the *Mojahedin-e Khalq* in Iran is the most prominent example.

An exception to these generalizations was the Palestinian nationalist movement, inside which Marxist organizations such as the Popular Front for the Liberation of Palestine and the Democratic Front for the Liberation of Palestine have wielded considerable influence. Among the Palestinians, Soviet and Chinese support for their cause and US support for Israel stimulated communist sympathies, and the religious factor was of less importance than elsewhere, as they included Christians as well as Moslems. It is significant that the only Marxist party which succeeded in taking power in an Arab country, the National Liberation Front, which ousted its rivals in the struggle for the leadership of the nationalist movement in South Yemen, had close links with the Popular Front for the Liberation of Palestine, with which it shared a common origin as a section of the Arab Nationalists' Movement.

Communism in Africa

Before World War II the only communist party in Africa south of the Sahara was the South African party, which was founded and originally led by whites. The Marxist regimes which emerged after 1963 fell into two main categories. Marxist organizations which had played a leading part in armed struggles against white rule were able to take power on the attainment of independence in the former Portuguese colonies of Angola, Guinea-Bissau and Mozambique in 1974–75 and in Zimbabwe in 1980. The Marxist regimes established in Congo in 1963, in Somalia in 1969 and in Benin and Ethiopia in 1974, on the other hand, came into being as the result of military coups led by small groups of officers, and the ruling parties were established only after the regime was already in existence. Elsewhere on the African mainland Marxist parties exercised little influence, although they had some success in the islands of Mauritius, Réunion and Seychelles, in the Indian Ocean.

2. INTERNATIONAL MARXIST ORGANIZATIONS AND CONFERENCES

The International Workingmen's Association (The First International)

The International Workingmen's Association was founded at a meeting of British and French trade union leaders in London in 1864, which elected a General Council of 34 members. Among them was Marx, who was deputed to draw up its Inaugural Address, and later drafted many of its most important documents. Despite his influential role in it, which is largely to be explained by the fact that he was able to act as an intermediary between British trade unionists and European socialists, the International was not an exclusively, or even predominantly, Marxist organization. In addition to Marxists, who were mostly German Social Democrats, its membership included British trade unionists, Owenites and former Chartists, French Proudhonists, who envisaged a society of producers' co-operatives, Irish, Italian and Polish nationalists and Bakuninist anarchists. It was largely owing to Marx's tact that this heterogeneous organization survived as long as it did.

In his Inaugural Address Marx attempted to draft a programme which would be acceptable to all sections of the International, and under his influence it gradually moved towards acceptance of more openly socialist aims. The Brussels congress of 1868 approved nationalization of the means of production, and the Basle congress of the following year common ownership of the land, despite the Proudhonists' opposition to both policies. The Paris Commune, however, split the International. Marx's defence of the Commune, *The Civil War in France* (see Appendix 2: Documents), written on behalf of the General Council, terrified the Liberal British trade union leaders, who withdrew their support. On the other flank Marx was confronted with the opposition of the anarchists, led by Mikhail Bakunin, whose adventurist policies threatened to wreck the International. At the 1872 congress in The Hague Bakunin was expelled, and in order to prevent the General Council from falling under anarchist control its headquarters were transferred to New York. Isolated from the European labour movement, the International lost its influence, and was dissolved in 1876.

The Second International

The Second International was founded at a congress which met in Paris on July 14, 1889, the centenary of the storming of the Bastille, with the German Social Democrat Wilhelm Liebknecht and Édouard Vaillant, a former Communard, as joint presidents. After the anarchists and syndicalists were excluded in 1896 it became, in theory at least, predominantly a Marxist organization, although parties which made no claim to be Marxist, such as the British Labour Party, were also admitted. In practice it was almost as heterogeneous as the First International, as was shown by the fact that its participants at various times included such very different figures as Karl Kautsky, Eduard Bernstein, Rosa

Luxemburg, Jules Guesde, Jean Jaurès, Pierre Laval, William Morris, Keir Hardie, Ramsay MacDonald, Lenin, Trotsky, Stalin and the young Benito Mussolini (then an Italian Socialist activist).

Following Millerrand's entry into the French government, the Paris congress of 1900 laid down that socialists should not enter bourgeois governments except in extraordinary circumstances, such as a threat to fundamental democratic institutions. The Amsterdam congress of 1904 condemned Bernstein's revisionist theories. From 1907 onwards the International was particularly concerned with the danger of a European war. The Stuttgart congress of 1907 adopted a resolution declaring that socialist parties should strive to prevent the outbreak of war, with an amendment sponsored by Rosa Luxemburg and Lenin which declared that if war broke out "socialists are obliged to intervene to bring it to an end as quickly as possible, and to exploit in every way the economic and political crisis created by the war to stir up the people and so to accelerate the overthrow of capitalist rule". Although this policy was reaffirmed at the Basle congress of 1912, when war broke out two years later most of the member parties supported the governments of their respective countries, and the International disintegrated.

The Zimmerwald Movement

In September 1915 an international socialist conference organized by the Italian Socialist Party, which had opposed Italy's entry into the war, met at Zimmerwald, in Switzerland, and was attended by delegates from 11 belligerent and neutral countries. Most of the delegates were "social-pacifists" who favoured a negotiated peace, but a minority, led by Lenin, advocated ending the war by revolutionary means. A second conference of delegates from 10 countries held at Kienthal, also in Switzerland, in April 1916 adopted a manifesto drafted by Lenin, which condemned the war as imperialist and called on the socialist parties and the working class to turn it into a proletarian revolution.

The Communist International (The Third International)

The Communist or Third International, known for short as the Comintern, was founded at a congress held in Moscow in March 1919 (see Appendix 2: Documents). Of the 35 delegates with voting powers, representing 19 parties and organizations, only five had come from abroad, the remainder being Russians, citizens of countries formerly included in the Russian Empire, prisoners of war and other foreigners resident in Russia. An Executive Committee, to which all member parties were to elect delegates, was established, with Grigory Zinoviev as chairman and Karl Radek as secretary.

The second congress, held in Petrograd and Moscow in July and August 1920, was attended by 169 delegates with voting powers, of whom 64 were Russians, 28 were foreigners resident in Russia and 77 came from abroad. It adopted the statutes of the International, which provided for the holding of annual congresses and the creation of trade union, youth and women's sections. The Executive Committee, which was the directing body of the International between congresses, would consist of five representatives of "the party of that country where, by decision of the world congress, the Executive Committee has its seat" and one representative each from the 10 to 13 most important communist parties. The congress also approved 21 conditions with which each party affiliated to the International must comply, including complete control of the party press by the leadership, the removal of "reformists and centrists" from all responsible positions, combination of legal and illegal work, the spreading of propaganda in the armed forces, the adoption of a centralized organization with "iron discipline" based on democratic centralism, the periodic purging of "petty-bourgeois elements", the adoption of a programme in conformity with the International's decisions, compliance with the decisions of congresses of the International and of its Executive Committee, and adoption of the name "Communist Party of such and such a country" (see Appendix 2: Documents).

The third congress (June–July 1921), which was attended by delegates from 48 countries, gave warning, in the light of the unsuccessful communist uprising in Germany three months before, that a communist party "should not let itself be forced into decisive struggles alone and isolated", and advocated the United Front policy, whereby "we must show the broad working masses that it is only the communists who fight for an improvement in their position". It also approved theses on party organization which stressed that all members must take an active part in the party's work and that the basic organization should be the factory cell.

The fourth congress (November–December 1922), at which 58 countries were represented, laid down that although the true realization of the United Front tactic could come only from below, communists might in certain circumstances negotiate with the leaders of other socialist parties and even form governments with them. A resolution on the reorganization of the Executive Committee was adopted whereby its members would not be delegated by the parties represented, as in the past, but elected by the congress.

Although the International's statutes provided for annual congresses, after 1922 they were held at increasingly long intervals. The fifth congress (June–July 1924) laid emphasis on the necessity for "bolshevization" of the affiliated parties on the Soviet model, with the result that many of their leaders were expelled in the next few years. Grigory Zinoviev, who had headed the International since its foundation, was replaced in 1926 by Nikolai Bukharin.

At the sixth congress (July–September 1928) Bukharin maintained in his report that, after the revolutionary period from 1917 to 1923 and the period of temporary stabilization of capitalism from 1923 to 1928, a "third period" of economic crises, increased internal tensions in capitalist states, imperialist wars and attacks on the Soviet Union was beginning. Hence he deduced that it was necessary to abandon the United Front policy and to win the working class away from the influence of the social democrats (now linked by the Labour and Socialist International), who were described as the "main enemy". The congress adopted the programme of the International, largely drafted by Bukharin, which had been under discussion since 1922. Bukharin was re-elected to the chairmanship, but a few months later was removed and replaced by Viacheslav Molotov.

The seventh and last congress was held in July and August 1935, two years after Hitler came to power. After the German communist Wilhelm Pieck had admitted that his party had underestimated the strength of Nazism and had laboured under "the absolutely false conception that all the bourgeois parties are fascist", the congress approved a report by the Bulgarian Georgi Dimitrov, which advocated the Popular Front policy and the building of the broadest possible unity against fascism (see Appendix 2: Documents). In response to complaints about interference in the member parties' internal affairs, a resolution was adopted directing the Executive Committee "to proceed, in deciding any question, from the concrete situation and specific conditions obtaining in each particular country, and as a rule to avoid direct intervention in internal organizational matters of the communist parties".

The Presidium of the Executive Committee voted in May 1943 to dissolve the International, as an assurance to the Soviet Union's allies in World War II that it did not intend to interfere in their internal affairs (see Appendix 2: Documents). The decision was subsequently ratified by all the affiliated parties.

Organizations affiliated to the Communist International

The Communist Youth International was founded in Berlin in 1919 as the youth section of the Comintern, and moved its headquarters to Moscow two years later. It was dissolved with the Comintern in 1943. A Communist Women's Organization was also established in 1919, but exercised little influence outside the Soviet Union.

The Red International of Labour Unions (also known as the Profintern, from the abbreviated form of its Russian name) was founded in 1920 as a rival to the social democratic International Federation of Trade Unions, and consisted of communist unions and communist factions in other unions. Although nominally independent, it was in reality controlled by the Comintern. It was dissolved in 1937 in accordance with the Popular Front policy of promoting unity between communists and socialists against fascism.

The Communist Information Bureau

The Communist Information Bureau (Cominform) was founded in September 1947 at a conference of the Soviet, Bulgarian, Czechoslovak, Hungarian, Polish, Romanian, Yugoslav, French and Italian Communist parties held at Szklarska Poreba, in Poland. Its aim was defined as "to organize interchange of experience among the parties, and if need be to co-ordinate their activities on the basis of mutual agreement" (see Appendix 2: Documents), and its headquarters were established at Belgrade. At its third meeting, held in Romania in June 1948, the Yugoslav party (which was not represented) was accused of pursuing an anti-Soviet and "nationalistic" policy and was expelled from the Cominform, whose headquarters were moved to Bucharest. Only one other meeting took place, in Hungary in November 1949, which adopted a resolution denouncing the Yugoslav leaders as a "clique of spies and fascists" and calling for their overthrow. Two of the signatories of the 1948 resolution, Traicho Kostov (Bulgaria) and Rudolf Slánský (Czechoslovakia), were themselves subsequently executed as "Titoists".

After Stalin's death in 1953 the Cominform became dormant, and the reconciliation between the Soviet and Yugoslav Communist parties in 1955 made it an embarrassment to the former. It was accordingly dissolved in April 1956, on the pretext that because of changes in the international situation it had "exhausted its function". Since then communist parties have had no international organizational structure (in contrast to social democratic and labour parties, which launched the Socialist International in 1951).

The Moscow Conference of Ruling Communist Parties (1957)

Representatives of the communist parties of the Soviet Union, China, Albania, Bulgaria, Czechoslovakia, East Germany, Hungary, North Korea, Mongolia, Poland, Romania and North Vietnam met in Moscow for discussions in November 1957 during the celebrations of the 40th anniversary of the Bolshevik revolution. A joint declaration adopted by the parties taking part (see Appendix 2: Documents) affirmed their support for peaceful coexistence, and stated that relations between the socialist countries were based on principles of complete equality, respect for territorial integrity, state independence and sovereignty, and non-interference in one another's internal affairs. It condemned revisionism as the main danger to the international communist movement, asserting that "the revisionists deny the historical necessity for a proletarian revolution and the dictatorship of the proletariat during the period of transition from capitalism to socialism, reject the principles of proletarian internationalism and call for the rejection of the Leninist principles of party organization and democratic centralism". It also condemned dogmatism and sectarianism, which, it said, could also be the main danger at different phases of development in one party or another. In conclusion, it recognized the possibility of achieving the socialist revolution peacefully by parliamentary means in certain countries, and called for co-operation between communist and socialist parties. Although the Yugoslav League of Communists was represented at the celebrations, it did not take part in the discussions or sign the declaration, with which it expressed its disagreement.

The Moscow Conference of Communist Parties (1960)

The Moscow conference of November 1960, the largest gathering of communist leaders since the Comintern's 1935 congress and the last at which the world's communist parties met as a united movement, was convened to consider the growing differences between the Soviet and Chinese parties. Delegations were present from 81 communist parties, but not from the Yugoslav League of Communists, which had not been invited. At the conference all the issues dividing the two sides were debated, including the inevitability of war under capitalism, the possibility of peaceful coexistence and a parliamentary transition to socialism, national liberation movements in the under-developed countries, the personality cult and the Chinese communes. Khrushchev, who put the Soviet case, was strongly supported by the Polish, Italian, French, British, Swedish and Swiss delegates; the West European spokesmen, who defended the parliamentary road to socialism and called for the abandonment of the phrase "the dictatorship of the proletariat", largely anticipated what later became known as the Eurocommunist position. Deng Xiaoping, the chief Chinese spokesman, was supported only by Hoxha (Albania) and the Burmese, Malayan and Australian delegates.

The conference adopted a 20,000-word declaration, which generally expressed the Soviet viewpoint, while making some concessions to the Chinese position (see Appendix 2: Documents). It held that war was not inevitable, in view of the strength of the socialist camp and the other forces opposing war, and that peaceful coexistence was possible, although this did not mean "conciliation of the socialist and bourgeois ideologies". It called for an "anti-imperialist, anti-feudal democratic revolution" in the colonial and under-developed countries, to be achieved by a united front of the workers, peasants and national bourgeoisie, and for joint action between communist and social democratic parties in support of common aims. It emphasized that "the choice of its social system is the inalienable right of the people of each country. Socialist revolution is not an item of export, and cannot be imposed from without." After reaffirming the 1957 declaration's statement on the possibility of a parliamentary transition to socialism and its condemnation of revisionism as the main danger and of dogmatism and sectarianism, it also condemned the personality cult and "the anti-Leninist ideas of the Yugoslav revisionists", and referred to the Soviet party as "the universally recognized vanguard of the world communist movement".

The Karlovy Vary Conference of European Communist Parties (1967)

This conference, held at Karlovy Vary (Czechoslovakia) in April 1967, was attended by delegations from 24 communist parties of Eastern and Western Europe, although the Albanian, Romanian and Yugoslav parties refused to take part. It adopted a statement on European security containing the following proposals: (i) recognition of the inviolability of the existing European frontiers; (ii) recognition of the existence of two German states; (iii) denial of nuclear weapons to West Germany; (iv) renunciation of the Munich Agreement of 1938; (v) conclusion by all European states of a treaty renouncing the use of force and interference in one another's internal affairs; (vi) normalization of relations between all states and East Germany; (vii) banning of neo-Nazi organizations in West Germany and legalization of the Communist Party; (viii) conclusion of a nuclear non-proliferation treaty; (ix) recognition of the principle of respect for the inviolability of neutral states; (x) elimination of economic barriers between socialist and capitalist states; (xi) withdrawal of foreign troops from European states and establishment of nuclear-free zones in Central Europe, the Balkans, the Danubian countries, the Mediterranean and Northern Europe; (xii) abolition of the military organizations of the Atlantic Pact and the Warsaw Treaty; (xiii) a conference of all European states on European security and peaceful co-operation; (xiv) a conference of representatives of all the European parliaments.

The Moscow Conference of Communist Parties (1969)

This conference took place in Moscow in June 1969 (after preparations lasting over a year), since when no further world conference of communist parties has been held (as at end-1985). Of the 86 parties invited 75 took part, including the Cuban and Swedish parties, which were represented only by observers. Five ruling parties (those of Albania, China, North Korea, North Vietnam and Yugoslavia) and several other parties which had either adopted a pro-Chinese position or wished to remain neutral in the Sino-Soviet controversy were not represented.

Leonid Brezhnev, the Soviet general secretary, in his speech strongly attacked both "right-wing opportunism" (i.e. Eurocommunism) and the "left-wing opportunism" of the Chinese party, which he accused of preparing for war with the Soviet Union; he declared that "genuine internationalism implies support for the existing socialist society by all fraternal parties". He was supported by the Bulgarian, Hungarian, Czechoslovak and Cuban representatives, who defended the Soviet intervention in Czechoslovakia. President Ceausescu of Romania, however, deplored attacks on China and called for non-interference in the internal affairs of other countries and parties; he maintained that there was no need for any leading centre of the international movement.

Enrico Berlinguer, the Italian delegate, appealed for a reconciliation with China and condemned the invasion of Czechoslovakia; he said that there could be no "guiding party or guiding state" for the movement, and affirmed his support for a pluralist and democratic system for Italy. The Australian, British, Spanish, Swedish and Swiss representatives also criticized the Soviet intervention in Czechoslovakia and emphasized each party's right to decide its own policy.

The document adopted by the conference had been drastically amended beforehand at a meeting of representatives of 68 parties, and contained no direct reference to China or the invasion of Czechoslovakia. The first of its four sections analyzed the international situation. The second stated that the successful development of the building of socialism in different countries, which took various forms, implied "strict adherence to the principles of proletarian internationalism, mutual assistance and support, equality, sovereignty and non-interference in each other's internal affairs", and that divergences between socialist countries must be settled through comradely discussion. It advocated co-operation in capitalist countries between communists and socialists, social democrats and "other democratic parties and organizations interested in the renewal of society", provided that the latter broke with "the policy of class collaboration with the bourgeoisie", and also between communists and religious believers. It called for close co-operation with other "patriotic and progressive forces" in the Asian and African countries which were struggling for independence or newly independent, and expressed support for the struggle in Latin America against US imperialism and internal reaction.

The third section, which laid down a programme of action, stated that "the policy of peaceful coexistence does not contradict the right of any oppressed people to fight for its liberation by any means it considers necessary, armed or peaceful", and "does not imply either the preservation of the socio-political status quo or a weakening of the ideological struggle". It called for a ban on nuclear, bacteriological and chemical weapons, a radical reduction in military budgets, general and complete disarmament under effective international control, and the simultaneous dissolution of NATO and the Warsaw Treaty Organization. Its proposals for Europe were similar to those contained in the Karlovy Vary statement (see above). It advocated the admission of China to the United Nations, the return of Taiwan to China and the evacuation by Israel of the territories occupied in 1967, and condemned racialism, Zionism and anti-semitism. The final section, on relations between communist parties, stated that "all parties have equal rights"; there was "no leading centre of the international communist movement", and each party worked out its own policy in full independence.

The statement was signed by 66 of the parties taking part in the conference, although the Romanian, Spanish, Swiss, Moroccan and Sudanese parties did so with reservations. The Italian, San Marinese, Australian and Réunion parties signed only the third section, and the Cuban, British, Norwegian, Swedish and Dominican parties did not sign any part of the statement.

The Berlin Conference of European Communist Parties (1976)

The conference of European communist parties held in East Berlin in June 1976, which was attended by 29 delegations representing all the European countries except Albania and Iceland, brought into the open the fundamental division between pro-Soviet, Eurocommunist and independent parties. In his speech on behalf of the Soviet party, which was conciliatory in tone, Brezhnev denied that there was any intention of creating a new organizational centre. While congratulating the Italian party on its electoral successes, however, he emphasized that "it is of special importance that when uniting in the struggles against reactionary imperialist circles with broad democratic streams, including social democrats and Christians, the communists remain revolutionaries, convinced champions of replacing the capitalist system by a socialist one". The Bulgarian, Czechoslovak and Hungarian spokesmen upheld the principle of proletarian internationalism (a term usually associated with acceptance of Soviet leadership) and condemned any criticism of the Soviet Union as "anti-Sovietism", and were supported by the Austrian, West German, Greek, Luxembourg, Norwegian, Portuguese and Turkish representatives. President Ceausescu of Romania and President Tito of Yugoslavia, on the other hand, strongly affirmed the principle of the independence of parties, and were supported by the Italian, French,

Spanish, British, Swedish and San Marinese speakers, who also declared their attachment to parliamentary democracy, the multiparty system and freedom of expression (for extract from Santiago Carrillo's speech on behalf of the Spanish party, see Appendix 2: Documents).

The declaration adopted by the conference had been the subject of heated controversy at the preparatory meetings of the drafting commission, consisting of representatives of 28 parties, the version finally approved being the seventh to be drafted. The Eurocommunist and independent parties had insisted that the declaration must first be approved by all the parties taking part, must recognize the complete independence of all communist parties and must not criticize the policies of the Chinese or any other party. They also secured the replacement of the phrase "proletarian internationalism" by "internationalist co-operation".

In its final form the declaration advocated complete disarmament under strict international control, a ban on nuclear, bacteriological and chemical weapons and dissolution of NATO and the Warsaw Treaty Organization. It put forward a number of demands relating to democracy and national independence in Europe, including an amnesty for Spanish political prisoners and émigrés, a peaceful solution of the Cyprus problem by negotiations between the two Cypriot communities under UN auspices, solidarity with the struggle of "the democratic forces of Northern Ireland" for civil rights and legalization of the Turkish Communist Party. It called for increased economic and cultural co-operation between all European states and recognition of the rights of migrant workers and national minorities. Finally, it advocated a settlement of the Middle Eastern conflict based on withdrawal of Israeli troops from occupied Arab territory, the independence and security of all states in the area and the establishment of a Palestinian state; support for the reconstruction of the Indo-Chinese countries; the ending of acts of terror against communists and democrats in Chile and other Latin American countries; peaceful reunification of Korea; support for the anti-imperialist struggles of the Arab and African peoples; and severance of relations with South Africa by all states.

The Sofia Conference of Soviet-bloc Parties (1976)

This conference, held in Sofia in December 1976, was attended by delegations from the communist parties of Bulgaria, Cuba, Czechoslovakia, East Germany, Hungary, Mongolia, Poland and the Soviet Union, nominally to discuss problems posed by their recent congresses. No statement was adopted, but the speeches were largely devoted to affirmations of loyalty to the concepts of proletarian internationalism, the dictatorship of the proletariat and the leadership of the Soviet party, and to condemnation of Eurocommunism as a bourgeois ideology.

World Marxist Review

World Marxist Review is the English-language title of the monthly magazine known in other languages as *Problems of Peace and Socialism*. Founded in Prague in 1958, it is described as "a theoretical and information journal of communist and workers' parties throughout the world", and is printed in 35 languages and distributed in 145 countries. The chief editor has always been a Russian, but 15 parties are represented on the editorial board and 65 on the editorial council. Inclusion on the editorial council is equivalent to recognition as a communist party by the Soviet party, although Eurocommunist and independent as well as pro-Soviet parties are represented. The editorial council thus constitutes the only formal organization linking the communist parties recognized by the Soviet party. The Yugoslav League of Communists has never been associated with the journal, and the Chinese and Albanian parties ended their connection with it in 1962.

World Marxist Review organizes periodical conferences, which have been the only conferences of communist parties on a world basis held since 1969. At a conference on its work held in Prague in 1981, attended by representatives of 81 communist and nine "revolutionary democratic" parties, strong criticism of the Soviet party's control of it was voiced by a number of Eurocommunist parties, including the Japanese, which advocated that it should cease publication.

The Fourth International

In 1929 Trotskyist groups in a number of countries formed the International Left Opposition, which was renamed the International Communist League four years later. This body regarded itself as an expelled faction of the Communist International, to which it frequently but unsuccessfully requested readmission. In September 1938 the League organized a congress near Paris, attended by 30 delegates from Europe, the United States and Latin America, which founded the Fourth International and adopted Trotsky's *The Death Agony of Capitalism and the Coming Tasks of the Fourth International* as its programme. On the outbreak of war the International Secretariat transferred its headquarters to the United States. After the murder of Trotsky in 1940 and the German occupation of Western Europe the International disintegrated, but in 1943 Michel Pablo set up a Provisional European Secretariat, which organized a conference of several of the European sections in the following year.

The International Secretariat was re-established under Pablo's leadership at the second congress, held in Paris in 1948, which was attended by 22 delegations from 19 countries. The third congress in 1951 welcomed the Yugoslav Communist Party's breach with the Cominform, and approved the tactic of entryism, i.e. infiltration of communist and socialist parties. At the fourth congress in 1953, however, a split occurred between Pablo and the British group led by Gerry Healy (later the Workers' Revolutionary Party), which at a conference in London formed the Fourth International—International Committee. This was joined by the (US) Socialist Workers' Party (SWP), the (French) Internationalist Communist Party and a number of smaller groups, although the majority of Trotskyist parties continued to support the International Secretariat. In 1963 the SWP returned to the International Secretariat, which was renamed the Fourth International—United Secretariat.

In addition to the United Secretariat and the International Committee, a number of international Trotskyist organizations exist, as detailed below.

(1) The Latin American bureau of the International Secretariat, led by Juan Posadas, broke away in 1962 and founded the Fourth International—International Secretariat (generally known as the Posadist Fourth International), with its headquarters in Argentina. It draws its support mainly from Latin America, but also has some followers in Western Europe.

(2) The Revolutionary Marxist Tendency was founded by Michel Pablo in 1964 after he had left the United Secretariat of the Fourth International.

(3) After being expelled from the International Committee in 1966, the (US) Spartacist League formed the International Spartacist Tendency, which has some support in other English-speaking countries.

(4) The (British) Militant Tendency in 1974 formed the Committee for the Workers' International, which has sections in a number of European and Asian countries.

(5) The (French) International Communist Organization (previously and later known as the Internationalist Communist Party) left the International Committee in 1971 and formed the Organizing Centre for the Reconstruction of the Fourth International (OCRFI). It joined with the (Argentinian) Workers' Socialist Party and other groups which had left the United Secretariat in 1980 to form the Fourth International—International Committee, which was renamed the Fourth International—International Centre of Reconstruction in the following year.

(6) The Fourth Internationalist Tendency was formed in 1979 by the (Argentinian) Workers' Politics and the (Bolivian) Workers' Revolutionary Party, which had left the OCRFI.

(7) The Trotskyist International Liaison Committee was formed in 1979 by the (British) Workers' Socialist League (now the Socialist Organizer Alliance) and Italian, Danish and US groups.

(8) The International Workers' League was formed in 1981 by the (Argentinian) Workers' Socialist Party, which had left the Fourth International—International Committee, and some European groups.

3. INTERNATIONAL COMMUNIST FRONT ORGANIZATIONS

The description "Communist front" is applied to an organization which, although including non-communists, is largely or entirely under communist control and serves the purposes of communist propaganda. A number of such organizations were formed by the Comintern between 1920 and 1923, including the Red International of Labour Unions (see above), the Red Sport International (Sportintern), the International Organization for Aid to Revolutionaries (International Red Aid) and the Peasants' International (Krestintern), all of which were dissolved between 1933 and 1947. The most important existing organizations are listed below.

Afro-Asian Peoples' Solidarity Organization (AAPSO)

History. The AAPSO was founded in 1957 to strengthen the African and Asian countries' struggle against imperialism and colonialism and to promote their economic, social and cultural development. It was divided by bitter controversy between the Soviet Union and China until China left it in 1967.

Leadership. Ahmad Hamrush (Egypt), pres.; Nuri Abdul Razzaq Husayn (Iraq), g.s. Neither is known to be a communist.

Structure. The conference meets at irregular intervals, and elects the Council, consisting of representatives from each national affiliate. The Presidential Board, which meets annually, consists of the president and eight vice-presidents. There is a permanent secretariat in Cairo, consisting of the general secretary, four deputy general secretaries and 11 secretaries.

Membership. 87 affiliated organizations from most of the African and Asian countries.

Publications. *Solidarity*, monthly; *Socio-Economic Development and Progress*, quarterly.

Christian Peace Conference (CPC)

History. The CPC was founded at a conference in Prague in 1958, with the aims of promoting social justice, disarmament and aid to the under-developed countries and combating exploitation, colonialism and racism.

Leadership. Bishop Károly Toth (Hungary), pres.; Dr Lubomir Mirejovsky (Czechoslovakia), g.s.

Structure. The Christian Peace Conference, meeting at irregular intervals, elects a Continuation Committee and a smaller Working Committee, and the latter elects the International Secretariat. The CPC has its headquarters in Prague.

Membership. Affiliates (churches, ecumenical bodies and individuals) in at least 80 countries.

Publications. *CPC*, quarterly; *CPC Information*, semimonthly.

International Association of Democratic Lawyers (IADL)

History. The IADL was founded in Paris in 1946, and has its headquarters in Brussels.

Leadership. Joe Nordmann (France, communist), pres.; Amar Bentoumi (Algeria, non-communist), g.s.

Structure. The congress, meeting at irregular intervals, elects its Council and Bureau.

Membership. Affiliates in over 80 countries; membership 25,000.

Publication. *International Review of Contemporary Law*, semi-annual.

International Organization of Journalists (IOJ)

History. The IOJ was founded in Copenhagen in 1946, and at first included associations from both Western and communist countries. As it passed under communist control, however, many Western associations withdrew, and in 1952 formed the rival International Federation of Journalists.

Leadership. Kaarle Nordenstreng (Finland), pres.; Jiří Kubka (Czechoslovakia), g.s.

Structure. The congress meets every five years, and elects the Executive Committee and a Presidium consisting of the president, 23 vice-presidents and the general secretary. There is an eight-member Secretariat in Prague.

Membership. Affiliates in over 120 countries; over 180,000 members.

Publications. *Democratic Journalist*, monthly; *IOJ News Letter*, semimonthly.

International Union of Students (IUS)

History. The IUS was founded in 1945 on the initiative of the (British) National Union of Students to promote friendship and co-operation among students, and held its founding congress in Prague in the following year. It subsequently came under communist control, and many Western student associations withdrew.

Leadership. Miroslav Stepan (Czechoslovakia), pres.; Georgios Michaelides (Cyprus), g.s.

Structure. The congress, meeting every three years, elects the Executive Committee, which meets at least three times between congresses. The congress also elects the president, 11 vice-presidents, the general secretary and nine secretaries. The IUS headquarters are in Prague.

Membership. 117 affiliates in 109 countries; over 10,000,000 members, mostly in the communist countries.

Publications. *World Student News*, monthly; *IUS News Service*, fortnightly.

Women's International Democratic Federation (WIDF)

History. The WIDF was founded in 1945 at a congress in Paris of women's organizations (mostly communist-controlled) from about 40 countries. It was expelled from France in 1951, and moved its headquarters to East Berlin.

Leadership. Freda Brown (Australia), pres.; Mirjam Vire-Tuominen (Finland), g.s.

Structure. The congress meets every five or six years, and elects a Council of 30, meeting annually, which elects the Bureau (meeting twice a year) and Secretariat.

Membership. 131 affiliates in 116 countries; over 200,000,000 members.

Publications. *Women of the Whole World*, quarterly; *Documents and Information*, published at irregular intervals.

World Federation of Democratic Youth (WFDY)

History. The WFDY, founded in London in 1945, aims to promote co-operation among youth organizations and international understanding among young people. Its headquarters, originally in Paris, were transferred to Budapest in 1951, when the WFDY was expelled from France. All the communist countries except Yugoslavia and most other countries are represented in it, but China and Cuba have boycotted some of its activities.

Leadership. Walid Masri (Lebanon), pres.; Vilmos Cserveny (Hungary), g.s.

Structure. The general assembly meets every three years and elects the Executive Committee. The Bureau/Secretariat consists of the president, nine vice-presidents, the general secretary, two deputy general secretaries, the treasurer and 20 secretaries.

Membership. Over 270 affiliates in 123 countries; over 150,000,000 members.

Publications. *World Youth*, monthly; *WFDY News*, semimonthly.

World Federation of Scientific Workers (WFSW)

History. The WFSW was founded in London in 1946 on the initiative of the (British) Association of Scientific Workers, with the aims of providing a liaison between organized scientific workers, improving their working conditions and promoting the peaceful application of scientific discoveries, but communist sympathizers soon obtained control.

Leadership. Jean-Marie Legay (France), pres.; R. Bird (Britain), g.s.

Structure. The general assembly, meeting every three years, elects an Executive Council of 30–35 members. Its headquarters are in London.

Membership. About 33 affiliates and 450,000 members in over 70 countries.

Publication. *Scientific World*, quarterly.

World Federation of Trade Unions (WFTU)

History. The WFTU was founded at a world congress of trade unions in Paris in 1945, with Sir Walter Citrine, then secretary of the (British) Trades Union Congress (TUC), as president, and originally consisted of 65 trade union organizations, representing 66,000,000 workers. As a result of friction between the communist and non-communist unions, however, the TUC, the (US) Congress of Industrial Organizations and the Dutch unions withdrew in 1949, and were quickly followed by most of the other Western trade union organizations. The French and Italian federations had already split into communist and non-communist organizations, only the former remaining in the WFTU. The seceding organizations subsequently formed the International Confederation of Free Trade Unions. The Yugoslav unions withdrew in 1950 in protest against the WFTU's support for Stalin's hostile policy towards Yugoslavia.

Expelled from France in 1951, the WFTU transferred its headquarters to Vienna. In 1956 it was again expelled, on the ground that it had not respected Austria's neutrality, and finally established its headquarters in Prague. The Italian General Confederation of Labour withdrew in 1978, in accordance with the Italian Communist Party's policy of independence from Moscow.

Leadership. Sándor Gáspár (Hungary), pres.; Ibrahim Zakariya (Sudan), g.s.

Structure. The congress, meeting every four years, elects the General Council, which elects the Executive Bureau and Secretariat.

Membership. 90 affiliates in 81 countries; 206,000,000 members. The great majority of the members are drawn from the (Soviet) All-Union Central Council of Trade Unions, with 130,000,000 members, and the trade union federations of other communist countries.

Publications. *World Trade Union Movement*, monthly; *Flashes from the Trade Unions*, weekly.

World Peace Council (WPC)

History. The WPC, founded at a congress held in Warsaw in 1950, established its headquarters in Paris, but was expelled from France in the following year. It then moved to Prague and in 1954 to Vienna, whence it was expelled in 1957 on the ground that its activities were incompatible with Austria's neutrality, and now has its headquarters in Helsinki.

Leadership. Romesh Chandra (India), pres.

Structure. The WPC meets annually and elects its Bureau and Secretariat.

Membership. More than 2,500 affiliates in 142 countries.

Publications. *New Perspectives*, bimonthly; *Peace Courier*, monthly.

SECTION TWO
COMMUNIST AND MARXIST PARTIES

1. Northern, Western and Southern Europe

2. Eastern Europe and the USSR

3. The Middle East and the Arab World

4. Asia and the Far East

5. Africa South of the Sahara

6. North America

7. Central America and the Caribbean

8. South America

9. Australasia and the Pacific

1. NORTHERN, WESTERN AND SOUTHERN EUROPE

Austria

Capital: Vienna   Pop. 7,579,000

The Austrian Social Democratic Party, founded in 1874, adopted a Marxist programme in 1889, and its theoreticians subsequently developed a distinctive system of thought known as Austro-Marxism which attempted to reconcile orthodox Marxism and revisionism. Following the abdication of the Emperor Karl in November 1918, Austria became a republic. After a period of coalition between the Social Democrats and the (Catholic) Christian Social Party in 1918–20, the latter emerged as the dominant party. The Christian Social Chancellor Engelbert Dollfuss ruled as a virtual dictator from 1933, and in the following year forcibly suppressed the Social Democratic Party. Occupied and annexed by Germany in 1938, Austria was liberated by the allies in 1945 and the republic re-established. The allied forces were withdrawn in 1955, when Austria declared its perpetual neutrality.

The Austrian Parliament consists of the 183-member National Council (*Nationalrat*), elected by proportional representation for a four-year term, and the 58-member Federal Council (*Bundesrat*), elected for a six-year term by the legislatures of the nine federal states. Austria was ruled by a coalition of the Austrian People's (Catholic), Socialist and Communist parties from 1945 to 1947; by a People's Party-Socialist coalition from 1947 to 1966; by the People's Party from 1966 to 1970; and by the Socialists from 1970 to 1983, when they formed a coalition with the Freedom (Liberal) Party.

Communist League of Austria
Kommunistische Bund Österreichs (KBÖ)

History. The KBÖ was founded in 1976 as a branch of the Communist League of West Germany (see under Federal Republic of Germany).

Leadership. Walter Lindner (ch.).

Orientation. Pro-Chinese.

Publication. *Klassenkampf* (Class Struggle), biweekly.

Communist Party of Austria
Kommunistische Partei Österreichs (KPÖ)

History. The KPÖ, founded in November 1918 by about 50 left-wing Social Democrats, rapidly reached 4,000 members, but an attempted uprising in Vienna in June 1919 failed completely. In the same year it became a founder member of the Comintern. After a period of internal dissension, it expanded its membership and influence from 1927 onwards, and obtained over 60,000 votes in the 1932 elections. It was banned in the following year, and when Dollfuss suppressed the Social Democratic Party in 1934 it took part in the fighting in Vienna. During the German occupation it organized national resistance, over 4,000 of its members being imprisoned.

The KPÖ was a co-founder, with the Socialist and Austrian People's parties, of the Second Republic, and during the years immediately after the war attained its greatest influence, its membership reaching 155,000. It won four seats in the *Nationalrat* in 1945, and was represented in the government until 1947. When the government increased food and other prices in 1950 it organized protest strikes and demonstrations, which the government denounced as an attempt to seize power. It won five seats in the 1949 elections, four in 1953 and three in 1956, in alliance with the Socialist Workers' Party, which had broken away from the Socialist Party and merged with the KPÖ in 1956.

After 1956 the KPÖ defined its policy as one of gradual and peaceful construction of socialism by parliamentary means. In 1967 it adopted a programme pledging support for the multiparty system and rejecting the term "dictatorship of the proletariat", and in the following year the Central Committee condemned the Soviet intervention in Czechoslovakia. The 1969 congress, however, approved a new programme which, while still envisaging a peaceful transition to socialism and a multiparty system, did not rule out the possibility of civil war and insisted that all parties must accept the socialist social system. A section of the party leadership was expelled in 1970 as anti-Soviet and "rightist", and in the following year the Central Committee repudiated its 1968 resolution on Czechoslovakia. The KPÖ has since pursued a consistently pro-Soviet policy.

Leadership. Franz Muhri (ch.).

Structure. The basic unit is the residential or workplace branch. The national congress, meeting every three years, elects a Central Committee of 64 members, which elects the 12-member Political Bureau and the three-member Secretariat. The party's youth organizations are the Communist Youth of Austria and the Communist Students' League. A court case in 1981 revealed that the KPÖ derives much of its finances from about 50 companies trading in coal and oil, with annual sales of nearly $500,000,000, which it acquired during the Soviet occupation of north-eastern Austria in 1945–55.

Membership. 12,000 (1983 estimate). Membership has steadily declined since 1955, and the majority of the members are over 50; support is strongest in Vienna.

Electoral influence. The KPÖ has not been represented in Parliament since 1959, and its vote has steadily declined since 1953. In the 1983 elections it fell to 31,408 (0.66 per cent).

Industrial influence. Communists operate inside the Socialist-controlled Austrian Trade Union Federation (*Österreichischer Gewerkschaftsbund,* ÖGB) through the Left Bloc Trade Union Fraction (*Fraktion Gewerkschaftliches Linksblock*), which is estimated to comprise 2.5 per cent of the 1,000,000 members of the ÖGB.

Orientation. Pro-Soviet.

Programme. The KPÖ advocates an "anti-monopolist democracy" that will eventually develop into socialism. Its ultimate aim is "the building of a socialist social system in accordance with general laws", which include "the establishment of the state power of the working class, the dictatorship of the proletariat and the broadest democracy for the working people, the guiding role of the Marxist–Leninist party on the basis of the closest alliance with the working class and all other working people, the nationalization of the fundamental means of production, a planned economy and the closest possible relations with the other socialist states".

Publications. Volksstimme (People's Voice), daily (16–17,000); *Weg und Ziel* (Path and Goal), monthly (4–5,000).

International affiliations. The KPÖ is represented on the editorial council of *World Marxist Review*, and maintains close relations with the Soviet-bloc parties.

League of Democratic Socialists
Bund Demokratischer Sozialisten (BDS)

History. This small group has close links with the Socialist Party of Great Britain (q.v.).

Orientation. Independent.

Publication. Internationales Freies Wort, quarterly.

International affiliations. World Socialist Movement.

Marxist–Leninist Party of Austria
Marxistisch–Leninistische Partei Österreichs (MLPÖ)

History. The MLPÖ was formed in 1966 as the Organization of Marxist–Leninists of Austria by Franz Strobl, who had been expelled from the Communist Party in 1963, and adopted its present name in 1967.

Leadership. Franz Strobl (first sec.).

Electoral influence. The MLPÖ contested a Vienna constituency in 1966, obtaining 486 votes.

Orientation. Pro-Chinese.

Programme. At its inaugural conference in 1967 the MLPÖ adopted a programme advocating the violent overthrow of capitalism and the establishment of the dictatorship of the proletariat.

Publication. Rote Fahne (Red Flag), bimonthly.

International affiliations. The MLPÖ has close links with the Chinese Communist Party.

Revolutionary Marxist Group
Gruppe Revolutionärer Marxisten (GRM)

History. Founded in 1972, the GRM contested the 1975 general election.

Leadership. Dr Hermann Dworczak.

Electoral influence. The GRM received 1,042 votes in Vienna in 1975, but in 1979 it failed to obtain the required number of signatures to qualify for participation in the elections.

Orientation. Trotskyist.

Publication. *Rotfront* (Red Front), monthly.

International affiliations. Fourth International, United Secretariat.

Belgium

Capital: Brussels   Pop. 9,920,000

Belgium was occupied by the Germans from 1940 to 1944, after King Leopold III had ordered the army to surrender. His action led to a crisis after the war, which ended only with his abdication in 1951 in favour of his son, King Baudouin. Since 1945 Belgium has been ruled by a succession of coalition governments formed from among the three main political tendencies—Christian Socials, Socialists and Liberals. The Belgian Parliament consists of the Chamber of Representatives, with 212 members elected for a four-year term by proportional representation, and the Senate, with 106 directly elected members, 50 elected by the provincial councils and 25 co-opted members, all of whom serve a four-year term.

Flemish (Dutch) is spoken in Flanders (the northern provinces of West Flanders, East Flanders, Antwerp, Limburg and the northern half of Brabant) and French in Wallonia (the southern provinces of Hainaut, Namur, Luxembourg, Liège and the southern half of Brabant), whilst Brussels, which lies in the northern half of Brabant, is bilingual. The three main tendencies, unlike the Marxist parties, are each divided into Flemish- and French-speaking parties. The linguistic question has been a source of controversy for many years, and has led to periodic outbreaks of violence. Plans for the establishment of regional governments and assemblies for Flanders, Wallonia and Brussels, in addition to the national government and Parliament, were approved in principle in 1978, but have not yet been fully implemented.

Communist Party of Belgium
Kommunistische Partij van België—Parti Communiste de Belgique (PCB)

History. The PCB was founded in 1921 by the merger of two left-wing groups which had broken away from the Belgian Workers' Party (later the Belgian Socialist Party), and first won two seats in the Chamber in 1925. Its membership and influence increased after its adoption of a Popular Front policy in 1935, and in the following year its parliamentary representation rose to nine seats. As a result of the leading role played by Communists in the wartime resistance movement, it won 12.7 per cent of the vote and 23 seats in the 1946 elections, and was represented in the government in 1946–47. It lost ground heavily in the years following, however, its membership falling from about 100,000 in 1945 to about 35,000 in 1950, and its parliamentary representation to four seats in 1954 and two in 1958. During the crisis leading to King Leopold's abdication it demanded the establishment of a republic; apparently as a result, its president, Julien Lahaut, was assassinated in 1950.

Since the 1960s the PCB has adopted a Eurocommunist position; it condemned the Soviet interventions in Czechoslovakia in 1968 and in Afghanistan in 1979 and the introduction of martial law in Poland in 1981, and has strongly criticized attacks on civil liberties in Eastern Europe. Its representation in the Chamber, after rising to six in 1965, fell to two in 1981, and in 1985 it lost its last remaining seats.

Leadership. Louis van Geyt (pres.); Claude Renard (vice-pres. and pres. of the French-speaking council); Jef Turf (vice-pres. and pres. of the Flemish-speaking council).

Structure. The basic units are the local sections and the workplace or university cells, which are organized into 24 district federations. There are three regional councils for Wallonia (13 federations), Flanders (10 federations) and Brussels. The national congress, meeting every three years, elects the president and a Central Committee of 72 members (37 from the French-speaking and 35 from the Flemish-speaking wing), which elects the Political Bureau of 14 members and the Secretariat. Auxiliary organizations are the Communist Youth of Belgium, the National Union of Communist Students and the (children's) Union of Belgian Pioneers.

Membership. 10,000 (1985 estimate). About two-thirds of the members are drawn from the French-speaking region, which includes the industrial and mining provinces of Liège and Hainaut.

Electoral influence. The PCB share of the vote fell from 138,992 (2.3 per cent) in the 1981 elections to 71,683 (1.2 per cent) in 1985.

Industrial influence. Communists play an important part in the Socialist-controlled General Workers' Federation of Belgium (*Fédération Génerale du Travail de Belgique*), especially in the Liège area.

Orientation. Eurocommunist, although there is a strong pro-Soviet element in the party, especially in Liège.

Programme. The PCB advocates the nationalization of the principal banks; control of the movement of capital; the acquisition by the state of a majority interest in enterprises of national importance; the conclusion of long-term trade agreements with the socialist and third-world countries; a public works programme to reduce unemployment; measures to assist small and middle-sized enterprises and small farmers; participation by the workers in the management of nationalized industries; and the establishment of regional councils with the powers and means to contribute to the balanced development of the regions. It regards these measures as a stage on "the peaceful and democratic road" to a distinctively Belgian form of socialism, which would nationalize the large-scale means of production and exchange, develop the economy and extend democratic liberties at all levels. In foreign policy it advocates the gradual abolition of both NATO and the Warsaw Pact and the ending of the arms race.

Publications. Le Drapeau Rouge (The Red Flag), French-language daily (14,500); De Rode Vaan (The Red Flag), Flemish-language weekly (11,000); *Les Cahiers Communistes* (Communist Notebooks), French-language monthly; *Vlaams Marxistisch Tijdschrift* (Flemish Marxist Chronicle), Flemish-language quarterly.

International affiliations. The PCB is represented on the editorial council of *World Marxist Review*. It maintains close relations with the French and other Eurocommunist parties and with the Yugoslav League of Communists, and has contacts with the Soviet-bloc parties. Relations with the Chinese party, suspended since 1965, were resumed in 1983.

Labour Party of Belgium
Partij van de Arbeid van België—Parti du Travail de Belgique (PTB)

History. The PTB was founded by former Flemish students of the Catholic University of Louvain as All Power to the Workers (*Alle Macht aan de Arbeiders— Tout le pouvoir aux ouvriers*), and adopted its present name in 1979. It has contested elections since 1974.

Leadership. Ludo Martens (1.).

Membership. Not known, but it is believed to be the largest party to the left of the Communist Party. It is well established in Antwerp, especially among the dockworkers.

Electoral influence. In the 1985 elections the PTB obtained 45,685 votes (0.8 per cent).

Orientation. Pro-Chinese.

Programme. The PTB is opposed to the "degeneration" of the Soviet Union and the Communist Party of Belgium, to state capitalism and "social fascism", and to the imperialism of the two superpowers, especially the Soviet Union. It advocates struggle against capitalism by both legal means, including elections, and "mass action". It opposes isolated acts of violence, but not the use of force against any force used against the workers by the bourgeoisie.

Publications. *Alle Macht aan de Arbeiders*, Flemish-language weekly; *Tout le pouvoir aux ouvriers*, French-language weekly.

International affiliations. The PTB has contacts with China, although it is not officially recognized by the Chinese Communist Party.

Marxist-Leninist Communist Party of Belgium
Parti Communiste Marxiste-Léniniste de Belgique (PCMLB)

History. The PCMLB, one of the oldest pro-Chinese parties in Europe, was founded in 1963 as the Communist Party of Belgium, Marxist-Leninist, by a group of Maoists who had been expelled from the Communist Party. In 1967 it split over the Cultural Revolution in China, its founder and first secretary, Jacques Grippa, being expelled for supporting Liu Shaoqi. It adopted its present name in 1970.

Leadership. Fernand Lefebvre (first sec.).

Membership. Under 100, mostly in Brussels and Liège.

Orientation. Pro-Chinese.

Publication. *Voix Communiste* (Communist Voice), weekly.

International affiliations. The PCMLB is officially recognized by the Chinese Communist Party.

Workers' Revolutionary League
Revolutionaire Arbeiders Liga—Ligue Révolutionnaire des Travailleurs (LRT)

History. The LRT was formed in 1971 by the merger of the Socialist Young Guards, a student organization, with a number of smaller Trotskyist groups.

Membership. At most 1,000.

Electoral influence. The LRT received 12,333 votes (0.2 per cent) in the 1981 general elections.

Orientation. Trotskyist.

Publications. *La Gauche* (The Left), French-language weekly; *Rood* (Red), Flemish-language weekly.

International affiliations. Fourth International, United Secretariat.

Terrorist Organizations

Fighting Communist Cells
Cellules Combattantes Communistes (CCC)

History. The CCC emerged in October 1984 with a series of bombings of the premises of multinational companies supplying arms or equipment to NATO and offices of the ruling Christian Social and Liberal parties. It was subsequently responsible for six explosions in December which damaged widely scattered sections of NATO's fuel pipeline, and for a number of bomb attacks in 1985 on NATO headquarters, government offices and employers' associations. A series of arrests of suspected CCC activists followed in December 1985.

Leadership. The suspected leader of the CCC, Pierre Carrette, who had run a secret printing press for the French organization Direct Action, went underground in 1984 but was one of those arrested in December 1985.

International affiliations. The CCC is believed to have links with Direct Action and the West German Red Army Faction.

Revolutionary Front for Proletarian Action
Front Révolutionnaire d'Action Prolétarienne (FRAP)

History. This hitherto unknown group claimed responsibility for bomb attacks in April 1985 on the parliamentary secretariat of the North Atlantic Assembly and the Brussels offices of the West German company AEG Telefunken. A suspected FRAP activist, Luc Van Acker, was arrested in January 1986 and charged with criminal conspiracy.

Cyprus

Capital: Nicosia   Pop. 662,000

Cyprus, which since 1570 had been ruled by Turkey, was placed under British administration in 1878 and annexed by Britain in 1914. A Legislative Council established in 1925 was abolished after an uprising in 1931 in support of union with Greece (*enosis*). A terrorist campaign launched in 1955 by the right-wing pro-Greek EOKA organization continued until 1958, and led to violent clashes between the Greek and Turkish communities. Under an agreement between Britain, Greece and Turkey, Cyprus became an independent republic in 1960 with a Greek President (Archbishop Makarios), a Turkish Vice-President, a

Cabinet containing representatives of both communities and a House of Representatives composed of 35 Greeks and 15 Turks (increased from the 1985 elections to 56 and 24 respectively). The agreement also provided for the retention of British bases on the island.

After further communal fighting in 1963 the Turkish Cypriots withdrew from the government and the House of Representatives, and have since held separate elections in their community. Supporters of *enosis* carried out a coup in 1974 with the Greek government's support and held power for eight days, whereupon Turkish troops invaded Cyprus and occupied the north of the island. A Turkish Cypriot Federated State was proclaimed in 1975 in the areas under Turkish occupation, and elections were held in the following year to a 40-member Legislative Assembly. The Assembly declared the Turkish Republic of North Cyprus an independent state in 1983, but the new state was officially recognized only by Turkey.

Progressive Party of the Working People
Anorthotikon Komma Ergazomenou Laou (AKEL)

History. The Communist Party of Cyprus, founded in 1926, was banned by the British authorities in 1933, many of its members being imprisoned. AKEL was founded in 1941 as its legal wing, and the two parties existed side by side until 1944, when the Communist Party was merged with AKEL. In the 1946 municipal elections AKEL won control of Nicosia and all the large towns.

While consistently opposing British rule, AKEL vacillated for some years between demands for union with Greece and for complete independence. It adopted a pro-*enosis* policy in 1949, and was banned in 1955, when 135 of its leading members were arrested. It condemned the EOKA campaign as "adventurist", however, and in 1958 a number of Communists were murdered by EOKA as "collaborators". The ban on AKEL was gradually relaxed in consequence, and was lifted in 1959.

Since 1960 AKEL has supported the policy of independence and non-alignment pursued by Archbishop Makarios and his successor, President Spyros Kyprianou. It contested the 1976 elections in alliance with the (centre-right) Democratic Front and the (socialist) United Democratic Union of the Centre, but fought the 1981 elections independently. In the 1983 presidential election it supported Kyprianou's candidature, on the basis of a minimum programme. Following disagreements between the President and the AKEL leaders over the handling of negotiations with the Turkish community, however, he terminated the co-operation agreement between his Democratic Party and AKEL in December 1984. In an attempt to force him to resign, AKEL and the conservative Democratic Rally secured in November 1985 the adoption of a motion for a premature dissolution of Parliament, but elections held in the following month proved disastrous for AKEL, whose vote dropped heavily.

Leadership. Ezekias Papaionnou (g.s.).

Structure. AKEL is organized in residential and workplace branches, representatives of which elect town and rural area committees. These in turn are subordinate to provincial committees, elected every three years. The congress, meeting every four years, elects the Central Committee, which elects the Political Bureau of 13 members and the Secretariat of three members. Auxiliary bodies include the United Democratic Youth Organization, with 10,000 members, and the Pan-Cypriot Workers' Federation (see below). AKEL derives much of its finances from enterprises which it controls, such as the Popular Distiller's Company and the People's Coffee Grinding Company, and has been described as "probably the major employer on the island".

Membership. 14,000 (1982 claim). AKEL is the largest party in Cyprus, and in proportion to the adult population is one of the largest communist parties in the non-communist world. 80 per cent of the members are Greeks, and about two-thirds are industrial workers and employees, the remainder being peasants, artisans, small businessmen and members of the professions. The Union of Greek Cypriots in England, the London branch of AKEL, has about 1,200 members.

Electoral influence. In the 1981 elections AKEL received 95,302 votes (32.8 per cent) and won 12 of the 35 seats in the House of Representatives. In 1985, however, its share of the vote fell to 27.4 per cent. and it obtained 15 seats in a House enlarged to 56 Greek members.

Industrial influence. AKEL controls the Pan-Cypriot Workers' Federation, the main trade union organization, which has about 45,000 members.

Orientation. Pro-Soviet. AKEL supported the Soviet intervention in Czechoslovakia in 1968 and in Afghanistan in 1979 and the declaration of martial law in Poland in 1981.

Programme. AKEL's policy is dictated by the need to secure a settlement of the constitutional question. After the conclusion of an electoral agreement with President Kyprianou's Democratic Party (DIKO) in 1982, AKEL stated that although the minimum programme included measures to reduce unemployment, the inflation rate and the deficit in the balance of payments, its aim at this stage was not to change the social system but "to make Cyprus truly independent, federated, non-aligned and demilitarized", and that the interests of the national bourgeoisie, represented by DIKO, and the working class were identical. In foreign policy it advocates the removal of all foreign troops and foreign bases, the ending of Cyprus' links with the European Communities and the strengthening of relations with the socialist, non-aligned and Arab countries.

Publications. *Kharavyi* (Dawn), daily (13,500); *Demokratia*, weekly.

International affiliations. AKEL is represented on the editorial council of *World Marxist Review*, and maintains close relations with the Soviet-bloc, Greek, Turkish and Arab Communist parties.

Turkish Republic of North Cyprus

Republican Turkish Party
Cumhuriyetçi Türk Partisi (CTP)

History. The CTP was founded in 1970 by Ahmed Mithat Berberoghlou, who unsuccessfully opposed Rauf Denktash in the 1973 election of the Vice-President of Cyprus. Its chairman, Özker Özgür, opposed Denktash in the 1976 election of the President of the Turkish Federated State of Cyprus. It won two of the 40 seats in the 1976 elections to the Legislative Assembly, and six in the 1981 elections. In a referendum held in March 1985 on the new constitution of the Turkish Republic, which it described as repressive and militaristic, it campaigned unsuccessfully for a "no" vote. Özgür again opposed Denktash in the presidential election in June, receiving 18.4 per cent of the vote. In the legislature elections in the same month the CTP won 12 of the 50 seats.

Leadership. Özker Özgür (ch.); Naci Usar (g.s.).

51

Structure. The CTP is organized in four districts, from which 12 elected members, together with the chairman and the members of the Central Committee, constitute the Party Council. The general congress is the supreme body.

Membership. 2,500 (1984 claim).

Electoral influence. The CTP's share of the vote rose from 15.1 per cent in the 1981 elections to 21 per cent in 1985.

Orientation. The CTP, which calls itself socialist, anti-imperialist and for the non-aligned movement, has been variously described as orthodox communist and left-wing socialist.

Programme. The CTP formerly advocated that Cyprus should become an independent, non-aligned, bicommunal federal republic, but supported the establishment of the Turkish Republic in 1983.

Publication. *Yenidüzen* (New Order), weekly.

Socialist Salvation (or Communal Liberation) Party
Toplumcu Kurtulus Partisi (TKP)

History. Founded in 1976, the TKP first contested elections in that year, becoming the second largest party in the Legislative Assembly with six seats. Its candidate, Ziya Rizki, took second place in the 1981 presidential election, and in the same year it won 13 Assembly seats. Its leader, Alpay Durduran, unsuccessfully contested the 1985 presidential election, taking third place with 9.2 per cent of the vote. After the legislature elections, in which it won 10 seats, it entered a coalition government with the centrist National Unity Party.

Leadership. Alpay Durduran (l.); Mehmet Altinay (g.s.).

Electoral influence. The TKP's share of the vote fell from 28.6 per cent in the 1981 elections to 16 per cent in 1985.

Orientation. The TKP describes itself as left of centre, but its opponents maintain that it is controlled by Maoist elements.

Programme. The TKP formerly advocated an independent, bizonal federal state of Cyprus free of British bases, but voted for the establishment of the Turkish Republic in 1983. It claims that its programme is based on Kemal Atatürk's reforms and social democratic principles.

Denmark

Capital: Copenhagen   Pop. 5,100,000

Since 1924 the Social Democrats have been the dominant party in Denmark, but after the introduction of the proportional representation system no party has ever obtained an absolute majority in Parliament. After the war, during which Denmark was occupied by Germany, the Social Democrats were in power, either as a minority government or in coalition with other parties, for most of the period from 1947 to 1982, when a centre-right coalition took office. The

Parliament (*Folketing*) consists of 179 members elected for a four-year term, 175 from metropolitan Denmark and two each from the Faroe Islands and Greenland. Under the electoral law a party must obtain 2 per cent of the vote to qualify for representation.

Communist Party of Denmark
Danmarks Kommunistiske Parti (DKP)

History. The DKP was founded in 1919 by left-wing Social Democrats and Syndicalists as the Left Socialist Party, and assumed its present name after joining the Comintern in the following year. It first won two seats in the *Folketing* in 1932, and increased its representation to three in 1939. During the German occupation it was engaged in active resistance as an illegal party , and in 1944 organized a general strike in Copenhagen which forced the German authorities to grant a number of concessions. Its following and prestige in consequence greatly increased, and it was represented by three ministers in a coalition government formed in May 1945. In elections held in the following October it obtained 255,000 votes (12.5 per cent) and 18 of the 149 seats in the *Folketing*, and by 1946 its membership had risen from the pre-war figure of 2,500 to 60,000. Its parliamentary representation, however, fell to nine seats in 1947 and to seven in 1950, and its membership to 22,500 in 1950. Following an increase in the size of the *Folketing* to 175 metropolitan seats, it won eight seats in 1953 on a reduced vote, and six in 1957.

The DKP passed through a crisis in 1956–58, after Aksel Larsen (its chairman since 1932) criticized the Soviet intervention in Hungary and advocated that it should refuse to support Soviet policies "slavishly". He was expelled for "Titoist revisionism" in 1958, and together with a number of his supporters, who had also been expelled or had resigned, formed the Socialist People's Party (see below). The DKP lost all its seats in the 1960 elections, and except for a short period in 1970–71, when a Left Socialist member defected to it, was not represented in the *Folketing* until 1973, when it won six seats. It obtained a seventh seat in 1975, but lost all its seats in 1979, and failed to recover them in the 1981 and 1984 elections. It won a seat in the 1979 elections to the European Parliament, however, which it contested as part of an alliance called the People's Movement against the Common Market, and retained it in the 1984 elections.

Leadership. Jørgen Jensen (ch.); Poul Emanuel (sec.).

Structure. The DKP has over 200 residential and workplace branches, which are grouped in 12 regional organizations in Copenhagen, 15 in its suburbs and 13 in the provinces. The congress, meeting every three years, elects the Central Committee (51 full and 15 candidate members), which elects the Executive Committee of 16 members, chairman and secretariat. The Communist Youth of Denmark and the Communist Students of Denmark are auxiliary organizations.

Membership. 10,000 (1985 claim). The DKP draws its support mainly from industrial workers, especially in the Copenhagen area.

Electoral influence. In the 1984 elections the DKP obtained 23,085 votes (0.7 per cent), its lowest vote since the war.

Industrial influence. The trade union federation (*Landsorganisationen*) is closely linked with the Social Democratic Party, but communists exercise considerable influence in certain sections, notably the metalworkers', typographers' and construction workers' unions. The DKP claimed in 1984 that its members held 3,000 elected posts in the trade union movement.

Orientation. Pro-Soviet. Although the DKP normally supports Soviet policies, it has criticized the Soviet intervention in Czechoslovakia and the persecution of dissidents in Eastern Europe.

Programme. The DKP advocates a "democratic policy directed against monopoly capitalism", the nationalization of industry, a planned economy, democratization of the constitution to permit full participation of the working class and their organizations in public affairs, and freedom for all parties which accept socialism. As immediate measures it calls for a 35-hour working week without reductions in pay and increased public investment in housing, public transport and education. In foreign affairs it opposes Danish membership of NATO and the European Communities, and proposes the formation of a neutral Northern Europe without nuclear weapons or bases.

Publications. Land og Folk (Country and People), daily (10,000); *Tiden-Verden rundt* (The Time-Around the World), monthly (3,200).

International affiliations. The DKP is represented on the editorial council of *World Marxist Review*, and has close ties with the Soviet-bloc parties, especially with the Socialist Unity Party of East Germany.

Communist Party of Denmark Marxist-Leninist
Danmarks Kommunistiske Parti Marxister-Leninister (DKP/ML)

History. Founded in 1978, the DKP/ML was refused electoral registration under that name and is obliged to contest elections as the Marxistisk-Leninistisk Parti (MLP).

Leadership. Klaus Riis (1st sec.).

Electoral influence. The MLP obtained fewer than 1,000 votes in the 1984 elections.

Orientation. Pro-Albanian.

Publications. Arbejderen (The Worker), daily; *Partiets Vej* (The Party's Way), quarterly.

International affiliation. The DKP/ML is officially recognized by the Albanian Party of Labour.

Communist Workers' Party
Kommunistisk Arbejderparti (KAP)

History. The KAP has its origins in a pro-Maoist group who defected from the Communist Party in the mid-1960s and in 1968 formed the Communist League (Marxist-Leninist) which became the KAP in 1976 (then under the leadership of Benito Scocozza). It first contested elections in 1979.

Leadership. Svend Aage Madsen (l.).

Electoral influence. The KAP received 4,223 votes (0.1 per cent) in the 1981 general election, but failed in 1984 to collect the required number of signatures ($\frac{1}{175}$th of the total valid vote in the previous election) to appear on the ballot. It has decided not to make this attempt in the next elections.

Orientation. Formerly pro-Chinese, now independent Maoist.

Publication. Arbejderavisen (Workers' News), weekly; *Kommunistisk Tidsskrift* (Communist Chronicle), quarterly.

Left Socialist Party
Venstresocialisterne (VS)

History. The VS was formed in 1967 by six *Folketing* members, who resigned from the Socialist People's Party in protest against its support for the Social Democratic government's policy of wage restraint. Except for the years 1971–75, when it was not represented in the *Folketing*, since 1967 it has held between four and six seats.

Leadership. Collective, the most influential member being Preben Wilhjelm.

Membership. 1,400. The VS enjoys substantial support among government employees, students and younger workers.

Electoral influence. The VS obtained 2.7 per cent of the vote and five seats in the 1984 elections. It is also represented on several city councils (with particular strength in Copenhagen) despite losing ground in the November 1985 local elections.

Orientation. Broadly Eurocommunist.

Programme. The VS occupies an intermediate position between the Socialist People's Party and the Communist Party, in common with both of which it opposes Danish membership of NATO and the European Communities. While not opposed in principle to co-operation with the Social Democratic Party, it demands greater concessions from the latter than does the Socialist People's Party (see below).

Socialist People's Party
Socialistisk Folkeparti (SF)

History. The SF was founded in 1958 by Aksel Larsen after his expulsion from the Communist Party, and won 11 seats in the 1960 elections. In the 1966–67 *Folketing*, in which it held 20 seats, it supported the minority Social Democratic government, but this arrangement broke down when its left wing defected to form the Left Socialist Party. The SF again supported a minority Social Democratic government in 1971–73. Its parliamentary representation fluctuated during the period 1968–81 between seven and 17 seats, but in the 1981 and 1984 elections it won 21. It also won a seat in the European Parliament in the 1979 and 1984 elections (and in 1985 was allotted a further seat following Greenland's withdrawal from the European Community).

Leadership. Gert Petersen (ch.); Lillian Ubbesen (sec.).

Membership. About 8,000.

Electoral influence. In the 1984 elections the SF received 11.5 per cent of the vote.

Industrial influence. The SF has some support in the trade unions, especially among provincial white-collar government employees.

Orientation. Eurocommunist.

Programme. The SF describes itself as a Marxist party, which works for socialism on the basis of the national tradition of parliamentary democracy. In foreign policy it opposes Danish membership of NATO and advocates neutrality and unilateral disarmament. It also opposes Danish membership of the European Communities, but favours less formal European political co-operation.

Publication. The party newspaper, *Socialistisk Dagblad* (Socialist Daily), ceased publication in 1982 for financial reasons.

International affiliations. The SF has close ties with the Socialist Left Party in Norway, the Left Party—Communists in Sweden and the Pacifist Socialist Party of the Netherlands, and maintains friendly relations with the Italian Communist Party. Its representatives in the European Parliament joined the Communist and Allies group, which also includes the French and Italian Communist members.

Socialist Workers' Party
Socialistisk Arbejderparti (SAP)

History. Formerly known as the Revolutionary Socialist Alliance, the SAP adopted its present name in 1980, and first contested elections in 1981. For electoral purposes it is obliged to use the name *Internationalen-Socialistisk Arbejderparti*.

Leadership. Collective.

Membership. 200.

Electoral influence. The SAP received 2,200 votes (less than 0.1 per cent) in the 1984 elections.

Orientation. Trotskyist.

Publication. *Klassekampen* (Class Struggle), weekly.

International affiliations. Fourth International, United Secretariat.

Faroe Islands

Capital: Tórshavn   Pop. 45,000

The Faroe Islands, though forming part of the Kingdom of Denmark, have their own government, which deals with internal affairs, and (currently) a 32-member Parliament, the *Lagting*. They return two representatives to the *Folketing*.

Faroese Communist Party

History. This party formed the Faroes section of the Communist Party of Denmark until 1975, when it became independent.

Leadership. Egon Thomsen (l.).

Electoral influence. The party failed to obtain the few hundred signatures necessary to appear on the ballot in the 1978 and 1980 elections to the *Lagting*.

Publication. *Friu Föroyar*, weekly.

Greenland

Capital: Nuuk (Godthåb)   Pop. 52,000

Since 1979 Greenland, while remaining part of the Kingdom of Denmark, has had its own government and Parliament (*Landsting*), which are responsible for internal affairs, and has also been represented by two members in the *Folketing*. Under the system of proportional representation employed the number of members in the *Landsting* may vary from 23 to 26.

Eskimo Community
Inuit Ataqatigiit (IA)

History. Founded in 1978, the IA campaigned unsuccessfully for a "no" vote in a referendum held in the following year on the Danish government's proposals for internal autonomy for Greenland. After the 1983 elections, in which it won two seats, it held the balance of power in the *Landsting* between the socialist *Siumut* and the non-socialist *Atassut*, each of which had won 12 seats, and by its support enabled the former to retain office. When new elections in 1984 again resulted in a tie between the two major parties, the IA, which had increased its representation to three, joined the *Siumut* in forming a coalition government.

Leadership. Aqqaluk Lynge (ch.); Ivalu Egede (sec.).

Electoral influence. The IA increased its share of the vote from 10.7 per cent in the 1983 elections to 12 per cent in 1984.

Programme. The IA advocates independence from Denmark, the restriction of Greenland citizenship to those with an Eskimo parent and the closure of US bases in Greenland. It also stands for the principle of property being communal.

Finland

Capital: Helsinki   Pop. 4,873,000

Formerly a Swedish dependency, Finland was ceded to Russia in 1809, while continuing to enjoy internal autonomy. The Finnish Social Democratic Party, formed in 1899 as the Finnish Labour Party, adopted a Marxist programme in 1903, and took a leading part in the agitation which forced the Russian government in 1906 to agree to the establishment of a single-chamber Parliament elected by universal suffrage. The independence of Finland was recognized by the Bolshevik government in 1917, but was followed in the early months of 1918 by a civil war between "reds" and "whites" which ended in the victory of the latter, over 8,000 "reds" being executed. Soviet demands for territorial concessions to ensure the security of Leningrad led to a war in 1939–40 in which Finland was defeated. When Germany invaded the Soviet Union in 1941 Finland entered the war as the ally of the Axis powers, but was forced to sue for peace in 1944. Since the armistice Finland has been ruled by a succession of coalition governments usually including at least two of the four main parties (the Social Democrats, the liberal Centre Party, the conservative National Coalition Party and the

Communist-dominated Finnish People's Democratic League), and has observed a foreign policy of strict neutrality.

The Parliament (*Eduskunta*) consists of 200 members elected by a proportional representation system for a four-year term. The President is elected for a six-year term by an electoral college chosen by universal suffrage.

Communist Party of Finland
Suomen Kommunistinen Puolue (SKP)

History. The SKP was formed in Moscow in 1918 by left-wing Social Democratic refugees from the white terror which followed the civil war in Finland, including Otto Kuusinen, and in the following year became a founder-member of the Comintern. A front organization, the Socialist Workers' Party, was established inside Finland in 1920, winning 27 seats in the 1922 elections, but was driven underground by anti-communist laws introduced in 1930. The SKP meanwhile retained its headquarters in Moscow, and many of its members suffered in the Soviet purges of 1936–39. During the war with the Soviet Union in 1939–40 a "Finnish People's Government" headed by Kuusinen was set up at the border town of Terijoki, but it disappeared when peace was signed. When the war was renewed in 1941 Communists were sent to concentration camps, and many were shot for treason.

Following the armistice with the Soviet Union, the SKP was legalized for the first time in 1944, and allied with the left wing of the Social Democratic Party to form the Finnish People's Democratic League (SKDL—see below). This alliance has continued to operate ever since, and SKDL ministers, including Communists, have served in coalition governments in 1944–48, 1966–70, 1970–71, 1975–76 and 1977–82.

Since 1966 the SKP has been divided into a Eurocommunist or moderate wing and a pro-Soviet or "hardline" wing, the former being led by Aarne Saarinen, who was elected party chairman in that year, and the latter by Taisto Sinisalo. In 1968 the majority of the Central Committee refused to approve the Soviet intervention in Czechoslovakia, and in the following year the party congress rejected the concept of the dictatorship of the proletariat and adopted a programme for the achievement of socialism by peaceful and democratic means. An open split was averted only through the mediation of the Soviet party, Saarinen and Sinisalo being elected chairman and vice-chairman respectively at an extraordinary congress in 1970, which decided that membership of the Central Committee, Political Bureau and Secretariat should be divided between the two factions in proportion to their strength. Controversy over policy and doctrine nevertheless continued; the hardliners opposed the SKDL's entry into the government in 1975, and 11 members were suspended from the SKDL parliamentary group in 1981 after they had voted against the budget.

An extraordinary congress in 1982 elected a Central Committee containing a Eurocommunist majority, meetings of which were boycotted by the hardliners. In their absence the committee elected Jouko Kajanoja and Arvo Aalto, who although Eurocommunists were acceptable to both wings, as chairman and general secretary, but negotiations continued for three months before a compromise was reached whereby a hardliner became vice-chairman and the Political Bureau was expanded to 11 members, four of whom were hardliners. In the 1983 elections the hardliners put forward a separate list in the Lapland electoral district; one member was elected, who was subsequently admitted to the SKDL parliamentary group. At a congress in May 1984 the hardliners rejected the Eurocommunists' terms for a new Central Committee; as a result, a Central

Committee and Political Bureau composed entirely of Eurocommunists were elected, and Aalto became chairman and Aarne Aitamurto general secretary. The hardline wing put forward its own candidates in local elections in October 1984, with the result that the SKDL lost a number of seats, whereupon the majority faction retaliated by establishing its own organizations in the districts controlled by the hardliners.

An extraordinary congress held in March 1985 unanimously re-elected Aalto chairman, elected Esko Vainionpää general secretary and amended the party rules to allow the Central Committee, instead of the congress as previously, to disband local or district organizations. The hardline wing, which had originally demanded the holding of the congress, boycotted it as a protest against the formation of parallel organizations, and refused to recognize its decisions. The Central Committee in September 1985 ordered the hardline faction to disband its rival organization within a month and close its newspaper; when this ultimatum was rejected, it expelled the eight minority-controlled district organizations.

Leadership. Arvo Aalto (ch.); Esko Vainionpää (g.s.).

Structure. The 1,350 residential and workplace branches are organized in 17 regional federations. The congress, normally meeting every three years, elects the Central Committee, which elects the chairman, vice-chairman, Political Bureau and Secretariat. The Central Committee elected in 1984 consisted of 50 full and 15 alternate members and the Political Bureau of nine members. Auxiliary bodies are the Finnish Democratic Youth League and the Women's Organization.

Membership. 34,000 (1985 estimate). The membership is mainly drawn from the lower-paid workers in the southern industrial centres and the northern rural areas, but in recent years the number of white-collar workers and intellectuals among the members has increased.

Electoral influence. See under "Finnish People's Democratic League" below.

Orientation. About 60 per cent of the membership are believed to be Eurocommunists and about 40 per cent pro-Soviet hardliners.

Programme. The programme adopted in 1969 states that "the socialist revolution will be realized in Finland in a peaceful and national way"; that "the transition to socialism will take place through social and economic reforms which will effect fundamental changes in the structure of the economy and social life and in power and ownership"; and that it will be possible "only in a situation in which the great majority of the people, and especially the working class, recognize the necessity for it and are prepared to take part in mass action against the reactionary forces".

Publications. *Kansan Uutiset* (People's News), daily (53,000); *Folktidningen* (People's News), Swedish-language weekly (4,000); *Kommunisti*, monthly. The hardline faction publishes the daily *Tiedonantaja*.

International affiliations. The SKP is represented on the editorial council of *World Marxist Review*, and maintains close relations with the Soviet Communist Party, which has consistently exercised its influence in support of the hardline faction. The Communist parties of Finland, Sweden, Norway and Denmark regularly exchange information, and their leaders meet periodically to co-ordinate their policies.

Finnish People's Democratic League
Suomen Kansan Demokraattinen Liitto (SKDL)

History. During the war with the Soviet Union in 1941–44 the left wing of the Social Democratic Party was expelled because of its opposition to the war; after the armistice it united with the Communists to form the SKDL, which won 45 seats in the 1945 elections and took part in a coalition government in 1944–48. In the 1958 elections it obtained the highest vote (23.17 per cent) and became the largest parliamentary group, with 50 seats, but its proposal that the socialist parties, which together had a majority in Parliament, should form a government was rejected by the Social Democratic Party and the independent Social Democrats. The SKDL subsequently served in centre-left coalition governments in 1966–70, 1970–71, 1975–76 and 1977–82. In the 1983 elections its representation fell from 35 to 26 seats, the smallest number which it had yet won.

Leadership. Esko Helle (ch.).

Membership. 172,000 (1984 claim).

Electoral influence. In the 1983 elections the SKDL obtained 400,930 votes (13.5 per cent).

Orientation. Eurocommunist. Although the Communist Party forms part of the SKDL and supplies most of its members of Parliament, the League has its own organization and programme, which is more moderate than the Communist Party's, and has successfully resisted attempts by the hardline Communists to obtain control of its organization.

Publications. *Kansan Tahto*, daily; *Hämeen Yhteistyö*, daily.

Marxist–Leninist Groups of Finland

History. This organization, founded in 1968 by dissident members of the Communist Party and the Finnish People's Democratic League, stages occasional anti-Soviet demonstrations, which are regularly reported in the Chinese press, but exercises little political influence.

Orientation. Pro-Chinese.

Publications. *Lakakuu*; *Aamulehti*.

France

Capital: Paris   Pop. 54,540,000

The French Socialist Party was formed in 1905 by the union of a Marxist party led by Jules Guesde and a non-Marxist party led by Jean Jaurès; officially called the French Section of the Workers' (i.e. Second) International (SFIO), it adopted an essentially Marxist programme. On the extreme left, however, the Marxists were less influential than the revolutionary syndicalists, who controlled the *Confédération Générale du Travail* (CGT) and advocated industrial rather than political action. The First World War, in which the majority of both the Socialist Party and the CGT leaders supported the war effort, split both organizations and led to the formation of the Communist Party.

After the war France was ruled by a succession of coalition governments, mostly of the right or right-centre. Fascist riots in Paris in 1934 were followed by the formation of the Popular Front of Communists, Socialists and Radicals, which was in power from 1936 to 1938, when the defection of the Radicals led to its collapse. War was declared on Germany in September 1939, but in June 1940 an armistice was signed after the Germans had overrun northern France. While the Germans occupied the north, including Paris, an extreme right-wing government at Vichy headed by Marshal Pétain ruled the rest of France. In London, however, General de Gaulle established the Free French movement to continue the struggle, and inside France active resistance was maintained until the allied landings in 1944.

The constitution of the Fourth Republic, adopted in 1946, vested supreme power in the National Assembly. The exclusion of the Communists, the largest party, from government after 1947 resulted in a series of weak governments, and the Algerian war led to a crisis in May 1958 which enabled de Gaulle to take power. The new constitution of the Fifth Republic greatly increased the powers of the President, who was to be elected for a seven-year term by an electoral college of members of Parliament and local councils; an amendment adopted in 1962 provided for his election by universal suffrage. De Gaulle was elected President in 1958 and re-elected in 1965, whilst Gaullist majorities were returned in elections in 1958, 1962 and 1967. Following student riots and a general strike in May 1968 new elections were held, which greatly increased the Gaullist majority. President de Gaulle resigned in 1969, and was succeeded by his former prime minister, Georges Pompidou. Elections in 1973 and 1978 again produced right-wing majorities, and when President Pompidou died in 1974 he was succeeded by the conservative centrist Valéry Giscard d'Estaing. In 1981, however, the Socialist leader, François Mitterrand, was elected President and called Assembly elections, which gave the Socialists an absolute majority.

The National Assembly consists of 577 members elected for five years, including 11 from the Overseas Departments (French Guiana, Guadeloupe, Martinique, Réunion, and St Pierre and Miquelon) and six from the Overseas Territories (French Polynesia, New Caledonia, the Wallis and Fortuna Islands, and Mayotte). Having for many years enjoyed an electoral system based on single-member constituencies, France reverted to a method of proportional representation for the 1986 National Assembly elections, in which the right-wing parties obtained a majority.

Communist Combat Organization
Organisation Combat Communiste (OCC)

History. The OCC was formed in 1974 by a group which had broken away from the "opportunist" Workers' Struggle organization.

Electoral influence. The OCC rejects participation in elections.

Orientation. Dissident Trotskyist. The OCC rejects the orthodox Trotskyist view that the Soviet Union is a degenerate workers' state, and maintains that there is no truly socialist country in the world.

Communist Committees for Self-management
Comités Communistes pour l'Autogestion (CCA)

History. The CCA was founded in 1976 by dissident sections of the Revolutionary Communist League and the Unified Socialist Party. It contested the 1978 elections in alliance with the Revolutionary Communist League and the Communist Organization of Workers, but fought the 1981 elections alone, putting forward 83 candidates.

Membership. 500.

Orientation. Trotskyist.

Programme. The CCA lays strong emphasis on workers' control of enterprises.

Communist Organization of France—Marxist-Leninist
Organisation Communiste de France—Marxiste-Léniniste (OCF–ML)

History. Although it rejects electoral processes as "bourgeois trickery", the OCF-ML put up six candidates in the 1978 elections. It did not contest the 1981 elections.

Leadership. Jacques Lucbert.

Membership. 500.

Orientation. Maoist.

Programme. The OCF-ML seeks to organize an avant-garde of the working class in opposition to both the right and the "false left".

Publication. *Drapeau Rouge* (Red Flag), monthly.

Communist Organization of Workers
Organisation Communiste des Travailleurs (OCT)

History. The OCT was formed in 1976 by a merger of Maoist and Trotskyist groups, and contested the 1978 elections in alliance with the Revolutionary Communist League and the Communist Committees for Self-management.

Membership. 1,800.

Orientation. The OCT occupies an intermediate position between Trotskyism and Maoism.

Programme. The OCT seeks to build a mass revolutionary party embracing new forms of struggle such as the campaigns for women's and soldiers' rights.

Publication. *Étincelle* (Spark), monthly. The name is a translation of that of *Iskra*, the underground newspaper run by Lenin in 1900–1903.

Communist Workers' Party of France
Parti Communiste Ouvrier de France (PCOF)

History. The PCOF was formed in 1979 after a split in the Marxist-Leninist Communist Party in the Strasbourg region.

Orientation. Pro-Albanian.

Publication. *La Forge*.

Democratic and Unitarian Communist Party
Parti Communiste Démocratique et Unitaire (PCDU)

History. The PCDU was founded in November 1983 by Henri Fiszbin, formerly a Communist deputy for Paris and secretary of the party's Paris federation. He was expelled from the Communist Party in 1981 for criticizing its policies, and subsequently formed a group called Communist Encounters, which achieved some success in the municipal elections of March 1983.

Leadership. Henri Fiszbin.

Orientation. Eurocommunist.

Programme. The PCDU advocates internal party democracy, independence of the Soviet Union and common action with the Socialist Party. Unlike the Communist Party, it supports President Mitterrand's austerity programme and the installation of cruise and Pershing missiles.

French Communist Party
Parti Communiste Français (PCF)

History. The PCF originated at the 18th Socialist Party congress, held at Tours in December 1920, when a motion for affiliation to the Comintern was adopted by 3,208 votes to 1,022. The new party—which adopted the name French Section of the Communist International, changed in 1921 to French Communist Party— was joined by 109,000 of the 178,000 Socialist Party members, but by only 13 of the 68 Socialist deputies. It also failed to obtain control of the *Confédération Générale du Travail* (CGT), and in 1933 founded the rival *Confédération Générale du Travail Unitaire* (CGTU).

During the 1920s the PCF pursued an anti-militarist and anti-imperialist policy, opposing the occupation of the Ruhr in 1923 and the wars against the Rif in Morocco and the Druse in Syria. Internal dissensions and Comintern interference led to frequent changes of leadership, until Maurice Thorez became secretary in 1930. The party's parliamentary representation declined from 26 in 1924 to 14 in 1928 and 12 in 1932, whilst by 1932 membership had fallen to about 25,000.

After the fascist riots of February 1934 the PCF called for a united front, and joint demonstrations were organized by the Communist and Socialist parties, the CGT and the CGTU. A pact for unity of action with the Socialists was signed in July, and this was later broadened in 1935 into the Popular Front, which also included the Radicals. As part of the same policy, the CGTU reunited with the CGT in 1935.

In the 1936 elections the Popular Front obtained a majority, the PCF winning 1,468,949 votes (15.3 per cent) and 72 seats, although it refused to join the new government formed by the Socialist leader, Léon Blum. During this period the PCF pursued a moderate and patriotic policy; it helped to negotiate a settlement of the mass strikes of June 1936, and supported French rearmament against the German threat. As a result its membership rose in 1937 to 328,547. Strains soon developed inside the Popular Front over foreign and colonial policy, however. During the Spanish Civil War, in which about 10,000 Frenchmen, most of them Communists, fought in the International Brigade, the PCF strongly opposed Blum's non-intervention policy, and after the Blum government was replaced in 1938 by an alliance of the Radicals and the right-wing parties it denounced the new government's appeasement policy, and especially the Munich Agreement.

The German-Soviet pact of August 1939, which the PCF defended, was followed by a period of confusion. On the outbreak of hostilities in September

1939, the PCF first declared its support for the war, then switched to a policy of opposition. It was immediately declared illegal, its press was banned, 3,400 Communists were arrested, 300 town councils were suspended, a number of Communist-controlled trade unions were dissolved and 42 Communist deputies were imprisoned, later being transferred to Algeria. Deserting from the army, Thorez escaped to Moscow. The great majority of the membership, including 21 deputies, resigned in protest against the change in policy. For a year after the fall of France the PCF pursued a vacillating policy which suggested that its underground leadership was divided; it unsuccessfully sought permission from the German authorities to republish *L'Humanité* and attacked both the Vichy government and General de Gaulle in its underground press, yet at the same time it organized resistance activities, including a successful miners' strike in the Nord and the Pas-de-Calais. When the Soviet Union entered the war it threw its whole weight behind the resistance movement, in which it played the dominant role through its military organization, the *Francs-Tireurs et Partisans*, thousands of Communists being executed by the Germans or killed in action. After the Allied landing in North Africa the PCF reached an agreement with de Gaulle in January 1943; the imprisoned Communist deputies were released, and in April 1944 two Communists entered his government-in-exile. In the following August the PCF was largely responsible for the uprising which expelled the Germans from Paris.

Because of its resistance record the PCF emerged from the war as the strongest party in France, with 804,229 members in 1946. In the elections of November 1946 it obtained 5,489,288 votes (28.6 per cent) and 166 seats, and from 1944 to 1947 it was represented in every government, except a short-lived Socialist ministry in 1946–47. Its opposition to the war in Vietnam and the government's incomes policy led to its exclusion from the government in 1947, however, and with the onset of the cold war its membership steadily fell, although in every election up to 1956 its share of the vote remained stable at about 25 per cent.

From 1956 the PCF entered a period of decline. The publication of the Khrushchev report (Thorez afterwards criticized Stalin's "mistakes", but did not refer to his "crimes" until 1961) and the party's support for the Soviet intervention in Hungary caused a heavy loss of membership. During the crisis of May 1958 a Communist attempt to organize a general strike in opposition to de Gaulle's coming to power failed because of the refusal of the Socialist and Catholic unions to support it, and in the Assembly only the Communists voted in a body against his investiture as Prime Minister. The elections held in November 1958, in which the two-ballot constituency-based system replaced proportional representation, reduced the PCF's representation in the Assembly to 10, and its share of the vote fell to 18.9 per cent. It regained some ground in the 1962 elections, with 41 seats and 21.7 per cent of the vote, and in each subsequent election until 1978 received between 20 and 22.5 per cent. Although no official figures were published during this period, membership is believed to have fallen below 200,000 by 1961, after which it began to rise again.

Under the leadership of Waldeck Rochet, who succeeded Thorez as general secretary in 1964, the PCF supported François Mitterrand (the candidate of the Federation of the Democratic and Socialist Left) in the 1965 presidential election, and reached an agreement with the Socialists and Radicals before the 1967 elections, in which it won 73 seats. From 1966 it adopted a more independent attitude towards the Soviet Union, notably when it condemned the Soviet intervention in Czechoslovakia. Its cautious policy during the crisis of May 1968 offended many of its supporters, however, and in the June elections its representation fell to 34. Its candidate in the 1969 presidential election, Jacques Duclos, received 21.27 per cent of the vote.

Georges Marchais, who became general secretary in 1972, further advanced the policy of unity of the left and independence of the Soviet Union. In 1972 the Communist and Socialist parties agreed on a common programme, and the Left Radicals later joined the alliance. The PCF subsequently won 73 seats in the 1973 elections, and in the 1974 presidential election supported Mitterrand, who was only narrowly defeated. In 1975 Marchais issued a joint declaration with Enrico Berlinguer (general secretary of the Italian Communist Party) affirming their parties' full support for democratic liberties, a multiparty system, co-operation between Communists, Socialists and Catholics, the European Communities and the gradual abolition of military blocs (see Appendix 2: Documents). The PCF shortly afterwards condemned the repression of dissidents in the Soviet Union. The 1976 party congress adopted a resolution calling for a peaceful and democratic advance to "socialism in the colours of France", and decided to omit the reference in the party statutes to the dictatorship of the proletariat, which, Marchais said, "does not correspond to the realities of our policy".

From late 1974 serious strains developed within the Union of the Left, as the steady growth of the Socialist Party was seen by the PCF as jeopardizing the equilibrium of the alliance and encouraging the Socialists to revert to a centrist strategy. The PCF accordingly launched a recruiting campaign, which raised its membership from 375,000 in 1971 to 632,000 in 1978, and the number of workplace cells from 5,050 in 1970 to 9,922 in 1978. Communist demands for the revision of the common programme were largely rejected by the Socialists and Left Radicals in 1977, with the result that the Union of the Left broke down. Although the PCF won 86 seats in the 1978 elections and 19 in the 1979 elections to the European Parliament, on each occasion its share of the vote fell below that of the Socialists, for the first time since 1936. Its support for the Soviet intervention in Afghanistan imposed further strains on relations with the Socialists.

Marchais, the Communist candidate in the 1981 presidential election, received only 15.34 per cent of the vote in the first round (following which the PCF swung behind Mitterrand's successful candidature in the second round), and in the subsequent general election Communist representation in the Assembly fell to 43. The new Socialist Prime Minister, Pierre Mauroy, included four Communists in his cabinet, but differences frequently arose between the Communists and Socialists, notably over the former's refusal to condemn the Soviet role in the imposition of martial law on Poland and their opposition to the government's austerity programme, cuts in the steel industry, French intervention in Chad and the introduction of US nuclear weapons into Europe. In the European elections of June 1984 the PCF won only 10 seats, and its share of the vote fell to 11.24 per cent, less than in any election since 1932. When Laurent Fabius formed a new Socialist government in July 1984 the Communists refused to enter it, on the ground that he had given unsatisfactory answers to their demands for a new policy which would promote employment and economic growth. The PCF broke with the parliamentary majority in September, and voted against the government for the first time in the budget debate in December 1984.

The PCF's setback in the European elections led to demands inside the party for changes in policy and leadership, greater internal democracy and the abandonment of the system of democratic centralism. At its congress in February 1985, however, Marchais was re-elected general secretary and his report and the final resolution were adopted, but not unanimously. The legislative elections of March 1986 proved even more disastrous for the PCF: its share of the vote dropped to 9.8 per cent and it won only 35 seats in an Assembly enlarged from 491 to 577 members.

Leadership. Georges Marchais (g.s.).

Structure. The PCF has about 28,000 residential and workplace cells, which are organized into local or enterprise sections and departmental federations. The congress, meeting every three years, elects the Central Committee of 142 members, which elects the Political Bureau (22 full members) and the Secretariat (seven full members). The party's youth section is the French Communist Youth Movement.

Membership. 610,000 (1984 claim). An analysis of the membership in 1978–79 showed that 51 per cent were industrial workers, 28 per cent white-collar workers, 13.5 per cent intellectuals and less than 3 per cent peasants, and that 35.7 per cent were women. The party's main strongholds are the Paris region, especially the industrial suburbs known as the "red belt", the north-eastern industrial departments of Pas-de-Calais and Nord, central France, and Marseilles and its industrial hinterland.

Electoral influence. The Communist vote has declined from 5,870,402 (20.6 per cent) in 1978 and 4,065,540 (16.17 per cent) in 1981 to 2,262,532 (11.24 per cent) in the 1984 European elections and to 2,724,381 (9.79 per cent) in 1986.

Industrial influence. The CGT, the largest trade union federation, which had a membership of 1,918,583 in 1980, is under Communist leadership. Its secretary, Henri Krasucki, is a member of the PCF Political Bureau.

Orientation. After 1966, and especially after 1975, the PCF moved towards a Eurocommunist position, but since 1980 it has tended to revert to its former pro-Soviet attitude in international affairs.

Programme. The joint programme approved by the Communist and Socialist parties in June 1981, when Communist ministers entered the Mauroy government, called for "new measures of social justice", including higher wages for the underpaid, shorter working hours, extension of the public sector of the economy, democratization of state planning, elaboration of a two-year recovery plan which would "create the conditions for new economic growth and an effective struggle against unemployment", and reduction of social inequalities. In foreign policy it supported respect for France's alliances; progressive dissolution of military blocs; international negotiations on the reduction of armaments in Europe, notably on Soviet SS-20 missiles and US Pershing II missiles; withdrawal of Soviet troops from Afghanistan and ending of all foreign interference there; Israel's right to existence and security; the Palestinians' right to a homeland; active French participation in the European communities, while respecting France's freedom of action and legitimate interests; "a successful conclusion of the process of economic, social and democratic renewal" in Poland; and "solidarity with the peoples of the Third World which, as in El Salvador and Nicaragua, are fighting for their national emancipation". After its break with the Socialist Party, on the ground that the government had abandoned this programme, the PCF stated in the resolution adopted at its 1985 congress that it was still prepared to enter into new agreements with the Socialist and other parties in pursuit of these aims.

Publications. L'Humanité, daily (150,000). Founded by Jaurès in 1904, the paper was taken over by the PCF when the Socialist Party split in 1920. Other periodicals include *L'Humanité dimanche*, Sunday newspaper (360,000); *Révolution*, weekly; *Cahiers du Communisme*, monthly.

International affiliations. The PCF is represented on the editorial board of *World Marxist Review*, and maintains close relations with both the Soviet-bloc and the

Eurocommunist parties. Relations with the Chinese party, broken off in 1965, were resumed in 1982.

Internationalist Communist Party
Parti Communiste Internationaliste (PCI)

History. The PCI, formed in 1944 by the merger of two small Trotskyist organizations, broke with the Fourth International in 1952, when it rejected a proposal that it should infiltrate the Communist Party. In the following year it joined with British and US Trotskyists in forming the Fourth International—International Committee. It adopted the name International Communist Organization in 1966, and was later joined by a number of student groups which had been active in the events of May 1968. Banned later in the same year, it was again legalized in 1970. It left the International Committee in 1971 and formed the Organizing Centre for the Reconstruction of the Fourth International, which in 1981 became the Fourth International—International Centre of Reconstruction. It reverted to its original name in 1981, to signify its intention to move from student- and union-oriented activity to a broader political role.

Leadership. Pierre Lambert.

Membership. 5,000, mostly students.

Industrial influence. Members are active in the Socialist trade union federation, *Force Ouvrière.*

Orientation. Trotskyist.

Publication. Jeune Révolutionnaire, monthly.

International affiliations. Fourth International—International Centre of Reconstruction.

Marxist-Leninist Communist Party
Parti Communiste Marxiste-Léniniste (PCML)

History. The PCML originated in the Federation of Marxist–Leninist Circles, formed in 1964 by Maoists in Marseilles and southern France who had been expelled from the Communist Party, and renamed the French Communist Movement, Marxist-Leninist, in 1966 and the Marxist-Leninist Communist Party of France in 1967. Banned in 1968, it continued a semi-legal existence until 1978, when it assumed its present name. It contested the 1978 and 1981 elections without success.

Leadership. Jacques Jurquet (g.s.).

Structure. The PCML is organized on the normal communist pattern, with cells, local and regional committees, a Central Committee, a Political Bureau and a Secretariat.

Membership. 3,000.

Orientation. Pro-Chinese.

Programme. The PCML advocates "struggle against the monopolist bourgeoisie as the principal enemy, rejection of revisionism and reformism, and struggle against the two superpowers preparing for war, and in particular against the more aggressive, Russian social-imperialism", in preparation for the defeat of the bourgeoisie and the establishment of the dictatorship of the proletariat.

Publications. *L'Humanité Rouge,* daily; *Prolétariat,* theoretical organ (6,000).

International affiliations. The PCML is officially recognized by the Chinese Communist Party.

Marxist–Leninist Union of Communists of France
Union des Communistes de France Marxiste-Léniniste (UCFML)

History. The UCFML was formed by a small group which broke away from the Unified Socialist Party in 1971.

Leadership. Alain Badieu.

Electoral influence. The UCFML advocates abstention in elections.

Orientation. Maoist.

Programme. The UCFML is hostile to both the Communist Party and the existing trade union movement, and seeks to create "a broad workers' avant-garde".

Revolutionary Communist League
Ligue Communiste Révolutionnaire (LCR)

History. The LCR, originally called the Communist League, was founded in 1969 as the successor to the Internationalist Communist Party and the Revolutionary Communist League, which had been banned in the previous year. Alain Krivine, one of the leaders of the 1968 student revolt, contested the 1969 presidential election as its candidate, receiving 239,106 votes (1.05 per cent). Banned in 1973 after a riot in Paris, the League was refounded under its present name, and has since contested elections without success, either alone or in alliance with other Trotskyist parties. Krivine contested the 1974 presidential election, receiving 93,990 votes (0.36 per cent), and was again put forward as a candidate for the presidency in 1981, but failed to obtain the required 500 sponsors. The LCR subsequently announced its support for President Mitterrand's government.

Leadership. Alain Krivine.

Structure. The annual congress elects the Central Committee, which elects the Political Bureau.

Membership. 6,000.

Orientation. Trotskyist.

Publication. *Rouge,* weekly.

International affiliations. Fourth International, United Secretariat.

Revolutionary Communist Party—Marxist-Leninist
Parti Communiste Revolutionnaire—Marxiste-Léniniste (PCRML)

History. The PCRML broke away from the Marxist-Leninist Communist Party of France in 1974, but fought the 1978 elections in alliance with it. Negotiations for their reunion in 1979 broke down, however, and they contested the 1981 elections separately.

Leadership. Max Cluzot (g.s.).

Structure. The party is based on cells (primarily in industrial enterprises), which are organized in federations covering several departments. The congress elects the Central Committee, which elects the Political Bureau and Secretariat.

Membership. 2,500.

Orientation. Pro-Chinese.

Programme. The PCRML "fights for the socialist revolution in France". It is critical of the French Communist Party, and denounces both the United States and the Soviet Union.

Publications. *Le Quotidien du Peuple*, daily (10,000); *Front Rouge*, theoretical review (5,000).

Unified Socialist Party
Parti Socialiste Unifié (PSU)

History. The PSU was formed in 1960 by the merger of three left-wing socialist groups, with the aim of uniting the left by drawing the Socialist Party farther to the left and democratizing the Communist Party, and won two seats in the Assembly in 1962 and four in 1967. During the crisis of May 1968 it adopted an extremist position, violently attacking the Communist Party for its moderation, and in the June elections it lost all its seats. Michel Rocard, its national secretary, contested the 1969 presidential election, receiving 816,471 votes (3.61 per cent), and in the 1973 elections it won three seats. It split in 1975, when a faction led by Rocard joined the Socialist Party, and its candidates in the 1978 and 1981 elections were all defeated. Mme Huguette Bouchardeau (national secretary since 1980), under whose leadership the PSU had identified itself with the feminist and ecological movements, was the party's candidate in the 1981 presidential election, and in 1983 entered Pierre Mauroy's government as Secretary of State for the Environment and Quality of Life, being promoted to ministerial rank in Laurent Fabius' government in the following year.

Leadership. Serge Depaquit (nat. sec.).

Structure. The PSU's supreme authority is its congress, which elects the National Council and National Secretariat.

Membership. 5,500. The PSU draws its main support from the Paris region, and especially from students.

Electoral influence. Mme Bouchardeau received 321,744 votes (1.11 per cent) in the 1981 presidential elections.

Orientation. Independent.

Programme. The PSU's 1981 election programme advocated labour-intensive economic growth; nationalization of the banks; increased taxation of higher incomes; creation of 100,000 jobs a year in the public services; reduction of the working week to 30 hours by 1988; abandonment of the nuclear energy programme; and concentration on energy conservation and the development of new sources of energy. It also supports industrial self-management (*autogestion*), decentralization, regional autonomy and women's rights.

Publication. *Tribune Socialiste*, monthly.

Workers' Struggle
Lutte Ouvrière (LO)

History. The LO, the most influential of the parties of the extreme left, was founded in 1968 as the successor to various earlier Trotskyist movements, and has unsuccessfully contested elections since 1973, either alone or in alliance with other Trotskyist parties. Its leader, Mlle Laguiller, was a presidential candidate in 1974 and 1981.

Leadership. Arlette Laguiller.

Membership. 5,000.

Electoral influence. Mlle Laguiller received 668,057 votes (2.3 per cent) in the 1981 presidential election.

Orientation. Trotskyist.

Programme. In her 1981 election campaign Mlle Laguiller called for the immediate introduction of a 35-hour working week and a national referendum on the high level of defence expenditure. The LO is opposed to the Mitterrand government.

Publication. *Lutte Ouvrière*, weekly.

Terrorist Organization

Direct Action
Action Directe (AD)

History. AD was founded in 1979 by a merger of Maoist and anarchist groups, and carried out a series of machine-gun and bomb attacks on government buildings, premises connected with arms manufacturers and symbolic targets such as the Atlantic Institute of International Affairs and the European Space Agency, as well as bank robberies to finance its activities. Jean-Marc Rouillan, believed to be its leader, was arrested in 1980, but was released in the following year under a general amnesty for political prisoners. Membership of the movement was declared a criminal offence in 1982. In January 1985 AD and the West German Red Army Faction announced that they had formed an alliance to carry out "attacks against the multinational structure of NATO, its bases, its military leaders, its plans and its propaganda". Gen. René Audran, the officer responsible for French arms exports, was shot dead in Paris 10 days later; AD claimed responsibility for the crime, its first attack on an individual rather than a building.

International affiliations. In addition to the Red Army Faction, AD is believed to co-operate with the Belgian Fighting Communist Cells, and has been suspected in the past of having connections with the Italian Red Brigades, the Basque ETA and Palestinian, Lebanese and Armenian terrorist groups.

Federal Republic of Germany

Capital: Bonn　　　　　　　　　　　　　　　　　　　　　　Pop. 61,770,000

The Social Democratic Party of Germany, founded in 1875, rapidly became the largest and most influential Marxist party in the world, with a membership in

1914 of 1,085,000. The leadership's decision in 1914 to support the German war effort as a defensive struggle against Russian aggression split the party, however; the anti-war deputies formed the Independent Social Democratic Party, and the extreme left organized the Spartacus League, which in 1918 became the Communist Party of Germany. The Weimar Republic of 1919–33, under attack from the Communists on the left and the Nationalists and Nazis on the right, proved politically unstable, and ended with the installation of Hitler as Chancellor in January 1933.

After World War II the occupying powers failed to agree on the future of a politically and economically united Germany, with the result that in 1949 the Federal Republic of Germany was established in the western zones occupied by US, British and French forces and the German Democratic Republic in the Soviet-occupied eastern zone. West Germany was ruled by the Christian Democrats (CDU–CSU) from 1949 to 1966, either alone or in coalition with the Free Democratic Party (FDP); by a coalition of the CDU–CSU and the Social Democratic Party (SPD) from 1966 to 1969; and by a coalition of the SPD and the FDP from 1969 to 1982, since when a CDU–CSU–FDP coalition has been in power.

The Federal Republic consists of 10 *Länder* (states), each with its own parliament. The Federal Parliament (*Bundestag*) normally contains 248 members elected for four years by majority vote in single-member constituencies, 248 elected by proportional representation and 22 nominated by the West Berlin House of Deputies (City Council), who do not exercise full voting rights.

Centre Faction
Zentrumfraktion

History. This group broke away from the Communist League in 1979, and largely controls the ecologist Green Party in Hamburg.

Leadership. Jürgen Reents.

Membership. 150 (1983 estimate), most of them in Hamburg.

Orientation. New Left.

Communist League
Kommunistischer Bund (KB)

History. The KB, founded in 1977, has been active in the anti-nuclear power movement and in the universities.

Membership. 500, of whom about 300 are in Hamburg (1985 estimate).

Orientation. Formerly Maoist, now New Left.

Publication. *Arbeiterkampf* (Workers' Struggle), monthly (6,000).

Communist League of West Germany
Kommunistischer Bund Westdeutschlands (KBW)

History. The KBW was founded in 1973, and contested the general elections in 1976 and 1980. It split in 1980, when about a quarter of the membership formed the League of West German Communists. Formerly the strongest of the German Maoist parties, by 1985 it was virtually inactive.

Leadership. Hans-Gerhart Schmierer (sec.).

Structure. The KBW is divided into three regional and 40 district units, and has a 14-member Central Committee and a five-member Standing Committee.

Membership. 500 (1983 estimate).

Electoral influence. The KBW obtained 8,285 votes in the 1980 elections. It won a seat on the Heidelberg city council in 1977.

Orientation. Pro-Chinese.

Programme. The KBW demands the arming of the people and the withdrawal of foreign troops from West Germany. Its ultimate aim is the revolutionary overthrow of the capitalist state, the destruction of the bourgeois state apparatus and the conquest of political power by the proletariat.

Publication. Kommune, monthly.

Communist Party of Germany—Marxist-Leninists
Kommunistische Partei Deutschlands—Marxisten-Leninisten (KPD—ML)

History. Founded in Hamburg in 1968, the KPD—ML was originally pro-Chinese, before adopting a pro-Albanian position.

Leadership. Horst-Dieter Koch (ch.).

Structure. Based on democratic centralism. The KPD—ML claims to have a section in West Berlin and an underground section in the German Democratic Republic.

Membership. 400 (1985 estimate).

Orientation. Pro-Albanian.

Programme. The KPD—ML aims at revolution, the establishment of the dictatorship of the proletariat and the creation of a unified socialist Germany.

Publications. Roter Morgen (Red Morning), weekly (6,000); *Der Weg der Partei* (The Way of the Party), bimonthly.

German Communist Party
Deutsche Kommunistische Partei (DKP)

History. The DKP can trace its origin to the Spartacus League, founded by Karl Liebknecht, Rosa Luxemburg and other left-wing Social Democrats in 1916 as an underground anti-war movement, which in December 1918 became the Communist Party of Germany (KPD). An attempted uprising in Berlin in the following month was easily crushed, and Liebknecht and Luxemburg were arrested and murdered. The left wing of the Independent Social Democratic Party joined the KPD in 1920, bringing its membership to nearly 400,000, but the party suffered from factional strife and frequent changes of leadership until Ernst Thälmann became its leader in 1925. In its policy it vacillated between ultra-leftism, unsuccessful uprisings being staged in central Germany in 1921 and in Hamburg in 1923, and attempts to co-operate with the Social Democrats. After 1928 it adopted an attitude of fierce hostility to the Social Democrats, whom it denounced as "social fascists"—a policy which facilitated Hitler's coming to power. It nevertheless remained the largest communist party outside the Soviet

Union and a major political force in Germany, and obtained over 5,980,000 votes (16.8 per cent) and 100 seats in the elections of November 1932.

Even after Hitler became Chancellor the KPD polled over 4,800,000 votes (12.1 per cent) in elections held in March 1933, and won 81 seats. A fire which destroyed the *Reichstag* building, however, was made the pretext for suppressing the party, many of its members, including Thälmann, being murdered and thousands more sent to concentration camps. Some of its leaders escaped to the Soviet Union, where a number of them were executed in Stalin's purges. Inside Germany underground Communist groups still continued to organize resistance, and formed the National Committee for a Free Germany, which after the war was banned by the US occupation authorities.

The KPD was revived in 1945, and made overtures for reunification to the Social Democratic Party, which rejected them in the western zones, although in the Soviet zone the two parties were merged in the Socialist Unity Party (SED). In the first federal elections, held in 1949, the KPD, which had separated itself organizationally from the SED shortly before, won 1,361,706 votes (3.73 per cent) and 15 seats in the *Bundestag*, but in the 1953 elections its vote fell to 607,413 (2.2 per cent) and it lost all its seats. In 1956 the KPD, whose membership had fallen from about 300,000 in 1946 to 70,000, was banned as unconstitutional and again went underground.

The party was again revived in 1968, under the new name of the German Communist Party (DKP), on the basis of undertaking to respect the constitution. In the first elections which it contested, in 1972, it obtained 113,891 votes (0.3 per cent), but its vote has since declined steeply. In 1972 Communists and left-wing sympathizers were banned from employment in the public services, but these regulations were overruled by two courts in 1985, and were revoked by the Social Democratic government in Saarland.

Leadership. Herbert Mies (ch.).

Structure. The DKP has over 1,400 residential and workplace groups, subordinated to 187 county organizations and 12 district organizations. The congress, meeting every two years, elects the chairman and vice-chairman and the Party Board, which elects the 15-member Presidium and the 11-member Secretariat. The party's youth organizations are the Socialist German Worker Youth, the Marxist Student Union and the Young Pioneers.

Membership. 50,482 (1984 claim). About 75 per cent of the members are industrial workers, especially from the Ruhr, the remainder being mostly white-collar workers, intellectuals and students.

Electoral influence. The DKP received 65,789 votes (0.2 per cent) in the 1983 federal elections. It has not been represented in the *Bundestag* since 1953, and has never been represented in the *Länder* parliaments.

Industrial influence. Communists play an active part in the Confederation of German Trade Unions. At the 1981 party congress 61.1 per cent of the 855 delegates were said to be union officials and 25.3 per cent shop stewards.

Orientation. Pro-Soviet.

Programme. The DKP defines socialism as the rule of the working class, in alliance with other working sections of the community, and collective ownership of the main means of production, to be achieved through unity of action between Communists, Social Democrats and all the progressive forces. It proposes to deal with the problems of unemployment and inflation by reducing working hours and overtime without reducing wages, lengthening paid holidays, lowering the pension age to 60 for men and 55 for women, freezing the prices of electricity, gas, water and public transport, and shifting the burden of taxation to the wealthy. In foreign policy it advocates recognition of the German Democratic Republic and the existing European frontiers, recognition of West Berlin as an independent political unit, a security system covering the whole of Europe and the simultaneous dissolution of NATO and the Warsaw Pact, and opposes the installation of cruise and Pershing missiles in Germany.

Publication. Unsere Zeit (Our Time), daily (25,000).

International affiliations. The DKP is represented on the editorial council of *World Marxist Review*, and has close relations with the Socialist Unity Party and the Soviet Communist Party.

International Marxist Group
Gruppe Internationaler Marxisten (GIM)

History. Founded in 1969, the GIM is the successor of the *Internationale Kommunisten Deutschlands*, which was established in 1931 and reorganized after World War II. It took part in elections for the first time in 1976.

Structure. The federal convention elects a 30-member Central Committee, which elects the nine-member Political Bureau.

Membership. 250 (1985 estimate). The GIM is the largest of 13 Trotskyist organizations in West Germany, which in 1985 were estimated to have a total of about 700 members.

Electoral influence. The GIM obtained 4,767 votes in the 1976 federal elections.

Orientation. Trotskyist.

Programme. The GIM aims at the establishment of a united socialist Germany as part of the United Socialist States of Europe.

Publications. Was Tun (What is to be done?), weekly; Die Internationale (The International), quarterly.

International affiliations. Fourth International, United Secretariat.

International Socialists of Germany
Internationale Sozialisten Deutschlands (ISD)

Structure. The ISD has its headquarters in Cologne.

Orientation. Trotskyist.

Publication. Sozialistische Rundschau (Socialist Observer).

League of Socialist Workers
Bund der Sozialistischen Arbeiter (BSA)

Membership. 150 (1983 estimate).

Orientation. Trotskyist.

Publication. Neue Arbeiterpresse (New Workers' Press), weekly.

League of West German Communists
Bund Westdeutscher Kommunisten (BWK)

History. The BWK broke away from the Communist League of West Germany in 1980, and contested the 1983 federal elections.

Membership. 450 (1985 estimate).

Electoral influence. The BWK obtained 2,553 votes in the 1983 elections.

Orientation. Maoist.

Publications. Politische Berichte (Political Reports), biweekly (1,500); *Nachrichtenheft* (Bulletin), biweekly (1,200).

Marxist Group
Marxistische Gruppe (MG)

Structure. The MG has a hierarchical structure, and enforces secrecy and strict discipline on its members.

Membership. 1,300 (1985 estimate), mostly students and academics.

Orientation. New Left.

Publication. Marxistische Zeitung (Marxist Chronicle), monthly. The MG also publishes university newspapers in editions of up to 14,000 copies and factory and local papers.

Marxist-Leninist Party of Germany
Marxistische-Leninistische Partei Deutschlands (MLPD)

History. The MLPD was founded in 1982 as the successor to the Communist Workers' League of Germany (*Kommunistischer Arbeiterbund Deutschlands*).

Structure. The MLPD has over 80 local groups, organized in 11 districts, and affiliated youth, student and intellectuals' organizations. Its headquarters are in Essen.

Leadership. Stefan Engel (ch.).

Membership. 1,000 (1985 estimate), plus 600–800 members of affiliated organizations. The MLPD is the largest and most active of the German Maoist organizations.

Orientation. Maoist.

Programme. The MLPD advocates the revolutionary overthrow of capitalism and the bourgeois state and the establishment of the dictatorship of the proletariat.

Publication. Rote Fahne (Red Flag), weekly (10,000). The MLPD also publishes over 80 factory newspapers.

Socialist Bureau
Sozialistische Büro (SB)

Membership. 700 (1985 estimate).

Orientation. New Left.

Programme. The SB aims to provide initiatives for common political action for the revolutionary change of society. Its members work inside the Social Democratic and Green parties, trade unions and social movements.

Publications. Links (Left), monthly (6,000); *Express*, monthly (3,000); *Widersprüche* (Contradictions), quarterly.

Terrorist Organizations

Red Army Faction
Rote Armee Fraktion (RAF)

History. This organization, formed in 1968, originated as an offshoot of the Socialist German Students' League, founded in 1946, which adopted revolutionary views after 1961, organized riotous demonstrations in West Berlin and other cities in 1967–68 and dissolved itself in 1970. The RAF, also known as the Baader-Meinhof Group, was responsible between 1968 and 1981 for many bomb explosions and acts of arson (directed mainly against US military installations, the judiciary, the police and the press), bank robberies and a number of assassinations of judges and businessmen. The group's best-known leaders, Ulrike Meinhof and Andreas Baader, committed suicide in prison in 1976 and 1977 respectively, and many of its members received heavy prison sentences.

By 1984 the RAF appeared to be moribund, and the police believed its active membership to have declined to about 20. In December, however, it launched a bombing campaign in support of demands by its imprisoned members for prisoner of war status; in January 1985 it announced that it had formed a common front against NATO with the French organization Direct Action (q.v.); and in the following month two of its members murdered the head of an engineering firm supplying equipment to NATO. The Ministry of the Interior estimated the number of RAF activists in May 1985 at about 500.

Orientation. Although the RAF claimed to be Maoists, its theories and practice had more in common with anarchism than with Marxism.

Programme. The RAF maintained that society could be changed only by violence under the leadership of a vanguard of revolutionary intellectuals. Meinhof defined their aims in 1974 as the destruction of the US military alliances throughout the world, the armed formations of the state, the economic power of the multinationals, and the governmental and non-governmental "bureaucracies, organizations and power structures (parties, trade unions and media) which rule the people".

International affiliations. The RAF had close connections with the Popular Front for the Liberation of Palestine, from which some of its members received training in guerrilla warfare, and the (Palestinian) Black September terrorist group, and also had links with the Red Brigades and Armed Proletarian Nuclei in Italy. In its 1985 anti-NATO campaign it was believed to be co-operating with both Direct Action and the Belgian Fighting Communist Cells.

Revolutionary Cells
Revolutionäre Zellen (RZ)

History. The RZ, an offshoot of the Red Army Faction, were responsible between 1973 and 1982 for numerous bomb explosions and acts of arson, most of them directed against US military installations or industrial property. They also admitted responsibility for the murder in 1981 of a member of the Hesse *Land* government, while claiming that they had intended only to maim him.

Structure. In contrast to the authoritarian structure of the RAF, the RZ are organized in small independent groups modelled on the Italian Red Brigades. Their membership has been estimated at about 200.

Orientation. The RZ accept Herbert Marcuse's theory that "outsiders" are the only true revolutionaries, and attempt to mobilize squatters, prisoners and other social outcasts.

West Berlin

The western sector of Berlin was occupied in 1945 by US, British and French forces and the eastern sector by Soviet forces, separate municipal governments for the two sectors being established in 1948. Whereas East Berlin has since been completely integrated into the German Democratic Republic, a four-power agreement of 1971 states that West Berlin is not part of the Federal Republic of Germany and is not governed by it, but that ties between them will be maintained and developed.

Socialist Unity Party of West Berlin
Sozialistische Einheitspartei Westberlins (SEW)

History. The SEW was formed in 1946 as the West Berlin section of the Socialist Unity Party of Germany, and first contested elections to the House of Deputies in 1954, receiving 2.7 per cent of the vote. It was refounded as an independent party in 1962 under the name Socialist Unity Party of Germany— West Berlin, which was changed to Socialist Unity Party of West Berlin in 1969.

Leadership. Horst Schmitt (ch.).

Structure. The SEW is based on workplace and residential groups, and organizations exist for each of the 12 administrative districts. The congress, meeting every two years, elects the 65-member Executive, which elects the 17-member Bureau and the seven-member Secretariat.

Membership. 4,500 (1985 estimate).

Electoral influence. In the 1981 elections to the House of Deputies the SEW received 8,216 votes (0.7 per cent), its lowest vote hitherto.

Orientation. Pro-Soviet.

Programme. The SEW advocates unity of action between Communists and Social Democrats, a common struggle by all the socialist and democratic forces against the power of the monopolies, nationalization of the most important means of production, and the rule of the working class and its Marxist–Leninist party.

Publication. *Die Wahrheit* (Truth), daily (16,000).

International affiliations. The SEW maintains close relations with the Soviet-bloc parties.

Great Britain

Capital: London

Pop. 54,850,000
(excluding N. Ireland)

The first Marxist party in Britain, the Democratic Federation, was founded by H. M. Hyndman in 1881 as a Radical organization, and was renamed the Social Democratic Federation (SDF) in 1883, when it adopted a Marxist programme. Hopes of forming a mass party, however, were frustrated by Hyndman's political opportunism and dictatorial methods, which led to a series of splits. A section of the leadership, including William Morris and Eleanor Marx, broke away in 1884 and founded the Socialist League, which fell under anarchist control in 1890 and soon disintegrated; a left-wing group in Scotland formed the Socialist Labour

Party (SLP) in 1903; and another group in London founded the Socialist Party of Great Britain in the following year. In 1900 the SDF co-operated with the non-Marxist Independent Labour Party (ILP) and Fabian Society and the Trades Union Congress to establish the Labour Representation Committee (LRC), but it withdrew in the following year because the LRC refused to adopt a socialist programme. The LRC won 29 seats in Parliament in 1906, and assumed the name of the Labour Party. The SDF merged with a dissident section of the ILP in 1912 in the British Socialist Party, which united in 1920 with sections of the SLP and ILP to form the Communist Party of Great Britain.

Communist Party of Britain—Marxist-Leninist (CPB—ML)

History. The CPB—ML was founded in 1968 by Reg Birch, a member of the executive of the Amalgamated Union of Engineering Workers, who had been expelled from the Communist Party in the previous year. The largest Maoist party in Britain, it was officially recognized by the Chinese Communist Party, but in 1979 adopted a pro-Albanian attitude.

Leadership. Reg Birch.

Membership. 400.

Electoral influence. The CPB—ML has not contested elections.

Orientation. Pro-Albanian.

Programme. The CPB—ML does not rule out the use of guerrilla warfare on behalf of the working class.

Publication. *The Worker*.

Communist Party of England, Marxist-Leninist (CPE–ML)

History. Formed in 1973, the CPE–ML has contested elections unsuccessfully since 1974.

Orientation. Maoist.

Communist Party of Great Britain (CPGB)

History. The CPGB was founded in 1920 at a convention of delegates from the British Socialist Party (BSP), the Socialist Labour Party (SLP) and other organizations, and was joined in the following year by most of the remaining Marxist groups except a section of the SLP, bringing its membership to about 3,000. The original members included one member of Parliament, Lt.-Col. C. J. L'Estrange Malone, who after being elected as a Liberal had joined the BSP, but he soon left the CPGB. Although the new party's application for affiliation to the Labour Party was rejected, individual Communists were allowed to become Labour Party members until 1925 and Labour candidates until 1924. Two Communists, Shapurji Saklatvala and J. T. Walton Newbold, sat in Parliament as Labour members in 1922–23, and Saklatvala was returned as a Communist to the 1924–29 Parliament.

During the 1920s the CPGB was active in the Minority Movement, which sought to organize the left inside the trade unions. In 1925, when the general strike was imminent, the Conservative government removed 12 leading

Communists from the industrial scene by charging them with sedition, sentences of six months' or a year's imprisonment being passed. After 1927 the CPGB abandoned its policy of co-operation with the Labour left for one of "class against class", and fought the 1929 elections on the slogan "Down with the three capitalist parties". In order to enforce the new policy, many of its leaders were dropped from the Political Bureau or the Central Committee in 1929, Albert Inkpin being replaced as general secretary by Harry Pollitt. This policy alienated many of its supporters, and membership dropped from 10,730 in 1926 to 2,555 in 1930.

After Hitler's coming to power in 1933 the CPGB again reversed its policy, calling for unity of all socialist parties and, after 1935, for a Popular Front of all anti-fascists, including Liberals and even Conservatives opposed to the National Government's appeasement policy. This appeal, although supported by the Labour left, was repeatedly rejected by the Labour Party leadership. The CPGB put forward only two candidates in the 1935 elections (William Gallacher, who was elected in West Fife, and Pollitt, who received 38 per cent of the vote in East Rhondda), and supported Labour candidates elsewhere. During the Spanish Civil War many British Communists fought in the International Brigade, over 250 being killed. The party's anti-fascist policy during this period attracted many new recruits, and by July 1939 membership had risen to 17,756.

On the outbreak of war in September 1939 the CPGB declared its support for "all necessary measures to secure the victory of democracy over fascism", but a month later it denounced the war as an imperialist war. Pollitt, who opposed this change of policy, was removed from the general secretaryship, although he was reinstated in 1941. The party's opposition to the war and its defence of the German–Soviet pact and the Soviet invasion of Finland made it extremely unpopular, and in January 1941 the party's paper, the *Daily Worker*, was banned.

After Hitler's invasion of the Soviet Union in June 1941 the CPGB announced its "wholehearted" support for the Churchill government and the war effort, and campaigned for the opening of a second front in Western Europe. The ban on the *Daily Worker* was lifted in 1942. Popular admiration for the Soviet resistance to the Germans brought a flood of recruits into the party, and by the end of 1942 membership reached 56,000, a level never attained before or since. In March 1945 the CPGB advocated that all-party government should be continued after the war, but this proposal was not supported by any other party. In the elections in July it put forward 22 candidates, who obtained 102,780 votes, the party's highest vote to date; Gallacher retained West Fife, Phil Piratin won Mile End and Pollitt polled over 15,000 votes in East Rhondda.

The CPGB at first supported the Labour government of 1945–51, but from 1947 onwards it adopted an increasingly critical attitude towards it. With the onset of the cold war its support and its membership slowly dwindled. The 100 candidates which it put forward for the 1950 elections received 91,815 votes, 97 of them forfeiting their deposits, and Gallacher and Piratin both lost their seats.

The events of 1956 precipitated a crisis in the party. At its congress in April Pollitt, who reported on Khrushchev's speech on Stalin's crimes at a secret session, was replaced as general secretary by John Gollan, and in July, on the insistence of the membership, a commission was appointed to report on "problems of inner-party democracy, including congress procedure". During the Hungarian uprising in October 1956 the *Daily Worker* suppressed the reports of its Budapest correspondent, who was later expelled from the party for publishing them in book form, and in November the Executive Committee declared its support for the Soviet invasion of Hungary. A special congress in 1957 upheld the leadership's line on Hungary; accepted the commission's report, which recommended that the existing system of "democratic centralism" should be retained; and rejected a minority report submitted by three of its members, which maintained that democratic centralism was "inappropriate to our party or to present British conditions" and attacked limitations on freedom of discussion within the party.

As a result of these developments thousands of members resigned, including prominent trade union leaders and academics, and membership fell from 33,095 in February 1956 to 24,670 two years later. It gradually rose again to 34,381 in 1964, but has since steadily declined. The party was further discredited when in 1961 a court ruled that elections in the Electrical Trades Union had been rigged by the Communist leadership.

Under Gollan's leadership the CPGB steadily moved towards a Eurocommunist position. It condemned the imprisonment of dissident Soviet writers in 1966 and the Soviet intervention in Czechoslovakia in 1968; declared in 1967 that there could be no single directing centre for the international communist movement; and refused to sign the document adopted by the Moscow conference of communist parties in 1969. This trend was intensified after Gordon McLennan succeeded Gollan as general secretary in 1975, both the Soviet intervention in Afghanistan in 1979 and the imposition of martial law in Poland in 1981 being condemned by the CPGB.

The movement towards Eurocommunism met with opposition from both a pro–Chinese group, which was expelled in 1967, and a pro–Soviet faction, which attempted unsuccessfully to reverse the party's position on Czechoslovakia at the 1969 and 1971 congresses and its policy on Poland at the 1983 congress. A pro–Soviet group which opposed the party's rejection of the theory of the dictatorship of the proletariat broke away in 1977 to form the New Communist Party.

By 1983 the CPGB was bitterly divided between the Eurocommunist majority and the pro–Soviet hardline minority. The former advocated that the party should seek to broaden its appeal by forming alliances with the peace, women's and ecological movements and the ethnic minorities, whereas the latter maintained that it should adhere to its traditional policy of giving priority to workplace agitation among the organized working class. This faction controlled the party's newspaper, the *Morning Star*, whilst its theoretical magazine, *Marxism Today*, acted as the organ of the Eurocommunist wing. At the 1983 party congress a resolution censuring the editorship of *Marxism Today* was defeated, and the editor of the *Morning Star*, Tony Chater, was not re-elected to the Executive Committee, this being the first time that the editor of the party paper had been excluded from this body. Attempts to remove him from the editorship at the 1984 meetings of the People's Press Printing Society were unsuccessful, but in January 1985 he and five other hardliners were expelled from the party for actively campaigning against its policies, the expulsions being upheld by a special congress in May. Ken Gill, general secretary of the Technical and Supervisory Section of the Amalgamated Union of Engineering Workers, and 11 other members of the management committee of the *Morning Star* were expelled in July.

Leadership. Gordon McLennan (g.s.).

Structure. The CPGB has about 1,000 constituency, workplace and college or university branches, which are controlled by district committees (15 in England and one each in Scotland and Wales). The biennial congress elects the 45-member Executive Committee, which elects the 16-Member Political Committee. All branches may submit nominations for the Executive Committee, but a "recommended list" of approved candidates is placed before the congress, and in practice is always elected. The party's youth organization is the Young Communist League (YCL).

Membership. 15,691 (1983). The party's traditional strongholds have been in London, Glasgow and the mining areas of Scotland and South Wales, but recent election results have shown a decline in support in all these areas. A survey published in 1969 showed that it consisted primarily of skilled and semi-skilled workers, especially engineers, miners and building workers, and teachers from similar backgrounds. The YCL has about 500 members.

Electoral influence. The 34 Communist candidates in the 1983 elections received 11,451 votes (0.037 per cent). The CPGB has not been represented in the House of Commons since 1950, although it has one member in the House of Lords, Lord Milford, a hereditary peer. It has a few councillors in local authorities in Scotland.

Industrial influence. The CPGB's influence in the trade unions has always been far greater than its political influence. Although it does not control any individual union, it is represented on most union executives, and in 1985 had one member on the General Council of the Trades Union Congress, Mick McGahey, vice-president of the National Union of Mineworkers.

Orientation. Eurocommunist.

Programme. The party programme adopted in 1977, *The British Road to Socialism* (see Appendix 2: Documents), envisages a peaceful transition to socialism, to be achieved through "a combination of a socialist parliamentary majority and mass struggle outside Parliament, ensuring a government that is determined and able to implement a socialist programme". Such a government would nationalize the key firms dominating the economy, the big banks, the major insurance companies, the oil industry, urban land, except that of owner-occupiers, and large agricultural estates, limited compensation being paid in the form of life annuities to individuals. Workers elected directly, and others appointed by the Trades Union Congress, would constitute a majority of the management boards of nationalized concerns. Controls would be instituted over the investment, production and employment policies of private firms, and the export of capital would be banned. A national economic plan would be adopted by Parliament after full consultation with the trade unions and other bodies. In private industry all important decision-making would be subject to collective bargaining with the unions. A wealth tax would be introduced, corporation tax increased and taxes on lower incomes and indirect taxation reduced. The monarchy and the House of Lords would be abolished, and Scottish and Welsh Parliaments established with adequate legislative, economic and financial powers. The freedom of all democratic parties, including those hostile to socialism, to contend for political support would be guaranteed, and a left-wing government would stand down if defeated in an election. In foreign policy the CPGB advocates withdrawal from NATO and the European Communities, the replacement of NATO and the Warsaw Pact by a European security system, and unilateral nuclear disarmament as a step towards general and complete disarmament.

Publications. *7 Days*, weekly; *Marxism Today*, monthly (13,500).
The party's newspaper was formerly the *Morning Star* (founded in 1930, and known until 1966 as the *Daily Worker*), which since 1948 has been controlled by the People's Press Printing Society, a co-operative, the members of which annually elect the management committee. The party's Executive Committee ruled in July 1985 that it had ceased to be a Communist paper, and in October *7 Days* replaced it as the party's official organ. The *Morning Star*'s sales fell in 1985 to about 10,000, and over half its daily print run of 30,000 was bought by the Soviet government for distribution in Eastern Europe. Sales of *Marxism Today*, on the other hand, have tripled since Martin Jacques became editor in 1978.

International affiliations. The CPGB is represented on the editorial board of *World Marxist Review*, and maintains friendly relations with both the Eurocommunist and the Soviet-bloc parties.

Militant Tendency

History. This organization, formed in 1954 as the Revolutionary Socialist League, adopted its present name in 1964, when it launched the weekly *Militant* and decided to conduct "deep entryist activities" inside the Labour Party. It was expelled from the Fourth International in 1965 for refusing to abandon "entryism". The report of an inquiry into its activities conducted by the national agent and general secretary of the Labour Party, which was published in 1982, concluded that it was "a well-organized caucus, centrally controlled, operating within the Labour Party . . . with its own programme and policy for distinctive and separate propaganda which is determined outside the structure of the Labour Party". The five members of the editorial board of *Militant* were expelled from the Labour Party in 1983, and following the discovery of the minutes of Militant branch meetings six other Militant members were expelled from the Blackburn Labour Party later in the same year. About 20 more Militant members were expelled from local Labour parties in 1985.

Leadership. Peter Taaffe (g.s. and editor of *Militant*).

Structure. Militant claims that it is "not an organization but a journal which . . . sets out to win support for its ideas and policies. There is no organizational structure or membership." The evidence of former members and Militant documents, however, shows that it is organized as a political party operating secretly outside the Labour Party. The organization is divided into 12 regions, 10 for England and one each for Scotland and Wales, each of which is subdivided into districts, generally covering a conurbation or county, and the 76 districts in turn are made up of 363 branches, often corresponding to a parliamentary constituency. Members are required to attend weekly branch meetings and caucus meetings in their trade unions, to pay very high weekly dues and to sell their quota of *Militant*. The organization has an estimated 160 full-time employees, about half of whom work in London on the production of the paper or in its specialized bureaux, while the remainder, officially described as "paper-sellers", work in the provinces as organizers and propagandists. The National Council, consisting of full-time employees and delegates from each region and district, meets annually to make policy decisions, which are always confirmed by the annual conference, officially described as a "readers' rally". The Central Committee of about 45 members, including representatives of the regions, meets every two or three months, whilst the Executive Committee of about 10 people, including the five members of the *Militant* editorial board, meets weekly and exercises similar functions to the Political Bureau of a Communist Party. Militant operates by attempting to gain control of constituency Labour parties and trade union branches and to secure the election of its members to Parliament and local authorities and to trade union offices.

Membership. 4,500 (1985 estimate). Support is particularly strong in Liverpool, where it dominates the district Labour Party and is strongly represented in the ruling Labour group on the city council, and inside the Labour Party Young Socialists, which is virtually controlled by Militant.

Electoral influence. Five Militant members contested the 1983 elections as Labour Party candidates, two of whom, Terry Fields and David Nellist, were elected.

Industrial influence. Militant caucuses are active in nearly 20 trade unions, including the Civil and Public Services Association, the Post Office Engineering Union, the National Union of Railwaymen and the General and Municipal Workers' Union. It normally operates inside the unions through a "broad left" alliance which also includes left-wing Labour Party members, Communists and members of other Trotskyist parties.

Orientation. Trotskyist.

Programme. Militant advocates abolition of the monarchy and the House of Lords, nationalization of "the top 200 monopolies", including newspaper printing plant, banks and insurance, a 35-hour week, nuclear disarmament and cuts in arms spending. *British Perspectives*, a document said to be used for the indoctrination of new recruits, envisages a general strike under Marxist influence which will result in "the coming to power of the working class".

Publications. *Militant*, weekly (40,000); *Militant International Review*, quarterly.

International affiliations. Militant founded in 1974 the Committee for the Workers' International, which has sections in Ireland, Belgium, West Germany, Sweden, Greece, Pakistan, Sri Lanka and South Africa, all working within other political parties.

New Communist Party (NCP)

History. The NCP was formed in 1977 by Communist Party members opposed to its Eurocommunist policy, under the leadership of Sid French, the party's Surrey organizer, who died in 1979. They objected in particular to its abandonment of the theory of the dictatorship of the proletariat, and the assurance given in the new party programme that a left-wing government would surrender power if defeated in a general election.

Leadership. Eric Trevett (g.s.).

Membership. 500, mostly in Surrey and Sussex. The NCP originally drew its main support from the mining and industrial areas of Yorkshire, but most of its members in these areas left it in 1981 to join the Labour Party.

Orientation. Pro-Soviet.

Programme. The NCP maintains that "working-class power, once gained, can only be held on to and consolidated by a proletarian dictatorship".

Publication. *New Worker*, weekly.

International affiliations. Although not officially recognized by the Soviet Communist Party, the NCP has received some support from East European countries, and especially from Czechoslovakia.

Revolutionary Communist Group (RCG)

History. The RCG broke away from the International Socialists (now the Socialist Workers' Party) in 1972.

Structure. RCG members live in communes and are required to adopt false names.

Membership. 30 (1985 estimate).

Orientation. Independent.

Programme. The RCG regards the young, the unemployed and the low paid as "the forces of the future", rather than the "reactionary and racist" Labour Party and trade union movement.

Publication. Fight Racism Fight Imperialism, monthly.

Revolutionary Communist League of Britain (RCLB)

History. The RCLB was formed in 1978 by the merger of the Communist Federation of Britain, Marxist-Leninist, founded in 1969, and the Communist Unity Association of Britain, Marxist-Leninist.

Orientation. Maoist.

Revolutionary Communist Party (RCP)

History. The RCP (known until 1981 as the Revolutionary Communist Tendency) was formed in 1977 by expelled members of the Revolutionary Communist Group, and contested the 1983 general election.

Structure. The RCP holds annual conferences on the theme of "preparing for power".

Membership. 60 (1985 estimate).

Electoral influence. The RCP's three candidates in the 1983 elections received a total of 934 votes.

Orientation. Trotskyist.

Publication. The Next Step, monthly.

Revolutionary Communist Party of Britain, Marxist-Leninist (RCPBM-L)

Leadership. David Williams (g.s.)

Orientation. Formerly Maoist, now pro-Albanian.

Publication. Workers' Weekly.

International affiliation. The RCPBM-L is officially recognized by the Albanian Party of Labour.

Revolutionary Workers' Party (RWP)

History. The RWP was founded in 1962.

Orientation. Trotskyist.

Publication. Red Flag, monthly.

International affiliation. Posadist Fourth International.

Socialist Federation (SF)

History. The SF was founded in Bradford (West Yorkshire) in 1984 by six expelled members of the Socialist Workers' Party (SWP) and their supporters.

Membership. The inaugural conference of the SF was attended by 60 ex-members of the SWP.

Orientation. Trotskyist.

Socialist League (SL)

History. The SL is the successor to a secret Trotskyist group inside the Labour Party formed in 1964, which came into the open in 1968 as the International Marxist Group (IMG) and contested the 1974 and 1979 elections. The IMG was dissolved in 1982 and refounded as the SL, its members being encouraged to penetrate the Labour Party and to become active in the trade unions. Differences over the SL's attitude to the Labour leadership led to a split in 1985, when a left-wing faction broke away.

Leadership. Bob Pennington (nat. sec.).

Membership. Estimated at 400 before the 1985 split, when about 150 members formed a rival organization.

Electoral influence. The IMG put forward nine "Socialist Unity" candidates for the 1979 elections, who obtained 2,681 votes. The SL did not contest the 1983 elections.

Industrial influence. The SL has had little success in its attempts to penetrate the trade unions because of the middle-class background of most of its members.

Orientation. Trotskyist.

Publication. Socialist Action, weekly.

International affiliation. Fourth International, United Secretariat.

Socialist Organizer Alliance (SOA)

History. The SOA was formed in 1982 by the merger of the Workers' Socialist League, established in 1974 by members expelled from the Workers' Revolutionary Party, and the International Communist League, founded in 1975 by the Workers' Fight group after its expulsion from the International Socialists.

Membership. 200 (1985 estimate).

Orientation. Trotskyist.

Publication. Socialist Organizer, weekly.

International affiliation. Trotskyist International Liaison Committee.

Socialist Party of Great Britain (SPGB)

History. The SPGB, which claims to be the oldest socialist party in Britain, was formed in 1904 by left-wing members of the Social Democratic Federation. It opposed both World Wars, and has consistently rejected all co-operation with other parties.

Leadership. Bill Valinas (g.s.).

Structure. Applicants for membership are required to undergo an examination in their knowledge of Marxism. Annual conferences attended by instructed delegates from the local branches take binding decisions. The SPGB is opposed to any form of leadership, and the general secretary and Executive Committee, elected annually by postal ballot of the whole membership, are answerable to the conference.

Membership. 700.

Electoral influence. The SPGB's one candidate in the 1983 elections received 85 votes.

Orientation. Independent. The SPGB describes itself as Marxist but not Leninist.

Programme. The SPGB advocates "the need for a majority of the population democratically to take control of the state and establish a system of common ownership", and "the establishment of a world-wide community based on the common ownership and democratic control of the means of wealth distribution and production".

Publications. *Socialist Standard*, monthly (3,000–4,000); *World Socialist*, twice yearly.

International affiliations. The SPGB has links with parties in Ireland, Austria, Canada, the United States, Australia and New Zealand and groups in Belgium and Sweden, which adhere to the same principles and together constitute the World Socialist Movement.

Socialist Workers' Party (SWP)

History. The SWP is the successor to the International Socialists, founded in 1950, which pursued a policy in the early 1960s of penetration of the Labour Party, and especially of the Labour Party Young Socialists. It was reorganized in 1976 as the SWP, with the aim of providing "the socialist alternative to the Labour Party". In 1976–77 it was involved in a number of unemployed and anti-fascist demonstrations which led to violent clashes with the police.

Leadership. Duncan Hallas (ch.); Jim Nichol (nat. sec.).

Structure. The SWP has numerous branches and 70 district committees. The annual conference elects the 40-member National Committee, which elects the 10-member Executive Committee.

Membership. 3,000–4,000 (1984 estimate). Until 1976 the SWP was predominantly composed of students, but the working-class membership, largely consisting of unemployed workers and immigrants, has since increased.

Electoral influence. The SWP has not contested recent general elections.

Industrial influence. The SWP exercises most influence in white-collar unions such as the National Union of Teachers and the National Association of Local Government Officers, but it also claims some support in the car industry, the docks, the railways and the mines. It attempts to organize "rank and file" movements independent of the existing union leadership.

Orientation. Trotskyist. The SWP differs from other Trotskyist parties in rejecting Trotsky's view that the Soviet Union is a "degenerated workers' state" and regarding it as a state capitalist society.

Programme. The SWP denies that socialism can be achieved by parliamentary means, and calls for mass action by the workers to seize control of the economy. It does not reject the use of force.

Publication. Socialist Worker, weekly (15,000).

Spartacist League (SL)

History. The SL was formed in 1976 by members of the US party of the same name.

Membership. Under 100 (1985 estimate).

Orientation. Trotskyist.

Publication. Workers' Hammer, monthly.

International affiliation. International Spartacist Tendency.

Workers' Power (WP)

History. WP originated as a left-wing faction inside the International Socialists (now the Socialist Workers' Party), from which it was expelled in 1975. After temporarily merging with the Workers' Fight group, which had also been expelled, to form the International Communist League (see under "Socialist Organizer Alliance"), WP became an independent organization in 1976.

Orientation. Trotskyist.

Programme. WP rejects all the existing Trotskyist international organizations, and advocates the formation of "fighting propaganda groups" as the basis for a new international.

Publication. Workers' Power, fortnightly.

Workers' Revolutionary Party (WRP)

History. The WRP, the oldest British Trotskyist party, can trace its descent from the Militant Group, formed by former Communists in the 1930s, from which the Workers' International League (WIL) broke away under the leadership of Gerry Healy. The WIL merged in 1944 with the Revolutionary Socialist League to form the Revolutionary Communist Party, which in 1949 became "The Club", a secret organization operating inside the Labour Party. This body broke with the Fourth International in 1953, and united with US and French Trotskyist parties to form the Fourth International, International Committee. Renamed the Socialist Labour League in 1959, it abandoned its "entryist" policy in 1965 after many of its members had been expelled from the Labour Party and the party's youth organization, the Young Socialists, had been dissolved. It adopted its present name in 1973, and has contested general elections since 1974.

A major split occurred in 1985, when Healy was expelled for alleged "systematic debauchery". He was supported by a minority of the Central Committee, including the actors Vanessa and Corin Redgrave, who attributed his expulsion to a right-wing faction led by Mike Banda which was "seeking a tactical orientation towards the Labour Party". This group was expelled, whereupon it formed a rival WRP.

Leadership. Mike Banda (g.s.).

Membership. Estimates of the WRP's membership before the 1985 split varied from 500 to 6,000–7,000.

Electoral influence. The WRP's 20 candidates in the 1983 elections received 3,657 votes.

Industrial influence. The WRP has had some influence in the engineering, mining and car industries. Before the 1985 split it was supported by a number of stage and television personalities, and attempted unsuccessfully to obtain control of Equity, the actors' union.

Orientation. Trotskyist.

Programme. The WRP advocates a revolutionary general strike, the formation of soviets, the replacement of the police by a workers' militia and the nationalization without compensation of financial institutions and major industries.

Publication. *Newsline*, daily. A rival edition of *Newsline*, appearing twice weekly, is published by the Healy-Redgrave faction.

International affiliation. Fourth International, International Committee. Since the withdrawal of the US and French sections this is virtually confined to the WRP.

Greece

Capital: Athens   Pop. 9,984,000

Greek politics between the two world wars were dominated by the struggle between monarchists and republicans, the monarchy being abolished in 1924 and restored in 1935. Elections in 1936 in which neither side obtained a majority were followed by the establishment of a military dictatorship by Gen. Metaxas. An Italian invasion in 1940 was repulsed, but in the following year the German army overran the country. A government-in-exile was established, and inside Greece the resistance forces, and especially the Communist-led National Liberation Army, conducted guerrilla operations. The Germans were expelled in 1944 with the assistance of British troops, which suppressed the Communist forces. A Communist rebellion in 1946–49 ended in defeat.

A series of right-wing governments held power from 1946 to 1963, when a centre-left government took office. Under pressure from the army King Constantine dismissed this in 1965, and a succession of short-lived governments followed until a military regime seized control in 1967. The King went into exile after an unsuccessful attempt to stage a counter-coup, and in 1973 a republic was proclaimed. After its attempt to organize a coup in Cyprus had led to a Turkish invasion of the island, the military regime resigned in 1974. Parliamentary government was restored, and the abolition of the monarchy confirmed by a referendum. The conservative New Democracy party held office from 1974 to 1981, when the Pan-Hellenic Socialist Movement was returned to power.

The 300-member Parliament is elected for a five-year term by a system of reinforced proportional representation, whereby 288 seats are filled from 56 electoral districts and 12 from national party lists.

Communist Party of Greece—Exterior
Kommunistikon Komma Ellados (KKE-Exterior)

History. The KKE originated as the Socialist Workers' Party of Greece, formed in 1918 by a number of small socialist groups and renamed the Socialist Workers' Party of Greece (Communist) in 1920. The party accepted the principles of the Comintern in 1924, and again changed its name to Communist Party of Greece—Greek Section of the Communist International. For several years it was divided by factional struggles, until in 1931 the Comintern secured the election of a new leadership headed by Nikos Zachariadis. After the elections of January 1936 the KKE, with 15 seats, held the balance of power in Parliament between the Monarchists and the Liberals, and an unstable situation ensued until in August Gen. Metaxas established his dictatorship, on the pretext that the Communists were planning a revolt, and banned all political parties.

Following the German invasion in 1941, the KKE formed the National Liberation Front (EAM), which organized the National Liberation Army (ELAS). With 70,000 members, ELAS constituted the main force in the resistance movement, and by 1944 controlled almost the whole country outside the towns. A Government of National Unity, which included six EAM representatives, was formed in Cairo, but after the liberation of Athens fighting broke out in the city, and ELAS was suppressed by British troops. The Communists began guerrilla warfare in 1946 under the leadership of Markos Vafiadis, who in the following year formed a "Free Greek Government", whereupon the KKE was declared illegal. In 1948 Vafiadis was replaced as the rebel commander by Zachariadis, and as head of the "government" by Dimitrios Partsalidis. The rebellion was crushed in 1949, and the leaders fled the country with thousands of their followers. During the civil war 1,223 Communists were executed and over 20,000 imprisoned.

A struggle ensued among the exiled leaders; Vafiadis and Partsalidis were expelled from the party, and Zachariadis, accused of fostering a personality cult, was replaced in 1957 by a collective leadership. Constantine Kolliyannis was elected first secretary in 1961, but after a section of the outlawed party inside Greece broke away in 1968 to form the KKE-Interior he was accused of being responsible for the split, and was replaced in 1973 by Kharilaos Florakis.

Legalized after the fall of the military regime in 1974, the KKE-Exterior contested the elections of that year in alliance with the United Democratic Left, winning five seats, and in 1977 fought alone, obtaining 11 seats. Its support for the Soviet intervention in Afghanistan led in 1980 to the resignation of over 400 of its members, who accused the leadership of pursuing policies dictated by the Soviet Communist Party and repressing all internal criticism. In the 1981 elections, however, it increased its share of the vote to 10.92 per cent and its parliamentary representation to 13, whilst in the elections to the European Parliament, held on the same day, it obtained 12.83 per cent of the vote and three of the 24 seats. After its overtures for representation in the new government had been rejected, it adopted a strongly critical attitude towards the ruling Pan-Hellenic Socialist Movement, which it accused of betraying its election promises. It won control of several major towns in the 1982 local elections, in which it obtained 19.5 per cent of the vote, and retained its three seats in the European Parliament in the 1984 elections. In the 1985 parliamentary elections 13 candidates were returned on the KKE list, including two who took their seats as independents, and the party recorded about 10 per cent of the vote.

Leadership. Kharilaos Florakis (1st sec.).

Structure. The residential and workplace branches are subordinate to the provincial or city committees, which in turn are subordinate to regional committees. The congress, meeting every four years, elects the Central Committee, which elects the nine-member Political Bureau. The party's youth organization is the Communist Youth of Greece.

Membership. 42,000 (1985 estimate). The majority of the members are concentrated in Athens, Piraeus, Salonika and other large cities.

Electoral influence. The KKE vote fell from 693,304 (11.64 per cent) in the 1984 European elections to 629,518 (9.89 per cent) in the 1985 elections.

Industrial influence. Unions affiliated to the KKE-Exterior won 17 of the 45 seats on the governing body of the General Confederation of Greek Workers in 1983.

Orientation. Pro-Soviet.

Programme. The KKE-Exterior holds that the revolution in Greece will pass through two phases, a democratic, anti-imperialist and anti-monopolist phase and a socialist phase, and advocates unity of the democratic, anti-imperialist and anti-monopolist forces, headed by the working class in alliance with the working peasantry, the middle classes and the progressive intellectuals. It calls for stricter controls over and heavier taxation of foreign and domestic monoplies, a more equitable taxation system favouring the working population, price controls, a shorter working week, an earlier retirement age, support for the agricultural co-operative movement and introduction of a voting system based on pure proportional representation. In foreign policy it supports the withdrawal of Greece from NATO and the European Communities, the removal of US and NATO bases and nuclear weapons from Greece, close economic relations with the socialist countries, and a negotiated settlement of the Cyprus question on the basis of an independent and united Cyprus and the withdrawal of all foreign troops.

Publications. *Rizospastis* (Radical), daily (20,000); *Kommunistiki Epitheorisi* (Communist Review), monthly.

International affiliations. The KKE-Exterior is represented on the editorial council of *World Marxist Review*, and maintains close relations with the Soviet-bloc parties.

Communist Party of Greece—Interior
Kommunistikon Komma Ellados, Esoteriku (KKE-Es.)

History. The KKE-Es. was formed by members of the banned Communist Party inside Greece and many of the Communist exiles in Romania and Czechoslovakia, who broke away in 1968 because they refused to accept the exiled leaders' view that the Soviet party was "the vanguard of the world communist movement", supported Dubček's reforms in Czechoslovakia and opposed the Soviet intervention in that country. In 1969 it declared that the international communist movement consisted of autonomous parties with equal rights, and that there could be no guiding state or party. After being legalized in 1974 the KKE-Es. merged with the United Democratic Left (EDA) for the general election, which it fought in alliance with the KKE-Exterior, winning two seats. The merger with the EDA was ended in 1975, but the two parties fought the 1977 elections in alliance, together with three smaller left-wing groups, the KKE-Es. obtaining one seat. It was unsuccessful in the 1981 elections, which it fought alone, but won a seat in the elections to the European Parliament, held on the same day. It generally supported the policies of the government formed in 1981 by the Pan-Hellenic Socialist Movement, in alliance with which it fought the 1982 local elections. It retained its seat in the European Parliament in the 1984 elections and won a seat in the national Parliament in 1985.

Leadership. Leonidas Kyrkos (l.).

Structure. The structure of the KKE-Es. is similar to that of the Communist Party of Greece—Exterior. The Executive Office, the highest party body, has 10 members.

Membership. 12,000 (1985 estimate). The membership, drawn largely from the cities, mainly consists of professional workers and intellectuals.

Electoral influence. The KKE-Es. vote fell from 203,813 (3.42 per cent) in the 1984 European elections to 117,050 (1.84 per cent) in the 1985 elections.

Industrial influence. Unions affiliated to the KKE-Es. won two of the 45 seats on the governing body of the General Confederation of Greek Workers in 1983.

Orientation. Eurocommunist.

Programme. The KKE-Es. advocates the unity of all anti-dictatorial forces in Greece to prevent the destabilization of democracy; the strengthening of civil liberties; the maximum cohesion between the people and the armed forces; and defence of national independence against US and NATO pressures and Turkish aggressiveness. It demands the nationalization of the energy industries, credit institutions, mines, heavy industry, the fertilizer, chemical and defence industries and public transport, reasonable compensation being paid, and state support for small enterprises. In foreign policy it favours withdrawal from NATO, as part of the process of abolition of military alliances; the removal of nuclear and military bases from the Balkans and of the US and Soviet fleets from the Mediterranean; multilateral co-operation between the Balkan countries; Greek membership of the European Communities, on condition that Greek agriculture and industry are protected; and a settlement of the Cyprus question through talks between the two communities without foreign interference.

Publication. Avgi (Dawn), daily (10,000).

International affiliations. The KKE-Es. has close relations with the Yugoslav and Romanian Communist parties and with the Eurocommunist parties of Western Europe. Relations with the Chinese Communist Party were established in 1983.

Greek Communist Party—Marxist-Leninist (KKE-ML)

History. The KKE-ML was formed in 1969, as the Organization of Greek Marxist-Leninists, by former members of the Organization of Marxist-Leninists of Greece, and adopted its present name in 1974. It contested the 1981 general elections and the 1984 European elections in alliance with the Revolutionary Communist Party (see below).

Orientation. Stalinist.

Organization of Marxist-Leninists of Greece (OMLE)

History. The OMLE was founded in 1964, and operated underground during the military regime of 1967–74.

Orientation. Pro-Chinese.

Pan-Hellenic Socialist Movement
Panellinion Socialistikou Kinema (Pasok)

History. Pasok was founded in 1974 by Andreas Papandreou, who had been a minister in 1964–65 in the Centre Union government led by his father, George Papandreou, and absorbed the Pan-Hellenic Liberation Movement and Democratic Defence, which had actively resisted the military dictatorship. After winning 12 seats in the 1974 elections, it became the strongest opposition party after the 1977 elections, with 93 seats, and took power after its victory in 1981, when it obtained 48.06 per cent of the vote and 172 seats. In the elections to the European Parliament, held on the same day, it obtained 40.17 per cent of the vote and 10 of the 24 seats, the discrepancy being attributed to its opposition to Greek membership of the European Communities. It retained its seats in the 1984 European elections, and was again returned to power in 1985, although with a reduced majority, its representation falling to 161 seats.

Leadership. Andreas Papandreou (ch.).

Structure. Pasok has local and district organizations. The congress elects the 80-member Central Committee, which elects the Executive Bureau and Secretariat.

Membership. 40,000 (1984 estimate).

Electoral influence. The Pasok vote increased from 2,476,491 (41.58 per cent) in the 1984 European elections to 2,916,450 (45.82 per cent) in 1985.

Industrial influence. Unions affiliated to Pasok won 26 of the 45 seats on the governing body of the General Confederation of Greek Workers in 1983.

Orientation. Independent; in 1975 Papandreou described Pasok as Marxist but not Leninist.

Programme. Pasok's 1985 election programme defined its economic policy as one of self-sustained development based on decentralization, socialization and workers' participation in decision-making. Private enterprise would be encouraged within the rules of healthy competition. It was planned to increase the competitiveness of the economy, expand its productive base and reduce unemployment through an aggressive programme of public and private investment, modernization and development of research. The credit system would be directed particularly to financing development programmes and strengthening small and medium-sized businesses. Agricultural and consumers' co-operatives would be encouraged. Pasok aimed to create a welfare state by development of the national health service, establishment of a national pensions scheme and the introduction of free family planning. It advocated an independent foreign policy actively contributing to détente and disarmament, the ultimate dissolution of both cold war blocs, co-operation with all the Balkan countries and creation of a nuclear-free zone in the region. US bases in Greece, in accordance with an agreement signed in 1983, would be removed in 1988. Sources of arms supplies would be diversified and a high-technology Greek arms industry developed. The armed forces would be strengthened, and would be deployed to confront "the real danger from the east" (i.e. from Turkey). Pasok was not opposed to a dialogue with Turkey, however, provided that Turkey recognized the existing legal regime in the Aegean and withdrew its troops from Cyprus.

Publication. *Exormisi*, weekly.

International affiliations. The Pasok members of the European Parliament sit with the Socialist group, but the party has declined to join the Socialist International.

Revolutionary Communist Party of Greece
Epanastatiko Kommunistiko Komma Ellados (EKKE)

History. The EKKE was formed in 1970, as the Revolutionary Communist Movement of Greece, by Greek students in West Berlin, and has contested elections since 1974.

Electoral influence. The share of the vote won by the EKKE and its ally the Greek Communist Party—Marxist-Leninist rose from 0.08 per cent in 1981 to 0.2 per cent in the 1984 European elections.

Orientation. Maoist.

United Democratic Left
Eniaia Demokratike Aristera (EDA)

History. The EDA was formed in 1951, when the Communist Party was illegal and its leaders in exile, as a cover for Communist activity inside Greece, and won 10 seats in the elections of that year. It lost them in 1952, after proportional representation had been replaced by a simple majority system, and fought the 1956 elections as part of the Democratic Union, an alliance of left and centre parties. In 1958, after proportional representation had been reintroduced, it obtained 24.3 per cent of the vote and 78 seats, becoming the largest opposition group in Parliament. It contested the 1961 elections as part of a left-wing alliance which won 24 seats, but fought the 1963 and 1964 elections without allies, obtaining 28 and 22 seats respectively. Banned under the military dictatorship of 1967–74, it merged in 1974 with the Communist Party of Greece—Interior (KKE-Es.), and contested the elections of that year in alliance with the Communist Party of Greece—Exterior, winning one seat. Although the EDA ended the merger with the KKE-Es. in 1975, it formed the Alliance of Progressive and Left-wing Forces with the KKE-Es. and three smaller groups for the 1977 elections, in which it again won one seat. It did not contest the 1981 elections, recommending its supporters to vote for the Pan-Hellenic Socialist Movement (Pasok). Its secretary, Manolis Glezos, was elected on the Pasok list in 1985, and sat in Parliament as an independent.

Leadership. Ilias Iliou (ch.); Manolis Glezos (sec.).

Structure. The EDA has basic organizations in districts, regions, trade unions, workplaces and universities.

Membership. 30,000 (1984 estimate).

Electoral influence. The EDA has not contested elections since 1977.

Orientation. Eurocommunist.

Programme. The EDA seeks to introduce "socialism with a human face", favours a multiparty system and rejects the dictatorship of the proletariat. It supports Greek membership of the European Communities.

Publications. The Greek Left (10,000); *EDA News* (10,000).

United Socialist Alliance of Greece (ESPE)

History. The ESPE was formed in 1984 by Stathis Panagoulis, previously Deputy Interior Minister in the Papandreou government, who had been expelled from the ruling Pan-Hellenic Socialist Movement in 1982 after accusing the leadership of reneging on its election promises. Panagoulis was re-elected in 1985 on the Communist Party of Greece—Exterior list, and. sat in Parliament as an independent.

Iceland

Capital: Reykjavik   Pop. 239,000

Iceland, formerly a dependency of the Danish crown, became a sovereign state under the King of Denmark in 1918, and adopted a republican constitution in 1944. It has since been ruled by a series of coalition governments formed by the four main parties—the conservative Independence Party, the liberal Progressive Party, the Social Democratic Party and the communist People's Alliance. The *Althing* (Parliament), elected by proportional representation for a four-year term, consists of 60 members, 20 of whom are elected by its members to form the Upper House.

Icelandic Communist Party—Marxist-Leninist

History. This party was formed in 1976.

Leadership. Gunnar Andresson (ch.).

Orientation. Pro-Chinese.

Publication. Stettabarattan (Class Struggle).

Organization of Icelandic Socialists

History. This organization was formed in 1969 by a group which had left the People's Alliance in the previous year after it had denounced the Soviet invasion of Czechoslovakia.

Electoral influence. The Organization received 448 votes (0.3 per cent) in the 1974 elections.

Orientation. Pro-Soviet.

People's Alliance
Althydubandalagid (AB)

History. A communist faction which had existed inside the Social Democratic Party since 1919 broke away in 1930, when it formed the Communist Party of Iceland and joined the Comintern. It first obtained representation in the *Althing* in 1937, winning three seats. Although a proposal for a merger was rejected by the Social Democratic Party in 1938, the left-wing Social Democrats united with the

Communists to form the United People's Party—Socialist Party (SA-SF), which left the Comintern and in 1942 won seven seats. When Iceland became independent in 1944 the SA-SF entered a coalition government with the Social Democrats and the Independence Party, but it withdrew in 1947, largely because of differences over the maintenance of US bases in Iceland. For the 1956 elections it combined with the small National Defence Party and a group of left-wing Social Democrats in the People's Alliance (AB), winning eight seats, and formed a coalition government with the Social Democrats and the Progressive Party which held office until 1958.

In 1968 the People's Alliance, which had fought elections since 1956 purely as an electoral alliance, became a single party, whereupon the non-Marxist section of the Alliance left it, declaring that the new party would be "the Communist Party under another name", and formed the Union of Liberals and Leftists. After the 1971 elections, in which it won 10 seats, the AB formed a coalition government with the Progressives and the Union of Liberals and Leftists, which resigned in 1974. It won 14 seats in the 1978 elections, and formed a coalition with the Progressives and Social Democrats. After new elections in the following year, in which its representation fell to 11, it entered a coalition with the Progressives and dissident Independence Party members early in 1980. It lost a seat in the 1983 elections, and was not represented in the new government.

Since 1968, when it strongly condemned the Soviet intervention in Czechoslovakia, the AB has pursued a Eurocommunist policy. The leadership denounced Soviet "military oppression against the countries of Eastern Europe and against Afghanistan" in 1982, and declared its support for the Solidarity movement in Poland.

Leadership. Svavar Gestsson (ch.); Helgi Gudmundsson (sec.).

Structure. The congress, meeting every three years, elects the 70-member Central Committee by a complex preference system. Between Central Committee meetings the 10-member Executive Committee is the highest authority. Leadership positions are limited to one term of office, and are equally divided between men and women.

Membership. 3,000 (1985 estimate). The AB draws its main support from industrial workers, fishermen and intellectuals in the Reykjavik area and the eastern fishing and processing towns.

Electoral influence. In each election since 1971 the AB has obtained between 17 and 23 per cent of the vote and between 10 and 14 of the 60 seats in the *Althing*, forming either the second or the third largest parliamentary group. In 1983 it received 17.3 per cent of the vote.

Industrial influence. The AB forms the largest element in the Icelandic Federation of Labour, but does not command a majority.

Orientation. Eurocommunist.

Programme. The AB put forward a programme to deal with the economic recession and the high inflation rate in 1982 which included limitation of imports, assistance to the fishing industry and agriculture, an increase in industry powered by hydroelectricity, reduction in government expenditures, establishment of a fund to raise the wages of low-paid workers and strengthening of price controls. In foreign policy it is strongly isolationist; it advocates withdrawal from NATO and closure of the US base at Keflavik, and opposes all proposals for Iceland's entry into the European Communities.

Publications. Thjodviljinn (Will of the Nation), daily (12,000).

International affiliations. Since 1968 the AB has not attended international communist meetings, and has avoided contacts with foreign communist parties. It maintains informal relations with the Socialist People's Party of Denmark and the Socialist Left Party of Norway.

Revolutionary Communist League
Fylking Bytingarsinnadhra Kommunista (FBK)

History. The FBK unsuccessfully put forward 24 candidates in the 1978 elections.

Membership. 200.

Orientation. Trotskyist.

Publication. Neisti (The Spark).

Ireland

Republic of Ireland
Capital: Dublin

Pop. 3,675,000

Northern Ireland
Capital: Belfast

Pop. 1,560,000

The first Marxist party in Ireland, the short-lived Irish Socialist Republican Party, was founded in 1896 by James Connolly, who was among the leaders of the Easter Rising in Dublin in 1916 and was afterwards executed. The national uprising of 1919–21 was ended by a treaty whereby the 26 overwhelmingly Catholic counties became the Irish Free State, an independent state within the British Empire, and the six predominantly Protestant counties of Northern Ireland remained a part of the United Kingdom, with representation in the Westminster Parliament, but with its own government and parliament at Stormont exercising responsibility for internal affairs. A civil war in the Free State between the supporters of the treaty and the republicans in 1922–23 ended in the victory of the former. The Free State (renamed Eire in 1937) became the Republic of Ireland in 1949, when it left the Commonwealth. Since 1932 power has alternated between the two main parties, *Fianna Fáil* and *Fine Gael*; the latter has always ruled in coalition with the Labour Party. The Irish Parliament consists of a House of Representatives (*Dáil Éireann*) of 166 members elected by proportional representation for a five-year term and a partly nominated and partly elected Senate.

From 1921 onwards Northern Ireland was ruled by the Unionist Party, representing the Protestant majority. Protest demonstrations in 1968–69 by the Northern Ireland Civil Rights Association against discrimination against the Catholic minority were followed by sectarian riots, the intervention of the British Army and a terrorist campaign by the Irish Republican Army (IRA) and other republican organizations which still continues. The Stormont Parliament was suspended and direct British rule introduced in 1972, and after a number of unsuccessful constitutional experiments a 78-member Northern Ireland Assembly with limited powers was elected by proportional representation in 1982 as a step towards devolution.

British and Irish Communist Organization

Orientation. This small neo-Stalinist group, with its headquarters in Dublin, is unique among the Irish Marxist parties in accepting the "two nations" theory, according to which the North should be recognized as forming a separate state.

Publication. Political Bulletin.

Communist Party of Ireland (CPI)

History. The original CPI was founded in 1921, when the Socialist Party of Ireland expelled its right wing and affiliated to the Comintern. In the complex situation created by partition and the civil war it was dissolved in 1923, and was replaced by the Irish Workers' League, which disappeared in the South in 1928 but continued to operate in the North. The CPI was re-established in 1933, and functioned throughout the country until 1941, when because of the difficulties created by the belligerent status of the North and the neutrality of the South the party's Southern organization suspended its activities. It was revived in 1948 as the Irish Workers' League, which changed its name in 1962 to the Irish Workers' Party and reunited with the Northern organization in 1970 as the CPI.

Leadership. Andrew Barr (ch.); James Stewart (g.s.).

Structure. The CPI is organized in residential and (in the North) in workplace cells. There are separate area committees for the North and the Republic. The congress, meeting every three years, elects the National Executive Committee of 23 members, which elects the National Political Committee. The party's youth organization is the Connolly Youth Movement.

Membership. 500 (1985 estimate). The CPI is slightly stronger among Northern Protestants than in the Republic, where its membership is mainly concentrated in Dublin.

Electoral influence. The CPI contests elections, but has never been represented in the *Dáil*, the Northern Ireland Parliament or the Westminster Parliament.

Industrial influence. The CPI has some influence in the Irish Congress of Trade Unions, of which Andrew Barr is a former president.

Orientation. Pro-Soviet.

Programme. The CPI advocates the establishment of a unified Irish socialist republic, to be attained through the united struggle of Catholic and Protestant workers, small farmers, small businessmen and intellectuals. It condemns terrorism as deepening the sectarian division between Catholic and Protestant workers, and seeks a peaceful and democratic solution of the Irish question through a phased withdrawal of the British forces. It opposes Irish membership of the European Communities and any Irish co-operation with NATO.

Publications. Irish Workers' Voice, weekly, Dublin; *Irish Socialist,* monthly, Dublin; *Unity,* monthly, Belfast.

International affiliations. The CPI is represented on the editorial council of *World Marxist Review.*

COMMUNIST AND MARXIST PARTIES

Communist Party of Ireland—Marxist-Leninist (CPI-ML)

History. This Maoist organization, with its headquarters in Dublin, operates on both sides of the border, and put forward one candidate in the elections to the Constitutional Convention in Northern Ireland in 1975.

Leadership. David Vipond.

Orientation. Pro-Albanian. The CPI-ML supports the use of violence.

Publication. Red Patriot.

Irish Marxist Society

History. This organization was formed in 1977 by a number of leading members of the Communist Party, who had resigned in protest against the lack of internal democracy and free discussion.

Orientation. Eurocommunist.

Publication. Socialist Quarterly.

Irish Republican Socialist Party (IRSP)
Pairtí Poblachtach Sóisialach na h-Éireann

History. The IRSP was founded in 1974 by a group favouring the resumption of military operations against the British in Northern Ireland, which broke away from Official *Sinn Féin* and the Official Irish Republican Army. Several people were killed in subsequent clashes between the two factions, the IRSP chairman, Seamus Costello, being shot dead in Dublin in 1977. The IRSP is closely linked with the Irish National Liberation Army (q.v.).

Leadership. Jim Laine (ch.); Anthony Doran (g.s.).

Membership. 2,457 in Ireland, 410 in Europe and the United States (1984 claim).

Electoral influence. The IRSP has contested elections in the Republic since 1977 without success, and won two seats in local elections in Belfast in 1981.

Orientation. Trotskyist.

Programme. The IRSP defines its aims as the ending of British rule in Northern Ireland and the establishment of a 32-county democratic socialist republic.

Publication. Starry Plough, monthly.

People's Democracy

History. People's Democracy was founded in 1968 by students at Queen's University, Belfast, as an offshoot of the Northern Irish Civil Rights Association, and played a leading part in the civil rights agitation of 1968–69. One of its members, Bernadette Devlin (Mrs McAliskey), represented Mid-Ulster in the Westminster Parliament from 1969 to 1974 as an Independent Unity member, and unsuccessfully contested the *Dáil* elections of February 1982 as a People's Democracy candidate.

Leadership. Eamonn McCann.

Structure. Although mainly active in Northern Ireland, People's Democracy also operates in the Republic. It has close associations with the Provisional IRA.

Orientation. Trotskyist.

International affiliations. Fourth International, United Secretariat.

Workers' Party
Pairtí na nOibrí

History. The Workers' Party is a successor party to *Sinn Féin* (Ourselves), the nationalist party founded by Arthur Griffith in 1905, which became the main republican organization after the 1916 rising. *Sinn Féin* split in 1922, when it became the party of the anti-treaty section led by Eamonn de Valera, and again in 1926 when he formed *Fianna Fáil*, leaving the diehard republicans in control of the party, with the Irish Republican Army (IRA) as its military wing. For many years *Sinn Fein* and the IRA were divided between a traditional nationalist and a socialist wing, until in 1969 the former broke away to form Provisional *Sinn Féin* (now known simply as *Sinn Féin*) and the Provisional IRA. The Official IRA suspended its military activities in 1972, and is believed to have been disbanded.

Official *Sinn Féin* (known in Northern Ireland as the Republican Clubs) changed its name in 1977 to *Sinn Féin*—The Workers' Party, and in 1982 dropped the prefix *Sinn Féin*. Having abandoned in 1971 its traditional policy of not taking seats in the Dublin, Stormont and Westminster Parliaments, it won a seat in the *Dáil* in 1981 and three in the elections of February 1982. In the new *Dáil*, in which it held the balance of power, it at first supported the minority *Fianna Fáil* government, but later voted against it on a motion of confidence as a protest against proposed cuts in the health service. In the subsequent elections, held in November, it won two seats.

Leadership. Tomás MacGiolla (pres.); Sean Garland (g.s.).

Structure. The Workers' Party is organized both in the Republic of Ireland and in Northern Ireland.

Electoral influence. In the Republic the Workers' Party has held between one and three seats in the *Dáil* since 1981, drawing its support mainly from industrial workers in Dublin and other towns. It obtained 2.29 per cent of the first-preference votes in the elections of February 1982, and 4.3 per cent in the 1984 elections to the European Parliament. It is also represented on 18 local authorities. In Northern Ireland it received 17,216 votes (2.72 per cent) in the 1982 elections to the Northern Ireland Assembly, and 14,650 votes in the 1983 general election.

Industrial influence. The Workers' Party exercises some influence in the trade union movement in the Republic.

Orientation. Independent.

Programme. The Workers' Party seeks to develop "anti-sectarian class politics" throughout Ireland, with the ultimate objective of establishing a single secular, democratic and socialist republic in which the working classes will own and control the country's wealth and resources. Its manifesto for the elections of November 1982 in the Republic stated that its priorities were the creation of full employment by 1991 and an increase in national income by an annual average of 5 per cent.

Publications. *Irish People*, weekly (30,000); *Workers' Life*, monthly (12,000); *Northern People*, weekly, Belfast.

World Socialist Party of Ireland

History. This small party, with its headquarters in Belfast, is closely linked with the Socialist Party of Great Britain (q.v.) and shares the same principles.

International affiliations. World Socialist Movement.

Terrorist Organization

Irish National Liberation Army (INLA)

History. The INLA was formed in 1974 as the military wing of the Irish Republican Socialist Party (q.v.), and has claimed responsibility for numerous acts of violence in Northern Ireland, England and the Republic of Ireland, including the murder in 1979 of Airey Neave, Conservative spokesman on Northern Ireland, by a bomb explosion in his car outside the House of Commons and an explosion in a public house at Ballykelly (Co. Londonderry) in 1982, in which 17 people were killed. It was proscribed in the United Kingdom in 1979 and in the Republic of Ireland in 1983. After a period of relative inactivity, the emergence of a new and younger leadership in 1984 was followed by an intensification of terrorist activities in the North.

Membership. 40–50 activists, centred on Belfast, Derry, Dundalk and Dublin (1985 estimate).

Italy

Capital: Rome   Pop. 57,000,000

Marxist thought has been influential in Italy since the formation of the Italian Socialist Party (PSI) in 1892, although the party was divided between reformists and revolutionaries, and the latter were often syndicalist rather than Marxist in their outlook. Italy's intervention in World War I, which the PSI opposed, was followed in 1919–20 by widespread industrial and agrarian unrest, and in 1921 the Marxist wing of the PSI broke away to form the Italian Communist Party (PCI). Both were suppressed by Mussolini's Fascist regime, which took power in 1922. Following Italy's entry into World War II and the allied invasion of Sicily in 1943 Mussolini was overthrown, and the King appointed a government headed by Marshal Badoglio, which signed an armistice with the Allies and declared war on Germany. The government was broadened in 1944 to include the PCI, the PSI, the Christian Democratic Party and the other anti-fascist parties. The Germans were expelled from Italy in 1945; the monarchy was abolished in the following year; and a new republican constitution came into force in 1948.

The left-wing parties were excluded from the government in 1947, since when the Christian Democrats have held power, either alone or in alliance with other parties. Since 1964 the PSI has served in a number of coalition governments, and in 1976–79 the PCI gave external support to a Christian Democratic government. The first coalition government with a Socialist Prime Minister was formed in 1983.

The Italian Parliament consists of the Senate of 315 members, elected for five years on a regional basis, and the Chamber of Deputies of 630 members, elected for five years by proportional representation. For administrative purposes Italy is divided into 20 regions, each with a regional council and *giunta* (executive).

Communist Party of Italy—Marxist-Leninist
Partito Comunista d'Italia—Marxista-Leninista (PCI-ML)

History. Founded in 1963 as the Italian Marxist-Leninist Movement, the PCI-ML adopted its present name in 1966. As the largest Maoist group in Italy it was officially recognized by the Chinese Communist Party, but in 1977 it adopted a pro-Albanian attitude.

Leadership. Fosco Dinucci.

Orientation. Pro-Albanian.

Publications. *Nuova Unità* (New Unity), daily; *Voce della Cella* (Voice from the Cell), weekly.

Continuous Struggle
Lotta Continua

History. Founded in 1968, this party was first organized on a national scale in 1972, and was involved in a number of clashes with right-wing extremists in 1972–73. It contested the 1976 elections in alliance with the Party of Proletarian Unity, winning one seat, and the 1979 elections in alliance with the Proletarian Democrats.

Leadership. Guido Vale.

Structure. The party is organized in autonomous groups, some of which in the 1970s had links with terrorist organizations.

Membership. *Lotta Continua* claimed 30,000 members in 1971 and 12,000 in 1977, but has since virtually disintegrated. It drew its support mainly from unskilled workers and students.

Orientation. Originally Trotskyist, *Lotta Continua* later adopted an independent attitude.

Publication. *Lotta Continua*, daily.

Italian Communist Party
Partito Comunista Italiano (PCI)

History. The PCI was founded in January 1921, when the left wing seceded from the Italian Socialist Party (PSI). The new party had about 55,000 members, and in elections in the following May obtained 300,000 votes and 15 seats. Despite the repressive measures of the Fascist regime which took power in 1922, it succeeded in winning 19 seats in the 1924 elections, but after 1925 repression was intensified, over 4,000 Communists being imprisoned.

The party leadership was divided between an ultra-leftist faction headed by Amadeo Bordiga, the PCI's first secretary, which advocated abstention from elections and the seizure of power through revolutionary action by the trade unions, and a group centred on the Turin paper *Ordine Nuovo*, which included Antonio Gramsci and Palmiro Togliatti. Gramsci, who succeeded Bordiga as general secretary, put forward in 1926 a programme for a common struggle by the northern industrial workers and the southern peasantry. Later in the same year, however, the party was banned and many of its leaders arrested, including Gramsci, who was sentenced to 20 years' imprisonment, and by 1934 its underground organization had been virtually destroyed and its membership reduced to 2,400. Even in prison Gramsci, who died in 1937, continued to write, and his *Prison Notebooks* are now regarded as a Marxist classic.

Under the leadership of Togliatti, Gramsci's successor, the PCI in 1934 concluded a pact for unity of action with the PSI, and in 1937 formed a broader alliance, the Italian Popular Union, with 45,000 members among the anti-fascist exiles in France. During the Spanish Civil War 5,000 Italians, commanded by the Communist Luigi Longo, fought in the International Brigades. The German–Soviet pact of 1939 destroyed the anti-fascist alliance, however, and on the outbreak of war many of the PCI leaders in France were arrested. The party headquarters were thereupon transferred to Moscow, where Togliatti arrived in 1940.

Underground activity inside Italy was revived in 1941, and a new pact was concluded with the PSI, which was later extended to include the other anti-fascist parties. Mass strikes against the war under Communist leadership in Turin and Milan in March 1943 prepared the way for the fall of Mussolini in July, and on returning to Italy in March 1944 Togliatti persuaded the anti-fascist parties to enter Marshal Badoglio's government. Meanwhile an anti-German partisan movement developed in central and northern Italy, mainly under Communist leadership, and made a major contribution to the allied victory. Primarily because of its role in the anti-fascist struggle, the PCI, which had probably had fewer than 3,000 members in 1940, most of them in prison or in exile, had 1,708,267 at the end of 1945 and 2,115,232 in 1948.

In the 1946 elections the PCI emerged as the third largest party, after the Christian Democrats and the PSI, with 19 per cent of the vote and 104 seats. The Communist and Socialist ministers were dropped from the government in 1947, and the elections in the following year resulted in an overwhelming victory for the Christian Democrats, although the PCI won 131 seats. Its attempts to secure the support of the southern peasantry, the lower middle class and the intellectuals for an "Italian road to socialism" had considerable success, however, and in 1953 it increased its share of the vote to 22.6 per cent and its parliamentary representation to 143.

The PCI had hitherto accepted Soviet leadership, and from 1947 to 1956 was one of the two West European parties included in the Cominform. After the publication of the "secret" Khrushchev report in June 1956, however, Togliatti put forward the demand for a "polycentric" communist movement without a "single guide", and affirmed his support for the possibility of achieving socialism by parliamentary means and the continuance of the multiparty system in a socialist society. The PCI's subsequent support for the Soviet intervention in Hungary led to a heavy loss of membership, which fell from 2,035,353 in 1956 to 1,792,974 in 1960, and the ending of its political alliance with the PSI. It nevertheless maintained its electoral position, winning 22.7 per cent of the vote and 140 seats in 1958 and 25.3 per cent and 166 seats in 1963.

Although the PCI supported the Soviet party after 1960 in its controversy with China, it continued to develop Togliatti's concept of polycentrism. In his "testament", written shortly before his death in 1964, he called for the liquidation of "old formulae which no longer correspond to present realities"; emphasized the necessity for the autonomy of communist parties; opposed the creation of any new centralized international organization; and advised the communist countries to abandon "the system of limitation and suppression of democratic and personal liberties introduced by Stalin". Longo, who succeeded him as general secretary, continued to assert the independence of the PCI, as was shown shortly afterwards when it criticized the manner in which Khrushchev had been removed from office, and still more strongly when it condemned the Soviet invasion of Czechoslovakia. At the Moscow conference of communist parties in 1969 the deputy general secretary of the PCI, Enrico Berlinguer, reaffirmed its opposition to the invasion; declared that there could not be "a guiding party or a guiding state" for the world communist movement; and stressed the PCI's support for "a pluralist and democratic system".

The PCI increased its support in successive elections, obtaining 26.9 per cent of the vote and 177 seats in 1968 and 27.1 per cent and 179 seats in 1972. Berlinguer, who succeeded Longo as general secretary in 1972, proposed in the following year the revival of the "historic compromise" between the three major forces in Italy—the Catholics, Socialists and Communists—which had existed in 1944–47; endorsed in 1974 Italian participation in the European Communities; and expressed support in 1975 for Italy's membership of NATO. In the same year he issued a joint statement with Georges Marchais, general secretary of the French party, affirming their full support for democratic liberties, a multiparty system, co-operation between Communists, Socialists and Catholics, the European Communities and the dissolution of military blocs (see Appendix 2: Documents).

These policies greatly increased the PCI's popular support, and its membership, which had fallen to 1,502,862 in 1969, rose to 1,814,740 in 1977. In the 1975 elections in 15 of the 20 regions its vote passed the 10,000,000 mark for the first time, and it emerged as the strongest party in Liguria, Piedmont, Emilia-Romagna, Tuscany, Umbria, the Marches and Latium, whilst in municipal elections held on the same day it received the highest vote in most of the major cities. The 1976 general election was an unprecedented success for the PCI, which obtained 12,620,509 votes (34.4 per cent) and 228 seats. After the elections it supported a minority Christian Democratic government from outside, but its demands for representation in the government were rejected, and in 1979 it returned to opposition.

Relations with the Soviet party meanwhile became increasingly strained. At the 1976 conference of European communist parties Berlinguer called for "the abandonment of obsolete methods" and "a socialist society which has as its foundation the value of individual and collective liberties and their guarantee, the principles of the secular non-ideological nature of the state and its democratic organization, the plurality of political parties and the possibility of alternation of government majorities, the autonomy of the trade unions, religious freedom and freedom of expression, culture and the arts and sciences". In 1980 the PCI strongly condemned the Soviet intervention in Afghanistan, and in 1981 the PCI delegate was refused permission to address the Soviet Communist Party congress because his speech called for the exclusion of foreign troops from that country. Following the declaration of martial law in Poland, the PCI Central Committee adopted in 1982 a resolution condemning "a system that does not permit real democratic participation in either the production or the political sphere", and declaring that "the phase in the development of socialism that began with the October Revolution has lost its driving force". The resolution was violently attacked in the Soviet and East European press. Although the PCI had condemned the Chinese invasion of Vietnam in 1979, relations with the Chinese Communist Party, which had been suspended since 1966, were resumed in 1980.

Support for the PCI declined after 1976, this being attributed in part to the public reaction against the terrorism of the Red Brigades, and in part to left-wing opposition to the "historic compromise" policy. In 1979 the PCI obtained 30.4 per cent of the vote and 201 seats in the parliamentary elections and 29.6 per cent and 24 seats in the elections to the European Parliament. It abandoned the "historic compromise" strategy in 1980, and put forward the new slogan of the "democratic alternative" based on an alliance between the PCI and PSI. Its advances were rejected by the PSI, and in the 1983 elections the PCI again lost ground, obtaining 29.9 per cent of the vote and 198 seats. In the European elections of June 1984, however, it received more votes than any other party for the first time in its history, obtaining 33.3 per cent of the vote as against 33 per cent for the Christian Democrats, and won 27 seats. Berlinguer, who had died a few days before the elections, was succeeded as general secretary by Alessandro Natta.

The Party of Proletarian Unity for Communism, founded by left-wing Socialists in 1972, which had fought the 1983 parliamentary elections and the 1984 European elections in alliance with the PCI, merged with it in November 1984. The PCI lost ground in the regional, provincial and municipal elections held in May 1985, its share of the vote in the regional elections falling to 30.2 per cent, and lost control of the Rome city council, which it had held since 1976, to the Christian Democrats.

Leadership. Alessandro Natta (g.s.).

Structure. The PCI is organized in about 12,000 residential and workplace cells, grouped in 108 provincial federations, which elect the 20 regional committees. The congress, meeting every four years, elects the 180-member Central Committee and the 57-member Central Control Commission, which jointly elect the chairman, the general secretary, the 33-member Directorate and the nine-member Secretariat.

Membership. 1,700,000 (1985 claim). Since the suppression of the Indonesian party in 1965 the PCI has been the largest communist party in any non-communist country. Although industrial workers form the largest element in the membership, the party also draws strong support from sections of the peasantry, the lower middle class and the intellectuals. The membership of the Communist Youth Federation has fallen from nearly 500,000 in the early 1970s to less than 50,000 in 1984.

Electoral influence. In 1983 the PCI obtained 29.9 per cent of the vote in elections to the Chamber of Deputies and 30.8 per cent in elections to the Senate. A year later it obtained 11,642,626 votes (33.3 per cent) in the elections to the European Parliament. In the 1985 regional elections it received 30.2 per cent of the vote nationally; between 44 and 47 per cent in the "red belt" of Emilia-Romagna, Tuscany and Umbria; over 30 per cent in Liguria and the Marches; and over 20 per cent in Latium, Piedmont, Lombardy, Abruzzi, Apulia, Campania, Basilicata, Calabria and Veneto. It has formed regional administrations in alliance with the PSI in Emilia-Romagna, Tuscany, Umbria, Liguria, Piedmont and Latium, and has been the ruling party, usually in alliance with the PSI, in Rome, Milan, Turin, Genoa, Venice, Bologna, Florence, Perugia, Naples and many smaller cities and towns.

Industrial influence. The PCI is the strongest force in the Italian General Confederation of Labour (*Confederazione Generale Italiana del Lavoro*, CGIL), the largest of the four main Italian trade union federations, with about 4,500,000 members. The CGIL withdrew from the Soviet-dominated World Federation of Trade Unions in 1978.

Orientation. Eurocommunist. A pro-Soviet faction exists inside the party, and is believed to be supported by about 25 per cent of the membership.

Programme. The PCI's programme for the 1983 elections included the following proposals: (1) Reform of the parliamentary system, the administration, local government, the administration of justice and the armed forces. Abolition of the Senate. Stronger measures against organized crime, drug trafficking and terrorism. (2) A programme of public investment in sources of energy, transport, housing and water supplies to combat unemployment, especially in the south; state assistance to co-operative enterprises; retraining schemes for the unemployed; an emergency programme to deal with youth unemployment. (3) A programme of state investment in industry and agriculture intended to promote technical innovations and exports. The establishment of a mixed system of private, co-operative and state farms which would facilitate technical assistance, irrigation, agrarian credits and alternative sources of energy. Reform of the structure of the banking system. (4) Reform of the taxation system, including the introduction of a graduated wealth tax. Introduction of a uniform pension system. Improvement of health services. (5) Adoption of a radical new housing policy which would safeguard both the rights of tenants and the legitimate interests of small proprietors. A 10-year housing plan, with the aim of building 10,000 new houses a year. Defence of the natural and historical environment. (6) Reform of the educational system and the universities, laying special emphasis on professional training and scientific and technological research. (7) Adoption of a Charter of Rights of the Citizen, which would be legally enforceable, and in particular would safeguard women, the young, the aged, the disabled and ethnic and linguistic minorities against all forms of discrimination. (8) International negotiations aimed at the reduction and destruction of Soviet missiles and the non-installation of Pershing and cruise missiles in Western Europe, as a step towards the banning and destruction of all nuclear weapons.

Publications. L'Unità (Unity), daily, founded by Gramsci in 1924 (200,000 daily, 600,000 on Sundays); *Rinascita* (Rebirth), weekly; *Critica Marxista* (Marxist Criticism) and *Politica ed Economia* (Politics and Economics), every two months.

International affiliations. The PCI is represented on the editorial board of *World Marxist Review*, and is recognized as a Communist Party by the Soviet-bloc parties. Although relations between them are strained, both sides suspended polemics in 1984. It also maintains relations with the Chinese and many other communist parties, and also with a number of Socialist parties, including the French Socialist Party and the British Labour Party.

Italian Communist Party, Marxist-Leninist
Partito Comunista (Marxista-Leninista) Italiano (PCM-LI)

History. The PCM-LI was founded in 1968 as the Union of Italian Communists (Marxist-Leninist) by the merger of four small Maoist groups, and adopted its present name in 1972. It contested the elections in the same year, receiving 85,000 votes.

Leadership. Aldo Bradirali.

Orientation. Maoist.

Publication. Servire il Populo (Serve the People). The name is taken from a well-known article by Mao Zedong.

Proletarian Democracy
Democrazia Proletaria (DP)

History. The name "Proletarian Democracy" was originally applied to the electoral alliance formed in 1976 by the Party of Proletarian Unity (PdUP),

Continuous Struggle and the pro-Chinese Workers' Vanguard movement (*Avanguardia Operaia*). The PdUP, which consisted of former Socialists and former Communists, split in 1977, when 8,000 former Socialists among its members, including two deputies, merged with the 25,000 Workers' Vanguard members to form the Proletarian Democracy party. It fought the 1979 elections in alliance with Continuous Struggle as part of the United New Left, which obtained 0.8 per cent of the vote. In the same year, however, it won a seat in the European Parliament, which it retained in the 1984 elections, and in the 1983 general election it won seven seats in the Chamber of Deputies.

Electoral influence. The DP obtained 497,751 votes (1.4 per cent) in the 1984 European elections.

Orientation. The DP occupies a position to the left of the Communist Party.

Revolutionary Communist Groups
Gruppi dei Comunisti Rivoluzionari (GCR)

Orientation. The GCR are the most important Italian Trotskyist organization.

Leadership. Livio Maitan.

International affiliations. Fourth International, United Secretariat.

Unified Communist Party of Italy
Partito Comunista Unificato d'Italia (PCUI)

History. Known until 1978 as the Organization of Communists of Italy, Marxist-Leninist, the PCUI is the largest pro-Chinese group in Italy. It is opposed to the use of terrorist methods.

Leadership. Osvaldo Pesce.

Workers' Autonomy
Autonomia Operaia

History. Workers' Autonomy was formed in 1969 by the left wing of Continuous Struggle, and absorbed the similar Workers' Power (*Potere Operaio*) group. A "New Left" movement with anarchist affinities, it sought "a new way of acting politically", such as the occupation of empty houses by the homeless. It drew its support largely from intellectuals, women, the young and the unemployed, and was organized in autonomous groups with no central leadership. During 1973–77, when the movement was most influential, some of its groups were involved in outbreaks of violence, with the result that it was subjected to rigorous repression. About 8,000 of its members were arrested in 1980 alone, 4,000 of whom were still held without trial four years later. Prof. Antonio Negri, a philosopher and its leading ideologist, was arrested in 1979 and charged with complicity in the murder of Aldo Moro by the Red Brigades (q.v.), but both this and another charge of "armed insurrection" had to be dropped for lack of evidence. Released in 1983 after being elected to Parliament as a Radical, he escaped to France, and in 1984 was sentenced *in absentia* to 30 years' imprisonment. 70 other members of the movement, most of them intellectuals, were tried at the same time on charges of subversive association and participation in armed groups, and after a trial which aroused widespread criticism 59 were sentenced to long terms of imprisonment.

Terrorist Organizations

Front Line
Prima Linea

History. Formed in Turin in 1976, Front Line was responsible for many murders of industrialists, factory executives, Christian Democratic politicians, magistrates and politicians, often in co-operation with the Red Brigades. Between 1981 and 1983 over 300 of its members received prison sentences, and by January 1983 it was no longer considered a serious threat.

Leadership. Sergio Segio, who was sentenced to life imprisonment *in absentia* in 1981 and was arrested in 1983, was reported to be the founder of Front Line and Corrado Alunni (also a prominent member of the Red Brigades), who was sentenced to life imprisonment in 1980, its leader.

Membership. The membership of Front Line, unlike that of the Red Brigades, largely consisted of industrial workers. It also contained some middle-class members, however, such as Marco Donat Cattin, the son of a Christian Democratic senator, who was sentenced to nine years' imprisonment in 1982.

Orientation. Front Line members described their terrorist activities as a means of expression of the struggle against capitalism.

International affiliations. Members of the organization stated during their trial in 1982 that it had had contacts since 1978 with the Basque Nation and Liberty (q.v.) organization in Spain, in co-operation with which a joint training camp had been set up in France.

Red Brigades
Brigate Rosse

History. Founded in 1969, the Red Brigades were active until 1972 mainly in Milan, but later extended their operations to Turin and Genoa, and after 1976 to most parts of Italy. Originally a propagandist organization, they began bombing the property of industrialists in 1970, and two years later turned to kidnapping. Since 1974 they have been responsible for numerous murders, mostly of Christian Democratic politicians, judges and magistrates, industrialists, journalists, policemen and prison guards. Their most sensational crimes were the kidnapping and murder in Rome in 1978 of Aldo Moro, president of the Christian Democratic Party and a former Prime Minister, and the kidnapping in Verona in 1981 of Brig.-Gen. James L. Dozier, the American deputy commander of NATO land forces Southern Europe, who was freed by the police six weeks later. Between 1977 and 1983 nearly 300 members of the Red Brigades received long prison sentences, including many life sentences. Following mass arrests, terrorist activity declined from 1981 onwards, and the Ministry of Justice stated in January 1983 that the Red Brigades no longer presented a serious threat. A number of murders were committed in 1983–84, however, by remnants of the organization calling themselves the Fighting Communist Party (*Partito Comunista Combatente*).

Leadership. Renato Curcio (sentenced to 15 years' imprisonment in 1978) was reported to be the leader of the Red Brigades and Alberto Franceschini (sentenced to 14½ years in 1978) their chief ideologist.

Structure. The Red Brigades were reported in 1977 to consist of cells of three to five members, only one of whom was in contact with another cell, whilst several cells constituted a city or regional column, activities being controlled by a strategic directorate.

Membership. The Red Brigades were estimated in 1980 to have about 500 activists and 10,000 supporters, but membership is believed to have greatly declined since then. The leaders and membership were largely young people and students with middle-class or upper-class backgrounds.

Orientation. Like the Red Army Faction (q.v.) in West Germany, the Red Brigades were a product of the "New Left" which emerged from the student unrest of 1968. They defined their aim as to provoke a fascist coup which would force the Communist Party to return to its revolutionary role; this in turn would lead to a civil war which would end in the establishment of the dictatorship of the proletariat.

International affiliations. In a statement issued in 1981 the Red Brigades proposed the formation of a terrorist international in which it would hold the central position, together with the Red Army Faction, and which Basque Nation and Liberty and the Irish Republican Army might also join if they abandoned "the stifling perspective of nationalism".

Luxembourg

Capital: Luxembourg-Ville   Pop. 366,000

After World War II, during which Luxembourg was occupied by Germany, a government of national union formed by all the parties which had taken part in the resistance movement held office from 1945 to 1947. There has since been a series of coalition governments, each formed by two of the three main parties—the Christian Social Party, the Socialist Workers' Party and the Democratic Party. The 64-member Chamber of Deputies is elected for a five-year term.

Communist Party of Luxembourg
Parti Communiste Luxembourgeois (PCL)

History. The PCL was formed in 1921 following a split in the Luxembourg Social Democratic Party (now known as the Luxembourg Socialist Workers' Party). Although its general secretary was elected to the Chamber of Deputies in 1934 his election was annulled by the majority, but a proposal to ban the party was rejected in a referendum in 1937. During the German occupation the PCL took an active part in resistance activities, several of its leaders being executed by the Germans. As a result its post-war membership rose to 5,000; it obtained nearly 14 per cent of the vote and seven seats in the 1945 elections, and from 1945 to 1947 was represented in the government. It subsequently lost much of its membership and its electoral support, however, winning five seats in 1948, four in 1951 and three in 1954 and 1959. Its representation rose to five in 1964 and six in 1968, when it obtained 15.45 per cent of the vote, but fell again to five in 1974 and two in 1979. It retained its two seats in the 1984 elections.

Leadership. René Urbany (ch.). The leadership is dominated by the Urbany family; the chairman and his father, Dominique Urbany, whom he succeeded in the post in 1977, are the two secretaries, and other members of the family or relations by marriage hold key positions.

Structure. The PCL is organized in residential and workplace groups and territorial sections. The congress, meeting every three years, elects the Central Committee of 31 full and seven candidate members, which elects the 10-member Executive and the Secretariat. The party's youth section is the Communist Youth Organization.

Membership. 600 (1985 estimate). The PCL draws its strongest support from the steelworkers in the south of the country.

Electoral influence. In the 1984 elections the PCL obtained 166,063 votes (5 per cent). It holds a number of seats on local councils.

Industrial influence. The Communist trade unions amalgamated in 1966 with the General Confederation of Workers, the largest of the three trade union federations, in which they exercise some influence, although it is dominated by the Socialist Workers' Party.

Orientation. Pro-Soviet. The PCL has consistently supported Soviet policies, and was one of the few West European communist parties which defended the invasion of Czechoslovakia in 1968.

Programme. The PCL holds that it is possible to achieve socialism peacefully, in accordance with national traditions, through collaboration between communists, socialists and the other democratic forces, but emphasizes that such collaboration cannot involve renunciation by the PCL of its Marxist-Leninist principles and programme. In foreign policy it opposes Luxembourg's membership of NATO and the European Communities, but considers it unrealistic for the time being to demand withdrawal from NATO.

Publication. *Zeitung vum Letzeburger Vollek* (Luxembourg People's Chronicle), daily (1,000–1,500).

International affiliations. The PCL is represented on the editorial council of *World Marxist Review*, and maintains close relations with the Soviet-bloc parties.

Malta

Capital: Valletta   Pop. 330,000

Formerly a British colony, Malta became independent in 1964, and adopted a republican constitution in 1974. The Nationalist Party held office until 1971, since when the Malta Labour Party has been in power. The 65-member House of Representatives is elected by proportional representation every five years.

Communist Party of Malta (CPM)

History. The CPM was founded in 1968 by former members of the Malta Labour Party (MLP).

Leadership. Anthony Baldacchino (ch.); Anthony Vassallo (g.s.).

Structure. The 11-member Central Committee is elected by the congress. The party's youth organization is the Communist Youth League.

Membership. 100 (1985 estimate).

Electoral influence. The CPM has not contested elections, in order to avoid splitting the MLP vote.

Industrial influence. Communists are active in the General Workers' Union, which comprises over half of the country's trade unionists.

Orientation. Pro-Soviet.

Programme. The new programme adopted by the 1984 congress called for the introduction of constitutional safeguards to ensure non-alignment, national sovereignty and independence, the conversion of the Mediterranean into a nuclear-free zone, measures to reduce unemployment and improved social services.

Publication. *Zminijietna* (Our Times), monthly.

International affiliations. The CPM maintains close relations with both the Soviet-bloc and the West European communist parties.

Monaco

Capital: Monaco-Ville   Pop. 30,000

The Principality of Monaco is ruled by an 18-member National Council elected for a five-year term.

Democratic Union Movement
Mouvement d'Union Démocratique (MUD)

History. The MUD, a Marxist party based on the trade unions, first won a seat in the National Council in 1963, which it lost in 1968 and regained in 1973. It was unsuccessful in the 1978 and 1983 elections.

The Netherlands

Capital: The Hague   Pop. 14,437,000

Since World War II, during which the Netherlands were occupied by Germany, a series of coalition governments have held power, formed mainly by the Labour Party, the (liberal) People's Party for Freedom and Democracy and the confessional parties (the Catholic People's Party and the two Protestant parties, the Christian-Historical Union and the Anti-Revolutionary Party), which in 1980 were merged in the Christian Democratic Appeal. The Parliament (States-General) consists of a 75-member First Chamber or Upper House elected by the 11 provincial councils for a six-year term, with half of its members retiring every three years, and a 150-member Second Chamber or Lower House, elected by proportional representation for a four-year term.

Alliance of Communists in the Netherlands
Verbond van Communisten in Nederland (VCN)

History. The VCN was formed in February 1984 by members of the Communist Party of the Netherlands (CPN) who opposed its new programme, and was originally intended to operate as a group inside it. The party's Executive Committee, however, ruled that VCN membership was incompatible with CPN membership, and at its first congress in October 1984 the VCN decided to form a new party in 1985.

Leadership. Laurens Meerten, Rene Dammen.

Structure. The VCN has a 10-member Executive Committee.

Orientation. Pro-Soviet.

Publication. *Manifest*, biweekly.

Communist Party of the Netherlands
Communistische Partij van Nederland (CPN)

History. The CPN originated in 1909, when the Marxist wing of the Social Democratic Workers' Party broke away and formed the Social Democratic Party. It changed its name to the Communist Party of Holland in 1918, thus becoming the first such in Western Europe, and adopted its present name in 1935. The party suffered from factional conflicts until in 1930 Paul de Groot became general secretary, retaining the post until 1962. It first achieved parliamentary representation in 1929, when two Communist deputies were elected.

During the German occupation the CPN was the strongest force in the resistance movement, losing about 60 per cent of its militants and many of its leaders. Despite these losses, it emerged from the war greatly strengthened, with a membership of 53,000, and in 1945 was offered a seat in the government, which it refused. In the 1946 general election it won 502,963 votes (10.5 per cent) and 10 out of the 100 seats in the Lower House, whilst in the provincial elections it obtained 31.5 per cent of the vote in Amsterdam. Its parliamentary representation, however, fell to eight in 1948, six in 1952 and four in 1956, which was subsequently increased to seven when the membership of the Lower House was enlarged to 150. The party joined the Cominform in 1947.

The Khrushchev Report and the Soviet intervention in Hungary gave rise to violent controversy in the CPN, which culminated in 1958 in the expulsion of four of the seven Communist deputies for "revisionism". After the 1960 World Communist Conference, at which the CPN emphasized the autonomy of individual parties, it adopted an increasingly independent attitude. It refused to support either side in the Sino-Soviet controversy; condemned the repression of civil liberties in the Soviet Union and the invasion of Czechoslovakia; and boycotted the Karlovy Vary conference of European communist parties in 1967 and the World Communist Conference in 1969. It ended this period of isolation when it attended the 1976 conference of European communist parties, but remained critical of the policies of the Soviet-bloc parties.

Communist representation in the Lower House fell to three in 1959, but thereafter rose to four in 1963, five in 1967, six in 1971 and seven in 1972.

Following its defeat in the 1977 elections, in which it obtained only 1.73 per cent of the vote and two seats, the CPN radically revised its policies in order to facilitate co-operation with the Labour Party and other left-wing parties, but won only three seats in the 1981 and 1982 elections. In December 1981 it was the first Dutch party to condemn the introduction of martial law in Poland, and its 1982 congress decided to break off relations with the Communist parties of Poland and Czechoslovakia and to support the Solidarity and Charter 77 movements in those countries. The congress also agreed to initiate discussions on a new party programme. These developments aroused considerable alarm among the more orthodox members, who formed the Horizontal Consultation of Communists (HOC), comprising about a quarter of the membership, to oppose what they regarded as non-Marxist and anti-Soviet tendencies.

The new programme, which aroused intense controversy, was adopted at an extraordinary congress in February 1984 by 392 votes to 142, with over 200 abstentions, whereupon a section of the HOC broke away and formed the Alliance of Communists in the Netherlands (see above). The CPN had previously held discussions in January with the Pacifist Socialist Party (PSP), the Radical Political Party (PPR) and a section of the Netherlands Federation of Trade Unions on the adoption of a joint electoral list and their possible merger in a single left-wing socialist party. For the 1984 European elections the three parties, together with the Green Party, formed the Green Progressive Accord, which received 5.6 per cent of the vote and won two of the 25 Dutch seats. The 29th CPN congress, held in March 1985, decided in favour of a common list with PSP, PPR and independent candidates for the 1986 parliamentary elections, but rejected the proposal for a merger.

Leadership. Elli Izeboud (ch.); John Geelen (sec.).

Structure. The CPN is organized in residential and workplace sections and in district federations. The congress, meeting every two years, elects the Central Committee of 46 members, which elects the chairman, the three-member Secretariat and the 10-member Executive Committee.

Membership. 10,000 (1985 estimate). The majority of the members are industrial workers, mainly in mining, textiles and shipbuilding, or agricultural workers from the northern provinces, but in recent years there has been a considerable influx of intellectuals and students. About one-third of the membership lives in Amsterdam.

Electoral influence. The CPN obtained 147,510 votes (1.9 per cent) in the 1982 elections. It holds some seats on local councils, including six on the Amsterdam city council and four in the Groningen provincial legislature.

Industrial influence. The CPN exercises some influence in the Netherlands Federation of Trade Unions, although Communists form less than 1 per cent of the membership.

Orientation. Eurocommunist.

Programme. The new programme adopted in 1984 stated that the CPN worked on the basis of Marxism and feminism, and dropped references to democratic centralism and proletarian internationalism. Minority opinions inside the party would be respected, and would no longer be subject to disciplinary methods. The CPN was committed to establishing a parliamentary democratic socialist form of government and to a socialism which was democratic, humane, progressive and committed to peace and freedom, and for this purpose hoped to achieve unity of action with other left-wing parties. In foreign policy it held that the United States and the Soviet Union shared responsibility for the arms race, and advocated withdrawal from NATO and the elimination of military blocs. It strongly opposed the deployment of nuclear missiles in the Netherlands. It supported dissident socialist groups in Eastern Europe seeking democracy and national independence.

Publications. *De Waarheid* (Truth), daily (13,000); *Politiek en Cultuur*, theoretical journal, 10 times a year.

International affiliations. Relations between the CPN and the Soviet-bloc parties are very strained, and it is not represented on the editorial council of *World Marxist Review*. It maintains friendly relations with the Italian, French and Belgian parties, and renewed contacts with the Chinese party in 1982.

Communist Workers' Organization—Marxist-Leninist

History. This party was formed in 1978 by the merger of three small Maoist organizations.

Orientation. Pro-Chinese.

Marxist-Leninist Party of the Netherlands
Marxistisch-Leninistisch Partij van Nederland

History. This Maoist party was founded in 1969.

Netherlands Communist Unity Movement—Marxist-Leninist
Kommunistische Eenheidsbeweging Nederland—Marxistisch-Leninistisch
(KEN-ML)

History. Founded in 1965 as the Marxist-Leninist Centre of the Netherlands, this party adopted its present name in 1970. Originally pro-Chinese, it has taken a more critical view of Chinese policies in recent years. Its membership mainly consists of students.

Orientation. Independent Maoist.

Publication. *Rode Tribune.*

Pacifist Socialist Party
Pacifistisch Socialistische Partij (PSP)

History. The PSP was founded in 1957 by about 300 former Labour Party members, and won two seats in the Second Chamber in 1959. Its parliamentary representation has since fluctuated between one and four seats. It fought the 1984 European elections in alliance with the Communist, Radical Political and Green parties, and in the same year entered into discussions with them on future co-operation (see under "Communist Party").

Leadership. Marko Mazeland (ch.); John Hontelez (g.s.).

Membership. 10,000 (1984 estimate).

Electoral influence. The PSP obtained 187,150 votes (2.3. per cent) in the 1982 elections.

Orientation. Independent.

Programme, The PSP combines Marxism with pacifism, which it holds to be inseparable from socialism. It advocates socialization of the economy, disarmament and the development of the United Nations into a world government.

Publication. Bevrijding (Liberation), (11,000).

Socialist Party
Socialistische Partij (SP)

History. Founded in 1971 as the Communist Party of the Netherlands—Marxist–Leninist, the SP assumed its present name in the following year. It has contested local elections since 1974 and parliamentary elections since 1977.

Electoral influence. The SP obtained 44,690 votes (0.5 per cent) in the 1982 elections.

Orientation. Maoist.

Socialist Workers' Party
Socialistische Arbeiderspartij (SAP)

History. The SAP was formed in 1974 as the International Communist League by a merger of the Revolutionary Communist Group, founded in 1972, and the Communist League Proletarian Left, a group expelled in the same year from the Pacifist Socialist Party. It adopted its present name in 1983.

Leadership. Rene Visser (nat. sec.).

Structure. The SAP is organized in cells, which elect regional committees. The congress, meeting every two years, elects the Central Committee, which elects the Political Bureau.

Membership. 600.

Orientation. Trotskyist.

Publications. Klassenstrijd (Class Struggle), biweekly (2,000); *De Internationale,* bimonthly (900).

International affiliations. Fourth International, United Secretariat.

Norway

Capital: Oslo   Pop. 4,145,000

The Norwegian Labour Party (DNA) was in office continuously from 1935 to 1981, except for the war years, when Norway was occupied by Germany, a short period in 1963 and the years 1965–71. The *Storting* (Parliament) consists of 155 members elected for a four-year term by proportional representation. Although the DNA remains substantially the largest and most influential single party, since 1981 it has been in opposition, latterly to a centre-right coalition headed by the Conservatives.

Communist Party of Norway
Norges Kommunistiske Parti (NKP)

History. The Norwegian Labour Party joined the Third International in 1919, but withdrew in 1923, whereupon its left wing, including 13 of its 28 members of Parliament, broke away and formed the NKP, which reaffiliated to the Comintern. The new party obtained 6.1 per cent of the vote and six seats in the 1924 elections, but thereafter its membership and influence steadily declined, and in 1936 it received only 0.3 per cent of the vote. Its active role in the resistance movement during the German occupation brought many new recruits into the party; its post-war membership rose to 40,000, and in the 1945 elections it obtained 176,535 votes (11.89 per cent) and 11 seats.

After the 1949 elections, in which it lost all its seats, Peder Furubotn, its general secretary and a former resistance leader, and eight other members of the Central Committee were expelled as "Trotskyists, bourgeois nationalists and Titoists". Many of their supporters left the party, the membership of which had fallen by 1950 to about 14,000, and many more resigned after it supported the Soviet invasion of Hungary. It won three seats in the 1953 elections and one in 1957, but from 1961 to 1973 it was not represented in the *Storting*.

Under the leadership of Reidar Larsen, who succeeded the Stalinist Emil Lovlien as Chairman in 1965, the NKP adopted a more independent line in its relations with other communist parties; it refused to take sides in the Sino-Soviet controversy, to participate in the Karlovy Vary conference of European parties in 1967 or to sign the document adopted by the World Communist Conference in 1969, and condemned the Soviet intervention in Czechoslovakia in 1968. It allied with other left-wing organizations in 1972 in the campaign which led to the rejection of Norwegian membership of the European Communities in a referendum. These organizations subsequently formed the Socialist Election Alliance, which returned 16 deputies, including Larsen, in the 1973 elections.

A proposal that the Alliance parties should dissolve themselves and merge into a single party was rejected in 1975 by the NKP congress, whereupon Larsen and a section of the membership resigned and joined the new Socialist Left Party. Since this split the NKP has consistently supported Soviet policies, including Soviet intervention in Afghanistan and the imposition of martial law in Poland, and has failed to win any seats in the *Storting*.

Leadership. Hans I. Kleven (ch.).

Structure. The congress, meeting every two years, elects the National Committee, which elects the Central Committee (14 full and six substitute members), the Secretariat and the chairman. The party's youth organization is the Norwegian Communist Youth League (NKU).

Membership. 500 (1985 estimate). The majority of the members are believed to be survivors from the wartime resistance period.

Electoral influence. The NKP vote fell from 7,154 (0.3 per cent) in the 1981 elections to 4,048 (0.2 per cent) in 1985.

Industrial influence. Communists operate inside the Labour-controlled Norwegian Trade Union Confederation, and exercise some influence at local levels inside the metalworkers', timber workers' and electrochemical unions.

Orientation. Pro-Soviet; there is some opposition to this policy inside the NKU.

Programme. The NKP's programme calls for a national plan to deal with unemployment, increased state subsidies for co-operative housing construction, price controls, higher social security payments, longer paid holidays, shorter working hours, additional workers' control over management and a redistribution of the burden of taxation. In foreign policy it opposes Norwegian membership of NATO and advocates the establishment of a Nordic nuclear-free zone.

Publication. Friheten (Freedom), semi-weekly (8,000).

International affiliations. The NKP maintains close relations with the Soviet-bloc parties.

Red Electoral Alliance
Rod Valgallians (RV)

History. The RV was formed in 1973 as an electoral alliance of the Workers' Communist Party (see below) and independent socialists, and has unsuccessfully contested each subsequent election.

Electoral influence. The RV vote fell from 18,602 (0.7 per cent) in the 1981 elections to 13,770 (0.5 per cent) in 1985.

Orientation. Independent.

Programme. The RV holds that socialism cannot be introduced in Norway through the ballot box, but only through a revolution in which the working class assumes state power after a prolonged struggle. A post-revolutionary socialist government must guarantee real and not merely formal democratic rights for working people, including freedom of speech and organization, independent trade unions, the right to strike and control by the workers over state and production organs. In foreign policy the RV regards the Soviet Union as the more aggressive of the two superpowers, and therefore advocates continued political (but not military) participation in NATO, strengthening the conventional defences of Western Europe and building an independent defence system outside NATO.

Socialist Left Party
Socialistisk Venstreparti (SV)

History. The SV is descended from the Socialist People's Party (SF), a left-wing group which broke away from the Labour Party in 1961 and won two seats in the 1961 and 1965 elections. The SF, the Communist Party and another dissident Labour group, the Labour Information Committee, campaigned successfully in 1972 against Norway's proposed entry into the European Communities, and in the following year formed the Socialist Election Alliance, which won 16 seats in the *Storting*. The groups composing the Alliance, with the exception of the majority of the Communist Party, merged in 1975 to form the SV, which won two seats in the 1977 elections, four in 1981 and six in 1985. The Alliance, and subsequently the SV, exercised some political influence between 1973 and 1981, when a minority Labour government was dependent on their votes to retain office.

Leadership. Theo Koritzinsky (ch.); Erik Solheim (sec.).

Structure. The congress, meeting every two years, elects the 29-member Central Committee and the seven-member Executive Committee. The party's youth organization is the Socialist Youth.

Membership. 2,000 (1985 estimate).

Electoral influence. The SV vote rose from 125,353 (5 per cent) in the 1981 elections to 135,191 (5.4 per cent) in 1985.

Orientation. Eurocommunist.

Programme. The SV, which defines its programme as one of "national independence, socialism and full employment", advocates expansion of the public sector, decentralization of government and workers' control of industry. In foreign policy it opposes Norwegian membership of NATO, and supports the establishment of a nuclear-free zone embracing Finland, Sweden, Norway, Denmark and Iceland.

Publication. *Ny Tid* (New Times), weekly.

International affiliations. The SV maintains close informal relations with the Socialist People's Party in Denmark, the Left Party—Communists in Sweden and the People's Alliance in Iceland.

Workers' Communist Party
Arbeidernes Kommunistiske Parti (AKP)

History. The AKP was formed in 1972 by the merger of several Maoist groups, including the youth organization of the Socialist People's Party, which had broken away in 1968. Since 1973 the AKP has contested elections as part of the Red Electoral Alliance.

Leadership. Paal Steigan (ch.); Sigurd Allen (sec.).

Membership. 1,000 (1985 estimate).

Electoral influence. See under "Red Electoral Alliance".

Orientation. Formerly pro-Chinese, now independent Maoist.

Programme. See under "Red Electoral Alliance".

Publication. *Klassekampen* (Class Struggle), daily.

Portugal

Capital: Lisbon   Pop. 10,300,000

The democratic republic established after the overthrow of the monarchy in 1910 was itself overthrown in 1926, when the army seized power. Under the authoritarian right-wing regime of Dr Antonio de Oliveira Salazar (Prime Minister from 1932 to 1968) Portugal was ruled by the National Union, the official party, which consistently won all the seats in the National Assembly, and his policies were continued by his successor, Dr Marcello Caetano. Internal opposition steadily increased from 1958 onwards, and after 1961 the government was confronted with armed revolts in its African colonies. Discontent with the conduct of the war led to the overthrow of the regime by a military revolt on April 25, 1974.

A Constituent Assembly elected in 1975 adopted a constitution which described Portugal as a democratic state based on pluralism "with the objective of ensuring the transition to socialism". In elections to the Legislative Assembly in 1976 the Socialists emerged as the largest party, and in presidential elections later in the same year Gen. Antonio dos Santos Ramalho Eanes, supported by the Socialists and the parties of the centre and right, defeated Major Otelo Saraiva de Carvalho, the candidate of the extreme left, and Octavio Pato, the Communist candidate. The minority Socialist government which then took power was defeated in 1978, and after a centre-left coalition and three non-party governments had held office elections in 1979 resulted in a victory for the centre-right Democratic Alliance, which retained power after new elections in 1980. President Eanes was re-elected later in the same year with Socialist and Communist support, defeating both right-wing and extreme left-wing candidates. The ruling alliance broke up in 1982, and after elections in 1983 a centre-left government was formed by the Socialist leader, Dr Mário Soares. New elections in 1985 were followed by the formation of a centre-right government, but in 1986 Soares was elected President.

The President is elected by universal suffrage for a five-year term, and the 250-member Assembly of the Republic for a four-year term.

Communist Party of Portugal—Marxist-Leninist
Partido Comunista de Portugal—Marxista-Leninista (PCP-ML)

History. The PCP-ML was formally constituted as a party in 1970 by a Maoist group which had broken away from the Communist Party in 1964. Legalized after the 1974 revolution, it did not contest the 1975 elections, and withdrew from the elections in the following year after taking part in the election campaign; it nevertheless received 0.29 per cent of the vote. For the 1979 elections it formed a joint front with the Workers' and Peasants' Alliance.

Leadership. Heduino Gomes (g.s.).

Structure. The PCP-ML is organized on the normal communist pattern, with cells, area, district and regional committees, a Central Committee, a Political Bureau and a Secretariat.

Membership. 4,500.

Orientation. Pro-Chinese.

Publications. Unidade Popular (Popular Unity) (10,000); *Estrêla Vermelha* (Red Star) (3,000).

Movement of the Socialist Left
Movimento de Esquerda Socialista (MES)

History. Formed in 1974 by a left-wing group which had broken away from the Socialist Party, the MES unsuccessfully contested the elections in 1975, when it obtained 1.02 per cent of the vote, and those in 1976 and 1979. It supported Major Carvalho in the 1976 presidential election.

Leadership. Collective.

Structure. The party's organization follows the usual communist pattern, with cells, factory, local and regional committees, a 24-member Central Committee and a five-member Political Bureau.

Membership. 1,000.

Orientation. Independent. The MES occupies an intermediate position between the Communist Party and the extreme left-wing Trotskyist and Maoist parties.

Publication. Poder Popular (People's Power).

Popular Democratic Union
União Democrática Popular (UDP)

History. The UDP, formed in 1974 by the merger of three Maoist groups, won a seat in the 1975 elections with 0.79 per cent of the vote. Although accused of complicity in an attempted coup in the following November, it retained its seat in the 1976 elections with an increased vote (1.69 per cent), having previously absorbed two other Maoist parties. It supported Major Carvalho in the 1976 presidential election. It again held its seat in the elections in 1979 (with 2 per cent of the vote) and 1980 (1.4 per cent), but lost it in 1983, when its share of the vote fell to 0.5 per cent.

Orientation. Maoist.

Popular Unity Forces
Forças de Unidade Popular (FUP)

History. The founder of the FUP, Lt.-Col. Otelo Saraiva de Carvalho, played a leading part in organizing the 1974 revolution, but was removed from his command after an attempted coup in November 1975 of which he was alleged to be the leader. After contesting the 1976 presidential election as the candidate of the extreme left, he formed the United Workers' Organization in 1978 from two small parties, the Popular Socialist Front, which had broken away from the Socialist Party, and the (Maoist) Proletarian Revolutionary Party. The United Workers' Organization was renamed the Popular Unity Force in 1980, and put forward Lt.-Col. Carvalho as its candidate in the presidential election of that year. Lt.-Col. Carvalho, Pedro Goulart, the party leader, and other members were arrested in June 1984 on suspicion of complicity in the terrorist activities of the Popular Forces of April 25 (see below), which the FUP had consistently refused to condemn.

Leadership. Pedro Goulart.

Electoral influence. Lt.-Col. Carvalho received 85,134 votes (1.48 per cent) in the 1980 presidential election.

Programme. The FUP (then called the United Workers' Organization) was formed in 1978 with the aims of defending the gains of the 1974 revolution, which according to Lt.-Col. Carvalho had been betrayed by the army and the "bourgeois" Communist Party, opposing the rebirth of fascism and achieving socialism, if necessary by force.

Portuguese Communist Party
Partido Comunista Português (PCP)

History. Founded in 1921 by a group which had broken away from the Socialist Party, the PCP was illegal from 1926 to 1974. During this period it proved the most active and best organized of the underground opposition groups, although many of its members were imprisoned or exiled. Alvaro Cunhal, its general secretary, was imprisoned in 1949 but escaped in 1960, spending the next 14 years in Prague and Moscow.

After the 1974 revolution the PCP was legalized, and held office in a series of provisional governments between May 1974 and July 1976. Its membership expanded from 15,000 in July 1974 to nearly 100,000 at the end of 1975, and with the support of sympathizers in the officer corps it extended its control over sections of the armed forces, the trade unions, the peasantry, the students, the news media and local government. In the elections of April 1975 it obtained 12.5 per cent of the vote and 30 of the 250 seats in the Constituent Assembly. Following an attempted left-wing coup in November, however, it came under attack from both the right and the extreme left, and found itself isolated. It obtained 14.5 per cent of the vote and 40 seats in the elections of April 1976, largely because its ally, the Portuguese Democratic Movement (MDP) did not contest the elections, but in June its candidate in the presidential election received only 7.5 per cent of the vote, and in the following month it was ousted from the government.

It contested the 1979 elections in alliance with the MDP, the two parties obtaining 19 per cent of the vote and the PCP 44 seats. In the elections of the following year their share of the vote fell to 16.9 per cent and communist representation to 39, but in 1983 the PCP, running alone, again obtained 44 seats. It did not contest the 1980 presidential election, in which it supported Gen. Eanes. In the 1985 elections it obtained 38 seats. In the 1986 presidential election it supported a dissident Socialist candidate in the first round and the victorious Socialist candidate in the second.

Leadership. Alvaro Cunhal (g.s.).

Structure. The PCP is organized in workplace, street and rural cells, which are subordinate to municipal, district and regional committees. The congress, meeting every three years, elects the Central Committee (91 full and 74 alternate members), which elects the 18-member Political Commission and the five-member Secretariat.

Membership. Over 200,000 (1984 estimate). The PCP has doubled its membership since 1976, and in proportion to population is the second largest communist party in Western Europe, after the Italian party. It draws its following mainly from the urban and industrial areas and from the agricultural labourers in the southern provinces of Alto and Baixo Alentejo, which are regions of large estates, but has little support among the smallholders of the northern provinces.

Electoral influence. The PCP share of the vote fell from 18.2 per cent in the 1983 elections to 15.46 per cent in 1985. In the 1983 municipal elections it received 20.7 per cent, and gained control of 55 of the 305 town councils.

Industrial influence. The PCP controls the General Confederation of Portuguese Workers (CGTP), the largest trade union federation, comprising 201 unions with 1,500,000 members.

Orientation. Pro-Soviet. The PCP has consistently defended Soviet policies, including the invasion of Czechoslovakia and Afghanistan and the introduction of martial law in Poland, and is hostile to Eurocommunism, which Cunhal described in 1982 as "communist in name and social democratic in ideology".

Programme. The PCP advocates the formation of a "government of national salvation" to defend the achievements of the 1974 revolution—nationalization measures, land reform, workers' control and democratic liberties. It opposes Portugal's entry into the European Communities.

Publications. Avante! (Forward), weekly (76,500); *O Militante* (The Fighter), theoretical journal. *Avante*, founded in 1931, was published illegally throughout the Salazar and Caetano regimes, except in 1939–41.

International affiliations. The PCP is represented on the editorial council of *World Marxist Review*, and maintains close relations with the Soviet-bloc parties.

Portuguese Communist Party, Reconstituted
Partido Comunista Português, Reconstituido

Orientation. Pro-Albanian.

Portuguese Democratic Movement
Movimento Democrático Português (MDP)

History. The MDP was founded in 1969 as the Democratic Electoral Committees, an alliance of Socialists, liberal Catholics and republicans which contested the elections in that year, obtaining 18,599 votes, but withdrew its candidates for the 1973 elections in protest against government repression during the campaign. After the revolution it became a legal political party under its present name, and was represented in two provisional governments in 1974–75. In the 1975 elections it obtained 4.12 per cent of the vote and five seats. Having fallen strongly under Communist influence, it did not contest the 1976 elections in order to avoid splitting the left-wing vote, and supported the Communist candidate in the presidential election of that year. It fought the next two general elections in alliance with the Communists, winning three seats in 1979 and two in 1980, but contested the 1983 elections alone, losing both its seats. The alliance with the Communists was renewed for the 1985 elections.

Leadership. José Manuel Tengarrinha (l.).

Orientation. The MDP is generally regarded as a Communist front organization.

Programme. The MDP advocates a socialist democracy, a non-aligned foreign policy and the abolition of military blocs.

Portuguese Workers' Communist Party
Partido Comunista dos Trabalhadores Portugueses (PCTP)

History. The PCTP was formed in 1970 as the Movement for the Reorganization of the Proletarian Party, with the object of "founding a real Communist Party", and adopted its present name in 1976. Legalized after the 1974 revolution, it organized a number of riotous demonstrations early in 1975, and was banned from taking part in the elections to the Constituent Assembly. It unsuccessfully contested the 1976 elections, when it obtained 0.67 per cent of the vote, and those of 1979, 1980 and 1983.

Leadership. Arnaldo Matos (g.s.).

Structure. The party's organization follows the normal communist pattern, with cells, local committees, a Central Committee and a Permanent Committee.

Membership. Several thousand.

Electoral influence. The PCTP has never been represented in the Assembly, but won several seats in the 1983 local elections.

Orientation. Formerly pro-Chinese, now independent Maoist. The PCTP is hostile to the post-1976 regime in China and the Hoxha regime in Albania, both of which it has condemned as "social fascist".

Programme. The PCTP has the short-term objective of establishing a people's democratic republic through a united people's democratic front, and the final objective of achieving communism.

Publication. *Luta Popular* (People's Struggle), (15,000).

Proletarian Revolutionary Party
Partido Proletario Revolucionario (PPR)

History. The PPR is the successor to the illegal Patriotic Front of National Liberation, formed in 1962 and based in Algeria. The Communist Party, which originally formed part of the Front, was excluded from it in 1970, when the Front announced its intention to conduct an armed struggle against the Caetano regime. During the next four years its military wing, the Revolutionary Brigades, was responsible for a number of bomb attacks, including an explosion at the regional army headquarters in Oporto in 1973. The PPR, which had replaced the Front in 1973, was legalized after the 1974 revolution. In June 1975 it demanded the immediate establishment of the dictatorship of the proletariat, and claimed to have set up revolutionary councils in about 250 enterprises. When in the following October the government ordered all civilians to surrender their weapons the PPR refused to do so until the working classes were in power, and the Revolutionary Brigades announced that they would return underground. The PPR thereafter combined political activities with bombings and bank robberies, for which several of its members received heavy prison sentences. Six PPR candidates contested the 1980 elections from prison, including two of the party's founders, Carlos Mela Antunes and Dr Isabel do Carmo, who had been sentenced to 15 and 11 years respectively, and were conditionally released in 1982 after going on hunger strike.

Orientation. Maoist.

Revolutionary Socialist Party
Partido Socialista Revolucionario (PSR)

History. Formed in 1978 as "a specific alternative to today's social democracy, Eurocommunism and Maoism", the PSR unsuccessfully contested the 1979 and 1980 elections.

Orientation. Trotskyist.

Workers' and Peasants' Alliance
Aliança Operária e Camponesa (AOC)

History. The AOC was banned in 1975 from taking part in political activities until after the elections to the Constituent Assembly. It unsuccessfully contested the general elections in 1976, when it received 15,671 votes (0.29 per cent), and in 1979, when it was allied with the Communist Party of Portugal—Marxist-Leninist.

Orientation. Maoist.

Workers' Party of Socialist Unity
Partido Obreiro de Unidad Socialista (POUS)

History. The POUS unsuccessfully contested the 1979 and 1980 elections, and put forward its own candidate in the 1980 presidential election, Aires Rodrigues, who obtained 12,612 votes (0.22 per cent).

Orientation. Trotskyist.

Workers' Socialist Organization
Organização Socialista de Trabhaladores (OST)

History. The OST was formed in 1978 by the merger of two Trotskyist organizations, the International Communist League, which had obtained 0.19 per cent of the vote in the 1975 elections and 0.3 per cent in 1976, and the Workers' Revolutionary Party.

Orientation. Trotskyist.

Terrorist Organization

Popular Forces of April 25
Forças Populares de 25 Abril (FP25)

History. This group, formed in 1980 and taking its name from the date of the 1974 revolution, claimed responsibility for 12 killings up to 1984, mainly of industrialists whom it accused of exploiting their employees, and a number of bombings and bank robberies. The police arrested 42 people suspected of involvement in its activities in June 1984, including Lt.-Col. Otelo Saraiva de Carvalho and other leading members of the Popular Unity Force (see above). Despite the arrests, FP25 intensified its activities from September onwards, and in the next six months was responsible for the murder of an industrialist, bomb attacks on the premises of foreign businesses, landowners' houses and an air base, and ineffective mortar attacks on the US embassy in Lisbon and NATO warships in the harbour. The trial of Lt.-Col. Carvalho and 71 others, 24 of whom were tried in absentia, on charges of direction or membership of a terrorist organization opened in July 1985.

Orientation. Many suspected FP25 members were reported to be former members of the Proletarian Revolutionary Party (see above), a Maoist organization.

International affiliations. FP25 has links with the Spanish organization Basque Nation and Liberty, and is believed to have co-operated with the West German Red Army Faction, the French Direct Action and the Belgian Fighting Communist Cells in a joint anti-NATO campaign in 1984–85.

San Marino

Capital: San Marino   Pop. 22,000

San Marino, which has been an independent republic since the 13th century, is governed by a Grand and General Council of 60 members elected for a five-year term, two of its members being elected every six months to act as Captains-Regent. From 1945 to 1957 a Communist-Socialist alliance held power, San Marino being the only West European country in which Communists remained in the government after 1948. A split in the Socialist Party led to a political crisis in 1957, and enabled a Christian Democratic-Social Democratic alliance to take power, with the assistance of the Italian government. A Christian Democratic-Socialist coalition took office in 1973 with Communist support, and after the 1978 elections a government was formed by the Communist, Socialist and Socialist Unity parties.

Marxist-Leninist Communist Party of San Marino
Partito Comunista Marxista-Leninista di San Marino

History. This party was formed in 1968 by defectors from the Communist Party; it contested the 1974 elections, obtaining 121 votes (0.8 per cent).

Orientation. Maoist.

San Marino Communist Party
Partito Comunista Sammarinese (PCS)

History. A section of the Italian Communist Party was formed in San Marino in 1921, and constituted itself into an independent party in 1941. It held power, in alliance with the Socialists, from 1945 to 1957 and again from 1978 onwards.

Leadership. Ermenegildo Gasperoni (pres.); Umberto Barulli (sec.).

Structure. The PCS is organized in 17 cells and five territorial sections. The congress elects the 35-member Central Committee and the seven-member Control Committee, which elect the 15-member Directorate and the five-member Secretariat. The party's youth organization is the Communist Youth Federation of San Marino.

Membership. 300 (1985 estimate).

Electoral influence. In each election since 1959 the PCS has obtained between 22 and 26 per cent of the vote and between 14 and 16 seats.

Orientation. Eurocommunist.

Programme. The PCS advocates collaboration with socialist and democratic parties in a broadly based government with a policy of economic, social, political and ideological renovation. It favours close co-operation with Italy on a basis of respect for San Marino's autonomy.

Publication. La Scintilla (The Spark), monthly (1,500).

International affiliations. The PCS collaborates closely with the Italian Communist Party.

Spain

Capital: Madrid   Pop. 38,435,000

The Spanish monarchy was overthrown in 1931, when a republic was proclaimed. After the victory of a left-centre alliance, the Popular Front, in the 1936 elections a military uprising led to civil war, which ended in 1939 in the establishment of the dictatorship of Gen. Francisco Franco. On his death in 1975 the monarchy was restored in the person of King Juan Carlos, grandson of the last king, and within less than two years parliamentary government and democratic liberties were re-established, political parties and free trade unions legalized and political prisoners released. Elections in 1977 and 1979 resulted in victories for the conservative Union of the Democratic Centre, but in 1982 the Spanish Socialist Workers' Party obtained a majority and formed a government.

The Spanish Parliament (*Cortes Generales*) consists of a Congress of Deputies of 350 members elected by proportional representation and a Senate of 208 members elected on a provincial basis by majority vote and 49 representing the autonomous regions, both chambers being elected for four-year terms.

Communist Party
Partido Comunista (PC)

History. The PC was founded in January 1984 by Ignacio Gallego, who had resigned from the Central and Executive Committees of the Communist Party of Spain (PCE) three months before as a protest against its Eurocommunist policies. The PC absorbed the Party of Catalan Communists, which had broken away from the Unified Socialist Party of Catalonia in 1982. Five other members of the PCE Central Committee defected to the PC in December 1984. In October 1985 Andalusian supporters of the PC formed the Communist Party of the Andalusian People (see below).

Leadership. Ignacio Gallego (g.s.).

Structure. The founding congress elected a 101-member Central Committee.

Membership. 25,000 (1984 claim).

Industrial influence. The PC claimed that 76 per cent of its members belonged to the Workers' Commissions, the trade union federation controlled by the PCE.

Orientation. Pro-Soviet.

Programme. The PC gave as one of its aims "to end the politico-ideological degeneration . . . which introduced Eurocommunism".

International affiliations. The PC's founding congress was attended by observers from the Soviet, Czechoslovak, East German and Polish Communist parties, but was boycotted by the Yugoslav, Romanian, Hungarian and most of the West European parties. The Soviet party welcomed the formation of the PC in *Pravda*, while continuing to maintain relations with the PCE.

Communist Party of Spain
Partido Comunista de España (PCE)

History. The PCE originated in 1920, when the majority of the Federation of Socialist Youth left the Spanish Socialist Workers' Party (PSOE) and formed the Spanish Communist Party. Another group which left the PSOE in April 1921 after it decided not to join the Third International formed the Spanish Communist Workers' Party, and in the following November the two groups merged to form the PCE. The new party was banned from 1923 to 1930. The leading left-wing members, who opposed all electoral alliances, were expelled or resigned in 1932, subsequently forming the Workers' Party of Marxist Unification (POUM), and in January 1936 the Socialist and Republican parties accepted the PCE's proposal for an alliance. In elections in the following month 286 Popular Front members, including 17 Communists, were returned, and a Republican government was formed. PCE membership grew rapidly from 35,000 to over 300,000, and in April 1936 the Communist and Socialist youth movements combined to form the Unified Socialist Youth, under the leadership of Santiago Carrillo.

After the Franco rebellion the PCE entered the government, in which it pursued a cautious policy, supporting the view of the Republicans and right-wing Socialists that the war took priority. It was thus ranged against the left-wing Socialists, Anarchists and POUM (who called for a social revolution) and was generally held responsible for the forcible suppression of the POUM in 1937. Franco's victory in 1939 was followed by wholesale executions of Communists, and the party leadership and thousands of their followers fled the country. Most settled in France, where they took a prominent part in the wartime resistance movement, while others went to Mexico or the Soviet Union. After 1948 the PCE abandoned attempts to maintain a guerrilla resistance inside Spain, and concentrated on infiltrating the state-controlled trade unions and building a broad alliance with other opposition groups. It played a leading role in a number of major strikes, including a general strike in Barcelona in 1951 and a widespread strike movement in Asturias, the Basque provinces and Catalonia in 1962, and gained control of the underground trade union movement, the Workers' Commissions. Julián Grimau, a member of the Central Committee, was executed in 1963 for "military rebellion", and many other Communists received heavy prison sentences for their political and trade union activities.

Under the leadership of Carrillo, who succeeded Dolores Ibárruri (La Pasionaria) as general secretary in 1960, the PCE adopted a strongly independent policy. It condemned the Soviet intervention in Czechoslovakia in 1968; expelled Enrique Lister, a former civil war commander who headed a pro-Soviet faction in the Central Committee, in 1970; and attempted in the following year to resume relations with the Chinese Communist Party, which had been suspended since 1966. Carrillo said in 1975 that the PCE could not accept a common line between the communist parties of Eastern and Western Europe, as that would give "not another communist party but another state the possibility of interfering", and at the European Communist Conference in 1976 he declared that Spanish Communists, who had learned the value of fundamental freedoms during the Franco dictatorship, could "in no circumstances, no matter what the social system and especially not in a socialist one", accept the idea of their disappearance (see Appendix 2: Documents). His exposition of his views in his book *Eurocommunism and the State* (1977) was bitterly attacked in the Soviet press.

The PCE and other groups of the left and centre formed the Spanish Democratic Junta in 1974 to press for reforms. After Franco's death this merged in March 1976 with a similar alliance formed by the PSOE in the Democratic Co-ordination, which demanded an amnesty for political prisoners, the return of political exiles and recognition of political rights for all parties. Having returned secretly to Spain, Carrillo publicly announced his presence in December and was arrested; he was released after a few days, however, and in April 1977 the PCE was legalized. It subsequently recognized the monarchy and the national flag, and ceased to use the republican flag as its symbol. Following its legalization, its membership increased from 15,000 in 1976 to 200,000.

In elections held in the following June the PCE obtained 9.22 per cent of the vote and 20 seats in the Congress of Deputies. At its 1978 congress, the first held legally inside Spain since 1932, it dropped the word "Leninist" from its official description, which henceforth qualified the party as "Marxist, democratic and revolutionary". It increased its share of the vote to 10.8 per cent in the 1979 elections and its parliamentary representation to 23. During this period it continued to maintain its independent position, condemning equally the Vietnamese invasion of Kampuchea, the Chinese invasion of Vietnam and the Soviet intervention in Afghanistan, and in 1980 it resumed relations with the Chinese Communist Party. After the introduction of martial law in Poland the Central Committee in January 1982 demanded the ending of Soviet interference in Poland, and Carrillo called for a new international alignment of socialist and communist parties and national liberation movements.

Carrillo's Eurocommunist policies and his authoritarian methods of leadership led to the emergence of three opposition factions: the "renovators", who demanded a stronger endorsement of Eurocommunism and greater internal democracy and decentralization; the "Leninists", who condemned the party's rejection of the dictatorship of the proletariat; and the pro-Soviet "Afghans". A number of splits followed; the leading "renovators" were expelled in 1981, the bulk of the Basque party broke away in the same year and a section of the Catalan party departed in 1982. After the 1982 elections, in which the PCE obtained only 3.8 per cent of the vote and four seats, Carrillo resigned the leadership in favour of Gerardo Iglesias, but internal dissensions continued. At the 1983 congress Iglesias was attacked by Carrillo, who had moved towards a more pro-Soviet position, but retained control with the support of about two-thirds of the new Central Committee. After the congress a pro-Soviet faction left the PCE to found the Communist Party (see above).

Violent polemics continued over Iglesias's proposal for the formation of an alliance of forces to the left of the Socialist Party (including Socialists and trade unionists disillusioned with the government's policies, ecologists and the peace movement) to fight the 1986 elections. This plan was opposed by Carrillo, who advocated instead a reconciliation with the pro-Soviet Communists who had left the PCE. A party conference in March 1985 was boycotted by his supporters, and while it was in progress he announced the formation of a "Communist Unity Platform" which in effect constituted a party within the party. He was thereupon removed from his post as the PCE's parliamentary spokesman, and after he and 18 of his supporters on the Central Committee had refused to conform to party discipline they were removed from all their party posts. His supporters subsequently formed the Communist Party of Spain, Marxist-Revolutionary (see below).

Leadership. Dolores Ibárruri (pres.); Gerardo Iglesias (g.s.).

Structure. The congress elects the 102-member Central Committee, which elects the 28-member Executive Committee and the 11-member Secretariat. The PCE includes the autonomous Unified Socialist Party of Catalonia and Communist Party of Galicia, each of which has its own Central Committee and is represented on that of the PCE. The bulk of the Basque Communist Party broke with the PCE in 1982.

Membership. 68,000 (1985 estimate). Membership has fallen by 170,000 since 1977. The party derives its main strength from the cities, especially Madrid and Barcelona, and from the Catalonia, Valencia and Andalusia regions.

Electoral influence. The PCE obtained 844,976 votes (3.8 per cent) in the 1982 elections. In municipal elections in 1983 it received 7 per cent of the vote but retained control of only one provincial capital, Córdoba.

Industrial influence. The PCE controls the Workers' Commissions (*Comisiones Obreros*, CCOO), probably the strongest of the four main trade union federations. In the elections of delegates to works councils in 1980 the CCOO returned 30.7 per cent of the delegates and the Socialist-controlled General Workers' Union (*Unión General de Trabajadores*, UGT) 29.6 per cent.

Orientation. Eurocommunist.

Programme. The PCE envisages a gradual transition to socialism, through an intermediate phase of "social and political democracy", to a stage where structural changes and the development of the productive forces "give rise to a qualitative leap from the bourgeois to the socialist order". Reforms proposed for this intermediate phase include nationalization of sources of finance and large monopolies, land redistribution and reorganization of agricultural production, tax reforms, workers' participation in management of the public and private sectors and a democratic system of economic planning. The PCE accepts the existence of a private sector, consisting of industries not controlled by monopolies and small and medium commerce; excessive profits would be taxed, but taxation would not be so high as to discourage private enterprise. It favours a high degree of regional self-government. In foreign policy it supports Spain's accession to the European Communities but opposes Spanish membership of NATO, advocating a non-aligned policy.

Publications. *Mundo Obrero* (Labour World), weekly; *Nuestra Bandera* (Our Flag), bimonthly.

International affiliations. The PCE is represented on the editorial council of *World Marxist Review*, but its relations with the Soviet-bloc parties are strained. It maintains close links with the other Eurocommunist parties, and especially with the Italian party.

Communist Party of Spain—Marxist-Leninist
Partido Comunista de España—Marxist-Leninista (PCE-ML)

History. Founded in 1964 by dissident members of the Communist Party of Spain, the PCE-ML was legalized in 1981 and contested the regional elections two years later.

Leadership. Raúl Marco (1st sec.).

Orientation. Formerly pro-Chinese, now pro-Albanian.

Publication. *Vanguardia Obrero* (Labour Vanguard).

International affiliation. The PCE-ML is officially recognized by the Albanian Party of Labour.

Communist Party of Spain, Marxist-Revolutionary
Partido Comunista de España, Marxista-Revolucionario (PCEMR)

History. The PCEMR was officially registered as a new party in October 1985 by supporters of Santiago Carrillo, the former general secretary of the Communist Party of Spain (PCE). Carrillo, who denied that he was personally responsible for its formation, stated that he would join it if he did not receive a favourable response to his appeal for the formation of an electoral alliance of the three main communist groups—his own followers, the supporters of Gerardo Iglesias (the PCE general secretary) and the Communist Party led by Ignacio Gallego.

Communist Unification of Spain
Unificación Comunista de España (UCE)

History. The UCE unsuccessfully contested the elections to the Andalusian Parliament in 1982.

Feminist Party
Partido Feminista (PF)

History. The PF was founded in 1979, and held its first congress in 1983.

Leadership. Lidia Falcón.

Structure. The party has a nine-woman executive.

Programme. The PF's programme is one of "active solidarity with all female, proletarian and oppressed peoples", and in particular of advancing the social, legal and political status of women.

Party for Communist Recovery and Unification
Partido por la Recuperación y la Unificación Comunista (PRUC)

History. The PRUC was founded in 1982.

Membership. 5,000 (1982 claim), 60 per cent of whom were said to be former members of the Communist Party of Spain.

Orientation. Pro-Soviet.

Progressive Federation
Federación Progresista (FP)

History. The FP was founded in 1984 by Ramón Tamames, formerly a leading member of the Communist Party of Spain.

Orientation. New Left.

Programme. The FP's statutes describe it as a federalist, radical, progressive and democratic party, in favour of external neutrality and opposed to military blocs, and state that it adopts "a critical position, inspired by the New Left, against the inequalities, injustice and corruption which are the hallmarks of capitalism as well as of bureaucratic socialism".

Reconstituted Spanish Communist Party
Partido Comunista Español Reconstituido (PCER)

History. The PCER, founded in Galicia in 1968 as an offshoot of the Communist Party of Spain—Marxist-Leninist, is best known for the activities of its terrorist wing, the October 1 Anti-fascist Resistance Group (see below).

Orientation. Maoist.

Revolutionary Communist League
Liga Comunista Revolucionaria (LDR)

History. The LCR, formed in 1970, merged in 1974 with the military wing of Basque Nation and Liberty (ETA VI—see below). It was announced in 1976 that the organization would be known as ETA VI in the Basque provinces and the LCR elsewhere.

Orientation. Trotskyist.

International affiliation. Fourth International, United Secretariat.

Spanish Workers' Communist Party
Partido Comunista de Obreros Españoles (PCOE)

History. The PCOE was formed at a congress in Paris in 1971 by dissident Communist Party members, who elected a Central Committee, repudiated the Communist Party's condemnation of the Soviet intervention in Czechoslovakia and declared support of the Soviet Union to be "the main criterion of proletarian internationalism". Legalized in 1979, it contested the 1983 regional elections.

Leadership. Gen. Enrique Lister (g.s.). One of the most distinguished republican commanders in the civil war, Lister was expelled from the Communist Party in 1970.

Structure. The congress elects the 81-member Central Committee, which elects the 11-member Executive Committee.

Orientation. Pro-Soviet.

Programme. The PCOE advocates the nationalization of the banks and key industries, land reform and rejection of Spain's entry into NATO and the European Community.

International affiliation. Although not officially recognized by the Soviet Communist Party, the PCOE is believed to receive covert Soviet support.

Unified Communist Party of Spain
Partido Comunista de España Unificado (PCEU)

History. The PCEU was founded in 1980 by a group of defectors from the Communist Party of Spain, and contested the 1983 regional elections in alliance with the Spanish Workers' Communist Party.

Orientation. Pro-Soviet.

Workers' Party of Spain
Partido de Trabajadores de España (PTE)

History. The PTE was formed in July 1979 by the merger of the Spanish Workers' Party, founded in 1968, which had obtained 200,000 votes (1 per cent) in the elections of March 1979, and the Workers' Revolutionary Organization, founded in 1969. It unsuccessfully contested the 1982 elections.

Orientation. Pro-Chinese.

Programme. The PTE's constitution describes its aim as to lead the working classes through the dictatorship of the proletariat to the establishment of a communist society.

Terrorist Organization

October 1 Anti-fascist Resistance Group
Grupo de Resistencia Antifascista Primero de Octubre (GRAPO)

History. GRAPO, the terrorist wing of the Reconstituted Spanish Communist Party (see above), takes its name from Oct. 1, 1975, when it shot dead four policemen in Madrid shortly before Gen. Franco made his last public speech. It was subsequently responsible for at least 65 murders of army officers, policemen, civil guards and businessmen, kidnappings of officials, bomb explosions and armed robberies in Madrid, Barcelona, Seville and other cities. After 17 of its members were arrested in 1985, the Ministry of the Interior claimed that all its known members were in prison.

Leadership. Mercedes Padrós Corominas, believed to be the leader of GRAPO, was arrested in 1985. Three previous leaders had been killed in gun battles with the police, a fourth had received prison sentences totalling 359 years and two others were under arrest.

Orientation. Maoist.

Andalusia

The Andalusian region, comprising the eight southern provinces of Almería, Cadiz, Córdoba, Granada, Jaén, Huelva, Málaga and Seville, was granted autonomy in 1981. Elections to the regional Parliament in 1982 resulted in a victory for the Spanish Socialist Workers' Party.

Andalusian Communist Movement
Movimiento Comunista Andaluz (MCA)

History. The MCA unsuccessfully contested the 1982 elections.

Communist Party of the Andalusian People
Partido Comunista del Pueblo Andaluz (PCPA)

History. This party was launched at a congress held in Seville in October 1985 by Andalusian supporters of Communist Party (PC) led by Ignacio Gallego, itself formed in January 1984 by pro-Soviet dissidents from the Communist Party of Spain (see above).

Leadership. Manuel Monereo Pérez (g.s.).

Basque Region

The Basque language is spoken in the provinces of Vizcaya and Guipúzcoa and in parts of Alava and Navarra, and also in part of the adjacent French department of Basses-Pyrénées. The autonomy which Vizcaya and Guipúzcoa had enjoyed since the Middle Ages was abolished in 1876 and re-established by the republican government in 1931. In consequence these provinces fought on the republican side in the civil war, and after they were conquered by Franco's forces in 1937 their autonomy, privileges, including tax concessions and control of the local police, and linguistic rights were again abolished. Resistance was kept alive by the Basque Nationalist Party (PNV), and after 1968 increasingly took the form of terrorism. A statute establishing a Basque Parliament with financial autonomy and its own police force for Vizcaya, Guipúzcoa and Alava, recognizing Basque as an official language and providing for the inclusion of Navarra in the Basque region if a referendum so decided was approved by a 90 per cent majority in the first three provinces in 1979, although 41 per cent of the electorate abstained from voting. In elections to the Basque Parliament in 1980 and 1984 the PNV emerged as the strongest party.

Basque Communist Party
Euzkadiko Partidu Komunista (EPK)

History. Although communist cells had existed in the Basque region since 1921, the EPK was not formed until 1935, when it became a constituent section of the Communist Party of Spain. It was represented in the Basque regional government formed in 1936, and subsequently in the Basque government-in-exile until 1947. After operating underground throughout the Franco regime it was legalized in 1977, and won a seat in the Basque Parliament in 1980. The EPK split in 1981, however, when the bulk of its members decided to merge with the Basque Revolutionary Party, and it lost its seat in the regional Parliament in 1984.

Electoral influence. The EPK obtained 1.3 per cent of the vote in the 1984 elections.

Orientation. Eurocommunist.

Programme. The EPK advocates a democratically governed Basque nation within a socialist Spain.

Publications. *Euzkadi Obrera* (Workers' Euzkadi), fortnightly; *Hemen eta Orain* (Here and Now), bimonthly.

Basque Left
Euzkadiko Ezkerra (EE)

History. This alliance of left-wing autonomist parties, with the Basque Revolutionary Party as its chief component, was formed in 1977 to fight the national elections and won one seat in the Congress of Deputies, which it retained in the 1979 and 1982 elections. It voted against the adoption of the new Spanish constitution in 1978 on the ground that it did not provide for adequate autonomy for the Basque region. In the elections to the Basque Parliament in 1980 it won six seats, which it retained in the 1984 elections.

Leadership. Juan María Bandrés Molet (l.); Mario Onaindía Machiondo (g.s.).

Electoral influence. The EE obtained 7.9 per cent of the vote in the 1984 elections.

Basque Left—Left for Socialism
Euzkadiko Ezkerra—Izquierda Socialista (EE-IS)

History. The EE-IS was formed in 1982 by the merger of the Basque Revolutionary Party (*Euskal Iraultzako Alerdia*, EIA), which had been founded in 1977 by the political-military wing of Basque Nation and Liberty (ETA) and had been legalized in 1978, with the bulk of the Basque Communist Party.

Leadership. Juan María Bandrés Molet (pres.); Mario Onaindía Machiondo (g.s.). Onaindia was sentenced to death in 1970 for his ETA activities, but his sentence was commuted to 30 years' imprisonment, and he was released in 1977.

Electoral influence. For electoral purposes the EE-IS forms part of the Basque Left (see above).

Programme. The EE-IS is strongly autonomist, but rejects the use of violence.

United People
Herri Batasuna (HB)

History. Formed in 1979 as an alliance of nationalist groups, the HB won three seats in the Congress of Deputies in the elections of that year and two in 1982, but refused to attend sessions as a protest against the government's policy on the Basque autonomy question, and advocated "active abstention" in the 1979 referendum on the autonomy statute because it did not incorporate Navarra into the Basque region. In the elections to the Basque Parliament it won 11 seats out of 60 in 1980 and 11 out of 75 in 1984, but refused to take its seats until an amnesty had been granted to imprisoned Basque terrorists.

Leadership. Juan Domínguez Lázaro (l.).

Electoral influence. The HB received 14.6 per cent of the vote in the 1984 elections.

Programme. The HB advocates the establishment of an independent Basque socialist state. It has close links with the military wing of Basque Nation and Liberty.

Terrorist Organization

Basque Nation and Liberty
Euzkadi ta Azkatasuna (ETA)

History. The ETA, which broke away from the Basque Nationalist Party in 1959, began a terrorist campaign of bomb explosions and murders of officials, policemen and civil guards two years later, and achieved its most spectacular success in 1973, when the Prime Minister, Admiral Luis Carrero Blanco, was killed by a bomb explosion in Madrid. Two ETA members were executed in 1975 for the murder of policemen.

The ETA had previously split in 1970 into the political-military wing (ETA-PM or ETA V), which concentrated on organizing a mass movement among the working class, and the military wing (ETA-M or ETA VI), which merged in 1974 with the Revolutionary Communist League (see above). The ETA-PM in 1975 formed the Patriotic Socialist Coalition (*Koordinadora Abertzale Sozialista,* KAS) with other left-wing autonomist parties, which in 1976 put forward the following conditions for a truce: (i) an amnesty for all political prisoners; (ii) legalization of all Basque political parties; (iii) withdrawal of the state security forces from the region; (iv) recognition of Basque as the official language of the region; (v) autonomy for the Basque provinces, including Navarra, the right to create an independent Basque state and recognition of the national links between the Spanish and French Basque regions. This programme, known as the KAS Alternative, was taken over by the ETA-M in 1978. The ETA-PM announced in 1976 that it would not use violence, in view of the changed situation since Franco's death, but would create a new nationalist party to work within the democratic framework, and in the following year formed the Basque Revolutionary Party. The two wings of the movement adopted opposing attitudes towards the

1979 referendum on the Basque autonomy statute; the ETA-M opposed it, whereas the ETA-PM regarded autonomy as a step towards independence.

Despite its renunciation of violence, the ETA-PM launched a bombing campaign designed to disrupt the tourist industry in 1979 in support of demands for the transfer of political prisoners to gaols in the Basque region, but abandoned it after explosions in Madrid had killed five people. Following an attempted military coup in Madrid, it announced in 1981 that it would observe an unconditional cease-fire, and urged the ETA-M to follow suit. A year later, however, it split into two wings, the larger of which, the ETA-PM (VIII), ended the cease-fire, whereupon the Basque Left (see above) renounced its ties with ETA-PM. The minority pacifist wing, the ETA-PM (VII), subsequently announced the dissolution of its military organization. The ETA-PM (VIII), which had kidnapped and murdered an army officer in 1983, merged in the following year with the ETA-M, which had meanwhile continued its terrorist campaign, 85 killings being attributed to it in 1980 alone. Its victims included the military governors of Madrid and Guipúzcoa, both assassinated in 1979, a Supreme Court judge, mayors, army officers, policemen and civil guards.

Structure. The ETA-M was reported in 1980 to be organized in cells, only one member of which communicated with other cells, and to have five operational regions each under a regional commander, in addition to cells outside the Basque region, e.g. in Madrid, Barcelona and Valencia. The leadership was believed to be living in France.

Programme. Both the ETA-M and the ETA-PM advocate the creation of an independent Basque socialist state, including the Basque regions of France; the latter, however, is prepared to accept autonomy inside Spain as an intermediate stage. ETA-M terrorism is believed to be intended to provoke a right-wing coup, which in turn would lead to a popular uprising in the Basque region.

International affiliations. Spanish police sources alleged in 1981 that ETA members had been trained in Algeria, South Yemen, Lebanon, Czechoslovakia, Ireland, Cuba and Uruguay, and that the organization had received economic aid from Libya, the Soviet Union and China.

Catalonia

Catalonia, comprising the four north-eastern provinces of Barcelona, Gerona, Lérida and Tarragona, was ruled by its semi-autonomous government, the *Generalitat*, from the 13th century to 1714. Re-established under the republic, its autonomy was again abolished by Franco in 1938. After his death the *Generalitat* was restored by decree in 1977, and a Catalan regional Parliament was established in 1980.

Unified Socialist Party of Catalonia
Partit Socialista Unificat de Catalunya (PSUC)

History. The PSUC was formed in 1936 by the merger of the Catalan Communist Party, the Catalan section of the Socialist Party and two smaller socialist organizations, and was represented in the Catalan government during the civil war. Banned under the Franco regime, it was again legalized in 1977, winning eight of the 47 Catalan seats in the elections of that year to the Congress of Deputies, and was included in the Catalan Executive Council which was subsequently established. In the 1980 elections to the Catalan Parliament it won 25 of the 135 seats. The PSUC was divided at this time between Eurocommunist and pro-Soviet factions; the latter obtained control at the party's 1981 congress, but the position was reversed a year later, whereupon the pro-Soviet wing broke away and formed the Party of Catalan Communists. In the 1984 elections the PSUC retained only six of its seats.

Leadership. Gregorio López Raimundo (pres.); Antoni Gutiérrez Díaz (g.s.).

Structure. The PSUC forms the Catalan section of the Communist Party of Spain.

Membership. 10,500.

Electoral influence. The PSUC share of the vote in the Catalan elections fell from 19 per cent in 1980 to 5.8 per cent in 1984.

Orientation. Eurocommunist.

Programme. The PSUC's programme is the same as that of the Communist Party of Spain, combined with strong support for Catalan autonomy.

Publications. Treball (Labour), weekly (10,000); *Nous Horitzons* (New Horizons), bimonthly (1,500).

Sweden

Capital: Stockholm   Pop. 8,335,000

The Social Democratic Labour Party has held office since 1932, either alone or in coalition with other parties, except for a short period in 1936 and during the years 1976–82. The *Riksdag* (Parliament), which is elected by proportional representation for a three-year term, was enlarged from 233 members to 350 in 1970, when the Second Chamber was abolished, the number being reduced to 349 in 1975 to prevent a tied vote of the whole membership.

Communist Party of Marxist-Leninist Revolutionaries
Kommunistiska Partiet Marxist-Leninisterna Revolutionärerna (KPMLR)

History. The KPMLR broke away from the Communist League of Marxist-Leninists (now the Communist Party of Sweden) in 1970, and was originally known as the Communist League of Marxist-Leninist Revolutionaries. It first contested elections in 1973, when it obtained 0.1 per cent of the vote.

Leadership. Frank Baude (ch.).

Membership. 1,500. The party draws its main support from Göteborg.

Electoral influence. The KPMLR won three seats in the 1982 local elections.

Orientation. Originally pro-Chinese, now pro-Albanian.

Publication. Proletären, weekly.

Communist Party of Sweden
Sveriges Kommunistiska Partiet (SKP)

History. The SKP was founded in 1967 as the Communist League of Marxist-Leninists by a small Maoist group which had broken away from the Left Party—Communists, and adopted its present name in 1973. It first contested elections in 1970, when it received 0.4 per cent of the vote.

Leadership. Roland Petersson (ch.); Jan-Olof Norell (sec.).

Structure. The SKP has about 120 local branches.

Membership. 2,000.

Electoral influence. In the 1979 elections, the last which it contested, the SKP obtained 10,862 votes (0.2 per cent). It won nine seats in the 1982 local elections.

Industrial influence. The SKP has strong support in the metalworkers' and teachers' unions.

Orientation. Pro-Chinese.

Publications. Gnistan (The Spark), weekly (5,000); *Marxistisk Forum,* quarterly (1,000).

International affiliations. The SKP is officially recognized by the Chinese Communist Party.

Communist Workers' Party of Sweden
Sveriges Arbetarpartiet Kommunisterna (SAK)

History. The SAK was founded in 1977 by about 1,500 dissident members of the Left Party—Communists, including its former chairman, Hilding Hagberg, and two members of the *Riksdag.* It unsuccessfully contested the elections in 1979, when it lost its two seats, and in 1982.

Leadership. Rolf Hagel (ch.).

Membership. 5,000 (1985 claim).

Electoral influence. The SAK obtained 0.1 per cent of the vote in the 1982 general election. In the local elections of the same year it won 12 seats, mainly in the northern provinces.

Orientation. Pro-Soviet.

Publication. Norrskenflamman (Northern Lights), daily.

International affiliations. The SAK has close links with the Soviet Communist Party.

Left Party—Communists
Vänsterpartiet Kommunisterna (VPK)

History. The VPK originated in 1917, when the left wing of the Social Democratic Labour Party (SAP) broke away and formed the Social Democratic Left Party, which joined the Third International in 1919 and changed its name to the Communist Party of Sweden (SKP) two years later. The new party suffered from frequent splits, as a result of which Sweden had two Communist parties from 1929 to 1934, the smaller of which was recognized by the Comintern. The SKP achieved its widest popular support at the end of World War II, obtaining 10.5 per cent of the vote and 15 seats in the 1944 general election and 11.2 per cent in the 1946 local elections, whilst its membership rose from about 10,000 in 1940 to 58,056 in 1944. Thereafter its support steadily declined, and in the 1958 elections it obtained only 3.4 per cent of the vote and four seats.

Demands for a more independent policy increased inside the party from 1956 onwards, and in 1964 the Stalinist chairman Hilding Hagberg was replaced by Carl Henrik Hermansson, under whose leadership the SPK criticized repressive measures inside the Soviet Union and adopted a neutral attitude towards the Sino-Soviet controversy. Its parliamentary representation rose to eight in 1964, but although it condemned the Soviet intervention in Czechoslovakia in 1968 it suffered heavy losses in the elections held shortly afterwards, winning only three seats. The party adopted its present name in 1967 to signify its aim of becoming "a forum for the whole socialist left". Internal dissensions nevertheless continued, a pro-Chinese group breaking away in 1967 and a pro-Soviet group in 1977. Lars Werner, who succeeded Hermansson as chairman in 1975, continued his Eurocommunist policy.

After the membership of the *Riksdag* was increased, the VPK won 17 seats in 1970, 19 in 1973, 17 in 1976, 20 in 1979 and 1982, and 19 in 1985. From 1970 to 1976, and again after 1982, it held the balance of power in the *Riksdag*, in which a minority SAP government depended on Communist support.

Leadership. Lars Werner (ch.); Bo Hammar (sec.).

Structure. The VPK is organized in 320 local or workplace sections and 22 districts. The congress, meeting every three years, elects the Party Board of 35 full and 15 candidate members, which elects the chairman and the nine-member Executive Committee. The party's youth organization is the Communist Youth.

Membership. 17,500 (1985 estimate). The party draws its strongest support from Stockholm, Göteborg and the northern provinces. It has a large following among miners, forestry workers, building workers and shipbuilders, and since 1967 has recruited an increasing number of white-collar workers and intellectuals.

Electoral influence. The VPK obtained 5.6 per cent of the vote in the 1979 and 1982 elections and 5.4 per cent in 1985.

Industrial influence. Although the Swedish Trade Union Confederation (*Landsorganisationen i Sverige*) is controlled by the SAP, the VPK exercises considerable influence at local level, especially in the miners', forestry workers' and building workers' unions.

Orientation. Eurocommunist. Werner said in an interview in 1979: "We reject all domination by strong communist states, particularly in Western Europe. We insist on going our own way and on communist parties being allowed to follow their own countries' traditions within the workers' movement. This includes democratic freedoms and rights, the multiparty system and the right to strike."

Programme. The VPK's programme for the 1982 elections included the creation of 100,000 new jobs, introduction of a six-hour working day, a freeze on rent increases, abolition of taxes on food, increased government aid to local authorities and dismantling of nuclear power stations. In foreign policy it advocates strict neutrality, abolition of military blocs and the creation of a zone free from nuclear weapons in Northern Europe.

Publications. Ny Dag (New Day), semiweekly (20,000); Socialistisk Debatt (Socialist Debate), monthly.

International affiliations. The VPK has close links with the Danish Socialist People's Party, the Norwegian Socialist Left Party and the Finnish, Italian and Spanish Communist parties. It has little contact with the Soviet-bloc parties, but relations with the Chinese Communist Party were resumed in 1982.

Socialist Party
Socialistiska Partiet (SP)

History. The SP was founded in 1953 as the Communist Workers' League by Set Persson, who had been expelled from the Communist Party, and assumed its present name in 1982.

Electoral influence. The SP received about 3,900 votes (0.07 per cent) in the 1982 elections.

Orientation. Trotskyist.

Publication. Internationalen.

International affiliations. Fourth International, United Secretariat.

World Socialist Movement, Swedish Group

Orientation. This small organization shares the same principles as the Socialist Party of Great Britain (q.v.).

Publication. *Varlssocialism* (World Socialism).

Switzerland

Capital: Berne   Pop. 6,477,000

The Swiss Confederation consists of self-governing cantons, 16 of which are predominantly German-speaking, six French-speaking and one Italian-speaking. The Federal Assembly comprises a Council of States (*Ständerat*), consisting of two members from each canton, and a National Council (*Nationalrat*) of 200 members elected for a four-year term in proportion to the population of the canton, the electoral system being decided by the canton. The President is elected annually by the Federal Assembly, which also elects the seven-member Federal Council (cabinet). Since 1959 Switzerland has been ruled by a coalition of the Social Democratic, Radical Democratic, Christian Democratic and Swiss People's parties.

Autonomous Socialist Party
Partito Socialista Autonomo (PSA)

History. Formed in 1969 by left-wing Social Democrats centred in the Italian-speaking canton of Ticino, the PSA has contested elections since 1975 in alliance with the Progressive Organizations of Switzerland, and since 1979 in alliance with the Swiss Labour Party. It has held one seat in the *Nationalrat* since 1975.

Leadership. Werner Carobbio (sec.).

Structure. The PSA has 65 local groups, five regional sections, a 39-member cantonal committee, a seven-member Political Bureau and a three-member Secretariat.

Membership. 1,000 (1985 estimate). Although based in Ticino, the PSA also has supporters in other cantons, and especially in Bern.

Electoral influence. The PSA won its parliamentary seat in Ticino, where it has eight representatives in the cantonal parliament.

Orientation. Independent. The PSA, which describes itself as "Marxist, revolutionary, anti-capitalist and internationalist", is considered to be more radical than the Swiss Labour Party.

Publication. *Politica Nuova* (New Politics), weekly.

Communist Party, Switzerland
Kommunistische Partei, Schweiz (KPS)

History. The KPS, which broke away from the Swiss Labour Party in 1963, was the first pro-Chinese party founded in Western Europe, but subsequently adopted both an anti-Soviet and an anti-Chinese attitude.

Membership. 100 (1982 estimate).

Electoral influence. The KPS does not contest elections, advocating direct action against the state and its institutions.

Orientation. Independent. The KPS describes itself as Marxist but not Leninist.

Publication. *Rote Fahne* (Red Flag), German-language monthly.

Communist Party, Switzerland—Marxist-Leninist
Kommunistische Partei, Schweiz—Marxistisch-Leninistische (KPS-ML)

History. The KPS-ML was founded in 1964 as the Organization of Communists of Switzerland—Marxist-Leninist by a Swede, Nils Andersson, who had been expelled from the Communist Party, Switzerland, and was officially recognized by the Chinese Communist Party. It adopted its present name in 1972.

Membership. 200 (1985 estimate).

Electoral influence. The KPS-ML does not contest elections.

Orientation. Pro-Chinese. The KPS-ML is strongly anti-Soviet, and advocates expanding the military budget.

Publication. *Oktober*, monthly in various languages.

Popular Workers' Party
Parti Ouvrier Populaire (POP)

History. This small communist formation operates in the French-speaking canton of Vaud, where it held eight seats on the Lausanne municipal council until losing them in the elections of October 1985.

Leadership. Dr. Forel.

Electoral influence. In the October 1985 cantonal elections the POP obtained 5 per cent. of the vote.

Progressive Organizations of Switzerland
Progressive Organisationen der Schweiz (POCH)

History. The POCH was formed in 1972 by a congress of local and cantonal groups which regarded the Swiss Labour Party as "stagnant" and its leaders as too elderly. It contested the 1975 elections unsuccessfully in alliance with the Autonomous Socialist Party (PSA) and the Revolutionary Marxist League, and the 1979 and 1983 elections in alliance with the PSA and the Swiss Labour Party, winning two seats in 1979 and three in 1983.

Leadership. Georg Degen (cent. sec.).

Structure. The POCH has sections in seven German-speaking cantons and informal organizations in other cantons. The national convention, held at irregular intervals, elects the Party Committee of about 50 members and the 10-member Managing Committee.

Membership. 10,000 (1985 estimate).

Electoral influence. The POCH–PSA alliance obtained 2.2 per cent of the vote in the 1983 elections. The POCH draws its strongest support from Basle and Lucerne.

Orientation. Independent.

Programme. The POCH describes itself as an independent party based on scientific socialism and ecological standpoints, campaigning for a classless society without exploitation and repression. Its new statutes, adopted in 1984, dropped references to Marxism-Leninism and to the Soviet Union as "the revolutionary power base", and laid greater emphasis on ecological questions.

Publication. POCH-Zeitung (POCH Chronicle), weekly.

Socialist Workers' Party
Sozialistische Arbeiter Partei (SAP)

History. The SAP, originally called the Revolutionary Marxist League, was formed in 1969 by about 100 young intellectuals from Vaud and Geneva who had been expelled from the Swiss Labour Party, and adopted its present name in 1980. It unsuccessfully contested the 1975 election in alliance with the Progressive Organizations of Switzerland, and fought the 1983 elections alone.

Leadership. The SAP refuses to divulge the names of its leaders. Its leading theoretician is Fritz Osterwalder.

Structure. The national congress elects the 34-member Central Committee, which elects the Political Bureau. Members are required to pay a substantial part of their incomes to the party.

Membership. 500 (1985 estimate).

Electoral influence. The SAP obtained 0.4 per cent of the vote in the 1983 elections.

Orientation. Trotskyist.

Publications. La Brèche (The Breach), French-language bimonthly; *Bresche* (Breach), German-language bimonthly.

International affiliations. Fourth International, United Secretariat.

Swiss Labour Party
Partei der Arbeit der Schweiz (PdA)—Parti Suisse du Travail

History. The Swiss Communist Party, to which the PdA is the successor, was formed in 1921 by the merger of the left wing of the Social Democratic Party with a Communist group founded in Zürich in 1918. Its membership, which had risen from an original 6,356 to 12,000 by 1930, fell to about 1,000 in 1938, and in 1940 it was banned by the federal government as a gesture of appeasement of Germany. It continued to operate underground, however, and in 1944 united with a group of left-wing Social Democrats to form the PdA.

The new party at first won considerable support; its membership reached 19,692 in 1945, and in the 1947 elections it obtained 49,404 votes (5.1 per cent) and seven seats. Thereafter its parliamentary representation, as well as its membership, steadily decreased, falling to three seats in 1959. It rose again to five in 1967 and 1971, but has since declined steeply; in 1983 the PdA won only one seat.

Leadership. Armand Magnin (g.s.); Jean Vincent (hon. pres.).

Structure. The PdA has local and workplace branches, organized on a cantonal basis. The national congress, held every four years, elects a Central Committee of 50 members, on which all linguistic regions are represented. The Central Committee elects the 14-member Political Bureau and the five-member Secretariat.

Membership. 4,500 (1985 estimate). The PdA is strongest in the French-speaking cantons of Geneva, Vaud and Neuchâtel, but also has some support in Zürich, Basle and Ticino.

Electoral influence. The PdA's share of the vote fell from 2.2 per cent in the 1979 elections to 0.9 per cent in 1983. Its parliamentary representatives in the past have mainly come from Geneva, where in 1967 it received more votes than any other party, Vaud and Neuchâtel. It has members on about 10 local councils.

Orientation. The PdA has normally taken a pro-Soviet line, but it sometimes adopted a more independent position, criticizing the Soviet intervention in Czechoslovakia and the introduction of martial law in Poland.

Programme. The party programme envisages the formation of a broad popular movement, based on unity of action between the Social Democratic Party and the PdA, to bring about the nationalization of large enterprises and reduction of the power of the monopolies as an intermediate stage in the struggle for socialism.

Publications. Voix Ouvrière (Workers' Voice), French-language weekly (8,000); *Vorwärts* (Forwards), German-language weekly (6,000); *Il Lavoratore* (The Worker), Italian-language weekly (3,000).

International affiliations. The PdA is represented on the editorial council of *World Marxist Review*.

Turkey

Capital: Ankara   Pop. 50,207,000

Acts of terrorism by both left-wing and right-wing extremists and clashes between them became increasingly common in Turkey from 1970 onwards. Martial law was proclaimed in 13 provinces in 1978 and was subsequently extended to seven more, but without effect, 3,710 people being killed in 1979 and the first nine months of 1980. The armed forces accordingly seized power on Sept. 12, 1980, dissolved Parliament, extended martial law to all the 67 provinces and suspended political activities, all the existing parties being dissolved in 1981. By the end of 1981 about 45,000 people had been arrested, many of whom were sentenced to death or to long terms of imprisonment, although up to October 1984 only 26 people were known to have been executed. A civilian government was formed in December 1983, after elections in which only parties approved by the military authorities were allowed to take part.

Communist Party of Turkey
Türkiye Komünist Partisi (TKP)

History. Founded in 1920, the TKP was banned in 1923, and has operated underground ever since. It has had its headquarters in East Berlin since World War II. Hundreds of its members and supporters were arrested after the 1980 coup, nine of whom were sentenced to death and 52 to terms of imprisonment in 1982–83. In 1984 the TKP and five other left-wing parties formed the Left Unity of Turkey and Turkish Kurdistan.

Leadership. Haydar Kutlu (g.s.).

Structure. The underground party inside Turkey is organized in workplace and residential cells, directed by provincial committees. A party congress, the first for over 50 years, held in 1983, elected a Central Committee, which re-elected Ismail Bilen (who died shortly after) chairman and Haydar Kutlu general secretary.

Membership. 2,000 (1977 claim). At the 1983 congress 42 per cent of the delegates were reported to be workers, 58 per cent intellectuals and 22 per cent Kurds.

Orientation. Pro-Soviet.

Programme. The TKP advocates a "national democratic revolution" to end the military dictatorship and establish a "government of national democratic forces", which would adopt a new constitution guaranteeing political rights and freedom of thought, religion and trade union activity, grant a general amnesty, end the oppression of the Kurdish people, carry out land reforms, expand the state sector of the economy, develop industrialization and withdraw from NATO. The struggle against the dictatorship must be led by the working class and must embrace the middle strata, patriotic elements in the army, progressive religious currents and the Kurdish national movement. Such a "national democratic revolution", which would use the most diverse forms of struggle while rejecting terrorism, would prepare the way for an "anti-imperialist people's democratic revolution".

Publications. *Atilim*, fortnightly, and *Durum*, fortnightly bulletin, published clandestinely.

International affiliations. The TKP is represented on the editorial council of *World Marxist Review*.

Turkish Communist Party—Marxist-Leninist (TKP-ML)

History. The TKP-ML, founded in 1973, conducted terrorist activities and attempted to set up a Turkish Revolutionary Peasants' Liberation Army. Many of its members were arrested in 1980–81, including its principal founder, Ibrahim Kaypakkaya, who died in custody. Over 80 of its members were sentenced to death and 168 to prison terms in 1984.

Orientation. Maoist.

Turkish Labour Party
Türkiye Isçi Partisi (TIP)

History. Founded in 1961 by trade union leaders and intellectuals, the TIP won 15 seats in the National Assembly in 1965, but retained only two in the 1969 elections, after a change in the electoral law to the disadvantage of the smaller parties. It was dissolved by the Constitutional Court in 1971 because of its support for Kurdish rights, and 21 of its leaders were imprisoned in the following year on a charge of propagating Marxism-Leninism. Amnestied in 1975, they were allowed to re-establish the party, but it failed to gain any seats in the 1977 elections. It was banned with the other parties in 1981, many of its leaders being arrested, and its chairman, Mrs Behice Boran, who had escaped abroad, was deprived of her citizenship for failing to return to stand trial.

Leadership. Mrs Behice Boran (ch.); Nihat Sargin (g.s.).

Structure. The TIP formerly held a biennial congress, which elected the 21-member Central Executive Committee.

Electoral influence. The TIP obtained 0.1 per cent of the vote in the 1977 elections.

Programme. The TIP advocated the democratization of political, economic and social life, the nationalization of foreign trade and foreign companies, agrarian reform, the abolition of foreign bases, the abrogation of treaties incompatible with national independence and the creation of an independent and socialist Turkey.

Worker–Peasant Party of Turkey
Türkiye Isci Köylü Partisi (TIKP)

History. The TIKP was founded in 1978, and organized a number of anti-Soviet demonstrations in the same year. Many of its members were arrested after the military coup in 1980. Its leader, Dogu Perinçek, was sentenced to a year's imprisonment in 1982, and in the following year 35 of its members were sentenced to death and 359 to terms of imprisonment on a change of attempting to establish a separate Kurdish state.

Leadership. Dogu Perinçek (ch.).

Structure. The TIKP claimed in 1979 to have established executive councils in 22 provinces and executive committees in 30 counties. The party congress elected the Party Assembly of 15 full and five alternate members, which elected the chairman.

Orientation. Pro-Chinese.

Programme. The TIKP described itself as the revolutionary party of the working class, guided by Mao Zedong thought and the three worlds theory and opposed to imperialism and Soviet social imperialism, its ultimate aim being the realization of the classless society.

Workers' Party of Turkey
Türkiye Emekçi Partisi (TEP)

History. The TEP broke away from the Communist Party of Turkey in 1975. The Constitutional Court ordered its dissolution in 1980 on the ground that its demand that Kurdish children should be educated in their own language contravened the constitution.

Leadership. Mihri Belli (ch.); Saban Ormanlar and Hamza Özkan (g.s.).

Structure. The TEP was organized at department and county level. The national congress elected the General Committee, which elected the chairman, general secretaries and Central Executive Committee.

Orientation. Independent.

Programme. The TEP advocated "an independent and genuinely democratic Turkey heading towards socialism".

Trade Union Organizations

Bank-Is

History. The general secretary of this small white-collar union, Atilla Onur, and 21 other leading members were sentenced to terms of imprisonment in 1982 for violating the anti-Communist articles of the penal code, the union being banned at the same time. The prosecution alleged that the defendants had taken instructions from the Albanian Party of Labour.

Confederation of Revolutionary Trade Unions of Turkey (DISK)

History. DISK was established in 1967, with about 70,000 members and a policy of "national independence and socialism". It was closely linked with the Turkish Labour Party (see above), of which its first chairman, Kemal Türkler, was one of the founders, and was regarded as influenced but not fully controlled by Marxists. Trade union legislation introduced in 1970 in an attempt to limit its influence led to protest demonstrations in Istanbul which developed into riots. By 1977 its membership had reached at least 550,000, organized in 27 unions, the largest of which, the metalworkers' union, had 80,000 members. It became a target, however, for right-wing terrorists, who in 1977 fired on a May Day rally in Istanbul organized by DISK, killing 34 people, and in 1980 murdered Türkler.

DISK was banned immediately after the 1980 coup, about 2,000 of its members being arrested, and charges of spreading Communist propaganda were subsequently brought against 52 of its leaders, for whom the prosecution demanded the death penalty. While on trial in 1982 Abdullah Bastürk and Fehmi Isiklar, its chairman and general secretary respectively, claimed to have been tortured since their arrest. The International Confederation of Free Trade Unions protested in 1981 against the authorities' actions against DISK as "completely unacceptable repression of human and trade union rights", and the case was one of the reasons for the suspension of Turkey from the European Parliament in the same year. Bastürk and 10 other leading DISK members were provisionally released in 1984.

Federation of Turkish Labour in Germany

History. This organization of Turkish workers in West Germany, which claims 20,000 members but is not recognized by the West German trade union movement, is believed to be controlled from East Berlin by the exiled leaders of the Communist Party of Turkey.

Turkish Teachers' Union (Tob-Der)

History. In 1972 prison sentences were passed on 59 *Tob-Der* members for conducting communist propaganda. The union was closed down and its property confiscated after the 1980 coup, and its president, Gultekin Gazioglu, who had escaped to West Germany, was deprived of his Turkish citizenship. A total of 55 of its officials were sentenced in 1981–82 to terms of up to nine years' imprisonment on charges of attempting to overthrow the state and propagating communism in schools.

Terrorist Organizations

Association of Revolutionary Youth (Dev-Genc)

History. This loose grouping of several extreme left-wing factions, established in 1969, was responsible for a number of bank robberies and acts of terrorism in 1971–72.

Marxist–Leninist Armed Propaganda Unit

History. This organization, which first emerged in Paris in 1973, was responsible for a number of attacks on US servicemen in Turkey in 1979–80 and for the murder in January 1980 of the Istanbul manager of the Israeli airline El Al, and was reported to have links with the Palestine Liberation Organization, which trained some of its members, the West German Red Army Faction and the Italian Red Brigades. In 1984 a military court found 67 of its members guilty of a total of 87 murders, 22 being sentenced to death and the rest to life imprisonment.

Revolutionary Left (Dev-Sol)

History. *Dev-Sol*, which broke away from Revolutionary Way (see below) in 1978, was responsible for many acts of terrorism, the most notorious being the murder of Dr Nihat Erim (a former Prime Minister) in July 1980, and was reported to have links with the Popular Front for the Liberation of Palestine, which supplied it with arms. A number of its members were condemned to death in 1981–84, six of them for the murder of Dr Erim, while others received long prison sentences.

Revolutionary Way (Dev–Yol)

History. Dev-Yol broke away from the Turkish People's Liberation Party (see below) in 1975, as it rejected the view of Mahir Çayan, the party's founder, that Turkish Marxists should rely on the communist countries for support, and regarded both the Soviet and Chinese regimes as revisionist. It was responsible for numerous acts of terrorism, and in 1980 attempted to set up a "liberated zone" at Fatsa, on the Black Sea coast. Over 1,000 of its members were arrested in 1980–82, of whom at least 21 were sentenced to death and 247 to prison terms. A member of the organization was hanged for murder in October 1984.

Dev-Yol was reported in 1981 to have moved its headquarters to Paris, where its six-member committee was headed by Çayan's widow, Mrs Gulten Çayan.

Turkish People's Liberation Army

See "Turkish People's Liberation Party".

Turkish People's Liberation Party (THKP)

History. The THKP, which broke away in 1970 from the Association of Revolutionary Youth (see above), was founded by Mahir Çayan, who held that the imperialists' control of the under-developed countries could be broken only through urban and rural guerrilla war. Its military wing, the Turkish People's Liberation Army, began operations in January 1971, and in the following March kidnapped and murdered the Israeli consul-general in Istanbul. Çayan was killed in a gun battle with troops in March 1972, and in May three members of the organization were hanged. Sporadic acts of violence nevertheless continued, and in 1976 the Liberation Army attempted to assassinate Bülent Ecevit (leader of the Republican People's Party and a former Prime Minister) while he was visiting the United States. Many THKP members were arrested in 1980–82, 14 of them being sentenced to death and 117 to long terms of imprisonment in 1984.

Kurdish Movements

The Kurdish minority in south-eastern Turkey is believed to number about 7,000,000. The Treaty of Sèvres, concluded between Turkey and the Western Allies in 1920, provided for the establishment of an independent Kurdish state, but was superseded in 1923 by the Treaty of Lausanne, which made no such provision. A Kurdish uprising in 1925 was ruthlessly crushed. Turkey does not recognize the Kurds as a cultural minority, and the use of the Kurdish language is forbidden, although many Kurds do not speak Turkish.

Kurdish Workers' Party (PKK or Apocular)

History. The PKK, founded in 1974, was given the name of *Apocular* after its founder, Abdullah Ocalan, and first became prominent in 1979, when it mounted an ambush in which a right-wing deputy was killed. Over 2,000 of its members were arrested after the 1980 coup, and many others took refuge in Iraq and Syria, from where they conducted guerrilla raids into Turkey. Although Turkish troops carried out a large-scale operation against Kurdish bases in Iraq in May 1983, PKK guerrillas coming from Iraq were believed to be responsible for a number of attacks on military and police posts in the Kurdish provinces in August 1984. The trial of 624 PKK members accused of attempting to set up a Marxist-Leninist state, which began in 1981, ended in 1985 when 22 were sentenced to death and 300 to prison terms.

Leadership. Nemesi Kiliç (g.s.).

Orientation. Kurdish nationalist.

Revolutionary Cultural Centres of the East

History. This movement, which was associated with the Turkish Labour Party (see above), began to set up cultural centres in Kurdish areas in 1969. It was banned in 1971, and 70 of its members received prison sentences of up to 16 years in the following year for founding "a secret society aimed at establishing an extreme left-wing regime".

Socialist Party of Turkish Kurdistan

History. This organization, which in order to avoid dissolution on charges of separation had operated under the name of the Socialist Party of Iraqi Kurdistan, was suppressed after the 1980 coup, 31 of its members being arrested, while its leadership escaped abroad.

Leadership. Kemal Burkay (l.).

Programme. The party was reported to aim at the establishment of an independent Kurdistan based on Marxist-Leninist principles.

2. EASTERN EUROPE AND THE USSR

Albania

Capital: Tirana   Pop. 2,906,000

The Kingdom of Albania was invaded and annexed by Italy in 1939. After Italy surrendered in 1943 it was occupied by German troops. From 1941 onwards the communist-led resistance movement, headed by Enver Hoxha, conducted a guerrilla struggle, which culminated in the expulsion of the Germans from Albania in 1944. A provisional government was established with Hoxha as Prime Minister, and in 1945 a Constituent Assembly was elected, which in the following year adopted a constitution abolishing the monarchy and declaring Albania a People's Republic. Industry, transport and banking were nationalized and land reforms carried out.

The new regime was dominated politically and economically by Yugoslavia until the break between the Soviet Union and Yugoslavia in 1948, when Albania adopted the violently anti-Yugoslav attitude which it has maintained ever since. Albania then passed under direct Soviet influence; a series of five-year plans on the Soviet model began in 1951, and agriculture was collectivized in 1958–61. However, Albania broke with the Soviet Union in 1961, after which it relied for its economic development largely on Chinese aid, until this ceased in 1978.

A new constitution adopted in 1976 describes Albania as a Socialist People's Republic and the Party of Labour as "the sole directing power in state and society", its first secretary being C.-in-C. of the armed forces. Private property, religion, the establishment of foreign bases and the stationing of foreign troops, and the acceptance of aid or credits from "capitalist or revisionist monopolies or states" are all forbidden.

Party of Labour of Albania (PLA)
Partia e Punës te Shqipërisë (PPS)

History. The communist groups which had existed in Albania since 1927 were organized in 1941 into a single Communist Party of Albania by representatives of the Yugoslav Communist Party, acting on the Comintern's instructions. The party, which had about 200 members, mostly students and young intellectuals, elected Enver Hoxha as secretary, and after playing the leading role in the resistance movement took power in 1944. A struggle ensued between a pro-Yugoslav group headed by Koci Xoxe, the Minister of the Interior, and Hoxha's faction, which sought to assert Albania's independence. After the expulsion of Yugoslavia from the Cominform in 1948 the "Titoists" were purged and Xoxe executed. The CPA was renamed the Party of Labour of Albania in the same year.

Khrushchev's denunciation of Stalin at the Soviet Communist Party congress in 1956 (for which the PLA was the last East European communist party to express support) led to criticisms of Hoxha's leadership and demands for the rehabilitation of Xoxe and other communists who had been executed or purged. This incident was followed by another purge, in which two former members of the Political Bureau, Dalli Ndreu and his wife, Liri Gega, were executed.

Relations between the PLA and the Soviet Communist Party deteriorated in 1960, as the former refused to support the Soviet Union in its controversy with China. A number of pro-Soviet members of the leadership were removed from their party and government posts and imprisoned, and in May 1961 the former C.-in-C. of the navy and three others were executed on a charge of plotting with Yugoslavia to overthrow the regime. The Soviet Union ended its economic aid to Albania in April 1961. At the Soviet Communist Party congress in October 1961 Khrushchev openly denounced the "bloody atrocities" of Hoxha and Mehmet Shehu (Prime Minister of Albania since 1954). He accused these leaders of having murdered almost all the founders of the PLA and the leaders of the wartime resistance movement, and called on the Albanian people to overthrow them. From 1961 onwards the PLA became the closest supporter of the Chinese Communist Party in its feud with the Soviet Union. A Cultural Revolution on the Chinese model was launched in 1966, the most striking feature of which was a campaign for the abolition of religion, Albania being declared "the first atheist state in the world". Purges and executions meanwhile continued; General Beqir Balluku, a former member of the Political Bureau, was reported to have been executed for conspiracy in 1975 with 14 other senior officers.

In July 1977 the PLA criticized the Chinese party's "three worlds" theory, and in subsequent statements it denounced the re-establishment of close relations between the Chinese and Yugoslav Communist parties. China in consequence terminated all economic aid to Albania in July 1978, since when the PLA has maintained a hostile attitude towards both China and the Soviet Union.

Shehu died in mysterious circumstances in December 1981, his death being officially attributed to suicide. He was succeeded as Prime Minister by Adil Çarçani, who dropped several of Shehu's close associates from the government, including Feçor Shehu (Minister of the Interior), Nesti Nase (Foreign Minister), Llambi Ziçishti (Health Minister) and Kadri Hazbiu (Defence Minister). In November 1982 Hoxha accused Mehmet Shehu of having been a US, Yugoslav and Soviet agent since the war, and of plotting to kill Hoxha and other Albanian leaders on Yugoslav orders. Feçor Shehu, Ziçishti and Hazbiu were reported to have been executed in September 1983, and several others, including Nase and Mehmet Shehu's widow and two sons, were sentenced to long terms of imprisonment. Hoxha died in April 1985, and was succeeded as first secretary by Ramiz Alia.

Leadership. The full members of the Political Bureau are President Ramiz Alia (1st sec.), Muho Asllani, Adil Çarçani, Hajredin Çeliku, Lenka Çuko, Hekuran Isai, Rita Marko, Pali Miska, Manush Myftiu and Simon Stefani.

Structure. The party congress, meeting every five years, elects the Central Committee, which elects the Political Bureau and Secretariat. At the 1981 congress a Central Committee of 81 full and 39 alternate members, a Political Bureau of 13 full members (three of whom, Hoxha, Mehmet Shehu and Kadri Hazbiu, have since died) and five alternate members and a Secretariat of five members were elected. The party's youth organization is the Union of Labour Youth of Albania.

Membership. 122,600 full and 24,363 candidate members (1981), of whom 38 per cent were workers, 29.4 per cent peasants, 32.6 per cent office workers and intellectuals and 30 per cent women.

Electoral influence. The People's Assembly consists of 250 members, elected every four years on a single list of candidates nominated by the Democratic Front, which is completely controlled by the PLA. According to the official returns for the 1982 elections, the entire electorate of 1,627,968 voted, only one vote being cast against the official candidates and eight votes being invalid.

Industrial influence. The PLA controls the Central Council of Albanian Trade Unions, which has 610,000 members.

Orientation. Independent. At the 1981 PLA congress Hoxha denounced Soviet socialism as "the most dangerous current of modern revisionism"; declared that under Mao Zedong "hegemonist ideas of world domination" had arisen in the Chinese Communist Party and since his death capitalism had been restored in China; and described Eurocommunism as "a degenerate bourgeois product of revisionism".

Programme. The PLA defines its aim as "wiping out the economic basis of feudalism and capitalism" in order "to build the economic basis of socialism, to liquidate the economic and cultural backwardness left over from the past and to set up a developed multi-branched economy with modern industry and mechanized agriculture". It lays great emphasis on preserving Albania's independence and territorial integrity and reliance on its own strength in building a socialist and communist society.

Publications. *Zëri i Popullit* (Voice of the People), daily, founded by Enver Hoxha in 1942 (105,500); *Rruga e Partisë* (The Party Road), theoretical monthly (10,000).

International affiliations. The only ruling communist parties with which the PLA maintains relations are those of Vietnam and North Korea. It acts as the theoretical centre for a number of splinter Marxist parties.

Bulgaria

Capital: Sofia   Pop. 8,969,000

Bulgaria, which had been under Turkish rule since the 15th century, became an independent kingdom in 1878. It took part in World War I as an ally of Germany. A left-wing Agrarian Party government which took office in 1920 was overthrown by a military coup in 1923. Parliamentary government was restored in 1926, but a second coup in 1934 was followed by a period of military dictatorship. In 1941 German troops entered Bulgaria, which declared war on Britain and the United States, although not on the Soviet Union. In September 1944, however, Soviet troops entered Bulgaria, which thereupon declared war on Germany, and the Communist-led Fatherland Front seized power in a bloodless coup. Following a plebiscite, the monarchy was abolished in 1946 and Bulgaria proclaimed a People's Republic. The opposition Agrarian leader, Nikola Petkov, was executed for treason in 1947; the Social Democratic Party was merged with the Communist Party in 1948; and the smaller Fatherland Front parties dissolved themselves in 1949. Although the Fatherland Front and the Agrarian Union nominally continued to exist, in practice from 1949 Communist control was complete. A new constitution adopted in 1971 describes the Communist Party as "the leading force in society and in the state".

Bulgarian Communist Party (BCP)
Bulgarska Komunisticheska Partiya

History. The Bulgarian Social Democratic Party, founded in 1891, split in 1903 into left-wing "narrow" and right-wing "broad" parties, the former taking the name Bulgarian Workers' Social Democratic Party (Narrow Socialists). After opposing Bulgaria's participation in World War I, it became a founder member of the Comintern in 1919, and changed its name to Bulgarian Communist Party (Narrow Socialists). In the 1920 elections it emerged as the second largest party, with 50 of the 229 seats in the National Assembly. It refused to co-operate with the Agrarian government, but after the coup of 1923 the two parties organized an unsuccessful uprising. After its failure most of the Communist leaders escaped abroad, and in the following year the BCP was banned. Reorganized in 1927 as the legal Workers' Party, it obtained 31 seats in the 1931 elections, and won the Sofia municipal elections in the following year. Again banned after the 1934 coup, it operated illegally for the next 10 years as the Bulgarian Workers' Party (Communist). Many of its exiled leaders living in the Soviet Union were executed in Stalin's purges.

In 1943 the Communists allied with the left-wing Agrarians and Social Democrats in the Fatherland Front, which organized partisan resistance to the German forces and seized power on Sept. 9, 1944. The Communists won 277 of the 465 seats in the 1946 elections, the last held on a multiparty basis, and the party leader, Georgi Dimitrov, formed a government. The Social Democratic Party was forced in 1948 to merge with the Bulgarian Workers' Party, which resumed its former name of the Bulgarian Communist Party (BCP). On his death in 1949 Dimitrov was succeeded as Prime Minister by Vasil Kolarov, who died in the following year and was succeeded by Vulko Chervenkov.

The breach between Yugoslavia and the Cominform was followed by a purge of "Titoists" in the BCP, and in 1949 Traicho Kostov, a former deputy premier and party secretary, was hanged on charges of treason and espionage. After Khrushchev's denunciation of Stalin in 1956, however, Kostov was rehabilitated; those imprisoned during the purge were released; and Chervenkov, who had already been replaced as first secretary by Todor Zhivkov in 1954, was accused of fostering a personality cult and replaced as Prime Minister by Anton Yugov.

During 1956–62 the leadership was divided by a conflict between a Stalinist and pro-Chinese faction headed by Chervenkov and a more liberal "Khrushchevist" faction headed by Zhivkov. A group accused of pro-Yugoslav sympathies was expelled from the Central Committee in 1957 and from the party in 1961; moreover, in 1958–59 attempts were made to reorganize the co-operative farms on the model of the Chinese communes, which Chervenkov openly praised, and to speed up the Five-Year Plan in imitation of the Chinese "great leap forward". After the split between China and the Soviet Union and Khrushchev's renewed denunciation of Stalin, however, Chervenkov was expelled from the Political Bureau in 1961 and from the party in the following year. Yugov, accused of responsibility for the execution of Kostov, was removed from the Central Committee in 1962 and replaced as Prime Minister by Zhivkov. Nine army officers and former partisans, some of whom had been purged as Titoists in 1950, were convicted in 1965 of plotting to seize power and sentenced to terms of imprisonment; although officially described as pro-Chinese, they were more probably "national communists" who wished Bulgaria to adopt a more independent attitude towards the Soviet Union.

Zhivkov was elected Chairman of the State Council (President of the Republic) in 1971 and was succeeded as Prime Minister by Stanko Todorov, who in turn was succeeded in 1981 by Grisha Filipov. The post of general secretary, abolished in 1954, was revived in 1981 for President Zhivkov. Georgi Atanasov succeeded Filipov as Prime Minister in 1986.

Leadership. The full members of the Political Bureau are President Todor Zhivkov (general secretary), Chudomir Aleksandrov, Milko Balev, Ognyan Doinov, Gen. Dobri Dzhurov, Grisha Filipov, Pencho Kubadinski, Petur Mladenov, Stanko Todorov and Yordan Yotov. There are also seven candidate members.

Structure. The party is organized in workplace and residential branches, which are grouped in district, city and regional organizations. The congress, meeting every five years, elects the Central Commitee, which elects the Political Bureau and Secretariat. The 1981 congress elected a Central Committee of 194 full and 138 candidate members, which elected a Political Bureau of 11 full and three candidate members and a Secretariat of 10 members.

Membership. 825,876 (1981), of whom 42.7 per cent were industrial workers. The Dimitrov Communist Youth League, the party's youth organization, has about 1,500,000 members.

Electoral influence. All candidates for the National Assembly are sponsored by the Fatherland Front, a single candidate being nominated for each constituency. According to the official returns for the 1981 elections, 99.96 per cent of the electorate voted, and 99.93 per cent of the votes were cast for the Fatherland Front candidates. Of the 400 members returned, 271 belonged to the BCP and 99 to the Agrarian Union (the other legal party), the remaining 30 being non-party candidates.

Industrial influence. The BCP controls the Central Council of Trade Unions, which has about 4,000,000 members. Its chairman, Petur Dyulgerov, is a candidate member of the Political Bureau.

Orientation. Pro-Soviet.

Programme. The BCP's programme as defined by President Zhivkov at the 1981 party congress concentrates on the development of the economy. According to Zhivkov, this would be most effectively achieved through (i) the intensification of automation and mechanization; (ii) the more efficient use of energy and raw materials; (iii) efforts to lessen the extent of bureaucracy; (iv) the development of new sources of energy such as nuclear power and solar and geothermal energy; (v) the development of co-operation with other members of the Council for Mutual Economic Assistance (Comecon); (vi) the reorganization of planning and management systems to give better co-ordination of centralized and decentralized powers; (vii) a general improvement in the quality and variety of manufactured goods, especially those intended for export; (viii) the closer alignment of production and market forces and the enhancement of the role of profit as an indicator of economic efficiency.

Publications. Rabotnichesko Delo (Workers' Cause), daily, founded in 1897 (750–800,000); *Novo Vremé* (New Times), theoretical monthly, founded in 1897 (32,000); *Partien Zhivot* (Party Life), monthly, founded in 1957 (42,000).

International affiliations. The BCP is represented on the editorial board of *World Marxist Review*, and maintains close relations with the other Soviet-bloc parties.

Czechoslovakia

Capital: Prague   Pop. 15,420,000

The Republic of Czechoslovakia was formed in 1918 by the union of Bohemia and Moravia (previously under Austrian rule) with Slovakia (hitherto part of Hungary). The first President, Tomáš Masaryk, was succeeded in 1935 by Eduard Beneš. An agitation among the German minority in western Bohemia led to the Munich Agreement of September 1938, by which Czechoslovakia was forced to cede the Sudetenland to Germany, and in March 1939 Bohemia and Moravia were occupied by Germany and declared a German protectorate, whilst Slovakia became a nominally independent German satellite. An uprising in Slovakia in August 1944 was crushed by the Germans, but in May 1945 Prague revolted four days before the Soviet army entered the city.

President Beneš, who had been forced to resign and go into exile after Munich, formed a provisional government in April 1945, in which all the six anti-fascist parties forming the National Front were included; this coalition was continued after elections in 1946, in which Communists and Social Democrats obtained 152 and the other parties 148 seats. Disagreements between the Communists and the right-wing parties, however, led to a cabinet crisis in February 1948, which enabled a Communist-dominated government to take power by a combination of constitutional methods with extra-parliamentary pressure. A new constitution was adopted, but President Beneš resigned rather than sign it, and was succeeded by the Communist leader, Klement Gottwald. Another constitution on the Soviet model was introduced in 1960, which described Czechoslovakia as a "Socialist Republic" instead of a "People's Democracy" and the Communist Party as "the leading force in society and the state".

The replacement of Antonín Novotný as Communist Party first secretary by Alexander Dubček in January 1968 and as President by Gen. Ludvík Svoboda in March, and the replacement of Jozef Lenárt as Prime Minister by Oldřich Černík in April, ushered in a period of reforms known as the "Prague Spring", which was ended by the Soviet invasion of Aug. 20–21. A treaty signed in October provided for the "temporary" stationing of Soviet troops in Czechoslovakia. The one permanent result of the Dubček interlude was the adoption (in October 1968) of legislation establishing a federal system of government. Gustáv Husák succeeded Dubček as first secretary in 1969 and Gen. Svoboda as President in 1976, whilst Lubomír Štrougal replaced Černík as Prime Minister in 1970.

Communist Party of Czechoslovakia (CPCz)
Komunistická Strana Československa (KSČ)

History. The CPCz was formally established in 1921, following a split in the Social Democratic Party, and then claimed 300,000 members, although by 1925 membership had fallen to under 100,000. It obtained almost 1,000,000 votes and 41 seats in the 1925 elections, but in 1929 its parliamentary representation fell to 30. Klement Gottwald became general secretary in 1929, and unsuccessfully opposed Masaryk in the 1934 presidential election. In the following year, however, the CPCz adopted a Popular Front policy, and when Masaryk resigned it supported Beneš' candidature. After the Munich Agreement, which it strongly opposed, it was banned as a gesture of appeasement to Germany, and its leaders escaped to the Soviet Union or to the West. It entered the National Front government in 1945, and after the 1946 elections, in which it emerged as the largest party with 93 of the 300 seats, in addition to 21 won by the Slovak Communists, Gottwald became Prime Minister. The crisis of February 1948 gave supreme power to the KSC, which absorbed the Social Democratic Party and the previously separate Communist Party of Slovakia. Gottwald took over the presidency, and was succeeded as Prime Minister by Antonín Zápotocký.

The breach between Yugoslavia and the Cominform was followed by a wholesale purge of the party, 169,544 members being expelled in six months in 1950–51, and by a series of political trials. Eleven leading Communists, including Rudolf Slánský (Gottwald's successor as general secretary) and Vladimir Clementis (a former Foreign Minister), were hanged in 1952 as "Trotskyist-Titoist-Zionist-bourgeois-nationalist traitors", and others were imprisoned, including Josef Smrkovský, leader of the Prague rising of 1945, and Gustáv Husák, formerly chairman of the Slovak Board of Commissioners. When Gottwald died in 1953 Zápotocký became President and Viliám Siroký Prime Minister. Antonín Novotný was elected first secretary later in the same year, the title of general secretary having been abolished after Slánský's disgrace in 1951; on Zápotocký's death in 1957 Novotný also assumed the presidency. After Khrushchev's denunciation of the Stalin cult in 1956 Novotný condemned the similar cult of Gottwald, but no serious attempt was made to introduce reforms.

Pressure for change steadily increased from 1960 onwards, both inside and outside the party. In 1963 Siroký was replaced as Prime Minister by Jozef Lenárt, and the victims of the 1952 trial were rehabilitated. Major economic reforms, largely inspired by Prof. Ota Šik, which aimed at greater decentralization and a "socialist market economy" were introduced in 1967. Faced with growing agitation inside the Writers' Union and among the students and demands for greater autonomy for Slovakia, Novotný resigned the post of party first secretary, and was replaced on Jan. 5, 1968 by Alexander Dubček.

Dubček's coming to power inaugurated the period of liberal and democratic reforms known as the "Prague Spring". The reformer Oldřich Černík replaced Lenárt as Prime Minister in April. The Central Committee in the same month elected a new Presidium dominated by reformers, from which Novotný was excluded, and adopted an "action programme" promising democratization of the system of government, freedom of assembly, the press, foreign travel and religion, restriction of the powers of the security police, rehabilitation of victims of injustice and autonomy for Slovakia. This policy of "socialism with a human face", however, deeply alarmed the Soviet Union and its allies, which brought pressure to bear on the Czechoslovak leaders from March onwards. During the night of Aug. 20–21 the country was occupied by Soviet, East German, Polish, Hungarian and Bulgarian troops, and Dubček, Černík, Smrkovsky and other leading reformers were taken to Moscow as prisoners. The party congress, which was due to meet in September, convened secretly in a Prague factory on Aug. 22, reaffirmed its support for Dubček's policies, elected a new Presidium composed entirely of reformers and demanded the withdrawal of the occupation forces (see Appendix 2: Documents).

On President Svoboda's insistence, the kidnapped leaders were released on Aug. 27, but the reform movement was largely reversed. In September the Central Committee repudiated the decisions of the secret congress, and press censorship was reintroduced. After anti-Soviet riots in March 1969 Husák replaced Dubček as first secretary in April, and a purge of the party began which reduced its membership from 1,600,000 in August 1968 to 1,200,000 in December 1970. The Central Committee, from which such reformers as Šik and Smrkovsky had been removed, announced in September 1969 its approval of the Soviet invasion, which it described as "actuated by the interests of the defence of socialism". In 1970 Lubomír Štrougal succeeded Černík as Prime Minister, and Dubček, Černík, Smrkovsky and many other reformers were expelled from the party. At the 1971 congress the party statutes were brought into line with Soviet practice by extending the period between congresses from four to five years, introducing candidate membership and reviving the title of general secretary, abolished in 1951. There have since been no significant changes in policy or leadership.

Leadership. The 11 full members of the Presidium are Gustáv Husák (g.s.), Vasil Bil'ák, Petr Colotka, Karel Hoffman, Alois Indra, Miloš Jakeš, Antonín Kapek, Josef Kempný, Josef Korčák, Jozef Lenárt and Lubomír Štrougal. There are also six candidate members.

Structure. The basic units are the workplace and residential branches, which are grouped in district and regional organizations. The congress, meeting every five years, elects the Central Committee, which elects the Presidium and Secretariat. The 1981 congress elected a Central Committee of 123 full and 55 candidate members and a Secretariat of nine secretaries and two members. The party's youth organization is the Socialist Union of Youth.

Membership. 1,623,000 (1984 claim).

Electoral influence. All candidates are nominated by the National Front, which nominally includes four other parties but in practice is completely controlled by the CPCz, for which 66 per cent of the seats are reserved. According to official figures 99.51 per cent of the electorate voted in the 1981 elections, and 99.9 per cent of the votes were cast for the National Front candidates.

Industrial influence. The CPCz controls the Revolutionary Trade Union Movement, the chairman of which, Karel Hoffman, is a member of the Presidium.

Orientation. Pro-Soviet.

Programme. In his report to the 1981 congress Husák advocated the improvement of labour productivity; advances in the automation and mechanization of production; the improvement of energy development; increased mechanization of agriculture and increased production of fertilizers; linking pay more closely with effort; the elimination of excessive bureaucracy; intensification of the propaganda functions of the media; and strengthening of the state security apparatus. Referring to the crisis in Poland, which he compared to that in Czechoslovakia in 1968, he declared that "the defence of the socialist system" was "a joint matter for states of the socialist community".

Publications. *Rudé Právo* (Red Justice), daily (950,000); *Tribuna* (Tribune), bimonthly (78,000); *Tvorba* (Creation), weekly (81,000). *Rudé Právo*, originally called *Právo Lidu* (The People's Justice), was the organ of the Social Democratic Party until it was taken over and renamed in 1920 by the left wing of the party, which in the following year formed the CPCz.

International affiliations. The CPCz is represented on the editorial board of *World Marxist Review*, and has close links with the other Soviet-bloc parties.

Communist Party of Slovakia
Komunistická Strana Slovenska (KSS)

History. A Slovak Soviet Republic proclaimed in June 1919, with the support of the Communist government then in power in Hungary, by repatriated Slovak prisoners of war who had been converted to communism in Russia was suppressed within three weeks. From 1921 to 1938 the Slovak Communists formed part of the Communist Party of Czechoslovakia, but after it was banned they set up their own clandestine organization, which played a leading part in the Slovak uprising of 1944. The Slovak Social Democratic Party merged with the KSS in the same year. After the war the KSS continued to operate independently, winning 21 of the 69 Slovak seats in the 1946 elections. In 1948, however, it was incorporated in the Communist Party of Czechoslovakia, of which it has since formed the regional organization.

Leadership. Jozef Lenárt (first secretary).

Structure. Although forming part of the Communist Party of Czechoslovakia, the KSS has its own congress, Central Committee of 91 full and 31 candidate members, and Presidium of 11 members.

Membership. 400,000 full and candidate members.

Publications. Pravda (Truth), daily (330,000); *Új Szó* (New Word), Hungarian-language daily (85,000).

Dissident Marxist Organizations

Charter 77

History. This movement takes its name from a manifesto signed by 242 people, which was published in Western newspapers (but not in Czechoslovakia) in January 1977. Recalling that Czechoslovakia had ratified the UN Covenants on Civil and Political Rights and on Economic, Social and Cultural Rights in 1976, it pointed out that in practice many rights guaranteed in these documents did not exist in Czechoslovakia, including the right of free expression of opinion, the right to education (infringed by the exclusion of many young people from higher education because of their own or their parents' opinions), the right to receive and impart information and ideas, religious freedom, freedom of assembly, the right to take part in the conduct of public affairs, equality before the law, the right to strike, the prohibition of arbitrary interference with privacy, family, home or correspondence, the rights of defendants and their defence, and the right freely to leave the country.

The movement subsequently issued numerous statements protesting against infringements of civil rights and on other subjects, including a protest against the declaration of martial law in Poland, demands for the withdrawal of Soviet troops from Czechoslovakia and a declaration on peace and disarmament. Many signatories and supporters of Charter 77 were imprisoned during 1977–84; others were detained without trial, and some who had been allowed to leave the country were deprived of their Czechoslovak citizenship.

Leadership. The movement has no leadership as such, but it periodically appoints spokesmen to represent it.

Structure. The original manifesto stated: "Charter 77 is a free, informal and open community of persons of varying convictions, religious and professions, joined together by the will to work individually and collectively for respect for civil and human rights. . . . Charter 77 is no organization and has no statutes, no permanent organs and no organized membership. Everyone belongs to it who agrees with its idea, takes part in its work and supports it. Charter 77 is no base for oppositional political activity. . . . It therefore does not intend to draw up its own programmes for political or social reforms or changes but wants to conduct, within its sphere of activity, a constructive dialogue with the political and state authorities. . . ."

Membership. The Ministry of the Interior was reported to estimate the number of Charter 77 sympathizers at 2,000,000.

Orientation. The majority of the signatories of Charter 77 were Marxists who had been expelled from the Communist Party since 1968, although they also included priests and other non-Marxists. Among them were Jiří Hajek (Foreign Minister in 1968), three former members of the party's Presidium (František Kriegel, Zdeněk Mlynár and Václav Slavik), a former candidate member of the Presidium (Bohumil Simon) and the widow and son of Rudolf Slánský, the former general secretary. The outlook of the Marxist members of the movement is similar to that of the Eurocommunist parties of Western Europe. Mlynár said in an open letter to Western communist and socialist leaders in 1977: "I am a communist, and I am convinced that socialism must give people more political and civil rights than capitalism. I thus share the conviction which many European communist parties represent today."

Programme. Charter 77 concentrates primarily on civil rights issues, but it also criticizes the centralized system of economic planning and advocates the withdrawal of Soviet troops and Soviet missiles from Czechoslovakia.

Publications. Charter 77 periodically issues statements on civil rights and other political questions.

International affiliations. Charter 77 has co-operated since 1978 with the Polish Social Self-defence Committee, and has appealed for support to Western communist and socialist parties. The government's repressive measures against its supporters have been condemned by the Italian, Spanish, French and British Communist parties.

Revolutionary Socialist Party

History. This organization, founded in 1968 as the Revolutionary Youth Movement, and later renamed the Revolutionary Socialist Party, took an active part in protest demonstrations in Prague on Aug. 21, 1969, the first anniversary of the Soviet invasion. At the trial in 1971 of 19 of its members, all students and intellectuals, it was described as a "clandestine subversive organization" inspired by the writings of Trotsky and the New Left, which had distributed "ultra-left propaganda". Petr Uhl, its leader, was sentenced to four years' imprisonment, and 15 others to shorter terms. It is not known whether the party still exists. Uhl was later associated with Charter 77, and in 1979 was sentenced to five years' imprisonment for his dissident activities.

Socialist Movement of Czechoslovak Citizens

History. This group, consisting of supporters of the 1968 reforms, issued a statement in 1973 calling for new policies, in which it said that the main causes of the country's stagnation and "the paralysis of its internal development", which threatened to divide the international communist movement, were the exclusion of thousands of skilled specialists, the suppression of all initiative except "initiative ordered from above", investment in projects with no future and a "a return to the outdated system of command management", and called on the Soviet leadership to show that it wanted to make good the consequences of the 1968 invasion. It is not known whether the organization still exists.

German Democratic Republic

Capital: East Berlin   Pop. 16,717,000

The German Democratic Republic was formed in 1949, when the Soviet-occupied zone of Germany was proclaimed an independent state, with Wilhelm Pieck as President and Otto Grotewohl as Prime Minister. Mass demonstrations against the regime in East Berlin in 1953 developed into serious riots, which were suppressed by the Soviet army. On his death in 1960 President Pieck was succeeded by Walter Ulbricht, with the title of Chairman of the Council of State. Grotewohl died in 1964, and was succeeded as Prime Minister by Willi Stoph. A new constitution was adopted in 1968 and amended in 1974; in its amended form the constitution no longer envisaged the eventual reunification of Germany, and declared that "the German Democratic Republic is linked irrevocably and for ever with the Soviet Union and other socialist states". Stoph succeeded Ulbricht as Chairman on the latter's death in 1973, and was succeeded as Prime Minister by Horst Sindermann; in 1976, however, Erich Honecker (general secretary of the Socialist Unity Party) was elected Chairman and Stoph resumed the premiership.

Socialist Unity Party of Germany
Sozialistische Einheitspartei Deutschlands (SED)

History. The SED was formed in 1946, when the Social Democratic Party in the Soviet zone was forced to merge with the Communist Party of Germany (for the earlier history of which see under Federal Republic of Germany). Originally Social Democrats and Communists were equally represented on the ruling committees, the Social Democrat Otto Grotewohl and the Communist Wilhelm Pieck being elected joint chairmen, and the party claimed that the position in Germany made possible a democratic "German road to socialism". After 1947, however, equal representation was abandoned, and the Russian road to socialism was declared to be the only one possible. Walter Ulbricht was elected to the new post of general secretary in 1950 (this being renamed first secretary under a new party statute introduced in 1963).

A number of leading party members were expelled in 1950 after the break between Yugoslavia and the Cominform, and others in 1953–54 after the Berlin riots. Several of these were rehabilitated in 1956, but the Hungarian revolt was followed by a new purge, Prof. Wolfgang Harich and others being imprisoned in 1957 and a number of leading Communists expelled from the Central Committee in the following year. Ulbricht resigned the post of first secretary in 1971 in favour of Erich Honecker, for whom the title of general secretary was revived in 1976.

Leadership. The full members of the Political Bureau are Erich Honecker (g.s.), Hermann Axen, Horst Dohlus, Werner Felfe, Kurt Hager, Joachim Herrmann, Werner Jarowinsky, Günther Kleiber, Egon Krenz, Werner Krolikowski, Erich Mielke, Günter Mittag, Erich Mückenberger, Alfred Neumann, Günter

Schabowski, Horst Sindermann, Willi Stoph and Harry Tisch. There are also seven candidate members.

Structure. There are over 74,000 workplace and residential primary organizations, which are subordinate to territorial, city and district committees. The congress, meeting every five years, elects the Central Committee, which elects the general secretary, Political Bureau and Secretariat. The Central Committee has 156 full and 51 candidate members, and the Secretariat 11 members. The party's youth organization is the Free German Youth, which has 2,300,000 members.

Membership. 2,202,277 (1983).

Electoral influence. All candidates for the People's Chamber (*Volkskammer*) are sponsored by the National Front, which although including four smaller parties and other groups is completely controlled by the SED, a single list of candidates being put forward. In the 1981 elections, in which the SED was allocated 127 of the 500 seats, 99.21 per cent of the electors were officially stated to have voted, 99.86 per cent of the valid votes being cast for the National Front candidates.

Industrial influence. The SED controls the Free German Trade Union Federation, which has 9,100,000 members. Its chairman, Harry Tisch, is a member of the Political Bureau.

Orientation. Pro-Soviet.

Programme. In his report to the 1981 SED congress, which largely concentrated on economic issues, Honecker said that the period up to 1990 would be characterized by (i) the growth of scientific development, particularly in the areas of microelectronics, automation and chemicals, (ii) a general increase in labour productivity, including rationalization and automation, (iii) greater efficiency in the use of energy and raw materials, (iv) the improvement in quality of goods produced, (v) an increase in national income in relation to expenditure, (vi) more extensive investment in technological processes.

Publications. Neues Deutschland (New Germany), daily (1,090,000); *Einheit* (Unity), theoretical monthly (245,000); *Neuer Weg* (New Road), organizational monthly (205,000).

International affiliations. The SED is represented on the editorial board of *World Marxist Review*, and maintains close relations with the other Soviet-bloc parties.

Dissident Marxists

Although no dissident Marxist organization is known to exist, a number of individuals have been penalized for advocating a more liberal form of Marxism than that practised by the ruling SED. In 1957 Prof. Wolfgang Harich of the Humboldt University of East Berlin was sentenced to 10 years' imprisonment and four other intellectuals to shorter terms for organizing underground cells. In a memorandum sent to Social Democrats in West Berlin, Harich claimed to be supported by many party officials and intellectuals, including the poet and dramatist Bertolt Brecht, who proposed to reform the SED from within by expelling the Stalinists, democratizing its organization and adopting an ideology which rejected Stalinism. Their political programme included restoration of the power of Parliament and freedom of thought; abolition of the security police and secret trials; organization of elections giving voters real choice; the introduction of profit-sharing; the establishment of workers' councils; and the ending of forced collectivization of agriculture. These reforms and the return of a Social Democratic majority in West Germany, it was hoped, would bring about the reunification of Germany and the German labour movement.

Prof. Robert Havemann, also of the Humboldt University, who had been a Communist since 1932 and a founder of the SED, expressed similar views in his lectures from 1956 onwards, and in consequence was expelled from both the party and the university, being held under house arrest from 1976 to 1979. In 1981, with 27 other East German citizens, he addressed a letter to President Brezhnev calling for the conclusion of a peace treaty and the withdrawal of all occupation troops from East and West Germany. He died in 1982.

Rudolf Bahro was sentenced to eight years' imprisonment in 1978 for allowing his book *Die Alternative*, in which he advocated a liberal form of Marxism, to be published in West Germany. Released under an amnesty in 1979, he left for West Germany and was deprived of his East German citizenship. He subsequently claimed in an interview that there existed in East Germany, even among high party officials, a strong tendency towards the political road described in his book.

Hungary

Capital: Budapest   Pop. 10,700,000

After the defeat of Austria-Hungary in World War I a republic was established in Hungary in November 1918, headed by Count Mihály Karolyi. In order to win Russian support against allied demands for territorial concessions he handed over power in March 1919 to a coalition government of Social Democrats and Communists, which proclaimed Hungary a soviet republic. This government was overthrown in August by invading Romanian troops, and a right-wing regime headed by Admiral Miklós Horthy took power. Hungary entered World War II in 1941 as the ally of Germany, and was overrun by the Soviet army in 1944–45. A coalition government of anti-fascist parties was formed, but by 1949, when a new constitution on the Soviet model was introduced, the Communist Party had succeeded in bringing the country completely under its control. Resentment of Soviet domination and the repressive policies of the Stalinist leadership led to a national uprising in 1956, which was crushed by Soviet troops. After a period of repression, the new regime headed by János Kádár adopted a policy of cautious liberalization in 1959, which it has since continued to pursue.

Hungarian Socialist Workers' Party (HSWP)
Magyar Szocialista Munkáspárt

History. A Hungarian section of the Russian Communist Party was formed in Moscow in March 1918 by Béla Kun and other prisoners of war, who on returning home in November founded the Communist Party of Hungary. The new party was allied with the Social Democrats in the left-wing government which held power from March to August 1919, Kun being given the Foreign Affairs portfolio. Under the Horthy regime the underground Communist Party exercised little influence, and many of its leaders who had escaped to Moscow, including Kun, were executed in Stalin's purges. In 1944 the party, renamed the Hungarian Communist Party, formed the National Independence Front with the Smallholders', Social Democratic and National Peasant parties, and after the 1945 elections, in which it obtained 70 of the 421 seats, it entered a coalition government with the other three parties. In the 1947 elections it emerged as the largest party, with 100 of the 411 seats, and in the following year it merged with the Social Democratic Party to form the Hungarian Workers' Party.

The party leadership was divided into a "Muscovite" group, including Mátyás Rákosi (the general secretary), Ernö Gerö and Mihály Farkas, who had been in Moscow during the war, and a "native" group, including Laszlo Rajk and János Kádár, who had remained in Hungary. In 1949 the "Muscovites" launched a massive purge, Rajk and other leading Communists being hanged on charges of plotting to overthrow the government with Yugoslav help, Kádár imprisoned and former Social Democrats removed from the leadership. In 1952 Rákosi took over the premiership, while remaining general secretary. After Stalin's death in the following year, however, Imre Nagy became Prime Minister and announced a programme of reforms, including the abandonment of enforced collectivization of agriculture, an amnesty for political prisoners and greater religious toleration. At the same time the title of general secretary was abolished, Rákosi becoming first secretary. A reaction followed in 1955, when Nagy was condemned as a "rightist deviationist", replaced as Prime Minister by András Hegedüs, and expelled first from the Political Bureau and the Central Committee and then from the party. Following Khrushchev's denunciation of Stalin in February 1956, Rajk was rehabilitated, Gerö succeeded Rákosi as first secretary, Farkas (the head of the secret police) was expelled from the party and Nagy was readmitted to party membership. These concessions, however, failed to appease the growing demand both inside and outside the party for fundamental changes.

Mass demonstrations demanding Nagy's reinstatement as Prime Minister, a return to democracy and the withdrawal of Soviet forces from Hungary took place in Budapest and other cities on Oct. 22–23, 1956, and an attempt by Soviet troops to suppress them provoked a popular uprising which spread throughout the country. As a concession, Nagy was appointed Prime Minister on Oct. 24, and Kádár succeeded Gerö as first secretary on the following day. Nagy announced on Oct. 31 that Hungary would leave the Warsaw Pact and pursue a policy of absolute neutrality, and on Nov. 3 formed a government in which all the parties existing in 1945 were represented. Kádár had previously announced on Nov. 1 that the Hungarian Workers' Party had been dissolved, and that a new party, the Hungarian Socialist Workers' Party, had been founded to lead the country to democratic socialism. On Nov. 4 the Soviet army launched a massive offensive, and by Nov. 10 the revolt was crushed. A new government headed by Kádár was set up, which promised in January 1957 to pursue a policy of democratization of the state system, although the HSWP would remain "the guiding force". Many "counter-revolutionaries", including Nagy, were executed in 1957–58; on the other hand, as a guarantee that there would be no return to the Stalinist past, Farkas was sentenced in 1957 to 16 years' imprisonment.

After the 1959 party congress, at which Kádár put forward the slogan "He who is not against us is with us", a more liberal policy was adopted, involving toleration of all elements which did not actively oppose the regime, the making of appointments on grounds of efficiency rather than ideology, the abolition of discrimination against those not of working-class or peasant origin, the adoption of a conciliatory attitude towards the Catholic Church and those who had taken part in the 1956 revolt, almost all of whom had been amnestied by 1963, greater intellectual and artistic freedom and more democracy in party affairs. This policy met with strong opposition inside the party, and in 1962 Rákosi, Gerö and 23 other leading Stalinists were expelled. Electoral reforms introduced in 1966 gave voters a limited choice of candidates. This policy of cautious liberalization, combined with complete support for Soviet foreign policy (exemplified by Hungarian participation in the invasion of Czechoslovakia in 1968), has been continued ever since.

The title of general secretary was revived in 1985, and the new post of deputy general secretary introduced.

Leadership. The Political Bureau consists of János Kádár (g.s.), Károly Németh (deputy g.s.), György Aczél, Sándor Gáspár, Károly Grosz, Csaba Hamori, Ferenc Havasi, György Lázár, Pál Losonczi, László Maróthy, Miklós Óvári, István Sarlós and István Szabó.

Structure. The membership is organized in over 20,000 workplace and residential basic units, which are subordinate to city, district and regional committees. The congress, meeting every five years, elects the Central Committee (105 members), which elects the Political Bureau and the eight-member Secretariat. The party's youth organization is the Communist Youth Union with 874,000 members.

Membership. 870,000 (1985 claim).

Electoral influence. A new electoral law adopted in 1983 made a choice of candidates mandatory in all parliamentary and local elections, but each candidate was required to accept the programme of the Patriotic People's Front (PPF), which is dominated by the HSWP. The majority of members of the National Assembly do not belong to the HSWP, and a number of independent candidates not nominated by the PPF were returned in the 1985 elections. Under the electoral law, in addition to the 352 ordinary members a "national list" of 35 public figures nominated by the PPF, which in 1985 included nine of the 13 members of the HSWP Political Bureau, is elected unopposed.

Industrial influence. The HSWP controls the Central Council of Trade Unions, which has 4,500,000 members. Sándor Gáspár, its president, is a member of the Political Bureau.

Orientation. Pro-Soviet.

Programme. The main features of the party's policy are described above. Changes in economic policy introduced since 1968 have reduced centralized planning; increased freedom for individual enterprises; broken up large trusts into smaller competing enterprises; given workers greater influence over the control of enterprises; related wages more closely to profits; permitted local councils and companies to issue bonds to supplement their development funds; authorized the creation of joint ventures by Hungarian and Western firms; and encouraged small-scale private enterprises.

Publications. *Népszabadság* (People's Freedom), daily (727,000); *Esti Hirlap* (Evening Paper), daily (239,000); *Társadalmi Szemle* (Social Review), theoretical monthly (45,000); *Pártélet* (Party Life), organizational monthly (95,000).

International affiliations. The HSWP is represented on the editorial board of *World Marxist Review*, and maintains close links with the other Soviet-bloc parties.

Dissident Marxists

The "Budapest School" of Marxists, which draws its inspiration largely from the events of 1956 and the writings of the Hungarian philosopher and literary critic György Lukács (1885–1971), regards the East European countries as societies of a new type which are neither capitalist nor socialist, but controlled by bureaucracies. Its activities have mainly taken the form of unauthorized publication of articles and books, private gatherings of small groups and a "flying university" which held private lectures. The movement, which is believed to have about 200 members, has been subjected to some harassment by the authorities, but this has been comparatively mild in form. The most prominent figure in the movement is László Rajk, the son of the Communist leader executed in 1949. The movement has expressed its support for the Charter 77 and Solidarity movements in Czechoslovakia and Poland.

Poland

Capital: Warsaw   Pop. 36,887,000

Poland, which had been partitioned between Russia, Prussia and Austria in 1795, regained its independence in 1918, and waged a war with Russia in 1920 which resulted in large acquisitions of territory. After a period of political instability Marshal Jozef Pilsudski carried out a military coup in 1926, and Poland passed under an authoritarian right-wing regime, although opposition parties were tolerated. In September 1939 Poland was overrun by Germany, while Soviet troops reoccupied the territories lost in 1920. A government-in-exile was formed in London, but in 1944 a rival provisional government, the Communist-dominated Lublin Committee, was set up in territory liberated by the Soviet army. Although representatives of both bodies formed a provisional government in 1945, by 1947 the Communists had obtained complete control.

Serious riots in Poznan in June 1956 were followed by major changes in the leadership of the Polish United Workers' Party (PUWP), despite Soviet threats of military intervention, Wladyslaw Gomulka being elected first secretary. A number of reforms were subsequently introduced, including the abandonment of enforced collectivization of agriculture and a greater degree of religious and intellectual freedom. In other respects, however, Gomulka's policy became increasingly conservative, and after riots in the Baltic ports in 1970 he was replaced by Edward Gierek. The new leadership's policy of financing industrial growth by borrowing abroad, combined with the low level of agricultural production and a series of bad harvests, led to a major economic crisis, which in the summer of 1980 became a political crisis. A wave of strikes in the Baltic ports and the Silesian coalfields resulted in the formation of an independent trade union federation, Solidarity, the membership of which had grown by September 1981 to nearly 10,000,000. Attempts to reach agreement between Solidarity, which put forward demands for democratization of the political system as well as economic demands, and the government failed, and in December 1981 martial law was declared, trade union activities banned and over 10,000 people interned. Martial law was suspended a year later and lifted in July 1983, but tensions remained.

Polish United Workers' Party (PUWP)
Polska Zjednoczona Partia Robotnicza (PZPR)

History. The PUWP traces its descent from the Polish Socialist Party, founded in 1892, which combined Marxism with Polish nationalism, and the Social Democracy of the Kingdom of Poland (SDKP), founded in 1893, which concentrated on socialist rather than nationalist aims, and in 1906 affiliated to the Russian Social Democratic Labour Party. A section of the Polish Socialist Party which objected to its use of terrorist tactics broke away in the same year and formed the Polish Socialist Party—Left, which united with the SDKP in 1918 to form the Communist Workers' Party of Poland. The new party, which was renamed the Communist Party of Poland in 1925, obtained 7 per cent of the vote in the 1928 elections, but by 1935 its membership had fallen to 10,000. In 1938 it was dissolved by the Comintern on the ground that its leadership had been infiltrated by the secret police; almost all the Polish Communists then in the Soviet Union were executed or sent to labour camps.

In 1941 the party was revived, as the Polish Workers' Party, by Polish Communist refugees in Moscow, who formed their own underground resistance organization inside Poland, the People's Army. It joined the provisional government formed in 1945, and in the 1947 elections, as a result of widespread rigging and intimidation, the Communists and their allies obtained 80 per cent of the vote. The Socialist Party merged with the Workers' Party in 1948 to form the Polish United Workers' Party. A massive purge of elements regarded as hostile to Soviet control followed, and Wladyslaw Gomulka (general secretary since 1945) was replaced by Boleslaw Bierut, expelled from the party and imprisoned.

The Soviet Communist Party congress in February 1956, during which the dissolution of the pre-war Polish Communist Party was officially declared to have been unjustified, led to a crisis in the PUWP. Bierut died in March, and was succeeded as first secretary by Edward Ochab. An amnesty was granted in April; the powers of the security police were limited by law; and in October the Central Committee elected a new Political Bureau from which the leading Stalinists were excluded, with Gomulka as first secretary. After September 1957, however, Gomulka largely abandoned the reforming policy which he had advocated, and a purge in 1957–58, in which over 200,000 members were expelled, was directed against "revisionists" as well as against Stalinists.

As Gomulka's popularity declined because of his failure to fulfil the hopes aroused by the events of 1956, his leadership was challenged by the "Partisan" faction headed by Gen. Mieczyslaw Moczar, Minister of the Interior. This group, which derived its support largely from former members of the resistance movement, was strongly nationalist, anti-liberal and anti-Semitic, and in 1968 it made student demonstrations in Warsaw a pretext for a purge of "Zionists" and "revisionists". Gomulka succeeded in bringing the anti-Zionist campaign to an end, but at the 1968 congress he was forced to admit representatives of the Partisans and other elements critical of his leadership to the party's leading bodies. After massive price increases in December 1970 had led to riots in the Baltic ports Gomulka resigned, and was succeeded as first secretary by Edward Gierek. At the 1971 congress Gomulka, Moczar and their supporters were excluded from the party leadership.

Following strikes in the summer of 1980, the Prime Minister, Edward Babiuch, resigned in August and Gierek in September, being replaced by Jozef Pinkowski and Stanislaw Kania respectively. Among the problems confronting the latter was the fact that something like a quarter of PUWP members had joined the new free trade union movement Solidarnosc (Solidarity) led by Lech Walesa. In subsequent changes in the leadership Gierek, Babiuch and their leading supporters were expelled from the Political Bureau and the Central Committee, and Piotr Jaroszewicz (Prime Minister from 1970 to February 1980) was expelled from the party. Pinkowski resigned in February 1981, and was succeeded as Prime Minister by Gen. Wojciech Jaruzelski, the Defence Minister.

In this crisis the PUWP was deeply divided. One faction, urging democratization of the party, held an unprecedented conference without the leadership's formal approval in April 1981; the other faction, of "hard-liners", organized in the Katowice Forum, which violently denounced "revisionism", "bourgeois liberalism" and "Trotsky-Zionism" inside the party. An extraordinary party congress was held in July 1981, at which the 1,964 delegates (who contrary to previous practice had been elected by secret ballot) included 421 Solidarity members. The congress expelled Gierek, Babiuch and their leading supporters from the party, and elected (also by secret ballot) a new Central Committee of 200 members which included only 19 members of the previous committee. The Central Committee then elected a Political Bureau with 15 full members, only four of whom (Kania, Jaruzelski, Kazimierz Barcikowski and Stefan Olszowski) had served on the previous Political Bureau. Kania was re-elected first secretary in a contest with Barcikowski, but he resigned in October 1981, Jaruzelski being appointed by the Central Committee to succeed him.

Having come to regard Solidarity as a threat to the regime, the government imposed a state of martial law on Dec. 13, 1981, and effectively banned Solidarity. Many leading party members were relieved of their posts and a number were detained for trial on various charges (including Gierek). Serious industrial and social disturbances ensued in many parts of the country, but gradually the government was able to re-establish control. The Solidarity movement was formally abolished in October 1982 and steps were taken to reassert party control over workers' organizations. In February 1983 Jaruzelski called on the PUWP to launch a campaign to eliminate "apathy" within the party.

Leadership. The full members of the Political Bureau are Gen. Wojciech Jaruzelski (1st sec.), Kazimierz Barcikowski, Tadeusz Czechowicz, Jozef Czyrek, Mrs Zofia Grzyb, Stanislaw Kalkus, Hieronim Kubiak, Zbigniew Messner, Stanislaw Opalko, Tadeusz Porebski, Jerzy Romanik, Albin Siwak and Marian Wozniak. There are also six candidate members.

Structure. The PUWP is organized in the normal way for a ruling communist party, with workplace and residential branches, city, rural and provincial committees, a congress normally meeting every five years, a Central Committee elected by the congress, and a Political Bureau and Secretariat elected by the Central Committee. Since 1980, however, the organization has been in a state of flux. The 1981 extraordinary congress introduced a number of innovations, including the election of the first secretary by secret ballot, and approved a draft of a new statute, which provided for some democratization of party procedures, limitation of terms of office and the practice of holding both government and party posts, and admission of religious believers to membership. The final text was to be submitted to a national conference which has not yet met. After the introduction of martial law the Political Bureau suspended the new statutes, and empowered higher-level bodies to dismiss and nominate party officials, to dissolve and replace local committees and branches and to expel members from the party.

Membership. 2,327,349 (1984 claim), of whom 40 per cent were workers. As a result of resignations and expulsions, membership had fallen from 3,149,000 in 1980. The party's youth organization, the Polish Socialist Youth Union, claimed 2,000,000 members in 1982, but this claim was regarded as greatly exaggerated.

Electoral influence. All candidates were formerly sponsored by the National Unity Front, which put forward a single list. Since 1957 voters have been allowed a limited degree of choice, as the number of candidates put forward has exceeded the number of seats. The National Unity Front was replaced in 1982 by the Patriotic National Regeneration Movement (PRON), which, like its predecessor, includes the PUWP, the United Peasants' Party, the Democratic Party and three lay Catholic groups. New electoral regulations adopted in 1984–85 provided for a choice between two candidates for 410 of the 460 seats in the *Sejm* (national parliament) on the basis of lists drawn up by the PRON formations, with the latter also nominating an unopposed "national list" of important public figures for the other 50 seats. These regulations were applied to *Sejm* elections for the first time in October 1985, when voter participation—which was not compulsory—was put at 79 per cent by the authorities but substantially lower by Solidarity.

Industrial influence. The PUWP formerly controlled the Central Council of Trade Unions, but this disintegrated in 1980 as the members of the official unions defected to Solidarity en masse, and was dissolved in 1981. New official unions were established under legislation introduced in 1982, and claimed in 1984 to have 5,000,000 members (including 600,000 retired workers), compared with 10,000,000 organized in Solidarity in 1981. The National Trade Union Alliance, which the new unions formed in 1984, soon adopted an independent attitude, opposing government proposals for price increases.

Orientation. Pro-Soviet.

Programme. The 1981 congress instructed the Central Committee to set up a Commission to prepare a new party programme. This has not yet been published.

Publications. *Trybuna Ludu* (People's Tribune), daily (1,000,000); *Nowe Drogi* (New Roads) and *Ideologia i Polityka* (Ideology and Politics), monthlies. A feature unique in communist-ruled countries is the publication of two weeklies representing opposing factions inside the party, the moderate *Polityka* and the hard-line *Rzeczywistość* (Reality).

International affiliations. The PUWP is represented on the editorial board of *World Marxist Review*, and maintains close ties with other Soviet-bloc parties.

Dissident Marxist Organizations

Clubs for a Self-governed Republic—Freedom, Justice, Independence

History. Jacek Kuron (the founder of this organization) and Karol Modzelewski were expelled from the ruling Polish United Workers' Party for "leftist deviations" in 1964, and sentenced in the following year to three and three and a half years' imprisonment respectively for circulating an open letter to the party, which advocated a new revolution to replace the rule of the bureaucracy by direct democracy through workers' councils. Following strikes and riots in June 1976 which forced the government to withdraw proposals for price increases, Kuron, Prof. Edward Lipinski, a leading economist, and other intellectuals formed the Workers' Defence Committee (KOR) to assist the families of workers who had been imprisoned or victimized, Lipinski subsequently being expelled from the PUWP.

In 1977 KOR was replaced by the Social Self-defence Committee (KSS), with the aim of pressing the government to honour its commitment to the UN covenants on human rights. This organization, which included Marxists, liberals and Catholics, agreed in 1978 to co-operate with the Charter 77 movement in Czechoslovakia, which had similar aims. It was dissolved in September 1981, as it considered that its work had been taken over by Solidarity, but in November Kuron and others, including Solidarity leaders, formed the Clubs for a Self-governed Republic—Freedom, Justice, Independence.

A manifesto adopted by the founders advocated the formation of clubs which would become the nuclei of political parties in a democratic state, and envisaged a society in which all citizens played a part in direct democracy; and the state, acting under the supervision of trade unions, consumer groups and co-operative movements, would intervene in social life only to the extent necessary to implement fundamental social aims, including primarily the insurance of a decent existence for everyone. Kuron was arrested, and with three of his associates was charged with conspiring to overthrow the state by force. Their trial opened in July 1984, but a few days later they were released under an amnesty.

Communist Party of Poland (CPP)

History. The CPP, founded in 1965, operated from Albania, and issued a number of statements denouncing the ruling Polish United Workers' Party as "counter-revolutionary", "social-democratic" and "a party of the bourgeoisie" and describing the Chinese Communist Party as "the vanguard of the world revolution". Kazimierz Mijal, who had been dropped from the Polish government as a Stalinist in 1957 and defected to Albania in 1966, was appointed its general secretary, and made regular broadcasts on Radio Tirana's Polish service. He re-entered Poland with forged papers in 1984, and was arrested on a charge of distributing illegal documents. It is uncertain whether the CPP still exists.

Experience and the Future (DiP)

History. This study group was formed in 1978 by a number of intellectuals, including senior members of the ruling Polish United Workers' Party (PUWP), and compiled three reports on the basis of questionnaires sent to leading academic, cultural and industrial figures. These attributed Poland's problems to the fact that the government had lost the trust of the public, as shown by the widespread mistrust of the reliability of the mass media. The group advocated greater powers and independence for the *Sejm* (Parliament), a new electoral system that would allow a choice between various PUWP candidates, the publication of complete and truthful information on the state of the country and a major programme of reforms, starting with the economy. In October 1981 DiP held a press conference, at which it advocated a coalition of the PUWP, Solidarity and the Catholic Church.

Romania

Capital: Bucharest   Pop. 22,683,000

Romania took part in World War I on the allied side, and under the peace settlement received Transylvania from Hungary and Bessarabia (Eastern Moldavia) from Russia. Following the rise of a powerful fascist movement, the Iron Guard, King Carol abolished the political parties in 1938 and established his own dictatorship. In 1940 Romania was forced to cede Bessarabia to the Soviet Union and Transylvania to Hungary, whereupon an Iron Guard coup compelled Carol to abdicate in favour of his son and set up a government headed by Gen. Ion Antonescu, which declared war on the Soviet Union in the following year. In August 1944, however, as Soviet troops were entering Romania, King Michael dismissed Antonescu, formed a coalition government including representatives of the National Peasant, National Liberal, Social Democratic and Communist parties, and declared war on Germany. By the peace treaty signed in 1947

Romania recovered Northern Transylvania but not Bessarabia, the population of which is predominantly Romanian.

Under Soviet pressure, King Michael accepted in 1945 a more left-wing government headed by Petru Groza, leader of the radical Ploughmen's Front, and during the next three years the Communist Party gradually assumed complete control. In 1947 the National Peasant and National Liberal parties were dissolved, the king was forced to abdicate and Romania was declared a People's Republic. Under a new constitution adopted in 1965 the official name of the country became the Socialist Republic of Romania.

Romanian Communist Party
Partidul Comunist Român (PCR)

History. The PCR was founded in 1921, when the left wing of the Social Democratic Party broke away and affiliated to the Comintern. Banned in 1924, it continued to operate illegally. The leadership was divided between the "Muscovites", such as Ana Pauker and Vasile Luca, who took refuge in the Soviet Union, where some of them were liquidated in Stalin's purges, and the "Romanians" working underground inside the country, such as Gheorghe Gheorghiu-Dej, who was sentenced to 12 years' imprisonment in 1933 for leading a railwaymen's strike, and Lucretiu Patrascanu. In 1944 the party was legalized and joined the government; Gheorghiu-Dej was elected general secretary, and membership rose within a few weeks from about 1,000 to several hundred thousand. The People's Democratic Front was formed by the Communist and Social Democratic parties and other left-wing organizations, and in elections in 1946 obtained 347 of the 414 seats in the Assembly, the Communists winning 73. The Social Democratic Party merged with the Communist Party in 1948 to form the Romanian Workers' Party, which became the only legal party.

A struggle for power followed inside the party, 192,000 members being expelled in a massive purge in 1948–50. Gheorghiu-Dej became Prime Minister in 1952, and at the same time Pauker, Luca and other leading "Muscovites" were removed from the leadership. Patrascanu, who favoured greater independence from Moscow, was executed in 1954 and Luca sentenced to life imprisonment. The post of general secretary was abolished in 1954, Gheorghe Apostol being elected first secretary. In the following year, however, Gheorghiu-Dej took over the post, and was succeeded as Prime Minister by Chivu Stoica. Members of the Political Bureau regarded as hostile to Gheorghiu-Dej were removed in 1957, and another purge of the membership followed. In 1961 Gheorghiu-Dej was elected President in succession to Ion Gheorghe Maurer, who became Prime Minister; the latter was succeeded in turn by Manea Mănescu (1974), Ilie Verdeţ (1979) and Constantin Dăscalescu (1982).

From the later 1950s onward the party increasingly asserted its independence of the Soviet Union. The withdrawal of Soviet troops from Romania was negotiated in 1958. In 1963–64 Romania strongly opposed proposals by the Council for Mutual Economic Assistance (Comecon) for "international socialist division of labour", which it feared would retard the development of its industry. It took up a neutral attitude in the Sino-Soviet controversy, and attempted unsuccessfully in 1964 to act as a mediator between the two sides. The Central Committee adopted a statement in April 1964 affirming Romania's independence and its right to decide its own political and economic policies.

When Gheorghiu-Dej died in 1965 Nicolae Ceauşescu succeeded him as first secretary and Stoica became President. Ceauşescu, who was elected President in 1967, continued Gheorghiu-Dej's independent policy, as was shown during 1966–

169

68 when Romania (i) opposed Soviet proposals for the strengthening of the Warsaw Treaty Organization, (ii) did not break off diplomatic relations with Israel after the Arab-Israel war of 1967, unlike the other Eastern European countries, (iii) refused to attend the Karlovy Vary conference of European communist parties and (iv) withdrew from the Budapest meeting of communist parties. During the Czechoslovak crisis of 1968 Romania supported Dubček's liberalization policy, and condemned both the Soviet invasion of Czechoslovakia and Brezhnev's assertion of the right of socialist countries to intervene in the affairs of another socialist country. A Soviet invasion of Romania was seriously feared at this time, and another period of tension occurred in 1971. Relations with the Soviet Union have since improved, however, although Romania has continued to maintain its independent attitude in its relations with Comecon and the Warsaw Treaty Organization.

In 1965 the party resumed its former name of the Romanian Communist Party and adopted new statutes, under which the Political Bureau was replaced by a Permanent Presidium (renamed the Permanent Bureau in 1974) and a larger Executive Political Committee and the title of general secretary was revived. The People's Democratic Front was replaced in 1968 by a new Socialist Unity Front. Patrascanu, Luca and other victims of repression were rehabilitated in the same year, and in 1969 the party congress condemned Gheorghiu-Dej's dictatorial methods. Only a limited degree of liberalization has been carried out, however, and in 1976 Ceauşescu reaffirmed the PCR's continued support for the theory of the dictatorship of the proletariat, on the ground that without it reactionary forces would sabotage the building of a new society.

Leadership. The Permanent Bureau consists of Nicolae Ceauşescu (g.s.), Emil Bobu, Mrs Elena Ceauşescu, Constantin Dăscălescu, Manea Mănescu, Gheorghe Oprea, Gheorghe Rădulescu and Ilie Verdeţ. There are 14 other full members of the Executive Political Committee and 28 alternate members.

The leadership is largely dominated by Ceauşescu's family, about 50 of whom hold senior party or government posts. His wife is a member of the Permanent Bureau and First Deputy Premier; his son Nicu Ceauşescu is an alternate member of the Executive Political Committee, first secretary of the Union of Communist Youth and Minister for Youth Problems; his brother-in-law, Manea Mănescu, is a member of the Permanent Bureau; his sister-in-law is a full member of the Executive Political Committee and a Deputy Premier; another brother-in-law is a Deputy Premier and yet another Minister of Mining; and his brother and daughter-in-law are full members of the Central Committee.

Structure. The PCR has over 70,000 workplace and residential branches, which are subordinate to the communal, district, municipal, city and regional organizations. The congress, meeting every five years, elects the general secretary and the Central Committee, which elects the Executive Political Committee and the Secretariat, and the Executive Political Committee elects its Permanent Bureau. The Central Committee consists of 265 full and 181 alternate members, and the Secretariat of 11 members.

Membership. 3,440,000 (1984 claim), representing 21.6 per cent of the adult population. In proportion to population, the PCR is the largest of the East European parties. In 1984 workers formed 55.76 per cent of the membership, peasants 15.76 per cent and intellectuals and clerical workers 20.63 per cent. The high proportion of women in the membership (31.61 per cent) and in the leading bodies (three full and four alternate members of the Executive Political Committee and 57 full and 73 alternate members of the Central Committee) is attributed to Mrs Ceauşescu's influence. The Union of Communist Youth has 3,200,000 members.

170

Electoral influence. All candidates for the Grand National Assembly are nominated by the Socialist Democracy and Unity Front, comprising the PCR and various mass organizations, although two or more candidates may be nominated for a seat. In the 1985 elections 99.99 per cent of the electorate were officially stated to have voted, of whom 97.73 per cent voted for the Front's candidates.

Industrial influence. The PCR controls the General Confederation of Romanian Trade Unions, with 7,000,000 members. Its chairwoman, Lina Ciobanu, is a full member of the Executive Political Committee of the PCR.

Orientation. Independent.

Programme. In his report to the 1984 PCR congress Ceauşescu envisaged a 34–37 per cent increase in industrial production during 1986–90, to be achieved mainly by modernizing existing capacity and applying advanced technologies. Priority would be given to developing the energy and raw materials base. Agricultural production would be developed through further mechanization, irrigation and land improvement and drainage. External economic policy would aim at the achievement of a positive trade and payments balance and the elimination of Romania's foreign debt. The national income was expected to rise by about 8 per cent annually, about 70 per cent being allocated to consumption and 30 per cent to development. The five-year plan for 1986–90 would aim to raise living standards, with a 10 per cent expansion in the volume of consumer goods sold, stability of service rates and retail prices, and improvements in health care. Planning policy would be based on an increase in the role played by the state; in this respect Romania conforms to the Stalinist model, in contrast to the policy of decentralization of management adopted in Hungary and Bulgaria. In foreign policy the PCR advocates the establishment of a zone free from nuclear weapons and foreign military bases in the Balkans and the simultaneous dissolution of NATO and the Warsaw Treaty Organization, while accepting the necessity of membership of the latter until this is achieved.

Publications. *Scînteia* (The Spark), daily (over 1,400,000); *Era Socialista* (Socialist Age), fortnightly (67,000).

International affiliations. The PCR is represented on the editorial board of *World Marxist Review*. While it has close though not always friendly relations with the Soviet-bloc parties, unlike them it has always maintained relations with the Chinese party. It also has close relations with the Yugoslav League of Communists and the Italian, Spanish and other Eurocommunist parties.

Dissident Marxists

Although no dissident Marxist organizations are known to exist, a number of prominent Communist Party members have protested against government discrimination against the Hungarian and other minority communities. Carol Kiraly, who until 1972 had been an alternate member of the Political Executive Committee, sent an open letter on this subject to the party leadership in 1977, and Prof. Lajos Takacs was reported to have delivered to the Central Committee, of which he was an alternate member, in the same year a memorandum containing detailed proposals for guarantees for minority rights. Kiraly claimed that his letter had received active support from prominent political figures, including Ion Gheorghe Maurer, the former Prime Minister, and Janos Fazekas, a Deputy Premier and member of the Political Executive Committee.

Union of Soviet Socialist Republics

Capital: Moscow   Pop. 274,860,000

Revolutionary opposition to the tsarist autocracy was organized from the 1860s onwards by the Narodniks (from the Russian *narod*, "people"), who advocated the establishment of a democratic republic and a form of socialism based on the village commune, and a section of whom practised terrorism. The Narodnik groups united in 1902 to form the Socialist Revolutionary Party. The first Russian Marxist organization, the Emancipation of Labour Group, was founded in 1883 by Georgi Plekhanov, and was followed by the League of Struggle for the Emancipation of the Working Class, formed by V. I. Lenin in 1895. These and other Marxist organizations merged in 1898 in the Russian Social Democratic Labour Party, which in 1903 split into a Bolshevik left and a Menshevik right. The Russian defeat in the Russo-Japanese war of 1904–05 precipitated the revolution of 1905, which forced Nicholas II to consent to the establishment of a Parliament, the Duma. During the revolution soviets (councils) of workers' deputies appeared for the first time.

Russia's defeat in World War I finally discredited the monarchy. After spontaneous demonstrations and strikes in Petrograd in March 1917 had been supported by the troops, the tsar was forced to abdicate, and a provisional government was formed. It forfeited popular support by attempting to continue the war, however, and its authority was challenged by the soviets of workers', peasants' and soldiers' deputies, which increasingly passed under Bolshevik control. On Nov. 7, 1917, the provisional government was overthrown, and a Bolshevik government, to which representatives of the Left Socialist Revolutionaries were later admitted, took power with the support of the soviets. A Constituent Assembly was elected, in which the Socialist Revolutionaries and Mensheviks had a majority; when it refused to ratify the Declaration of the Rights of the Toiling and Exploited People submitted to it by the government it was dissolved in January 1918.

Peace was concluded with Germany in March 1918, whereupon the Left Socialist Revolutionaries staged an unsuccessful uprising in Moscow and were suppressed. During 1918–20 White armies led by former tsarist officers waged war on the soviet government, with the active support of Britain, France, the USA and Japan, but were defeated by the Red Army, organized by Leon Trotsky. Russia was renamed the Russian Soviet Federated Socialist Republic in 1918, and the Union of Soviet Socialist Republics in 1922. In the latter year the Mensheviks, Socialist Revolutionaries and other left-wing parties, which had continued to operate legally and had sometimes co-operated with the Bolsheviks, were banned, the Communist Party becoming the only legal party.

During the civil war, the government pursued a policy of "war communism", whereby economic administration was highly centralized, private trade was forbidden and grain was forcibly requisitioned from the richer peasants. However, a serious mutiny at the Kronstadt naval base in 1921 was followed by the introduction of the New Economic Policy, which abolished compulsory grain deliveries, restored small industrial enterprises to their former owners and permitted private trade. This policy was abandoned in 1928, when the first five-year plan for the industrialization of the country began. In 1929–30 the peasants were forced to enter collective farms, and the rich peasants (kulaks) were "liquidated", over 1,000,000 being banished to remote areas. These measures, which were fiercely resisted by the peasants, resulted in a widespread famine in 1932–34 in which thousands died. By the end of the 1930s, however, the task of industrialization had largely been completed.

A new and more democratic constitution was introduced in 1936, but was immediately followed by a reign of terror in which at least 4,000,000 people were executed or sent to labour camps. After unsuccessful attempts to form an alliance with Britain and France, the Soviet Union signed a non-aggression pact with Germany in August 1939. In accordance with secret clauses of this treaty, Eastern Poland was annexed a month later, and Estonia, Latvia, Lithuania and Bessarabia in 1940. In June 1941, however, the German army invaded the Soviet Union, and was finally expelled only after a struggle in which about 20,000,000 Soviet citizens lost their lives.

Some liberalization of the regime took place after Stalin's death in 1953, and especially after the 20th Communist Party congress in 1956, although civil liberties remained severely restricted. A new constitution was adopted in 1977, which claimed that "having fulfilled the tasks of the dictatorship of the proletariat, the Soviet state has become a state of the whole people"; it described the Communist Party as "the leading and guiding force of Soviet society and the nucleus of its political system, of all state and public organizations".

Communist Party of the Soviet Union (CPSU)
Kommunisticheskaya Partiya Sovietskogo Soiuza

*History.*The Russian Social Democratic Labour Party, the forerunner of the CPSU, was founded at a secret congress in Minsk in 1898, and two years later began publishing *Iskra* (the Spark), which was printed abroad and smuggled into Russia, with Vladimir Ilyich Lenin as one of its editors. At its second congress, held in Brussels and London in 1903, the party split into supporters and opponents of Lenin's conception of the party as a highly centralized organization of professional revolutionaries, the former becoming known as Bolsheviks ("majority") and the latter as Mensheviks ("minority"). After several attempts to re-establish unity had failed, the Bolsheviks formed themselves into a separate party in 1912, with its own central committee and newspaper, *Pravda*. They strongly opposed Russia's participation in World War I, unlike the Mensheviks (who were divided between "defencists" and "internationalists"), and put forward the slogan "Turn imperialist war into civil war".

After the revolution of March 1917 the Bolshevik leaders, almost all of whom had been living in exile or banished to Siberia, returned to the capital, Petrograd (previously St Petersburg and subsequently Leningrad). In opposition to Joseph Stalin and Lev Kamenev, who had advocated pressure on the provisional government to force it to make peace, Lenin demanded its overthrow and replacement by a soviet republic; he was supported by Leon Trotsky, who had previously occupied an intermediate position between the Bolsheviks and the Mensheviks and had frequently attacked Lenin but who now joined the Bolsheviks. Lenin's policy prevailed and on Nov. 7, 1917, the provisional government was overthrown in an almost bloodless revolution, for the organization of which Trotsky was mainly responsible; it was replaced by a Council of People's Commissars, with Lenin as its chairman and Trotsky and Stalin as Commissars for Foreign Affairs and Nationality Affairs respectively.

The membership of the party, which was renamed the Russian Communist Party (Bolsheviks) in 1918 and the All-Union Communist Party (Bolsheviks) in 1925, rose from under 24,000 at the beginning of 1917 to 240,000 at the end of the year and 730,000 in 1921. Meanwhile, its organization developed rapidly. The Central Committee, which in April 1917 consisted of nine full and five candidate members, was gradually expanded, reaching 63 full and 43 candidate members in 1925. The eighth party congress decided in 1919 that the Central Committee should appoint from among its members a Political Bureau (Politburo) of five members to decide "matters which admit of no delay", an Organizational Bureau (Orgburo) of five and a Secretariat of six. The original Politburo consisted of Lenin, Trotsky, Stalin, Kamenev and N. N. Krestinsky, with Grigori Zinoviev, Nikolai Bukharin and Mikhail Kalinin as candidate members. Stalin was elected in 1922 to the new post of general secretary, which enabled him to place his supporters in key positions. The "unlimited authority" which Stalin had concentrated in his hands deeply disturbed Lenin, who in his "testament", dictated during his final illness in 1922–23, proposed that he should be removed from the post (see Appendix 2: Documents). When this document was placed before the Central Committee after Lenin's death in January 1924, however, it decided to ignore this recommendation, on the proposal of Zinoviev and Kamenev.

In 1921, when a controversy over the role of the trade unions had divided the party into opposing factions, the 10th party congress adopted a resolution drafted by Lenin which banned the formation of factional groups. A purge followed, which reduced the membership to 472,000, although a recruitment campaign in memory of Lenin again increased the number of full and candidate members to 1,148,000 by 1927. Despite the ban, four factional groups with representation on the Politburo existed in 1924; a leftist group led by Trotsky, Stalin's faction, the Leningrad group led by Zinoviev and Kamenev, and a moderate group led by Bukharin, Alexei Rykov (Lenin's successor as Prime Minister) and Mikhail Tomsky. During Lenin's illness Zinoviev and Kamenev allied with Stalin to ensure that Trotsky did not succeed him in the leadership; they broke with Stalin in 1925, however, fearing his growing power, and in the following year formed the "united opposition" with Trotsky, while Stalin allied with Bukharin's group. The 15th congress in December 1927 expelled Trotsky, Zinoviev, Kamenev and 74 of their leading supporters from the party, although many of them, including Zinoviev and Kamenev, were subsequently readmitted. Trotsky was expelled from the country in 1929, and his attempts to continue the struggle against Stalin from exile had no influence on political life in the Soviet Union.

The factional struggle largely turned on economic issues. Trotsky and the left advocated a policy of accelerated industrialization, financed at the expense of the peasantry, whereas Bukharin, who was supported by Stalin, favoured conciliation of the peasantry, who were to be encouraged to form co-operatives voluntarily. After the defeat of the left opposition, however, Stalin turned against the "right deviation", and in 1929 launched his new policy of collectivization of agriculture. In November 1929 Bukharin, Rykov and Tomsky were expelled from the Politburo, leaving Stalin as the unchallenged leader of the party. The former leaders were replaced on the Politburo by Viacheslav Molotov, who succeeded Rykov as Prime Minister in 1930, Marshal Kliment Voroshilov, Lazar Kaganovich, Anastas Mikoyan, Sergei Kirov and other supporters of Stalin.

During the 17th congress in January 1934 suggestions were put forward that Stalin should be replaced by Kirov, who had succeeded Zinoviev as secretary of the Leningrad Party. In December of that year Kirov was assassinated, probably on Stalin's orders. His death was made the pretext in 1936–38 for a reign of terror, in which it has been estimated that 500,000 people were shot and millions more sent to labour camps, most of them without trial. Many of those executed were party members, including five full or candidate members of the Politburo and 98 of the 139 members of the Central Committee elected in 1934. At three public trials many of the former opposition leaders, including Zinoviev, Kamenev, Bukharin and Rykov, were condemned to death after making obviously false "confessions" of treason and terrorism. Trotsky was also sentenced to death *in absentia*, and was murdered by an agent of Stalin in Mexico in 1940. As a result of the terror, the number of full and candidate members of the party fell from about 2,809,000 in 1934 to 2,477,666 in 1939, although over 1,000,000 candidate members had been admitted during 1936–39. The membership was replenished by recruiting campaigns and by the admission of soldiers on specially easy terms during the war of 1941–45; despite the heavy wartime casualties, the total had risen to 6,882,145 by 1952.

After the purges Stalin's domination of the party became complete. He assumed the prime ministership in 1941, while retaining the general secretaryship. No party congresses were held between 1939 and 1952, and the Central Committee rarely met. The personality cult of Stalin, which had been steadily increasing since 1929, reached its height 20 years later with the celebrations of his 70th birthday. Sporadic executions of party leaders meanwhile continued. In 1948 the death occurred in mysterious circumstances of Andrei Zhdanov, who was regarded as Stalin's probable successor; thereafter most of his associates in the Leningrad party were shot, including Nikolai Voznesensky, a member of the Politburo. At the 19th party congress, held in 1952, the party was renamed the Communist Party of the Soviet Union (the name "Bolsheviks" being dropped), the Politburo was replaced by a Presidium and the Orgburo was abolished.

When Stalin died in March 1953 a collective leadership was established, headed by Georgi Malenkov, who succeeded him as both Prime Minister and first secretary (the title of general secretary being abolished), Molotov and Lavrenti Beria, the notorious head of the secret police. However, Malenkov was replaced as first secretary a few days later by Nikita Khrushchev, and in July Beria was expelled from the party and arrested, subsequently being shot for treason after a secret trial. In 1955 Malenkov also resigned the premiership, and was succeeded by Nikolai Bulganin.

At the 20th party congress in 1956 Khrushchev bitterly attacked Stalin's dictatorial methods, his use of terrorism and the personality cult surrounding him (see Appendix 2: Documents). The following year the Stalinist "anti–party group" in the leadership made an unsuccessful attempt to depose Khrushchev, whereupon Molotov, Malenkov and Kaganovich were expelled from the Presidium and the Central Committee; moreover, in 1958 Bulganin was replaced as Prime Minister by Khrushchev, subsequently being dropped from the Presidium. The 22nd congress in 1961, at which Khrushchev intensified his criticism of Stalin and the "anti–party group", adopted a new party programme and party rules, which condemned the personality cult, provided for periodic renewal of leading bodies and affirmed the right of members to criticize the leadership, while maintaining the ban on factional groups.

Khrushchev's erratic international and economic policies aroused strong opposition, and in 1964 his critics in the leadership brought about his replacement as first secretary by Leonid Brezhnev and as Prime Minister by Alexei Kosygin. The 23rd congress in 1966 revived the use of the terms general secretary and Politburo, and abolished the provision for periodic replacement of officials. The new leadership largely reversed Khrushchev's comparatively liberal policies and carried out a limited rehabilitation of Stalin; moreover, after the invasion of Czechoslovakia in 1968 the so-called Brezhnev Doctrine enunciated the right of the Soviet Union to intervene in socialist countries where there was a danger of restoration of capitalism. Brezhnev in 1977 assumed the post of President of the Presidium of the Supreme Soviet (head of state). Kosygin was succeeded as Prime Minister in 1980 by Nikolai Tikhonov.

After Brezhnev died in 1982 Yury Andropov was elected general secretary and subsequently President. Andropov died in 1984, however, and was succeeded in both posts by Konstantin Chernenko. On his death in the following year Chernenko was succeeded as general secretary by Mikhail Gorbachev and as President by Andrei Gromyko. Tikhonov was replaced as Prime Minister by Nikolai Ryzhkov in September 1985. In late 1985 and early 1986 Gorbachev moved to consolidate his authority by appointing his supporters to key party and government posts in place of representatives of the "old guard".

Leadership. The full members of the Politburo in March 1986 were Mikhail Gorbachev (g.s.), Geidar Aliev, Gen. Viktor Chebrikov, Andrei Gromyko, Dinmukhamed Kunaev, Yegor Ligachev, Nikolai Ryzhkov, Vladimir Shcherbitsky, Eduard Shevardnadze, Mikhail Solomentsev, Vitaly Vorotnikov and Lev Zaikov. The candidate members were, Piotr Demichev, Vladimir Dolgikh, Nikolai Slyunkov, Marshal Sergei Sokolov, Yury Solovev, Nikolai Talyzin and Boris Yeltsin.

Structure. The basic unit is the primary party organization or branch, the membership of which varies between a minimum of three and several thousand. The great majority of branches are based on factories, offices, farms and other places of work, although branches may also be formed in blocks of flats or small villages. In 1982 there were 419,670 branches, of which only 75,679 were organized on a territorial basis. In large enterprises or organizations branches are divided into smaller groups, e.g. workshop groups in factories. Branches elect delegates to the provincial or city conference. The conferences at each level elect the town, district, borough, provincial or city committee, which elects a bureau from among its members to conduct day-to-day business between its meetings. In all the 15 union republics, except the largest, the Russian Soviet Federative Socialist Republic (RSFSR), the provincial and city conferences elect delegates to the republican congress; this elects its Central Committee, which elects a Politburo and Secretariat.

The provincial and city conferences in the RSFSR and the republican congresses in the other republics elect delegates to the all-union congress. About 5,000 delegates took part in the 1986 congress, in addition to fraternal delegations from communist parties throughout the world. The proceedings, which normally last about a week, open with the Central Committee's report, delivered by the general secretary, which includes a survey of the international situation, internal political and economic developments and inner-party matters. From 1919 to 1924 congresses were held annually, and four more took place between 1926 and 1934; during the next 22 years, however, only two were held, in 1939 and 1952. Since 1961 congresses have taken place every five years, and in 1971 the party rules were amended to make this the regular practice, in order that congresses might approve the new five-year plan.

The congress elects the Central Committee, a body which has steadily increased in size; that elected in 1986 consisted of 307 full and 170 non-voting candidate members. It has been estimated that 48 per cent of these were full-time party officials, 26.4 per cent national or regional government officials, 7 per cent members of the armed forces and only 5 per cent workers or peasants. Although the full committee normally meets only twice a year, it can play a decisive role when differences arise inside the Politburo, as in 1957, when it supported Khrushchev against the "anti-party group", and in 1964, when it removed him from office.

176

At the end of the congress the new Central Committee elects the Politburo and the Secretariat at its first meeting. The Politburo consists of about 20 full and candidate members, headed by the general secretary, who meet at least once a week to lay down guidelines on policy. The Secretariat meets weekly and consists of some 10 members (including the general secretary), about half of whom are also members of the Politburo. Normally each member of the Secretariat is responsible for one aspect of policy, such as party organization, ideology, foreign relations, industry or agriculture.

Membership. Over 19,000,000 including candidate members (1986 claim). An applicant for membership must submit references from three party members of five years' standing who have known him for at least a year; if he is under 24 one of these must come from the Komsomol (youth organization—see below) district or city committee. If his application is approved by a general meeting of his branch he becomes a candidate member, and is required to take part in party activities and to pay dues proportionate to his earnings, but is not qualified to vote at meetings or to hold any party office. After a year, if his application is again approved by a two-thirds vote at a branch meeting, he is admitted to full membership. At regular intervals a review of the membership takes place; between 1971 and 1976 the membership of nearly 347,000 people who had "allowed themselves to depart from the rules of party life, committed breaches of discipline and lost touch with their party branches" was not renewed.

In 1984 industrial workers formed 44.1 per cent of the membership, peasants 12.4 per cent and white-collar workers, professional personnel and members of the armed forces 43.5 per cent. The proportion of women members has steadily risen, reaching 27.6 per cent in 1984. Over 100 national groups are represented, but the great majority of the members are Russians (60 per cent) or Ukrainians (16 per cent).

The party's youth organization, the All-Union Leninist Communist League of Youth, generally known as the Komsomol, which caters for young people between the ages of 14 and 28, had 42,000,000 members in 1984, and forms the party's main source of recruits.

Electoral influence. All candidates for the Supreme Soviet and lower elected bodies campaign as members of the "bloc of Communists and non-party people", the electors being required to approve or reject the single candidate in each constituency. In the 1984 elections to the Supreme Soviet 99.99 per cent of the electorate were officially stated to have voted, 99.94 per cent of them in favour of the candidates. Of the 1,499 deputies elected 1,071 were party members.

Industrial influence. The CPSU completely controls the All-Union Central Council of Trade Unions, which has about 130,000,000 members, comprising virtually the entire workforce. Attempts to establish unofficial trade unions in 1977 and 1978 were suppressed, their leaders being sent to labour camps on various charges or to psychiatric hospitals or expelled from the country.

Programme. The CPSU (then known as the Russian Social Democratic Labour Party) adopted its first programme in 1903 and its second in 1919, after the revolution. Its third programme, adopted in 1961 (see Appendix 2: Documents), contained a highly optimistic forecast of the country's economic development, which became a source of embarrassment as its predictions remained unfulfilled. It envisaged that by 1970 the Soviet Union would surpass the United States in production per head of population, and that by 1980 industrial output would increase by 500 per cent, agricultural production by 250 per cent and real income per head of population by over 250 per cent, every family would have a comfortable flat or modern house, housing, public transport, heating and other services would be provided free, the working week would be reduced to 34 hours or less, the minimum annual paid holiday would be increased to a month and taxation would be abolished. It also contained references to relations with China, Albania and Yugoslavia which reflected the circumstances then prevailing but quickly became out of date.

The fourth programme was published in 1985 and adopted by the 27th party congress in February-March 1986 (see Appendix 2: Documents). Unlike its predecessor, it is couched in very general terms and avoids detailed forecasts and specific references to foreign communist parties. It states that the correctness of the third programme's main guidelines has been confirmed, but that it is now possible to define the prospects for the development of Soviet society more precisely. It condemns both "the personality cult and deviations from Lenin's norms of party and state leadership" and "errors of a subjectivist and voluntarist nature" (the shortcomings attributed to Stalin and Khrushchev respectively), and also comments that there were "certain unfavourable tendencies", such as failure to carry out necessary changes, in the 1970s and early 1980s (i.e. under Brezhnev).

The programme states that by the year 2000 the country's production potential must be doubled. This will be achieved by the renewal of the production apparatus on the basis of advanced technology, including comprehensive mechanization, automation and the use of computers, thereby increasing labour productivity by 130–150 per cent. Investment will be shifted away from new construction to the technical re-equipment and modernization of existing enterprises. This will require the further development of heavy industry, but growth of the production of consumer goods must also be accelerated. Scientific farming systems and intensive techniques must be introduced everywhere, land use improved and its fertility increased.

The programme promises that full employment will be ensured and manual labour reduced, and that the growth of labour productivity will open up opportunities for shortening the working day and lengthening paid holidays. Minimum wages will be increased and taxes reduced as public wealth increases, and the provision of every family with a flat or house by the year 2000 will be regarded as a matter of particular significance. The quality of the medical service will be radically improved, and pension scales will be raised periodically.

On the political system the programme declares that with the elimination of the exploiting classes the dictatorship of the proletariat has fulfilled its historical mission, and the proletarian state has developed into a state of the whole people. At the present stage the main political task is "improving soviet democracy and implementing increasingly fully the socialist people's self-management". The leading force in this process, the programme adds, is the party, under whose leadership the state, the trade unions, the Komsomol, the co-operatives and other social organizations function.

Turning to foreign policy, the programme affirms that the CPSU upholds the principle of the peaceful coexistence of states with different social systems, which presupposes the renunciation of the use or threat of force as a means of resolving disputes, non-interference in other states' internal affairs, strict respect for the sovereignty and territorial integrity of states, co-operation on the basis of full equality and discharge of commitments arising from the principles of international law and international treaties. The party favours normal, stable relations with the United States, and attaches great significance to co-operation among the states of Europe on a basis of "respect for the territorial and political realities which came about as a result of World War II". It will work for general and complete disarmament under strict international control; the exclusion of weapons of mass destruction from space; the implementation of steps leading to the total elimination of nuclear weapons, including the ending of tests and production, renunciation of first use of them and destruction of all nuclear arsenals; the banning of other weapons of mass destruction, including chemical weapons; reductions in armed forces; and the elimination of military bases on foreign territory. The CPSU proposes the simultaneous dissolution of NATO and the Warsaw Treaty, or as a first step the dismantling of their military organizations and the conclusion of a treaty between them on the mutual non-use of force.

On the world communist movement the programme says that the CPSU accepts that the communists of each country determine their own policies autonomously, and that when differences exist these should not prevent international co-operation between parties. The CPSU, however, will continue to rebuff opportunism and reformism, dogmatism and sectarianism, and "any attempts to emasculate the class meaning of communists' activity or to distort the revolutionary nature of the goals and means of the struggle to achieve them" (an obvious reference to Eurocommunism).

Publications. *Pravda* (Truth), the party daily (over 11,000,000), was founded by Trotsky in 1905 and passed under Bolshevik control in 1912. The other main party organs are *Kommunist*, its theoretical journal, appearing 18 times a year (over 1,000,000), and *Partiinaya Zhizn* (Party Life), a fortnightly dealing with internal party affairs (over 1,160,000). Party newspapers are published in each union republic in local languages and in Russian. It was stated in 1976 that the CPSU published 386 newspapers in 86,000,000 copies and 273 journals in 81,000,000 copies. *Izvestiya* (News), founded in 1917 as the organ of the Petrograd soviet, is the official government daily (9,000,000).

International affiliations. The CPSU is represented on the editorial board of *World Marxist Review*. It maintains relations with over 100 communist parties, although relations with some of the Eurocommunist and independent parties, such as the Yugoslav, Romanian, Italian and Japanese, are often strained. Relations with the Chinese and Albanian parties were broken off in the 1960s.

Dissident Marxists

No dissident Marxist organizations are known to operate inside the Soviet Union, although in 1972 a number of small underground groups were reported to exist, with such names as the Party of True Communists and the Marxist Party of a New Type, which accepted the Soviet system but called for implementation of the guarantees of human rights contained in the constitution. A New Left movement was formed in Leningrad in 1976 by students, who distributed leaflets demanding "socialism with a human face"; a member of this group, Arkadi Tsurkov, was sentenced in 1979 to five years in a labour camp for taking part in the editing of *Perspectives*, a clandestine left-wing opposition journal. Underground journals which criticized the Soviet system from a Marxist viewpoint and reproduced documents of West European communist parties were reported to be in circulation in 1982.

Individual Marxists, together with liberals and Christians, have taken a prominent part in the civil rights movement which developed after 1966. The best-known is the historian Roy Medvedev, the son of a Marxist philosopher executed under Stalin, who was expelled from the Communist Party in 1969. In his *Let History Judge*, published in Britain in 1972, he made a detailed analysis of the origins and consequences of Stalinism, which he regarded as a perversion of Leninism. In his subsequent writings he envisaged the democratization of the Soviet Union as being brought about by "initiatives coming from above and supported from below", like Khrushchev's denunciation of Stalin, and advocated that Soviet dissidents should look for support primarily to left-wing circles in the West. An attempt to nominate him as an independent candidate in the 1979 elections to the Supreme Soviet was rejected by the authorities.

Leonid Plyushch, a mathematician, was detained in a psychiatric hospital in 1973, but was allowed to leave the country in 1976 after the French Communist Party had protested. In an open letter, in which he described himself as an "opposition communist", he appealed to the Western communist parties to "adopt a firm and uncompromising position in support of the democratization of the 'socialist' countries and an amnesty for political prisoners in those countries", and declared that "socialism without democracy is anti-socialism". Prof. Lev Kopelev, a literary historian, was expelled from the Communist Party in 1968 and from the Writers' Union in 1977 for his dissident activities, and while visiting West Germany in 1981 was deprived of his Soviet citizenship.

Marxists have also been prominent in the movement for the defence of the Ukrainian language and culture against forcible Russification. Levko Lukyanenko, a lawyer, was condemned to death in 1961 for trying to set up a Marxist group demanding self-determination for the Ukraine, the sentence being commuted to 15 years in a labour camp; after his release he was again sentenced in 1978 to 10 years in a labour camp, to be followed by five years' internal exile, for his part in the civil rights movement. Vyacheslav Chornovil, then a Komsomol official, was sentenced to three years' imprisonment in 1967 for protesting against the imprisonment of 15 Ukrainians for opposing Russification, and to seven years in a labour camp, followed by five years' internal exile, in 1973 for involvement in producing an underground magazine, *The Ukrainian Herald*, which its editors emphasized was neither anti-Soviet nor anti-Communist. Geli Snegiryov, a writer and film producer, was expelled from the Communist Party and the Writers' Union in 1974, and in 1977 renounced his Soviet citizenship, declaring that the new constitution was "a lie from beginning to end" and that the state had "destroyed the élite of my Ukrainian people". In an open letter he challenged Brezhnev to abolish the KGB (security police), strip Marxism of its "aura of dogma", dissolve the co-operative and state farms, restore the land to the peasants, permit emigration and allow the constituent republics to secede. He died in 1978 while under arrest.

Union Republics

Given below are details of the Communist parties in 14 of the 15 Union Republics which makes up the USSR (the party organization in the Russian Soviet Federative Socialist Republic being an integral part of the CPSU).

Armenia

Capital: Yerevan   Pop. 3,222,000

History. The Union of Armenian Social Democrats, founded in 1902, subsequently split into Bolshevik and Menshevik factions, the former of which in 1920 formed the Communist Party of Armenia. The nationalist Armenian Revolutionary Federation (Dashnaks) in 1918 established an independent Armenian Republic, but two years later, fearing Turkish occupation, it peacefully accepted Soviet rule. Many of the party's leaders were executed in 1937 on charges of Trotskyist or Dashnak activities.

Leadership. Karen S. Demirchyan (1st sec.).

Membership. 170,500.

Publications. Sovetakan Hayastan (Soviet Armenia), daily; *Leninyan Ugiov* (Lenin's Way), monthly.

Azerbaijan

Capital: Baku   Pop. 6,400,000

History. The Social Democratic movement in Baku, which had originated in the 1890s, split after 1905 into Bolshevik and Menshevik sections, with the former (the leaders of which included Stalin) in the majority. A Bolshevik government was established in Baku in 1918, but was forced to resign three months later, 26 of its members subsequently being shot. The Musavat (Moslem nationalist) government which then took power was overthrown by the Red Army in 1920. The Communist Party of Azerbaijan was formed in the same year.

Leadership. Kyamran Bagirov (1st sec.).

Membership. 330,000.

Publications. Kommunist, daily; *Bakinski Rabochi* (Baku Worker), daily; *Azerbaijan Kommunisti,* monthly.

Byelorussia

Capital: Minsk   Pop. 9,806,000

History. The north-western committee of the Russian Social Democratic Labour Party, formed in 1904, became the party's north-western regional organization in 1917 and the Byelorussian Communist Party in the following year. The party suffered heavily during Stalin's terror, when almost all the leadership were executed and the membership fell by more than a half.

Leadership. Nikolai Slyunkov (1st sec.).

Membership. 600,000.

Publications. Zvyazda (The Star), daily; *Sovietskaya Byelorussia,* daily; *Kommunist Belorussi,* monthly.

Estonia

Capital: Tallinn   Pop. 1,507,000

History. The Russian Social Democratic Labour Party in 1904 established an organization in Tallinn, which became the Estonian Communist Party in 1920. A soviet regime was established in November 1917, which was overthrown in

February 1918 when Estonia was occupied by German troops and re-established after their withdrawal in November the same year. It was again overthrown in 1919 with the aid of British naval forces and an independent Estonian Republic established, which was recognized by Russia in the following year. The Communist Party attempted an uprising in 1924, which was immediately crushed. When Estonia was annexed by the Soviet Union in 1940 the Estonian Communist Party became a section of the Soviet party.

Leadership. Karl Vaino (1st sec.).

Membership. 95,000.

Publications. Sovietskaya Estonia, daily (49,000); *Rahva Hääl* (Voice of the People), daily (161,000); *Eesti Kommunist,* monthly (20,000).

Georgia

Capital: Tbilisi   Pop. 5,137,000

History. A Marxist group was formed in Georgia in 1893, which later merged with the Russian Social Democratic Labour Party. When the party split the majority of its members supported the Mensheviks, and in 1918 an independent Georgian Republic was established with a Menshevik government. This was recognized by Russia in 1920, but in the following year Georgia was invaded by the Red Army and annexed. The Georgian Communist Party, which was founded in 1920, suffered heavily from Stalin's terror, 425 of the 644 delegates to its 1937 congress being arrested, exiled or shot. After Eduard Shevardnadze became first secretary in 1972 another sweeping purge took place, in which several thousand people were arrested on corruption charges and many party and government officials dismissed.

Leadership. Dzhumbar Tatiashvili (1st sec.).

Membership. 318,000.

Publications. Kommunisti, daily; *Zarya Vostoka* (Eastern Dawn), daily; *Sakartvelos Kommunisti* (Georgia Communist), monthly.

Kazakhstan

Capital: Alma-Ata   Pop. 15,470,000

History. The Communist Party of Kazakhstan was formed in 1921, after the establishment of the Kazakh Autonomous Soviet Socialist Republic in the previous year. It absorbed a large Moslem nationalist element, which was eliminated in Stalin's terror, every member of its Politburo being shot in 1937.

Leadership. Dinmukhamed Kunaev (1st sec.).

Membership. 700,000.

Publications. Kazakhstanskaya Pravda (Kazakhstan Truth), daily; *Sotsialistik Kazakstan,* daily; *Kazakstan Kommunisti,* monthly.

Kirghizia

Capital: Frunze   Pop. 3,803,000

History. The Communist Party of Kirghizia originally formed part of the Communist Party (Bolsheviks) of Turkestan, founded in 1920, and became a separate organization in 1937 after the establishment of the Kirghiz Soviet Socialist Republic.

Leadership. Absamat Masaliyev (1st sec.).

Membership. 126,000.

Publications. *Sovietskaya Kirgizia*, daily; *Sovetik Kyrghyzstan,* daily; *Kommunist,* monthly.

Latvia

Capital: Riga   Pop. 2,568,000

History. The Latvian Social Democratic Labour Party, formed in 1900, collaborated with the Russian Social Democrats, and in 1914 passed under Bolshevik control. The Latvian Soviet Republic proclaimed in December 1917 was overthrown in February 1918, when German troops occupied Latvia, and after their withdrawal in November an independent republic was set up. The Red Army occupied Riga in January 1919, when a soviet regime was temporarily established, but was driven out in June. The Communist Party of Latvia, formed in March 1919, operated underground until the Soviet occupation of Latvia in June 1940, and after its annexation by the Soviet Union became part of the Soviet Communist Party.

Leadership. Boriss Pugo (1st sec.).

Membership. 160,000.

Publications. *Tsinya* (Struggle), daily; *Sovietskaya Latvia,* daily; *Padomyu Latviyas Komunists,* monthly (24,000).

Lithuania

Capital: Vilnius   Pop. 3,504,000

History. The Social Democratic Labour Party of Lithuania and Byelorussia was formed in 1918 and subsequently renamed the Communist Party of Lithuania and Byelorussia. A soviet regime was established in December 1918, but was overthrown by Polish, German and Estonian nationalist forces in the following summer. The Communist Party was divided into separate Lithuanian and Byelorussian parties in 1920, when Russia recognized Lithuania's independence. The army seized power in 1926, claiming to have forestalled a Communist coup, executed four leading communists and established a dictatorial regime which lasted until 1940, when Soviet troops occupied the country. The Communist

Party then emerged from underground, and after the annexation of Lithuania by the Soviet Union was incorporated into the Soviet party.

Leadership. Piatrus Griskevicius (1st sec.).

Membership. 170,000.

Publications. *Tiesa* (Truth), daily (300,000); *Sovietskaya Litva,* daily (76,000); *Komunistas,* monthly (77,000).

Moldavia

Capital: Kishinev   Pop. 4,053,000

History. A Moldavian autonomous republic was formed within the Ukrainian Soviet Socialist Republic in 1924; it was merged with Bessarabia in 1940, after the latter was annexed from Romania, to form the Moldavian Soviet Socialist Republic. A separate Communist Party of Moldavia was then established as a section of the Soviet party.

Leadership. Semyon Grossu (1st sec.).

Membership. 175,000.

Publications. *Moldova Sochialiste,* daily (270,000); *Sovietskaya Moldaviya,* daily (143,000); *Tribuna,* monthly (31,000); *Kommunistul Moldovei,* monthly (20,000).

Tajikistan

Capital: Dushanbe   Pop. 4,236,000

History. The Bolshevik organizations in Tajikistan were merged in 1920 in the Communist Party of Turkestan, and became a separate section of the Soviet party in 1929, when the Tajik Soviet Socialist Republic was established.

Leadership. Kakhar Makhkamov (1st sec.).

Membership. 97,000.

Publications. *Kommunisti Tajikistan,* daily; *Tochikistoni Sovieti,* daily; *Kommunisti Tochikiston,* monthly.

Turkmenistan

Capital: Ashkhabad   Pop. 3,045,000

History. Social Democratic groups existed in Turkmenistan from 1902, and were incorporated in the Russian Social Democratic Labour Party in 1905. A soviet regime was established in 1917, overthrown by opposition groups backed by British troops in July 1919, and re-established in 1920. A separate Communist Party of Turkmenistan within the Soviet party was formed when Turkmenistan became a Union Republic in 1924.

Leadership. Saparmurad Niyazov (1st sec.).

Membership. 103,000.

Publications. *Turkmenskaya Iskra* (Turkmenistan Spark), daily; *Soviet Turkmenistani,* daily; *Turkmenistan Kommunisti,* monthly.

Ukraine

Capital: Kiev   Pop. 50,456,000

History. Although there were many Ukrainians in the Bolshevik Party before the revolution, no separate Bolshevik organization existed until 1918, when the Communist Party (Bolsheviks) of the Ukraine was founded. A complex civil war was fought in the Ukraine in 1918–21 between Bolsheviks, Whites, Ukrainian nationalists and anarchists before the Bolsheviks established their control. As a result of the government's fear of Ukrainian nationalism, control of the Ukrainian party was kept firmly in Russian hands, and during Stalin's terror a sweeping purge of alleged nationalists took place, with the result that the party's membership fell from 453,500 in 1934 to 285,800 in 1938. Aleksei Kirichenko, appointed in 1953, was the first Ukrainian to hold the post of first secretary.

Leadership. Vladimir Shcherbitsky (1st sec.).

Membership. 2,900,000.

Publications. *Radyanska Ukraina* (Soviet Ukraine), daily; *Pravda Ukrainy,* daily (555,000); *Rabochaya Gazeta,* daily (481,000); *Kommunist Ukraini,* monthly (96,000).

Uzbekistan

Capital: Tashkent   Pop. 17,044,000

History. The Russian Social Democratic Labour Party formed an organization in Tashkent in 1903, which in 1918 was incorporated in the Communist Party (Bolsheviks) of Turkestan. The Communist Party of Uzbekistan was formed in 1925, after Uzbekistan became a Union Republic, and suffered a drastic purge in 1935–37, both the first secretary and the Prime Minister being among those executed.

Leadership. Inamszhan Usmankhodzhayev (1st sec.).

Membership. 490,000.

Publications. *Soviet Uzbekistani,* daily; *Pravda Vostoka* (Eastern Truth); *Partiya Turmushi* (Party Life), monthly.

Yugoslavia

Capital: Belgrade   Pop. 22,997,000

Yugoslavia was formed in 1918 by the merger of the former Austro-Hungarian territories of Slovenia, Croatia and Bosnia-Hercegovina with the kingdoms of

Serbia and Montenegro under the Serbian monarch. King Alexander's centralizing policy and the dominant position given to the Serbs aroused strong opposition in Croatia, and in 1934 he was assassinated by Croat terrorists. German troops overran Yugoslavia in April 1941; much of its territory was partitioned between Germany, Italy, Hungary, Bulgaria and Albania, a nominally independent state of Croatia was established and Serbia came under German administration. Two guerrilla movements developed, the royalist Chetniks in Serbia, led by Col. Draža Mihailović, and the Communist Partisans led by Tito. After attempts at co-operation between them had broken down, the Chetniks often collaborated with the Axis forces against the Partisans, and in 1943 Allied support was transferred from Mihailović to Tito. A provisional government, the Council of Liberation, was established in 1943 with Tito as Prime Minister; it took power in 1945 after the Germans had been expelled from Belgrade.

The monarchy was abolished in November 1945, and two months later a constitution modelled on that of the Soviet Union was adopted, under which Yugoslavia became a People's Republic consisting of the six federal republics of Serbia, Croatia, Slovenia, Montenegro, Bosnia-Hercegovina and Macedonia and the two autonomous provinces of Kosovo and Vojvodina. During the next three years agrarian reforms were carried out, the collectivization of agriculture begun, industry, transport and banking nationalized and a five-year plan introduced.

The break with the Soviet Union in 1948 was followed by major changes in the political and economic system, management of industry by elected workers' councils being introduced in 1950, economic planning decentralized and the collectivization of agriculture abandoned. Relations with the Western powers were improved in 1950–51 and US economic and military aid accepted. A more democratic constitution came into force in 1953, Marshal Tito being elected to the new office of President, which combined the functions of head of state and Prime Minister. After Stalin's death relations with the Soviet Union were normalized in 1955, although further periods of strain followed in 1957–62 and 1968–71. Since 1953 Yugoslavia had cultivated relations with Egypt, India and other African and Asian countries, and in 1961 it became a founder-member of the non-aligned movement.

A third constitution, adopted in 1963, described Yugoslavia as a Socialist Federal Republic; reintroduced the office of Prime Minister; and remodelled the Federal Assembly, which would consist of a Federal Chamber elected on a territorial basis and four chambers each dealing with a specialized subject. Constitutional amendments adopted in 1971 limited the powers of the federal government to defence, foreign affairs, foreign trade and the unity of the economic and social system, and established a Presidency of 22 members on which each republic was represented by three members and each autonomous province by two. A fourth constitution, promulgated in 1974, incorporated these amendments, but reduced the size of the Presidency to nine members, consisting of one representative of each republic and autonomous province and the president of the League of Communists. The five-chamber system introduced in 1963 was replaced by two indirectly elected chambers, the Federal Chamber, composed of delegates of self-managing organizations and communities and of socio-political organizations, and the Chamber of Republics and Provinces, consisting of delegates of the Republican and Provincial Assemblies. Since Tito's death in 1980 the post of President has rotated annually among the members of the Presidency.

League of Communists of Yugoslavia (LCY)
Savez Komunista Jugoslavije

History. The Socialist Workers' Party of Yugoslavia (Communist), formed by left-wing Social Democrats in 1919, joined the Third International, and was renamed the Communist Party of Yugoslavia (CPY) in the following year. It rapidly grew to over 60,000 members, and in the 1920 elections to the Constituent Assembly obtained 12.4 per cent of the vote and 59 of the 419 seats. After the Minister of the Interior was assassinated by Communists in 1921, however, the party was banned and went underground. At first it favoured Yugoslav unity, but in 1924, on the Comintern's orders, it demanded independence for Croatia, Slovenia and Macedonia. An abortive attempt at insurrection in 1929 was followed by severe repression, and by 1932 its membership had fallen to 200. Many of its leaders escaped to the Soviet Union, where most of them were executed in Stalin's terror. It abandoned its secessionist policy in 1935, and under the leadership of Josip Broz (Tito), who was appointed general secretary by the Comintern in 1937, slowly built up its membership, which reached 12,000 in 1940. Over 500 Yugoslavs served in the International Brigades in the Spanish Civil War, some of whom later distinguished themselves as Partisan leaders.

The CPY's leadership of the Partisan movement won it mass support; although 9,000 of its 12,000 members in 1941 were killed in the war, by 1945 its membership had risen to 141,000. During 1945–47, as the ruling party, it pursued an orthodox Stalinist policy and co-operated closely with the Soviet Communist Party, but from the beginning of 1948 relations between the two parties rapidly deteriorated. In June the CPY was expelled from the Cominform, on the grounds that it had "taken an entirely wrong line on the principal questions of foreign and internal policy", "pursued a hateful policy in relation to the Soviet Union", failed to carry on the class struggle in rural areas, subordinated the party to the People's Front, established a "bureaucratic regime" inside the party, rejected criticism by the Cominform and "taken the path of nationalism". While categorically rejecting those accusations, the CPY at first attempted to re-establish friendly relations with the Soviet Union, but the Cominform countries' economic blockade of Yugoslavia, threats of Soviet intervention and the trials of László Rajk in Hungary and Trajko Kostov in Bulgaria, at which the Yugoslav leaders were accused of being Western agents, made this impossible. The break with Moscow was followed by a rapid increase in membership, from 483,000 members in 1948 to 773,000 in 1952.

The 1952 party congress, at which Tito vigorously denounced Stalinism as a "revisionist deviation", abandoned the names of Communist Party and Political Bureau in favour of League of Communists (as used by Marx) and Executive Committee. Differences continued, however, over how complete the break with Stalinism should be, and in 1954 Milovan Djilas, a member of the Executive Committee who had advocated the "withering away" of the LCY, was expelled from the Central Committee and subsequently resigned from the party.

The 1958 party congress adopted a new programme, which condemned the bureaucratic state and the "merging of the state and party apparatus", and suggested that the state should become an apparatus of experts subordinated to elected bodies. It also condemned the view that "communist parties have a monopoly over every aspect of the movement of society towards socialism and that socialism can only find its representatives in them and through them", and denied that any one party was entitled to a monopoly in the sphere of ideology. This programme was violently attacked by the Soviet, Chinese and other ruling communist parties, which boycotted the congress. The 1960 Moscow conference of 81 communist parties, to which the LCY was not invited, condemned "the Yugoslav variety of international opportunism", and declared that "active struggle to safeguard the communist and working-class movement from the anti-Leninist ideas of the Yugoslav revisionists remains an essential task of the Marxist-Leninist parties". Friendly relations with the Soviet party were re-established in 1962, although the Chinese and Albanian parties remained violently hostile to

Yugoslavia. After the LCY had declared its unconditional support for the Czechoslovak reforms of 1968 and strongly condemned the Soviet-led invasion, relations with the Soviet party passed through another period of tension, which continued until 1971, whilst relations with the Chinese party showed a marked improvement.

Political and economic rivalries between the federal republics led to a series of crises after 1966. Vice-President Aleksander Ranković, the leading spokesman for the centralizing Serb nationalist faction, was expelled in 1966 from the Central Committee and subsequently from the LCY. Nationalist agitation in Croatia was followed in 1971 by major changes in the leadership of the Croation League of Communists, and in 1973 the president and secretary of the Serbian party resigned after being accused by Tito of excessive liberalism. During the period 1969–74 a total of 143,756 members were expelled for ideological reasons or for inactivity, and the membership fell from 1,146,084 to 1,076,711. Following riots among the Albanian population of Kosovo province in 1981, many of the provincial party officials were removed from their posts.

Changes in the party structure introduced in 1966 established a new body, the Presidium; limited the Executive Committee's powers to organizational affairs; introduced the new office of president of the party, to which Tito was elected; and abolished the post of general secretary and the Secretariat. The 1969 party congress replaced the Central Committee by an annual conference and the Executive Committee by an Executive Bureau consisting of the party president, two representatives from each republic and one from each autonomous province. The 1974 congress, however, reintroduced the Central Committee, and the 1978 congress replaced the Presidium and Executive Committee by a smaller Presidium of 24 members. After Tito's death in 1980 the post of president of the LCY was abolished; instead the post of the president of the Presidium would rotate annually among its members.

After its reconciliation with the Soviet and the Chinese parties the LCY continued to maintain its independent position in its relations with other communist parties, a policy which Tito strongly defended at the conference of European parties in 1976. It condemned the Vietnamese invasion of Kampuchea, the Soviet intervention in Afghanistan and the declaration of martial law in Poland, but regarded the Chinese invasion of Vietnam as partly provoked by Vietnam's action in Kampuchea.

Leadership. The highest party body is the Presidium, consisting of three members from each republic, two from each autonomous province and one from the army. The Presidium elects its president from among its members for a one-year term and its secretary for a two-year term. Its membership is as follows: Nikola Stojanović, Franjo Herljević, Hamdija Pozderac (Bosnia-Hercegovina); Jure Bilić, Dušan Dragosavac, Josip Vrhovec (Croatia); Dimče Belovski (sec. 1984–86), Kiro Hadži-Vasilev, Krste Markovski (Macedonia); Vidoje Zarković (pres. 1985–86), Miljan Radović, Dobroslav Ćulafić (Montenegro); Dragoslav Marković, Dobrivoje Vidić, Dušan Čkrebić (Serbia); Mitja Ribičič, Milan Kučan, Andrej Marinc (Slovenia); Ali Šukrija, Ilijaz Kurteši (Kosovo); Petar Matić, Slavko Veselinov (Vojvodina); Gen. Georgije Jovicić (army).

Structure. Basic organizations, which in 1985 numbered over 70,000, are formed in places of work, local communities and army units, and operate within the local commune organization. Each republic and province has its own party organization, headed by its Central or Provincial Committee and Presidium, which are elected at its congress (or conference in the case of a province). The national congress, meeting every four years, elects the 165-member Central Committee, consisting of 20 members from each republican and 15 from each provincial party and 15 from the army, and the Central Committee elects the Presidium.

Membership. 2,500,000 (1984 claim). Nearly 75,000 members left the LCY in 1984, less than 20 per cent of whom were expelled; most of the remainder were believed to have resigned because of discontent over falling living standards, caused by foreign debts, a high inflation rate and mass unemployment. The League of Socialist Youth of Yugoslavia, the LCY's youth organization, had 3,800,000 members in 1981.

Electoral influence. All candidates for the Federal Assembly are nominated by the Socialist Alliance of Working People, which is dominated by the LCY. Members of the Assembly are chosen by a complicated system of indirect elections, so that the voter has a free choice only at the local level.

Industrial influence. The LCY controls the Confederation of Trade Unions of Yugoslavia, which has 5,500,000 members.

Orientation. Independent.

Programme. The programme adopted in 1958 (see above), which remains in force, emphasizes that the basic principle governing the LCY's work "is not that of command but rather of stimulation of activity and initiative among citizens", and that "with the lessening of social antagonisms and the consolidation and development of socialist social relations, the LCY will decreasingly be a factor of power and will increasingly tend to become a factor in the formation and development of socialist consciousness among the working masses which take a direct part in the exercise of power". The LCY continues to adhere to the principles laid down by Tito, of socialist self-management, equality of the nationalities of Yugoslavia, non-alignment in international affairs and opposition to bureaucracy, centralization and disruptive nationalism.

Publications. Komunist, weekly (50,000); Socijalizam, monthly (10,000). Borba (Struggle) is the daily organ of the Socialist Alliance of Working People.

International affiliations. Although the LCY is recognized by the Soviet-bloc parties as a Communist party, its relations with them are often strained, and it is not represented on the editorial council of *World Marxist Review*. It has close relations with the Romanian and Italian parties, and relations with the Chinese party, suspended in 1958, were resumed in 1978.

Dissident Marxist Organizations

Albanian Groups

History. The Kosovo region, about 77 per cent of the population of which is of Albanian origin, forms an autonomous province within the Serbian Republic. Riots centring on the University of Pristina occurred in November 1968 and again in March 1981, during which demands were reported to have been put forward for the upgrading of the province to the status of a full republic within the Yugoslav Federation or for its incorporation into Albania. The following clandestine organizations were reported to have been involved in the disturbances or to have conducted Albanian nationalist propaganda: (i) the **Albanian Marxist-Leninist Communist Party in Yugoslavia**, which official spokesmen accused of having initiated the 1981 riots; (ii) the **Red Front** (said to be closely linked with the Albanian Party of Labour and the Albanian intelligence services), five members of which were sentenced to three to eight years' imprisonment in January 1982; (iii) the **People's Liberation Movement of Kosovo**, three members of which were sentenced to six to eight years' imprisonment in July 1981; (iv) the **Marxist-Leninists of Kosovo**, 18 members of which were sentenced to four to 15 years' imprisonment in July 1982; (v) **Independence**, nine members of which were sentenced to one to four years' imprisonment in July 1982.

Five members of the Albanian community in the Macedonian Republic, which comprises about 20 per cent of its population, were sentenced to seven to 13½ years' imprisonment in May 1981 for forming an organization called the **National Party of Labour** to campaign for the secession of the Albanian region of Macedonia.

Communist Party of Yugoslavia (CPY)

History. A number of leading Communist Party members who supported the Cominform at the time of its break with the Yugoslav party in 1948 (generally known as "Cominformists") fled the country, while others were arrested and sentenced to terms of imprisonment, including Cols. Vlado Dapčević and Mileta Perović. Both were amnestied in 1956 and left Yugoslavia, Perović settling in Kiev and Dapčević in Brussels, but continued to attempt to organize opposition to the Tito government. The CPY was founded by their supporters at a secret congress held in 1974 at Bar in Montenegro, Perović being elected its general secretary. In September of the same year 27 people accused of forming the party were sentenced in Kosovo and five in Montenegro to terms ranging from one to 14 years' imprisonment, and a number of others were sentenced to prison terms during 1975–78. Perović was expelled from the Soviet Union in 1975 and from France in the following year, after attempting to set up the headquarters of the CPY in Paris. Dapčević was condemned to death in 1976, the sentence being immediately commuted to 20 years' imprisonment, and Perović to 20 years in 1978; although they were officially said to have been arrested in Yugoslavia, both claimed to have been kidnapped, Dapčević in Romania and Perović in Switzerland, and brought to Yugoslavia by force. Official spokesmen claimed that the CPY had been involved in the riots in Kosovo in 1981.

Orientation. Although the Cominformist movement was originally pro-Soviet, the CPY apparently adopted a pro-Albanian attitude. Col. Dapčević, who declared himself in 1967 to be an opponent both of Tito and of Brezhnev, then general secretary of the Soviet party, was accused at his trial of receiving financial aid from Albania and advocating the cession to Albania of parts of Kosovo and Macedonia.

Programme. The programme adopted at the 1974 congress advocated (i) formation of a united front of all socialist and democratic groups opposed to Tito; (ii) formation of an all-party provisional government; (iii) disbandment of the secret police and abolition of political prisons; (iv) abolition of the Presidency and removal of Tito from all political functions; (v) nationalization of the principal means of production; (vi) a new electoral law giving all adults the right to vote and election of a constituent assembly; (vii) withdrawal from agreements with Western governments.

Membership. Unknown. The Croatian government claimed in 1975 to have dossiers on some 2,900 Cominformists.

Marxist-Leninist Communist Party of Yugoslavia

History. Nine Cominformists were sentenced in Bosnia in 1976 to terms of three to 12 years' imprisonment for forming this party to overthrow Tito, seize power and bring Yugoslavia under foreign influence. They were also accused of maintaining contact with groups in the Soviet Union, Bulgaria, Czechoslovakia, Hungary and Romania.

Trotskyists

History. Attempts were made in 1971–72 to establish a branch of the Fourth International in Belgrade, three students being given prison sentences of up to two years in 1972 for attempting to form a Trotskyist terrorist group and an architect sentenced to two years in 1973 for having had contacts with representatives of the International. It is not known whether any Trotskyist organization still exists.

Eurocommunists

History. Liberal Marxist views similar to those of the Eurocommunist parties have been advocated by a number of Yugoslav intellectuals, including Milovan Djilas, Mihajlo Mihajlov and the group associated with the journal *Praxis*.

After his resignation from the League of Communists in 1954 (see above) Djilas advocated the formation of a democratic socialist party in an interview with the *New York Times*, and was subsequently given a suspended sentence of 18 months' imprisonment for conducting propaganda hostile to Yugoslavia. In 1956 he was sentenced to three years' imprisonment for attacking the government's attitude to the Hungarian crisis in statements to the foreign press. In his book *The New Class*, which was published abroad in 1957, he contended that in the communist countries the party bureaucracy had developed into a new ruling class (see Appendix 2: Documents), and in consequence he was sentenced to an additional seven years. Released in 1961, he was sentenced to eight years' imprisonment in the following year for revealing state secrets in his book *Conversations with Stalin*. He was finally released in 1966.

Mihajlo Mihajlov, then assistant professor of Slavonic literature in the University of Zadar, was sentenced to nine months' imprisonment in 1965 for publishing an article on Soviet labour camps, the sentence being suspended. After he had announced in the following years his intention of founding a magazine as the nucleus of a democratic socialist party he was sentenced to a year's imprisonment for spreading false information about Yugoslavia, and in 1967 he received a further sentence of four and a half years on a charge of conducting hostile propaganda. Released in 1970, he was sentenced in 1975 to seven years' imprisonment for criticizing the regime in articles published abroad, but was released under an amnesty in 1977.

The sociological and philosophical journal *Praxis*, founded in 1964, made itself the organ of the liberal Marxists, and came under strong criticism from official spokesmen in 1966. Eight members of the staff of the philosophical faculty of the University of Belgrade, all of whom were associated with the journal, were suspended by the Serbian government in January 1975, and *Praxis* ceased publication in the following month, as the printers had refused to produce it any longer. Unrest among intellectuals nevertheless continued; a government spokesman in April 1984 criticized those who "openly support a multi-party system", and a week later Djilas and 27 other people conducting an informal political discussion in a Belgrade flat were arrested. They were released after questioning, but four of the group were later brought to trial.

Dr Vojislav Seselj, a sociologist and a former LCY member, was sentenced to eight years' imprisonment in Sarajevo (Bosnia-Hercegovina) in November 1984 for "counter-revolutionary activities, anarcho-liberalism, nationalism and attempting to overthrow the power of the working class", the sentence being reduced to four years on appeal. The charges referred to an unpublished manuscript found in his flat, in which he called for the "de-Titoization" of the "bureaucratic and Stalinist" political system. Three other members of the group received sentences of one to two years' imprisonment in Belgrade in February 1985 for disseminating hostile propaganda, but were released pending appeal.

3. THE MIDDLE EAST AND THE ARAB WORLD

Algeria

Capital: Algiers (El Djezaïr)   Pop. 21,351,000

A French colony since 1830, Algeria became part of France in 1944. An uprising launched in 1954 by the National Liberation Front, headed by Ahmed Ben Bella, ended in 1962 with the establishment of an independent republic, with Ben Bella as President. He was overthrown in 1965 by a military coup led by Col. Houari Boumedienne, who succeeded him as President. After Boumedienne's death in 1978 Col. Bendjedid Chadli was elected to the post. Public life is dominated by the ruling National Liberation Front (FLN), an avowedly socialist formation which has succeeded in relegating communist/Marxist groups to the fringes of the political arena.

International Communist Party

History. Three army cadets and two civilians were sentenced in 1980 to terms of imprisonment ranging from three to 10 years for forming a cell of this party in the army, with the support of left-wing movements in certain European countries. The leader of the group, Mohammed Benssada, who had escaped to France, was sentenced to 10 years' imprisonment in absentia.

Socialist Vanguard Party
Parti de l'Avant-Garde Socialiste (PAGS)

History. The Communist Party of Algeria, formed in 1920 as a section of the French Communist Party, became an independent party in 1935 and changed its name to the Algerian Communist Party in the following year. Banned in September 1939, it was legalized in 1943 after the Allied landings in Algeria. At this time it advocated autonomy but not complete independence for Algeria, and drew its support mainly from the European section of the population. After the outbreak of the nationalist uprising it was again banned in 1955, and in the following year formed its own military organization, which co-operated with the forces of the FLN in the struggle against the French.

It resumed public activities after the attainment of independence in 1962, but was banned for the third time a few months later. In 1964 it dissolved itself, and its members joined the FLN as individuals. After Col. Boumedienne's coup in the following year, however, fearing that this marked a swing to the right, the Communists and other dissident left-wing elements in the FLN formed the Popular Resistance Organization, which was renamed the Socialist Vanguard Party in 1966. From 1971 it gave qualified support to the socialist policies pursued by President Boumedienne, but since 1981 it has adopted a critical attitude towards President Chadli's more conservative approach.

Leadership. Sadiq Hadjeres (1st sec.).

Membership. 450 (1985 estimate).

Electoral influence. The FLN is the only party permitted to put forward candidates.

Industrial influence. The PAGS has cells in factories, which compete with the official trade union organization, the General Union of Algerian Workers.

Orientation. Pro-Soviet.

Programme. The PAGS programme, adopted in 1981, includes defence of the state sector of the economy, the ending of anti-democratic measures, the strengthening of co-operation with socialist states and an end to attempts to buy weapons from imperialist countries.

Publication. *Sawt al-Sha'b* (Voice of the People), issued at infrequent intervals.

International affiliations. The PAGS is represented on the editorial council of *World Marxist Review*.

Bahrain

Capital: Manama   Pop. 400,000

Formerly a British-protected territory, the Emirate of Bahrain became fully independent in 1971. A National Assembly was established, but was dissolved in 1975. There are no legal political parties.

National Liberation Front of Bahrain (NLFB)

History. This clandestine organization was formed in 1955. A number of its members were arrested and arms seized in 1975, following the discovery of NLFB cells in Kuwait, Lebanon and Syria.

Leadership. Yusuf al-Hassan al-Ajajai (ch.).

Industrial influence. The NLFB controls the Bahrain Workers' Union.

Orientation. Pro-Soviet. The NLFB has defended the Soviet intervention in Afghanistan.

Programme. The NLFB advocates the formation of a united front of "national forces" to ensure freedom from imperialist domination and the establishment of democratic liberties.

International affiliations. The NLFB has close relations with the Soviet Communist Party (which regards it as a revolutionary democratic party on its way to becoming a communist party) and with the Arab communist parties.

Popular Front for the Liberation of Bahrain

History. Little is known of this clandestine organization, a number of members of which were arrested in 1975. It formed an alliance with the National Liberation Front of Bahrain in 1981.

Publication. Fifth of March.

International affiliations. The Front co-operates with other Arab communist and revolutionary organizations.

Djibouti

Capital: Djibouti   Pop. 350,000

Formerly a French overseas territory, known until 1967 as French Somaliland and subsequently as the French Territory of the Afars and Issas, Djibouti became an independent republic in 1977, Hassan Gouled Aptidon being elected president. The ruling party, the Popular Rally for Progress, was declared the only legal party in 1981. About 40 per cent of the population are Issas (Somalis) and about 35 per cent Afars (a people akin to the Ethiopians), the remaining 25 per cent being made up of Arab and Somali immigrants.

Democratic Front for the Liberation of Djibouti
Front Démocratique pour la Libération de Djibouti (FDLD)

History. The Popular Liberation Movement, a Marxist–Leninist Afar organization, boycotted the negotiations with France on the attainment of independence in 1977, and was subsequently banned by President Gouled Aptidon, who accused it of carrying on terrorist activities with Ethiopian support. It merged in 1979 with an Afar faction of the National Union for Independence (the ruling party before 1977) to form the FDLD.

Egypt

Capital: Cairo   Pop. 47,049,000

Following Egypt's defeat in the war of 1948 with Israel, King Farouk was forced to abdicate in 1952 in favour of his infant son by a military coup organized by the "Free Officers" movement. In the following year a republic was established with Gen. Mohammed Neguib as President. He was overthrown in 1954, and was succeeded by Col. Gamel Abdel Nasser, who pursued a policy of socialist reforms at home and Arab unity, support for the Palestinian cause, non-alignment and friendship with the Soviet Union abroad. On his death in 1970 he was succeeded by Vice-President Anwar Sadat, who reversed many of his policies, concluding peace with Israel in 1979 and adopting an increasingly pro-Western foreign policy. He also introduced a multiparty system at home (for the first time since the 1952 revolution), although opposition formations have so far made only limited headway against the ruling National Democratic Party (NDP). President Sadat was assassinated by Moslem fanatics in 1981, and was succeeded by Vice-President Hosni Mubarak, who has largely continued his predecessor's policies.

Egyptian Communist Party (ECP)
Al-Hizb al-Shuyu'i al-Misri

History. The Socialist Party of Egypt was founded in 1921 and renamed the Communist Party of Egypt in 1923, when it joined the Comintern. It drew its membership mainly from Italians, Greeks, Jews and other minorities, but virtually disappeared after 1925, when it was banned and its leaders imprisoned. Communist groups revived after 1941, and in 1958 a number of them formed the Unified (Second) Communist Party of Egypt. The new party was persecuted by the Nasser regime, about 2,000 of its members being held in detention camps, and dissolved itself in 1965, most of its members joining the Arab Socialist Union, then the only legal party. In 1972, however, many of the imprisoned Communists were released, and the party was again clandestinely revived as the Egyptian Communist Party. The ban on the party imposed in 1925 remains in force, the ECP being specifically excluded from the law of 1977 authorizing the formation of political parties. Arrests and trials of Communists have frequently been reported since 1974.

Leadership. Farid Muhajid (g.s.).

Membership. 500 (1985 estimate).

Orientation. Pro-Soviet.

Programme. At its 1980 congress, the first which it had held on Egyptian territory, the ECP adopted a programme focusing on "the liberation of the whole Arab homeland from imperialism and Zionism".

International affiliations. The ECP is represented on the editorial board of *World Marxist Review*, and co-operates closely with the other Arab communist parties.

Egyptian Communist Party—8 January

History. The Prosecutor-General claimed in 1977 that this group had been "smashed", but the arrest of 31 of its members on charges of incitement through printing and circulating opposition leaflets was announced in February 1982.

Egyptian Communist Workers' Party (ECWP)

History. The ECWP, an offshoot of the Egyptian Communist Party, first became prominent in January 1977, when the Prosecutor-General claimed that it had been "smashed" following widespread price riots in that month. Six of its members were sentenced to terms of one to five years' imprisonment in 1978 for belonging to an illegal organization, and the party was officially declared dissolved. Further arrests and trials of ECWP members have periodically been reported since.

Programme. The ECWP opposes the normalization of relations with Israel and advocates a rapprochement with the Soviet Union.

International affiliations. The ECWP was reported in 1977 to have links with the ruling National Liberation Front of South Yemen (now the Yemen Socialist Party) and the Palestinian Rejection Front, headed by the Popular Front for the Liberation of Palestine.

National Progressive Unionist Party (NPUP)

History. The NPUP originated as the National Progressive Unionist Group in March 1976, when President Sadat announced that the Arab Socialist Union, the only legal party, would be permitted to have three different groupings—a liberal right, a governmental centre and a Marxist left. Following elections in the following October, in which it won two of the 340 elective seats in the People's Assembly, it was reconstituted as an independent party. It strongly criticized President Sadat's policies, and especially his conclusion of a peace treaty with Israel in March 1979, and in consequence was subjected to considerable harassment, many of its members being arrested for alleged Communist activities and its newspaper, *Al Ahali*, suspended from 1979 to 1982. It lost both its seats in the 1979 elections, but regained one in a by-election in Alexandria in January 1984. In general elections in the following May it failed to win a seat, as it had not obtained the 8 per cent of the vote necessary to obtain representation; President Mubarak, however, appointed an NPUP representative as one of the 10 nominated members of the Assembly.

Leadership. Khalid Muhyi al-Din (g.s.); Dr Rifaat al-Said (deputy g.s.). Khalid Muhyi al-Din was one of the original 10 members of the "Free Officers" organization, which was responsible for the 1952 revolution.

Electoral influence. The NPUP obtained 4.17 per cent of the vote in the 1984 elections.

Industrial influence. About 70 NPUP members, out of about 200 nominated, were elected to trade union posts in 1979, after a court had overruled a government attempt to have their nominations declared invalid.

Orientation. Independent. Muhyi al-Din stated in 1981 that the NPUP united all left-wing forces, including "Nasserist, Marxist, religious enlightenment, Arab patriotic, socialist and democratic currents".

Programme. The NPUP advocates increased democratization, state ownership of industry, exclusion of foreign investment and greater support for the Palestinian cause.

Publication. Al Ahali (The People), weekly (100,000).

People's Movement

History. Sixteen alleged members of this clandestine organization were arrested in 1983 and tried in the following year on a charge of advocating violent revolution.

Revolutionary Current

History. Little is known of this clandestine Maoist group. Although the Prosecutor-General claimed in 1977 that it had been "smashed", it is believed to still exist.

Iran

Capital: Tehran   Pop. 43,820,000

During World War I, when parts of Iran were occupied by Russian and British troops despite the government having declared its neutrality, nationalist guerrillas harassed the occupying forces, and in 1920 set up a soviet republic in the northern province of Gilan. A military coup in 1921 established the virtual dictatorship of Col. Reza Khan, who suppressed the Gilan Republic and in 1925 deposed the Shah, seizing the crown for himself. Soviet and British troops again occupied Iran in 1941, and forced the Shah, who had displayed pro-German sympathies, to abdicate in favour of his son, Mohammed Reza. In the Soviet zone independent republics were proclaimed in the Azerbaijani and Kurdish areas in 1945, but were suppressed after the Soviet troops withdrew in the following year. The nationalization of the British-controlled oil industry in 1951 and the formation of a government by the radical nationalist Dr Mohammed Mossadeq was followed by a political crisis, which ended only when the government was overthrown by a military coup in 1953.

The Shah's increasingly autocratic rule, his Westernizing policies and the corruption of his entourage aroused strong and widespread opposition, which was brutally suppressed. Guerrilla activities by the Marxist opposition began in 1971, and throughout 1978 mass demonstrations, strikes and riots kept Iran in turmoil. The Shah fled the country in January 1979, and after heavy fighting between the army and the revolutionary forces in the following month Iran was proclaimed an Islamic republic in April. The new regime was at first supported by an alliance of Shi'ite Moslem fundamentalists (led by Ayatollah Ruholla Khomeini), liberals and Marxists, and in 1980 a liberal, Abolhassan Bani-Sadr, was elected President. In June 1981, however, Khomenei's followers gained complete control; Bani-Sadr was deposed and escaped to France, and Marxist and other opponents of the regime were subjected to a reign of terror, in which thousands were executed. A frontier dispute with Iraq led to war in 1980, and inside the country the Kurds rose in revolt in support of their demand for autonomy.

Battle
Peykar

History. This small Maoist organization was virtually wiped out in 1981–82, its members being given the choice between recantation and execution.

Communist Party of Iran (CPI)

History. The CPI was formed in September 1983 by the merger of several Marxist organizations, including the *Komala* (see below), in opposition to the pro-Soviet *Tudeh* Communist party.

Leadership. Abdullah Mohtadeh (l.).

Orientation. Independent.

Communist Union of Iran
Tashkilat-e Ettehadiye-ye Komunistha-ye Iran

History. This small party was formed in 1979 by members of the *Tudeh* Communist Party, who considered that it was discredited by its connection with Moscow. It was virtually wiped out in 1982, over 100 of its members, including the entire leadership, being arrested or killed.

Orientation. Independent.

Party of the Masses
Hezb-e Tudeh-ye Iran

History. The Communist Party of Iran was founded in 1920 at Enzeli, on the Caspian coast, which was occupied by Soviet troops who had entered Iran in pursuit of retreating White forces. After the suppression of the Gilan Republic it operated underground, and was banned in 1931. Refounded in 1941 as the Party of the Masses (usually known as the *Tudeh* party), it soon became the largest party in the country, with over 400,000 members, and in 1946–47 was represented in the government by three ministers. After an attempt on the Shah's life in 1949 it was banned and many of its members imprisoned, but it resumed open political activity during the crisis of 1951–53, at first opposing and then supporting Dr Mossadeq's government. Many of its members were executed or imprisoned after the coup of 1953; its network inside the army was broken up, 26 officers being executed, and communist propaganda was made a capital offence. Most of its leaders escaped to East Germany, where it had its headquarters until 1979.

The party again resumed public activities in May 1978, when it began organizing demonstrations against the Shah. After the 1979 revolution, which it regarded as "a people's revolution of religious tendency", it strongly supported Ayatollah Khomenei, denouncing President Bani-Sadr, the Kurdish revolt and rival Marxist organizations such as the *Mojahedin*. In consequence it was tolerated for a time by the regime, although its newspaper was periodically suspended, but from August 1982 its support for a negotiated peace with Iraq brought it increasingly under attack. About 400 of its members were arrested in November 1982 and 30 more in February 1983, including its general secretary, Nureddin Kianuri. After Kianuri and other *Tudeh* leaders had made televised confessions (believed to have been obtained by torture) to having spied for the Soviet Union, the party was banned in May 1983 and over 1,000 of its members and sympathizers arrested. Ten senior members of the party's military wing, including a former commander of the navy, were executed for treason and espionage in February 1984, but the trial of Kianuri and its other civilian leaders, which was due to open in November, was postponed indefinitely. A meeting of exiled members of the Central Committee held in East Germany in January 1984 elected Ali Khavari as the provisional party leader pending convocation of a congress.

Leadership. Ali Khavari (provisional l. in exile).

Structure. The party is believed to operate clandestinely through small autonomous cells.

Membership. The *Tudeh* was estimated in early 1983 to have about 2,000 active members and over 10,000 sympathizers, but by the end of the year virtually all its activists were in prison or in exile.

Electoral influence. The *Tudeh* received 60,000 votes (3 per cent) in the 1980 elections.

Orientation. Pro-Soviet.

Programme. A resolution adopted by the 1984 Central Committee meeting held that the clergy had prevented the transformation of the political revolution of 1979 into a social revolution, and had "established a medieval theocratic despotism to revive the system of dependent capitalism". It stated that the party's main task was the revival of its organization inside Iran, and called for the unity of all revolutionary, democratic and anti-imperialist forces, particularly the *Mojahedin*.

Publications. *Mardom* (The People); *Rah-e Tudeh* (Way of the Masses). Both are published in Europe.

199

International affiliation. The *Tudeh* is represented on the editorial council of *World Marxist Review*.

Revolutionary Workers' Party
Hezb-e Kargaran-e Enqelabi (HKE)

History. The HKE was founded in Tehran in 1978, and draws its support mainly from intellectuals and students.

Leadership. Babak Zahraie (l.).

Orientation. Trotskyist.

Programme. The HKE calls for a workers' and peasants' government, equality for women, self-determination for ethnic minorities and the separation of church and state.

Publication. *Kargar* (The Worker), weekly.

International affiliations. Fourth International, United Secretariat.

Socialist Workers' Party
Hezb-e Kargaran-e Sosialist (HKS)

History. The HKS, which draws its membership largely from intellectuals, was formed in Tehran in January 1979. Fourteen of its members were tried in the following August for supporting the Arab minority's demand for autonomy.

Orientation. Trotskyist.

Programme. The HKS advocates government by the workers and peasants, equality for women, political and cultural autonomy for ethnic minorities and a secular socialist state.

Publication. *Che Bayad Kard?* (What is to be done?), fortnightly.

International affiliations. Fourth International, United Secretariat.

Workers' Unity Party
Hezb-e Vahdat-e Kargaran (HVK)

Orientation. Trotskyist.

Programme. The HVK has called for the ending of executions of members of opposition groups, autonomy for ethnic minorities, land reform and equality for women.

Publication. *Hemmat* (Aspiration), weekly.

International affiliations. Fourth International, United Secretariat.

Guerrilla Organizations

People's Fighters
Fedayin-e Khalq

History. This organization originated with a Marxist group formed in 1963, which began guerrilla operations against the Shah's regime in 1971 with an attack on a police post at Siahkal, in the Elburz Mountains north of Tehran, and later in the same year united with other groups to form the *Fedayin*. Although several hundred of its members were killed in action, executed or imprisoned, it continued its war against the army and police until February 1979, when it played a crucial role in the fighting which led to the overthrow of the monarchy. It split in 1980, the majority of its members adopting a pro-government position similar to that of the *Tudeh* party, whilst a minority resumed guerrilla operations and gave active support to the Kurdish revolt.

Membership. 5,000 (1981 estimate).

Orientation. Independent.

People's Holy Warriors
Mojahedin-e Khalq

History. The *Mojahedin* conducted a guerrilla war against the Shah's regime from 1974 onwards, and took part in the uprising of February 1979. They supported the establishment of the Islamic Republic, their leader, Mas'ud Rajavi, being elected to the Constituent Council of Experts which drafted the constitution. He was not allowed to stand as a candidate in the presidential election in January 1980, however, and in the course of the year the *Mojahedin* were subjected to increasing harassment by Moslem fundamentalist elements. They supported President Bani-Sadr in his conflict with Ayatollah Khomenei, and after his deposition in June 1981 Rajavi escaped with him to France, where they formed the National Resistance Council for Liberty and Independence. Inside Iran the *Mojahedin* resumed guerrilla operations, and were responsible for the assassination of a number of government leaders in 1981–82. Mussa Khiabani, their military leader, was killed in 1982 with almost all his staff, and thousands of their members were executed or killed in action; the *Mojahedin* claimed in September 1984 that nearly 9,000 of their members and sympathizers had been executed, including 130 army officers. By 1984 they had been forced to abandon the armed struggle, except in Kurdistan, where nearly 3,000 *Mojahedin* co-operated with the Kurdish nationalist rebels.

Leadership. Mas'ud Rajavi, Mohsen Reza'i.

Membership. 100,000 (1981 claim). The *Mojahedin* draw their support mainly from the young, the educated middle class, the workers in the oilfields, the Kurds and other ethnic minorities, and were believed in 1981 to enjoy majority support in the traditionally left-wing provinces bordering the Caspian Sea.

Orientation. Islamic Marxist. The *Mojahedin* maintain that the practice of Islam, although not its fundamental principles, must be updated in order to bring about a just and classless society.

Kurdish Party

Kurdish Communist Party of Iran
Komala

History. This Kurdish nationalist party, founded in 1969, has waged a guerrilla war against the government forces since 1979 in support of its demand for Kurdish autonomy. It formerly co-operated with the Kurdish Democratic Party of Iran (KDPI), although clashes between the two organizations sometimes occurred, and since January 1985 they have been at war. Unlike the KDPI, the *Komala* has refused to join the National Resistance Council formed in 1981 by ex-President Bani-Sadr and the *Mojahedin-e Khalq*, on the ground that its programme does not aim at social revolution. It was one of the organizations which merged in 1983 to form the Communist Party of Iran (see above), of which it constitutes the Kurdish section.

Orientation. Islamic Marxist.

Iraq

Capital: Baghdad   Pop. 15,000,000

The Iraqi monarchy was overthrown in 1958 by a military revolt and a republic established, with Gen. Abdul Karim Qasim as Prime Minister. He was himself overthrown and murdered in 1963, when a Baathist–Nasserist government was formed, but after fierce conflicts between the Nasserists and rival Baathist factions it was removed eight months later by a coup organized by the President, Col. Abdul Salam Aref. On his death in 1966 he was succeeded by his brother, Maj.-Gen. Abdul Rahman Aref, who was removed in 1968 by a Baathist coup. Maj.-Gen. Ahmed Hassan Bakr, who then became President, resigned in 1979 and was succeeded by Saddam Hussein.

The Democratic Party of Kurdistan and other Kurdish nationalist organizations have conducted a guerrilla war since 1961, except for intervals of peace in 1965–69, 1970–74 and 1975–76, in support of their demand for autonomy. Since 1980 a war between Iraq and Iran over divergent frontier claims has been in progress.

Iraqi Communist Party (ICP)
Al-Hizb al-Shuyu'i al-Iraqi

History. Founded in 1934 as the Committee for Struggle against Imperialism, the ICP assumed its present name in the following year. After growing rapidly in the 1940s it was suppressed, its general secretary, Yusuf Salman, and three of its other leaders being hanged in 1949. It emerged from underground after the 1958 revolution, and for a time exercised considerable influence in the trade unions and among students. It was discredited, however, by the excesses of its followers, who in 1959 massacred alleged supporters of a Nasserist revolt at Mosul and "reactionary" Turcomans at Kirkuk, and in consequence split into two factions, only the minority faction being recognized by Gen. Qasim's government. The 1963 coup was followed by wholesale executions of Communists, including eight of the 26 members of the party's Central Committee.

Leading Communists continued to be imprisoned or murdered under the regimes of the Aref brothers and President Bakr, until in 1971 the government agreed to end the persecution of the ICP in return for its support. Two Communist ministers were appointed in the following year, and in 1973 an agreement was concluded whereby the ICP was legalized, for the first time since its formation, and formed the National Progressive Front with the ruling *Baath* Party on the basis of a common programme. In 1978, however, 21 Communists were hanged on a charge of forming secret cells within the armed forces; hundreds of Communists were reported to have been arrested, and many others fled the country or took refuge in the areas controlled by the Kurdish rebels. The ICP withdrew from the National Progressive Front in 1979, whereupon the

Communist ministers were dropped from the government. In 1980 the ICP allied with the Democratic Party of Kurdistan, the Socialist Party of Kurdistan and other organizations to form the National Democratic Front, with the aim of overthrowing the Saddam government.

Leadership. Aziz Muhammad (1st sec.).

Membership. 2,000 (1983 estimate).

Orientation. Pro-Soviet.

Programme. The charter of the National Democratic Front, which the ICP supports, states that its aim is to replace the existing dictatorial regime by a national coalition government which will achieve democracy for Iraq and autonomy for Kurdistan within the framework of Iraqi sovereignty. The Front is described as "part of the Arab liberation movement and the world revolutionary movement", and as aiming at "an alliance of the working class, the peasants, the petit bourgeoisie in the cities and the progressive patriotic factions among the bourgeois middle class".

Publication. *Tariq al Sha'b* (People's Road), published clandestinely.

International affiliations. The ICP is represented on the editorial board of *World Marxist Review*, and maintains close relations with Arab communist parties.

Israel

Capital: Jerusalem*   Pop. 4,060,000†

Palestine, formerly part of the Ottoman Empire, became a British mandate in 1920. Zionist immigration, which had begun before World War I, greatly increased under British rule and led to frequent clashes between the Palestinian population and the immigrants. The United Nations General Assembly decided in 1947 in favour of the partition of Palestine into Arab and Jewish states, but this proposal, although accepted in principle by the Jews, was rejected by the Palestinians. When the British mandate ended in 1948 the Jewish National Council proclaimed the new state of Israel within the boundaries proposed by the United Nations, whereupon the armies of Egypt, Transjordan, Syria, Lebanon and Iraq invaded Israel with the aim of establishing an independent united Palestine. The Israeli forces repelled the invaders, however, and overran much of the territory allocated to the Palestinians by the United Nations. Under armistice agreements signed in 1949 Israel was left in control of three-quarters of Palestine, while the southern coastal strip around Gaza came under Egyptian administration and the central area west of the River Jordan, including the Old City of Jerusalem, was incorporated into Transjordan, which was renamed Jordan.

Israel invaded Egypt in 1956, occupying the Gaza Strip, the Sinai Peninsula and the Suez Canal Zone, but subsequently withdrew. In a surprise attack in 1967 Israel captured the Gaza Strip and the Sinai Peninsula from Egypt, the West Bank and the Old City of Jerusalem from Jordan and the Golan Heights from Syria, Jerusalem being proclaimed the unified capital of Israel. A fourth war in 1973, following an attack on Israel by Egypt and Syria, was less decisive. Under a peace treaty with Egypt signed in 1979 Israel evacuated the Sinai Peninsula, but

---

* not recognized as such by the United Nations
† excluding the population of the "administered territories"

the other territories occupied in 1967 remained under Israeli administration. In order to eliminate Palestinian guerrillas operating from Lebanese territory, Israeli troops occupied southern Lebanon from 1982 to 1985.

As no party has ever obtained a majority in the *Knesset* (Parliament) under the prevailing proportional representation system, which guarantees representation to any party obtaining 1 per cent of the vote, Israel has been ruled by a series of coalition governments, dominated until 1977 by the Israeli Labour Party, and from 1977 to 1984 by the right-wing Consolidation (*Likud*) party. After the 1984 elections, as neither could secure sufficient support to form a government, the two major parties formed a national unity government with the support of six of the minor parties.

Communist Party of Israel

History. The Socialist Workers' Party of Palestine, from which the Communist Party is descended, was founded in 1919, assumed the name of Communist Party of Palestine in 1921 and joined the Third International in 1924. Again renamed the Communist Party of Israel (*Miflaga Kommunistit Isra'elit—Maki*) on the foundation of the state of Israel in 1948, it won between three and six of the 120 seats in the *Knesset* in each of the elections between 1949 and 1961. Throughout its history it was weakened by divisions between its Palestinian and its Jewish members, and in 1965 most of the former seceded to form the New Communist List (*Reshima Kommunistit Hadasha—Rakah*). *Maki* won only one seat in the 1965 and 1969 elections, and ceased to exist as a separate party in 1975, when it merged with Focus (*Moked*), a Zionist socialist organization.

The New Communist List is now officially known as the Communist Party of Israel, although inside the country it is still generally referred to as *Rakah*, the abbreviation of its former name. After winning three seats in 1965 and 1969 and four in 1973, it contested the 1977 elections as part of the Democratic Front for Peace and Equality (*Hadash*), which also included a section of the Black Panthers (an organization of Afro–Asian Jews protesting against alleged discrimination by European Jews) and the leaders of Arab local councils. The Front won five seats in 1977 and four in 1981 and 1984.

Leadership. Meir Vilner (g.s.); Tawfiq Toubi (deputy g.s.).

Structure. The party is organized in workplace and residential cells, local branches and regional committees. The congress, meeting every four years, elects the Central Committee, which consists of 31 full and five candidate members. The Central Committee elects the Political Bureau, which consists of nine full and four alternate members.

Membership. 1,500 (1985 estimate). Although many of the leaders are Jewish, about 80 per cent of the members are Palestinians.

Electoral influence. The Democratic Front for Peace and Equality, of which *Rakah* forms the strongest component, obtained 3.4 per cent of the vote in both the 1981 and the 1984 elections. *Rakah* controls most of the town councils in Palestinian areas.

Orientation. Pro-Soviet.

Programme. *Rakah*'s long-term aim is the establishment of a socialist society in Israel. In the short term it calls for a reshaping of economic and social policy in the interests of the working people and the middle strata; a substantial reduction of the military budget; the continued existence of Israel within its pre-1967 frontiers; withdrawal from the occupied territories; acceptance of the Palestinians' right to self-determination and their own state; the ending of discrimination against Arabs; and the right of Palestinian refugees to return.

Publications. *Zo-Ha-Derekh* (This is the Way), Hebrew weekly; *Al-Ittihad* (Union), Arabic biweekly; *Al-Jadid* (The New), Arabic monthly.

International affiliations. *Rakah* is represented on the editorial council of *World Marxist Review.*

Democratic Front for Peace and Equality
Hazit Democratit le-Shalom ve-Shivayon (Hadash)

See under "Communist Party of Israel".

Israeli New Left
Smol Yisrael Chadish (Siah)

History. Founded in 1968, this organization joined the Peace and Equality Movement on its formation in 1977.

Membership. Siah draws its membership mainly from students.

Orientation. Independent.

Programme. Siah advocates the formation of an independent Palestinian state alongside Israel.

Publication. *Siah* (Dialogue), published at irregular intervals.

Israeli Socialist Organization (ISO)
Irgun Sotziyalisti Isra'eli

History. The ISO was formed in 1962 by a group which had been expelled from the Communist Party of Israel.

Orientation. Independent. The ISO adopts a critical attitude towards both the Soviet and the Chinese Communist parties.

Programme. The ISO advocates "de-Zionification" and the integration of Israel into a unified socialist Middle East.

Publication. *Matzpen* (Compass), monthly.

Palestinian Communist Party

See under main heading "Palestinian Movements".

Peace and Equality Movement
Shalom-Shivyon le-Israel (Shelli)

History. *Shelli* was formed in 1977 as an electoral alliance of left-wing groups, including Focus (*Moked*), which had absorbed the *Maki* section of the Communist Party of Israel (q.v.), the Israeli New Left and a section of the Black Panther movement of oriental Jews. It won two seats in the elections of that year, but failed to obtain representation in 1981. For the 1984 elections it joined forces with other left-wing groups to form the Progressive List for Peace, which won two seats.

Leadership. Ran Cohen (ch.).

Structure. The movement's supreme organ is its congress, which meets every four years. There are an 85-member Council and a 13-member Leadership Committee.

Membership. 1,600.

Electoral influence. The Progressive List for Peace, which included *Shelli*, obtained 1.8 per cent of the vote in the 1984 elections.

Industrial influence. Shelli is represented on the executive committee of the Israeli Federation of Labour (*Histadrut*) and a number of trade unions and labour councils.

Orientation. Independent. While including Marxist elements. *Shelli* advocates a democratic humanist socialism.

Programme. Shelli seeks a peace settlement with the Arab peoples and with the Palestinian people based on mutual recognition of the right of all peoples to self-determination and to a sovereign state, and opposes any discrimination on national, communal, class, religious or sexual grounds.

Publication. Acheret (Another Path).

Progressive List for Peace

See under "Peace and Equality Movement".

Revolutionary Communist Alliance
Brit Kommunistit Mahapkhanit

History. This party originated as the result of a split in the Israeli Socialist Organization (q.v.).

Orientation. Maoist.

Publication. Ma'avak (Struggle).

Revolutionary Communist League
Brit Kommunistit Mahapkhanit

History. This party broke away from the Israeli Socialist Organization (q.v.) in the 1970s.

Orientation. Trotskyist.

International affiliations. Fourth International, United Secretariat.

Workers' League
Brit ha Po'alim

History. The Workers' League originated as a breakaway from the Israeli Socialist Organization.

Orientation. Trotskyist.

Publication. Avant-garde.

International affiliations. Fourth International—International Centre of Reconstruction.

Jordan

Capital: Amman   Pop. 3,500,000

The Emirate of Transjordan was established as a British mandate in 1923, and became an independent kingdom in 1946. After the war of 1948 with Israel the Arab territories on the west bank of the Jordan river were annexed, the name of the kingdom being changed to Jordan, and a constitution adopted in 1952 established a House of Representatives with 30 members each from the East and West Banks. Elections in 1956 gave a majority to the Nasserist, Baathist and other Arab nationalist parties, but in the following year King Hussein dissolved Parliament and banned all political parties. The West Bank territories were occupied by Israel in 1967. After heavy fighting with the royal troops in 1970–71 the Palestinian guerrilla organizations, which had used Jordan as a base for operations against Israel, were expelled from the country. In accordance with a decision of the Arab heads of state, King Hussein ceded responsibility for the West Bank to the Palestine Liberation Organization in 1974, but proposals were put forward in 1984 for the appointment of members from the occupied territories to the House of Representatives.

Communist Party of Jordan (CPJ)
Al-Hizb al-Shuyu'i al-Urdunni

History. Founded in 1943 as the National Liberation League, the CPJ assumed its present name in 1951. A Communist was returned to the House of Representatives as an independent from Nablus in 1954, and in 1956 a Communist was elected "independent Christian" member for Bethlehem. The 1957 ban imposed on the CPJ, along with the other parties, still remains in force, membership being punishable by up to 15 years' imprisonment, but the party's activities through front organizations have at times been tolerated.

Leadership. Faiq Warrad (1st sec.).

Structure. The CPJ is organized in a network of small cells.

Membership. 200 (1983 estimate).

Orientation. Pro-Soviet.

Programme. The CPJ advocates the establishment of an independent Palestinian state and the development of Palestinian–Jordanian relations "on the basis of equality . . . under conditions of freedom, democracy and social progress".

Publications. Al Jamahir (The Masses), clandestine newspaper appearing once or twice a month; *Al Haqiqah* (Truth), monthly.

International affiliations. The CPJ is represented on the editorial council of *World Marxist Review*, and maintains close relations with the other Arab communist parties.

Communist Party of Jordan—Leninist Cadre

History. This left-wing group broke away from the Communist Party in 1970.

Leadership. Fahmi Salfiti, Rushdi Shahin.

Publication. *Al Haqiqah* (not to be confused with the Communist Party's journal of the same name).

Lebanon

Capital: Beirut   Pop. 2,601,000

Formerly a French mandate, Lebanon became an independent republic in 1943. Political leaders of the Maronite Christians and Sunni Moslems, then the two largest religious communities, reached an agreement that the President and the army commander should always be Maronites, the Prime Minister should be a Sunni, the cabinet should include representatives of all the main religions of the country and parliamentary representation should be divided between Christians and Moslems in a ratio of six to five. This distribution reflected the position in 1932, when the last census was held; it is believed, however, that Moslems now outnumber Christians and that Shi'ites form the largest Moslem community.

Relations between the many religious communities (Maronites, Greek Orthodox, Greek Catholics, Armenian Orthodox, Armenian Catholics, Sunnis, Shi'ites, Druses and others) have always been tense, and led to a short civil war in 1958. Tension was increased by the influx of Palestinian refugees after the war with Israel in 1948 and especially by the activities of the Palestinian guerrillas, who made Lebanon their main military base after their expulsion from Jordan in 1970–71. An attack on Palestinians by the (right-wing Maronite) Phalangist Party sparked off a civil war in 1975–76 between alliances of right-wing Christian and left-wing and Moslem parties, in which Syria intervened on the side of the former. Although a United Nations force was introduced into southern Lebanon in 1978 to maintain order, clashes continued not only between Christians and Moslems but also between rival Christian and rival Moslem groups and between both and the Syrian and UN forces, while Israel carried out numerous raids on Palestinian bases. In 1982 Israeli troops invaded Lebanon and occupied most of the southern half of the country, withdrawing in 1985.

Lebanese Communist Party (LCP)
Al-Hizb al-Shuyu'i al-Lubnani

History. The Lebanese People's Party, founded in 1924, was renamed the Syrian–Lebanese Communist Party in the following year, when it affiliated to the Third International, and subsequently the Communist Party of Syria and Lebanon. Separate parties for Lebanon and Syria were formed in 1944, reunited in 1948 and finally separated in 1958. The LCP first received legal recognition in 1972. During the civil war of 1975–76 it joined the alliance of Moslem and left-wing parties, the Lebanese National Movement, and raised a force of about 5,000 volunteers. As a result it lost much of its support among the Greek Orthodox Christians, from whom it had mainly been recruited, while greatly increasing its following among Shi'ite Moslems. Recruitment rivalries between the LCP and the Shi'ite fundamentalist *Amal* movement led to clashes in southern Lebanon in

1981–82 which caused heavy casualties. During the Israeli invasion the LCP conducted guerrilla activities against the occupation forces.

Leadership. George Hawi (g.s.).

Structure. In normal circumstances the LCP is organized in residential and workplace branches, with district and regional organizations, and the congress, meeting every four years, elects the Central Committee, which elects the Political Bureau and the Secretariat. In fact, only four congresses have been held, the last in 1979, and in areas controlled by the Phalangists the party is organized in small underground groups.

Membership. 14,000–16,000 (1981 claim). It is estimated that about 50 per cent of the membership are Shi'ites, 30 per cent Christians and 15–20 per cent Sunnis.

Orientation. Pro-Soviet.

Programme. The LCP's immediate objectives are to safeguard Lebanon's territorial integrity, independence and sovereignty and to strengthen co-operation with the other Arab countries, the socialist countries and the non-aligned and third-world countries. Its final aim is to establish a national democratic regime to open the road to transition to socialism.

Publications. Al-Nida (The Call); daily; Al-Akhbar (The News), weekly; Al-Tariq (The Road), quarterly.

International affiliations. The LCP is represented on the editorial council of *World Marxist Review*, and co-operates closely with the other Arab Communist parties.

Organization of Communist Action in Lebanon (OCAL)

History. The OCAL was founded in 1970 by Muhsin Ibrahim, formerly a leading member of the Arab Nationalists' Movement, and has close links with the Democratic Front for the Liberation of Palestine (see under main heading "Palestinian Movements"). It took an active part in the civil war as a member of the Lebanese National Movement.

Leadership. Muhsin Ibrahim (g.s.).

Membership. 2,000 (1985 estimate). The OCAL is mainly composed of students, but also draws support from Shi'ites in Beirut.

Orientation. Formerly pro-Chinese, now independent.

Publication. Al-Hurriya, weekly.

Morocco

Capital: Rabat   Pop. 23,565,000

The Kingdom of Morocco, which had been divided in 1912 into French and Spanish protectorates, regained its independence in 1956 after a violent struggle. A parliamentary constitution was introduced in 1962. An agreement for the division of the Spanish colony of Western Sahara between Morocco and Mauritania was concluded in 1975, but Mauritania abandoned its claim in 1979, and attempts to impose Moroccan rule met with armed resistance from the Polisario Front, which in 1974 proclaimed the Saharan Arab Democratic Republic.

Forward
Ilal Amam

History. This clandestine organization was formed by Abraham Serfaty and Prof. Abdellatif Laâbi after the banning in 1969 of the Party of Liberation and Socialism (see under "Party of Progress and Socialism"), which they had left because of their Maoist views. At the trial in 1973 of Laâbi and 79 others, 66 of whom received prison sentences, it was alleged that Forward had formed an alliance with two other underground Marxist groups, the March 23 Group and Rally (*Al Moutakalinine*), and had plotted to overthrow the monarchy and set up a people's democratic republic under Serfaty's leadership. In a second mass trial in 1977 Serfaty and 43 others were sentenced to life imprisonment and another 132 to shorter terms. The accused, most of whom were intellectuals or students, denied the charges, while admitting their Marxist beliefs and affirming their support for self-determination for Western Sahara. Three students were given prison sentences in 1980 for attempting to reconstitute Forward.

March 23 Group

See under "Forward".

Party of Progress and Socialism
Parti du Progrès et du Socialisme (PPS)

History. The Moroccan section of the French Communist Party, founded in 1931, to which the PPS is the successor, was banned with the French party in 1939 and refounded as a separate Moroccan Communist Party in 1943, about 80 per cent of its members at this time being Europeans. It returned one member to the French Constituent Assembly in 1945. After it issued a manifesto in 1946 demanding the abrogation of the protectorate treaty and the evacuation of French troops its European support declined, and in 1952 it was banned by the French authorities for its support of the independence movement.

On the attainment of independence in 1956 it resumed its activities, but was banned by the royal government in 1959. It nevertheless enjoyed a measure of toleration, and unsuccessfully put forward three candidates, who stood as independents, in the 1963 elections. Refounded in 1968 as the Party of Liberation and Socialism, it was again banned in the following year after its general secretary, Ali Yata, had attended the Moscow world conference of Communist parties. In 1974 it was renamed the Party of Progress and Socialism, and was granted legal status. It returned 26 candidates in communal and municipal elections held in 1976, and in elections to the Chamber of Representatives in the following year Yata was elected in Casablanca. When a 10-member defence council was appointed in 1979 to advise the King on the situation in Western Sahara, Yata was included as the representative of the PPS. It gained a second seat in the 1984 elections.

Leadership. Ali Yata (g.s.).

Structure. The PPS is organized in the normal Communist way, with workplace and residential cells, sections and regional organizations. The national congress elects the 65-member Central Committee, which elects the 12-member Political Bureau and the four-member Secretariat.

Membership. 2,000 (1985 estimate).

Electoral influence. In the 1984 elections the PPS obtained 102,314 votes (2.3 per cent).

Orientation. Pro–Soviet.

Programme. The PPS advocates nationalization of the main sectors of the economy, consolidation of the public sector, use of private capital to develop the economy, promotion of social security and public health services and of education and vocational training, and the freezing and control of prices. It strongly supports Morocco's claim to Western Sahara.

Publication. *Al-Bayane* (The Bulletin), published daily in Arabic and French editions.

International affiliations. The PPS maintains relations with the East European, West European and Arab communist parties, but is not represented on the editorial council of *World Marxist Review*.

Oman

Capital: Muscat   Pop. 1,500,000

The Sultanate of Oman (known until 1970 as Muscat and Oman) is an independent state with close treaty relations with Britain. There are no legal political parties.

Popular Front for the Liberation of Oman (PFLO)

History. The PFLO was originally a nationalist movement known as the Popular Front for the Liberation of the Occupied Arabian Gulf and directed against British influence in the Arab states on the Persian Gulf. It launched a guerrilla campaign in 1965 in the western province of Dhofar, operating from bases in South Yemen, and in 1968 passed under Marxist control. It merged in 1972 with a similar organization, the National Democratic Front for the Liberation of the Occupied Arabian Gulf, to form the Popular Front for the Liberation of Oman and the Arabian Gulf. In the following year it announced that it intended to "liberate" all the Emirates on the Gulf, and claimed that it controlled about one-sixth of Omani territory, excluding desert areas, the strength of its forces at this period being estimated at about 3,000. In 1974, however, it changed its name to the Popular Front for the Liberation of Oman, as an indication that it intended to confine its activities to Oman in future. By the end of 1975 the Sultan's troops, assisted by small British and larger Iranian forces, had virtually eliminated the rebels, although sporadic incidents continued until 1979. Oman and South Yemen agreed in 1982 not to allow their territories to be used for hostile activities against each other. A PFLO delegation visited Syria in 1984 for talks with leaders of the ruling *Baath* Party.

Palestinian Movements

Over 1,000,000 Palestinians were expelled or fled from the territories controlled by the Israeli forces during the Arab-Israeli war of 1948, most of them being housed in refugee camps in the West Bank (the area of Palestine then controlled by Jordan) and the Gaza Strip (then controlled by Egypt). The Palestinian Liberation Organization (PLO) estimated the total number of Palestinians in 1982 at 4,642,900, of whom 1,825,500 were living in Palestine (530,500 in Israel, 818,300 in the West Bank and 476,700 in the Gaza Strip), 1,160,800 in Jordan, 600,000 in Lebanon, 278,800 in Kuwait, 215,000 in Syria and 127,000 in Saudi Arabia, the remainder being scattered through the other Arab countries and the rest of the world. Slightly different estimates were given by the Israeli government and the US State Department.

The PLO was founded in 1964, with the support of the Arab League, at a conference of Palestinian organizations, including the largest and most important, *Al Fatah*, which gained control of the PLO in 1969, its leader, Yasser Arafat, being elected chairman. Guerrilla operations against Israel were begun at the end of 1964 by *Al Fatah*, operating from the West Bank, Lebanon and Egypt, and after 1966 from Syria. In 1967 Israeli troops overran the West Bank and the Gaza Strip, which thereafter remained under Israeli military administration. The guerrilla organizations subsequently operated mainly from Jordan and Syria, and after their expulsion from Jordan by King Hussein in 1970–71 from Lebanon, while some resorted to hijacking of airliners and attacks on Israeli targets outside the Middle East. In 1974 the PLO was divided by proposals for the establishment of a Palestinian state in the West Bank and the Gaza Strip, which were supported by *Al Fatah* and the Democratic Front for the Liberation of Palestine but opposed by a number of its constituent organizations grouped in the Rejection Front. It was further weakened by the involvement of some guerrilla organizations in the Lebanese civil war of 1975–76 and by repeated Israeli raids on Lebanon, culminating in a full-scale invasion in 1982. The Palestinians' defeat in Lebanon was followed in 1983 by a split in *Al Fatah*, one section of which rebelled against Arafat's leadership, with other guerrilla organizations either supporting the rebels or attempting to act as mediators.

Democratic Front for the Liberation of Palestine (DFLP)

History. The DFLP (known until 1974 as the Popular Democratic Front for the Liberation of Palestine) originated in 1969, when a left-wing section of the Popular Front for the Liberation of Palestine (PFLP) led by Nayef Hawatma, a Jordanian Christian, seceded in protest against its policy of conducting hijackings and other spectacular operations outside Israeli territory. It advocated the establishment of a democratic Palestinian state for both Arabs and Jews, in which Jewish culture would be respected, and succeeded in establishing friendly relations with some Israeli left-wing organizations. In 1973 it proposed as an intermediate step the establishment of a Palestinian state in the West Bank and the Gaza Strip, which although opposed by the Rejection Front was adopted by the PLO as its official policy in the following year. The DFLP's attempts to secure Israeli support for its policies, however, were frustrated by its continuation of guerrilla operations inside Israel, and especially by its raid on the town of Maalot in 1974, in which 20 schoolchildren were killed. It took part in the Lebanese civil war of 1975–76 on the Moslem side, while opposing proposals to impose a military solution to the conflict. In 1983 it announced its decision to merge with the PFLP, but for the time being the two organizations continued to operate separately, while co-operating in attempts to mediate between the hostile factions in *Al Fatah*.

Leadership. Nayef Hawatma (g.s.).

Orientation. Originally pro-Chinese, the DFLP moved after 1970 towards a pro-Soviet position.

Palestinian Communist Party (PCP)
Al-Hizb al-Shuyu'i al-Filastini

History. The PCP was formed in 1982 to include Palestinian Communists living in the West Bank, the Gaza Strip and other countries, but not those who lived in Jordan or held Jordanian citizenship and were therefore eligible for membership of the Communist Party of Jordan. In 1984 it joined the Democratic Alliance, which attempted to heal the split in the PLO caused by the revolt against Arafat's leadership.

Leadership. Bashir al-Barghuti (g.s.).

Membership. 200 (1985 estimate).

Orientation. Pro-Soviet.

Programme. The PCP advocates the withdrawal of Israel from the occupied territories, the establishment of an independent Palestinian state and the return of Palestinian refugees to their homeland.

Publication. *Al-Tali'ah* (The Vanguard).

International affiliations. The PCP is represented on the editorial council of *World Marxist Review*, and maintains close relations with the other Arab Communist parties.

Palestinian National Front (PNF)

History. The PNF was formed in 1973, with the support of the Palestinian Liberation Organization (PLO), to co-ordinate the activities of the resistance organizations in the occupied West Bank, and in its first communiqué described itself as "an integral part of the Palestinian national movement as represented by the PLO". It had considerable success in organizing strikes and demonstrations in 1973–74, to which the Israeli authorities replied with mass arrests and the deportation of PNF leaders to Lebanon, and secured an overwhelming victory in municipal elections held in 1976, in which pro-PLO candidates obtained control of nearly all the local councils. It was subsequently weakened, however, by dissensions between its pro-*Fatah* and pro-Communist wings.

Membership. 100–500 (1983 estimate).

Programme. The PNF advocates the establishment of an independent Palestinian state in the West Bank and the Gaza Strip, to be brought about by mass political struggle and armed resistance.

Popular Front for the Liberation of Palestine (PFLP)
Al-Jabhat al-Shabiyya al-Tahrir al-Filastiniyya

History. The PFLP is an offshoot of the Arab Nationalists' Movement (ANM), a pan-Arab organization founded in Beirut in 1950 by George Habash, a Christian Palestinian, with the aim of creating a united Arab state extending from the Persian Gulf to the Atlantic. Expelled from Lebanon in 1954, the ANM leaders transferred their headquarters to Cairo, and subsequently co-operated closely with

President Nasser's regime. A Palestinian branch of the ANM formed in 1964, the National Front for the Liberation of Palestine, began guerrilla operations against Israel soon after, and in 1967 merged with two other groups to form the PFLP.

The ANM had originally been hostile to socialism, which it regarded as divisive in the national movement, but after 1960 a section of its membership adopted Marxist views and became increasingly critical of Nasserism. In consequence President Nasser in 1968 cut off all aid to the PFLP, which moved its headquarters to Jordan. In the same year it adopted the tactic of hijacking Israeli and Western airliners to force Israel to release Palestinian prisoners, with disastrous consequences, as the hijacking in 1970 of three airliners, which were flown to Jordan and blown up, provoked King Hussein into expelling the Palestinian guerrillas from Jordan. The PFLP decided in 1972 to abandon this tactic as non-Marxist and as hampering them in their task of building a mass organization.

In 1974 the PFLP, together with three smaller guerrilla organizations, formed the Rejection Front, which opposed what it regarded as tendencies towards a compromise settlement of the Palestinian question, but which broke up in 1978 when the PFLP re-established good relations with *Al Fatah* led by Yasser Arafat. During the Lebanese civil war of 1975–76 the PFLP fought on the side of the Lebanese Moslem and left-wing forces. Following the split in *Al Fatah* in 1983, the PFLP and the Democratic Front for the Liberation of Palestine, which announced their decision to merge, attempted to act as mediators between the two sides, and in 1984 formed the Democratic Alliance for this purpose, together with the Palestinian Liberation Front and the Palestinian Communist Party. In 1985, however, the PFLP joined the Palestinian National Salvation Front, an alliance of anti-Arafat organizations.

Leadership. George Habash (g.s.).

Saudi Arabia

Capitals: Riyadh (royal capital)
Jeddah (administrative capital)   Pop. 10,794,000

Saudi Arabia was formed in 1926, after the conquest of the Kingdom of the Hejaz by Abdul-Aziz ibn Sa'ud, Sultan of Nejd, and assumed its present name in 1932. It is an absolute monarchy, with no parliament or legal political parties.

Communist Party of Saudi Arabia (CPSA)

History. The National Reform Front, founded in 1954, was renamed the Saudi National Liberation Front in 1958 and the Communist Party of Saudi Arabia in 1975. It operates from South Yemen, and its activities inside Saudi Arabia are believed to be confined to distributing clandestine leaflets.

Leadership. Ahmad Musa (g.s.).

Membership. Believed to be very small.

Orientation. Pro-Soviet.

Programme. The CPSA has defined its policy as "establishing a broad fatherland front, including all national and opposition forces in Saudi Arabia and abroad, with the purpose of toppling the King's regime and liquidating the influence of US imperialism and the international monopolies that control our national resources".

International affiliations. Although not represented on the editorial council of *World Marxist Review*, the CPSA is recognized as a communist party by the Soviet-bloc parties.

Somali Democratic Republic

Capital: Mogadishu   Pop. 5,500,000

Somalia became an independent republic in 1960, when the former Italian Somaliland was united with the British Somaliland Protectorate, and was renamed the Somali Democratic Republic after a military coup in 1969. A Supreme Revolutionary Council headed by Gen. Mohammed Siyad Barreh held power from 1969 to 1976, when it was replaced by the Somali Revolutionary Socialist Party (SRSP), and was temporarily revived in 1980–82 while a state of emergency was in force. Under a new constitution adopted in 1979 Somalia was declared to be a socialist nation with the SRSP as its sole party and supreme ruling body. A longstanding territorial dispute with Ethiopia over the Ogaden region, which is inhabited by ethnic Somali nomads, led to a short war in 1977–78, when Somali troops invaded the Ogaden in support of local guerrillas but were forced to withdraw.

Democratic Front for the Salvation of Somalia (DFSS)

History. The Somali Salvation Front (SSF), to which the DFSS is the successor, was formed in 1979 by Col. Abdullahi Yusuf Ahmad, who had escaped into Kenya with about 30 other officers after an attempted coup in the previous year, and was supported by the Ethiopian government. Based at Warder, in the Ogaden, it conducted guerrilla operations against the Somali army from 1980 onwards, and was responsible for bomb explosions in Mogadishu in 1981.

The SSF united in October 1981 with two other dissident organizations, the Somali Workers' Party, which operated from South Yemen, and the Democratic Front for the Liberation of Somalia, to form the DFSS. According to reports from Somali dissidents, which were confirmed in part by Western diplomatic sources, after DFSS guerrillas attacked the border town of Bohotleh in January 1982 11 senior officers were executed without trial for alleged collaboration with the guerrillas, whereupon a mutiny occurred which was crushed only after several days' fighting. During the following summer DFSS forces were reported to be holding positions 20 miles inside Somalia, and sporadic clashes continued in the border area at least until 1984.

Leadership. Col. Abdullahi Yusuf Ahmad (ch.).

Membership. The SSF claimed in 1981 to have 10,000 active members, and the DFSS claimed shortly after its formation in the following October that hundreds of Somali soldiers had deserted to its forces. A large number of DFSS guerrillas were reported in 1984 to have surrendered, however.

Orientation. The DFSS is believed to be pro-Soviet.

215

Programme. The DFSS advocates the overthrow of President Siyad Barreh's regime; the establishment of a democratic system under a new constitution; the holding of free elections; the removal of all US bases from Somalia; a non-aligned foreign policy; good-neighbourly relations with other East African countries; and support for the Palestine Liberation Organization and all movements fighting against apartheid.

International affiliations. The DFSS has received support from Ethiopia, South Yemen and Libya.

Somali Revolutionary Socialist Party (SRSP)

History. The Supreme Revolutionary Council established in 1969 with Gen. Siyad Barreh as chairman, to which the SRSP is the successor, adopted strongly socialist policies, including the nationalization of foreign-owned banks and oil companies, transport, shipping and the import and distribution of consumer goods. The SRSP was founded at a congress in June 1976, at which President Siyad Barreh, who was elected its general secretary, declared his support for scientific socialism and his conviction of "the historic inevitability of the eventual victory of the socialist system". The Supreme Revolutionary Council was dissolved, and its members appointed to the new party's Central Committee.

Relations with the Soviet Union, from which Somalia had been receiving military aid since 1963, became increasingly close after the 1969 coup, and a treaty of friendship and co-operation was signed in 1974. As a protest against the support given to Ethiopia by the Soviet Union and Cuba during the Ogaden war, however, the Somali government abrogated the treaty in November 1977, broke off diplomatic relations with Cuba and expelled all Soviet and Cuban advisers. It has since largely relied on China and the United States for aid.

Leadership. The Political Bureau consists of President Mohammed Siyad Barreh (g.s.), First Vice-President Mohammed Ali Samater, Second Vice-President Hussein Kulmiye Afrah, Brig.-Gen. Ahmed Suleman Abdulla and Col. Ahmed Mahmoud Farah.

Structure. The SRSP has a 57-member Central Committee.

Electoral influence. In the 1979 elections to the People's Assembly the SRSP candidates were officially stated to have received 99.91 per cent of the vote.

Orientation. Independent.

Programme. The SRSP claims to pursue a Marxist policy adapted to local conditions. The constitution describes the country's economy as a socialist one based on state, co-operative, private and joint state-private enterprises, and its foreign policy as one of non-alignment, co-operation with all peoples and support for liberation movements all over the world.

International affiliation. The SRSP in 1981 became a founder member of Socialist Inter-African (the international organization of African parties claiming to be democratic socialists), in which it is the only thoroughly Marxist party.

Sudan

Capital: Khartoum   Pop. 21,103,000

Sudan, which had been an Anglo–Egyptian condominium since 1899, became an independent republic in 1956. Gen. Ibrahim Abboud seized power in 1958, but was forced to resign in 1964 by a popular uprising. The civilian government then formed was itself overthrown in 1969 by a military coup led by Col. Jaafar Mohammed al-Nemery, who was elected President in 1971 and re-elected in 1977 and 1983. Although three attempts to overthrow him were defeated between 1971 and 1976, the situation remained unstable until a national reconciliation agreement with his right-wing opponents was signed in 1978. A revolt in the non-Arab and non-Moslem southern provinces, which had broken out in 1963, was ended by an agreement signed in 1972 which established an autonomous Southern Region, but guerrilla activities began again in 1983.

While President Nemery was visiting the United States in March 1985 mass demonstrations and riots occurred in Khartoum and other major cities, and were followed in April by a general strike intended to bring down the government. The armed forces then assumed control, declared President Nemery deposed and set up a military transitional council headed by Gen. Abdel Rahman Swar el Dahab. It was stated that following the adoption of a new constitution elections would be held and a civilian government formed in a year's time.

Sudanese Communist Party (SCP)
Al-Hizb al-Shuyu'i al-Sudani

History. Founded in 1946 by a group of intellectuals at Khartoum University, the SCP in 1951 helped to form the Anti-Imperialist Front, which led the struggle for independence and won a seat in the House of Representatives in 1953 and again in 1958. It was driven underground after Gen. Abboud's coup, many of its leaders being arrested, and in 1964 largely organized the uprising in Khartoum and the general strike which overthrew his dictatorship. The civilian government which replaced him included one Communist and three Communist sympathizers, but they were dropped after a cabinet crisis four months later. In the 1965 elections 11 Communists were returned, including the only woman member of the Assembly. Alarmed by the party's growing influence, the conservative majority in the Assembly dissolved it, expelled the Communist deputies and refused to reinstate them when the High Court declared the ban illegal. In the 1968 elections the party's general secretary, Abdul Khaliq Mahjub, was the only Communist returned.

The SCP supported Col. Nemery's coup in 1969, and was represented in his government by three Communists or sympathizers. Its refusal to disband and merge into a single national party aroused his suspicions, however, and in 1970 the Communist ministers were dropped from the government. The SCP at this time was at the height of its influence, with between 5,000 and 10,000 members, and was regarded as the strongest and best-organized communist party in Africa and the Arab world. It enjoyed strong support inside the trade unions, and especially the railwaymen's union, among professional workers, intellectuals and students, and inside the army, and was the only Arab communist party with a large following among the peasantry. It was divided, however, into three factions: a pro-Soviet faction led by Mahjub, a more radical pro-Chinese faction and a group advocating "local Sudanized Marxism" which would be independent of foreign parties.

In July 1971 Nemery was overthrown by a coup organized by left-wing officers, but succeeded in regaining power three days later. Although it was doubtful whether the SCP was responsible for the coup, over 2,000 Communists were arrested, the party was banned, several of its leaders were hanged, including Mahjub and Shafei Ahmed al-Sheikh, general secretary of the Sudan Workers' Trade Union Federation, and most of the remaining leaders were driven into exile. The government subsequently accused the SCP of organizing a series of disturbances in alliance with the *Baath* Party and the Moslem Brotherhood, including a military plot and student demonstrations in 1973 and an attempted military revolt in 1975. The last Communist detainees were released in 1978, but further trials of Communists on subversion charges were reported in 1979–80.

In 1984 the SCP joined the National Salvation Front, a secret alliance of opposition organizations which also included the Umma and Democratic Unionist parties. This body, renamed the Alliance of National Forces for National Salvation, led the demonstrations and strikes in March–April 1985 which brought about President Nemery's overthrow, and afterwards pressed the army leaders for a speedy return to civilian rule. After the revolution the SCP emerged from underground, and the ban on it automatically lapsed.

Leadership. Muhammad Ibrahim Nugud Mansur (g.s.).

Structure. The SCP has a Central Committee of 12 members, six of whom form the Political Bureau and, with one other member, also constitute the Secretariat.

Membership. 1,500 (1985 estimate).

Industrial influence. The SCP exercises a strong influence in the Sudan Workers' Trade Union Federation.

Orientation. Pro-Soviet.

Programme. The charter of the Alliance of National Forces for National Salvation, which is supported by the SCP, calls for the guarantee of basic human rights, regional self-government for the South, development of Sudan's natural wealth to cope with the economic crisis, a non-aligned foreign policy, decentralization of government and a new constitution, to be ratified by a democratically-elected body at the end of the transitional period.

International affiliations. The SCP is represented on the editorial council of *World Marxist Review*, and co-operates closely with the other Arab communist parties.

Syria

Capital: Damascus   Pop. 10,075,000

A French mandate since 1920, Syria became an independent republic in 1941. To counter increasing Communist influence in the armed forces a union with Egypt was rushed through in 1958, but this was ended by Syria in 1961. The *Baath* Party seized power in 1963, but conflict followed between the left and right wings of the party, and then between opposing factions inside the left, which obtained control in 1966. Lieut.-Gen. Hafez al-Assad expelled the rival faction from power in 1970, and was elected President in the following year and re-elected in 1978 and 1985. The Progressive Front of National Union was formed in 1972 by the *Baath*, Communist and Arab Socialist parties, the Arab Socialist Union and the Socialist Unionist Movement, which became the only legal parties, although the *Baath* Party, which alone was allowed to operate inside the armed forces and among students, remained the dominant political force. A new constitution declaring Syria a "socialist popular democracy" was adopted in 1973, under which a People's Council elected for a four-year term was established.

Party of Communist Action (PCA)

History. The PCA, founded in 1976, has suffered considerable persecution. About 180 of its members were reported in 1984 to have been imprisoned without trial, some of them for eight years.

Orientation. The PCA is independent of the Soviet and Chinese Communist parties and of all the Arab regimes.

Publication. Al-Rai al-Ahmar (The Red Flag).

Syrian Communist Party (SCP)
Al-Hizb al-Shuyu'i al-Suri

History. The SCP was founded in 1925 as the Syrian section of the Syrian-Lebanese Communist Party, and became a separate party in 1944. The Syrian and Lebanese parties were again united in 1948 and finally separated in 1958. Driven underground in 1949, the Syrian party resumed legal activities in 1954. In the elections of the same year Khalid Bakhdash, its general secretary since 1944, was returned for a Damascus constituency, becoming the first Communist elected as such to an Arab Parliament. When all parties were dissolved after the union with Egypt in 1958 he went into exile and the SCP was forced to go underground, many of its members being arrested. Although it supported the break with Egypt in 1961, all its candidates were defeated in the subsequent elections and Bakhdash was refused permission to return. He was finally readmitted after the left-wing Baathist coup of 1966, when a Communist entered the government in a personal capacity.

The ties between the SCP and the left-wing Baathists were strengthened after Gen. Assad took power in 1970, and each subsequent government has included two representatives of the party. It achieved legal status when it joined the Progressive Front of National Union in 1972, and won seven seats in the People's Council in 1973 and six in 1977. In the 1981 elections, however, which it contested independently of the other parties in the Front, it lost all its seats.

The SCP has suffered several splits since 1971, when it divided into a pro-Soviet faction led by Bakhdash, which supported the establishment of a Palestinian state alongside Israel, and a dissident faction which demanded a more independent policy and the forcible overthrow of Israel, which would be incorporated into a Palestinian state. Although the two factions were reconciled in 1973, a section of the dissidents led by Riyad al-Turk were expelled, and in the following year formed a rival Communist Party which according to some sources enjoys more support than the official party. Another breakaway group led by Yusuf Murad, a former Central Committee member, formed the Base Organization in 1980.

Leadership. Khalid Bakhdash (g.s.).

Structure. The SCP is organized in the normal communist way, with a Central Committee, an eight-member Political Bureau and a Secretariat.

Membership. 5,000 (1985 estimate).

Electoral influence. In the 1981 elections the SCP obtained 0.78 per cent of the vote.

Orientation. Pro-Soviet.

Programme. The SCP supports the *Baath* Party's policy of Arab unity and socialism, while claiming to speak for "the interests of the broadest strata of the population". Recent statements by SCP leaders have criticized the government's social and economic policies and called for greater democracy.

Publication. *Nidal al Sha'ò* (People's Struggle), fortnightly.

International affiliations. The SCP is represented on the editorial council of *World Marxist Review*, and maintains close relations with Arab communist parties.

Tunisia

Capital: Tunis   Pop. 7,202,000

A French protectorate since 1881, Tunisia became independent in 1956 after a struggle combining strikes, terrorism and guerrilla warfare. The monarchy was abolished in 1957 and Habib Bourguiba (leader of the Neo-Destour, which had headed the struggle for independence) elected President. After being re-elected three times he was proclaimed President for life in 1974. The Neo-Destour, which was renamed the Destour Socialist Party in 1964, was the only legal party from 1963, when the Communist Party was banned, to 1981, when a multiparty system was introduced.

Tunisian Communist Party
Parti communiste tunisien (PCT)

History. The Tunisian section of the French Communist Party, founded in 1920, became a separate party in 1937. Banned two years later, the PCT resumed legal activities in 1943 and took an active part in the struggle for independence, many of its members being imprisoned in 1952–54. It was ordered to cease its activities in 1963, its press being banned, although it continued to operate underground. It nevertheless gave critical support to the Bourguiba government until 1969, when the Destour Socialist Party abandoned its policy of collectivization of agriculture. In 1981 the PCT was legalized, and unsuccessfully contested 37 of the 136 seats in the National Assembly in the elections of that year.

Leadership. Muhammad Harmel (g.s.).

Structure. The 1981 PCT congress elected a 12-member Central Committee, six members of which constituted the Political Bureau and three the Secretariat.

Membership. 4,000 (1984 claim).

Electoral influence. According to the official returns, the PCT obtained 0.78 per cent of the vote in the 1981 elections. It claimed, however, that the results had been rigged, and that it had received 15–25 per cent in Tunis, a majority in Gafsa and a large vote in Gabes. Independent sources estimated its share of the vote at 5 per cent.

Orientation. Pro-Soviet.

Programme. The PCT operates as a "loyal opposition" to the Destour Socialist Party, supporting progressive reforms and the introduction of a multiparty system while opposing repressive measures against the opposition.

Publication. Al-Tarik al-Jadid (The New Path), weekly.

International affiliations. Although not represented on the editorial council of *World Marxist Review*, the PCT is recognized by the Soviet-bloc parties as a communist party.

Yemen Arab Republic

Capital: Sana'a   Pop. 9,000,000

The deposition of the Imam and the establishment of the republic in 1962 led to civil war, which was ended in 1970 by a compromise agreement between the republicans and royalists. The agreement was opposed by the left-wing republicans, who received support from the People's Democratic Republic of (South) Yemen. Fighting on the border in 1979 was followed by an agreement for the eventual unification of the two states, negotiations on which continue.

National Democratic Front (NDF)

History. The NDF was formed in 1977 by left-wing republican exiles in South Yemen, and began guerrilla operations in the same year. Although its general secretary, Sultan Ahmad Omar, was a Marxist, the leadership also included Baathists, and it was joined in 1978 by Major Abdallah Abdel Aalim, a former member of the Presidential Council, who had escaped to Aden after leading an unsuccessful revolt. It launched a rebellion in February 1979 with South Yemeni support, during which it occupied the towns of Qataba, Al Bayda and Harib and was joined by defecting government troops, but withdrew its forces into South Yemen after a cease-fire in March. An agreement was reached in the spring of 1980 whereby NDF representatives were to be admitted to the government, but was repudiated in the summer by President Ali Abdullah Saleh in return for a promise of financial aid from Saudi Arabia. The NDF thereupon resumed guerrilla operations, which despite two cease-fire agreements in 1981–82 were still in progress in 1984, although it was no longer receiving aid from South Yemen.

Leadership. Sultan Ahmad Omar (g.s.).

Membership. The NDF draws its main support from the Shafi'i (Sunni Moslem) areas in the southern provinces.

Orientation. The NDF is pro-Soviet in its outlook, but is not supported by the Soviet Union, which has supplied large quantities of arms to the government.

Programme. The NDF advocates free elections, an amnesty for political prisoners, land reform, nationalization of industry, greater independence of Saudi Arabia and union with South Yemen.

Popular Unity Party of Yemen (PUPY)

History. The PUPY was formed in 1982, with headquarters in Aden. Dr Abdul Karim Ali al-Iryani, then Prime Minister, described it as "100 per cent Marxist-Leninist" and as the strongest and most active opposition force in the country; alleged that it was not distinct from the Yemen Socialist Party, the ruling party in South Yemen; and stated that it was carrying on guerrilla warfare from bases in that country. These allegations were not confirmed by independent sources, however.

Leadership. Dr Iryani named Yahya al-Shami, Mohammed Kassem al-Thawr and Jarallah Omar as leaders of the PUPY.

People's Democratic Republic of Yemen

Capital: Aden   Pop. 2,147,000

The town of Aden was annexed by Britain in 1839, and a protectorate was established in 1873 over the neighbouring sultanates and sheikhdoms. These were united in 1959 as the South Arabian Federation, which Aden joined in 1963. After a terrorist campaign in Aden and tribal revolts in the sultanates the federation became independent in 1967 as the People's Republic of Yemen, which was renamed the People's Democratic Republic in 1970. The country is a one-party state dominated by the Yemen Socialist Party, within which a struggle for power between hardline and more moderate elements developed into a state of virtual civil war in early 1986.

People's Democratic Union (PDU)

History. The PDU was founded in 1961 by the brothers Abdallah and Ali Abd ar-Razzaq Ba Dhib, with the former as general secretary. Abdallah Ba Dhib in 1969 entered the government, in which the PDU has been represented ever since, and on his death in 1976 was succeeded as general secretary by his brother. In 1975 the PDU joined the United Political Organization of the National Front, which in 1978 became the Yemen Socialist Party (YSP), with Ali Ba Dhib as a member of its Political Bureau and Secretariat. He was dropped from both posts and from the PDU leadership in 1980, being succeeded by his brother Abu Bakr Ba Dhib, but was readmitted to the YSP Political Bureau in 1984.

Leadership. Abu Bakr Abd ar-Razzaq Ba Dhib (g.s.).

Structure. The PDU has a youth organization, *Shabiba* (Youth), and is often referred to by that name.

Membership. Under 500 (1983 estimate).

Orientation. Pro-Soviet.

Yemen Socialist Party (YSP)

History. The National Liberation Front, to which the YSP is the successor, was formed in 1963 as the Aden branch of the Arab Nationalists' Movement, the pan-Arab movement founded by George Habash (see entry "Popular Front for the Liberation of Palestine" in the main section "Palestinian Movements"). It organized the terrorist campaign in Aden in 1963–67, and in the summer of 1967 seized power in all the 16 sultanates and sheikhdoms in the South Arabian Federation. When the federation became independent as the People's Republic of Yemen on Nov. 30 it took power, with Qahtan as-Shaabi (its general secretary) as President, and changed its name to the National Front.

At its congress in 1968 the party split into a nationalist faction led by President Shaabi and a Marxist faction, most of the Marxist leaders being arrested. In 1969, however, President Shaabi was removed from office, subsequently being expelled from the party, and was replaced by Salem Rubayya Ali. Following this change of leadership, which marked the triumph of the Marxist wing of the National Front, the government was broadened to include members of the People's Democratic Union (PDU) and the (Baathist) Popular Vanguard Party (PVP); foreign banks and companies were nationalized; and in 1971 almost all businesses still in private hands were taken over by workers' committees.

In 1975 the National Front, the PDU and the PVP formed the United Political Organization of the National Front, with a view to the eventual creation of a single Marxist–Leninist party, despite opposition from President Ali, who contended that the formation of such a party would accentuate South Yemen's isolation in the region. He was overthrown by a coup in June 1978 and executed on a charge of attempting to establish his own dictatorship; it was widely suggested, however, that the real reason for his execution was his desire to reduce Soviet influence in South Yemen and to establish closer relations with North Yemen, Saudi Arabia, Iran, China and the United States. He was succeeded as President by Ali Nasir Muhammad, the Prime Minister. The three parties comprising the United Political Organization formed the Yemen Socialist Party in the following October as a vanguard party based on Marxist-Leninist principles, although the PDU and the PVP continued to exist as separate parties.

Abd al-Fattah Ismail, then general secretary of the YSP, was elected President in December 1978 in place of Nasir Muhammad, who retained the premiership. Ismail's policy of assisting revolutionary movements in neighbouring states, such as the National Democratic Front in North Yemen and the Popular Front for the Liberation of Oman, isolated South Yemen in the Arab world and led to a short war with North Yemen in 1979. In the following year he was replaced in both his posts by Nasir Muhammad, and was sent into exile in the Soviet Union. Nasir Muhammad ended support for foreign revolutionary movements, established normal relations with North Yemen, Oman and Saudi Arabia, and pursued a pragmatic economic policy, encouraging private trade and investment and easing import restrictions. His policies, however, met with opposition from a hardline faction in the YSP leadership, and in February 1985 he resigned the premiership in favour of Haider Abu Bakr al Attas, while retaining the presidency and the general secretaryship. Ismail, who had recently returned from exile, was appointed to the YSP Secretariat, though not to the Political Bureau.

At the third YSP congress in October 1985 the Central Committee and Political Bureau were enlarged to include supporters of all factions, and although Nasir Muhammad retained his posts he was opposed by the majority of the new 16-member Political Bureau, to which Ismail had been elected. A fierce struggle continued between the Ismail and Nasir Muhammad factions, erupting into open warfare in January 1986, when heavy fighting in Aden resulted in hundreds of casualties and widespread destruction. At least four members of the Political Bureau were killed, including Ismail. After a fortnight the fighting ended in the victory of the hardline faction, and Nasir Muhammad fled the country. In February the Assembly elected Haider Abu Bakr al Attas as President and Yassin Said Numan as Prime Minister, while Ali Salim al Bidh became general secretary of the YSP.

Leadership. Members of the Political Bureau in March 1986 included Ali Salim al Bidh (g.s.), Salim Saleh Muhammad (assistant g.s.), Haider Abu Bakr al Attas, Dr Abdul Aziz ad-Dali and Saleh Munassar as-Siyali, (all of whom had been elected or re-elected prior to the fighting) as well as Yassin Said Numan,

Muhammad Said Abdullah Mohsen, Fadel Mohsen Abdullah and Said Saleh Salim (who were elected after the fighting).

Structure. The YSP congress elects the Central Committee, which elects the Political Bureau and Secretariat.

Membership. 26,000 (1985 claim).

Electoral influence. All candidates for the People's Supreme Assembly are sponsored by the YSP.

Industrial influence. The party controls the General Confederation of Workers.

Orientation. Pro-Soviet.

Publications. *Ar-Rabi Ashar Min Oktubar* (October 14), daily (20,000); *Qadaya al Asr* (Questions of Our Time), weekly.

Programme. The YSP describes its policy as one of "scientific socialism adapted to local conditions".

International affiliations. The YSP has close relations with the Soviet, Arab and African Communist parties, but is not represented on the editorial council of *World Marxist Review*.

4. ASIA AND THE FAR EAST

Afghanistan

Capital: Kabul   Pop. 14,200,000

A constitution was granted in 1964 by King Muhammad Zahir Shah, under which an elected Parliament, the *Loya Jirga*, was established. In 1973, however, the monarchy was overthrown by a coup led by Lieut.-Gen. Sardar Muhammad Daoud Khan, who became President, but was himself overthrown in 1978 by a coup organized by the People's Democratic Party. The new Marxist regime, under which the country was renamed the Democratic Republic of Afghanistan, met with fierce resistance from tribal guerrillas, and in 1979 Soviet troops entered Afghanistan in support of the government forces. By 1985 a military stalemate had been reached, with the government and Soviet troops controlling the towns and the rebels most of the countryside.

People's Democratic Party of Afghanistan (PDPA)
Jamiyat-e-Demokratiki Khalq-e-Afghanistan

History. The PDPA was founded in 1965 by Nur Mohammed Taraki and Babrak Karmal, the latter, with four supporters, being returned in the first elections to the *Loya Jirga*, held in the same year. It split in 1967 into two factions named after the journals produced by each, *Khalq* (The People), led by Taraki and Hafizullah Amin, and *Parcham* (The Flag), led by Karmal. The split largely reflected the social and ethnic divisions in Afghan society, *Khalq* drawing its support from rural areas and the dominant Pathan community and *Parcham* from the towns and the smaller ethnic groups. In the 1969 elections the Marxist group in the *Loya Jirga* was reduced to three members, who included Amin.

After the 1973 coup the *Parcham* group at first supported President Daoud's regime, whereas the larger *Khalq* group opposed it. President Daoud, however, began to purge the Marxists from the army and the administration in 1975 and was suspected of being responsible for the assassination of a number of them, with the result that the two PDPA factions reunited in 1977. On April 27, 1978, he was overthrown and shot, together with many of his supporters, in a coup led by Col. Abdul Qader, deputy C.-in-C. of the air force, and a government largely drawn from the PDPA was formed, with Taraki as President and Prime Minister and Karmal and Amin as Deputy Premiers.

Despite their formal reunion, tensions between the *Khalq* and *Parcham* factions continued, and in the summer Karmal and other prominent Parchamis were sent into exile as ambassadors. Control now passed into the hands of Amin, who succeeded Taraki as Prime Minister in March 1979 and, when the latter died in mysterious circumstances in September, became President and PDPA general secretary. His ruthless suppression of all opposition, however, completely alienated public opinion, even among the government's supporters. Soviet troops, which had begun entering Afghanistan in small numbers in September 1979, apparently at Amin's invitation, were flown into Kabul in strength on Dec. 25–26. On Dec. 27 it was announced that Amin had been executed and that Karmal, who had returned from exile, had succeeded him in all his offices.

The new government, in which Sultan Ali Keshtmand succeeded Karmal as Prime Minister in 1981, and the PDPA Political Bureau were drawn mainly from the *Parcham* faction, although the *Khalq* faction was also represented in both. Conflict between them nevertheless continued, several of Amin's ministers and associates being executed in 1980 and Khalqis purged from the army, the administration and the party leadership. A party congress scheduled for March 1982 was downgraded to a conference, which lasted only two days, apparently because of factional disagreements over the election of delegates. In an attempt to conciliate public opinion, the government drastically modified in 1981–82 the radical agrarian reform programme introduced in 1978, established the National Fatherland Front in 1981 as a broad alliance of political parties, trade unions, mass organizations and religious and tribal bodies, and emphasized its respect for Islam and traditional customs. These measures appeared to have some effect in building support for the regime, and several thousand of the *mujaheddin* guerrillas were reported to have abandoned the struggle and accepted a government amnesty in 1985–86.

Leadership. The Political Bureau consists of Babrak Karmal (g.s.), Sultan Ali Keshtmand, Dr Mohammed Najibullah, Nur Ahmad Nur, Maj.-Gen. Mohammed Rafi, Dr Anahita Ratebzad, Lieut.-Gen. Mohammed Aslam Watanjar and Dr Saleh Mohammed Zeary (full members); Brig.-Gen. Nazar Mohammed, Abdul Zahoor Razmjo, Mahmoud Baryalai and Solayman La'eq (alternate members).

Structure. The PDPA claims to have about 3,000 primary organizations, 61 city and superdistrict committees and 207 district and subdistrict committees. There is a Central Committee of at least 52 full and 27 alternate members, and a six-member Secretariat. Subsidiary organizations include the Democratic Youth Organization of Afghanistan and the Democratic Women's Organization of Afghanistan, which claim to have 120,000 and 25,000 members respectively.

Membership. 150,000 full and candidate members (1985 claim). This figure is widely regarded as exaggerated. Whereas the membership formerly consisted almost entirely of intellectuals, since 1978 great efforts have been made to recruit workers, peasants and soldiers, who are admitted to full membership after six months as a candidate instead of the year required of other applicants.

Industrial influence. The PDPA controls the Central Council of Trade Unions, which claims to have 170,000 members.

Orientation. Pro-Soviet.

Programme. The PDPA plans to establish a mixed economy, in which the state would control the main levers of economic power, while leaving light industry and trade largely in private hands. Particular emphasis is laid on the development of industry, mining, energy (including oil and natural gas), transport and communications. Its agricultural policy is aimed at the elimination of the feudal system, the redistribution of land, the development of irrigation, the mechanization of agriculture and the formation of production and marketing co-operatives, membership of which would be voluntary. It plans to eliminate illiteracy by 1990.

Publications. Haqiqat-e-Enqelabe Saur (The Truth about the April Revolution), daily; *Kabul New Times*, English-language daily.

International affiliations. The PDPA is aligned with the Soviet-bloc parties.

Bangladesh

Capital: Dhaka   Pop. 99,585,000

The eastern and predominantly Moslem section of Bengal was included in Pakistan when India was partitioned in 1947, being known as East Bengal until 1955 and subsequently as East Pakistan. In elections held in December 1970 the Awami League, led by Sheikh Mujibur Rahman, obtained 151 of the 153 East Pakistan seats and a majority in the National Assembly, but its demand for autonomy for East Pakistan was rejected by President Yahya Khan. On March 25–26, 1971, the army occupied Dhaka, whereupon the Awami League proclaimed East Pakistan an independent republic, under the name of Bangladesh. The ensuing civil war ended in December, when the Indian army intervened in support of the rebels and overran East Pakistan.

The Awami League formed a government in Bangladesh, with Sheikh Mujib as Prime Minister and after January 1975 as President. He was overthrown and murdered in a military coup on Aug. 15, and after two further coups on Nov. 3 and 7 Maj.-Gen. Ziaur Rahman took control as Chief Martial Law Administrator, assuming the presidency in 1977. Parliamentary government was restored in 1979, when elections were held, but in 1981 President Zia was murdered in an attempted coup. After a brief period of civilian government, Lieut.-Gen. Hossain Mohammad Ershad seized power and dissolved Parliament in 1982, and in the following year proclaimed himself President. An alliance of 15 left-wing and centrist parties headed by the Awami League had previously been formed to press for a return to democratic government.

Bangladesh Communist Party, Marxist-Leninist
Bangladesher Samyabadi Dal, Marxist-Leninist (BSDM-L)

History. The East Pakistan Communist Party, Marxist-Leninist, of which the BSDM-L is an offshoot, was formed in 1966 as a Maoist organization by Muhammad Toha and Abdul Haq, who had left the pro-Soviet Communist Party of Pakistan. In compliance with the Chinese government's policy, it opposed the secession of Bangladesh from Pakistan in 1971; a section of the membership led by Toha thereupon formed the BSDM-L, which conducted guerrilla operations in the Noakhali district of the Ganges delta and attempted unsuccessfully to seize the leadership of the liberation movement. After the establishment of Bangladesh it called for the overthrow of the Awami League government, and when Sheikh Mujibur Rahman was murdered in 1975 emerged as a legal party, Toha being elected to the Parliament of 1979–82. The BSDM-L joined the 15-party alliance in 1983.

Leadership. Muhammad Toha (ch.); Sukhendu Dastidar (g.s.).

Structure. The national congress elects the 15-member Central Committee, which elects the five-member Political Bureau.

Membership. 1,400 (1984 estimate).

Orientation. Formerly Maoist, now pro-Soviet.

Bangladesh Peasants' and Workers' People's League
Bangladesh Krishak-Sramik Awami League (Baksal)

History. The Baksal was formed in 1983 by a group of leading Awami League members who had been expelled. It is a member of the 15-party alliance, and co-operates closely with the Communist Party.

Leadership. Abdur Razzak (g.s.).

Orientation. Pro-Soviet.

Communist Party of Bangladesh (CPB)

History. Originally part of the Communist Party of India, the Communist Party of Pakistan became an independent organization in 1948. It won four seats in the East Bengal Provincial Assembly in 1954, but was banned two months later. Its East Pakistan section took an active part in the 1971 uprising, forming guerrilla units, and again became a legal organization, as the Communist Party of Bangladesh, on the attainment of independence. It unsuccessfully contested four seats in the 1973 elections, and later in the same year formed an alliance with the ruling Awami League and the pro-Soviet wing of the National Awami Party to combat terrorism and corruption. It was banned by President Zia after an attempted coup in 1977, the ban being lifted a year later, and a number of its leaders were arrested after a strike by government employees in 1980 and again after student demonstrations in Dhaka in 1983. The CPB is a member of the 15-party alliance.

Leadership. Moni Singh (pres.), Muhammad Farhad (g.s.).

Structure. The CPB has a 26-member Central Committee and a 10-member Secretariat.

Membership. 3,000 (1985 estimate).

Orientation. Pro-Soviet.

Programme. The CPB has defined its policy as one of "building up unity and understanding among the parties of left-progressive orientation, at the same time forging unity with broad democratic forces in the struggle for democracy and constitutional rights and freedoms".

Publication. Ekota.

East Bengal Communist Party, Marxist-Leninist (EBCPM-L)

History. The EBCPM-L was founded in 1968 by Alauddin Ahmed, Abdul Matin and Tipu Biswas after they had been expelled from the East Pakistan Communist Party, Marxist–Leninist, and became the largest Maoist party in East Pakistan, with about 2,000 members. It conducted guerrilla operations during the 1971 revolt in the Rajshahi-Pabna area, north-west of Dhaka, and after the attainment of independence attempted to organize peasant revolts against the Awami League government. Biswas was killed and Matin arrested during the struggle, and after Ahmed's arrest in 1975 the revolt collapsed.

Orientation. Pro-Chinese.

228

National Socialist Party
Jatiya Samajtantrik Dal (JSD)

History. The JSD was formed in 1972 by the majority of the student section of the Awami League and members of the resistance movement, with Maj. M. A. Jalil and Abdur Rab, two former guerrilla leaders, as chairman and general secretary. In the 1973 elections it contested 236 seats, obtaining 1,195,572 votes (6.5 per cent), but won only one seat. After riots in Dakha in 1974 the JSD was banned and its leaders imprisoned. Its underground military wing, the People's Revolutionary Army, led by Col. Abu Taher, which had strong support in the armed forces, was responsible for the coup of Nov. 7, 1975, which placed Maj.-Gen. Ziaur Rahman in power. Its leaders, who were immediately released, called on Nov. 15 for the formation of councils of soldiers, workers and peasants to carry out a socialist revolution, and were again arrested on Nov. 23–24. Col. Taher was hanged in 1976 and the other leaders sentenced to long prison terms, and after an attempted coup in 1977 the JSD was banned, the ban being lifted a year later. It won nine seats in the 1979 elections, but its candidate in the 1981 presidential election, Maj. Jalil, who had been released with the other imprisoned leaders in the previous year, polled negligibly. The JSD joined the 15-party alliance in 1983.

Leadership. Shahjahan Siraj (l.).

Orientation. Independent.

Publication. Gonokantha (Voice of the People).

Burma

Capital: Rangoon   Pop. 37,100,000

Burma, which had been under British rule since 1885, was occupied by the Japanese in 1941–42. An alliance of nationalist parties, the Anti-Fascist People's Freedom League (AFPFL), formed a resistance movement, and co-operated with the British in expelling the Japanese in 1945. When Burma became an independent republic outside the British Commonwealth in 1948 the AFPFL took office, but was confronted almost immediately with armed revolts by the two Communist parties, the Karens and the Arakanese. Other ethnic minorities, such as the Kachins, Karennis, Shans and Mons, later joined in the civil war, which was still continuing in 1986.

After a military coup in 1962 a Revolutionary Council headed by Gen. Ne Win seized power and established the Burma Socialist Programme Party (BSSP). A new constitution adopted in 1973 declared Burma a Socialist Republic, with the BSSP as "the only political party leading the state". Gen. Ne Win served as Chairman of the Council of State (President) until 1981, when he was succeeded by Gen. San Yu.

Burmese Communist Party (BCP)

History. Founded in 1939, the BCP was one of the organizations which in 1943 formed the Anti-Fascist People's Freedom League, from which it was expelled in

1946. It launched an armed rebellion in 1948, operating at first mainly in Central Burma, and subsequently in the Arakan mountains and the Irrawaddy delta. It has frequently attempted to form alliances with the rebel ethnic groups, but they have rarely proved lasting. Peace negotiations with the government in 1958 and 1963 produced no result.

In the early 1960s the BCP adopted a strongly pro-Chinese attitude, and in 1967 the Chinese Communist Party openly declared its support for the rebels. In the following year the BCP transferred its headquarters to the Chinese border area, and began receiving large quantities of military aid from China. In imitation of the Chinese Cultural Revolution, it carried out a wholesale purge of "revisionists" in 1967–68 in which many of its leaders were murdered, including three of the eight members of the Political Bureau. The party chairman, Thakin Than Tun, was assassinated in 1968 by a follower who feared for his life, and his successor, Thakin Zin, was killed in 1975 in an engagement in the Pegu Yoma mountains which marked the end of the BCP's activities in Central Burma. He was succeeded as chairman by Thakin Ba Thein Tin, who has lived in Beijing since 1953.

Peace negotiations in 1980–81 broke down, as the government refused to accept the BCP's demands that it should allow the party and its armed forces to continue to exist and should recognize their base areas as an autonomous region. To offset a decline in Chinese aid, the BCP has been actively involved since the late 1970s in the international drug traffic. The party held its third national congress on Sept. 9–Oct. 2, 1985, "in a liberated area of Burma".

Leadership. Thakin Ba Thein Tin (ch.).

Structure. Little is known of the BCP's organization. It has a Central Committee of 29 members and an eight-member Political Bureau.

Membership. 3,000, including candidate members (1979 claim). No membership figures have since been published. Estimates of the strength of its armed forces range from 8,000 to 15,000.

Orientation. Pro-Chinese.

Programme. The BCP defined its programme in 1982 as (i) to end the civil war and establish peace in the country; (ii) to win full democratic rights for the people; (iii) to build national unity; (iv) to raise the people's living standards; (v) to oppose the two superpowers, and particularly Soviet social imperialism; (vi) to preserve world peace. In its recent propaganda it has demanded expansion of the private sector, payment of compensation for nationalized enterprises, liberalization of export and import controls, a multiparty system, freedom of the press and religious freedom.

Publications. The BCP radio station, the Voice of the People of Burma, broadcasts from Yunnan province, in southern China.

International affiliation. The BCP has close links with the Chinese Communist Party.

Communist Party of Burma (CPB)

History. The CPB broke away from the Burmese Communist Party in 1946, and began guerrilla operations in the Irrawaddy valley two years later. Its armed strength, estimated at one stage at 1,000 men, had declined by 1961 to about 500.

Thakin Soe, its general secretary, was captured in 1970 and sentenced to death, since when it has ceased to exercise any influence.

Orientation. Trotskyist.

China

Capital: Beijing

Pop. 1,059,800,000

The revolution of 1911–12, which overthrew the imperial dynasty and established a republic, was followed by a period of chaos. Sun Yat-sen, the founder of the Kuomintang (People's National Party), formed a government at Canton in 1923, but northern China remained under the control of rival generals. The Kuomintang army, commanded by Gen. Chiang Kai-shek, defeated the northern warlords in 1926–28 and occupied Beijing, but civil war followed between the Kuomintang government and the Communists, with whom Chiang had broken in 1927. The Japanese, who had overrun Manchuria in 1931, invaded China in 1937, whereupon Chiang was forced to conclude an alliance with the Communists. After the defeat of Japan in 1945 the civil war was renewed, and concluded in 1949 with the victory of the Communists, the establishment of the Chinese People's Republic and the flight of the Kuomintang government to Taiwan.

Communist Party of China (CPC)
Zhongguo Gongchan Dang

History. The CPC was founded in 1921, with Chen Duxiu as general secretary, at a congress in Shanghai of 12 delegates, including Mao Zedong, from small Marxist groups in Beijing, Shanghai and other cities. The membership, which originally totalled only 57, at first grew very slowly, reaching 1,000 only in the spring of 1925. In 1923, however, the Kuomintang and the CPC agreed to co-operate against the northern warlords, and Communists were permitted to join the Kuomintang as individuals. The active part taken by the Communists in the campaigns of 1926–27 greatly increased their influence, and by April 1927 CPC membership had reached 58,000.

In March 1927 a Communist-led insurrection in Shanghai enabled Chiang Kai-shek to enter the city unopposed, whereupon he turned on his allies, 5,000 of whom were massacred within two days. A period of confusion followed, Chen Duxiu being replaced as general secretary by Qu Qiubai, who in turn was replaced in 1928 by Li Lisan. Attempted uprisings in the later months of 1927 at Nanchang and Canton were suppressed. Mao Zedong meanwhile organized a peasant revolt in Hunan, and after its defeat established his headquarters on Chingkanshan, a mountain on the Hunan-Jiangxi border. Here he was joined in 1928 by troops which had taken part in the Nanchang uprising, headed by Zhu De, which formed the nucleus of the Chinese Red Army. From this base the Communists gradually extended their control over a great part of Jiangxi and large areas of Hunan and Fujian. After an unsuccessful occupation of Changsha in 1930 Li Lisan was removed from the leadership; the policy of combining uprisings in the cities with attacks on them from outside was abandoned, and Mao's concept of a revolution based primarily on the poor peasants rather than the industrial proletariat gradually won acceptance.

In 1931 a Chinese Soviet Republic was established in the Communist-controlled area, with Mao as chairman and Zhu as C.-in-C. After the Central Committee, which had been operating underground in Shanghai, joined Mao in Jiangxi in 1931, however, differences arose over political and military policy, and he was removed from his military posts in 1932 and from his political posts in 1934. Four offensives by the Kuomintang forces were defeated during 1930–33, but a fifth, for which over 900,000 troops were mobilized, compelled the Communists to evacuate Jiangxi in October 1934 and set out on the "Long March" to the north-west. During the march a conference was held in January 1935 at Zunyi (in Guizhou), at which Mao was elected chairman of the party's Military Affairs Committee, becoming in effect party leader, and Zhang Wentian general secretary. After a 6,000-mile march, only 4,000 people out of 86,000 who had set out reached Shaanxi in October 1935, and established their new headquarters at Yenan. The post of general secretary was abolished in 1937.

In December 1936 Chiang Kai-shek was arrested at Zian by rebellious officers, who demanded the ending of the civil war and a policy of resistance to Japanese aggression, but was released on the intercession of a Communist delegation headed by Zhou Enlai. Negotiations followed between the Kuomintang and the CPC, and after the outbreak of war with Japan in July 1937 an agreement was reached for co-operation between them. This broke down in 1940, when Kuomintang troops attacked a Communist unit, and from then on Chiang combined passive resistance to the Japanese with military operations against the Communist forces, which by 1944 were holding down 64 per cent of the Japanese troops in China. By 1945 the Communists controlled most of Shaanxi, Shanxi, Hebei and Shandong and part of Inner Mongolia; the population under Communist rule had increased from 1,500,000 in 1937 to 90,000,000, and the strength of the Communist forces from 80,000 in 1937 to 900,000 regulars and 2,200,000 militia. The seventh CPC congress, held at Yenan in 1945, when the party's membership had grown to 1,210,000, elected Mao chairman of the Central Committee, a post which he retained until his death, and adopted a new party constitution which declared Mao Zedong Thought to be the guide for the party's work.

After the Japanese surrendered the CPC proposed that the Kuomintang and the Communists should form a coalition government, but this offer was rejected by Chiang. Civil war broke out in 1946, in which the Kuomintang forces' overwhelming numerical superiority at first gave them the advantage. By the end of 1948, however, the Communists controlled Manchuria and much of the north, and in the course of the following year they overran the rest of mainland China. The People's Republic of China was proclaimed in Beijing on Oct. 1, 1949, with Mao as Chairman (President), and a coalition government was formed by the CPC and four smaller opposition parties, with Zhou Enlai as Prime Minister.

During 1950–55 large estates were divided among the landless peasants; the formation of agricultural co-operatives was encouraged; industry and commerce were left largely in private hands; and a five-year plan was begun for the development of heavy industry. The collectivization of agriculture was carried out in 1955, and in the following year private enterprises were transferred to joint state-private ownership. Following Khrushchev's criticism of the Stalin cult at the 20th Soviet Communist Party congress, the eighth CPC congress in 1956 adopted a new party constitution from which the references to Mao Zedong Thought were omitted. The post of general secretary was revived for Deng Xiaoping, and a new body was created, the Standing Committee of the Political Bureau, consisting of Mao, Liu Shaoqi, Zhou Enlai, Zhu De, Chen Yun and Deng. The party's membership was given as 10,734,385.

Mao had already put forward the slogan "Let 100 flowers blossom, let 100 schools of thought contend" in a speech in May 1956 advocating greater intellectual and artistic freedom. He developed this theme in a speech in February

1957 in which he distinguished between "contradictions between ourselves and the enemy", which were "antagonistic", and "contradictions among the people", which were "non-antagonistic" and should be solved by democratic methods (see Appendix 2: Documents). A "rectification campaign" was launched in April, in which the public were encouraged to criticize government and party officials who ignored popular grievances, but this met with such an enthusiastic response that the campaign was transformed in June into one against "rightists". The non-Communist ministers were subsequently dropped from the government.

In 1958 the Great Leap Forward policy was adopted on Mao's initiative, whereby industrial and agricultural targets were repeatedly raised, the agricultural co-operatives were grouped into large communes combining agriculture with small-scale industry and over 2,000,000 "backyard furnaces" were established for the local production of iron and steel. This policy, which failed to achieve the desired results, led to a political and economic crisis. At a Central Committee meeting in December a resolution was adopted criticizing the mistakes made in its application, and Mao was forced to resign the chairmanship of the Republic in favour of Liu Shaoqi. The Defence Minister, Marshal Peng Dehuai, strongly criticized in 1959 the "empty boasting", "hot-headedness" and "leftist errors" accompanying the Great Leap Forward, and was replaced by Marshal Lin Biao. As a result of the increasingly strained relations between the Chinese and Soviet Communist parties, the Soviet Union withdrew all technical aid to China in 1960, and a succession of disastrous harvests added to the country's economic problems. Liu, Zhou Enlai and Deng Xiaoping tried to solve the crisis by a policy whereby the peasants were allowed to cultivate private plots of land, a free market developed in the villages and increased use was made of bonuses and other material incentives in industry.

Differences between the Chinese and Soviet parties on internal and international policies and on ideological questions, which had been increasing since 1956, came into the open in 1959. Although a temporary compromise was reached at the Moscow conference of Communist parties in 1960, an acrimonious exchange of correspondence between the two parties took place in 1963–64 (see Appendix 2: Documents), in which the Chinese party accused the Soviet party of revisionism and opportunism, and relations between them were broken off by the CPC in 1966. As a result the CPC found itself virtually isolated, with the Albanian Party of Labour its only supporter among the major Communist parties.

Mao, who had played only a secondary role since the fiasco of the Great Leap Forward, regarded the economic policy pursued since then as likely to lead to a return to capitalism, and formed the idea that the party was undergoing a degeneration similar to that which, he believed, had occurred in the Soviet party. Although in a minority in the leadership, he was supported by Lin Biao, who promoted the Mao cult by launching a campaign in the army for the study of his thought and issuing the "little red book" of quotations from his writings. After repeated attempts by Mao during 1962–65 to impose his views on the party had had little success, he left Beijing for Shanghai, which he made his base for his campaign against his colleagues. With the backing of the army, he forced the Political Bureau, meeting in Shanghai, to issue on May 16, 1966, a circular calling for a purge of "those representatives of the bourgeoisie who have sneaked into the party, the government, the army and various spheres of culture", which marked the beginning of the Cultural Revolution. Demonstrations against Mao's opponents began in Beijing University in the same month, and were followed by the formation of the Red Guard units, composed of students and schoolchildren, who terrorized anyone suspected of bourgeois tendencies. Returning to Beijing, Mao presided on Aug. 1–12 over a Central Committee session which issued instructions for the conduct of the Cultural Revolution, and while it was meeting published a poster headed "Bombard the Headquarters" which held up the students' actions as an example. He found his main supporters among the leadership in Lin Biao, who guaranteed the army's support and who replaced Liu Shaoqi as the second in the party hierarchy, and Zhou Enlai, who consistently acted as a moderating influence and sought to limit the damage caused by the Cultural Revolution.

In 1967 the Red Guards, whose excesses had aroused uneasiness, were replaced as the main agents of the Cultural Revolution by the Revolutionary Rebels, consisting of adult workers. Pitched battles between rival factions followed in many cities and provinces, and throughout 1967–68 China was reduced to a state of virtual anarchy. The party and the government disintegrated, as almost all their leading members came under attack and were repeatedly replaced. The most virulent campaign was directed against Mao's rival Liu Shaoqi, denounced as the "No. 1 capitalist-roader", who was expelled from the party and removed from the chairmanship of the Republic in 1968 and died in prison in the following year. In these circumstances Mao was obliged to fall back on the support of the army; the revolutionary committees which replaced the old local authorities in 1967–68 and the new provincial CPC committees formed in 1970–71 were largely under military leadership, and the army took control of many ministries.

The ninth CPC congress, held in 1969, adopted a new party constitution which named Lin Biao as Mao's successor, reinstated the reference to Mao Zedong Thought and abolished the office of general secretary, and elected a new Political Bureau dominated by Lin's military associates and politicians who had risen to prominence during the Cultural Revolution. The new leadership soon split over foreign policy questions, however. In view of the growing hostility between China and the Soviet Union, Mao and Zhou Enlai favoured a détente with the United States, which although opposed by Lin was achieved when President Nixon visited China in 1972. After an unsuccessful attempt to organize a coup Lin fled the country in 1971 and was killed when his plane crashed in Mongolia, whereupon his supporters on the Political Bureau were arrested.

The change in China's international relations was reflected in the three worlds theory put forward by the CPC in 1974, which rejected the earlier conception of the world as divided into the "imperialist camp" dominated by the United States, the "socialist camp" and the developing countries, on the ground that the Soviet Union had degenerated into an aggressive "social imperialist" superpower and the "socialist camp" no longer existed. Instead it maintained that the world was divided into the two superpowers, the United States and the Soviet Union, which constituted the main threat to peace; the developed countries of Western and Eastern Europe, Canada, South Africa, Australia, New Zealand and Japan, which were struggling to free themselves from US or Soviet domination; and the developing countries of Asia, Africa and Latin America, including China, with which the developed countries should ally themselves to oppose the superpowers. This theory, however, was rejected by many of the pro-Chinese Communist parties throughout the world, including the Albanian Party of Labour.

After the 10th congress, held in 1973, at which Lin's followers were dropped from the Political Bureau, conflict continued between the moderate faction led by Zhou and the extremist "gang of four" headed by Mao's wife, Jiang Qing. Zhou secured the rehabilitation of many of those disgraced during the Cultural Revolution, including Deng Xiaoping, who was appointed a Deputy Premier in 1973 and readmitted to the Political Bureau in the following year, and in 1975 put forward a programme for the modernization of agriculture, industry, defence and science and technology ("the four modernizations"). After Zhou died in January 1976, however, he was succeeded as Prime Minister by Hua Guofeng, who represented a centrist group in the leadership, and Deng, whom Zhou had intended as his successor, was removed from all his offices as an "unrepentant capitalist-roader".

When Mao died in September Hua took over as party chairman. The "gang of four" were arrested, as were many of their supporters, and in 1981 were sentenced to long terms of imprisonment, together with Lin Biao's leading associates. Deng was readmitted to the Political Bureau in 1977, and after a struggle between the left and right wings of the leadership, headed by Hua and Deng respectively, Hua was replaced as Prime Minister in 1980 by Zhao Ziyang and as chairman in 1981 by Hu Yaobang, both close associates of Deng who had been disgraced during the Cultural Revolution. The office of chairman was abolished under a new party constitution adopted in 1982 by the 12th congress, Hu being elected to the post of general secretary, which had been revived in 1980. The new Central Committee elected a Political Bureau from which Hua was excluded.

From 1978 onwards the theories and practices adopted during the Great Leap Forward and the Cultural Revolution were gradually abandoned. The theories on revisionism put forward during the exchange of polemics with the Soviet Union in 1963–64 were admitted in 1980 to be incorrect. The communes were virtually dismantled, land being allocated to households on a contract basis and the communes' administrative functions transferred to the local authorities. Economic planning was relaxed, and greater responsibilities allocated to individual enterprises. Wages were related more closely to output. The formation of small private enterprises was encouraged. Former capitalists' confiscated property was restored to them. Loans were accepted from foreign governments and banks, and foreign investment in joint ventures was sought. Religion, suppressed during the Cultural Revolution, was again tolerated. About 100,000,000 people disgraced since 1957 were rehabilitated, many of them posthumously, including Liu Shaoqi and Peng Dehuai. A resolution on Mao adopted by the Central Committee in 1981 (see Appendix 2: Documents) stated that his contribution to the Chinese revolution far outweighed his mistakes, but condemned many of the policies which he had pursued since 1957, including the anti-rightist campaign, the Great Leap Forward and the Cultural Revolution. The 1982 party constitution retained the reference to Mao Zedong Thought, but defined it as representing the crystallized collective wisdom of the party.

Leadership. The Political Bureau consists of Hu Yaobang (g.s.), Deng Xiaoping, Zhao Ziyang, Li Xiannian and Chen Yun (Standing Committee); Fang Yi, Yu Qiuli, Ni Zhifu, Peng Zhen, Wan Li, Xi Zhongxun, Yang Shangkun, Gen. Yang Dezhi, Hu Qiaomu, Wu Xueqian, Li Peng, Yao Yilin, Tian Jiyun, Hu Qili and Qiao Shi (other full members); Miss Chen Muhua and Gen. Qin Jiwei (alternate members).

Structure. Primary party organizations are formed on a workplace or residential basis, and also in units of the armed forces, where there are three or more members. Above them organizations exist at branch, county, provincial and regional level. The national congress, normally meeting every five years, elects the Central Committee (210 full and 133 alternate members), which elects the Political Bureau, the Secretariat (11 members), the general secretary and the Military Commission. A unique feature of the CPC is the Central Advisory Commission, established in 1982, consisting of 172 party members of at least 40 years' standing, elected by the congress. Its chairman (Deng Xiaoping) is a member of the Standing Committee of the Political Bureau, and its three vice-chairmen are entitled to attend Political Bureau meetings and its members to attend Central Committee sessions as non-voting participants.

Membership. The CPC is the largest Communist Party in the world, with over 40,000,000 members. The Communist Youth League, the party's youth organization, has 50,000,000 members.

Electoral influence. All candidates for the National People's Congress (Parliament) are approved by the CPC.

Industrial influence. The CPC controls the All-China Federation of Trade Unions, the chairman of which, Ni Zhifu, is a member of the Political Bureau.

Programme. The 1982 constitution states that the party's task at the present stage is "to unite the people of all nationalities in working hard and self-reliantly to achieve, step by step, the modernization of our industry, agriculture, national defence and science and technology and make China a culturally advanced and highly democratic socialist country", with the ultimate aim of the realization of Communism. In his report to the 1982 congress Hu Yaobang said that the CPC would strive to bring about an all-round upsurge of the economy, to "build a high level of socialist spiritual civilization" and to "attain a high level of socialist democracy". It would pursue an independent foreign policy directed against the hegemonism of the two superpowers; seek to secure the reunification of Taiwan with China through talks with the Kuomintang; and co-operate with the Third World countries, the friendly socialist countries (North Korea, Romania and Yugoslavia) and Japan.

Publications. *Renmin Ribao* (The People's Daily); *Jiefangjunbao* (Liberation Army Daily); *Hongqi* (Red Flag), theoretical monthly; *China Daily*, English-language daily; *Beijing Review*, weekly published in English and other languages.

International affiliations. The CPC's leadership is accepted by a number of small communist parties, such as those of Burma, Malaya and Thailand. Relations with the Soviet-bloc parties (except the Romanian) have been suspended since 1966, and with the Albanian Party of Labour since 1978. On the other hand, relations with the Yugoslav League of Communists and the Italian, French, Spanish and other Eurocommunist parties have been resumed in recent years.

India

Capital: Delhi   Pop. 746,388,000

After a long struggle against British rule led by the Indian National Congress, India attained independence in 1947, and a Congress government headed by Jawaharlal Nehru took office. Under the constitution adopted in 1949 India became a federal republic, and now consists of 22 states, each with its own Legislative Assembly and a ministry headed by a Chief Minister, and nine union territories, each with a legislature with more limited powers. The Parliament consists of two houses, the directly-elected *Lok Sabha* (House of the People) and the *Rajya Sabha* (Council of States).

The Congress obtained a majority in the *Lok Sabha* in elections held in 1951–52, 1957, 1962, 1967 and 1971. Border disputes with China led to a short war in 1962. On his death in 1964 Nehru was succeeded as Prime Minister by Lal Bahadur Shastri, who died two years later and was succeeded by Mrs Indira Gandhi, Nehru's daughter. The Congress split in 1969, when the right wing, led by Morarji Desai, broke away and formed the Congress (O). Following the development of a strong agitation against government corruption and the defeat of the Congress in the Gujarat state elections, Mrs Gandhi in 1975 proclaimed a state of emergency, under which habeas corpus and other fundamental rights were suspended, many opposition leaders were imprisoned, the press was censored and elections were postponed.

In the 1977 elections the Congress was defeated by the Janata Party, formed by the Congress (O) and three other opposition parties, and Desai formed a government. A crisis followed inside the Congress, from which Mrs Gandhi and her supporters broke away in 1978 to form the Congress (I). The Janata Party disintegrated into several rival parties in 1979–80, and in elections in 1980 Mrs Gandhi was returned to office. She was assassinated in October 1984, and was succeeded as Prime Minister by her son, Rajiv Gandhi. Elections held two months later resulted in an overwhelming victory for the Congress (I), which won 403 of the 513 constituencies in which voting took place.

All-India Communist Party (AICP)

History. The AICP was formed in 1980 by former members of the Communist Party of India (CPI), who disagreed with its policy of opposition to the Congress (I), and was joined in the following year by S. A. Dange, the former chairman of the CPI. It contested the West Bengal elections in 1982 in alliance with the Congress (I), without winning any seats.

Leadership. Shripad Amrit Dange (g.s.).

Membership. 70,000 (1982 claim). This figure is generally regarded as exaggerated.

Orientation. Pro-Soviet.

Programme. The AICP supports the Congress (I), on the ground that it represents the national bourgeoisie and is striving to strengthen democratic socialism.

All-India Forward Bloc (AIFB)

History. The AIFB was founded in 1939 as a left-wing group inside the Congress by Subhas Chandra Bose, who subsequently organized the Indian National Army, which collaborated with the Japanese against the British during the war in Burma, and was killed in an air crash in 1945. Banned in 1942, the AIFB was legalized after the war, and became an independent party in 1946. Two years later it split into Marxist and non-Marxist wings, which fought the 1952 elections as separate parties, the Marxist wing winning one seat in Madras, and in 1953 the non-Marxist wing merged with the Praja Socialist Party. The AIFB split again in 1954, when its only member of Parliament was expelled for advocating closer relations with the Communist Party, whereupon his supporters formed the Forward Bloc—Marxist. In each general election since 1957 the AIFB has won between one and three seats, all in West Bengal or Tamil Nadu (formerly known as Madras).

In West Bengal, its main stronghold, the AIFB has been represented in the Assembly since 1952, its strength varying from three members in 1971–72 to 28 in the Assembly elected in 1982, and joined the United Front ministries of 1967 and 1969–70 and the Left Front ministries formed in 1977 and 1982. It has also been represented in the Tamil Nadu Assembly in 1952–57, 1962–67 and 1971–77 and since 1980, and in the Bihar Assembly in 1952–57 and since 1980.

Leadership. Prem Dutta Paliwal (ch.); Chitta Basu (g.s.).

Electoral influence. The AIFB won two seats in the 1984 elections, both in West Bengal.

Orientation. Independent.

Programme. The AIFB advocates nationalization of key industries and redistribution of the land.

Communist Party of India (CPI)

History. Although individual Indian communists took a prominent part in the work of the Third International from 1920 onwards, the CPI was not founded until 1925. Thirty-one of its leading members were arrested in 1929 on a charge of conspiring to overthrow British rule, being sentenced to long terms of imprisonment, and in 1934 the CPI was banned. It co-operated closely with the Congress from 1935 to 1942, when it announced its support for the British war effort and refused to join the "Quit India" agitation, being legalized in consequence in 1943. In 1948 it organized a number of peasant revolts, notably in the Telengana region of Hyderabad, but it abandoned this policy two years later for one of peaceful competition with the Congress. In the elections of 1951–52 it emerged as the strongest opposition party, with 23 seats in the *Lok Sabha*, which increased to 29 in the 1957 and 1962 elections.

In the 1957 state elections the CPI obtained representation for the first time in all the Legislative Assemblies. In Kerala it won 60 of the 126 seats, and E. M. S. Namboodiripad formed a ministry, described as "the first Communist government in the world through the ballot box", with the support of five independents. The government was overthrown in 1959, however, as the result of a violent campaign organized by the Congress, and in elections in the following year the CPI was defeated by a Congress-led alliance of parties, although its share of the vote rose from 39 to 43.3 per cent.

Longstanding differences inside the party came to a head at the 1961 congress, when the right wing advocated an alliance with the left wing of the Congress to work for socialist policies, and the left unity of the socialist parties against the Congress. When the general secretary, Ajoy Ghosh, died in 1962 the centrist Namboodiripad was chosen to succeed him as a compromise candidate, and the rightist Shripad Amrit Dange was elected to the new office of chairman. During the war with China later in the same year the CPI's National Council announced its full support for the government, but a section of the left adopted a pro-Chinese attitude, about 1,000 of them being interned. In 1964 the left wing broke away and formed the Communist Party of India—Marxist (CPM).

The CPI won 23 seats in the 1967 *Lok Sabha* elections, and following the state elections of the same year joined coalition governments with the CPM in Kerala and West Bengal. Co-operation between them soon broke down, however, and the West Bengal government fell a few months later and the Kerala government in 1969. After elections in West Bengal a new left-wing coalition government was formed in 1969, but this also disintegrated in the following year. In the 1971 *Lok Sabha* elections the CPI again obtained 23 seats, although it lost ground to the CPM in West Bengal and Kerala.

After the split in the Congress in 1969 the CPI moved closer to Mrs Gandhi's wing of the party. C. Achutha Menon, the CPI leader in Kerala, formed a minority government in that year with Congress support, and in 1971 the Congress entered his ministry. The CPI fought the Assembly elections in West Bengal and a number of other states in 1972 in alliance with the Congress, on a basis of opposition to "right reaction and left adventurism", and during the emergency of 1975–77 was the only major opposition party which supported the government's measures. As a result, it obtained only seven seats in the 1977 *Lok Sabha* elections, and also lost many seats in the 1977–78 state elections, except in Kerala, where it increased its representation and entered a Congress-led ministry.

Following these setbacks, the CPI abandoned its policy of co-operation with the Congress, and admitted that its support for the emergency had been a mistake. It fought the 1980 *Lok Sabha* elections in alliance with the CPM, winning 11 seats, and was represented in CPM-led governments in Kerala in 1980–82 and in West Bengal from 1982. Its change of policy, however, was opposed by a pro-Congress faction inside the party, which broke away and formed the All-India Communist Party in 1980, and by Dange, who was expelled in the following year, the post of chairman being abolished. In the 1984 elections it suffered its worst electoral defeat hitherto, winning only six seats.

Leadership. C. Rajeswara Rao (g.s.).

Structure. Branches are formed on a residential or workplace basis, and are organized at district and state level. State party conferences elect the State Council, which elects its Executive Committee and Secretariat. The party congress, meeting every three years, elects the 124-member National Council, which elects the 11-member Central Executive Council, Secretariat and general secretary.

Membership. 478,500 (1984 claim). Membership is strongest in Bihar, Andhra Pradesh, Kerala and Tamil Nadu.

Electoral influence. The CPI obtained 2.73 per cent of the vote in the 1984 elections and won six seats (three in West Bengal, two in Bihar and one in Andhra Pradesh).

Industrial influence. The CPI controls the All-India Trade Union Congress, which has about 1,200,000 members.

Orientation. Pro-Soviet. The 1982 CPI congress condemned Maoism and Eurocommunism, and described the Soviet party as the vanguard of the world communist movement.

Programme. The CPI advocates unity of the "left and democratic forces" against the "reactionary and authoritarian" internal policies of the Congress (I), while supporting its foreign policy of non-alignment and friendship with the Soviet Union. This policy is opposed by a section of the party, however, which favours the establishment of a "national patriotic front" with the Congress (I) against the right-wing parties.

Publications. *New Age* (weekly), *Party Life* (fortnightly). The CPI also publishes daily papers in Kerala, Andhra Pradesh, West Bengal, Punjab and Manipur, and over 20 weeklies in various languages.

International affiliations. The CPI has close ties with the Soviet Communist Party, and is represented on the editorial board of *World Marxist Review*.

Communist Party of India—Marxist (CPM)

History. The CPM was formed in 1964 by the left wing of the Communist Party, with E. M. S. Namboodiripad as its general secretary, and was supported by 11 of the 29 Communist members of *Lok Sabha*. At its first congress it adopted a programme stating that it would strive to "achieve the establishment of people's democracy and socialist transformation through peaceful means", and that Parliament and state legislatures could serve as "instruments of the people in their struggle for democracy". Most of its leaders were subsequently arrested, not being released until 1966. In the 1967 elections it won 19 *Lok Sabha* seats, and following the state elections of the same year was represented in coalition governments in Kerala, where Namboodiripad became Chief Minister, in 1967–69 and in West Bengal in 1967 and in 1969–70.

The CPM was divided from the first between moderates, who favoured the use of parliamentary methods, and Maoists, who opposed the policy of entering coalition governments and advocated the establishment of rural bases for armed struggle on the Chinese model. The Maoists, who organized a peasant revolt in 1967 in the Naxalbari area of West Bengal, were expelled in 1967–68, and subsequently formed the Communist Party of India—Marxist-Leninist.

In the 1971 elections the CPM obtained 25 seats, becoming the largest opposition group in the *Lok Sabha*, and in the 1977 elections it won 22. It made sweeping gains in the state elections in 1977 in West Bengal, where it obtained 178 of the 294 seats, in 1978 in Tripura, with 49 of the 60 seats, and in 1980 in Kerala, with 35 of the 140 seats. Left Front ministries under CPM leadership were subsequently formed in West Bengal by Jyoti Basu, in Tripura by Nripen Chakravorty and in Kerala by E. K. Nayanar. The Kerala government was defeated in elections in 1982, but the Left Front ministries retained office after elections in West Bengal in 1982 and in Tripura in 1983. In the *Lok Sabha* elections the CPM obtained 35 seats in 1980 and 22 in 1984.

Leadership. E. M. S. Namboodiripad (g.s.).

Structure. The structure of the CPM is similar to that of the Communist Party of India. It has a Central Committee of 45 members and a Political Bureau of nine members.

Membership. 267,000 (1983 claim). About 60 per cent of the membership are in West Bengal and Kerala.

Electoral influence. The CPM obtained 5.8 per cent of the vote in the 1984 elections and won 22 seats (18 in West Bengal, two in Tripura and one each in Kerala and Andhra Pradesh).

Industrial influence. The CPM controls the Centre for Indian Trade Unions, with about 1,500,000 members, and the All-India *Kisan Sabha* (Peasants' League), representing 5,700,000 agricultural workers.

Orientation. Independent. Originally pro-Chinese, the CPM adopted in 1967 a policy of equidistance between the Soviet and Chinese parties; its 1978 congress approved a resolution criticizing both Soviet "revisionism" and the Chinese three worlds theory. The 1982 congress, however, adopted resolutions supporting Soviet intervention in Afghanistan and Vietnamese intervention in Kampuchea, opposing Eurocommunism and the Polish Solidarity movement, and criticizing Chinese collaboration with the United States.

Programme. The CPM advocates making the right to work a fundamental right; expansion of the powers of the states; nationalization of monopolies; abolition of landlordism; a just and equitable incomes and wages policy; a minimum wage based on need; safeguards for the rights of Moslems; and equality for all Indian languages. It calls for a united front of left-wing parties and co-operation with "democratic bourgeois" parties against the Congress. In West Bengal the CPM-led government has pursued a policy of land reform, village development, including the provision of roads, schools and water supply, and suppression of corruption.

Publications. People's Democracy, weekly (17,500); *Lok Lahar*, Hindi weekly; daily papers in Andhra Pradesh, Kerala and West Bengal.

International affiliations. Relations with the Chinese party, the only party to recognize the CPM when it was founded, were broken off by the Chinese in 1967 and re-established in 1983. Talks with the Soviet party on the establishment of relations took place in the same year.

Communist Party of India—Marxist-Leninist (CPML)

History. The CPML was formed in 1969 by Maoists who had resigned or been expelled from the Communist Party—Marxist, with Kanu Sanyal (leader of the Naxalbari revolt of 1967) as its leader and Charu Mazumdar as general secretary. Its programme denounced "the hoax of parliamentarianism", and defined its aims as "to liberate the rural areas through armed agrarian revolution and encircle the cities, and finally to liberate the cities and thus complete the revolution throughout the country". It concentrated at first on attempting to organize peasant revolts in West Bengal, Andhra Pradesh and other states, but in 1970 it launched a terrorist campaign in Calcutta and other towns in West Bengal against "class enemies" such as businessmen, policemen and government officials, over 800 of whom were murdered in 15 months.

Mazumdar was expelled in 1971 as a "Trotskyist adventurist", and died in prison in the following year. His followers subsequently split into a pro-Lin Biao faction, who maintained that since Marshal Lin's death the Chinese Communist Party had been taken over by revisionists, and an anti-Lin Biao faction, led by Sanyal, which accepted the Chinese party's leadership. These groups broke up in turn into numerous smaller factions, which were estimated in 1983 to number nearly 50, and while continuing their terrorist activities in West Bengal, Kerala and other states also waged war on one another. Several factions united in 1982 to form the Central Reorganization Committee of the CPML, which said in a statement that despite Mazumdar's mistakes his revolutionary programme would still form the basis of the movement's activities, but criticized "one-sided emphasis on armed struggle" and the movement's failure to produce a concrete programme, which had isolated it from the people. While proclaiming support for Mao Zedong Thought, the statement condemned the "Deng-Hua clique" which had "usurped" power in China after Mao's death.

The anti-Mazumdar faction, led by Satya Narain Singh, rejected terrorism, and advocated a combination of legal and illegal activities and participation in mass movements launched by other left-wing parties. After the emergency of 1975–77, during which the CPML had been banned, Singh's faction adopted a policy of participating in elections, winning a seat in the West Bengal Assembly in 1977 and another in the Assam Assembly in the following year. It supported the Janata Party in the 1980 general election, on the ground that the other main parties were all pro-Soviet, and contested the 1982 West Bengal elections independently of other parties, without success.

Naxalites

History. The term "Naxalites" (from Naxalbari, in West Bengal, the centre of a peasant revolt in 1967) is applied to Maoists who use guerrilla or terrorist tactics, usually in rural areas, and covers some sections of the Communist Party of India-Marxist-Leninist (see above) and also independent Maoist groups. The movement is strongest in West Bengal, Bihar, Andhra Pradesh and Kerala, but Naxalite groups have also operated in Assam, Punjab and Maharashtra.

Revolutionary Socialist Party (RSP)

History. The RSP is an offshoot of the *Anushilan Samiti*, a nationalist terrorist organization later renamed the Hindustan Republican Socialist Army, and adopted its present name in 1938. It worked at first inside the Congress Socialist Party, which was affiliated to the Congress, but broke away in 1940, and operated underground until 1946.

It has obtained between one and four seats in each general election since 1952, all of them in West Bengal or Kerala. The policies of its organizations in these two states, whence it draws its main support, have not always been consistent, however, and in 1971 and 1977 it contested the general elections in alliance with the Congress in Kerala and as an opposition party in West Bengal. In Kerala it joined the United Front government of 1967–69 together with the Communist Party—Marxist (CPM) and the Communist Party of India (CPI); the CPI-led government of 1970–77, which was first supported and later joined by the Congress; and the CPM-led government of 1980–82. In West Bengal it joined the United Front government of 1969–70, and has been represented in the CPM-led government since 1977. It has also been represented in the CPM-led government in Tripura since 1978.

Leadership. Tridib Chowdhury (g.s.).

Structure. The national conference, consisting of delegates from district and state units, elects the Central Committee, the Central Executive Council and the general secretary. The Central Committee elects the seven-member Central Secretariat.

Membership. 17,500 (1984 claim).

Electoral influence. The RSP won three seats in the 1984 elections, all in West Bengal.

Orientation. Independent.

Programme. The RSP's aim is the establishment of socialist rule and working people's power.

Publications. *The Call* (5,000); *Ganavarta*, in Bengali (17,000); *Pravaham*, in Malayalam (3,500).

Socialist Unity Centre of India (SUCI)

History. The SUCI, founded in 1948, was represented in the *Lok Sabha* by one member in 1967–71. In West Bengal it held two seats in the Assembly in 1957–62, and since 1967 has held between one and seven seats. It was represented in the United Front ministries of 1967 and 1969–70, but since 1977 has refused to co-operate with the other left-wing parties. It held two seats in the Assam Assembly in 1978–83, and won one in the Orissa Assembly in 1985.

Leadership. Nihar Mukherjee (g.s.).

Structure. The SUCI is organized in the normal Communist way with a Central Committee and Political Bureau.

Membership. 165,304 (1983 claim).

Electoral influence. The SUCI's 10 candidates in the 1984 elections obtained 196,767 votes (0.78 per cent of the votes cast in West Bengal).

Orientation. Independent. The SUCI regards all other Communist parties as revisionist.

Programme. The SUCI stands for "the establishment of socialism and ultimately communism as a means to achieve a world communist society".

Publications. Organs in English, Bengali, Oriya, Assamese, Malayalam and Hindi (total circulation 200,000).

State Parties

MAHARASHTRA

Peasants' and Workers' Party of India (PWPI)

History. The PWPI, which broke away from the Congress in 1948, held two seats in the *Lok Sabha* in 1952–57, four in 1957–62 and five in 1977–80, and won one in 1984. In Maharashtra (formerly known as Bombay) it has been represented in the Assembly since 1952, its strength varying between 31 and seven members, and took part in a coalition ministry headed by the Janata Party in 1978–80.

Leadership. Dajiba Desai (g.s.).

Membership. 10,000 (1984 claim).

Orientation. Independent.

Programme. The PWPI aims to establish a people's democracy, nationalize basic industries, promote industrialization and establish a unitary state with provincial boundaries drawn on a linguistic basis.

MANIPUR

People's Liberation Army (PLA)

History. The PLA has conducted terrorist operations since its formation in 1979, and since 1981 has co-operated with the National Socialist Council of Nagaland (see below). It was declared an illegal organization in 1981. Its C.-in-C., Biseswar Singh, was captured in 1981, and his successor, Kunj Behari Singh, was killed in a clash with troops in the following year.

Membership. The PLA draws its support from the Meteis, a tribal people who represent 60 per cent of the population of Manipur.

Orientation. Maoist.

Programme. The PLA demands independence for the whole north-eastern region of India.

International affiliations. PLA members are believed to have received military training from the Chinese in Tibet.

NAGALAND

All-Nagaland Communist Party (ANCP)

History. The ANCP, formed in 1979, was believed to have its headquarters in Burmese territory, and to have close links with a force of Naga separatists which had been encamped in Burma since it returned in 1977 from receiving military training in China, and also with Naga and Arakanese separatist organizations in Burma. It was thought to be responsible for an ambush near the Burmese border in March 1979 in which seven Indian soldiers were killed.

Orientation. Maoist.

National Socialist Council of Nagaland (NSCN)

History. The NSCN broke away in 1978 from the Naga separatist movement led by A. Z. Phizo, and by 1980 was reported to have seized control of the Naga rebel forces in Burma. Heavy fighting occurred in the same year between the NSCN and the pro-Phizo forces, who collaborated with the Burmese security forces in operations against them. Since 1981 the NSCN has co-operated with the People's Liberation Army in Manipur (see above).

Leadership. Muivah Tangkul; Issak Swu.

Orientation. Maoist.

WEST BENGAL

Bolshevik Party of India (BPI)

History. The BPI was founded in 1933 as the Bengal Labour Party, and adopted its present name in 1939. It was represented in the West Bengal Assembly in 1969–71, and had one minister of state in the United Front government of 1969–70.

Orientation. Independent.

Forward Bloc—Marxist (FBM)

History. The FBM was formed in 1954 by a left-wing group which had broken away from the All-India Forward Bloc (see above). In West Bengal it has held one or two seats in each Assembly since 1957 except those of 1962–67 and 1972–77, and was represented by a minister of state in the United Front ministry of 1969–70.

Orientation. Independent.

Revolutionary Communist Party of India (RCPI)

History. The RCPI was founded in 1934 by former members of the Communist Party who opposed its policy of co-operation with the Congress. For some years after the attainment of independence it pursued a policy of armed struggle, the most notable example of which was a raid on Dum Dum airport (Calcutta) in 1949, but it later abandoned this strategy. In West Bengal, where it has held two or three seats in the Assembly in 1969–72 and again since 1977, it was included in the United Front ministry of 1969–70 and has held office in the Left Front government since 1977. It also held a seat in the Assam Assembly in 1957–67.

Leadership. Sudhin Kumar (sec.).

Orientation. Independent.

Indonesia

Capital: Jakarta   Pop. 169,442,000

The Netherlands East Indies were occupied by the Japanese from 1942 to 1945. The independent Republic of Indonesia, with Dr Achmed Sukarno as President, was proclaimed by the nationalists when Japan surrendered, and after an armed struggle was recognized by the Netherlands in 1949. President Sukarno attempted to govern through an alliance of nationalist, Moslem and Communist parties, but following the attempted Communist coup of 1965 he was removed from office in 1967 and succeeded by a military regime headed by Gen. Suharto.

Communist Party of Indonesia
Partai Komunis Indonesia (PKI)

History. The Indies Social Democratic Organization, founded in 1914, was renamed the Communist Party of the Indies in 1920, becoming the first communist party in Asia, and assumed its present name in 1924. It organized unsuccessful armed uprisings in West Java and Central Sumatra in 1926–27, and was subsequently banned, some of its members being executed and over 10,000 others imprisoned or deported to Dutch New Guinea. After the Japanese occupation, during which it took part in the resistance movement, it emerged from underground in 1945 and joined the nationalist revolt against Dutch rule. In 1948, however, it staged an abortive coup against the nationalist government in East Java, with the result that most of its leaders were killed or executed.

Under the leadership of Dwipa Nusantara Aidit, M. H. Lukman and Njoto, who took control in 1951, the PKI adopted a strongly nationalist policy, supporting the demand for the annexation of Dutch New Guinea and the government's opposition to the formation of the Malaysian Federation. Popular support grew rapidly; in the 1955 elections the PKI obtained 6,176,914 votes (16.4 per cent), emerging as the fourth strongest party, and its membership increased from 7,900 in 1952 to an estimated 1,750,000 in 1962. It also won the support of President Sukarno, who appointed Aidit and Lukman ministers without portfolio in 1962 and Njoto a minister in 1964. In May 1965 Aidit claimed that the PKI had 3,000,000 members, making it the largest Communist Party in the world outside China and the Soviet Union, in addition to 3,000,000 members of its youth movement and 20,000,000 sympathizers. In the Sino-Soviet controversy the PKI strongly supported China.

On Oct. 1, 1965, a group of Communist officers, believing a right-wing coup to be imminent, themselves carried out a coup in Jakarta in which six generals were murdered. The revolt, for which the PKI had declared its support, was almost immediately crushed, and a massacre followed in which at least 500,000 known or suspected Communists, including Aidit and most of the other party leaders, were murdered by Moslem mobs or by the army. About 700,000 people were arrested, and in 1966 the PKI was banned, although it maintained a guerrilla resistance in Central and East Java and West Borneo until 1968. Arrests and trials of Communists continued for many years; 37,000 were officially stated to be still detained in 1981, and executions of Communists sentenced years earlier were still continuing in 1985.

The PKI now consists of small groups of exiles living in China or Eastern Europe, who are divided into pro-Chinese and pro-Soviet factions. It is not known whether any underground organization exists in Indonesia.

Leadership. Jusuf Adjitorop (g.s., pro-Chinese faction); Satiadjaya Sudiman (g.s., pro-Soviet faction).

Membership. Pro-Chinese faction 200; pro-Soviet faction 50 (1983 estimate).

Orientation. Divided.

International affiliations. The pro-Soviet faction is represented on the editorial council of *World Marxist Review*.

East Timor

After the revolution of 1974 the Portuguese government announced that elections would be held in 1976 in East Timor, hitherto a Portuguese colony, and that Portuguese sovereignty would end not later than 1978. Civil war broke out in 1975 between pro- and anti-Indonesian forces, however, whereupon Indonesian troops invaded East Timor, which was annexed in the following year.

Revolutionary Front for the Independence of East Timor
Frente Revolucionaria de Timor Leste Independente (Fretilin)

History. Founded in 1974 as the Timorese Social Democratic Association, *Fretilin* advocated full independence for East Timor, and in September 1975 defeated the pro-Indonesian parties and took control of the colony. Two months later it proclaimed the Democratic Republic of East Timor, with Francisco Xavier do Amaral as President. After the Indonesian invasion, during which 60,000–100,000 suspected *Fretilin* supporters were massacred, it maintained a guerrilla resistance which was still in progress in 1986. Amaral was expelled from the party in 1977 as a "capitulationist", and was succeeded as President by Nicolau dos Reis Lobato, who was killed in battle in 1979.

Leadership. José Gusmao Sha Na Na (leader of the Revolutionary Council of the Resistance).

Membership. *Fretilin* claimed in 1982 to have six regular companies (about 6,800 men) fighting in central and southern East Timor. An Indonesian military spokesman, however, estimated its strength in December 1984 at between 500 and 700 armed men.

Japan

Capital: Tokyo

Pop. 119,400,000

After World War II Japan was occupied by US and British Commonwealth forces. A democratic constitution was introduced in 1946, the first elections under it being held in the following year. Since 1948 the conservative Liberal–Democratic Party has been in office.

The occupation regime was ended in 1951, when a peace treaty was signed with the Western allies, although a separate treaty with the United States permitted the retention of US forces in Japan. This was superseded in 1960 by a security treaty providing for the maintenance of US military bases. The state of war between Japan and the Soviet Union was ended in 1956, but no peace treaty has been signed, as the Soviet Union has consistently refused to return the southern Kurile Islands, which it has occupied since 1945.

Communist Party—Marxist–Leninist (CPM–L)

History. The Japanese Communist Party (Left), to which the CPM–L is the successor, was founded in 1969 by Maoists who had resigned or been expelled from the Japan Communist Party. Originally pro-Chinese, it condemned "the counter-revolutionary renegade line of Chinese revisionism, represented by the theory of three worlds", at its 1978 congress. It adopted its present name in 1980, when it merged with the Japanese Communist Party—Marxist–Leninist, another small Maoist organization.

Leadership. Chaji Harada (ch.); Takaharu Samioka (g.s.).

Orientation. Independent Maoist.

Publication. *Jinmin Shinpo*.

Japan Communist Party (JCP)
Nihon Kyosanto

History. Founded in 1922, the JCP remained illegal until 1945, its membership never exceeding 1,000. After the war it pursued a moderate policy, and its membership grew rapidly, reaching 100,000 in 1947. It won four seats in the House of Representatives in 1947 and 35 in 1949, when it received 9.6 per cent of the vote. In 1950, however, it was criticized by the Cominform for believing that a peaceful transition to socialism was possible in the presence of the US occupation forces, whereupon it began advocating the use of force, and in 1952 was responsible for anti-US riots in Tokyo. Its membership fell heavily in consequence, and in the 1952 elections it lost all its seats. The leadership admitted its "leftist errors" in 1956, and the 1961 congress adopted a programme which advocated the attainment of power through parliamentary means.

The JCP adopted a pro-Chinese attitude in the Sino–Soviet controversy in 1963, the pro-Soviet section of the leadership, including two members of the House of Representatives, being expelled in the following year. In 1967, however, it took up an independent position, the pro-Chinese leaders in turn being expelled, and has since been extremely critical of both the Soviet and the Chinese parties. A special party convention in 1976 dropped the phrase "dictatorship of the proletariat" from its programme, replaced the term "Marxism–Leninism" by "scientific socialism" and adopted a declaration of respect for human rights, freedom of speech and thought, personal property and the multiparty system. It has since condemned the Chinese invasion of Vietnam in 1979, Soviet policies in Afghanistan and Poland, and the North Korean government's use of terrorist methods.

After the defeat of 1952 the JCP's parliamentary representation gradually increased, reaching 14 seats in 1969 and 38 in 1972. It fell to 17 in 1976, rose to

39 in 1979, and again fell to 29 in 1980 and 26 in 1983. Its membership, which in 1958 was only 30,000, rose to 195,000 in 1966 and over 370,000 in 1976.

Leadership. Kenji Miyamoto (ch. of the Central Committee); Tetsuzo Fuwa (ch. of the Presidium).

Structure. The JCP is organized in residential and workplace branches, which are subordinate to district and prefectural organizations. The congress, meeting every three years, elects the Central Committee of 189 full and 22 candidate members, which elects the chairman and Presidium. The Presidium elects the Permanent Bureau and Secretariat.

Membership. 480,000 (1984 estimate).

Electoral influence. In each election since 1972 the JCP has received between 9 and 10.5 per cent of the vote. In 1983 it received 5,302,485 votes (9.34 per cent).

Orientation. Eurocommunist.

Programme. The JCP envisages the achievement of socialism through parliamentary means, and advocates the nationalization of key industries but not of small enterprises, agriculture or fisheries. It calls for the adoption of a non-aligned foreign policy, abrogation of the US–Japanese security treaty, the return to Japan of the southern Kurile Islands, and reduced defence spending.

Publications. *Akahata* (Red Banner), daily (620,000, Sunday circulation 2,480,000); *Zen'ei* (Vanguard), monthly.

International affiliations. The JCP has close relations with the Eurocommunist parties of Western Europe and the Yugoslav and Romanian Communist parties, but its relations with the Soviet, Chinese and North Korean parties are strained. Although represented on the editorial council of *World Marxist Review*, it has criticized the magazine's pro-Soviet bias.

Voice of Japan

History. This small party was formed in 1964 by pro-Soviet Communists expelled from the Japan Communist Party.

Leadership. Yoshio Shiga.

Orientation. Pro-Soviet.

International affiliations. The Voice of Japan has been supported in the past by the Soviet Communist Party.

Terrorist Organization

United Red Army (URA)
Rengo Sekigun

History. The URA was formed in 1969 as an offshoot of the Communist League, a Trotskyist organization. Between 1970 and 1977 it was responsible for a number of hijackings and acts of terrorism inside and outside Japan, some of which were carried out in co-operation with the Popular Front for the Liberation of Palestine (PFLP—see under main heading "Palestinian Movements"), the most notorious being the murder of 26 people at Lod airport (Israel) in 1972 by three

URA members who opened fire indiscriminately. The URA, which has its headquarters in Lebanon, was reported in 1982 to have announced that it had given up terrorism because it had failed to win international support.

Leadership. Miss Fusako Shigenobu (supreme commander).

Membership. The Japanese police estimated in 1978 that the URA had 30 members and over 100 sympathizers.

Programme. URA statements have called for a revolution in Japan, the overthrow of the monarchy and the establishment of a people's republic.

International affiliations. Apart from the PFLP, the URA was reported in the 1970s to have links with terrorist movements in other countries, including the Red Army Faction in West Germany and Basque Nation and Liberty (ETA) and the Revolutionary Anti-fascist Patriotic Front (FRAP) in Spain.

Kampuchea

Capital: Phnom-Penh   Pop. 6,118,000

The Kingdom of Kampuchea (Cambodia), which since 1867 had been a French protectorate, in 1948 became an independent state within the French Union, from which it withdrew in 1955. As head of state Prince Norodom Sihanouk attempted to pursue a neutral policy, which brought him into conflict with the United States, South Vietnam and Thailand, and in 1970 was overthrown by a military coup, a republic being established. A civil war followed, in which the republicans were supported by the United States and South Vietnam and Prince Sihanouk by the Kampuchean Communists and North Vietnam. After the defeat of the republicans in 1975 a coalition government was formed, with Prince Sihanouk as head of state; in the following year, however, he was replaced by Khieu Samphan, a Communist constitution was adopted, under which the country was renamed Democratic Kampuchea, and a Communist government was formed, with Pol Pot as Prime Minister. Its repressive policies led to a series of revolts, and repeated Kampuchean attacks on Vietnamese territory developed into war in 1977. Vietnamese troops occupied Kampuchea at the beginning of 1979, expelled the Pol Pot government from Phnom-Penh and set up a government headed by Heng Samrin, Kampuchea again being renamed the People's Republic of Kampuchea. Fighting continued in the Thai border area, however, and in 1982 an alliance was formed between Pol Pot's supporters and two non-Communist resistance groups headed by Prince Sihanouk and Son Sann.

Kampuchean People's Revolutionary Party (KPRP)

History. The Communist Party of Indo-China, to which the KPRP is a successor, was founded in 1930 and divided into separate parties for Vietnam, Kampuchea and Laos in 1951, the Kampuchean party calling itself the Kampuchean People's Revolutionary Party. The party was split, however, between a pro-Vietnamese faction, nicknamed the Vietminh Khmers, which favoured collaboration with Prince Sihanouk against the French, and a faction led by Pol Pot (then known as Saloth Sar) which advocated his overthrow. After the defeat of the French in 1954 many of the former faction settled in North Vietnam, enabling their opponents to gain control of the party. As a cover for its activities a legal party, the Party of the Masses (*Pracheachon*), was founded, but this achieved little success, and a policy was adopted of infiltrating the Popular Socialist Community (*Sangkum*), the government party founded by Prince Sihanouk.

At its second congress, held in secret in Phnom-Penh in 1960, the KPRP changed its name to the Communist Party of Kampuchea (CPK), and decided to combine revolutionary armed violence with "legal, semi-legal and illegal struggle". The Sino–Soviet controversy led to a conflict between the supporters of North Vietnam, which sought to play a mediating role between China and the Soviet Union, and the Maoists led by Pol Pot. The general secretary, Tou Samout, was assassinated in 1962, allegedly by supporters of Pol Pot, who was elected his successor in the following year. In 1968 the CPK led a peasant revolt in Battambang province, which rapidly spread to many of the other provinces, and the rebels were joined by Khieu Samphan and other *Sangkum* members of Parliament who were secret Communists.

On the outbreak of civil war in 1970 the CPK formed an alliance with Prince Sihanouk's supporters, and Khieu Samphan and other Communists joined the government-in-exile which he had set up in Beijing. Hundreds of the Vietminh Khmers returned to Kampuchea to take part in the struggle, but in 1973 Pol Pot launched a purge of the pro-Vietnamese faction, many of whom took refuge in Vietnam. The CPK government which took power in 1976 (see under "Party of Democratic Kampuchea") was drawn entirely from Pol Pot's supporters.

A military revolt against the Pol Pot regime broke out in May 1978 in the south-eastern provinces under the leadership of Vice-President Sau Phim, who was killed in the fighting, and in December the Kampuchean National United Front for National Salvation was formed in the "liberated zone" by Vietminh Khmers and disillusioned Pol Pot supporters to work for the overthrow of the regime, under the leadership of Heng Samrin, a CPK official who had joined the revolt. After the overthrow of the Pol Pot government in January 1979 a provisional government was formed in Phnom-Penh, with Heng Samrin as President. A reorganization congress of the CPK was held in the same month, at which it was decided that the party should revert to its original name of the KPRP, to distinguish it from Pol Pot's party, Pen Sovan being elected general secretary. He was removed from his post in 1981, officially for health reasons, and was succeeded by Heng Samrin.

Leadership. The Political Bureau consists of Heng Samrin (g.s.), Chea Sim, Hun Sen, Say Phuthang, Bou Thang, Chea Soth, Men Samon, Mat Ly and Nay Pena (full members), Chan Seng and Nguon Nhel (alternate members).

Structure. The 1985 congress elected a 31-member Central Committee, which elected the Political Bureau and Secretariat.

Membership. 700 (1985 estimate).

Electoral influence. All candidates in the 1981 elections were put forward by the Kampuchean National United Front for National Salvation (later renamed the Kampuchean United Front for National Construction and Defence), which is dominated by the KPRP.

Orientation. Pro-Soviet.

Programme. The programme adopted by the 1981 KPRP congress envisaged a mixed economy, with three sections: the state section, covering major industries, transport, communications and trade; the collective section, consisting of "solidarity teams" in agriculture, fishing, forestry and craftsmanship; and the private section, covering small-scale agriculture, industry, craftsmanship and trade.

Publications. Kampuchea; *Kaset Kantoap Padivoat* (Revolutionary Army).

International affiliations. The KPRP has close links with the Communist parties of Vietnam and Laos.

Party of Democratic Kampuchea (PDK)

History. For the early history of the Communist Party of Kampuchea (CPK), the predecessor of the PDK, see entry for "Kampuchean People's Revolutionary Party" above. The CPK joined in 1970 the government-in-exile formed by Prince Sihanouk, which took control after the fall of Phnom-Penh in 1975. When Prince Sihanouk's supporters were ousted in the following year Khieu Samphan became President and Pol Pot formed a CPK government, which introduced a form of communism more radical than in any other country. The inhabitants of the towns were forced to leave for the countryside; communes on the Chinese model were established; private property and money were abolished; families were broken up; the practice of religion was forbidden; and the intellectuals and the middle classes were virtually wiped out by mass executions. All opposition was ruthlessly suppressed, many leading members of the government, the CPK and the army being executed in a series of purges. The total number of deaths under the regime has been estimated at over 2,700,000.

After the Vietnamese invasion in 1979 the Pol Pot government transferred its headquarters to the Thai frontier area, where it maintained a guerrilla resistance with the aid of military supplies from China reaching Kampuchea through Thailand. In September 1979 it announced the foundation of the "Patriotic and Democratic Front of the Great National Union of Kampuchea", with a programme of expulsion of the Vietnamese and establishment of a democratic and non-aligned Kampuchea, and in December a new government was formed with Khieu Samphan as Prime Minister, Pol Pot becoming C.-in-C. The CPK was officially stated in 1981 to have been dissolved "to conform with the new strategic line, which does not pursue socialism and communism", although Prince Sihanouk maintained a year later that it still existed, with Pol Pot as its general secretary. After its alleged dissolution the CPK was referred to as the Party of Democratic Kampuchea, the official name of the country in 1976–79, or as the Red Khmers (*Khmers Rouges*). The PDK formed a coalition government in 1982 with Prince Sihanouk's supporters and the Khmer People's National Liberation Front, led by Son Sann, in which the three parties were equally represented, Prince Sihanouk becoming President, Khieu Samphan Vice-President and Foreign Minister and Son Sann Prime Minister. Pol Pot was officially stated in 1985 to have been replaced as C.-in-C. of the PDK forces by Son Sen.

Leadership. Khieu Samphan (ch.); Son Sen (vice-ch.).

Membership. The PDK armed forces are estimated at 10,000 to 30,000 men.

Orientation. Pro-Chinese.

Programme. The PDK officially supports the programme of the Patriotic and Democratic Front, which calls for the expulsion of the Vietnamese, the election of a National Assembly under UN supervision, a multiparty system, freedom of speech, the press and religion, and an economy based on "individual or family production activity", in which private property would be guaranteed.

International affiliations. The PDK has close links with the Chinese Communist Party.

Democratic People's Republic of Korea

Capital: Pyongyang   Pop. 19,630,000

Korea, which had been annexed by Japan in 1910, was occupied in 1945 by Soviet troops north of the 38th parallel and US troops south of it. Although this division had been intended to be temporary, separate elections were held in the North and the South in 1948 and separate constitutions adopted, under which North Korea was named the Democratic People's Republic of Korea and South Korea the Republic of Korea. The Soviet occupation forces were withdrawn in the same year, and the US forces in 1949. North Korean troops invaded the South in 1950, and a war followed in which the South Koreans were assisted by US, British Commonwealth and other Western forces and the North Koreans by Chinese troops. An armistice was concluded in 1953, the new division between the North and South following the cease-fire line. Talks on reunification took place between representatives of North and South Korea in 1972–73 and 1979–80, but without success.

Korean Workers' Party (KWP)
Choson Nodong-dang

History. The Korean Communist Party, founded in 1925, was virtually destroyed three years later by mass arrests. It subsequently split into three main groups: the "domestic faction", led by Pak Hon Yong, which continued to work underground inside Korea; the "Manchurian group", led by Kim Il Sung, which conducted a guerrilla war against the Japanese in Manchuria from 1934 onwards, was forced to retreat to Siberia in 1940 and returned with the Soviet army in 1945; and the "Yenan group", which escaped to China, where they collaborated with the Chinese Communists against the Japanese.

In South Korea the Communist Party was revived in 1945 by Pak Hon Yong, and merged in the following year with the People's Party under the name of the South Korean Workers' Party. A separate North Korean Communist Party was formed in 1945 by the Manchurian group and the "Soviet group", consisting of Koreans who had lived in Siberia, under the leadership of Kim Il Sung, who became Prime Minister in the following year, and merged in 1946 with the New People's Party, which had been formed by the Yenan group, in the North Korean Workers' Party. The South Korean Communist leaders subsequently took refuge in the North, and in 1949 the North and South Korean Workers' parties were united in a single party. Many of the Communists who had remained in the South were executed during the war of 1950–53 or fled to the North; after the war the survivors attempted to organize guerrilla bands, but by 1955 these had all been wiped out.

In North Korea a number of leaders of the domestic faction were executed in 1953 on a charge of being US spies, and Pak Hon Yong suffered the same fate two years later. The Soviet group was purged in 1956 after it had demanded a slowing of the pace of collectivization and industrialization and attacked the cult of Kim Il Sung, and the Yenan group was also purged in 1958, leaving Kim's Manchurian group in control of the party; the leaders of the two factions were allowed to return to the Soviet Union or China, however, following Soviet intercession.

During the Sino–Soviet controversy the KWP at first supported China, but in 1966 it issued a statement accusing the Chinese party of attempting to dictate to other parties, and declaring that no Communist Party must be "ideologically chained to anyone". It has since combined an independent attitude with the maintenance of friendly relations with both China and the Soviet Union, although on some questions, such as the war between Vietnam and Kampuchea, it has adopted a position closer to that of the Chinese party. It has neither condemned nor endorsed the Soviet intervention in Afghanistan.

After Kim Il Sung's election as President in 1972 a struggle is believed to have taken place over the succession. The election of his eldest son, Kim Chong Il, in 1980 to the KWP's Presidium, Political Bureau, Secretariat and Military Commission was regarded as equivalent to his formal recognition as President Kim's successor. Although opposition continued at least until 1983, when over 1,000 political and military leaders were reported to have been purged, by 1984 Kim Chong Il had effectively taken power.

Leadership. The Presidium of the Political Bureau, the highest party body, consists of President Kim Il Sung (g.s.), Kim Chong Il and Gen. Oh Jin Wu. There are also 14 other full members of the Political Bureau and 18 alternate members.

Structure. The KWP is organized in residential and workplace cells, which are subordinate to the regional and provincial organizations. The party congress, which nominally meets every four years, although in fact only two congresses have been held since 1961, elects the Central Committee (145 full and 103 alternate members), which elects the Political Bureau, the 12-member Secretariat and the general secretary. A new body, the Presidium of the Political Bureau, was created in 1980.

Membership. 3,000,000 (1985 claim).

Electoral influence. All candidates for the Supreme People's Assembly are approved by the KWP. It is regularly claimed after each election that the entire electorate has voted for the official candidates.

Industrial influence. The KWP controls the General Federation of Trade Unions of Korea, which has about 2,000,000 members.

Orientation. Independent.

Programme. The KWP bases its policy on the principle of *juche*, variously translated as "self-reliance" and "national identity". President Kim defined this in 1975 as involving an ideological revolution, aimed at "revolutionizing and 'working-classizing' all members of society to make them men of a communist type"; a technical revolution to "free the working people from heavy labour"; and a cultural revolution to "intellectualize the whole of society". It proposes to solve the Korean question by the formation of a confederation, in which the North and South would each exercise regional autonomy and would retain its own ideology and social system, with a Supreme National Confederal Assembly containing equal numbers of representatives from the North and the South, a Confederal Standing Committee which would decide on defence, foreign policy and other matters of common concern, and a single national army.

Publications. Nodong Sinmun (Workers' Daily), daily (1,000,000); *Kulloja* (Working People), monthly (100,000).

International affiliations. While insisting on its independence, the KWP maintains relations with pro-Soviet, pro-Chinese, Eurocommunist and independent communist parties. It is not represented on the editorial council of *World Marxist Review.*

Laos

Capital: Vientiane   Pop. 3,732,000

The Kingdom of Laos, a French protectorate since 1895, was occupied by the Japanese in 1941. The Free Lao movement, which originated as a resistance movement during the Japanese occupation, continued to oppose the French after their reoccupation of Laos in 1945. It split in 1949, however, when a treaty was signed recognizing Laos as an independent state within the French Union, the majority of its leaders joining the government while the Communists continued to maintain a guerrilla resistance.

A government of national union was formed in 1957, but was replaced by a right-wing government in the following year. A civil war broke out in 1960, in which the centrist group or "neutralists" were allied with the Lao People's Party (Communists) against the right-wing forces, and ended with the formation of a new government of national union in 1962, but this arrangement broke down in the following year, when the neutralists split into left- and right-wing factions. A new civil war ensued in 1964, in which the right and the right-wing neutralists were supported by the United States and Thailand and the Communists and left-wing neutralists by North Vietnam, and continued until 1973, when a cease-fire agreement was signed.

A third government of national union was formed in 1974, but disintegrated in the following year, when the right-wing ministers fled the country. The Communists thereupon seized control of the towns, the King abdicated and Laos was proclaimed a People's Democratic Republic, with Prince Souphanouvong as President. A government was then formed by Kaysone Phomvihan, the Communist leader.

Lao People's Revolutionary Party (LPRP)
Phak Pasason Pativat Lao

History. The Lao section of the Communist Party of Indo-China, founded in 1930, to which the LPRP is the successor, formed in 1944 its own military organization, the *Pathet Lao,* which operated inside the anti-Japanese and anti-French Free Lao movement, and in 1953 seized control of the north-eastern provinces of Phong Saly and Sam Neua. The Lao People's Party was founded in 1955, with Kaysone Phomvihan as general secretary, and took part in the governments of national union of 1957–58, 1962–63 and 1974–75. Renamed the Lao People's Revolutionary Party in 1975, it seized power in the same year.

Leadership. The Political Bureau consists of Kaysone Phomvihan (g.s.), Nouhak Phoumsavan, President Souphanouvong, Phoumi Vongvichit, Khamtai Siphandon, Phoun Sipaseut and Sisomphon Lovansai.

Structure. The LPRP has a Central Committee of 47 full and six alternate members, a seven-member Political Bureau and a nine-member Secretariat.

Membership. 35,000 (1985 estimate).

Electoral influence. All candidates in the 1975 elections, the last held, were approved by the LPRP.

Orientation. Pro-Soviet. Until 1978 the LPRP attempted to maintain a neutral attitude towards the controversies between the Soviet Union and Vietnam on the one hand and China and Kampuchea on the other, but since the Vietnamese intervention in Kampuchea and the Chinese invasion of Vietnam in 1979 its relations with China have been strained.

Programme. The LPRP envisages a gradual transition to socialism in a series of stages covering a long period. In the present stage the economy consists of five sectors: state enterprises (mining, railways, the state airline, exports and major factories), co-operatives, joint state-private enterprises, the individual sector (farmers, craftsmen and small traders) and capitalist enterprises. A policy of rapid formation of agricultural co-operatives adopted in 1978 was abandoned in the following year. Government policy has largely concentrated on the attainment of self-sufficiency in food production and the elimination of illiteracy.

Publication. Pasason (The People), daily (10,000).

International affiliations. The LPRP has close relations with the Vietnamese Communist Party and the Kampuchean People's Revolutionary Party.

Malaysia

Capital: Kuala Lumpur   Pop. 15,330,000

Malaya was overrun in 1941–42 by the Japanese, who surrendered in 1945. The British-protected Malay States and the crown colony of the Straits Settlements were united in 1948 in the Federation of Malaya, which became independent in 1957. Malaya in turn united in 1963 with Singapore, Sarawak and Sabah (British North Borneo) to form the Federation of Malaysia, from which Singapore seceded two years later. Since then the Malaysian government's policy of promoting the economic interests of the ethnic Malay community has been criticized by non-Malay groups amid continuing underlying inter-communal tensions from which left-wing parties have derived some political benefit.

Communist Party of Malaya (CPM)

History. The South Seas Communist Party, formed in Singapore in 1928, was renamed the Communist Party of Malaya two years later, and although illegal acquired considerable influence in the trade union movement. During the Japanese occupation it organized the Malayan People's Anti-Japanese Army, which led the resistance movement. Legalized in 1945, it was banned three years later when it launched a guerrilla campaign against British rule, and a state of emergency was declared. Peace talks in 1955 between Chin Peng, the CPM general secretary, and the Chief Ministers of Malaya and Singapore produced no result, as the Communists refused to dissolve their party. The revolt was virtually crushed by 1960, when the state of emergency was ended, after 6,710 of the rebels had been killed, and in 1961 Chin Peng settled in Beijing, while retaining the general secretaryship. Small bands nevertheless continued guerrilla activities in the jungle areas on either side of the Thai border, often in co-operation with the Communist Party of Thailand, and joint operations have periodically been launched against them by Malaysian and Thai troops since 1977. Musa bin Ahmad, the CPM chairman, who had lived in Beijing since 1956, returned to Malaysia in 1980 and surrendered to the authorities.

Leadership. Chin Peng (g.s.).

Membership. 2,000 guerrillas in Thailand and 260 in Malaysia (1985 estimate). The great majority of the members are drawn from the Chinese community, which forms about 35 per cent of the population.

Orientation. Pro-Chinese.

Programme. A new party constitution adopted in 1980 described the CPM as a proletarian party guided by Marxism–Leninism–Mao Zedong Thought, and declared that the revolution could attain victory not through parliamentary democracy, armed uprising in the cities or urban guerrilla war, but only by "using the countryside to encircle the cities and seize political power by armed force". In a policy statement issued in 1984, however, it adopted a much more moderate attitude, advocating free distribution of land to landless peasants, respect for the power of the sultans over the management of state land, protection of the land of landlords who supported the establishment of a democratic coalition government, and protection of estates and industrial enterprises owned by small or medium national capitalists. The CPM retains its pre-1963 name because it does not recognize the existence of the Federation of Malaysia or the independence of Singapore, where it also operates.

Publication. The CPM broadcasts through the "Voice of Malayan Democracy", which is believed to operate from southern China.

International affiliations. The CPM has close relations with the Chinese Communist Party, although the latter claims that it gives the CPM only "moral support".

Communist Party of Malaysia (MCP)

History. The MCP was formed in 1983 by the merger of the Communist Party of Malaya—Revolutionary Faction and the Communist Party of Malaya—Marxist–Leninist (CPMM–L), which broke away from the Communist Party of Malaya (CPM) in 1970 and 1974 respectively. Both groups rejected the Maoist theory of using the countryside to encircle the cities as unworkable in Malaysia, where the rural population is predominantly Malay, whereas the CPM membership is mainly Chinese, and advocated rallying support among the Chinese population in the towns and the use of urban guerrilla warfare. Fighting occurred between CPM and CPMM–L forces in southern Thailand in 1982.

Leadership. Ah Leng (g.s.); Huang Chen (deputy g.s.).

Membership. 800 (1985 estimate).

Orientation. Pro-Chinese.

Programme. The MCP, unlike the CPM, recognizes the existence of Malaysia and the independence of Singapore, and seeks to win the support of both the Malay peasantry and the urban Chinese.

Publication. The MCP broadcasts through the "Voice of the People of Malaysia", a clandestine radio station the location of which is unknown.

Islamic Brotherhood Party (*Paperi*)

History. The *Paperi*, founded in 1965, is a front organization for the Communist Party of Malaya, intended to appeal to dissident Moslems and ethnic Malays.

Malayan People's Liberation Front (MPLF)

History. The MPLF, founded in 1968 as the Malayan National Liberation Front and renamed in 1984, describes itself as a revolutionary mass underground group armed with Marxism–Leninism–Mao Zedong Thought and led by the Communist Party of Malaya, of which it constitutes the urban wing.

Malayan People's Liberation League (MPLL)

History. The MPLL, known until 1983 as the Malayan People's Liberation Union, is a front organization for the Communist Party of Malaysia.

Malay Nationalist Revolutionary Party of Malaya (MNRPM)
Partai Kebangsaan Melayu Revolusioner Malaya

History. The MNRPM, founded in 1981, is a front organization for the Communist Party of Malaya, intended to secure the support of the Moslem community.

Leadership. C. D. Abdullah (ch.).

Orientation. Pro-Chinese.

Programme. The MNRPM advocates unity of Communists, Socialists, nationalists and religious groups in an anti-imperialist national united front, to form a national democratic coalition government and pursue a non-aligned foreign policy. It lays great emphasis on Islamic teachings in its propaganda.

North Kalimantan Communist Party (NKCP)

History. The NKCP, founded in the 1950s, has conducted guerrilla operations in Sarawak. It has no organizational connection and little contact with the Communist Party of Malaya.

Membership. 100 (1985 estimate).

Orientation. Pro-Chinese.

Programme. The NKCP demands independence for Sarawak.

Mongolia

Capital: Ulan Bator   Pop. 1,860,000

Outer Mongolia, previously a Chinese province, declared itself an independent state in 1911, with the Living Buddha of Urga as the Bogdo Gegen (head of state). It was occupied in 1919 by Chinese troops, who were expelled in 1921 by White Russian forces. The White regime was overthrown a few months later by

Mongolian nationalists, aided by the Soviet army, and the Bogdo Gegen's government was re-established. On his death in 1924 the Mongolian People's Revolutionary Party took power, and a constitution on the Soviet model was introduced under which Mongolia was declared a People's Republic, thus becoming the second oldest Communist state in the world.

Mongolian People's Revolutionary Party (MPRP)
Mongol Ardyn Khuvagalt Nam

History. The Mongolian People's Party was formed in 1921 by the merger of two nationalist groups led by Sukhe Bator and Choibalsan, and organized a small force which co-operated with the Soviet army in overthrowing the White Russian regime. The party, which was renamed the Mongolian People's Revolutionary Party in 1924, was represented in the new government only by Sukhe Bator, who died in 1923, but after the Bogdo Gegen's death in the following year Soviet support enabled it to concentrate power in its own hands. Although the 1925 party congress adopted a resolution declaring that Mongolia would be transformed to a socialist country without passing through a capitalist stage, no radical changes were made until 1928, when a policy was adopted of collectivization of agriculture, confiscation of the estates of princes and lamas, banning private trade and opposition to religion. These measures aroused such strong resistance that they were abandoned or modified in 1932. A series of purges took place between 1922 and 1939, in which many party leaders who advocated greater independence of the Soviet Union were executed.

Choibalsan, the only member of the original leadership who survived the purges, became Prime Minister in 1939, and on his death in 1952 was succeeded by Yumjaagyin Tsedenbal, who also took over the general secretaryship of the MPRP in 1958. After attempting to remain neutral in the Sino–Soviet controversy, the party adopted a pro-Soviet attitude in 1961, with the result that relations with China have since been extremely strained. Tsedenbal was elected President in 1974, but resigned all his posts for health reasons 10 years later; Jambyn Batmounkh succeeded him as Prime Minister in 1974 and as general secretary and President in 1984, and was himself succeeded as Prime Minister in 1984 by Dumaagiyn Sodnom.

Leadership. The Political Bureau consists of Jambyn Batmounkh (g.s.), Bat-Ochirym Altangerel, Dumaagiyn Sodnom, Tumenbayaryn Ragchaa, Damdiny Gombojav, Demchigiyn Molomjants, Bujyn Dejid, Tserendashiyn Namsray and two candidate members.

Structure. Branches are formed on a residential or workplace basis, and organizations exist at regional, city and district level. The congress, meeting every five years, elects the Central Committee (91 full and 71 candidate members), which elects the Political Bureau and Secretariat. The party's youth organization is the Mongolian Revolutionary Youth League.

Membership. 76,240 (1981 claim).

Electoral influence. In the 1981 elections to the People's Great Hural the single list of MPRP and non-party candidates was officially stated to have received 99.9 per cent of the votes.

Industrial influence. The MPRP controls the Central Council of Mongolian Trade Unions, which has 400,000 members.

Orientation. Pro-Soviet.

Programme. MPRP policy statements concentrate on increasing agricultural and industrial production, enlargement of the area under cultivation and development of the mining industry.

Publication. Unen (Truth), daily.

International affiliations. The MPRP has always had close associations with the Soviet party. It is represented on the editorial board of *World Marxist Review*.

Nepal

Capital: Katmandu   Pop. 17,000,000

The Kingdom of Nepal was ruled by the Rana family, who held the hereditary office of Prime Minister, from 1846 to 1950, when they were overthrown by a popular revolt and the King resumed an active political role. A Parliament was elected in 1959, but in December 1960 King Mahendra dissolved it, arrested most of its members and dismissed the government, all political parties being banned in the following month. A "basic democracy" system was introduced in 1962, whereby village and town councils (*panchayats*) elected district councils, which in turn elected members to the National Council, other members of which were nominated by the King. Indirect election of the National Council was replaced in 1980 by direct election, but the ban on parties remained in force.

Communist Party of Nepal (CPN)

History. The CPN was founded in Calcutta in 1949 by a group of Nepalese exiles led by Pushpa Lal. After the revolution of 1950 it operated openly in Nepal, but was banned in 1952 for alleged complicity in an attempted left-wing coup in Katmandu. It nevertheless received over half the votes in the Katmandu municipal elections in the following year, winning five of the 18 seats. Legalized in 1956, it obtained 7.5 per cent of the vote and four of the 109 seats in the 1959 parliamentary elections.

After the royal coup of 1960 and the banning of political parties a section of the CPN leadership, including Pushpa Lal, escaped to India, where they issued a statement calling for the overthrow of the royal regime. Another section led by Keshar Jung Raimajhi, the general secretary, however, offered to co-operate with the regime and formally dissolved the party, although in fact it continued to operate underground. The split became complete in 1962, when Pushpa Lal's group set up a separate organization. Although the differences between them were concerned with tactics rather than ideology, Pushpa Lal's faction adopted a pro-Chinese and Raimajhi's a pro-Soviet attitude.

In the 1963 elections to the National Council, although they were not contested on party lines, at least three Communists were returned as independents, and Raimajhi's section of the party has since continued to agitate, in alliance with the Nepali Congress and other banned parties, for the legalization of political parties, the release of political prisoners and the restoration of human rights. In recent years, however, it has split into three factions, led by Raimajhi, Bishnu Bahadur Manandhar and Tulsi Lal Amatya respectively, all three of whom regard the restoration of democracy rather than the overthrow of the monarchy as their primary aim, take part in *panchayat* elections and are prepared to co-operate with the Nepali Congress.

The pro-Chinese section of the party, which represented the majority of the membership, split into four factions. Two of these, led by Mrs Sahana Pradhan (Pushpa Lal's widow) and Man Mohan Adhikari respectively, abandoned their pro-Chinese line and adopted an independent attitude. Both are prepared to co-operate with the Nepali Congress to bring about the restoration of democracy, although the PL (for Pushpa Lal) Group led by Mrs Pradhan lays greater emphasis on the overthrow of the monarchy. In 1984 they formed an alliance with the two pro-Soviet groups led by Manandhar and Amatya, the Leftist Unity Front.

Another pro-Chinese faction led by Mohan Bikram Gharti, the Fourth Congress Group, decided in 1984 that since Mao Zedong's death the Chinese party had abandoned Marxism–Leninism, and that no communist state existed anywhere. This conclusion was rejected, however, by the Mashal Group, named after its paper and led by Nirmal Lama, which broke away from Gharti's group and continued to maintain its pro-Chinese attitude. Both groups regard the monarchy and the Nepali Congress as enemies of equal importance, and therefore reject any form of co-operation with the latter.

Membership. 5,000, of which the pro-Soviet groups constitute about 25 per cent (1985 estimate).

Orientation. Three pro-Soviet, one pro-Chinese, one independent Maoist and two independent factions.

Publications. Samikshya Weekly, pro-Soviet; *Naya Janabad* (New Democracy) and *Nepal Patra,* independent; *Mashal* (Torch), pro-Chinese.

Communist Party of Nepal—Marxist–Leninist (CPNM–L)

History. The CPNM–L, an offshoot of the Indian Naxalite movement, originated in the early 1970s, when it launched a "class annihilation" movement against landowners in eastern Nepal. Its leaders, Mohan Chandra Adhikari and Radha Krishna Mainali, were subsequently sentenced to life imprisonment.

Leadership. The CPNM–L is reported to be divided into three factions, headed by Prakash Chandra Mainali, Mod Nath Prasrit and Durga Bahadur Singh respectively.

Membership. Unknown. The CPNM–L exercises some influence among students.

Orientation. Independent Maoist. The CPNM–L derives its theories largely from Lin Biao and the "gang of four".

Programme. The CPNM–L's primary aim is the overthrow of the monarchy, but it rejects co-operation for this purpose with the Nepali Congress, which it regards as an instrument of both capitalism and the Indian government.

Publication. Barga Sangharsha (Class Struggle).

Pakistan

Capital: Islamabad   Pop. 96,900,000

Pakistan was formed in 1947 by the union of the former Indian provinces of West Punjab, Sind, the North-West Frontier Province, Baluchistan and East Bengal (later renamed East Pakistan), which seceded in 1971 to become the independent state of Bangladesh. For most of its existence Pakistan has been ruled by a succession of military regimes, headed by Gen. Ayub Khan (1958–69), Gen. Yahya Khan (1969–71) and Gen. Mohammad Zia ul-Ḥaq (since 1977).

Communist Party of Pakistan (CPP)

History. Originally a section of the Communist Party of India, the CPP became an independent organization in 1948. Ten officers and three civilians, including Sajjad Zaheer, the party's general secretary, and another member of its Executive, were sentenced to prison terms in 1953 on charges of conspiring to seize power and set up a government on the communist model but under military domination. After elections in East Bengal in which four Communists were returned the CPP was banned in 1954, and has remained illegal ever since. It was greatly weakened by the secession in 1971 of Bangladesh, from which it drew most of its support.

Leadership. Ali Nazish (g.s.).

Membership. Under 200 (1985 estimate).

Orientation. The CPP moved in the late 1970s from a pro-Chinese to a pro-Soviet attitude.

People's Movement
Awami Tehrik

History. Founded in the late 1960s as the *Sindhi Awami Tehrik*, this party built up a strong organization in the rural areas of Sind, where it conducted an agitation in defence of the tenant farmers' interests against the landlords. It played a prominent part in the civil disobedience campaign launched in 1983 by the Movement for the Restoration of Democracy (MRD—an alliance of parties opposed to President Zia's regime) in support of its demands for immediate elections and the ending of martial law, and formally joined the MRD in 1984, when it dropped the word "Sindhi" from its name.

Leadership. Rasool Bux Pallejo (pres.); Imtiaz Alam (g.s.).

Orientation. Maoist.

Philippines

Capital: Quezon City (Manila)   Pop. 55,528,000

A US colony from 1898, the Philippines were occupied by the Japanese from 1941 to 1945, and became an independent republic in 1946. Faced with both communist and Moslem guerrilla movements, President Ferdinand Marcos ruled as a virtual dictator from 1971 onwards. Following disputed presidential elections in February 1986, he was forced to flee the country by a military revolt and was succeeded by the opposition presidential candidate, Mrs Corazon Aquino, who released political prisoners and offered to negotiate with the guerrillas.

Communist Party of the Philippines
Partido Komunista ng Pilipinas (PKP)

History. Founded in 1930, the PKP was banned two years later after peasant riots for which it was held responsible, but was legalized in 1938. During the Japanese occupation it organized the People's Anti-Japanese Army (*Hukbalahap*), which played a prominent part in the resistance movement. After the war the PKP resumed legal activities, but the six Communists who were returned in the 1946 elections were not allowed to take office. The *Hukbalahaps*, who had refused to disband or surrender their weapons, thereupon launched a guerrilla campaign in Luzon, but by 1954 their revolt had been contained and their numbers reduced from a post-war maximum of 10,000 to about 2,000. The PKP was banned in 1948, and a law of 1957 made its leaders and organizers liable to the death penalty and its members to imprisonment.

The party split in 1968, when its pro-Chinese wing broke away and formed the Communist Party of the Philippines—Marxist–Leninist (see below). The leaders of the PKP gave themselves up in 1974, in response to an amnesty offer by President Marcos, since when the party, although nominally still illegal, has been allowed to operate virtually unmolested.

Leadership. Felicismo Macapagal (g.s.).

Structure. The PKP's basic unit is the nucleus, organized on a workplace or residential basis. The national congress elects the Central Committee, which elects the Political Bureau and Secretariat.

Membership. 400 (1985 estimate).

Orientation. Pro-Soviet.

Programme. The PKP advocates the restoration of democratic liberties such as habeas corpus and the right to strike; the release of all political prisoners; a comprehensive price control system; interest-free amortization payments for family farms; the formation of co-operative farms for landless workers and marginal farmers; the withdrawal of US military bases; and the establishment of a nuclear-weapons-free zone in South-East Asia.

Publication. *Ang Komunista* (The Communist), published at irregular intervals.

International affiliations. The PKP is represented on the editorial council of *World Marxist Review*.

Communist Party of the Philippines—Marxist–Leninist (CPP-ML)

History. The CPP-ML was founded in 1968 by the pro-Chinese faction of the Communist Party of the Philippines, and declared its adherence to Marxism–Leninism and Mao Zedong Thought. It has since pursued a policy of combining peaceful agitation conducted through the National Democratic Front with guerrilla warfare waged by the New People's Army.

Leadership. Rodolfo Salas (ch.); Rafael Baylosis (g.s.).

Structure. The CPP-ML is organized in the normal Communist way, with a Central Committee elected by the national congress and a Political Bureau and Secretariat elected by the Central Committee. There are 17 regional committees, which exercise considerable autonomy, and five commissions which direct and co-ordinate their political and military activities.

262

Membership. 30,000 (1984 claim).

Industrial influence. The CPP-ML is believed to exercise considerable influence in the trade unions through the May 1 Movement, which it controls.

Orientation. Originally pro-Chinese, the CPP-ML has moved towards an independent position in recent years. In particular, it is strongly opposed to the presence of US bases in the Philippines, which China supports as a counterweight to "Soviet expansionism".

Programme. The CPP-ML sought to unite the national bourgeoisie, petty bourgeoisie, workers and peasants in a common struggle for the overthrow of the Marcos dictatorship and the establishment of a revolutionary coalition government.

Publication. Ang Bayan (The Nation), monthly.

International affiliations. The former close relations between the CPP-ML and the Chinese Communist Party have been suspended since 1975, when China established diplomatic relations with President Marcos' government.

National Democratic Front (NDF)

History. The NDF, which has been active at least since 1972, is an underground alliance of movements and is generally regarded as a front organization for the Communist Party of the Philippines—Marxist-Leninist.

Leadership. Antonio Zumel (ch.).

Membership. 1,000,000 (1983 claim).

Publication. Liberation, monthly.

Guerrilla Organization

New People's Army (NPA)

History. The NPA is an offshoot of the *Hukbalahap* movement (see under "Communist Party of the Philippines"), which survived in remote areas of Luzon after the suppression of its revolt of 1946–54. Following the split in the Communist Party, the Communist Party of the Philippines—Marxist–Leninist founded the NPA in 1969 as its military wing, and secured the support of the majority of the "Huks". Originating in Luzon, the NPA had extended its activities by 1972 to Mindanao, where it has sometimes co-operated with the Moro National Liberation Front (Moslem separatist guerrillas). By 1985 it largely controlled the rural areas of Mindanao, where it had tied down 60,000 government troops, and was also active in Luzon, Samar, Negros, Panay and other islands.

Leadership. Juanito Rivera (commander).

Structure. The NPA is organized in regular mobile forces, operating in units up to 500 strong, which carry out assaults on towns, army camps and other targets; guerrilla forces, which defend existing guerrilla zones and create new ones; militia and self-defence corps, which combine defence duties with productive work; and city partisans, operating in groups of up to 100, which disrupt governmental activities and assassinate policemen, soldiers and suspected informers.

Membership. The NPA claims to have 22,000 guerrillas, excluding village militias, and several million sympathizers. Other estimates of the number of guerrillas vary between 5,000 and 16,000.

Programme. The NPA pusues the classical Maoist strategy of gradually expanding its control of the countryside in preparation for taking over the cities.

Singapore

Capital: Singapore　　　　　　　　　　　　　　　　Pop. 2,531,000

Singapore, previously a British colony, was granted internal self-government in 1959 and joined the Federation of Malaysia in 1963. It seceded two years later, however, when it became an independent state. The People's Action Party has been in office since 1959, and held every seat in Parliament from 1968 to 1981.

Communist Party of Malaya (CPM)

History. The CPM (for fuller details of which see under "Malaysia") also operates underground in Singapore, where it has been banned since 1948.

Membership. 200–500 (1985 estimate).

Orientation. Pro-Chinese.

Programme. The CPM advocates the dissolution of the Malaysian Federation and the union of Singapore with Malaya.

Socialist Front
Barisan Socialis

History. The Socialist Front was formed in 1961, when the left wing of the ruling People's Action Party broke away. Most of its leaders were arrested in February 1963 on a charge of "pro-Communist agitation" and detained without trial, some of them for many years, but it obtained 30 per cent of the vote and 13 of the 51 seats in the Legislative Assembly in elections held in the following September. It opposed the secession of Singapore from Malaysia in 1965, and subsequently boycotted the sessions of the Assembly and the 1968 elections. Since 1972 it has contested each general election without success.

Electoral influence. In the 1984 elections, when it contested four of the 79 seats, the Socialist Front obtained 24,212 votes (2.7 per cent of the total vote and 38.2 per cent of the vote in those constituencies).

Programme. The Socialist Front advocates the formation of a unified democratic Malaya, including Singapore.

Sri Lanka

Capital: Colombo　　　　　　　　　　　　　　　　Pop. 15,925,000

Sri Lanka (known until 1972 as Ceylon), which had been a British colony since 1802, was granted a parliamentary constitution in 1931 and attained dominion status in 1948. The conservative United National Party (UNP) held office until 1956, the social democratic Sri Lanka Freedom Party (SLFP) from 1956 to 1965, except for a short period in 1959–60, and the UNP from 1965 to 1970. The United Front, consisting of the SLFP and the (Marxist) Lanka Equal Society and Communist parties, took power in 1970, and two years later introduced a new constitution under which Sri Lanka was proclaimed a democratic socialist republic. The UNP won an overwhelming victory in the 1977 elections, and adopted an amendment to the constitution whereby a popularly elected President would be head of the government. The Prime Minister, J. R. Jayawardene, assumed the Presidency in the following year. He was re-elected by popular vote in 1982, and another constitutional amendment extended the life of the Parliament elected in 1977 until 1989.

Political life has largely been dominated by relations between the Sinhalese majority, who are Buddhists, and the large Tamil minority, living mainly in the north of the island, who are Hindus. Friction between the two communities has led to frequent outbreaks of rioting, notably in July 1983, and to demands by the Tamils for the establishment of either a federation or a separate Tamil state. Terrorist activities by Tamil separatists have become increasingly widespread since 1978.

Communist Party of Sri Lanka (CPSL)

History. The CPSL originated in 1940, when the Stalinist wing of the Lanka Equal Society Party (LSSP) broke away and formed the United Socialist Party. Because of its support for the war effort after 1941, it was legalized in 1943, when it adopted the name of Communist Party of Ceylon. It won three seats in the 1947, 1952, 1956 and March 1960 elections, and four in July 1960 and 1965. It fought the 1970 elections in alliance with the Sri Lanka Freedom Party and the LSSP, winning six seats, and subsequently joined the United Front government. The Communist ministers resigned in February 1977, and the CPSL fought the elections in the following July in alliance with the LSSP, losing all its seats. It gained one seat in a by-election in 1981, however. The party was banned after communal riots in 1983, but the ban was lifted three months later.

Leadership. Pieter Keuneman (pres.); Kattorge P. Silva (g.s.).

Structure. Branches are organized on a residential or workplace basis, and there are area and district committees. The national congress, held every two years, elects the 50-member Central Committee, which elects the president, the general secretary, the 11-member Political Bureau and the Secretariat.

Membership. 6,000 (1985 estimate).

Electoral influence. The CPSL obtained 1.9 per cent of the vote in the 1977 elections.

Industrial influence. Almost all trade unions in Sri Lanka are linked to a political party through the trade union federation to which they are affiliated. The CPSL controls the Ceylon Federation of Trade Unions, which has a strong following in the public and especially in the private sector.

Orientation. Pro-Soviet.

Programme. The CPSL advocates the nationalization of banks, estates and factories and regional autonomy for the Tamils, but opposes the creation of a separate Tamil state.

Publications. Aththa (Truth), Sinhala daily; *Mawbima* (Homeland), Sinhala weekly; *Deshabimani* (Patriot), Tamil weekly; *Forward*, English weekly.

International affiliations. The CPSL is represented on the editorial council of *World Marxist Review.*

Communist Party of Sri Lanka—Marxist–Leninist (CPSLML)

History. The CPSLML was formed by a Maoist faction in the Communist Party of Sri Lanka, which broke away in 1964.

Orientation. Pro-Chinese.

Lanka Equal Society Party
Lanka Sama Samaja Pakshaya (LSSP)

History. The LSSP was founded in 1935 as a broadly-based Marxist party, with freedom from British rule and the achievement of socialism as its aims, and won two seats in the elections in the following year. It adopted Trotskyist views in 1939, and two years later joined the Fourth International. Because of its anti-war policy, it was banned during World War II and its leaders detained. In the 1947 elections 10 seats were won by the LSSP and five by the Bolshevik–Leninist Party, which had broken away in 1945 but reunited with it in 1950, and in subsequent elections the LSSP obtained nine seats in 1952, 14 in 1956, 10 in March 1960 and 12 in July 1960.

In 1964 it formed a coalition government with the Sri Lanka Freedom Party (SLFP), being expelled from the Fourth International in consequence, but the government was defeated in elections in the following year, in which the LSSP won 10 seats. It fought the 1970 elections in alliance with the SLFP and the Communist Party, winning 19 seats, and subsequently entered the United Front government; as a result of differences with the SLFP leadership, however, the LSSP ministers were dropped from the government in 1975. The LSSP failed to win any seats in the 1977 elections, which it fought in alliance with the Communist Party, and has not since been represented in Parliament.

Leadership. Athauda Seneviratne (pres.); Bernard Soysa (g.s.).

Structure. The national congress elects the Central Committee, which elects the general secretary and the Political Bureau.

Membership. 20,000 (1984 estimate).

Electoral influence. Dr Colvin de Silva, the LSSP candidate in the 1982 presidential election, obtained 0.9 per cent of the vote.

Industrial influence. The LSSP controls the Ceylon Federation of Labour, one of the strongest trade union federations.

Orientation. Formerly Trotskyist, now independent.

Programme. The LSSP seeks "the building of a socialist society with a multiparty political system, where the fullest democracy is enjoyed by the people both in the political and the economic fields".

Publications. Samasamajaya (Equal Society), Sinhala weekly; *Samadharmam*, Tamil weekly; *Samasamajist*, English weekly.

New Equal Society Party
Nava Sama Samaja Pakshaya (NSSP)

History. The NSSP was formed by the left wing of the Lanka Equal Society Party, from which it broke away in 1979. It contested the 1982 presidential election, but was banned in the following year.

Leadership. Vasudeva Nanayakkara (l.).

Electoral influence. Nanayakkara, the NSSP candidate in the 1982 presidential election, obtained 0.26 per cent of the vote.

Orientation. Trotskyist.

People's Liberation Front
Janatha Vimukthi Peramuna (JVP)

History. The JVP was founded in 1967 by a group led by Rohana Wijeweere, who had left the Communist Party of Sri Lanka—Marxist–Leninist because they rejected its theory that in under-developed countries a "people's democratic revolution" must precede the socialist revolution, and quickly won wide support among the young. Although it supported the United Front in the 1970 elections, Wijeweere and over 4,000 of its members were arrested by the United Front government in March 1971. In consequence it launched a revolt in April, which was quickly crushed, Wijeweere being sentenced to life imprisonment in 1974. The JVP was legalized in 1977, however, and on his release later in the same year Wijeweere repudiated the use of violent methods. In local elections held in 1981 it won 18 seats on six district councils, including four of the 16 seats in Colombo, and in the 1982 presidential election Wijeweere took third place after the United National Party and Sri Lanka Freedom Party candidates. The JVP was banned after communal riots in 1983.

Leadership. Rohana Wijeweere (ch.); Lionel Bopage (g.s.).

Electoral influence. Wijeweere, the JVP candidate, obtained 4.2 per cent of the vote in the 1982 presidential election.

Orientation. Independent.

People's United Front
Mahajana Eksath Peramuna (MEP)

History. The MEP is the successor to the Revolutionary Equal Society Party (*Viplavakari Sama Samaja Pakshaya*, VSSP), led by Philip Gunawardene, which broke away from the Lanka Equal Society Party in 1951. The VSSP fought the 1956 elections in alliance with the Sri Lanka Freedom Party, winning five seats, and was represented in the government until 1959. It then merged with a Buddhist organization to form the MEP, with a programme of nationalization of banks, tea and rubber plantations and foreign-owned industry and defence of the supremacy of Buddhism and the Sinhala language against Christianity and English. It won 10 seats in the elections of March 1960, three in July 1960 and two in 1965, and supported the United National Party government of 1965–70. After 1970 it was not represented in Parliament until 1983, when it won a seat in a by-election.

Leadership. Dinesh P. R. Gunawardene (g.s.).

Orientation. Independent.

Programme. The MEP, which combines Marxism with Buddhism and Sinhalese communalism, advocates nationalization of foreign-owned estates and a self-reliant national economy.

Thailand

Capital: Bangkok   Pop. 51,724,000

The Kingdom of Thailand (known until 1939 as Siam) was ruled by a succession of military regimes, with short intervals of parliamentary government, from 1932, when the absolute monarchy was overthrown by a coup, to 1973, when a student revolt in Bangkok led to the establishment of a civilian government and the adoption of a democratic constitution. During the war in Indo-China Thai troops served in South Vietnam and Laos, and US aircraft used Thai bases to bomb North Vietnam. A military coup in October 1976 was followed by the establishment of an extreme right-wing regime and mass arrests of Socialists, trade unionists, intellectuals and students; parliamentary government was restored in 1979, however.

Communist Party of Thailand (CPT)

History. The CPT, founded in 1942 by ethnic Chinese, was represented in Parliament in 1946–47 by its general secretary, Prasad Sabsunthorn, but was banned in 1952. Its third congress, held in 1961, at which Charoen Wan-Ngam was elected general secretary, adopted a strongly pro-Chinese attitude towards the Sino–Soviet controversy, and decided to adopt Maoist guerrilla war tactics. Guerrilla operations were begun in 1965 in the north-eastern provinces bordering on Laos, where the CPT had won the support of the Meo tribesmen, and subsequently spread to the northern provinces and to the extreme south, where Malayan Communist guerrillas were already active. The "Thai People's Liberation Army" received considerable aid after 1970 from China and North Vietnam, and during the Vietnamese war carried out a number of raids on US bomber bases in Thailand.

Outside aid was greatly increased after the Communists took control of South Vietnam, Kampuchea and Laos in 1975; 1,500 guerrillas were reported in 1978 to be operating from bases in Kampuchea. The coup of October 1976 forced thousands of Socialists and students to flee to the "liberated zones", and in the following year the Socialist Party and the United Socialist Front, which had been driven underground, formed an alliance with the CPT, the Co-ordinating Committee for Patriotic and Democratic Forces (CCPDF), to conduct a revolutionary struggle against the government. By 1978 it was estimated that about 12,000 guerrillas and 10,000–15,000 members of village militia groups were operating in 46 of the 72 provinces.

The split in 1978 between China and Vietnam and the Vietnamese occupation of Kampuchea in the following year greatly weakened the CPT. It at first attempted to maintain a neutral position, but in 1979 it adopted a pro-Chinese attitude and offered to co-operate with the government against the alleged threat of a Vietnamese invasion, this offer being rejected. Sections of the CPT and many of the Socialists in the CCPDF were pro-Vietnamese in their sympathies,

268

however, and fighting was reported to have taken place between the two factions. Both China and Vietnam, which were anxious to improve their relations with Thailand, ended their aid to the guerrillas in 1979, and the CPT radio, the "Voice of the People of Thailand", which had operated from southern China, ceased to broadcast in the same year. After the Vietnamese occupation the guerrillas lost the use of their bases in Kampuchea, and the pro-Chinese Thai Communists were expelled from Laos.

Thousands of the guerrillas, including most of the non-Communists who had joined them in 1976, defected from 1979 onwards, taking advantage of the government's offer of an amnesty. The CPT's fourth congress, held in 1982, led to a split on ideological and tactical questions between the Maoist leadership and the younger members, and a number of the latter defected, including Udom Srisuwan, a member of the Political Bureau and chairman of the CCPDF. Fearing that the CPT would switch from guerrilla warfare to urban terrorism, the police arrested a number of leading Communists in Bangkok in the summer of 1984, and claimed to have discovered evidence that they had sought support from the Soviet Union, Vietnam and the Irish Republican Army. The strength of the guerrillas was reported in October 1984 to have declined to 1,200–1,500 in the south, 50–80 in the north and 30–40 in the north-east, and after further mass defections it was officially claimed in August 1985 that the CPT no longer existed in the southern border provinces, although "small groups of criminal bandits" were still operating there.

Leadership. Virat Angkhathavorn, who is reported to be responsible for the CPT's finances, is its best-known leader. A new general secretary is believed to have been elected at the 1982 congress in succession to Charoen Wan-Ngam, who had recently died, but his name was not divulged.

Membership. 1,200–1,500 (1985 estimate).

Orientation. Since 1961 the CPT has followed a pro-Chinese policy, but in recent years it has moved towards an independent attitude. The 1982 congress was reported to have rejected the Chinese party's three worlds theory.

Programme. The CPT is believed to be divided between those who favour continuation of the Maoist strategy of rural guerrilla war and advocates of a shift to urban struggle.

New Party
Pak Mai

History. The New Party was formed in 1979 by pro-Vietnamese Thais living in Laos, under the leadership of Bunyen Wothong, a former Socialist member of Parliament and vice-chairman of the Co-ordinating Committee for Patriotic and Democratic Forces (see under "Communist Party of Thailand"), who had taken refuge in the Communist-controlled area of Thailand after the 1976 coup. By the beginning of 1982 it was conducting guerrilla operations in both the north-eastern provinces bordering on Laos and the extreme south, and was reported to have been involved in clashes with the Communist Party of Thailand (CPT).

Leadership. Bunyen Wothong.

Membership. 200–1,000 (1982 estimates). The original membership consisted largely of ethnic Thais, unlike that of the largely Chinese CPT.

Orientation. Pro–Soviet.

Vietnam

Capital: Hanoi   Pop. 60,000,000

The French invaded and annexed Cochin China (in southern Vietnam) in 1859, and after a second war in 1883 established a protectorate over Tonkin and Annam (in the north and centre). Vietnam was occupied by the Japanese in 1941, with the connivance of the Vichy French authorities, but a guerrilla resistance was maintained by the *Viet Minh*. After the Japanese surrender in 1945 the *Viet Minh* proclaimed the independent Democratic Republic of Vietnam, and a National Assembly was elected in January 1946. Although the French recognized Vietnam in March as a free state within the French Union, they declared war in November by shelling Haiphong, and in 1948 set up a government in Saigon headed by Bao Dai, the former Emperor of Annam. The war ended in 1954 with the French defeat at Dien Bien Phu.

The Geneva Conference of 1954, at which France, Britain, the Soviet Union, China, the United States and the two Vietnamese governments were represented, temporarily divided Vietnam into two zones at the 17th parallel, the North being controlled by the *Viet Minh* government and the South by the Bao Dai regime, and provided that the country should be reunited following elections in 1956. All North Vietnamese proposals for the holding of elections, however, were rejected by President Ngo Dinh Diem, who had deposed Bao Dai in 1955 and declared South Vietnam a republic, and the country remained divided into a Communist North and a US-supported South.

Local revolts against Diem's regime, which began in 1957 and from 1959 were supported by the North Vietnamese government, gradually developed into a major civil war. The resistance movement, which included both Communist and non-Communist elements, united in 1960 to form the National Liberation Front (NLF), which in 1969 set up the Provisional Revolutionary Government of South Vietnam (PRG). US "advisers" were sent in increasing numbers after 1961 to assist the South Vietnamese forces, and in 1964 the United States began clandestine military operations against North Vietnam by land, sea and air. Large-scale bombing of North Vietnam began in February 1965, and in the following month US combat troops were sent to South Vietnam; their strength reached 540,000 in 1968, but thereafter was steadily reduced. In response, North Vietnamese troops began entering South Vietnam through Laos and Kampuchea in May 1965. Under a cease-fire agreement concluded in 1973 the US forces were withdrawn and the bombing of North Vietnam ended, but fighting continued, and attempts to reach a political settlement through talks between the South Vietnamese government and the PRG broke down in 1974. When the North Vietnamese and NLF forces launched an offensive in March 1975 the South Vietnamese troops' resistance collapsed; Saigon fell in April, and the PRG took control of the South.

North and South Vietnam were reunited in 1976 as the Socialist Republic of Vietnam, and in 1980 a new constitution was adopted which declared Vietnam "a state of proletarian dictatorship" and the Communist Party "the only force leading the state and society". In 1978 Vietnam came under pressure from China, with which its relations had become increasingly cool since 1972; clashes occurred on the border, Vietnamese territory was attacked from Kampuchea (then ruled by the pro-Chinese Pol Pot government) and China cut off economic and technical aid to Vietnam. In December 1978 Vietnam invaded Kampuchea and overthrew Pol Pot; the Chinese army subsequently invaded Vietnam in February 1979, but was forced to withdraw.

Vietnamese Communist Party (VCP)
Dang Cong San Viet Nam

History. The Communist Party of Indo-China (CPIC), to which the VCP is a successor, was founded by Ho Chi Minh in 1930, with 211 members, and later in the same year organized a rising against French rule in Tonkin, which was suppressed. A second rising in the Mekong delta in 1940 was also unsuccessful. In 1941 Ho organized the Revolutionary League for the Independence of Vietnam (*Viet Nam Doc Lap Dong Minh Hoi*), usually known as the *Viet Minh*, an alliance of Communists and nationalists which conducted a guerrilla war against the Japanese occupation forces, with assistance from the United States. After the defeat of Japan the Democratic Republic of Vietnam was proclaimed in Hanoi on Sept. 2, 1945, with Ho as President and Prime Minister. War with France followed in 1946.

The second congress of the CPIC, held in 1951, divided the party into separate parties for Vietnam, Kampuchea and Laos, and the Vietnamese Workers' Party (VWP) was formed, with Ho as chairman and Truong Chinh as general secretary and a programme of national independence and agrarian reform. After the partition of Vietnam by the Geneva Agreements the VWP became the ruling party in the North. Ho resigned the Premiership in 1955, while retaining the Presidency, and was succeeded in this post by Pham Van Dong. Attempts to impose collectivization led to peasant revolts in the following year; Truong Chinh, who was particularly associated with this policy, was then replaced as general secretary by Ho, who resigned the post in 1960 in favour of Le Duan.

The VWP adopted a neutral attitude towards the Sino–Soviet controversy, and Ho attempted to use his prestige in the world communist movement to act as a mediator. In his political testament, published after his death in 1969, he appealed for the restoration of the unity of the international movement; its publication was directly responsible for the holding of talks between the Soviet and Chinese Prime Ministers, Alexei Kosygin and Zhou Enlai, but produced no permanent effect. Ho was succeeded as President by Ton Duc Thang.

After the reunification of Vietnam the VWP, which was renamed the Vietnamese Communist Party in 1976, absorbed the Revolutionary Workers' Party, which had been founded in 1962 as a separate Communist Party for South Vietnam. Friction between pro-Soviet and pro-Chinese factions inside the party led to the exclusion from the Central Committee in 1976 of a number of pro-Chinese members, including Hoang Van Hoan, who was also dropped from the Political Bureau. China's hostile attitude finally forced the VWP in 1978 to abandon its neutral position and to align itself openly with the Soviet Communist Party. Hoang Van Hoan defected to China in the following year, and in 1980 was sentenced to death in absentia. Following the death of Ton Duc Thang, Truong Chinh was elected Chairman of the Council of State (President) in 1981.

Leadership. The Political Bureau consists of Le Duan (g.s.), Truong Chinh, Pham Van Dong, Pham Hung, Le Duc Tho, Gen. Van Tien Dung, Gen. Chu Huy Man, To Huu, Vo Chi Cong, Vo Van Kiet, Do Muoi, Le Duc Anh, Nguyen Van Linh and Nguyen Duc Tam (full members); Nguyen Co Thach and

Dong Sy Nguyen (alternate members). The chairmanship has been left vacant since the death of Ho Chi Minh.

Structure. The VCP in 1982 had 120,654 cells and 35,146 primary organizations (branches). The national congress, normally held every five years, elects the Central Committee (116 full and 36 alternate members), which elects the Political Bureau and the 10-member Secretariat. The party's youth organization is the Ho Chi Minh Communist Youth Union.

Membership. 1,730,214 (1984 claim).

Electoral influence. All candidates are nominated by the Vietnam Fatherland Front, comprising political parties, trade unions and mass organizations, which is dominated by the VCP. The number of candidates put forward exceeds the number of seats (in the 1981 elections there were 614 candidates for 496 seats), and successful candidates are required to receive at least 50 per cent of the votes. The proportion of electors voting in 1981 was officially given as 97.96 per cent.

Industrial influence. The VCP controls the Vietnam Confederation of Trade Unions.

Orientation. Pro-Soviet.

Programme. In his report to the 1982 congress, Le Duan defined the party's tasks as "to carry out three revolutions: the revolution in relations of production, the scientific and technological revolution and the ideological and cultural revolution; to step up socialist industrialization, build the material and technological foundations of socialism and take our country's economy from small-scale production to large-scale socialist production; and to give priority to heavy industry on the basis of developing agriculture and light industry".

Publications. Nhan Dan (The People), daily (300,000); *Tap Chi Cong San* (Communist Review), monthly.

International affiliations. The VCP has close relations with the Soviet Communist Party, the Kampuchean People's Revolutionary Party and the Lao People's Revolutionary Party. It is represented on the editorial council of *World Marxist Review.*

5. AFRICA SOUTH OF THE SAHARA

Angola

Capital: Luanda   Pop. 8,000,000

After a 14-year struggle conducted by three nationalist organizations—the Popular Movement for the Liberation of Angola (MPLA), the National Union for the Total Independence of Angola (UNITA) and the National Front for the Liberation of Angola (FNLA)—the Portuguese colony of Angola achieved its independence in November 1975, when rival governments were established by the MPLA and by the UNITA and FNLA. Civil war between them had already begun, and in October 1975 South African troops invaded Angola in support of UNITA, which was also receiving supplies from the United States and was assisted by Chinese and North Korean military advisers. In response to the MPLA's appeal for help against the South African intervention, the Cuban government sent troops to Angola and persuaded the Soviet Union to send military advisers and supplies. By February 1976 the MPLA government controlled the greater part of the country, and was recognized by the Organization of African Unity and many other countries, including the members of the European Community, although not by the United States. Most of the South African troops were withdrawn in March 1976, but UNITA has continued to conduct a guerrilla resistance in the south and east with the support of South Africa, which has repeatedly carried out military incursions into Angola.

Popular Movement for the Liberation of Angola—Labour Party
Movimento Popular de Libertação de Angola—Partido do Trabalho
(MPLA-PT)

History. The Popular Movement for the Liberation of Angola (MPLA) was formed in 1956 by the merger of an already existing Angolan Communist Party with a nationalist organization, the Party of Struggle of the Africans of Angola, under the leadership of Mario de Andrade, who resigned the party chairmanship in 1962 in favour of Agostinho Neto. It played the leading part in the revolt against Portuguese rule, sometimes in collaboration with the other two nationalist movements (see above), although at other times fighting occurred between them. Neto's leadership was challenged in 1973 by Daniel Chipenda, the vice-chairman, and in May 1974 by Andrade, who formed the Active Revolt (*Revolta Activa*) faction; a compromise was reached in September, when Chipenda and Andrade became joint vice-chairmen, but three months later Chipenda and his supporters were expelled, subsequently joining the National Front for the Liberation of Angola.

The People's Republic of Angola was proclaimed on Nov. 11, 1975, with Neto as President, and a government headed by Lopo do Nascimento was formed three days later. Dissension continued inside the party, however; Andrade and other leaders of Active Revolt were arrested in 1976, and another dissident faction attempted to stage a coup in Luanda in the following year. At its first congress, held in 1977, the MPLA was renamed the Popular Movement for the Liberation of Angola—Labour Party. Do Nascimento was removed from the premiership and the party Secretariat in 1978, the office of Prime Minister being abolished. On his death in 1979 Neto was succeeded as President and MPLA-PT chairman by José Eduardo dos Santos.

Conflict ensued between President dos Santos' supporters, who favoured a negotiated settlement of the civil war, a non-aligned foreign policy and closer economic relations with the West, and a hardline pro-Soviet faction, which maintained that only a military solution was possible. The President's position was strengthened by an extraordinary congress held in 1980, and by the removal in 1984 of the Foreign Minister, Paulo Teixeira Jorge, who opposed negotiations with South Africa. At the second party congress, held in December 1985, the Central Committee was enlarged to give President dos Santos' faction a majority, his opponents being dropped or demoted to candidate membership, and similar changes were made in the new Political Bureau, from which three veteran guerrilla leaders were dropped, including Lucio Lara, the former organization secretary of the MPLA.

Leadership. The Political Bureau consists of José Eduardo dos Santos, Afonso Pedro Van Dunem Mbinda, António dos Santos Franca Ndalo, Francisco Magalhaes Paiva Ngumba, Julião Mateus Paulo Dino Matross, Kundi Payama, Manuel Alexandre Duarte Rodrigues Kito, Pascoal Luvualu, Pedro de Castro dos Santos Van Dunem Loy, Pedro Maria Tonha Pedale and Roberto António Francisco de Almeida. There are also two candidate members.

Structure. Congresses are held every eight years, and extraordinary congresses between them to assess progress. The congress elects the Central Committee, which was enlarged from 55 members to 75 in 1980 and to 90 in 1985, and the Central Committee elects the Political Bureau.

Membership. 35,000 (1985 estimate). Only those living exclusively by their work are eligible, and new members are required to serve a probationary period of varying length, depending on their social category.

Electoral influence. All candidates must be approved by the MPLA-PT.

Industrial influence. The MPLA-PT controls the National Union of Angolan Workers, which includes 90 per cent of the nation's workers.

Orientation. Pro-Soviet.

Programme. The MPLA-PT is a Marxist-Leninist "vanguard party of the proletariat", uniting workers, peasants and revolutionary intellectuals, the state being "an instrument capable of applying the orientations defined by the party". Strategic industries are government-controlled, but the private sector is encouraged and supported by the state as long as it respects the general economic and labour policies defined by the MPLA-PT. Angola is non-aligned, and prohibits the installation of foreign military bases on its territory.

Publications. A Célula.

International affiliations. The MPLA-PT has close links with the Soviet-bloc and Cuban Communist parties.

Benin

Capital: Porto Novo   Pop. 3,910,000

The former French colony of Dahomey (renamed Benin in 1975) became an independent republic in 1960. After 1963 it passed through a period of political instability until 1972, when Major Kerekou seized power and established a military regime, which came to be based politically in the Benin People's Revolutionary Party as the sole legal political party.

Benin People's Revolutionary Party
Parti de la Révolution Populaire du Bénin (PRPB)

History. The PRPB is the successor to the 67-member National Council of the Revolution set up by the military regime in 1973. President Kerekou announced in 1974 that a socialist society would be established in Dahomey, with Marxism-Leninism as its philosophy, and that the National Council, which had been given a 14-member Political Bureau, would be transformed into a party. In the following year he announced that Dahomey had been renamed the People's Republic of Benin, and that the ruling party would be known as the Benin People's Revolutionary Party. The PRPB held its first congress in 1976.

Leadership. President Ahmed Mathieu Kerekou (ch.).

Structure. The party's supreme organ is its congress, but congresses are convened only when the Political Bureau deems it necessary, the most recent being held in November 1985. The congress elects the 45-member Central Committee, which elects the Political Bureau.

Membership. 200 (1984 claim).

Electoral influence. Candidates for the Revolutionary National Assembly are selected at public meetings from a list presented by the PRPB, and the electorate are then required to vote for or against the resulting single list of candidates.

Industrial influence. The PRPB's attempts to establish control over the trade unions have met with considerable resistance, especially from the teachers' unions.

Orientation. Independent. The PRPB has avoided taking sides in the Sino-Soviet dispute.

Programme. President Kerekou defined the tasks of the movement in 1974 as the elimination of foreign domination; struggle against racialism, apartheid, regionalism, tribalism, imbalances between regions and social injustice; the building of the national economy on the basis of scientific socialism by relying on the country's own strength and resources; and "the scientific organization of the social and productive forces for the defence of the revolution". He stated in 1977 that the regime would have to pass through three phases: a revolutionary national liberation movement, a democratic people's revolution and a socialist revolution.

Publication. *Ehuzu* (Things have changed), daily (1,000).

Burkina Faso

Capital: Ouagadougou   Pop. 7,400,000

The former French colony of Upper Volta, which became an independent republic in 1960, was dominated from 1966 to 1980 by its President, Lt.-Col. Sangoule Lamizana. He was removed in 1980 by a coup led by Col. Saye Zerbo, who was himself overthrown two years later, when Maj. Jean-Baptiste Ouedraogo became head of state and Capt. Thomas Sankara Prime Minister. Capt. Sankara and other radical members of the ruling People's Salvation Council were arrested in May 1983, but were released a month later under pressure from the army. Another coup in August 1983 placed Capt. Sankara in power as head of state and chairman of the National Revolutionary Council, which replaced the People's Salvation Council. The name of the country was changed in 1984 to Burkina Faso, meaning "democratic land of honest men".

Patriotic League for Development
Ligue Patriotique pour le Développement (Lipad)

History. This Marxist party, founded in 1973 from the (pro-Soviet) African Independence Party (PAI), was represented in Capt. Sankara's first (1982) government by Emmanuel Dadjouari (Education) and Ibrahima Koné (Youth and Sports), both of whom were removed after his arrest in May 1983. They were reinstated when Capt. Sankara took power in August 1983, after which Lipad became the dominant governmental influence. Koné was dismissed in May 1984, however, allegedly for using his position to promote his party, and four other Lipad ministers were dropped when Capt. Sankara formed a new cabinet in August. This development signalled a marked diminution in the influence of Lipad, which had hitherto had some success with its strategy of attracting intellectuals and young army officers to a "progressive" formation which was not ostensibly a communist party.

Leadership. Dr Hamilton Coulibaly (l.).

Industrial influence. Lipad has close links with the Confederation of Voltaic Trade Unions.

Orientation. Pro-Soviet.

Union of Communist Struggles
Union des Luttes Communistes (ULC)

History. This splinter group was formed in 1980 as a result of a scission in the students' union (UGEV). It is basically pro-Chinese, although its adherents include some of the Trotskyite persuasion. The ULC participated in the first Sankara government (formed in 1982) and appeared to increase its influence in September 1984 when its representation in the cabinet increased from two to five ministers. The most notable of these was the ULC leader, Basile Laita Guissou, who became Minister of Foreign Affairs.

Leadership. Basile Laita Guissou (l.).

Orientation. Pro-Chinese.

Voltaic Revolutionary Communist Party
Parti Communiste Révolutionnaire Voltaïque (PCRV)

History. The PCRV, a pro-Albanian grouping, refused to participate in the 1982 Sankara government, arguing that a military takeover was not the same thing as a popular revolution. At the time of the 1982 coup it had strong support within trade union and student organizational structures. In the September 1984 cabinet reshuffle the PCRV again refused to participate in a government which it regarded as reactionary. However, one PCRV faction was not similarly convinced, since it formed the *Groupe Communiste* (GC) and accepted one cabinet seat.

Orientation. Pro–Albanian.

Cameroon

Capital: Yaoundé   Pop. 8,600,000

The former French trust territory of Cameroon became an independent republic in 1960. Since 1966 the ruling Cameroon National Union has been the only legal party.

Union of Cameroonian Peoples
Union des Populations Camerounaises (UPC)

History. Founded in 1947, with Félix Moumié as president and Ruben Um Nyobé as general secretary, the UPC claimed in 1955 to have 80,000 members, but was banned by the French authorities in the same year after riots in Douala for which it was held responsible. Um Nyobé began guerrilla operations in 1956, and was killed two years later. A wing of the party led by Théodore Mayi Matip, who was returned to the Legislative Assembly in a by-election in 1959, attempted to act as a legal opposition; after the attainment of independence in 1960 the UPC was legalized, and in the subsequent general election it won 22 of the 106 seats. This policy was denounced by Moumié, who urged the continuation of guerrilla warfare; he was poisoned in Geneva in 1960, however, allegedly by French terrorists. The party split in 1961 into a pro-Soviet faction led by Ernest Ouandié and a pro-Chinese faction led by Osende Afana, both of which conducted guerrilla operations. After Afana was killed in 1966 and Ouandié was captured in 1970 and executed the rebellion collapsed. The UPC now has its headquarters in Paris.

Cape Verde

Capital: Praia   Pop. 310,000

The former Portuguese colony of the Cape Verde Islands became an independent republic in 1975, when the African Party for the Independence of Guinea and Cape Verde took power with a programme of ultimate union with Guinea-Bissau. This aim was abandoned in 1981, however.

African Party for the Independence of Cape Verde
Partido Africano da Independência de Cabo Verde (PAICV)

History. The PAICV originated as the Cape Verdian section of the African Party for the Independence of Guinea and Cape Verde (PAIGC—see under "Guinea-Bissau"), founded in 1956. In elections held in June 1975 the PAIGC was the only contesting party, and on the attainment of independence in the following month the People's Assembly elected Aristides Maria Pereira (general secretary of the party) President of the Republic. Following the coup in Guinea-Bissau in November 1980, the Cape Verdian branch of the PAIGC formed itself in January 1981 into a separate party, the PAICV.

Leadership. President Aristides Maria Pereira (g.s.).

Structure. The party congress elects the 42-member National Council, which elects the nine-member Political Commission and the Secretariat.

Membership. 5,985 (1983).

Electoral influence. All candidates for the National People's Assembly are returned on the PAICV list, although not all are party members. The official candidates in the 1985 elections were stated to have received 94 per cent of the vote on a 69 per cent poll.

Orientation. Independent.

Programme. The PAICV describes itself as a liberation movement in power and the vanguard of the Cape Verdian people, endeavouring to associate the mass of the people with the decision-making process, and standing for non-alignment, a new international economic order, peaceful coexistence, peace and complete disarmament, and African unity.

Congo

Capital: Brazzaville   Pop. 1,745,000

The former French Congo became an independent republic in 1960, with the Abbé Fulbert Youlou as President. He was forced to resign by popular demonstrations in 1963, when Alphonse Massemba-Débat became President and a Marxist–Leninist regime, the oldest in Africa, was established. Massemba-Débat resigned after a coup in 1968, and was succeeded in the following year by Maj. Marien Ngouabi, Congo being proclaimed a People's Republic. Ngouabi was assassinated in 1977, and his successor, Col. Joachim Yhombi-Opango, was compelled to resign two years later in favour of Col. Denis Sassou-Ngouesso.

Congolese Labour Party
Parti Congolais du Travail (PCT)

History. The National Movement of the Revolution, founded in 1964 as the sole legal party, was replaced by the PCT in 1969, and a new constitution was adopted under which the party chairman also acted as head of state. Throughout its history the PCT has suffered from factional struggles. After an attempted coup by the left wing of the party in 1972 a massive purge took place which reduced the membership to about 200, the Central Committee to five members and the Political Bureau to three. The first secretary, Ambroise Noumazalay, and his predecessor, Claude-Ernest Ndalla, were condemned to death, although the sentences were commuted to life imprisonment and they were amnestied in the following year. By 1975 the membership had again increased to about 1,500, but a strike in 1976 led to another mass purge, Pierre Nze, a leading member of the Political Bureau, being among those expelled. Following the assassination of President Ngouabi in 1977, ex-President Massemba-Débat was executed and

Ndalla again sentenced to life imprisonment on charges of complicity in the crime. The new President, Col. Yhombi-Opango, was removed from office by the Central Committee in February 1979 and replaced by Col. Sassou-Ngouesso; a party congress in the following month expelled Yhombi-Opango as the leader of a "rightist" faction and re-elected Nze to the Political Bureau. President Sassou-Ngouesso met with opposition from a leftist faction led by Nze and Jean-Pierre Thystère Tchikaya, the party's leading ideologist; the latter was removed from all his party posts in 1984, however, and Nze was dropped from his post as Foreign Minister shortly after.

Leadership. President Denis Sassou-Ngouesso (ch.).

Structure. The party congress, held every five years, elects the Central Committee of 75 members, which elects the 13-member Political Bureau. The party's youth organization is the Union of Congolese Socialist Youth, membership of which is compulsory.

Membership. 8,685 (1984 claim). New members are required to serve a probationary period of up to two years.

Electoral influence. In theory candidates for the National People's Assembly may be nominated by the PCT, by trade unions and other mass organizations and by groups of individuals, but in practice all candidates are approved by the PCT. In the 1984 elections 95 per cent of the electorate were stated to have voted for the official candidates.

Industrial influence. The Congolese Trade Union Confederation formerly played an independent role, and in 1976 called a strike against the government's price policies, but has since been brought under PCT control.

Orientation. Independent. The PCT has avoided involvement in the Sino–Soviet controversy, and maintains friendly relations with both countries. It has expressed support for the Soviet intervention in Afghanistan.

Programme. The PCT holds that Congo is passing through a stage of national and democratic revolution, in which it is necessary to rally all the anti-imperialist forces, including the national bourgeoisie (as opposed to the comprador bourgeoisie), and to pave the way for the transition to socialism. The key sectors of the economy are controlled by the state, but small enterprises are permitted and foreign investment encouraged. The PCT seeks to encourage mass involvement in social affairs, but regards the one-party system as necessary to prevent tribal warfare and to act as a "general staff and vanguard" of the nation.

Publication. Etumba (Combat), weekly (a few thousand).

Ethiopia

Capital: Addis Ababa   Pop. 42,000,000

Following mutinies in the armed forces and the police, strikes, land seizures by the peasantry and student demonstrations, the Ethiopian armed forces seized control in June 1974. The Emperor Haile Selassie was deposed in September in favour of his son, and a military government headed by Lt.-Gen. Aman Andom took power. Andom was killed two months later while resisting arrest, and was succeeced by Brig.-Gen. Teferi Benti. It was announced in December that

Ethiopia would become a unitary socialist one-party state, and in March 1975 the monarchy was abolished. Benti in turn was killed by his colleagues in 1977, and was succeeded as head of state by Lt.-Col. Mengistu Haile Mariam. Throughout its existence the military regime (generally known as the *Derg*) has been engaged in military operations against separatist revolts in Eritrea, Tigre province, Ogaden and other regions, and since 1982 the country has suffered from a disastrous drought and resultant famine.

Ethiopian Communist Party (ECP)

History. The ECP, founded in 1976, accused the *Derg* of having replaced feudalism by a "petty-bourgeois system", and was subsequently suppressed. It is doubtful whether it still exists.

Orientation. Pro-Chinese.

Programme. The ECP demanded the election of a People's Assembly; the formation of a government controlled by the Assembly; freedom of the press; the right to strike and to form trade unions and political parties; and the right to self-determination, including secession, by different nationalities.

Ethiopian People's Revolutionary Party (EPRP)

History. The EPRP, founded in 1976 and drawing its support mainly from intellectuals in Addis Ababa, denounced the military regime as "fascist" and denied that a military junta could achieve a genuine people's revolution. It launched a terrorist campaign in the autumn of 1976, in which it attempted to assassinate Lt.-Col. Mengistu and killed a number of government officials, and claimed to have a military branch, the Revolutionary People's Army, fighting in several provinces. The government, which accused the EPRP of drawing support both from China and from the US Central Intelligence Agency, replied to its "white terror" with a "red terror", many EPRP members being executed during 1976–79. In 1981 the EPRP joined the liberal Ethiopian Democratic Union (EDU) and other left-wing organizations in forming the Ethiopian Democratic Front. Nothing more was heard of this organization, but in 1983 EPRP and EDU members were reported to have formed the Ethiopian People's Democratic Movement, which was co-operating with the secessionist Tigre People's Liberation Front.

Marxist All-Ethiopian Socialist Movement (MAESON)

History. The MAESON, drawing its membership mainly from intellectuals, was founded in February 1977 as the sole legal political party, but in April a section of its members, who objected to the regime's pro-Soviet orientation, decided to adopt an attitude of "revolutionary opposition". The party was gradually discarded by the regime from July onwards, and many of its leading members went into hiding. The executive committee of the All-Ethiopian Trade Union, who were said to favour the return to power of MAESON members, were dismissed in 1978.

Workers' Party of Ethiopia (WPE)

History. The decision to establish a single political party on a nationalist and socialist basis was announced in December 1974. The Marxist All-Ethiopian

Socialist Movement (see above) was named as the official party in February 1977, but from July onwards it was replaced by another organization, Flame (*Seded*). Lt.-Col. Mengistu stated in 1978 that a third body, the Union of Ethiopian Marxist–Leninist Organizations (UEMLO), would form the nucleus of a mass Workers' Party, but a year later he said that all applications for membership of the new party would be screened on an individual basis, apparently indicating that both Flame and the UEMLO had been dissolved. A Commission for Organizing the Party of the Working People of Ethiopia (COPWE) was set up in December 1979, with Lt.-Col. Mengistu as its chairman, and was dissolved at the founding congress of the WPE, held in September 1984.

Leadership. The full members of the Political Bureau are Lt.-Col. Mengistu Haile Mariam (g.s.), Fikre Selassie Wogderess, Fissheha Desta, Brig.-Gen. Tesfaye Gebre Kidan, Berhanu Bayih, Addis Tedla, Legesse Asfaw, Ato Hailu Yimenu, Ato Emanuel Amde-Mikhail, Alemu Agebe and Shimelis Mazengia. There are also six alternate members.

Structure. The WPE has 6,500 cells, 240 district, 70 sub-regional and 33 regional organizations, a Central Committee of 136 full and 64 alternate members and an eight-member Secretariat.

Membership. 30,000–50,000 (1984 estimate). Of the 1,900 delegates to the founding congress 69 per cent were members of the armed forces or civil servants.

Industrial influence. The WPE controls the All-Ethiopian Trade Union, the country's only trade union organization.

Orientation. Pro-Soviet.

Programme. The founding congress adopted a 10-year plan for economic and social development, aimed at self-sufficiency in food, reafforestation, soil conservation, expansion of irrigated farming, establishment of co-operative and state farms and promotion of industrial development. The plan envisages the continuation of a mixed economy in agriculture, trade and small-scale industry.

Publications. Serto Ader (The Working People); *Meskerem* (September).

International affiliations. The WPE has close relations with the ruling parties of the Soviet-bloc countries, Cuba, South Yemen, Angola, Mozambique and Zimbabwe.

Eritrean Separatist Movement

The former Italian colony of Eritrea was united with Ethiopia in 1952 on a federal basis, enjoying internal autonomy, but in 1962 its federal status was abolished and it was incorporated in Ethiopia as a province. Eritrea secessionists have since conducted a guerrilla resistance, under the leadership first of the Eritrean Liberation Front and subsequently of a number of breakaway movements, of which the Eritrean People's Liberation Front is the strongest.

Eritrean People's Liberation Front (EPLF)

History. The EPLF broke away from the traditionalist Eritrean Liberation Front in 1970, and by 1977 had overrun the greater part of Eritrea, including numerous towns, and set up its own administration. In 1978, however, the Ethiopian government launched an offensive and succeeded in recapturing all the major towns except Nakfa. An EPLF proposal for a cease-fire and a referendum on Eritrea's future status, made in 1980, was ignored by the government. Another government offensive in 1982 failed to take Nakfa, and in 1984 the EPLF took the offensive, recapturing the town of Tessenei and inflicting a number of major defeats on the government forces. By 1985 the EPLF claimed to control 85 per cent of Eritrea.

Leadership. Ramadan Mohammed Nur (g.s.); Isaias Afewerki (deputy g.s. and military commander).

Structure. A congress held in 1977 elected a 43-member Central Committee and a 13-member Political Committee.

Membership. The EPLF was estimated in 1985 to have 30,000–40,000 fighters.

Orientation. Independent. The EPLF is hostile to the Soviet Union and Cuba, which have given military aid to the Ethiopian government, but some communist parties, including those of Yugoslavia, Italy and France, have adopted a sympathetic attitude towards the Eritreans' struggle.

Programme. The EPLF's aims have been defined as a national democratic revolution without ethnic or religious discrimination, a state at the service of the people and an independent Eritrean nation which would be "nobody's satellite".

The Gambia

Capital: Banjul
Pop. 610,000

The former British colony of The Gambia became an independent state within the Commonwealth in 1965 and a republic in 1970. Since independence it has been ruled by the People's Progressive Party, the leader of which, Sir Dawda Jawara, has been President since 1970. In 1982 The Gambia joined Senegal, within which it forms an enclave, in the Confederation of Senegambia. Both states retain their independence and sovereignty, but their armed forces and security forces are integrated and their foreign and communications policies co-ordinated.

Socialist and Revolutionary Labour Party (SRLP)

History. The SRLP was founded in 1978 by Kukli Samba Sanyang. During the absence abroad of President Jawara, it seized power in Banjul in July 1981 with the support of the majority of the Field Force, the police and the civilian population. A National Revolutionary Council of nine civilians and three officers headed by Sanyang was established, which accused the Jawara government of corruption, tribalism and social oppression, and announced that it would introduce a dictatorship of the proletariat led by a Marxist-Leninist party to promote revolutionary socialism. President Jawara, however, invoked a mutual defence agreement with Senegal, and the revolt was suppressed within a week by

Senegalese troops. Sanyang escaped abroad, but 63 people were sentenced to death for participating in the revolt.

Guinea-Bissau

Capital: Bissau Pop. 840,000

The Portuguese colony of Guinea was declared an independent republic, under the name of Guinea-Bissau, in 1973 by the African Party for the Independence of Guinea and Cape Verde, which had been conducting an armed struggle since 1961. Following the Portuguese revolution of 1974, the independence of Guinea-Bissau was recognised by the new Portuguese government. President Luis de Almeida Cabral was overthrown in 1980 by a coup led by the Prime Minister, Maj. João Bernardo Vieira, who succeeded him as head of state.

African Party for the Independence of Guinea and Cape Verde
Partido Africano da Independência da Guiné e do Cabo Verde (PAIGC)

History. The PAIGC was founded in 1956 by Amilcar Cabral, a Cape Verdian *mestiço* (half-caste), and launched an armed revolt in Portuguese Guinea in 1961. Cabral was assassinated in 1973, and was succeeded as general secretary by Aristides Maria Pereira, also a Cape Verdian. The PAIGC had previously organized elections in 1970 in the areas under its control to a National Assembly, which in 1973 proclaimed the independence of Guinea-Bissau, with Luis de Almeida Cabral (the brother of Amilcar Cabral) as its President. He was overthrown in 1980, however, in a coup largely provoked by resentment among Guinean blacks of the predominance of Cape Verdian *mestiços* in government and party circles; as a result the Cape Verdian section of the PAIGC broke away and formed an independent party led by Pereira, who since 1975 had been President of Cape Verde (see under main heading "Cape Verde"). A PAIGC congress in 1981 decided to retain the party's existing name, and expelled President Pereira and ex-President Cabral, the former being succeeded as general secretary by President João Bernardo Vieira. A new constitution adopted in 1984 declared the PAIGC the leading political force in society and the state, which defined the bases for state policy in all fields. In January 1986 a number of prominent figures were expelled from the PAIGC in consequence of their alleged involvement in an attempt to overthrow President Vieira the previous November.

Leadership. President João Bernardo Vieira (g.s.); Dr Vasco Cabral (perm. sec. of the High Council).

Structure. The PAIGC has a 51-member High Council and a 24-member Executive Committee.

Orientation. Independent.

Publication. O Militante.

Lesotho

Capital: Maseru Pop. 1,474,000

The former British High Commission Territory of Basutoland, which forms an enclave inside South Africa, became the independent Kingdom of Lesotho in

1966. Having been a multi-party parliamentary democracy (with a constitutional monarchy), the country underwent a military coup in January 1986 in which the government of Dr Leabua Jonathan (Basotho National Party) was overthrown by Maj.-Gen. Justin Lekhanya.

Communist Party of Lesotho (CPL)

History. The CPL, founded in 1962, was the only legal communist party in southern Africa until it was banned shortly after contesting the 1970 general election. The ban was partly lifted in 1984 so that the CPL could contest the coming elections, but like the other opposition parties it boycotted the elections held in the following year.

Leadership. R. Matji (ch.); Jacob M. Kena (g.s.).

Structure. The CPL has a Central Committee and district and village committees.

Membership. Unknown. The CPL is believed to derive its support mainly from migrant workers in South Africa, but it also has a following in Maseru and certain areas of southern Lesotho.

Orientation. Pro-Soviet.

Programme. The CPL has defined its immediate task as the struggle, in the framework of a national liberation front, for the establishment of a national democratic state with a non-aligned and anti-imperialist foreign policy, and its ultimate aim as the setting up of the dictatorship of the proletariat and a socialist society.

Mauritius

Capital: Port Louis   Pop. 1,000,000

The former British colony of Mauritius became an independent state within the Commonwealth in 1968, with the British monarch, represented by a Governor-General, as head of state. The island of Diego Garcia, previously administered by Mauritius, had been separated from it in 1965 to provide defence facilities for the British and US governments. The Mauritius Labour Party, in alliance with smaller parties, held office from 1967 to 1982, when it was defeated by the Mauritian Militant Movement. The government split in 1983, however, and after new elections a government was formed by the Mauritian Socialist Movement and the Labour and Social Democratic parties.

Mauritian Militant Movement
Mouvement Militant Mauricien (MMM)

History. The MMM, founded in 1970 by Paul Bérenger, won 30 of the 62 elective seats in the 1976 elections, becoming the largest parliamentary group, and in municipal elections in the following year gained control of three of the five town councils, including Port Louis. In the 1982 general election the MMM and allied parties won all the elective seats, and subsequently formed a government headed by Aneerood Jugnauth, the MMM president. The party split in the following year over economic and linguistic policies, however, and Jugnauth was expelled and formed the Mauritian Socialist Movement. In the subsequent elections the MMM won only 19 seats.

Leadership. Paul Bérenger (l.); D. Fokeer (pres.); Ponapar Naiker (g.s.).

Electoral influence. The MMM obtained 46 per cent of the vote in the 1983 elections. It drew its support mainly from the towns, winning 19 of the 30 urban seats.

Industrial influence. The General Workers' Federation is affiliated to the MMM.

Orientation. Independent.

Programme. The MMM's ultimate aim is the introduction of self-managing socialism. It advocates nationalization of public transport, the national airline and 20,000 acres of land, to be distributed among rural workers and cultivated on a co-operative basis, an expanded welfare state, job creation schemes and a wealth tax. It proposes to amend the constitution in order to make Mauritius a republic within the Commonwealth and to enable compensation for nationalized property to be paid in instalments, on condition that it is used for economic development in Mauritius. In foreign policy it supports strict non-alignment and the restoration of Diego Garcia to Mauritian sovereignty.

Mauritian Militant Socialist Progressive Movement
Mouvement Militant Mauricien Socialiste Progressiste (MMMSP)

History. The MMMSP was formed in 1973 by left-wing dissidents in the Mauritian Militant Movement, and unsuccessfully contested the 1976 elections.

Leadership. Dev Virahsawmy (ch.).

Structure. The MMMSP has cells, a party congress, a Central Committee and a Political Bureau.

Industrial influence. The MMMSP claims to control the 10,000-member United Workers' Federation.

Orientation. Maoist.

Programme. The MMMSP defines its aim as the creation of a united front to free the country from imperialist domination and to build the base for the construction of socialism.

Publication. *Soley Ruz* (Red Sun), weekly (10,000).

Mauritian Socialist Movement
Mouvement Socialiste Mauricien (MSM)

History. The MSM was formed in 1983 by Aneerood Jugnauth, the Prime Minister, after his expulsion from the Mauritian Militant Movement (MMM), and was later joined by the bulk of the Mauritian Socialist Party, which had broken away from the Labour Party in 1979 and had formed a coalition with the MMM in the previous year. The MSM fought the ensuing elections in alliance with the Labour Party, the alliance winning 37 of the 62 elective seats, and afterwards formed a government led by Jugnauth, in which the Mauritian Social Democratic Party was also included.

Leadership. Aneerood Jugnauth (l.).

Membership. The MSM draws its membership mainly from the Hindu community.

Orientation. Independent.

Programme. The MSM's programme is similar to that of the MMM, but it is regarded as more pragmatic in its application.

Mozambique

Capital: Maputo   Pop. 13,413,000

The Front for the Liberation of Mozambique (Frelimo) began an armed struggle against Portuguese rule in 1964, and gradually extended its control over a large part of the country. After the Portuguese revolution of 1974 the new government agreed to recognize Mozambique's independence from 1975, a transitional government of Frelimo and Portuguese representatives holding office in the interim. The People's Republic of Mozambique became independent on June 25, 1975, with Samora Machel, the Frelimo president and military commander, as President and a constitution which recognized Frelimo as "the directing power of the state and society".

Front for the Liberation of Mozambique
Frente da Libertação de Moçambique (Frelimo)

History. Frelimo was formed in 1962, with Eduardo Mondlane as president, by the merger of three nationalist organizations which had been founded in the previous two years. It launched an armed struggle in the northern provinces in 1964, and by 1966 claimed to control one-fifth of Mozambique. From the beginning, however, it suffered from internal disputes over its policy and methods; some of its early leaders defected to the Portuguese, and in 1969 Mondlane was murdered, as the result of a conspiracy between the Portuguese secret police and the internal opposition. He was succeeded by a presidium of Uria Simango, Samora Machel and Marcelino dos Santos, but in 1970 Simango was expelled, Machel and dos Santos becoming president and vice-president respectively. On the achievement of independence in 1975 Machel also became President of the Republic. The third party congress, held in 1977, declared Frelimo a Marxist-Leninist vanguard party of selected cadres based on the industrial workers and peasants, aimed at the development of scientific socialism.

Leadership. The Political Bureau consists of Samora Moisés Machel (g.s.), Marcelino dos Santos, Joaquim Alberto Chissano, Alberto Chipande, Armando Emilio Guebuza, Jorge Rebelo, Mariano de Araújo Matsinhe, Sebastião Marcos Mabote, Jacinto Soares Veloso, Mário de Graça Machungo and José Óscar Monteiro.

Structure. The national congress elects the 118-member Central Committee, which elects the Political Bureau and the six-member Secretariat.

Membership. 110,323 (1983 claim). New members must live by their own labour and possess "outstanding political and moral qualities", must be approved by a mass meeting of their workmates and must serve a year's probationary period.

Electoral influence. All the 226 members of the National People's Assembly are elected from Frelimo lists by an elaborate system of indirect election.

Orientation. Independent. During the struggle for independence Frelimo adopted a neutral position in the controversy between the Soviet Union and China, from both of which it received aid. It has since maintained friendly relations with the Communist parties of both countries.

Programme. Frelimo's objectives are the consolidation of independence and the construction of a socialist society with an independent, planned and advanced economy able to satisfy the people's growing needs (see Appendix 2: Documents). It follows an independent foreign policy based on the struggle for peace, democracy and progress.

Publications. *Noticias*, daily; *O Tempo*, weekly; *Voz da Revolução*, Central Committee organ.

Niger

Capital: Niamey   Pop. 5,800,000

The former French colony of Niger became an independent republic in 1960, with Diori Hamani as President. He was overthrown in 1974 by a coup led by Lt.-Col. Seyni Kountché, who succeeded him as head of state and who dissolved the country's existing political institutions.

Independence
Sawaba

History. The Niger Democratic Union, formed by Djibo Bakary in 1951, won the elections to the Territorial Assembly in 1957, when Bakary formed a government. Renamed Independence in 1958, it was defeated in new elections in that year and banned in 1959, a number of its leaders being imprisoned. Groups of *Sawaba* guerrillas who entered Niger from Ghana in 1964 were wiped out, and an attempt on President Hamani's life in 1965 was unsuccessful. Bakary was allowed to return from exile after the 1974 coup, but was arrested in the following year on a charge of conspiracy, not being released until 1984. It is doubtful whether *Sawaba* still exists.

Nigeria

Capital: Lagos   Pop. 88,148,000

The former British colony of Nigeria became independent in 1960, with the British sovereign as head of state, and a federal republic within the Commonwealth in 1963. Following a coup in 1966, it was ruled by a series of military regimes, all political parties being banned until 1978. After elections in 1979 civilian rule was restored. New elections in 1983, which were widely believed to have been rigged, were followed by a coup and the establishment of another military regime, under which parties were again banned.

Socialist Working People's Party (SWPP)

History. The SWPP, founded in 1963 as the Socialist Workers' and Farmers' Party, was banned with the other parties in 1966 and went underground. Revived under its present name in 1978, it was refused registration by the Federal Electoral Commission, and in consequence was unable to contest the 1979 and 1983 elections. It was again banned with the other parties in 1983.

Leadership. Chaika Onozie (ch.); Wahab Goodluck (deputy ch.); Dapo Fatogun (g.s.).

Structure. The party has a four-member Political Bureau.

Industrial influence. The SWPP has considerable influence in the Nigerian Labour Congress, the country's only trade union organization, the president of which, Hassan Sunmonu, is a member of its Political Bureau.

Orientation. Pro-Soviet.

Programme. "To organize the working people of Nigeria towards winning political power and building a socialist state founded on the ideas of scientific socialism".

Publication. *New Horizon*, the Nigerian edition of *World Marxist Review*.

Réunion

Capital: Saint-Dènis   Pop. 535,000

The island of Réunion has been a French overseas department since 1946, and is represented in the French Parliament by three deputies and two senators. It has an Assembly of 45 members.

Movement for the Independence of Réunion
Mouvement pour l'Indépendance de la Réunion (MIR)

History. The MIR, founded in 1981, is the successor to the Marxist-Leninist Communist Organization of Réunion, formed by Maoist defectors from the Communist Party in 1975, and the Movement for the Liberation of Réunion.

Programme. The MIR advocates complete independence for Réunion.

Réunion Communist Party
Parti Communiste Réunionnais (PCR)

History. The PCR, formed in 1945 as the Republican Committee for Democratic and Social Action, became the Réunion federation of the French Communist Party in 1949 and an independent party in 1959. Its general secretary, Paul Vergès, was elected to the European Parliament in 1979 and 1984.

Leadership. Paul Vergès (g.s.).

Structure. The PCR has a 32-member Central Committee, a 12-member Political Bureau and a six-member Secretariat.

Membership. 10,000 (1981 claim).

Electoral influence. In the 1983 elections to the Réunion Assembly the PCR obtained 64,800 votes (32.73 per cent) and 16 of the 45 seats.

Industrial influence. The PCR controls the General Confederation of Réunion Workers, the general secretary of which is a member of its Secretariat.

Orientation. Eurocommunist.

Programme. The PCR advocates increased autonomy for Réunion, a more balanced economy as a means of redressing the inequality between social benefits in France and on the islands, and the removal of foreign military forces from the Indian Ocean.

Publication. Témoignages (Records), daily (10,000).

International affiliations. The PCR has close relations with the Communist parties of France and the other French overseas departments.

São Tomé and Príncipe

Capital: São Tomé   Pop. 105,000

The former Portuguese colony of São Tomé and Príncipe consists of two islands off the coast of Gabon with a total area of 372 square miles. After the Portuguese revolution of 1974 a transitional government was established, and independence was achieved in the following year on the basis of a one–party–state system.

Movement for the Liberation of São Tomé and Príncipe
Movimento de Libertação de São Tomé e Príncipe (MLSTP)

History. The MLSTP, which was founded in 1960 as the Committee for the Liberation of São Tomé and Príncipe and assumed its present name in 1972, conducted underground agitation from its base in Gabon until 1974, when it was recognized by the Portuguese government as the sole representative of the people of the islands and a transitional government was formed, consisting of four MLSTP members and a nominee of the Portuguese government. On the attainment of independence in 1975 Dr Manuel Pinto da Costa, the party's general secretary, became President, and an MLSTP government took office with Miguel dos Anjos da Cunha Lisboa Trouvoada as Prime Minister. The post of Prime Minister was abolished in April 1979, and Trouvoada, who had retained his other portfolios, was arrested in September on a charge of attempting to seize power, although he was released two years later. The premiership was revived in 1980, when President Pinto da Costa assumed the post. In 1984–85 the government's policy moved sharply to the right; the more radical and pro-Soviet ministers were dismissed or demoted, many economic controls were dismantled and a military training agreement was signed with the United States.

Leadership. President Manuel Pinto da Costa (g.s.).

Structure. The congress elects the Central Committee of 41 full and 10 alternate members, which elects the Political Bureau.

Electoral influence. All the 40 members of the National People's Assembly, who are elected by the People's District Assemblies, are MLSTP nominees.

Orientation. Independent. The government emphasizes its non-alignment, and maintains friendly relations with the Soviet Union, Cuba, Yugoslavia, China and North Korea.

International affiliations. The MLSTP has close relations with the ruling parties in Angola, Guinea-Bissau and Mozambique.

Senegal

Capital: Dakar   Pop. 6,541,000

Since becoming an independent republic in 1960 the former French colony of Senegal has been ruled by the Senegalese Progressive Union, which in 1976 was renamed the Socialist Party of Senegal. A constitutional amendment adopted in 1976 limited the number of political parties to three (a socialist, a liberal and a Marxist party); the number was increased to four in 1978 to allow for the existence of a conservative party, and in 1981 most restrictions on the official recognition of parties were lifted, although electoral alliances were forbidden.

African Independence Party
Parti Africain de l'Indépendance (PAI)

History. The PAI was founded by Majhemout Diop in 1957 as a federal party campaigning for the independence of the French African colonies, but after the attainment of independence it decided in 1962 to restrict its activities to Senegal. It was banned in the same year after riots for which it was held responsible, and 29 of its members were sentenced to terms of imprisonment on conspiracy charges in 1965. It was legalized under the 1976 constitutional amendment, but a pro-Soviet wing of the party continued to operate clandestinely, and broke away in 1981 to form the Independence and Labour Party. The PAI contested the 1978 and 1983 elections without success.

Leadership. Majhemout Diop (pres.); Bara Goudiaby (g.s.).

Structure. The PAI has a Central Committee and an Executive Secretariat.

Membership. 2,000 (1982 estimate).

Electoral influence. The PAI obtained 5,146 votes (0.47 per cent) in the 1983 elections.

Orientation. Independent.

Publications. *La Lutte* (The Struggle), monthly (1,000); *Momsareew* (Independence), weekly (1,000).

Democratic League—Movement for the Labour Party
Ligue Démocratique—Mouvement pour le Parti du Travail (LD-MPT)

History. The LD-MPT was registered in 1981 and contested the 1983 elections.

Leadership. Babacar Sané, Mamadou Ndoye, Abdoulaye Bathily (leaders).

Electoral influence. The LD-MPT obtained 12,204 votes (1.12 per cent) in the 1983 elections.

Industrial influence. The LD–MPT has close ties with several trade unions, including the principal teachers' union, of which Mamadou Ndoye is general secretary.

Orientation. Independent.

Publication. Vérité (Truth).

Independence and Labour Party
Parti de l'Indépendance et du Travail (PIT)

History. The PIT, formerly the clandestine pro-Soviet wing of the African Independence Party, became a separate party in 1981, and contested the 1983 elections without success.

Leadership. Amath Dansoko (g.s.).

Structure. The PIT has a 55-member Central Committee, a 14-member Political Bureau and a seven-member Secretariat.

Electoral influence. The PIT obtained 5,929 votes (0.55 per cent) in the 1983 elections.

Orientation. Pro-Soviet.

Publication. Daan Doole, Gestu.

International affiliations. The PIT since 1981 has replaced the African Independence Party as the Marxist party recognized by the Soviet-bloc parties, and is represented on the editorial council of *World Marxist Review*.

Popular Democratic Movement
Mouvement Democratique et Populaire (MDP)

History. The MDP was founded in 1981 by Mamadou Dia (Prime Minister in 1959–62), and contested the 1983 elections.

Leadership. Mamadou Dia (l.).

Electoral influence. The MDP obtained 12,447 votes (1.14 per cent) in the 1983 elections.

Orientation. Independent.

Programme. The MDP advocates socialist self-management of the economy.

Revolutionary Movement for the New Democracy
Mouvement Révolutionnaire pour la Démocratie Nouvelle (MRDN)/And-Jëf

History. The MRDN was legalized in 1981, but boycotted the 1983 elections as a protest against the ban on electoral alliances.

Leadership. Landing Savane (l.).

Orientation. Pro-Chinese.

Publication. Jaay Doolé Bi.

Union for People's Democracy
Union pour la Démocratie Populaire (UDP)

History. The UDP, which had broken away from the Revolutionary Movement for the New Democracy, was registered in 1981, but boycotted the 1983 elections.

Leadership. Hamedine Racine Guisse (l.).

Orientation. Pro-Albanian.

Workers' Socialist Organization
Organisation Socialiste des Travailleurs (OST)

History. The OST, founded and registered in 1982, boycotted the 1983 elections.

Leadership. Mbaye Bathily (l.).

Orientation. Trotskyist.

Seychelles

Capital: Victoria   Pop. 66,000

The British colony of Seychelles became an independent republic within the Commonwealth in 1976. As a result of a coup in June 1977, the country became a one-party state with a presidential form of government, as confirmed under the 1979 constitution.

Seychelles People's Progressive Front (SPPF)

History. The SPPF was founded in 1963 as the Seychelles People's United Party (SPUP), and won three of the eight elective seats in the Legislative Council in 1967 and five of the 15 elective seats in the Legislative Assembly in 1970. In the 1974 elections its representation fell to two seats, although it obtained 47.6 per cent of the vote. Its pressure for complete independence, however, forced the ruling Seychelles Democratic Party (SDP) to adopt a similar policy, and in 1975 the two parties formed a coalition government. On the achievement of independence in the following year James Mancham, the SDP leader, became President and was succeeded as Prime Minister by France Albert René, the SPUP leader. In 1977 Mancham was deposed by a coup while absent abroad, whereupon René replaced him as President and formed a new government drawn entirely from the SPUP. Although he promised to introduce "a non-Marxist form of socialism appropriate to Seychelles", the SPUP, which was renamed the Seychelles People's Progressive Front in 1978, has since become increasingly Marxist in its theory and policies. A new constitution adopted in 1979 declared Seychelles a socialist state, with the SPPF the only legal party.

Leadership. France Albert René (g.s.); Maj. James Michel (deputy g.s.).

Structure. The SPPF has 23 branches, corresponding to the country's 23 districts. Branch committees, previously elected, have since 1982 been nominated by the Central Executive Committee. The party congress meets annually, and every three years elects the 13-member Central Executive Committee.

Membership. Over 8,000 (1981 claim). New members are required to serve a six months' probationary period, and must be approved by the Central Executive Committee.

Electoral influence. Although only SPPF branch offices may nominate candidates, subject to the Central Executive Committee's approval, electors may be given a limited choice. The 23 elective seats in the People's Assembly were contested by 55 SPPF candidates in 1979 and by 30 in 1983.

Industrial influence. The SPPF controls the National Workers' Union, the country's only trade union organization.

Orientation. Independent.

Programme. The SPPF has defined its main objectives as preserving the economic and political independence of Seychelles, promoting people's democracy and creating a socialist state in which all citizens will enjoy equal opportunities and be guaranteed the satisfaction of their vital requirements. It pursues a foreign policy of positive non-alignment, and demands that the Indian Ocean become a zone of peace in which foreign military bases are not permitted.

Publication. *The People* (1,000).

South Africa

Capitals: Pretoria (administrative)
Cape Town (legislative)
Bloemfontein (judicial) Pop. 32,460,000

South Africa, formerly a dominion within the Commonwealth with the British sovereign as head of state, became a republic and left the Commonwealth in 1961. Africans, who form 70 per cent of the population, were formerly represented by four members in the Senate and by three in the House of Assembly; in the Cape, Coloured (mixed-race) voters were included in the general register, although membership of both houses was limited to whites. The National Party, which came to power in 1948 with a policy of *apartheid* (separate development) and has held office ever since, first placed the Cape Coloureds on a separate register and provided for their representation by four members, but later abolished both African and Coloured representation. Ten "Bantu homelands" with limited internal autonomy were created, four of which were subsequently declared independent states, although they have not been recognized by any other government. In 1983 a new constitution was adopted, under which the Senate was abolished and separate chambers established for whites, Coloureds and Indians; elections to the Coloured and Indian chambers held in 1984, however, were boycotted by the great majority of the electorate. The government's policies have met with continuous resistance from the African population, which has taken the form of peaceful agitation, strikes, boycotts, riots, sabotage and guerrilla warfare.

South African Communist Party (SACP)

History. The SACP was founded in 1921, as the Communist Party of South Africa (CPSA), by the merger of the International Socialist League, which had broken away from the South African Labour Party in 1915, and a number of smaller Marxist groups. Although it was open to all races, its original membership mainly consisted of English-speaking whites, and considerable controversy took place before, in 1924, it decided to concentrate on recruiting African workers. By 1928 it had about 1,750 members, of whom 1,600 were Africans, but factional disputes and purges reduced its membership in 1933 to only 150. During the later 1930s and early 1940s, however, it extended its influence to all sections of the population, including Indians, Coloureds and Afrikaners, and its membership rose to several thousand. Sam Kahn was returned to the House of Assembly as a natives' representative by an overwhelming majority in 1948 and Fred Carneson to the Cape Provincial Council in the following year, while other Communists were elected to the Cape Town and Johannesburg city councils.

The Suppression of Communism Act, passed in 1950, declared the CPSA an illegal organization and made membership or support of it punishable by up to 10 years' imprisonment. While the bill was still before Parliament the CPSA dissolved itself, but the Communist members of Parliament and the provincial and city councils were deprived of their seats, and Communist trade union officials were removed from their posts. Two Communists in succession were elected by large majorities in 1952 and 1954 to the seat previously held by Kahn, but both were expelled from the House of Assembly. A number of African and Indian leaders, including both Communists and non-Communists, were convicted under the Suppression of Communism Act in 1952 for advocating equal political rights for all races; the judge explained that they had been convicted of "statutory communism", which had "nothing to do with communism as it is commonly known".

The CPSA was refounded, as the South African Communist Party, at a secret conference in Johannesburg in 1953, although its underground existence was not revealed until 1960. Its members operated inside a number of opposition organizations, including the African National Congress (ANC), the (white) Congress of Democrats, the South African Coloured People's Organization and the South African Indian Congress, which together formed the Congress Alliance. The Congress of the People, organized by the Alliance in 1955, adopted the Freedom Charter, which called for the right to vote and to be elected for people of all races, the nationalization of the mines, the banks and major industries, and the redivision of the land among those who worked it. The police arrested 156 people who had been involved in the congress, including Moses Kotane (the former general secretary of the CPSA), Carneson and other Communists, in 1956 on a charge of treason; after a trial lasting over two years 28 of the accused were acquitted in 1961, and the charges against the rest were dropped.

After the Sharpeville massacre of 1960, when the police fired on a peaceful demonstration against the pass laws, killing 69 people, ANC and SACP leaders co-operated in forming a clandestine organization, *Umkhonto we Sizwe* (Zulu for "Spear of the Nation"), which began a sabotage campaign in 1961. Eight alleged leaders of *Umkhonto*, including Nelson Mandela, general secretary of the ANC, and Ahmed Kathrada, a Communist, were sentenced to life imprisonment in 1964. In a series of trials in 1965–66, which revealed that the SACP had been penetrated by secret police agents, 22 people were sentenced to prison terms on charges of SACP membership, including two members of its Central Committee, Abram Fischer, who was also charged with conspiracy to commit sabotage and received a life sentence, and Carneson, who stated at his trial that he had been tortured three times by the security police. Prosecutions of Communists thereafter declined, although three whites were sentenced to prison terms for Communist activities in 1975–76. Ahmed Timol, said to be the leader of the SACP's "main unit" in South Africa, died in 1971 while in police custody, allegedly by committing suicide.

The government's campaign against the radical opposition, the SACP later admitted, "almost decimated the movement, smashed the party headquarters and penetrated deeply into its membership cells, and finally made the retreat of the party and the ANC leadership into temporary exile abroad essential if anything was to be saved for rebuilding". Most of the SACP leaders still at liberty escaped to friendly African countries or to Europe, and were joined by others who had been permitted to leave South Africa on condition that they did not return. Guerrilla operations by *Umkhonto* nevertheless continued inside South Africa, usually taking the form of bomb explosions or sabotage.

Leadership. The party chairman, Dr Yusuf Dadoo, died in exile in 1983, and the general secretary, Moses Mabhida, in 1986. The names of other members of the Political Bureau and Central Committee are not published.

Membership. 1,000 (1978 estimate).

Orientation. Pro-Soviet. SACP publications have attacked Maoism and Eurocommunism and defended the declaration of martial law in Poland in 1981.

Programme. The SACP regards itself as "a vital part of the liberation forces headed by the ANC", which aim "to unite all sections and classes amongst the oppressed and other truly democratic forces for a revolution . . . whose main content is the national liberation of African and other black oppressed groups, and which must put an end to race discrimination in all its forms, restore the land and wealth of our country to the people and guarantee democracy, freedom and equality of rights and opportunities to all".

Publication. African Communist, quarterly, published in London.

International affiliations. The SACP is represented on the editorial council of *World Marxist Review,* and maintains close relations with the Soviet-bloc parties. The South African government alleges that *Umkhonto we Sizwe* members have received military training in the Soviet Union.

Zimbabwe

Capital: Harare   Pop. 8,400,000

The self-governing British colony of Rhodesia, in which the franchise was restricted to whites and a comparatively small number of Africans possessing certain income and educational qualifications, was declared independent of Britain by the ruling Rhodesian Front in 1965 and a republic in 1970. After a prolonged guerrilla struggle by African nationalist organizations, an agreement was reached in 1979 under which Rhodesia became the independent Republic of Zimbabwe in the following year, with a House of Assembly of 100 members, 80 of whom are elected by universal suffrage on a common roll and 20 on a separate roll for whites, Coloureds and Asians. Elections held in 1980 were won by the Zimbabwe African National Union—Patriotic Front (ZANU-PF), which formed a coalition government which also included members of the Patriotic Front—Zimbabwe African People's Union (PF-ZAPU) and white members. Most of the PF-ZAPU ministers were dropped in 1982, and after the 1985 elections a new government was formed drawn entirely from ZANU-PF, which had increased its majority, with the exception of one white minister.

Zimbabwe African National Union—Patriotic Front (ZANU-PF)

History. The Zimbabwe African National Union (ZANU), led by Ndabaningi Sithole, broke away in 1963 from the Zimbabwe African People's Union (ZAPU), which had been formed by Joshua Nkomo two years earlier, and began guerrilla operations in 1966, at first with little success. With the assistance of the Front for the Liberation of Mozambique (see under "Mozambique"), however, it organized the Zimbabwe African National Liberation Army (ZANLA), which from 1972 onwards played the leading role in the nationalist uprising. A prolonged struggle in 1974–76 between Sithole and the more radical elements in the party, who were supported by ZANLA, resulted in his replacement as leader by Robert Mugabe, whereupon he formed his own organization, known as ZANU (Sithole). ZANU and ZAPU in 1976 formed an alliance, the Patriotic Front (PF), although they retained their separate military wings; ZANLA, which was based on the majority Shona tribes and constituted about 80 per cent of the guerrillas, was supported by China and operated from Mozambique, while the ZAPU military organization, the Zimbabwe People's Revolutionary Army, which was based on the Ndebele of Matabeleland, was supported by the Soviet Union and operated from Zambia.

The PF took part in the 1979 Lancaster House conference, at which the independence agreement was reached, but the two parties fought the 1980 elections separately, as ZANU-PF and PF-ZAPU. They resulted in a major victory for the former, which won 57 of the 80 black seats, against 20 for PF-ZAPU and three for the United African National Council, and Mugabe subsequently formed a government dominated by ZANU-PF. His cautious economic policies led to considerable criticism, and in 1981 Edgar Tekere, the party's general secretary, who had demanded "revolutionary" changes, was removed from his post. ZANU-PF's second congress, held in 1984, adopted a new party constitution, which increased the size of the Central Committee from 33 to 90 and established a Political Bureau, and adopted resolutions in favour of increased socialization and the establishment of a one-party state. In the 1985 elections ZANU-PF increased its parliamentary representation to 64 seats.

Leadership. The Political Bureau consists of Robert Mugabe (pres. and 1st sec.), Simon Muzenda (vice-pres. and 2nd sec.), Maurice Nyagumbo, Enos Nkala, Emmerson Munangagwa, Dr Nathan Shamuyarira, Didymus Mutasa, Dr Dzingai Mutumbuka, Mrs Teurai Ropa Nhongo, Ernest Kadungure, Lt.-Gen. Rex Nhongo, Mayor Urimbo and Maj.-Gen. Josiah Tungamirai.

Structure. The Central Committee consists of 42 members elected from the eight provinces, 38 from the provincial executives, the Women's League and the youth wing, and 10 nominated by the party president. The Political Bureau is nominated by the president in consultation with the vice-president. The Central Committee elects five standing committees (the political and policy, economic, social and welfare, national security, and legal and constitutional committees) to supervise the work of government departments.

Electoral influence. The ZANU-PF vote increased from 1,668,992 (63 per cent) in 1980 to 2,199,057 (78 per cent) in 1985.

Industrial influence. The Zimbabwe Congress of Trade Unions was established in 1981 as the national trade union federation under the leadership of Albert Mugabe, the Prime Minister's brother, but attempts by ZANU-PF to control it have met with considerable resistance.

Orientation. Independent. The government has warm relations with China, which supported ZANU during the liberation struggle; relations with the Soviet Union, which supported ZAPU, are cool.

Programme. The 1984 congress adopted resolutions in favour of intensifying "the socialization of the economy through state ownership of the means of production" and the establishment of a one-party state "in the fullness of time and in accordance with the law and the constitution". In his speech to the congress Mugabe said that the government's aim was "the achievement of a socialist, egalitarian and fully democratic society", and that it would move rapidly towards state participation in strategic industries such as chemicals and engineering as part of a strategy designed to increase "the degree of local ownership and control of the means of production", establish a state trading corporation to co-ordinate imports and exports, and set up state farms alongside the existing white-dominated commercial farming sector.

Publication. Moto.

6. NORTH AMERICA

Canada

Capital: Ottawa   Pop. 25,142,000

Canada has a nominated Senate of 104 members and an elected House of Commons of 282 members. Each of the 10 provinces has its own legislature and government. The Liberal Party was in power in 1921–30, 1935–57, 1963–79 and 1980–84, and the Conservative Party (renamed the Progressive Conservative Party in 1942) in 1930–35, 1957–63, 1979–80 and since 1984. The third national party is the socialist New Democratic Party (NDP), which was known until 1961 as the Co-operative Commonwealth Federation. In the September 1984 federal elections the Progressive Conservatives won 211 seats in the Commons, the Liberals 40 and the NDP 30 (one independent also being elected).

Communist Party of Canada (CPC)

History. The CPC, founded in 1921 as an underground party, formed the Workers' Party of Canada in the following year as a cover organization, and was legalized in 1924. It was banned in 1931, eight of its leaders being arrested, and worked underground until it was legalized again in 1934. Because of its anti-war policy it was again banned in 1940, over 100 of its leading members being interned; they were released in 1942, however, the CPC having switched to a pro-war policy after the German invasion of the Soviet Union. In 1943 it was reorganized as the Labor Progressive Party (LPP); Fred Rose won a Montreal seat in the House of Commons in the same year, and LPP candidates also won two seats in the Ontario Assembly and one in the Manitoba Assembly. Rose was convicted in 1946 of spying for the Soviet Union, being expelled from the House of Commons in the following year, and the LPP lost one of its Ontario seats in 1951, the other in 1955, and its Manitoba seat in 1958. Following Khrushchev's denunciation of Stalin, a section of the leadership in 1956 demanded the adoption of a more independent attitude towards the Soviet Union and the resignation of Tim Buck, the Stalinist general secretary, but without success. The LPP reassumed the name of Communist Party of Canada in 1959.

Leadership. William Kashtan (g.s.).

Structure. Party clubs are organized on a residential or workplace basis, and on a linguistic basis among immigrants. District or city committees are established where more than two clubs exist, and there are committees for each province. The national convention, held every two years, elects the 20-member National Committee, which elects the Central Executive Committee. Communists in Quebec are organized in the *Parti Communiste du Québec*, which develops its own policies on the basis of the CPC's programme.

Membership. 2,500 (1985 estimate). Support is strongest in Ontario, Manitoba and British Columbia.

Electoral influence. The CPC has not been represented in the Federal Parliament since 1947, or in the provincial legislatures since 1958. Its 52 candidates in the 1984 elections received just over 8,000 votes. It holds a number of seats in the Winnipeg and Vancouver city councils.

Industrial influence. The CPC exercises some influence in several trade unions.

Orientation. Pro-Soviet.

Programme. While critical of the New Democratic Party, the CPC advocates co-operation with it, particularly in local politics. It calls for Canada's withdrawal from NATO, and opposes the testing of cruise missiles in Canada.

Publications. Canadian Tribune and *Pacific Tribune,* weeklies, published in Toronto and Vancouver respectively; *Combat,* French-language semimonthly; *Communist Viewpoint,* quarterly.

International affiliations. The CPC is represented on the editorial council of *World Marxist Review.*

Communist Party of Canada—Marxist-Leninist (CPC-ML)

History. The CPC-ML, founded in 1970 as a pro-Chinese party, has since adopted a pro-Albanian attitude.

Leadership. Hardial Bains (1st sec.).

Membership. 500–1,000 (1985 estimate).

Electoral influence. The CPC-ML received 0.1 per cent of the vote in the 1980 elections, and did not contest the 1984 elections.

Industrial influence. CPC-ML supporters in the unions are organized in the Revolutionary Trade Union Opposition.

Orientation. Pro-Albanian. CPC-ML publications have described the Soviet Union as "a fascist dictatorship of the bourgeoisie", and China as "the most reactionary warmongering social-imperialist power".

Programme. The CPC-ML believes that objective conditions in Canada are ripe for revolution, and advocates revolutionary violence as the means of establishing a communist regime.

Publication. The Marxist-Leninist, daily.

International affiliations. The CPC-ML has close relations with the Albanian Party of Labour.

Forward Readers' Group (FRG)

Structure. This Trotskyist group, centred on the monthly *Forward,* operates inside the New Democratic Party.

Revolutionary Workers' League (RWL)

History. The RWL was founded in 1977 by the merger of three Trotskyist groups.

Leadership. John Riddell (g.s.).

Membership. Several hundred (1985 estimate).

Orientation. Trotskyist.

Programme. The RWL supports the New Democratic Party (NDP), but is critical of its leadership and calls on it to adopt more socialist policies. RWL members have been expelled from the NDP.

Publications. Socialist Voice and *Lutte Ouvrière* (Workers' Struggle), both bimonthly.

International affiliations. Fourth International, United Secretariat.

Socialist Party of Canada (SPC)

History. The SPC was founded in 1931 as an offshoot of the Socialist Party of Great Britain (SPGB).

Leadership. L. G. Jenkins (g.s.).

Membership. 20 (1984 estimate).

Orientation. Independent.

Programme. The SPC's principles are similar to those of the SPGB. It opposes co-operation with any other party.

Publication. Socialist Fulcrum, quarterly.

International affiliations. World Socialist Movement.

Trotskyist League (TL)

Orientation. Trotskyist.

Programme. The TL occupies a position to the left of the Revolutionary Workers' League, which it criticizes for its support of the New Democratic Party and its unwillingness to use violence.

Publication. Spartacist Canada, monthly.

International affiliations. International Spartacist Tendency.

Workers' Socialist Group
Groupe Socialiste des Travailleurs (GST)

Structure. The GST operates only in Quebec.

Orientation. Trotskyist.

Programme. The GST advocates independence for Quebec and the creation of a workers' party there.

Publication. Tribune Ouvrière (Workers' Tribune).

International affiliations. Fourth International, International Committee.

Mexico

Capital: Mexico City Pop. 77,659,000

After a period of violent revolutionary struggles beginning in 1910, Mexico has been ruled since 1929 by the National Revolutionary Party, which was renamed the Party of the Mexican Revolution in 1938 and the Institutional Revolutionary Party (PRI) in 1946. The executive President is elected for a single six-year term. The Chamber of Deputies, which is elected every three years, contains 400 seats, of which 300 are filled by members elected by majority vote in single-member constituencies and 100 are distributed among parties which have won fewer than 60 seats in proportion to their share of the vote.

In parliamentary elections held on July 7, 1985, the PRI won 289 of the directly elective seats, the (right-wing) National Action Party (PAN) nine and the (pro-government) Authentic Party of the Mexican Revolution (PARM) two. Of the 100 proportional seats, the PAN obtained 32, the (right-wing) Mexican Democratic Party (PDM) 12 and the PARM seven, while on the left the Unified Socialist Party of Mexico (PSUM) took 12, the Socialist Workers' Party (PST) 12, the Popular Socialist Party (PPS) 11, the Revolutionary Workers' Party (PRT) six and the Mexican Workers' Party (PMT) six.

Libertarian Communist Movement
Movimiento Comunista Libertario

History. This group was formed by Communist Party members who refused in 1981 to join the Unified Socialist Party of Mexico.

Leadership. Evaristo Pérez Arreola (l.).

Popular Socialist Party
Partido Popular Socialista (PPS)

History. The PPS was founded in 1948 as the Popular Party by the trade union leader Vicente Lombardo Toledano, who contested the 1952 presidential election but received only 2 per cent of the vote. It was renamed the Popular Socialist Party in 1960, and three years later absorbed the Mexican Worker-Peasant Party, which had broken away from the Communist Party in 1940. It has had close ties with the left wing of the ruling Institutional Revolutionary Party, whose presidential candidates it supported in the 1964, 1976 and 1982 elections. In February 1985, however, the PPS entered into an electoral alliance with other left-wing and progressive parties, including the Mexican Workers' Party, the Revolutionary Workers' Party, the Socialist Workers' Party, the Unified Socialist Party of Mexico and (the liberal) Unification and Progress.

Leadership. Jorge Cruickshank García (g.s.).

Structure. Base units of three or more members, who must serve a probationary period of six months, are formed at places of work or residence. The national assembly, meeting every three years, elects the Central Committee, which elects the national leadership and general secretary. Its youth organization is the Socialist Popular Youth.

Electoral influence. The PPS won 11 of the 100 proportionally distributed seats in the Chamber in 1979, 1982 and 1985.

Industrial influence. The PPS controls the General Union of Workers and Peasants of Mexico (UGOCM).

Orientation. Pro-Soviet.

Programme. The PPS defines its aim as "building socialism in Mexico, developing the Mexican revolution through the unity of the patriotic and democratic forces to confront North American imperialism and the country's oligarchic bourgeoisie".

Publications. El Combatiente (The Fighter), weekly (25,000); *Nueva Democracía* (New Democracy), quarterly (5,000).

International affiliations. The PPS has links with the Soviet-bloc parties through the World Federation of Trade Unions and the World Federation of Democratic Youth, to which the General Union of Workers and Peasants of Mexico and the Socialist Popular Youth respectively are affiliated.

Revolutionary Workers' Party
Partido Revolucionario de los Trabajadores (PRT)

History. The PRT contested the 1982 presidential and congressional elections without success, but won six of the proportionally distributed seats in 1985. In the latter elections the PRT was allied with other left-wing and progressive parties (see entry for "Popular Socialist Party" above).

Leadership. José Manuel Aguilar Mora (g.s.).

Electoral influence. Sra Rosario Ibarra de la Piedra, the PRT candidate in the 1982 presidential election, obtained 1.85 per cent of the vote.

Orientation. Trotskyist.

International affiliations. Fourth International, United Secretariat.

Socialist Workers' Party
Partido Socialista de los Trabajadores (PST)

History. The PST, founded in 1973, developed out of the National Committee of Investigation and Organization, an unofficial body set up to investigate the events of Oct. 2, 1968, when troops fired on demonstrators in Mexico City, causing many casualties. It was given official recognition in 1978, and won 10 of the proportionally distributed seats in the 1979 elections, 11 in 1982 and 12 in 1985 (when it was allied with other left-wing and progressive parties—see entry for "Popular Socialist Party" above).

Leadership. Rafael Aguilar Talamantes (pres.); Graco Ramírez Abreu (g.s.).

Structure. The national assembly elects the Central Committee, which elects the Political Commission and Executive Commission.

Electoral influence. The PST candidate, Candido Díaz Cerecedo, obtained 1.5 per cent of the vote in the 1982 presidential election.

Orientation. Independent.

Programme. The PST advocates nationalization of all foreign companies and banks, with control by workers' councils of nationalized industries; government control of basic industries and natural resources; a government monopoly of foreign trade; collectivization of the land; and a general amnesty for political prisoners.

Publication. El Insurgente Socialista (The Socialist Rebel).

Unified Socialist Party of Mexico
Partido Socialista Unificado de Mexico (PSUM)

History. The PSUM was formed in 1981 by the merger of the Mexican Communist Party (PCM) with four smaller parties, the Revolutionary Socialist Party (PSR), the Mexican People's Party (PPM), the Socialist Action and Unity Movement (MAUS) and the Popular Action Movement (MAP). A sixth party, the Mexican Workers' Party, originally decided to join it but later withdrew, as it objected to the name "Socialist".

The PCM, founded in 1919, was banned in 1929 for participating in an abortive revolt, and although legalized in 1935 was not registered as a political party for electoral purposes until 1978. In the 1979 elections it obtained 5 per cent of the vote and 18 of the proportionally distributed seats. Since 1968, when it condemned the Soviet invasion of Czechoslovakia, it has adopted a Eurocommunist position. The formation of the PSUM met with considerable opposition inside the PCM, many members of which refused to join it or afterwards withdrew. The new party won 17 seats in the 1982 elections and 12 in 1985 (when it was allied with other left-wing and progressive parties—see entry for "Popular Socialist Party" above).

Leadership. Pablo Gómez Alvarez (g.s.).

Structure. The national congress, held every three years, elects the 75-member Central Committee, which elects the 21-member Political Commission and the seven-member Secretariat.

Membership. 40,800 (1984 claim).

Electoral influence. The PSUM candidate in the 1982 presidential election, Arnaldo Martínez Verdugo, obtained 3.65 per cent of the vote. In the 1985 elections the PSUM obtained 3.1 per cent.

Orientation. Eurocommunist. Before the Political Commission was expanded in 1984 from 17 to 21 members, the Eurocommunist PCM and MAP held 10 and four seats respectively and the pro-Soviet PSR, PPM and MAUS one each.

Programme. The PSUM advocates the establishment of a left-revolutionary government through the ballot, and to this end favours the merger of revolutionary parties with similar programmes, an alliance of the left and co-operation with non-leftist groups on specific issues. It calls for the replacement of the presidential system of government by one ensuring the supremacy of the legislature, the introduction of proportional representation, an economic policy allowing for periodic increases in wages and agricultural prices, nationalization of enterprises with worker participation and a moratorium on Mexico's foreign debt.

Publication. Asi Es, weekly.

International affiliations. The PSUM is represented on the editorial council of *World Marxist Review*, and has relations with both the Soviet and the Chinese Communist parties.

Unity of the Communist Left
Unidad de Izquierda Comunista (UIC)

History. The UIC broke away from the Communist Party in 1973, and was officially registered as a political party in 1978.

Orientation. Pro-Soviet.

Programme. The UIC supports "the fight for political power for the workers and the people of Mexico and participation of the working classes and democratic forces in government at all levels".

Guerrilla Organization

Party of the Poor
Partido de los Pobres (PLP)

History. The PLP was founded in 1967 by Lucio Cabañas, who had been expelled from the Communist Party for advocating the use of violent methods, and operated in the mountains of Guerrero, one of the poorest states in the country, kidnapping local landowners, whom it held to ransom, and ambushing army patrols. In May 1974 it kidnapped Senator Rubén Figueroa, who had been sent to negotiate with Cabañas; after a ransom had been paid he was freed by the army in September, and one of the kidnappers, Félix Bautista, fled the country after leaving part of the ransom money with the Communist Party. Cabañas was killed in a clash with the army in December. Little was heard of the PLP between 1975 and 1984, when its deputy leader, Francisco Fierro Loza, who had recently accepted a government amnesty, was assassinated. Arnaldo Martínez Verdugo (a former general secretary of the Communist Party and a member of the Political Commission of the Unified Socialist Party of Mexico) and Bautista were kidnapped by the PLP in 1985 and held prisoners until part of Figueroa's ransom was handed over.

United States of America

Capital: Washington, D.C.   Pop. 236,413,000

Marxist ideas were introduced into the USA after the European revolutions of 1848 by German immigrants, who formed a number of local organizations, the earliest being the Proletarian League, established in New York in 1852. The first American Marxist party was the Workingmen's Party of America, founded in 1874 and later renamed the Socialist Labor Party, a dissident section of which united in 1901 with the Social Democratic Party, founded three years earlier by Eugene Debs, to form the Socialist Party of America. After 1912, when its membership reached 120,000 and Debs polled 897,000 votes in the presidential election, its influence declined as the result of a series of splits, and in 1919 its Marxist wing broke away to form the Communist Party of America.

Congress has adopted three measures directed against the Communist Party and other Marxist organizations. The Smith Act of 1940 made it an offence punishable by up to 10 years' imprisonment to advocate the overthrow of the government by force or violence, the maximum penalty being increased in 1956 to 20 years. The Voorhis Act, also adopted in 1940, made the affiliation of American parties to international organizations illegal. The Internal Security or McCarran Act of 1950 required all communist or "communist front" organizations and their members to register with the Justice Department, and provided for the internment of "subversives" in time of war or insurrection. The Supreme Court, however, ruled in 1965 that the section requiring individual communists to register was unconstitutional under the Fifth Amendment, which provides that "no person shall be compelled in any criminal case to be a witness against himself", thereby rendering the Act virtually unenforceable.

Communist Party USA (CPUSA)

History. The CPUSA originated in 1919, when two Marxist groups broke away from the Socialist Party of America and founded the Communist Labor Party and the Communist Party of America. Both were driven underground in 1920 by the Palmer raids (named after the then Attorney-General, A. Mitchell Palmer), in which 10,000 people were arrested, including most of the two parties' leaders. They merged in 1921 as the Communist Party of America, and formed the Workers' Party of America (WPA) as a legal cover organization. The Communist Party formally merged in 1923 with the WPA, which was renamed the Workers' (Communist) Party in 1925 and the Communist Party of the USA in 1930. Under its different names the party contested each presidential election from 1924 to 1932, with William Z. Foster as its candidate.

From 1923 to 1929 the party was torn by factional struggles, a Trotskyist group headed by James P. Cannon being expelled in 1928 and a right-wing "Bukharinist" group headed by Jay Lovestone (the executive secretary) in the following year. As a result its membership fluctuated widely, falling from 25,000 in 1923 to 9,642 in 1929. Under the leadership of Earl Browder (the Communist candidate in the 1936 and 1940 presidential elections) the CPUSA at first pursued an ultra-leftist policy, denouncing President Roosevelt's New Deal as "fascist" and demanding the right of self-determination for areas of the southern states with a Negro majority. With the adoption of the Popular Front policy in 1935 it swung to the right, announcing its support for the New Deal, and in a bid for popular support Browder put forward the slogan "Communism is 20th-century Americanism". During this period of moderate policies its membership rose to 75,000. On the outbreak of war in 1939, however, it again swung to the left, demanding that the USA should keep out of the "imperialist war" and denouncing Roosevelt for his support for Britain. After the adoption of the Voorhis Act in 1940 it formally disaffiliated from the Third International.

When Germany invaded the Soviet Union in 1941 the CPUSA immediately demanded full US support for the Soviet Union and Britain, and after the USA entered the war it put forward the slogan "Everything for national unity". In 1944 it reached its maximum membership of 80,000, including 15,000 whose membership had been suspended while they were in the forces. On Browder's proposal the party was officially dissolved in 1944 and converted into an educational organization, the Communist Political Association (CPA), members of which were free to join either the Democratic or the Republican Party. The CPA, which supported Roosevelt in the 1944 presidential election, advocated peaceful settlement of internal disputes and opposed raising the issue of socialism in the post-war period, in order not to weaken the national unity necessary to enable the Allied leaders' decisions to be put into effect. In 1945, however, the French Communist leader Jacques Duclos denounced Browder's policies, whereupon the CPA was dissolved and the CPUSA reconstituted with Foster as chairman and Eugene Dennis as general secretary, Browder being expelled from the party in 1946 for "deserting to the side of the class enemy". In the 1948 presidential election the CPUSA supported Henry Wallace, the Progressive Party candidate.

Between 1947 and 1956 the party was subjected to violent persecution. In 1949 Dennis and nine other national leaders were sentenced to five years' imprisonment and another to three years under the Smith Act, and after the sentences had been upheld by the Supreme Court 83 leaders of the state parties received similar sentences between 1952 and 1956. Many Communists were imprisoned for contempt of Congress for refusing to testify before the House of Representatives Committee on Un-American Activities; some states passed sedition laws making CPUSA membership punishable by 20 years' imprisonment; "Communist-infiltrated" trade unions were deprived of their legal standing; and in some states Communists were forbidden to teach in schools. A reaction began when the Supreme Court ruled in 1956 that state sedition laws were superseded by the Smith Act, and reversed in 1957 the convictions of some leading Communists, on the ground that CPUSA membership was not sufficient evidence for conviction under the Smith Act; in consequence many other convictions were reversed and some indictments were dropped.

Khrushchev's denunciation of Stalin in 1956 led to a split in the CPUSA. The 1957 national convention (the first since 1950) attributed the party's past mistakes to "left-sectarianism", and admitted that it had "viewed uncritically developments in the Soviet Union and other socialist countries". Foster denounced the resolutions as "revisionist", and was subsequently removed from the chairmanship. A controversy developed, however, between a liberal faction led by John Gates, the editor of the *Daily Worker*, and the dominant hard-line faction. Publication of the *Daily Worker* was discontinued, despite Gates' opposition, and in 1958 he and most of his supporters left the party. Membership fell in consequence from 20,000 in 1956 to under 7,000 in 1958.

Gus Hall succeeded Dennis as general secretary in 1959. He was the Communist candidate in the 1968 presidential election, the first which the party had contested since 1940, and in each subsequent election.

Leadership. Henry Winston (nat. ch.); Gus Hall (g.s.).

Structure. The basic organization is the shop, industrial or community party club. The party is organized in most of the 50 states, with state committees elected at state congresses, and in large states there may be two district committees. The national convention, meeting every four years, elects the 83-member Central Committee, which elects the nine-member Political Bureau. The party's youth organization is the Young Communist League.

Membership. 17,500 (1985 claim). The membership, which is mainly concentrated in a few industrial states, is largely middle-aged or elderly.

Electoral influence. The CPUSA has never been represented in Congress or in any state legislature. In the 1984 presidential election its candidate received 35,561 votes (0.03 per cent).

Industrial influence. Communist influence in the trade unions, which was considerable in the 1930s and 1940s, is now insignificant.

Orientation. Pro-Soviet.

Programme. The CPUSA seeks to play "a vanguard role in the struggle for advanced social legislation, for world peace and in solidarity against US imperialism, for working-class internationalism . . . and to end all forms of racist and political repression and oppression". It advocates a massive job-creation programme, a six-hour day with no reduction in pay, a higher minimum wage, cuts in the military budget, increased expenditure on social services, ending tax benefits for the rich, abolition of income tax on incomes below $30,000 a year and termination of interest payments on the federal debt.

Publications. *Daily World*, published five times a week (100,000); *Political Affairs*, monthly (20,000).

International affiliation. The CPUSA is represented on the editorial board of *World Marxist Review*.

Revolutionary Communist Party (RCP)

History. The RCP, founded in California in 1967 as the Bay Area Revolutionary Union, adopted its present name in 1975. Originally pro-Chinese, it denounced the Chinese leadership as revisionist after the arrest of the "gang of four" in 1976, and staged violent demonstrations in Washington in 1979 during the visit of Deng Xiaoping, whom it described as "a posturing, bootlicking and sawed-off pimp". It has also organized demonstrations against the Soviet representatives at the United Nations.

Leadership. Bob Avakian (ch.), who lives in exile in France and faces a long prison sentence if he returns to the USA.

Membership. Estimated in the late 1970s at 2,000, but now much smaller.

Electoral influence. The RCP advocates a boycott of elections, which it regards as meaningless.

Orientation. Independent Maoist.

Programme. The RCP advocates revolutionary war and an armed seizure of power by the working class.

Publications. *Revolutionary Worker*, weekly; *Revolution*, bimonthly.

International affiliation. In 1984 the RCP and a number of other small Maoist groups formed the Revolutionary Internationalist Movement.

Socialist Labor Party of America (SLPA)

History. The SLPA, the oldest socialist party in the USA, was founded in 1874 as the Workingmen's Party of America, changed its name to the Socialist Labor Party in 1877 and adopted its present name in 1890. Under the leadership of Daniel De Leon (1852–1914) it developed a combination of Marxist and syndicalist theory, whereby the party would gain power through the ballot and industrial unions would then take control of industry. It contested each presidential election from 1892 to 1976.

Leadership. Robert Bills (nat. sec.).

Structure. Based on local sections, the SLPA has a seven-member National Executive, elected for a two-year term by the annual national convention. All major policy decisions are subject to a referendum of the membership.

Membership. 550–650 (1984 estimate).

Orientation. Marxist-De Leonist.

Programme. The SLPA advocates "peaceful civilized change from capitalism to socialism via the ballot box" and the establishment of socialist government based on worker management and control of industry.

Publication. The People, weekly (10,000).

Socialist Workers' Party (SWP)

History. The SWP, founded in 1938, is the successor to the Communist League of America (Opposition), formed by James P. Cannon after his expulsion from the Communist Party as a Trotskyist in 1928. One of the original member-parties of the Fourth International, it withdrew from formal membership in 1940 in compliance with the Voorhis Act, while maintaining "fraternal affiliation". It opposed US participation in World War II, and in 1941 Cannon and 17 other leading members were imprisoned under the Smith Act. Since 1948 it has contested each presidential election, receiving its highest vote (91,314) in 1976. When the Fourth International split in 1953 it joined the International Committee, but in 1963 it transferred its support to the United Secretariat. Since 1981 it has moved away from orthodox Trotskyist ideology and has adopted a less hostile attitude towards existing communist regimes, with the result that several of its leading members have resigned or been expelled.

Leadership. Jack Barnes (nat. sec.).

Membership. Under 1,000 (1985 estimate), mainly concentrated in the industrial states.

Electoral influence. Mel Mason, the SWP presidential candidate in 1984, received 24,687 votes (0.02 per cent).

Orientation. Trotskyist.

Publication. Militant, weekly.

International affiliation. The SWP co-operates with the Fourth International, United Secretariat, although not formally affiliated to it.

Spartacist League (SL)

History. The SL was formed in 1964 after the expulsion of its leaders from the Socialist Workers' Party.

Orientation. Trotskyist.

International affiliation. After being expelled from the Fourth International, International Committee, in 1966 the SL founded the International Spartacist Tendency.

Workers' League (WL)

History. This Trotskyist organization contested the 1984 presidential election, its candidate, Ed Winn, receiving 10,800 votes.

Workers' World Party (WWP)

History. The WWP broke away from the Socialist Workers' Party in 1958.

Leadership. Sam Marcy (ch.).

Electoral influence. The WWP's presidential candidate in 1984, Larry Holmes, received 15,000 votes.

Orientation. Trotskyist.

World Socialist Party of the United States (WSPUS)

History. This small party shares the principles of the Socialist Party of Great Britain.

Orientation. Independent.

Publication. *The Western Socialist*.

International affiliations. World Socialist Movement.

Terrorist Organizations

May 19th Communist Organization

History. This group, established in 1978, was originally the East Coast faction of the Prairie Fire Organizing Committee, a successor to the Weather Underground (see below), and took its name from the birthday of Ho Chi Minh and the Black Muslim leader Malcolm X. It has been linked with armed robberies and "expropriations", including a holdup in New York in 1981 in which a security guard and two policemen were killed.

Weather Underground

History. This group was founded in 1969 by a militant faction inside Students for a Democratic Society, a radical student movement formed in 1962 which organized demonstrations against the Vietnamese war and racism. Originally known as the Weathermen, it took its name from a line by Bob Dylan, "You don't need a weatherman to know which way the wind blows". Organized in cells of four or five members, it was responsible for a large number of bomb explosions in New York and other cities between 1969 and 1975, after which it declined in size and activity.

7. CENTRAL AMERICA AND THE CARIBBEAN

Antigua and Barbuda

Capital: St John's   Pop. 77,000

The islands of Antigua and Barbuda became an independent state within the Commonwealth in 1981, with the British sovereign, represented by a Governor-General, as head of state. In the 1984 elections the ruling Antigua Labour Party won all the 16 Antigua seats in the House of Representatives, the Barbuda seat being retained by an independent.

Antigua Caribbean Liberation Movement (ACLM)

History. The ACLM, founded in 1977 as the Afro-Caribbean Liberation Movement, unsuccessfully contested the 1980 elections. After the failure of negotiations on an opposition united front it did not put forward candidates for the 1984 elections, which had been caused by allegations of governmental corruption and maladministration published in its newspaper *Outlet.* The ACLM's chairman was imprisoned for six months in late 1985 for libelling a government minister.

Leadership. Tim Hector (ch.); Conrad Luke (vice-ch.).

Electoral influence. In the 1980 elections the ACLM received less than 1 per cent of the vote.

Orientation. Caribbean "new left".

Publication. Outlet (weekly).

Costa Rica

Capital: San José   Pop. 2,550,000

The Republic of Costa Rica is governed by a President and a Legislative Assembly of 57 members, both elected for four years by universal suffrage. Unlike most Latin American countries, its recent history has been peaceful, except for a short civil war in 1948 following a disputed presidential election. Since 1949 power has alternated between social democratic and centre-right parties. In the February 1982 elections (in which the social democratic National Liberation Party retained power) two left-wing blocs shared less than 2 per cent of the vote.

311

Costa Rican Communist Party
Partido Comunista Costarricense (PCC)

History. The PCC was officially registered in 1984, but had its registration withdrawn by the Electoral Tribunal later in the year.

Leadership. Manuel Enrique Delgado Cascante (pres.).

Costa Rican People's Party
Partido del Pueblo Costarricense (PPC)

History. The PPC, founded by Manuel Mora Valverde in 1984 after his expulsion from the Popular Vanguard Party (PVP), claimed to be the genuine PVP and often used the name. In preparation for the 1986 elections it formed the Patriotic Alliance, together with the Costa Rican Socialist Party, the New Republic Movement and the Radical Democratic Party.

Leadership. Manuel Mora Valverde (g.s.).

Orientation. Pro-Cuban.

Costa Rican Socialist Party
Partido Socialista Costarricense (PSC)

History. The PSC, founded in 1972, contested the 1978 and 1982 elections as part of the People United alliance (see under Popular Vanguard Party). Although it did not win any seats, by previous agreement one of the PVP deputies resigned after the 1982 elections in favour of the PSC leader, Alvaro Montero Mejía. In 1984 it joined the Patriotic Alliance (see under Costa Rican People's Party).

Leadership. Alvaro Montero Mejía (pres.); Alberto Salom Echeverría (sec.).

Membership. The PSC draws its support mainly from public employees and intellectuals.

Industrial influence. Mejía is the leader of the public employees' union.

Orientation. The PSC describes itself as Marxist-Leninist, but is considered more flexible in its approach than the other People United parties.

New Republic Movement
Movimiento de la Nueva Republica (MNR)

History. The MNR was formed in 1984 by members of the People's Revolutionary Movement, which originated in 1970 as a radical student movement, and was alleged to have acted as a support group for the Sandinistas during the Nicaraguan revolution of 1978–79. In 1984 it joined the Patriotic Alliance (see under Costa Rican People's Party).

Leadership. Sergio Erick Ardón (l.).

Popular Vanguard Party
Partido Vanguardia Popular (PVP)

History. Founded in 1931 as the Communist Party of Costa Rica by Manuel Mora Valverde, the PVP adopted its present name in 1943. It won strong support in the trade unions in the 1940s, and by 1948 had 3,000 members and seven deputies in the Assembly. After the 1948 civil war, however, it was banned under the constitution adopted in the following year, and subsequently operated through front organizations such as the Popular Socialist Alliance and the Socialist Action Party until it was again legalized in 1975. For the 1978 elections, together with the Costa Rican Socialist, Workers' and Socialist Action parties, it formed the People United (*Pueblo Unido*) alliance, which unsuccessfully put forward Rodrigo Roberto Gutiérrez as its presidential candidate but won three seats in the Assembly. In the 1982 elections, fought in alliance with the Costa Rican Socialist and Workers' parties, the PVP returned three deputies, one of whom resigned in favour of a Socialist. Mora, who had been the party's general secretary since its foundation, was replaced in 1983 by Humberto Vargas Carbonell, and refused to accept the new honorific post of president. He was expelled in 1984 with his leading supporters, and formed the Costa Rican People's Party. His expulsion was variously attributed to rivalry between the older and younger PVP leaders and the victory of a hardline pro-Soviet faction over a more moderate pro-Cuban wing. The PVP later left the People United coalition and formed the Popular Democratic Union (UDP).

Leadership. Arnoldo Ferreto Segura (pres.); Humberto Vargas Carbonell (g.s.).

Structure. The PVP claims to have 5,000 cells. The congress elects the 35-member Central Committee, which elects the Political Commission and Secretariat.

Membership. Over 10,000 (1983 claim). Other sources estimated the membership before the 1984 split at about 3,500.

Electoral influence. The PVP has not contested elections independently under its own name since 1948. In the 1982 presidential election the PVP-supported candidate, Rodrigo Roberto Gutiérrez, obtained 3.2 per cent of the vote.

Industrial influence. The PVP controls the General Workers' Confederation.

Orientation. Pro-Soviet.

Programme. The PVP programme adopted in 1971 envisages a democratic, agrarian and anti-imperialist revolution followed by a socialist revolution as a single uninterrupted process.

Publication. Libertad, weekly (21,500).

International affiliations. The PVP is represented on the editorial council of *World Marxist Review*.

Socialist Action Party
Partido de Acción Socialista (PAS)

History. The PAS, formed as a front organization for the banned Popular Vanguard Party, contested the 1970 and 1974 elections; on the latter occasion, when the PVP leader Manuel Mora Valverde was its presidential candidate, it won two seats in the Assembly. In the 1978 elections it formed part of the People United alliance. The Electoral Tribunal suspended its recognition of the PAS in 1979, since when it has remained inactive.

Leadership. Marcial Aguiluz Orellana (pres.); Arnoldo Ferreto Segura (sec.).

Workers' Party
Partido de los Trabajadores (PT)

History. The PT originated as the political wing of the People's Revolutionary Movement, the majority of which has become the New Republic Movement. It contested the 1978 and 1982 elections as part of the People United alliance, winning one seat on the latter occasion.

Leadership. Johnny Francisco Araya Monge (pres.); Ilse Acosta Polonio (sec.).

Orientation. Independent. The PT rejects the description "Marxist-Leninist", and has criticized the Popular Vanguard Party's pro-Soviet attitude.

Workers' Socialist Organization
Organización Socialista de los Trabajadores (OST)

History. The OST was founded in 1976, and unsuccessfully contested the 1978 elections.

Leadership. Marta Trejos Montero (pres.); Rosendo Fujol Mesalles (sec.).

Orientation. Trotskyist. The OST condemns both "the opportunism of the Latin American Communist parties" and "the adventurism of guerrilla groups".

Programme. The OST aims at world revolution through the seizure of power by workers' and peasants' councils.

Publication. *Qué Hacer*, fortnightly (4,000).

International affiliations. Fourth International, United Secretariat.

Cuba

Capital: Havana   Pop. 10,000,000

Cuban politics were dominated from 1933 to 1958 by Sgt. (later Gen.) Fulgencio Batista, who served as President from 1940 to 1944 (pursuing a liberal policy) and seized power in 1952, when he established a dictatorship widely regarded as brutal and corrupt. He was overthrown by a guerrilla revolt led by Fidel Castro Ruz, and fled the country on Jan. 1, 1959. Castro assumed the premiership in the following month.

The United States almost from the first adopted a hostile attitude towards the new regime. Economic aid to Cuba was ended in 1960; an unsuccessful invasion by Cuban exiles was organized in 1961 by the Central Intelligence Agency (CIA); an economic blockade of Cuba was imposed in 1962 through the Organization of American States; and according to later official US statements at least eight plots to assassinate Castro and other Cuban leaders were organized by the CIA between 1960 and 1965. As a result the Castro government, which had originally been non-communist, was forced to turn to the Soviet Union for economic and military aid, and after 1961 adopted communist policies.

The new constitution adopted in 1976 describes Cuba as "a socialist state of working people and other manual and intellectual workers", and recognizes the leading role of the Communist Party. The 499-member National Assembly is elected indirectly for a five-year term by the municipal assemblies, which are elected by universal suffrage. The National Assembly elects the 30-member

314

Council of State, the president of which is head of state and government. Castro has held this post since 1976.

Communist Party of Cuba
Partido Comunista de Cuba (PCC)

History. The PCC was formed by the merger of three distinct organizations, the Popular Socialist Party (formerly the Communist Party), Fidel Castro's July 26 Movement and the Revolutionary Directorate. The Communist Party, founded as an underground organization in 1925, was legalized in 1938, and changed its name to the Popular Socialist Party (PSP) in 1944. It returned 10 deputies in the 1940 elections, and was represented in Batista's government of 1940–44 by Juan Marinello, the first Communist in Latin America to hold ministerial office. Its influence declined after 1944, however, and in 1953 Batista banned it.

On July 26, 1953, Castro led an armed revolt against the Batista regime, which was easily crushed. Released under an amnesty in 1955, he went to Mexico, where he organized the July 26 Movement. In December 1956 he returned in the yacht *Granma* with 81 followers, 70 of whom were killed by government troops on landing. The survivors launched a guerrilla campaign in the Sierra Maestra, which gradually spread and gained the support of the anti-Batista student movement, the Revolutionary Directorate. The government's resistance collapsed in December 1958, many of its troops deserting to the insurgents, and in the following month the Fidelistas took power.

The July 26 Movement was democratic, socialist and nationalist rather than Marxist, and was hostile to the PSP, which had given no support to the revolt until the summer of 1958. US hostility, however, compelled Castro to ally himself with the PSP, then the best organized party in Cuba. The July 26 Movement, the PSP and the Revolutionary Directorate formed an alliance, the Integrated Revolutionary Organizations, early in 1961, and in December Castro announced his adhesion to Marxism-Leninism and the theory of the dictatorship of the proletariat. The United Party of the Socialist Revolution was established in the following year as the sole legal party, and was renamed the Communist Party of Cuba in 1965.

After attempting to remain neutral in the Sino-Soviet controversy, the PCC adopted a pro-Soviet attitude in 1963. Relations between the PCC and the Soviet Communist Party were extremely strained during 1964–68, however, as Castro insisted on the PCC's independence, declaring that "we are not and never will be anybody's satellite", and criticized both the Soviet and the Chinese party for attempting to seek supporters inside the PCC. During this period he pursued a policy of active assistance to guerrilla movements in Latin America, such as Ernesto "Che" Guevara's unsuccessful attempt to organize a revolt in Bolivia in 1966–67; attacked the Bolivian and Venezuelan Communist parties for refusing to support such movements; and denounced the Soviet Union's policy of extending diplomatic and economic relations with Latin American governments irrespective of their political complexion, as well as its internal economic policies, which he described as "capitalistic". The leading "old Communists" (former PSP members) were purged from the government in 1964–65 and replaced by Fidelistas from the July 26 Movement, and 37 of them were expelled from the PCC in 1968 and imprisoned for forming a pro-Soviet "anti-party group".

The failure of Guevara's revolt and Cuba's economic difficulties forced Castro to modify his policies. Relations with the Soviet Union improved after he supported the Soviet intervention in Czechoslovakia in 1968, and in 1972 Cuba entered the Council for Mutual Economic Assistance (Comecon). At the first

315

PCC congress, held in 1975, Castro admitted that the Cuban leaders had been guilty of "utopian attitudes" and "disregard for the experience of other processes", and the PCC subsequently supported the Soviet intervention in Afghanistan and the imposition of martial law in Poland.

In 1984–85 the party moved towards a more independent policy. A number of "old Communists", including a member of the Secretariat, were removed from their posts and replaced by younger officials who favoured limited encouragement of the private sector; home ownership was transferred from the state to the tenant; official attitudes towards the Catholic church were softened; and attempts were made to improve relations with the United States and to expand trade with Western countries. At the third PCC congress, held in February 1986, 10 of the 24 Political Bureau members and about a third of the 225 Central Committee members were replaced in order to bring more women, blacks and youth into the leadership; a new party programme received provisional approval.

Leadership. The full members of the Political Bureau are Fidel Castro Ruz (1st sec.), Raúl Castro Ruz (2nd sec.), Juan Almeida Bosque, José Ramón Machado Ventura, Carlos Rafael Rodríguez, Pedro Miret Prieto, Armando Hart Dávalos, Jorge Risquet Valdés, Julio Camacho Aguilera, Osmany Cienfuegos Gorrián, Sra Vilma Espin de Castro, Esteban Lazo Dávalos, Abelardo Colome and Roberto Veiga. There are also 10 alternate members.

Structure. The PCC has about 20,000 branches, 169 municipal and 14 provincial committees. The congress elects the Central Committee (146 full and 79 alternate members), which elects the Political Bureau and the nine-member Secretariat. The party's youth organization is the Union of Communist Youth.

Membership. 523,639, including candidate members (1986 claim).

Electoral influence. All candidates for the municipal assemblies and the National Assembly are approved by the PCC, although at least two candidates are put forward in each election.

Industrial influence. The PCC controls the Confederation of Cuban Workers, the general secretary of which, Roberto Veiga, is a member of the Political Bureau.

Orientation. Pro-Soviet.

Programme. The PCC seeks to reduce Cuba's economic dependence on sugar production by promoting the diversification of agriculture and the development of both heavy and light industry. The formation of agricultural co-operatives is encouraged. Emphasis is laid on the development of education and health services and on the mobilization of the entire population for national defence against the threat of US intervention. The PCC prides itself on its "revolutionary internationalism", as exemplified by its prominent role in the non-aligned movement, its economic and military aid to the Sandinista regime in Nicaragua and the New Jewel Movement government in Grenada, and its military assistance to the Angolan and Ethiopian governments against hostile guerrilla movements.

Publications. Granma, daily (600,000); *Juventud Rebelde* (Rebel Youth), daily organ of the Union of Communist Youth (200,000).

International affiliations. The PCC is represented on the editorial council of *World Marxist Review.*

Dominica

Capital: Roseau   Pop. 76,000

The former British colony of Dominica became an independent republic within the Commonwealth in 1978. Formed since 1980 by the conservative Dominica

Freedom Party, the government has accused the opposition Labour Party of Dominica (LPD) of being led by communists and funded by communist states, but the LPD rejects such allegations.

Dominica Liberation Movement Alliance (DLMA)

History. The DLMA (also known as the Dominica Liberation Movement) was formed from four left-wing groups in 1979 by Atherton Martin, who had recently been dropped from the Dominica Labour Party government for advocating closer ties with Cuba, and unsuccessfully contested the 1980 elections. In 1981 it accepted an offer from the Cuban Communist Party for university scholarships in Cuba to be provided for students from Dominica. The movement did not contest the 1985 general election in its own right, but claimed the support of two of the five victorious Labour candidates.

Leadership. Atherton Martin (l.); Bill Riviere (g.s.).

Electoral influence. In the 1980 elections the DLMA obtained 2,464 votes (8.02 per cent).

Orientation. Caribbean "new left".

Dominican Republic

Capital: Santo Domingo   Pop. 6,416,000

The Dominican Republic was subjected to the dictatorship of Gen. Rafael Trujillo from 1930 to 1961, when after his assassination democratic government was restored. Juan Bosch Gaviño, leader of the moderate socialist Dominican Revolutionary Party (PRD), was elected President in 1963, but was overthrown by a military coup seven months later. A revolt by his supporters in 1965 led to a civil war, which was ended by US military intervention. Joaquín Balaguer, a former supporter of Trujillo, was elected President in 1966 and twice re-elected, but was defeated in 1978 by the candidate of the PRD, which has since held power.

The Dominican Marxist parties, which are all very small (their total membership being estimated at about 5,000), emerged from underground after Trujillo's death, and supported Bosch in the 1965 civil war. Under the right-wing Balaguer regime Maoist tendencies became dominant in most of them, and some parties attempted to launch a guerrilla war. For the 1982 elections they formed two electoral alliances, Socialist Unity, headed by the Dominican Communist Party, and the United Left, neither of which succeeded in gaining any seats in Congress.

Anti-Imperialist Patriotic Union
Union Patriotica Antiimperialista (UPA)

History. The UPA contested the 1982 elections as part of the United Left alliance. Together with the PCD and the PTD (see below) and the Socialist Bloc (*Bloque Socialista*), it represented the Dominican Republic at a pan-Caribbean socialist conference held in Cuba in 1984.

Leadership. Franklin Franco (l.).

Communist Party of the Dominican Republic
Partido Comunista de la República Dominicana (PCRD)

Leadership. Luis Montas (l.).

Communist Workers' Nucleus
Núcleo de los Trabajadores Comunistas (NTC)

History. The NTC contested the 1982 elections as part of the United Left alliance. Its leader was arrested in August 1984.

Leadership. Rafael Taveras (l.).

Orientation. Maoist.

Dominican Communist Party
Partido Comunista Dominicano (PCD)

History. The PCD, founded clandestinely by students in 1944 as the Dominican Revolutionary Democratic Party, was legalized in 1946 as the Popular Socialist Party, but was banned in the following year, its leaders being imprisoned or exiled. After Trujillo's death it resumed its activities, being banned again in 1963, and took part in the 1965 civil war. It resumed the name PCD in the same year. Legalized again by President Balaguer in 1977, in an attempt to split the opposition vote in the coming elections, it contested the 1982 elections, with Narciso Isa Conde as presidential candidate, in the Socialist Unity alliance with the Movement for Socialism.

Leadership. Narciso Isa Conde (g.s.).

Structure. The PCD's organization follows the normal communist pattern, the 27-member Central Committee and the Secretariat being elected by the congress.

Membership. 500–1,000 (1985 estimate).

Electoral influence. The PCD obtained 7.1 per cent of the vote in the 1982 elections.

Orientation. Pro-Soviet.

Publication. Hablan los Comunistas (The Communists Speak), weekly.

International affiliation. The PCD is represented on the editorial council of *World Marxist Review*.

Dominican Popular Movement
Movimiento Popular Dominicano (MPD)

History. Founded by exiles in Cuba in 1956, the MPD began activities in the Dominican Republic after Trujillo's death, and adopted a pro-Chinese orientation. It was banned in 1963, but continued to operate underground. It contested the 1982 elections as part of the United Left alliance.

Leadership. Julio de Peña Valdés (l.).

318

Dominican Workers' Party
Partido de los Trabajadores Dominicanos (PTD)

History. The PTD contested the 1982 elections as part of the United Left alliance. It later merged with the (pro-Albanian) Labour Communist Party of the Dominican Republic (*Partido Obrero Comunista de la República Dominicana*, POCRD) led by Rafael Chaljub Mejía.

Movement for Socialism
Movimiento por Socialismo (MPS)

History. The MPS contested the 1982 elections in alliance with the Dominican Communist Party.

Socialist Party
Partido Socialista (PS)

History. The PS originated as an offshoot of the Camilo Torres Revolutionary Committee, which attempted to organize guerrilla warfare against the Balaguer regime. It contested the 1982 elections as part of the United Left alliance.

Workers' Revolutionary Party
Partido Revolucionario de los Trabajadores (PRT)

History. The PRT contested the 1982 elections as part of the United Left alliance.

Workers' Socialist Movement
Movimiento Socialista de los Trabajadores (MST)

History. Like the Socialist Party, the MST is an offshoot of the Camilo Torres Revolutionary Committee, and contested the 1982 elections as part of the United Left alliance.

El Salvador

Capital: San Salvador   Pop. 4,829,000

The greater part of the cultivated land in El Salvador, a densely populated country with the highest population growth rate in Central America, is owned by a small number of wealthy families, and peasants are employed on the coffee, cotton and sugar plantations on a seasonal basis, having little or no land of their own and no guarantee of employment. Laws providing for the redistribution of land were adopted in 1975 and 1980, but were neutralized by amendment or suspension, and produced practically no result. El Salvador is the most industrialized Central American state, with a considerable urban working class.

From 1932, when a peasant revolt was suppressed and between 15,000 and 30,000 of the rebels massacred, to 1979 El Salvador was under military rule. Although after 1962 presidential elections were held every five years, they were marked by massive electoral fraud, and always resulted in the return of the candidates of the official National Reconciliation Party. Persons suspected of disaffection were frequently murdered by the security forces or extreme right-wing terrorist groups; the victims included the Archbishop of San Salvador, Mgr Oscar Arnulfo Romero y Galdames, who was shot in 1980, and many priests who sympathized with the peasants' grievances. In this situation guerrilla movements directed against the regime developed rapidly in the 1970s.

President Carlos Humberto Romero was deposed by a coup in October 1979, when a military-civilian junta took power and a government was formed including representatives of the left and centre parties. The junta's failure to control the excesses of the security forces and the extreme right, however, led to the resignation in January 1980 of the civilian ministers, who were largely replaced by representatives of the right wing of the Christian Democratic Party, and in December the Christian Democratic leader, José Napoleón Duarte, was appointed President. The Marxist, social democratic and radical Catholic parties had meanwhile formed in April the Democratic Revolutionary Front (FDR), which subsequently allied with the Farabundo Martí Liberation Front (FMLN), formed in October by the guerrilla organizations, and sporadic fighting developed into civil war when the FMLN launched an offensive in January 1981. Elections to a Constituent Assembly held in March 1982, which were boycotted by the FDR parties, were followed by the formation of a coalition government by the Christian Democrats and two right-wing parties. Duarte, who was elected President by popular vote in May 1984, entered into negotiations with the FDR in October, but without result.

Democratic National Union
Unión Democrática Nacional (UDN)

History. The UDN, formed as a legal front organization for the illegal Communist Party of El Salvador, allied with the Christian Democratic Party and the National Revolutionary Movement to form the National Opposition Union, which put forward a single candidate in the 1972 and 1977 presidential elections. It joined the Revolutionary Co-ordination of the Masses on its formation in January 1980 and the Democratic Revolutionary Front in April. Although it is still nominally legal, its leader, Mario Aguiñada Carranza, went underground in 1981 after an attempt on his life.

Leadership. Mario Aguiñada Carranza (g.s.).

Orientation. Pro-Soviet.

Popular Liberation Movement
Movimiento de Liberación Popular (MLP)

History. This small party joined the Revolutionary Co-ordination of the Masses shortly after its formation, and is linked with the Central American Workers' Revolutionary Party.

Leadership. Fabio Castillo Figueroa (g.s.).

Orientation. Independent.

Popular Revolutionary Bloc
Bloque Popular Revolucionaria (BPR)

History. The BPR was founded in 1975 by former members of the Unified Popular Action Front, who rejected its policy of alliance with non-proletarian parties and advocated a strategy of independent working-class action, and developed into a mass movement of peasants, agricultural workers, trade unions, teachers and students, which by 1980 claimed 100,000 members. It established links in 1979 with the Farabundo Martí Popular Liberation Forces, and in the following year helped to form the Revolutionary Co-ordination of the Masses.

Leadership. Facundo Guardado y Guardado (g.s.).

Membership. 50,000 (1983 estimate). The BPR is the largest Marxist party in El Salvador.

Industrial influence. The strongest of the organizations supporting the BPR is the Catholic Federation of Salvadorean Peasants—Agricultural Workers' Union.

Orientation. Independent. Guardado has stated that "we abide by Marxist–Leninist ideology adjusted to El Salvador's specific conditions".

Salvadorean Revolutionary Party
Partido Revolucionario Salvedoreño (PRS)

History. The PRS was formed in 1977 as the Popular Leagues of February 28, largely under student leadership, and took its name from the date of popular demonstrations against the notoriously fraudulent elections of that year, which were violently suppressed. It allied itself in 1978 with the People's Revolutionary Army (ERP). After the coup of October 1979 it temporarily broke with the ERP and announced its support for the new government, but in January 1980 it joined the other Marxist parties in forming the Revolutionary Co-ordination of the Masses. It adopted its present name in 1984.

Leadership. José Leoncio Pichinte (g.s.).

Orientation. Independent.

Unified Popular Action Front
Frente de Accion Popular Unificada (FAPU)

History. The FAPU was formed in 1974 by left-wing Christian Democrats, and at first pursued a policy of alliance with the Christian Democratic Party, the National Revolutionary Movement, the Democratic Nationalist Union and dissident sectors of the military. It subsequently established links with the National Resistance Armed Forces (see below), however, and helped to form the Revolutionary Co-ordination of the Masses (CRM) in January 1980. It broke away a few months after to throw its support behind a dissident member of the ruling junta, Col. Adolfo Arnoldo Majano, but later returned to the CRM.

Leadership. Alberto Ramos (g.s.).

Membership. After the Popular Revolutionary Bloc, the FAPU is the largest of the Salvadorean Marxist parties. It draws its support largely from industrial workers and the lower middle class in the towns.

Orientation. Independent.

Party Alliances

Democratic Revolutionary Front
Frente Democrático Revolucionario (FDR)

History. The FDR was formed in April 1980 as an alliance of the five Marxist parties comprising the Revolutionary Co-ordination of the Masses with the

Salvadorean Democratic Front, which had been formed shortly before by the social democratic National Revolutionary Movement (MNR), the Popular Social Christian Movement (MPSC) and trade union, professional and student organizations, and organized a partially effective general strike in August. Enrique Alvarez Córdova (MPSC), the general secretary of the FDR, and five of its other leaders were kidnapped and murdered in November by right-wing terrorists. In January 1981 the FDR established a Political Diplomatic Commission in Mexico City, consisting of one representative from each of its seven constituent parties, which acted as a government-in-exile and was subsequently recognized by the Mexican, French and Dutch governments as a representative political force which must participate in negotiating a settlement. After the government had rejected several appeals by the FDR for peace talks, negotiations between President Duarte and FDR leaders took place in October 1984, but without success.

Leadership. The Political Diplomatic Commission consists of Guillermo Manuel Ungo (MNR) as chairman, Fabio Castillo Figueroa (MLP), Mario Aguiñada Carranza (UDN), Rubén Ignacio Zamora Rivas (MPSC), José Napoleón Rodríguez Ruíz (FAPU), Ana Guadalupe Martínez (PRS), Salvador Samayoa (BPR) and Héctor Oqueli.

Orientation. The FDR is an alliance of Marxists, radical Catholics, social democrats and liberals.

Programme. The FDR's programme calls for a popular democratic government based on the working class, the peasantry, the advanced sections of the middle class and all those among medium-sized industrialists, merchants, artisans and farmers who support its programme; defence of democratic liberties; reconstruction of the army, with liberal elements of the officer corps serving alongside ex-guerrillas; agrarian reforms based on the expropriation of the large landowners, with guarantees for medium and small farmers; nationalization of public utilities; expanded social and welfare services; and independence from the United States.

Revolutionary Co-ordination of the Masses
Coordinadora Revolucionario de Masas (CRM)

History. The CRM was formed in January 1980 by the Popular Revolutionary Bloc, the Unified Popular Action Front, the Popular Leagues of February 28 (now the Salvadorean Revolutionary Party) and the Democratic Nationalist Union, and was later joined by the Popular Liberation Movement. In April it merged with the Salvadorean Democratic Front to form the Democratic Revolutionary Front, within which it continued to operate.

Guerrilla Organizations

Central American Workers' Revolutionary Party
Partido Revolucionario de Trabajadores Centroamericanos (PRTC)

History. This small organization, founded in 1975, is linked with the Popular Liberation Movement, and has sections in Guatemala and Honduras. It began guerrilla operations in 1979, and joined the Farabundo Martí National Liberation Front in December 1980.

Leadership. Roberto Roca (commander).

Communist Party of El Salvador
Partido Comunista de El Salvador (PCES)

History. The PCES was founded by Agustin Farabundo Martí in 1930, and two years later organized a peasant revolt in the western departments—the first attempted revolution by a Latin American Communist Party. In the repression which followed Farabundo Martí and most of the other PCES leaders were executed, and the party was practically wiped out. Reorganized in 1936 as an underground party, it devoted itself mainly to the formation of urban trade unions, and sought to bring about the peaceful removal of the military dictatorship by forming electoral alliances through front parties such as the Democratic Nationalist Union. This policy led to a split in 1970, when Salvador Cayetano Carpio (then its general secretary) broke away, subsequently forming the Farabundo Martí Popular Liberation Forces. Although the PCES finally adopted a policy of armed struggle at a clandestine congress in May 1979, after the coup in the following October it decided to support the new civilian-military junta, and one of its members, Gabriel Gallegos Valdés, entered the government as Minister of Labour and Social Security. He resigned with the other civilian ministers in January 1980, however, and the PCES then announced its reorganization as a guerrilla movement, with the Democratic National Union as its political wing.

Leadership. Jorge Schafik Handal (g.s.); Américo Mauro Araujo (deputy g.s.).

Membership. 500 (1984 est.).

Orientation. Pro-Soviet.

International affiliations. The PCES is represented on the editorial council of *World Marxist Review*.

Farabundo Martí National Liberation Front
Frente Farabundo Martí para la Liberación Nacional (FMLN)

History. Four guerrilla organizations (the FPL, ERP, FARN and PCES) formed a Unified Revolutionary Directorate (*Directorio Revolucionario Unificado*, DRU) in June 1980, which was replaced in October by the FMLN, its leading body being known as the DRU. The FMLN, which originally consisted of the FPL, ERP and PCES, was later joined by the FARN, which had temporarily broken away, and by the PRTC. The Front takes its name from the leader of the 1932 peasant revolt.

The FMLN launched a general offensive in January 1981, during which it secured control of much of the northern departments of Morazán and Chalatenango, as well as large areas elsewhere. By February 1982 the FMLN was estimated to control one-fourth of the country, and by the end of 1983 it also held large stretches of the coast. In 1984, however, the army, which had received large supplies of US military aid, secured the military initiative, and the FMLN subsequently reduced its guerrilla activities in rural areas, dispersed its forces into small units and transferred the bulk of its members to the towns, in order to build up its civilian support.

Leadership. The DRU consists of Leonel González (FPL), Joaquín Villalobos (ERP), Fermán Cienfuegos (FARN), Jorge Schafik Handal (PCES) and Roberto Roca (PRTC).

Membership. 6,000–15,000 (1985 estimates).

Farabundo Martí Popular Liberation Forces
Fuerzas Populares de Liberación Farabundo Martí (FPL)

History. The FPL was founded in 1970 by Salvador Cayetano Carpio after his break with the Communist Party with a policy of "prolonged popular war" on the Vietnamese model, and adopted the Popular Revolutionary Bloc as its political wing in 1979. It became one of the founding organizations of the Unified Revolutionary Directorate and the Farabundo Martí National Liberation Front (FMLN) in 1980. A split developed early in 1983 between a faction working for greater unity in the FMLN and negotiations with the government and a hardline group which adhered to the policy of prolonged war, and led to the murder of Mélida Anaya Montes (the FPL second-in-command) in Nicaragua in April and the suicide six days later of Carpio, who supported the hardline faction and was believed to have arranged her assassination.

Leadership. Leonel González (C.-in-C.); Dimas Rodríguez (2nd-in-command).

Membership. The FPL is by far the largest of the guerrilla organizations.

National Resistance Armed Forces
Fuerzas Armadas de Resistencia Nacional (FARN)

History. The FARN was formed in 1975 by Ernesto Jovel and Fermán Cienfuegos, who had broken away from the People's Revolutionary Army. They contended that organization and political education of the masses must precede armed insurrection, and established links with the Unified Popular Action Front. The FARN helped to found the Unified Revolutionary Directorate in June 1980, but later left it to support the military faction led by Col. Majano; after Jovel's death in September, however, it joined the Farabundo Martí National Liberation Front.

Leadership. Fermán Cienfuegos (commander).

Membership. The FARN is the third largest guerrilla organization, after the Farabundo Martí Popular Liberation Forces and the People's Revolutionary Army.

People's Revolutionary Army
Ejército Revolucionario del Pueblo (ERP)

History. The ERP was formed in 1971 by a group of left-wing Christian Democrats, led by Ernesto Jovel, Roque Dalton García, Joaquín Villalobos and Fermán Cienfuegos, and later adopted Trotskyist views. It rejected the policy of prolonged popular war favoured by the Farabundo Martí Popular Liberation Forces as unduly cautious, and advocated open war, in preparation for which it carried out a number of kidnappings to raise money. Policy differences led to a serious of murders in 1975, Dalton being among the victims, whereupon Jovel and Cienfuegos broke away and formed the National Resistance Armed Forces. The ERP allied in 1978 with the Popular Leagues of February 28, but a temporary breach between them occurred after the coup of October 1979, when the ERP launched an attempted insurrection, suffering heavy casualties. It was among the founders of the Unified Revolutionary Directorate in June 1980 and the Farabundo Martí National Liberation Front in October. In the ensuing civil war it operated mainly in the eastern departments of Morazán, San Miguel, Usulatán and La Unión, and in September 1983 launched a major offensive, during which it briefly occupied the city of San Miguel and captured 60 other towns and villages. Its large formations proved to be vulnerable to government firepower, however, and it subsequently broke up its forces into small groups.

Leadership. Joaquín Villalobos (commander); Ana Guadalupe Martinez (2nd-in-command).

Membership. The ERP is the second largest guerrilla organization, after the Farabundo Martí Popular Liberation Forces.

Revolutionary Workers' Movement—Salvador Cayetano Carpio
Movimiento Obrero Revolucionario—Salvador Cayetano Carpio (MOR-SCC)

History. This hardline group broke away from the Farabundo Martí Popular Liberation Forces (FPL) after the murder of Mélida Anaya Montes and the suicide of Carpio in April 1983, and was responsible for the murder of a US military adviser in the following month, apparently with the object of sabotaging a proposal for talks with the US government. It was condemned by the new FPL leadership in December as maintaining Carpio's "sectarian anti-unitarian positions", denying the Farabundo Martí National Liberation Front's vanguard role and "proclaiming itself the sole representative of the working class".

Grenada

Capital: St George's   Pop. 120,000

The former British colony of Grenada became an independent state within the Commonwealth in 1974, with the British monarch, represented by a Governor-General, as head of state. The Grenada United Labour Party government, headed by Sir Eric Gairy, was overthrown by a coup in 1979, when a People's Revolutionary Government headed by Maurice Bishop took power. Bishop was overthrown and murdered in 1983, whereupon US forces occupied the island. Elections held in 1984 resulted in a victory for the conservative New National Party, which formed a government.

Maurice Bishop Patriotic Movement (MBPM)

History. The MBPM is the successor to the Movement for the Assemblies of the People, founded by Maurice Bishop and Kendrick Radix in 1972, and the JEWEL (Joint Endeavour for Welfare, Education and Liberation) movement, founded in the same year by Unison Whiteman and Selwyn Strachan, which merged in 1973 to form the New Jewel Movement (NJM). The NJM contested the 1976 elections in alliance with two other parties, winning three of the 15 seats in the House of Representatives. In 1979 it overthrew the repressive Gairy government in an almost bloodless coup, and established a People's Revolutionary Government with Bishop as Prime Minister.

Although the new government carried out a number of useful reforms in the fields of health, education, housing and employment, its close ties with Cuba alienated the USA and the more conservative Caribbean states, while inside the NJM Bishop's moderate policies aroused strong opposition from a more left-wing faction led by Bernard Coard, the Deputy Premier. On Oct. 13, 1983,

Bishop was overthrown by this faction and placed under arrest, and six days later he was shot, together with Whiteman and two other members of the government. US troops, supported by contingents from six Caribbean countries, invaded Grenada on Oct. 25, and despite strong resistance established control in a few days. Coard, Strachan and a number of their supporters were arrested and charged with Bishop's murder.

The MBPM was founded in May 1984 by Radix and George Louison, another former member of Bishop's government, and unsuccessfully contested the elections in the following December.

Leadership. Kendrick Radix (ch.); George Louison.

Electoral influence. The MBPM obtained 2,024 votes (5 per cent) in the 1984 elections.

Publications. The Indies Times, weekly; *The Democrat*, biweekly.

International affiliations. The MBPM has support groups in Britain, the United States, Canada and Sweden, and maintains close relations with Cuba.

Guadeloupe

Capital: Pointe-à-Pitre   Pop. 332,000

Guadeloupe is a French overseas department, and has three representatives in the National Assembly and two in the Senate. It has a 42-member General Council elected by majority voting over two rounds and a 41-member Regional Council elected by proportional representation. An agitation for the independence of Guadeloupe, accompanied by acts of violence, has been in progress since the mid-1960s, and has dominated political life since 1980.

Guadeloupe Communist Party
Parti Communiste Guadeloupéen (PCG)

History. Founded in 1944 as a federation of the French Communist Party, the PCG became an independent party in 1958. It won a seat in the French National Assembly in 1981, and 11 seats in the Regional Council in 1983.

Leadership. Guy Daninthe (g.s.); Henri Bangou.

Structure. The PCG has residential and workplace branches. The congress, meeting every four years, elects the Central Committee, which elects the 12-member Political Bureau and the Secretariat. The youth branch is the *Jeunesses Communistes*.

Membership. 3,000 (1985 estimate).

Electoral influence. The PCG received 20,776 votes (22.65 per cent) in the 1983 Regional Council elections, and in 1985 it held eight of the 42 General Council seats. It controls six of the 34 municipal councils, and two others are controlled by a Communist-Socialist alliance.

Industrial influence. The PCG plays a leading role in the General Confederation of Labour of Guadeloupe, the island's largest trade union federation.

Orientation. Eurocommunist.

Programme. The PCG advocates revitalization of the economy through the diversification of agriculture, modernization of the sugar industry, import substitution and the expansion of tourism, and improved health, education and transportation programmes. It supports the maximum internal autonomy for Guadeloupe but not immediate independence, and condemns the use of terrorist methods.

Publication. L'Etincelle (The Spark), weekly (5,000).

International affiliations. The PCG has close ties with the French Communist Party, but does not automatically follow its lead. It refused to support the Communist list in the 1979 and 1984 European elections and advocated abstention, on the ground that EEC policies operated against Guadeloupe's interests.

Guatemala

Capital: Guatemala City   Pop. 8,400,000

Guatemala was ruled by a succession of despotic *caudillos* until 1944, when President Jorge Ubico was overthrown. After 1945 President Juan José Arévalo attempted to deal with the agrarian problem (arising from the fact that 70 per cent of the cultivable land is owned by about 4 per cent of the population) by initiating a land reform programme, and this was carried farther by his successor, President Jacobo Arbenz Guzmán, who alienated the US government by expropriating the American-owned United Fruit Company. In 1954 forces financed and armed by the US Central Intelligence Agency invaded Guatemala from Honduras; Arbenz was overthrown, and the new regime returned all expropriated lands to their former owners. For the next 31 years Guatemala was ruled by right-wing governments, civilian or military, except for the years 1966–70, when the reformist Revolutionary Party held office, and the army periodically intervened to prevent the return of presidential candidates of whom it disapproved, either by seizing power, as in 1963–66 and 1982–85, or by falsifying the election results. After 1960 opposition took the form of guerrilla warfare, to which the regime responded with wholesale killings of dissident elements, including opposition politicians, peasant leaders, trade unionists, students, intellectuals and priests, carried out by the security forces or by government-supported terrorist groups; according to one estimate, which was regarded as conservative, 138,000 people "disappeared" in this way between 1954 and 1985. A new period of civilian rule began in 1985, when Vinicio Cerezo, of the centre-right Christian Democratic Party, was elected President.

Guatemalan Committee of Patriotic Unity
Comité Guatemalteco de Unidad Patriótica (CGUP)

History. The CGUP was formed in February 1982 by Guatemalan exiles in Mexico City representing the principal opposition organizations, including the Democratic Front against Repression, the January 31 Popular Front and the United Revolutionary Front.

Leadership. The eight-member co-ordinating committee includes Luis Cardoza y Aragón (a member of the Arbenz government of 1951–54), Guillermo Toriello Garrido (Foreign Minister in the Arbenz government), Pablo Geto (a member of the Committee for Peasant Unity) and Carlos Gallardo Flores (leader of the Democratic Socialist Party).

Orientation. The CGUP is an alliance of Marxists, Catholics, social democrats and liberals.

Programme. The CGUP's founding document stated that although it had no direct link with the guerrillas it endorsed the basic programme of the Guatemalan National Revolutionary Unity organization, and believed that popular revolutionary war was the only path left open against "the bloodiest dictatorship that Latin America has ever known".

Guatemalan Labour Party
Partido Guatemalteco del Trabajo (PGT)

History. The Socialist Labour Unification, founded in 1921, was reorganized as the Communist Party of Guatemala in 1924, but was suppressed after the peasant revolt of 1932 in El Salvador and almost ceased to exist. Revived in 1947 as the Democratic Vanguard, it was renamed the Communist Party of Guatemala in 1949 and the Guatemalan Labour Party in 1952. Under the Arbenz government it dominated the trade union movement and exercised considerable political influence, although holding only four seats in Congress. After the 1954 coup it was banned and most of its leaders murdered or driven into exile, since when it has worked underground. It has suffered severely from right-wing terrorists, two of its general secretaries, 19 Central Committee members and the leader of its youth wing, the Patriotic Labour Youth, having been murdered during 1972–83. At its fourth congress, in 1969, it adopted the position that the revolution could triumph only through the use of force, but differences over tactics led to a series of splits, and the party did not commit itself fully to armed struggle until 1981.

Leadership. Carlós González (g.s.).

Membership. 750 (1984 estimate).

Industrial influence. The PGT controls the Guatemalan Autonomous Federation of Trade Unions, an underground organization of about 50 small unions, and has some influence in the National Committee for Labour Unity, the most important trade union federation.

Orientation. Pro-Soviet.

Programme. The PGT advocates the formation of an alliance of all revolutionary forces, combining armed struggle with legal activity through mass fronts, to carry out an agrarian democratic revolution as a step towards the socialist revolution.

International affiliations. The PGT is represented on the editorial council of *World Marxist Review*.

Guatemalan Labour Party—Leadership Nucleus (PGT-CN)

History. The PGT-CN broke away from the Guatemalan Labour Party in 1978, advocating that the party should reconstitute itself as a guerrilla organization, and was one of the four groups which founded Guatemalan National Revolutionary Unity in 1982.

Leadership. Mario Sánchez (l.).

January 31 Popular Front
Frente Popular 31 de Enero (FP-31)

History. FP-31 was formed in 1981 as an alliance of peasant, trade union, student and revolutionary Christian organizations, and helped to form the Guatemalan Committee of Patriotic Unity in the following year. It takes its name from an incident on Jan. 31, 1980, when Indian peasants occupied the Spanish embassy in Guatemala City as a protest against military excesses in El Quiché department, whereupon the police stormed the building, 39 people being killed.

Orientation. FP-31 includes both Marxist and non-Marxist opponents of the regime.

Programme. FP-31 has defined its aim as "the removal from power of the military, economic and political forces which sustain the dictatorship and the establishment of a revolutionary, popular and democratic government".

Guerrilla Organizations

Armed People's Organization
Organización del Pueblo en Armas (ORPA)

History. The ORPA was formed in 1972 by former members of the Rebel Armed Forces, but did not begin guerrilla activities until 1979. It originally operated in both urban and rural areas, but its network in Guatemala City was destroyed by the security forces in 1981. It has since conducted operations in the countryside, especially in the western and northern departments, with considerable success.

Leadership. Gaspar Ilóm (commander).

Guatemalan National Revolutionary Unity
Unidad Revolucionaria Nacional Guatemalteca (URNG)

History. The URNG was formed in February 1982 by the Guerrilla Army of the Poor, the Rebel Armed Forces, the Armed People's Organization and the Guatemalan Labour Party–Leadership Nucleus to provide a unified military command for the guerrilla forces.

Programme. The URNG's basic programme defines its aims as (i) an end to repression and a guarantee of life, peace and fundamental human rights for all citizens; (ii) provision for the basic needs of the majority of the people; (iii) equality for the Indian and white populations; (iv) creation of a new society in which all sections of the population will be represented in the government; (v) a foreign policy based on non-alignment and international co-operation.

Guerrilla Army of the Poor
Ejército Guerrillero de los Pobres (EGP)

History. The EGP was formed in 1972 by former members of the Rebel Armed Forces, and began military operations in 1975, with an initial membership of about 300. It has been most active in the north-western mountains, the central highlands and the Pacific coastal area, combining guerrilla warfare with political propaganda, especially among the Indian population. In 1981 it attempted to launch a general insurrection and to establish "liberated zones", but after suffering heavy losses in a government offensive in the following year it reverted to guerrilla tactics.

Leadership. Rolando Morán (C.-in-C.).

Structure. The EGP has six independent commands in the rural areas and one in Guatemala City.

Membership. 2,000 combatants (1986 estimate). The EGP is the largest and most active of the guerrilla organizations.

Rebel Armed Forces
Fuerzas Armadas Rebeldes (FAR)

History. The FAR was formed in 1962 as an alliance of the November 13 Revolutionary Movement of radical officers (MR-13), members of the Guatemalan Labour Party (PGT) and students. MR-13 withdrew from the alliance in 1965, and the FAR broke with the PGT in 1968. It was almost wiped out by a government offensive in 1970, and also lost members to the newly-formed Guerrilla Army of the Poor and Armed People's Organization, but its activities revived in the later 1970s. In recent years it has operated mainly in the north, the central highlands and Guatemala City.

Leadership. Pablo Monsanto (commander).

Membership. Under 200 combatants, plus several hundred sympathizers (1984 estimate).

Haiti

Capital: Port-au-Prince

Pop. 5,800,000

In the period from 1957 to 1986 Haiti was a dictatorship, headed originally by President François Duvalier and after his death in 1971 by his son, Jean-Claude Duvalier, who held office as President for life. The only legal party was the official National Unity Party. Communist activity was banned in 1949 and declared punishable by death in 1969. Following a popular revolt, Duvalier fled the country in February 1986 and a military-civilian government headed by Gen. Henri Namphy took power.

Haitian Workers' Party
Parti des Travailleurs Haïtiens (PTH)

History. The PTH, founded in 1966, was pro-Chinese until 1976, when it decided that the Chinese leaders had adopted a revisionist position.

Membership. 350 (1983 estimate).

Orientation. Independent Maoist.

Programme. The PTH describes itself as "an anti-capitalist party that is carrying out an anti-imperialist, anti-feudal and anti-dictatorial struggle", and considers it necessary to prepare for an armed struggle.

Unified Party of Haitian Communists
Parti Unifié des Communistes Haïtiens (PUCH)

History. A communist party was formed in 1930 by Max Hudicourt, but died out after its leaders were exiled in the same year. It was revived in 1946 as the Popular Socialist Party under the leadership of Hudicourt, who was elected to the Senate but was assassinated in 1947, and in 1949 the party was banned. Two successor parties were subsequently formed, the People's National Liberation Party in 1954 and the Popular Unity Party in 1959, and merged in 1968 to form the PUCH. It operated underground and in exile until the overthrow of the Duvalier regime in 1986, when its general secretary returned to Haiti.

Leadership. René Théodore (g.s.).

Structure. The congress elects the Central Committee, which elects the Political Bureau.

Membership. 350 (1983 estimate).

Orientation. Pro-Soviet.

Publication. *Boukan*, published sporadically.

Honduras

Capital: Tegucigalpa   Pop. 4,424,000

Honduras was ruled by the conservative National Party from 1932 to 1956 and by the Liberals from 1957 to 1963, and passed under military rule from 1963 to 1980, except for a short period under a National Party government in 1971–72. The Liberal Party regained power in 1980. After 1979 the political situation was complicated by the Sandinista revolution in Nicaragua and the civil war in El Salvador, as the government allowed anti-Sandinista rebels to establish bases in Honduras and co-operated with the Salvadorean army against the Farabundo Martí National Liberation Front. The Honduran Marxist parties retaliated with hijackings, bombings and attempts to organize guerrilla warfare, with little success, while many opposition politicians, peasant leaders and trade unionists were kidnapped or murdered by the security forces or by right-wing terrorist organizations.

Communist Party of Honduras
Partido Comunista de Honduras (PCH)

History. The original PCH, founded in 1927, was suppressed after the peasant revolt of 1932 in El Salvador. Revived in 1944 as the Democratic Revolutionary Party of Honduras, it was banned in 1946–48 and again in 1953, when its leaders were exiled. It was refounded as the PCH in 1954, and although declared illegal three years later has at times functioned openly, depending on the attitude of the government in power. A split occurred in 1971, when a pro-Chinese faction broke away. Rigoberto Padilla Rush, the PCH general secretary, escaped to Cuba in 1982 after an attempt to arrest him, and the deputy general secretary, Herminio Deras, was murdered in the following year by right-wing terrorists.

Leadership. Mario Sosa Navarro (head of the Political Commission). Rigoberto Padilla Rush was removed from his post as general secretary in 1984, as he was living abroad.

Structure. Workplace or residential cells are formed where there are at least three Communists. The congress elects the Central Committee, which elects the Political Commission and Secretariat.

Membership. 1,500 (1983 estimate).

Orientation. Pro-Soviet.

Programme. The PCH, which has been divided for many years by controversies over whether it should use constitutional or violent means, finally committed itself to a policy of guerrilla warfare when it joined the Honduran Revolutionary Movement in 1983.

Publication. *Vanguardia Revolucionaria*, monthly.

International affiliations. The PCH is represented on the editorial council of *World Marxist Review*.

Communist Party of Honduras—Marxist-Leninist
Partido Comunista de Honduras—Marxista-Leninista (PHC-ML)

History. The PCH-ML was formed in 1971 by Maoists who had broken with the Communist Party over the question of armed struggle.

Orientation. Pro-Chinese.

Honduran Revolutionary Movement
Movimiento Hondureño Revolucionario (MHR)

History. The MHR was formed in April 1983 as an alliance of the Communist Party of Honduras, the Central American Workers' Revolutionary Party, the Lorenzo Zelaya Popular Revolutionary Forces, the Revolutionary Unity Movement, the Cinchonero Popular Liberation Movement and the Morazanista Honduran Liberation Front.

Leadership. "Manuel Federico" (g.s.).

Structure. The National Unified Directorate of the MHR consists of representatives of the six affiliated organizations.

Programme. The MHR plans to form a single army under one command to conduct a guerrilla war and to "play an active part in the event of a regionalization of the Central American crisis".

People's Revolutionary Union
Unión Revolucionaria del Pueblo (URP)

History. The URP was formed in 1978 by former members of the Communist and Socialist parties, and announced the beginning of its armed struggle in 1980. Tomás Nativí, its president, was abducted and Fidel Martínez, its general secretary, killed by the security forces in 1981. The Cinchonero Popular Liberation Movement is believed to be its military wing.

Revolutionary Unity Movement
Movimiento de Unidad Revolucionario (MUR)

History. Little is known of this organization, which was among the founders of the Honduran Revolutionary Movement in 1983.

Guerrilla Organizations

Central American Workers' Revolutionary Party
Partido Revolucionario de Trabajadores Centroamericanos (PRTC)

History. The PRTC, which also has sections in El Salvador and Guatemala, was founded in 1975 and emerged from underground in 1979. Its leader, José María Reyes Matos, was reported to have been killed in 1983 while leading a force of 300 guerrillas in the northern Olancho province.

Cinchonero Popular Liberation Movement
Movimiento de Liberación Popular Cinchonero (MLP)

History. The MLP, founded in 1978 as the military wing of the People's Revolutionary Union, secured the release of 15 Salvadorean and Honduran political prisoners in 1981 by hijacking an airliner, and has since claimed responsibility for a number of bomb explosions. The name "Cinchonero" is believed to be derived from the nickname of a 19th-century peasant leader.

Lorenzo Zelaya Popular Revolutionary Forces
Fuerzas Populares Revolucionarias Lorenzo Zelaya (FPR-LZ)

History. The FPR-LZ was formed by the Communist Party of Honduras—Marxist-Leninist in 1981, and takes its name from a peasant leader killed by the security forces in 1965. It hijacked an airliner in April 1982 in an unsuccessful attempt to secure the release of political prisoners, and claimed responsibility for a number of bomb explosions in Tegucigalpa in the same year.

Leadership. Efraín Duarte (l.).

Morazanista Honduran Liberation Front
Frente Morazanista de Liberación Hondureña (FMLH)

History. The FMLH, founded in 1979, takes its name from the Honduran revolutionary leader Francisco Morazán (1792–1842). It has engaged in sporadic terrorist activities since 1980.

Leadership. Fernando López (spokesman).

Programme. The FMLH stated in 1980 that it aimed to seize power in order to establish a people's government on the basis of a large-scale agrarian reform.

Jamaica

Capital: Kingston   Pop. 2,338,000

The former British colony of Jamaica became an independent state within the Commonwealth in 1962, with the British monarch, who is represented by a

Governor-General, as head of state. Since independence Jamaica has been ruled by the conservative Jamaica Labour Party (JLP) from 1962 to 1972 and since 1980, and by the socialist People's National Party (PNP) from 1972 to 1980. The 1983 general election, which was fought on an outdated register, was boycotted by the major opposition parties, the JLP winning all the 60 seats in the House of Representatives.

Jamaica Communist Party (JCP)

History. The JCP was founded in 1975, and gave critical support to the PNP government of 1972–80.

Leadership. Chris Lawrence (g.s.).

Electoral influence. The JCP has not contested elections.

Industrial influence. The JCP is active in the Independent Trade Union Action Council, which is affiliated to the World Federation of Trade Unions.

Revolutionary Marxist League (RML)

History. The RML was formed in the late 1970s.

Membership. Under 50 (1985 estimate).

Electoral influence. The RML advocated abstention in the 1980 and 1983 elections.

Orientation. The RML describes itself as Trotskyist, but rejects the orthodox Trotskyist view that the Soviet Union is a degenerated workers' state.

Workers' Party of Jamaica (WPJ)

History. The WPJ was founded in 1974 as the Workers' Liberation League, and reconstituted under its present name in 1978. Although it gave critical support to the PNP government of 1972–80, its proposals for an electoral alliance in the 1980 elections were rejected by the PNP, and relations between the two parties have since become increasingly strained. Two WPJ members were shot dead by police on Feb. 25, 1985, in disputed circumstances.

Leadership. Dr Trevor Munroe (g.s.).

Membership. 50 (1985 estimate). The WPJ is highly selective in its recruiting, and claims to accept less than half of those who apply for membership.

Electoral influence. The WPJ has not contested elections.

Industrial influence. The University and Allied Workers' Union, of which Dr Munroe is general secretary, is affiliated to the WPJ, and enjoys some support among farm and factory workers.

Orientation. Pro-Soviet.

Publication. Struggle.

International affiliation. The WPJ is represented on the editorial council of *World Marxist Review*.

Martinique

Capital: Fort-de-France   Pop. 330,000

Martinique is a French overseas department, with three representatives in the National Assembly and two in the Senate. It has a 36-member General Council elected by majority voting over two rounds and a 41-member Regional Council elected by proportional representation. An agitation for the independence of Martinique, accompanied by acts of violence, has been in progress since 1980.

Communist Party for Independence and Socialism
Parti Communiste pour l'Indépendance et le Socialisme (PCIS)

History. The PCIS was formed in 1984 by dissidents who had resigned or been expelled from the Communist Party over the independence issue.

Leadership. Dany Emmanuel, Léandre Marimoutou.

Programme. The PCIS advocates immediate independence for Martinique. It refuses to condemn pro-independence violence.

Martinique Communist Party
Parti Communiste Martiniquais (PCM)

History. Founded in 1925 as a federation of the French Communist Party, the PCM received over 60 per cent of the vote in the 1946, 1951 and 1956 elections and returned two deputies to the National Assembly, including the poet Aimé Césaire. Its influence declined, however, after Césaire resigned in 1956 and founded the Martinique Progressive Party (PPM), which many Communists joined. The PCM became an independent party in 1957, and abandoned its former policy of assimilation for one of autonomy. Together with the PPM and the Socialist Party it formed the Martinique National Front for Autonomy in 1975, but by 1980 this alliance had effectively collapsed. The three parties fought the 1983 Regional Council elections independently, and together obtained 21 seats, including four for the PCM. Césaire then formed a ruling bureau (administration), in which all three parties were represented. The PCM split in 1984, when two of the Communist members of the Regional Council, Dany Emmanuel and Léandre Marimoutou, resigned from the party to form the Communist Party for Independence and Socialism.

Leadership. Armand Nicolas (g.s.).

Structure. The PCM is organized in workplace and residential branches. The congress, meeting every four years, elects the 33-member Central Committee, which elects the 13-member Political Bureau and the four-member Secretariat.

Membership. Under 1,000 (1985 estimate). A large proportion of the members are teachers and civil servants.

Electoral influence. The PCM obtained 10,283 votes (9.04 per cent) in the 1983 Regional Council elections. In 1985 it held three seats on the General Council. It controls two of the 34 municipal councils and is represented on nine others.

Industrial influence. The PCM controls the Martinique General Confederation of Labour, the largest trade union federation, the general secretary of which, Philibert Duféal, is a member of its Political Bureau.

Orientation. Eurocommunist.

Programme. The PCM advocates autonomy for Martinique as a first step towards eventual independence, but condemns the use of terrorist methods.

International affiliations. The PCM has close ties with the French Communist Party.

Socialist Revolution Group
Groupe Révolution Socialiste (GRS)

History. The GRS broke away from the Communist Party in 1971, and unsuccessfully contested the 1983 elections to the Regional Council.

Leadership. Gilbert Pago (g.s.).

Membership. 100 (1982 estimate).

Electoral influence. The GRS obtained 2,229 votes (1.96 per cent) in the 1983 Regional Council elections.

Orientation. Trotskyist.

Programme. The GRS advocates immediate independence.

Publication. *Révolution Socialiste*, weekly (2,500).

Nicaragua

Capital: Managua   Pop. 3,100,000

Nicaragua was occupied almost continuously by US marines from 1909 onwards, until a guerrilla struggle headed by Augusto César Sandino forced them to withdraw in 1933. Sandino was assassinated in the following year by order of Anastasio Somoza García, the commander of the National Guard, who seized power in 1936. For the next 43 years Nicaragua was ruled by Somoza and, after his assassination in 1956, by his sons Luis and Anastasio Somoza Debayle, either directly or through puppet Presidents.

Growing opposition to the repressive and notoriously corrupt Somoza regime was brought to a head by the assassination of a leading Conservative editor in January 1978. Protest demonstrations, strikes, spontaneous popular insurrections in the towns and attacks on the towns by the Sandinista National Liberation Front (FSLN) guerrillas continued throughout the year and the first half of 1979, and in June 1979 a five-person junta representing all sections of the opposition from the Conservatives to the FSLN was formed in Costa Rica as a government-in-exile. President Anastasio Somoza fled the country on July 17, and three days later the junta established a provisional government in Managua. A Council of State, consisting of representatives of political parties, trade union federations and employers' organizations, was set up in 1980 to act as an interim legislature pending the holding of elections.

The new government, which like the junta included representatives of all the main political tendencies, nationalized the banks, mines, fisheries, forests and the property of the Somoza family and confiscated unused land for redistribution, but left the greater part of the economy in private hands. The regime came under attack, however, both from the right-wing parties, which accused the FSLN of seeking to establish a Marxist-Leninist dictatorship, and from the smaller Marxist parties, which criticized its policies as insufficiently socialist. The FSLN was supported by the Independent Liberal, People's Christian Social and Nicaraguan Socialist parties, which joined it in 1980 in forming the Patriotic Revolutionary Front.

Armed attacks on Nicaragua from Honduras were launched from late in 1979 by former members of the Somozist National Guard, and from 1980 by conservative elements which had supported the 1979 revolution but opposed the FSLN's socialist measures. A similar attitude was adopted by Eden Pastora Gómez, formerly a prominent FSLN commander, who formed a separate guerrilla organization operating from Costa Rica in 1982. The counter-revolutionaries were actively assisted by the US government, which from 1981 became increasingly hostile towards the Nicaraguan regime, accusing it of assisting the rebels in El Salvador, and in 1984 US agents organized the mining of Nicaraguan ports.

Presidential elections held in November 1984, which were boycotted by three right-wing parties but were considered free and fair by foreign observers, resulted in a victory for the FSLN candidate, Daniel Ortega Saavedra. In elections to the National Assembly held at the same time, which were conducted by proportional representation, the FSLN won 61 of the 96 seats, the Democratic Conservative Party 14, the Independent Liberal Party nine, the People's Christian Social Party six and the three smaller Marxist parties two each.

Communist Party of Nicaragua
Partido Comunista de Nicaragua (PCN)

History. The PCN broke away from the Nicaraguan Socialist Party in 1967. Legalized after the 1979 revolution, it soon came into conflict with the Sandinista regime, which it attacked as insufficiently radical, and a number of its leading members were imprisoned in 1981–82 for organizing strikes and land seizures. It contested the 1984 presidential and parliamentary elections, winning two seats in the National Assembly.

Leadership. Elí Altamirano (g.s.).

Membership. The PCN claimed 1,200 members in 1979, but independent sources estimated its membership at about 150.

Electoral influence. The PCN obtained less than 2 per cent of the vote in the 1984 elections.

Industrial influence. The PCN controls the Council of Action and Labour Unity, which has considerable influence in the trade union movement.

Orientation. Pro-Chinese.

Publication. *Avance*, daily.

Nicaraguan Socialist Party
Partido Socialista Nicaragüense (PSN)

History. Founded in 1937, the PSN was banned two years later, allowed to resume its activities during World War II and again banned in 1945. Its 1973 congress held that although it was impossible to eliminate the Somoza regime without armed struggle, conditions for such a struggle were still lacking; hence it did not support the Sandinista guerrillas, but formed a series of political alliances with the non-socialist opposition parties. Legalized in 1979, it has since generally supported the government's policies, and joined the Patriotic Revolutionary Front in 1980. It contested the 1934 presidential and parliamentary elections, winning two seats in the National Assembly.

Leadership. Luis Sánchez Sancho (g.s.).

Membership. 250 (1983 estimate).

Electoral influence. The PSN received less than 2 per cent of the vote in the 1984 election.

Industrial influence. The PSN controls the Independent General Confederation of Labour, which has about 5,000 members.

Orientation. Pro-Soviet.

International affiliations. The PSN is recognized by the Soviet-bloc Communist parties, but is not represented on the editorial council of *World Marxist Review*.

Popular Action Movement—Marxist-Leninist
Movimiento de Acción Popular—Marxista-Leninista (MAP-ML)

History. The MAP-ML was formed in 1967 by pro-Chinese members of the Nicaraguan Socialist Party, and later adopted a pro-Albanian attitude. Its trade union wing, the Workers' Front (*Frente Obrero*, FO), formed in 1974, organized the Anti-Somozist People's Militias (Milpas), which played an active part in the struggle against the dictatorship. After the Sandinistas took power *El Pueblo*, the MAP-ML newspaper, denounced the 1979 revolution as "not a workers' but a bourgeois revolution", and encouraged strikes and illegal land seizures; in consequence Milpas was disarmed, and in 1980 *El Pueblo* was temporarily closed down and several MAP-ML and FO leaders imprisoned for three months. In the 1984 elections the MAP-ML put forward Isidoro Téllez, the FO general secretary, as its presidential candidate, and won two seats in the National Assembly.

Membership. The MAP-ML's membership in 1979–80 was believed to be about 25, but it exercised a much wider influence through *El Pueblo* and the FO.

Electoral influence. The MAP-ML obtained less than 2 per cent of the vote in the 1984 elections.

Industrial influence. The MAP-ML controls the Workers' Front.

Orientation. Pro-Albanian.

Publication. *El Pueblo* (The People), daily.

Sandinista National Liberation Front
Frente Sandinista de Liberación Nacional (FSLN)

History. The FSLN, which is named after the national hero Augusto César Sandino, was founded in 1962 by a small group of intellectuals, including Carlos

Fonseca Amador and Tomás Borge Martínez, and began guerrilla operations in the following year. After suffering a series of defeats, it abandoned all military activity from 1970 to the end of 1974. Fonseca, the FSLN's leading theoretician, was killed in action in 1976, and after 1975 disagreements on strategy split the movement into three factions. The Protracted People's War (GPP) group favoured the creation of liberated zones on the Chinese and Vietnamese model, which would provide bases from which to attack the towns; the Proletarian Tendency maintained that the FSLN should concentrate on winning the support of the urban working class; and the Third Force (*Terceristas*) advocated a combination of an armed offensive and broad political alliances with other opposition organizations, which would lead to a general insurrection. A synthesis of all three strategies was finally agreed upon, and in March 1979 a National Directorate was formed, consisting of the three main leaders of each faction. This plan was subsequently put into effect, with complete success.

Although the FSLN's decisive role in the overthrow of the Somoza dictatorship inevitably made it the dominant political force after the revolution, it was represented only by Daniel Ortega Saavedra in the five-person junta which took power in July 1979, and by three of the 18 ministers in the government formed at the same time. FSLN representation in the government was subsequently increased, but both the junta and the government remained multiparty bodies. In the 1984 elections Daniel Ortega was elected President, and the FSLN obtained a majority in the National Assembly.

Leadership. The National Directorate consists of Daniel Ortega Saavedra, Humberto Ortega Saavedra and Víctor Manuel Tirado López (*Terceristas*); Tomás Borge Martínez, Henry Ruiz Hernández and Bayardo Arce Castano (GPP); and Jaïme Wheelock Román, Carlos Núñez Téllez and Luís Carrión Cruz (Proletarian Tendency).

Structure. The FSLN was essentially a guerrilla organization when it took power, and has only since developed into a political party. Emphasis has been laid on the building up of mass organizations to provide a source for recruits; these include the Sandinista Defence Committees, which are responsible for security, education and public health programmes, the Sandinista Youth, the Nicaraguan Women's Association, the Sandinista Workers' Central and the Farmworkers' Association. New FSLN members are required to prove their participation in the pre-1979 revolutionary struggle and their good record since.

Membership. 200,000 (1985 estimate).

Electoral influence. The FSLN received 66.9 per cent of the vote in the 1984 elections, on a 75.4 per cent turnout.

Industrial influence. The FSLN controls the Sandinista Workers' Central, which claims 100,000 members.

Orientation. Independent. The FSLN adheres to the principle laid down by Fonseca that "we identify with socialism, while retaining a critical attitude to the socialist experiences".

Programme. The FSLN advocates democratic government, with a multiparty system and popular participation in decision-making; a mixed economy containing a strong socialist element; and a foreign policy based on national independence and non-alignment.

Publication. Barricada, daily (30–35,000).

International affiliations. The FSLN has always maintained close relations with the Cuban Communist Party, while pursuing its own internal policies. It has been represented at congresses of the Socialist International, although it is not a member.

Panama

Capital: Panama City Pop. 2,134,000

Formerly part of Colombia, Panama became an independent republic in 1903 after a revolt encouraged and assisted by the United States. A treaty signed a fortnight later gave the United States the right to construct the Panama Canal, to control a zone five miles wide on either side of it and to intervene in Panama's internal politics, although the right of intervention was given up in 1936. Popular resentment at the privileged position enjoyed by the United States in the Canal Zone led to violent rioting in 1964.

A junta headed by Col. (later Brig.-Gen.) Omar Torrijos Herrera seized power in 1968, abolished political parties and established an Assembly of Community Representatives elected on a non-party basis. Gen. Torrijos, who was granted special powers as head of government in 1972, pursued a reformist policy, and in 1977 negotiated a new treaty with the United States, under which Panama was given jurisdiction over the Canal Zone and would take full control of the canal and the Canal Zone by the year 2000. He resigned his special powers in 1978, and a law was adopted granting legal recognition to political parties which collected the signatures of 30,000 supporters. Full democratic civilian government was re-established in 1984, when presidential and legislative elections were held.

Communist Party—Marxist-Leninist
Partido Comunista—Marxista-Leninista (PC-ML)

History. The PC-ML broke away from the People's Party of Panama in 1973.

Orientation. Pro-Chinese.

People's Party of Panama
Partido del Pueblo de Panama (PPP)

History. Founded in 1930 as the Communist Party of Panama, the PPP assumed its present name in 1943, and for some years exercised considerable influence in the trade union and student movements. It was banned in 1950, although it continued to operate more or less openly, depending on the attitude of the government in power, and was formally abolished with the other parties in 1968. It strongly supported Gen. Torrijos' internal reforms and his demand for Panamanian control of the Canal Zone, and under his regime a number of PPP members held influential government positions. The PPP was granted legal registration in 1981, but this was withdrawn after it failed to obtain the required percentage of votes in the 1984 elections.

Leadership. Rubén Darío Sousa Batista (g.s.).

Structure. The PPP is organized in workplace and residential branches, and has local, zonal and regional committees. The congress, meeting every four years, elects the Central Committee, which elects the Political Bureau and Secretariat.

Membership. 36,000 (1983 claim). Independent sources estimate the active membership at about 750.

Industrial influence. The PPP largely controls the Workers' National Centre, which is affiliated to the World Federation of Trade Unions.

Orientation. Pro-Soviet.

Programme. The PPP believes that since 1968 Panama has been passing through a "democratic national-liberation revolution" which can prepare the way for a socialist revolution. It therefore advocates a political alliance of all parties supporting Gen. Torrijos' programme, a mixed economy with state and co-operative property playing the dominant role, and a foreign policy based on non-alignment and anti-imperialism.

Publication. *Unidad* (Unity), weekly.

International affiliations. The PPP is represented on the editorial council of *World Marxist Review*.

Tendency
Tendencia

History. The Tendency, also known as the Fraction (*Fracción*), was formed in 1975 by leading members of the People's Party's youth and student organizations, and held its first congress in 1978.

Membership. 1,500 (1984 estimate).

Workers' Revolutionary Party
Partido Revolucionario de los Trabajadores (PRT)

History. The PRT received legal registration in 1983, and for the elections in the following year formed the United People's Front in alliance with several trade union groups. Its registration was subsequently withdrawn, as it had not received the required quota of votes.

Leadership. Graciela J. Dixon (pres.); Egbert Wetherborne (g.s.).

Orientation. Trotskyist.

Workers' Socialist Party
Partido Socialista de los Trabajadores (PST)

History. The PST joined the National Opposition Front formed in 1979 to demand immediate elections and full freedom of expression. It received legal registration in 1983, but this was withdrawn after it failed to obtain the required percentage of votes in the 1984 elections.

Leadership. Virgilio Arauz (l.).

Orientation. Trotskyist.

Programme. The PST advocates nationalization of the Panama Canal and the banks and the withdrawal of the US garrison from the Canal Zone.

Puerto Rico

Capital: San Juan   Pop. 3,300,000

Puerto Rico, which was annexed from Spain by the USA in 1898, has since 1952 been "a free state in association with the United States". It enjoys internal autonomy, but the USA is responsible for its defence. Executive power is vested in the Governor, elected every four years, and there is a 27-member Senate and a 51-member House of Representatives. Since 1928 there has been an active nationalist movement, which demands complete independence for Puerto Rico and in 1950 organized an abortive insurrection. In recent years nationalist activities have been mainly confined to bombing incidents in the United States.

Puerto Rican Communist Party
Partido Comunista Puertorriqueño (PCP)

History. The PCP, founded in 1934, dissolved itself in 1944 and was reconstituted two years later, on both occasions following the example of the Communist Party USA. In 1954 10 of its leaders were prosecuted under the Smith Act (see under "United States of America").

Leadership. Franklin Irrizarry (g.s.).

Structure. The PCP is organized in residential and workplace branches. The congress, held every five years, elects the Central Committee, which elects the Political Commission.

Membership. 125 (1985 estimate).

Orientation. Pro-Soviet.

Programme. The PCP advocates complete independence for Puerto Rico.

Publication. El Pueblo, monthly (3,000).

International affiliations. The PCP has ties with the US Communist Party.

Puerto Rican Socialist League
Liga Socialista Puertorriqueña (LSP)

History. The LSP was founded in 1964.

Leadership. Juan Antonio Corretjei (g.s.).

Orientation. Trotskyist.

Puerto Rican Socialist Party
Partido Socialista Puertorriqueño (PSP)

History. The PSP was founded in 1971 by the conversion into a political party of the Pro-Independence Movement, established in 1959, and had one member in the House of Representatives in 1974–76.

Leadership. Juan Mari Bras (g.s.); Carlos Gallisá (pres.).

Structure. The congress elects the Central Committee, Political Commission and Secretariat.

Membership. 150 (1985 estimate).

Electoral influence. In the 1984 elections the PSP received 0.3 per cent of the vote.

Orientation. Pro-Cuban.

Programme. The PSP's aim is the establishment of an independent socialist republic.

Publications. *Claridad*, weekly; *Tribuna Roja* and *Nueva Lucha*, bimonthly.

International affiliations. The PSP has close ties with the Cuban Communist Party.

Guerrilla Organization

Armed Forces of National Liberation
Fuerzas Armadas de Liberación Nacional (FALN)

History. This separatist organization, which is believed to have no more than 20 members, claimed responsibility for 120 bombing incidents in New York and other US cities between 1974 and 1983, in which five people were killed. Its then leader, William Morales, was arrested in Mexico City in 1983 after a gun battle in which two people were killed, and four of its members were convicted of seditious conspiracy in Chicago in 1985.

Leadership. Carlos Alberto Torres (l.).

St Vincent and the Grenadines

Capital: Kingstown   Pop. 130,000

The former British colony of St Vincent and the Grenadines has had internal self-government since 1969, and became an independent state in 1979, with the British monarch, represented by a Governor-General, as head of state. The conservative St Vincent Labour Party held office, alone or in coalition, from 1967 to 1984, except for the years 1972–74, but was defeated in the 1984 elections by the centrist New Democratic Party.

United People's Movement (UPM)

History. The UPM was formed in 1979 as an electoral alliance of (i) the Youlou United Liberation Movement (Yulimo), a left-wing party founded in 1974 which contained both Black Power and Marxist elements, (ii) the People's Democratic Movement, a social democratic party formed in 1978 by the merger of the Democratic Freedom Movement and the People's Democratic Congress, and (iii) Arwee, a radical rural movement which subsequently merged with Yulimo. Ralph Gonsalves, the leader of Yulimo, resigned in 1982 as a protest against its increasingly Marxist orientation and formed the Movement for National Unity. The UPM was reconstituted for the 1984 elections, but failed to win any seats.

Leadership. Oscar Allen (l.).

Electoral influence. The UPM's share of the vote fell from 14.4 per cent in the 1979 elections to 3.2 per cent in 1984.

Orientation. Independent. The UPM claims to accept scientific socialism adapted to St Vincent conditions, but rejects the label "communist".

Publication. Freedom.

Trinidad and Tobago

Capital: Port of Spain   Pop. 1,100,000

The former British colony of Trinidad and Tobago became an independent state within the Commonwealth in 1962 and a republic in 1976. The People's National Movement has been in power continuously since 1956.

Communist Party of Trinidad and Tobago (CPTT)

History. The CPTT was founded in 1979.

Orientation. Pro-Albanian.

February Eighteenth Movement (FEM)

History. The FEM was founded in 1972. It was represented at a pan-Caribbean socialist conference held in Cuba in 1984.

Leadership. James Millette.

Orientation. Pro-Soviet.

National Movement for the True Independence of Trinago (NMTIT)

History. The NMTIT was founded in 1974.

Leadership. Teddy Belgrave.

Industrial influence. The NMTIT is linked with the Oilfield Workers' Trade Union.

Orientation. Maoist.

People's Popular Movement (PPM)

History. The PPM was founded in 1981. It was also represented at the Cuban conference in 1984.

Leadership. Michael Als (ch.).

Membership. 100 (1982 estimate). The PPM is believed to be the country's strongest Marxist party.

Orientation. Pro-Soviet.

United Revolutionary Organization (URO)

History. The URO was founded in 1971.

Orientation. Pro-Soviet.

Workers' Revolutionary Committee (WRC)

History. The WRC was founded in 1980.

Leadership. James Poon.

Orientation. Pro-Soviet.

8. SOUTH AMERICA

Argentina

Capital: Buenos Aires   Pop. 30,097,000

Argentina was ruled by the Radical Civic Union from 1916 to 1930, when the first of a long series of military coups ushered in a period of Conservative government. After another coup in 1943 Col. Juan Domingo Perón as Labour Minister gained the support of the majority of the trade unions, and was elected President in 1946 and re-elected in 1951. In office he pursued a policy of asserting Argentina's political and economic independence, nationalizing banks and public utilities, developing industry, raising working-class living standards and extending social services. His increasingly dictatorial methods brought him into conflict with the Church and the army, however, and in 1955 he was overthrown and driven into exile.

For the next 18 years attempts to restore democratic government were blocked by the leaders of the armed forces, who feared that free elections would restore Perón to power, two elected civilian Presidents and three military Presidents placed in office by the army being removed by force during this period. The Peronist movement meanwhile split into opposing factions, ranging from the extreme right to the extreme left; while the Peronist left largely adopted Marxist views, the Marxist parties moved towards a more sympathetic attitude to Perón's populist nationalism, to which they had previously been hostile. A guerrilla campaign by Peronists and Marxists forced the military regime to permit free elections in March 1973, in which the Peronist candidate, Héctor Cámpora, was elected President. He resigned after seven weeks in office, and in new elections in September Perón received an overwhelming majority.

Friction soon developed between Perón and his left-wing supporters, and intensified after his death in 1974, when he was succeeded in the presidency by his widow, María Estela Martínez de Perón. Guerrilla activity was resumed, while right-wing extremists launched a terrorist campaign against the left. A military junta seized power in 1976, and established a reign of terror in which up to 30,000 people disappeared. The failure of the junta's attempt to recover the Malvinas (the Falkland Islands) in 1982 led to the collapse of the regime, and elections were held in 1983 in which the Radical candidate for the presidency, Raul Alfonsín Foulkes, defeated his Peronist opponent.

Communist Party of Argentina
Partido Comunista de la Argentina (PCA)

History. The PCA, the oldest Communist Party in the western hemisphere, was founded in 1918 as the Internationalist Socialist Party by a dissident group which had been expelled from the Socialist Party in the previous year, and adopted its present name in 1920. It was driven underground after the 1930 coup, but regained its legal status in 1945. In the 1946 elections it allied with the

346

Conservatives, Radicals and Socialists to oppose Perón, and in the years following its influence declined as the Peronists secured control of most of the trade unions. After Perón's fall the Peronist and Communist-led unions frequently co-operated, however, and the PCA was banned on several occasions between 1959 and 1971. It supported the left-centre Popular Revolutionary Alliance in the elections of March 1973, two Communists being returned as Alliance deputies, but threw its support behind Perón in the presidential election in September. Under the military regime of 1976–82 it was banned with the other political parties. In the 1983 elections it supported the Peronist presidential and gubernatorial candidates, while putting forward its own candidates for Parliament and the local councils.

Leadership. Athos Fava (g.s.).

Structure. The national congress, held every four years, elects the Central Committee (92 full and 33 alternate members), which elects the general secretary, Executive Committee (eight members) and Secretariat.

Membership. 200,000 (1984 claim). Independent sources estimate the membership at about 70,000.

Electoral influence. Communist candidates received 1.3 per cent of the vote in the 1983 elections.

Industrial influence. The PCA has little influence in the trade unions, most of which are under Peronist control.

Orientation. Pro–Soviet.

Publication. ¿*Qué Pasa?* (What is happening?), weekly.

International affiliations. The PCA is represented on the editorial board of *World Marxist Review.*

Communist Vanguard
Vanguardia Comunista

History. This small pro-Chinese party, which broke away from the Communist Party in 1964, achieved some influence among students and workers in the early 1970s, but has shown few signs of activity since 1976.

Labour Party
Partido Obrero (PO)

History. The PO, founded in 1982, unsuccessfully contested the elections in the following year.

Leadership. Gregorio Flores (l.).

Membership. 60,875 (1983 claim).

Orientation. Trotskyist.

Marxist–Leninist Communist Workers' Party
Partido Obrero Comunista Marxista-Leninista (POCML)

History. The POCML was formed by a pro-Chinese section of the Socialist Party, and was originally known as the Vanguard Socialist Party.

Movement to Socialism
Movimiento al Socialismo (MAS)

History. The MAS was founded in 1982, and unsuccessfully contested the elections in the following year.

Leadership. Luis Zamora (l.).

Membership. 55,173 (1983 claim).

Orientation. Trotskyist.

Popular Left Front
Frente de Izquierda Popular (FIP)

History. The FIP was founded in the 1950s, as the Socialist Party of the National Left, by Marxists who favoured an alliance with the Peronists, and adopted its present name in 1973. It put forward the historian Jorge Abelardo Ramos as its candidate in the presidential election of March 1973, obtaining less than 1 per cent of the vote, but supported Perón in the September election. Unlike other Trotskyist-Peronist groups, the FIP has strongly opposed political violence.

Leadership. Jorge Abelardo Ramos (l.).

Orientation. Trotskyist-Peronist.

Revolutionary Communist Party
Partido Comunista Revolucionario (PCR)

History. The PCR was formed in 1968 by pro-Chinese members of the Communist Party who accused it of "class conciliation", and was officially recognized by Peking.

Workers' Revolutionary Party
Partido Revolucionario de los Trabajadores (PRT)

History. The PRT, formed in 1965, organized the People's Revolutionary Army (see below) as its military wing in 1969, and because of its advocacy of violence was not legalized after the fall of the military regime in 1982.

Leadership. Luis Mattini (g.s.).

Orientation. Trotskyist.

International affiliations. The PRT was formerly affiliated to the Fourth International, United Secretariat, from which it withdrew in 1973.

Guerrilla Organizations

Montoneros

History. The Montoneros, who derived their name from the irregular troops which took part in the 19th-century Argentinian civil wars, originated in a group of 12 young revolutionists formed in 1968 under the leadership of Mario Eduardo

Firmenich. After carrying out a number of bank robberies and thefts of arms, in 1970 they kidnapped and murdered ex-President Pedro Eugenio Aramburu as a reprisal for the execution of Peronists during his term of office, and in 1971–72 raised funds by kidnapping foreign business executives. After the Peronist victories in the 1973 elections they abandoned the use of violence, but the increasingly right-wing policies pursued by President Perón led to a split between the President and the Montoneros, who had developed into a mass movement. They went underground after his death in 1974, and launched a campaign of attacks on military targets or police premises, hijackings, kidnappings and assassinations which helped to provoke the military seizure of power in 1976. Over 2,000 Montoneros were killed between January 1976 and June 1977 in clashes with the military, and in 1977 Firmenich and most of the other leaders went into exile. Guerrilla activities continued under the leadership of Horacio Mendizábal, who was killed in 1979, but in 1981 Firmenich ordered the abandonment of armed struggle. He was arrested in Brazil in 1984 and extradited to Argentina for trial on charges of murder and kidnapping. Another Montonero leader, Ricardo Obregón Cano, was sentenced to 10 years' imprisonment in 1985.

Leadership. Mario Eduardo Firmenich (C.-in-C.).

Orientation. Although the Montoneros claimed to be Peronists, and in 1975 founded the Authentic Peronist Party as the political wing of their movement, their views had more in common with Castroism, Trotskyism and Maoism than with orthodox Peronism.

People's Revolutionary Army
Ejército Revolucionario del Pueblo (ERP)

History. The ERP was formed in 1969 as the armed wing of the Workers' Revolutionary Party (see above), and began operations in the following year, under the leadership of Mario Roberto Santucho. It pursued a strategy of urban guerrilla warfare, including kidnappings, bank robberies, hijackings and assassinations of officers and businessmen, and in 1974 opened a rural front in Tucuman province. Santucho was killed in 1976, and in the following year the movement was virtually destroyed and its members driven into exile. ERP members were believed to be responsible for the assassination of ex-President Anastasio Somoza Debayle of Nicaragua in Paraguay in 1980.

Orientation. Trotskyist.

International affiliations. The ERP in 1974 formed the Revolutionary Co-ordinating Junta, which linked it with similar guerrilla movements in Bolivia, Chile and Uruguay.

Bolivia

Capital: La Paz   Pop. 6,400,000

Bolivian politics since World War II have been dominated by the Revolutionary Nationalist Movement (MNR), founded in 1941. Víctor Paz Estenssoro, the MNR leader, won the largest vote in the 1951 presidential election, whereupon a military junta seized power and cancelled the election results. A popular uprising in 1952, however, overthrew the junta and established an MNR government, which introduced universal suffrage, nationalized the tin mines and divided the large estates among the peasantry. President Paz Estenssoro was removed by a coup in 1964, and a series of military regimes followed, including a left-wing government headed by Gen. Juan José Torres which held power in 1970–71 and a right-wing regime headed by Col. Hugo Bánzer Suárez which succeeded it. Presidential elections in 1978 and 1979 produced inconclusive results, and after a third election in 1980 was won by Hernán Siles Zuazo, leader of the Revolutionary Nationalist Movement of the Left (a radical offshoot of the MNR), the army seized power. The resistance of the political parties and the trade unions, however, forced the military leaders in 1982 to allow President Siles to take office. The 1985 elections resulted in a victory for Paz Estenssoro.

Bolivian Workers' Revolutionary Party
Partido Revolucionario de los Trabajadores Bolivianos (PRTB)

History. The PRTB is an offshoot of the National Liberation Army (*Ejército de Liberación Nacional*, ELN) established by Ernesto (Che) Guevara in 1966 and suppressed in the following year. The ELN was revived in 1969 as an urban guerrilla organization, and in 1975 formed the PRTB as its political wing, with the object of opposing President Banzer's dictatorship through "a wide resistance movement combining legal, semi-legal and clandestine organizations". The party was responsible for some bomb explosions in the later 1970s, but made little impact either as an urban guerrilla or a political organization. It contested the 1985 presidential election but polled insignificantly.

Leadership. Antonio Peredo (l.).

Communist Party of Bolivia
Partido Comunista de Bolivia (PCB)

History. The PCB was formed in January 1950 by dissident members of the youth wing of the Party of the Revolutionary Left, and was banned three months later. Legalized after the 1952 revolution, it unsuccessfully contested the 1956 and 1960 presidential elections. Although it refused in 1967 to co-operate in Che Guevara's attempt to launch a guerrilla struggle in Bolivia, it was again banned in the same year. The ban was subsequently lifted, but under the Banzer regime the PCB was driven underground. In the elections of 1978, 1979 and 1980 it formed part of the Democratic Popular Unity Front, together with the Revolutionary Nationalist Movement of the Left and the Movement of the Revolutionary Left (MIR), which supported Hernán Siles Zuazo's candidature for the presidency. The PCB was represented in President Siles' government by two ministers, holding the Labour and Mines portfolios, from October 1982 to November 1984, when they resigned in protest against its economic policies. For the 1985 elections it formed the United People's Front, together with the Revolutionary Party of the National Left and two dissident factions of the MIR, and won four seats in Congress.

Leadership. Simón Reyes Rivera (g.s.).

Structure. The national congress elects the Central Committee, which elects the general secretary and the Political Commission.

Membership. 300 (1985 estimate).

Electoral influence. The PCB has not contested elections independently of other parties since 1960.

Industrial influence. The PCB exercises a strong influence in the Bolivian Workers' Central (COB), the national trade union federation, and especially in the Miners' Federation. Its influence declined in 1983–84, however, because of its support for the Siles government's austerity programme, and at the 1984 COB congress it lost three of its seven leadership positions.

Orientation. Pro-Soviet.

International affiliation. The PCB is represented on the editorial council of *World Marxist Review.*

Communist Vanguard of the Revolutionary Workers' Party
Vanguardia Comunista del Partido Obrero Revolucionario (VCPOR)

History. A dissident group which broke away from the Revolutionary Workers' Party in 1975 split two years later, one section forming the VCPOR. This in turn divided into three in 1978, two sections breaking away to form the Workers' Vanguard and the Workers' Socialist Organization.

Leadership. Victor Sossa (l.).

Orientation. Trotskyist.

Marxist-Leninist Communist Party of Bolivia
Partido Comunista de Bolivia Marxista-Leninista (PCBML)

History. The PCBML broke away from the Communist Party in 1965. For the 1978 elections it formed the Left Revolutionary Front, together with the Revolutionary Party of the Nationalist Left and the Revolutionary Workers' Party, but in 1979 and 1980 it supported Víctor Paz Estenssoro, leader of the right-wing faction of the Revolutionary Nationalist Movement

Leadership. Oscar Zamora Medinacelli (1st sec.).

Membership. 150 (1985 estimate).

Industrial influence. The PCBML has some influence in the trade unions, especially among the miners.

Orientation. Pro-Chinese.

International affiliation. The PCBML is recognized by the Chinese Communist Party.

Movement of the Revolutionary Left
Movimiento de la Izquierda Revolucionaria (MIR)

History. The MIR was formed after the right-wing coup in 1971 by members of the youth section of the Christian Democratic Party, and conducted guerrilla activities against President Banzer's regime. In the 1978, 1979 and 1980 elections it formed part of the Democratic Popular Unity Front, which supported Hernán Siles Zuazo's candidature, with its leader, Jaime Paz Zamora, as vice-presidential candidate. The MIR was represented in President Siles' government from October 1982 to January 1983, when it withdrew because of disagreements on policy, and again from April to December 1984, when Vice-President Paz and the MIR ministers resigned. The party split in the following month, when its general secretary, Antonio Araníbar Quiroga, formed the MIR—Free Bolivia. The main body of the MIR fought the 1985 elections alone, with Paz Zamora as its presidential candidate, and won 16 seats in Congress. Two dissident factions, the MIR—Free Bolivia and the MIR—Masses, led by Walter Delgadillo (general secretary of the Bolivian Workers' Central), on the other hand, joined the Communist Party and the Revolutionary Party of the National Left to form the United People's Front, which put forward Araníbar Quiroga as its presidential candidate, but won only four seats.

Leadership. Jaime Paz Zamora (l.).

Electoral influence. The MIR obtained 153,143 votes (8.8 per cent) in the 1985 elections, more than any other left-wing party.

Orientation. Independent. The MIR contains both Marxists and left-wing Catholics who aim to radicalize Catholic opinion.

Programme. The MIR seeks to organize the working class, the peasants and the middle classes into a single revolutionary bloc with a view to the national and social liberation of the Bolivian people.

Party of the Revolutionary Left
Partido de la Izquierda Revolucionaria (PIR)

History. The PIR, founded in 1940 as a pro-Soviet party but with no formal links with Moscow, exercised considerable influence for some years, especially among the miners. This greatly declined after its youth wing broke away in 1950 to form the Communist Party, and in 1952 it dissolved itself. Revived in 1956, it gradually moved to the right, while still claiming to uphold "pure Marxism". Its leader, Ricardo Anaya Arce, accepted government office under the military dictatorships of Gen. René Barrientos Ortuño in 1964–69 and Gen. Juan Pereda Asbún in 1978, and in the 1979 and 1980 elections it supported Gen. Banzer's candidature.

Leadership. Ricardo Anaya Arce (l.).

Posadist Trotskyist Revolutionary Workers' Party
Partido Obrero Revolucionario Trotskista Posadista (PORTP)

History. The PORTP broke away from the Revolutionary Workers' Party—Struggle in 1963.

Leadership. Carlos Flores Bedregal (l.).

Orientation. Trotskyist.

International affiliation. Posadist Fourth International.

Revolutionary Workers' Party
Partido Obrero Revolucionario (POR)

History. The POR, founded in 1934, is the oldest Marxist party in Bolivia. Banned in 1949, it was legalized after the 1952 revolution, in which it supported the Revolutionary Nationalist Movement (MNR). Most of its members joined the MNR in 1954, however, and a split occurred in 1957, when González Moscoso's faction broke away, with the result that the vote for its presidential candidate fell from nearly 3,000 in 1956 to 637 in 1960. The POR was again banned after Che Guevara's revolt in 1967, subsequently legalized, and again banned under President Banzer's dictatorship. In the 1978 elections it supported the Left Revolutionary Front's candidate.

Leadership. Guillermo Lora Escóbar (l.).

Industrial influence. The POR has considerable influence in the Bolivian Workers' Central (COB), and especially in the Miners' Federation, although this has declined in recent years. At the 1984 COB congress it failed to win a seat on the executive.

Orientation. Trotskyist.

International affiliation. Fourth Internationalist Tendency.

Revolutionary Workers' Party—United
Partido Obrero Revolucionario—Unificado (PORU)

History. The PORU was formed in 1984 by the merger of two existing organizations: (i) the Revolutionary Workers' Party—Struggle (POR-*Combate*), led by Hugo González Moscoso, which broke away from the Revolutionary Workers' Party (POR) in 1957 and pursued a policy of guerrilla struggle, with little success; (ii) the Workers' Vanguard, another offshoot of the POR led by Filemón Escobar, which contested the 1979 presidential election, receiving 1.13 per cent of the vote.

Orientation. Trotskyist.

Publication. Bandera Socialista (Socialist Flag).

International affiliation. Fourth International, United Secretariat.

Socialist Party
Partido Socialista (PS)

History. The PS, founded in 1971 by the merger of three small socialist organizations, subsequently split into a left wing led by Marcelo Quiroga Santa Cruz (later known as "Socialist Party One"—PS-1), which contested the 1978, 1979 and 1980 elections with Quiroga as its presidential candidate, and a right wing which supported Siles Zuazo's candidature. PS-1 obtained five seats in Congress in 1979 and 11 in 1980, but after the death of Quiroga, who was murdered by troops during the 1980 military coup, its influence declined. In the 1985 elections its presidential candidate, Ramiro Velasco, took sixth place, and its congressional representation fell to five.

Leadership. Walter Vázquez (l.).

Electoral influence. The PS-1 vote fell from 113,309 (8 per cent) in 1980 to 38,782 (2.2 per cent) in 1985.

Orientation. Independent.

Workers' Socialist Organization
Organización Socialista de los Trabajadores (OST)

History. The OST broke away in 1978 from the Communist Vanguard of the Revolutionary Workers' Party, and contested the 1979 elections in alliance with the Socialist Party.

Leadership. Sonia Montaño (l.).

Orientation. Trotskyist.

Brazil

Capital: Brasília   Pop. 134,380,000

Following a revolution in 1930, Getúlio Vargas assumed the presidency, and in 1937 introduced a new constitution which gave him dictatorial powers. He was deposed by the army in 1945 and democratic government reintroduced, but in 1964 the left-wing President João Belchior Marques Goulart was overthrown and a military government established. The existing political parties were dissolved in 1965 and replaced by the pro-government Alliance for National Renewal and the opposition Brazilian Democratic Movement as the only legal parties. Popular pressure forced the regime to adopt more liberal policies from 1978 onwards; the formation of new parties was permitted, and elections in 1985 resulted in the return of the opposition candidate, Tancredo de Almeida Neves, as the first civilian president since 1964. He died shortly after his election, and was succeeded by Vice-President José Sarney.

Brazilian Communist Party
Partido Comunista Brasileiro (PCB)

History. The PCB was founded in 1922 as the Communist Party of Brazil (PCdoB), and was banned a few months later. Luis Carlos Prestes, a former army officer who had achieved fame through his leadership of a military revolt in 1924–26 and had since become a Communist, was elected general secretary in 1935. A few months later he launched an unsuccessful uprising against the Vargas dictatorship, hundreds of Communists, including Prestes, subsequently being imprisoned. The PCdoB was legalized in 1945, and its membership rapidly reached 150,000; in the 1945 elections it polled 570,000 votes (10 per cent of the total vote) and returned 14 deputies and one senator. Alarmed by further Communist election successes, the government banned the party in 1947, ending the only period of legality until 1985, and Congress cancelled the mandates of all Communists elected to state or national office. In an unsuccessful attempt to obtain legal recognition, the PCdoB changed its name in 1960 to the Brazilian Communist Party and dropped international slogans from its statutes. Although not officially recognized, it operated openly under the Goulart government of 1961–64, but after the 1964 coup it was driven underground and many Communists arrested. The 1974 elections, in which the opposition Brazilian Democratic Movement made substantial gains with Communist support, were followed by a period of severe repression, over half the PCB leadership being killed by the police. After the adoption of a more liberal policy by the government Prestes was allowed to return from exile in 1979, but was replaced as general secretary by Giocondo Gervasi Dias in the following year. Major policy differences developed between Prestes and the other leaders, whom he accused of "right-wing opportunism", and in 1982 he was expelled from the party.

Leadership. Giocondo Gervasi Dias (g.s.).

Structure. The 1984 party congress elected a 66-member National Provisional Committee, which elected a 12-member National Executive Committee (also referred to as the National Committee for Legalization of the PCB).

Membership. 8,000 (1984 estimate).

Electoral influence. The PCB is represented in Congress, although it did not contest the 1982 elections under its own name.

Orientation. Pro-Soviet.

Programme. The political resolution adopted by the 1984 PCB congress called for the restoration of democracy, ending Brazil's dependence on imperialism, breaking the power of the monopolies and landowners and opening the road to socialism, and declared that the proletariat must assure the unity of the patriotic national forces while preserving its political, ideological and organizational independence. Its immediate demands included the abolition of anti-democratic laws, freedom of party and trade union activity, the adoption of anti-monopoly laws, the channelling of investment into areas which enlarged the domestic market and created jobs, the rescheduling of debts at fixed rates, cost of living and productivity adjustments for wages, administration of welfare services by the trade unions and price controls on essential goods and services.

Publication. *Voz de Unidade* (Voice of Unity), weekly.

International affiliation. The PCB is represented on the editorial council of *World Marxist Review*.

Communist Party of Brazil
Partido Comunista do Brasil (PCdoB)

History. The PCdoB was founded by a pro-Chinese faction which broke away from the Brazilian Communist Party in 1962 and revived the party's former name. After the arrest of the "gang of four" in 1976 it adopted a pro-Albanian attitude. It was responsible for the organization of unemployed demonstrations in São Paulo in 1983 which led to serious rioting.

Leadership. João Amazonas (g.s.).

Membership. 7,000 (1984 estimate).

Electoral influence. The PCdoB is represented in Congress, although it did not contest the 1982 elections under its own name.

Orientation. Pro-Albanian.

Publication. *Tribuna de Luta Operária* (Tribune of Working-class Struggle), weekly.

International affiliation. The PCdoB is officially recognized by the Albanian Party of Labour.

Communist Revolutionary Party
Partido Revolucionário Comunista (PRC)

History. The PRC was founded and adopted its programme at a congress held in January 1984.

Leadership. Genuíno Neto (g.s.).

Orientation. Independent. The PRC is opposed to social democracy, reformism, Stalinism and Trotskyism, and has no international connections.

Programme. The PRC's programme defined its objective as "the revolutionary overthrow of the military dictatorship, carrying down the bourgeois state with it, and then building a workers' and people's democracy upon the rubble".

Freedom and Struggle
Liberdade e Luta (Libelu)

History. Libelu operates inside the non-socialist Workers' Party (*Partido dos Trabalhadores*), which was founded in 1980.

Leadership. Clara Ant (l.).

Orientation. Trotskyist.

October 8 Revolutionary Movement
Movimento Revolucionário do Outubre 8 (MR-8)

History. MR-8 was formed in 1968 by a dissident student group which broke away from the Brazilian Communist Party (PCB), and took its name from the date of Ché Guevara's death in the previous year. In 1969 it kidnapped the US ambassador, whom it held as a hostage until the government released 15 named political prisoners, many of its members subsequently being arrested in police raids. At its fourth congress in 1983 MR-8 renounced its former "anti-Soviet and leftist" positions and decided to return to the PCB, but a section of the membership continued to operate as a separate party.

Membership. 1,500 (1984 estimate).

Publication. Hora do Povo, weekly.

Revolutionary Brazilian Communist Party
Partido Comunista Brasileiro Revolucionário (PCBR)

History. The PCBR was founded in 1967 by Mário Alves de Souza Vieira and Apolônio Pinto de Carvalho, who had been expelled from the Brazilian Communist Party for advocating an armed insurrection against the military regime. They were arrested in 1970; Vieira died under torture, whilst Carvalho was released in exchange for the West German ambassador, who had been kidnapped by urban guerrillas, and went into exile. The PCBR still exists, but exercises little influence.

Orientation. Maoist.

Socialist Youth Foundation
Alicerce da Juventude Socialista (AJS)

History. The AJS was formed in 1983 by the merger of two organizations, Foundation and Socialist Convergence, and like Freedom and Struggle operates inside the Workers' Party, of which the two organizations form the left wing.

Orientation. Trotskyist.

Chile

Capital: Santiago   Pop. 11,878,000

The Liberal President Arturo Alessandri, elected in 1920, was overthrown in 1925 by Col. (later Gen.) Carlos Ibañez, who ruled as President and virtual dictator from 1927 but was himself overthrown in 1931. A period of confusion ensued, during which a group of officers established a shortlived socialist republic, until in 1932 Alessandri was re-elected President. The Radical Party held power from 1938 to 1952, until 1947 with Communist and Socialist support, but in 1952 Gen. Ibañez was re-elected. The Conservative-Liberal candidate Jorge Alessandri was elected President in 1958, and the Christian Democrat Eduardo Frei Montalva in 1964.

Salvador Allende Gossens, the Socialist leader, was elected President in 1970 as the candidate of Popular Unity, an alliance of Socialists, Communists and left-wing Radicals and Christian Democrats, and formed a government which nationalized the banks and copper mines and carried out a programme of land reforms. His government was overthrown in 1973 by a military coup, Allende dying during the fighting, and a junta headed by Gen. Augusto Pinochet Ugarte took power. Congress was dissolved, the Marxist parties banned and political activities by other parties suspended until 1977, when they were also banned. Popular discontent with President Pinochet's dictatorship led to mass protest demonstrations in 1983–85, which were supported by all the political parties.

Communist Party of Chile
Partido Comunista de Chile (PCCh)

History. The Socialist Workers' Party, founded in 1912, was renamed the Communist Party of Chile in 1922, when it joined the Third International. It was banned by President Ibañez in 1927, and when legalized in 1931 split into the PCCh and the Communist Left, a Trotskyist organization, both of which put forward candidates for the presidential elections of that year. In 1936 the PCCh, together with the Socialist and Radical parties, formed the Popular Front, which made large gains in the 1937 congressional elections and secured the return of the Radical Pedro Aguirre Cerda as President in the following year. Although the Popular Front was dissolved in 1941, the PCCh supported the Radical candidates in the 1942 and 1946 presidential elections, and President Gabriel González Videla in 1946 included three Communists in his cabinet. Alarmed at the growing influence of the PCCh, which by 1947 had 50,000 members, five representatives in the Senate and 15 in the Chamber of Deputies, however, he dismissed the Communist ministers after five months, and in 1948 banned the PCCh and excluded known Communists from the electoral registers. The PCCh contested the 1949 congressional elections as the National Democratic Front, retaining six seats in the Chamber, and after the ban was lifted in 1958 increased its representation to 15 in 1961, 18 in 1965 and 22 in 1969. During this period it developed into the largest Communist Party in Latin America and the third largest in the non-communist world, after the Italian and French, with 200,000 members in 1972.

In 1969 the PCCh helped to form the Popular Unity coalition, which in the following year secured the election of President Allende, whom the PCCh had already supported in the 1952, 1958 and 1964 presidential elections. Inside his government, which included three Communist ministers, the PCCh acted as a moderating influence, opposing demands by the Socialists and the Movement of the Revolutionary Left (MIR) for a speeding up of the revolutionary process and advocating concessions to middle-class opinion and the opening of a dialogue with the Christian Democrats.

After the 1973 coup the PCCh was banned and its leaders sent to concentration camps; most were later allowed to go into exile, however, including the general secretary, Luís Corvalán Lepe, who was exchanged in 1976 for the Soviet dissident Vladimir Bukovsky. The PCCh attempted to maintain the Popular Unity alliance and to develop co-operation with the Christian Democrats, but in 1982 a split occurred between those sections of the opposition advocating armed struggle against the regime, as the PCCh had done since 1980, and those opposed to such tactics. In 1983 the PCCh formed the Popular Democratic Movement, an alliance which also included the MIR, a left-wing faction of the Socialist Party, the Christian Left and the Movement for United Popular Action. The PCCh played a prominent part in the mass anti-government demonstrations of 1983–85, the first of which was organized by its youth section.

Leadership. Luís Corvalán Lepe (g.s.).

Structure. The PCCh maintains a clandestine organization inside Chile, based on 5,000 cells. It has a Political Bureau of 20 and a Secretariat of five members, all of whom are living in exile.

Membership. 20,000 (1984 estimate).

Electoral influence. In the 1973 congressional elections, the last held, the PCCh received 16 per cent of the vote.

Industrial influence. The PCCh dominates the illegal but active National Trade Union Co-ordinating Committee, founded in 1980.

Orientation. Pro-Soviet.

Programme. The PCCh advocates the formation of the broadest possible alliance against the Pinochet dictatorship, use of all forms of struggle, including armed force, and the establishment of a "national people's democratic government" representing all anti-fascist forces.

Publication. El Siglo (The Age), published clandestinely at irregular intervals.

International affiliation. The PCCh is represented on the editorial council of *World Marxist Review*.

Revolutionary Communist Party of Chile
Partido Comunista Revolucionario de Chile (PCRC)

History. The PCRC was founded in 1966 by Maoists who had been expelled from the Communist Party. Originally pro-Chinese, it later adopted a hostile attitude towards both the Soviet and the Chinese regimes, which it regarded as revisionist.

Orientation. Independent Maoist.

International affiliation. The PCRC has links with the US Revolutionary Communist Party.

Socialist Party
Partido Socialista (PS)

History. The PS was formed in 1933 by the merger of six small parties which had supported the shortlived socialist republic established in the previous year, and adopted a declaration of principles in which it affirmed its support for Marxism and the theory of the dictatorship of the proletariat. It was joined in 1937 by the Communist Left, a Trotskyist breakaway from the Communist Party of Chile (PCCh), and contested the elections of that year as part of the Popular Front, winning 19 seats in the Chamber of Deputies. In 1948 it split into the Socialist Party of Chile, which supported the banning of the PCCh, and the Popular Socialist Party, led by Salvador Allende, which opposed the ban and proclaimed itself a Marxist-Leninist party, but when in 1952 the Popular Socialists decided to support Gen. Ibañez's candidature Allende returned to the Socialist Party of Chile, which adopted him as its presidential candidate. The two parties reunited in 1957 as the Socialist Party, which was declared to be a Marxist-Leninist party.

The reunited PS increased its representation in the Chamber to 13 seats in 1961, 15 in 1965 and 1969 and 28 in 1973. It joined the Popular Unity alliance in 1969, and in the following year Allende, who had been its candidate in 1958 and 1964, was elected President. Inside his government, in which the PS held four portfolios, it pressed for a speedy advance to socialism, in opposition to the more cautious policies advocated by the PCCh, and opposed proposals for a dialogue with the Christian Democrats.

After the 1973 coup the PS split into a large number of factions, as a result of disagreements over the reasons for the failure of the Allende government and how democracy could be restored. The principal Socialist leaders in exile issued a declaration in Rome in 1982 reaffirming their acceptance of Marxism as a framework of historical analysis, while declaring their support for democracy, a multiparty system and human rights and condemning Soviet intervention in Afghanistan and Poland. The leaders of three Socialist factions joined with the Christian Democratic, Republican, Social Democratic and Radical parties in the following year to form the Democratic Alliance, from which the PCCh was excluded on the ground that it advocated the violent overthrow of the regime, but a left-wing faction of the PS led by Clodomiro Almeyda Medina a month later joined the Communist-led Popular Democratic Movement.

Leadership. Carlos Briones (g.s.).

Orientation. Independent.

Guerrilla Organizations

Manuel Rodríguez Patriotic Front
Frente Patriótico Manuel Rodríguez (FPMR)

History. The FPMR, which is named after an early 19th-century revolutionary, first emerged in March 1984, when it occupied a radio station and broadcast an anti-government statement, and was subsequently responsible for a series of bomb explosions. It is believed to be linked with the Communist Party.

Leadership. Daniel Huerta (commander).

Movement of the Revolutionary Left
Movimiento de la Izquierda Revolucionaria (MIR)

History. The MIR was founded in 1965 by students at the University of Concepción, and began accumulating funds by means of bank robberies in 1967. It gave President Allende conditional support during and after the 1970 election, and pursued a policy of forcibly taking over farms and factories in order to compel the government to adopt a more radical policy. After the 1973 coup, to which it offered armed resistance, many of its members were executed, including the peasant leader Gregorio José Liendo ("Commandante Pepe"). Its general secretary, Miguel Enríquez, was killed in a gun battle with troops in 1974, and was succeeded by Andrés Pascal Allende (the former President's nephew), who was allowed to leave Chile in 1976 after taking refuge in the Costa Rican embassy. MIR resistance nevertheless continued inside Chile, taking the form of assassinations of persons associated with the regime and bomb attacks on government buildings. In 1983 the MIR joined the Popular Democratic Movement (see under "Communist Party of Chile").

Leadership. Andrés Pascal Allende (g.s.).

Orientation. Independent. The MIR drew its inspiration primarily from the teachings of Castro and Guevara, but was also influenced by Maoist and Trotskyist thought.

Colombia

Capital: Bogotá   Pop. 31,000,000

A Liberal President was elected in 1930, for the first time since 1884, but in 1946 the Conservatives regained power. The murder in 1948 of the left-wing Liberal leader Jorge Eliécer Gaitán was followed by five years of civil war between Liberals and Conservatives in which up to 300,000 people were estimated to have been killed. Gen. Gustavo Rojas Pinilla seized control in 1953, but was overthrown in 1957, when the Liberal and Conservative parties agreed to avoid further conflict by sharing power until 1974, with the presidency alternating between the two parties. Guerrilla warfare by left-wing groups, which began during the civil war, continued until 1984, when the Conservative President Belisario Betancur Cuartas concluded ceasefire agreements with the main guerrilla organizations. The situation remained precarious, however, because of clashes between the army and the guerrillas and the activities of right-wing terrorists, who murdered many guerrilla leaders, and the truce with one of the largest guerrilla forces, M-19, broke down in the summer of 1985.

Communist Party of Colombia
Partido Comunista de Colombia (PCC)

History. The Socialist Revolutionary Party, founded in 1926, affiliated to the Third International two years later, and was renamed the Communist Party of

Colombia in 1930. From 1944 to 1947 it operated under the name of the Social Democratic Party. Banned by President Rojas in 1956, it regained semi-legal status after his fall in the following year. Since 1972 it has been allowed to participate in elections under its own name, and has done so in alliance with other left-wing parties.

Leadership. Gilberto Vieira (g.s.).

Structure. The national congress, meeting every four years, elects the Central Committee (80 members), which elects the 14-member Executive Committee and the Secretariat.

Membership. 12,000 (1984 estimate). The Communist Youth of Colombia, the PCC's youth organization, claims to have 2,000 members.

Electoral influence. In the 1984 municipal and state assembly elections the PCC obtained 2 per cent of the vote.

Industrial influence. The PCC controls the Trade Union Confederation of Colombian Workers, one of the four main trade union federations, which claims to have 300,000 members.

Orientation. Pro-Soviet.

Programme. The PCC advocates the formation of a broad anti-monopoly and anti-imperialist front, with a programme of agrarian reform aimed at a fundamental change in the system of land tenure, nationalization of oil and coal resources, and free health, education and social security services.

Publications. *Voz Proletaria* (Proletarian Voice), weekly (45,000); *Documentos Políticos*, monthly.

International affiliation. The PCC is represented on the editorial council of *World Marxist Review*.

Communist Party of Colombia, Marxist-Leninist
Partido Comunista de Colombia, Marxista-Leninista (PCC-ML)

History. The PCC-ML was founded in 1965 by Maoist elements expelled from the Communist Party, and in 1968 formed its own guerrilla organization, the People's Liberation Army. It has not attempted to gain legal status, but contested the 1978 elections as part of the United Popular Front.

Membership. 1,000 (1984 estimate).

Orientation. Pro-Chinese.

Publication. *Revolución*.

International affiliation. The PCC-ML is officially recognized by the Chinese Communist Party.

Independent Revolutionary Workers' Movement
Movimiento Obrero Independiente Revolucionario (MOIR)

History. The MOIR, founded in 1971, fought the 1974 and 1978 elections in alliance with the Communist Party and other left-wing parties. It subsequently denounced the Communist Party as reformist, however, and since 1982 has contested elections on its own, with little success.

Leadership. Francisco Mosquera (g.s.).

Electoral influence. The MOIR obtained 0.04 per cent of the vote in the 1984 municipal and state assembly elections.

Orientation. Pro-Chinese.

Publication. Tribuna Roja (Red Tribune), quarterly.

International affiliation. The MOIR has links with the Chinese Communist Party.

Patriotic Union
Unión Patriótica (UP)

History. The UP was founded in 1985 as the political wing of the Revolutionary Armed Forces of Colombia (see below).

Programme. The UP programme emphasizes political and trade union liberties, agrarian reform, decentralization of the administration and opposition to US interference in foreign policy.

Guerrilla Organizations

April 19 Movement
Movimiento 19 de Abril (M-19)

History. M-19, which first appeared in 1974, originated as the armed wing of the National Popular Alliance (ANAPO), the populist party founded by ex-President Rojas, and derived its name from the date of the 1970 presidential election in which he was defeated, his followers maintained, by fraudulent counting of the votes. The ANAPO leadership repudiated M-19, however, and it gradually adopted a Marxist ideology. It began guerrilla operations in 1976, and developed into one of the largest guerrilla organizations in the country. In August 1984 it signed a one-year ceasefire agreement, and announced its intention of constituting itself as a political party. It took advantage of the truce to secure control of zones in the south of the country and to set up camps on the outskirts of the main cities, which it used as recruiting centres. After the army had retaliated by attacking its camps in the jungle and several of its leaders had been murdered by right-wing terrorists, M-19 announced in June 1985 that it was ending the truce. In November 41 guerrillas occupied the Palace of Justice in Bogotá; the army then stormed the building, over 100 people being killed, including 12 judges and all the guerrillas.

Leadership. Alvaro Fayad Delgado, the M-19 leader, was killed in March 1986.

Membership. 6,000 (1984 claim).

Orientation. Independent.

International affiliations. An M-19 spokesman said in 1985 that the movement had links with revolutionary organizations in Ecuador, Venezuela, El Salvador, Panama and Nicaragua.

National Liberation Army
Ejército de Liberación Nacional (ELN)

History. The ELN was founded by Fabio Vásquez Castaño in 1964, and began guerrilla operations in the following year. In 1966 it was joined by Camilo Torres

Restrepo, a former priest, who was killed in action a month later and became a legendary hero among left-wing Catholics. Regarded in the 1960s as the strongest of the guerrilla forces, it suffered heavily from an army offensive in 1973, and was further weakened by the defection of Vásquez in 1976. It nevertheless rejected President Betancur's ceasefire offer in 1984, and denounced the guerrilla leaders who had accepted it as "traitors to the revolutionary cause".

Leadership. Nicolás Rodríguez Bautista (l.).

Membership. 350 (1984 estimate).

Orientation. Castroist.

International affiliations. The ELN was reported in 1983 to have links with a number of foreign guerrilla groups, including Red Flag (Venezuela), Shining Path (Peru) and the Farabundo Martí National Liberation Front (El Salvador).

Pedro León Arboleda (PLA)

History. The PLA operated as the urban section of the People's Liberation Army, and took its name from a former general secretary of the Communist Party of Colombia, Marxist–Leninist, who was killed by the police in 1975. It was reported in 1983 to be co-operating with the National Liberation Army, with which it had reached a political agreement.

Membership. 100 (1983 estimate).

Orientation. Pro-Chinese.

People's Liberation Army
Ejército Popular de Liberación (EPL)

History. The EPL, which was founded by the Communist Party of Colombia, Marxist–Leninist in 1968 and was the first Maoist guerrilla organization in Latin America, conducted only limited operations after 1975. It signed a one-year ceasefire agreement in August 1984, but sporadic clashes between the guerrillas and the army continued. After an EPL leader, Oscar William Calvo, was murdered in Bogotá by right-wing terrorists in November 1985, it withdrew from the agreement.

Leadership. Francisco Caraballo (l.).

Membership. 350 (1984 estimate).

Orientation. Pro-Chinese.

Revolutionary Armed Forces of Colombia
Fuerzas Armadas Revolucionarias de Colombia (FARC)

History. The FARC originated as the armed forces of the republic of Gaitania, covering 2,000 square miles in the high Andes south of Bogotá, which was founded in 1949 during the civil war by Fermin Charry Rincón, a peasant leader and a member of the Central Committee of the Communist Party of Colombia (PCC). On his death in 1960 control passed to Manuel Marulanda Vélez, also a PCC Central Committee member, and the republic was renamed Marquetalia. Although it was occupied by the army in 1964, the guerrillas continued their resistance, and in 1966 were officially recognized by the PCC and given their present name. The FARC, which became one of the strongest of the country's guerrilla forces, conducted operations with considerable success until 1984, when it signed a one-year ceasefire agreement. Although it strictly observed the truce, it suffered heavily from right-wing terrorists, who murdered over 70 of its leading members in 1984–85.

Leadership. Manuel Marulanda Vélez (l.).

Membership. 4,000–5,000 (1984 claim).

Orientation. Pro-Soviet.

Ricardo Franco Front
Frente Ricardo Franco (FRF)

History. The FRF was formed in February 1984 by dissident members of the Revolutionary Armed Forces of Colombia (FARC) who opposed acceptance of President Betancur's ceasefire proposals, and was responsible for several bomb explosions in May at US diplomatic and commercial buildings in Bogotá and for a number of attacks in 1985 on army bases and police stations. It was condemned both by the FARC, which in May 1985 declared war on all groups opposed to the restoration of peace, and by the Communist Party of Colombia (PCC); as a reprisal the FRF attempted in June to assassinate Hernando Hurtado, a member of the PCC Executive Committee.

Leadership. Javier Delgado (l.).

Workers' Self-defence Movement
Movimiento de Autodefesa Obrero (MAO)

History. The MAO, an urban movement specializing in kidnappings and assassinations, emerged in 1978. It was almost wiped out in 1982, when its principal leaders in Bogotá were arrested, and signed a ceasefire agreement in 1984.

Orientation. Trotskyist.

Ecuador

Capital: Quito Pop. 9,500,000

Ecuador passed through a period of political instability between 1925 and 1948, during which 22 heads of state held office. The Liberal President Carlos Arroyo del Río was deposed in 1944 by an insurrection in which Conservatives, dissident Liberals, Socialists and Communists were allied, and was succeeded by President José María Velasco Ibarra. Forced to resign three years later, he was re-elected in 1952 and 1960, but was overthrown by a popular revolt in the following year. His successor, President Carlos Julio Arosemena Monroy, was deposed in 1963, when a military junta seized power, only to be overthrown three years later. Re-elected for a fifth term in 1968, President Velasco assumed dictatorial powers in 1970 and was removed by a coup in 1972. A "revolutionary and nationalist" military regime then held power until 1979, when civilian government was restored.

Ecuadorean Communist Party
Partido Comunista Ecuatoriano (PCE)

History. The Ecuadorean Socialist Party, founded in 1926, was admitted to the Communist International as a fraternal member two years later. In 1931 it was renamed the Communist Party and became a full member of the Comintern, whilst a dissident group reconstituted the Socialist Party. The PCE took part in the 1944 insurrection, and was subsequently represented for a few months by one minister in President Velasco's government. Under the junta which held power in 1963–66 it was banned and its leaders imprisoned. It contested the presidential and congressional elections of 1978–79 and 1984 as the leading party in an alliance known as the Broad Left Front, which won one seat in Congress in 1979 and two in 1984.

Leadership. René Maugé Mosquera (g.s.).

Structure. The party congress elects the eight-member Central Committee, the functions of which are similar to those discharged by the Political Bureau or corresponding body in other communist parties.

Membership. 500 (1985 estimate).

Electoral influence. Maugé, the PCE candidate, obtained 3.2 per cent of the vote in the 1978 presidential election and 3.6 per cent in 1984.

Industrial influence. The PCE controls the Ecuadorean Workers' Confederation, which contains about 20 per cent of the country's trade unionists.

Orientation. Pro-Soviet.

Programme. The party programme adopted in 1968 states that its objective is national liberation through an anti-imperialist, anti-feudal, democratic revolution which will develop into a socialist revolution.

Publication. *El Pueblo* (The People), daily.

International affiliation. The PCE is represented on the editorial council of *World Marxist Review*.

Ecuadorean Communist Party, Marxist-Leninist
Partido Comunista Ecuatoriano, Marxista-Leninista (PCE-ML)

History. The PCE-ML was founded in 1963 by Maoist dissidents expelled from the Communist Party. It contested the 1979 congressional elections and the 1984 presidential and congressional elections as the leading party in the Democratic Popular Movement, which won one seat in 1979 and three in 1984.

Membership. 100 (1985 estimate).

Electoral influence. Jaime Hurtado González, the candidate supported by the PCE-ML, received 6.1 per cent of the vote in the 1984 presidential election.

Orientation. Pro-Chinese.

Ecuadorean Revolutionary Socialist Party
Partido Socialista Revolucionario Ecuatoriano (PSRE)

History. The PSRE was founded in 1960 by left-wing dissidents who broke away from the Socialist Party and adopted a Castroist ideology. It contested the

1984 presidential and congressional elections in alliance with the Socialist and Ecuadorean People's parties, winning one seat.

Leadership. Jorge Chiriboga Guerrero (g.s.).

Membership. 200 (1985 estimate).

Electoral influence. Manuel Salgado Tamayo, the presidential candidate supported by the PSRE in 1984, received 0.7 per cent of the vote.

Orientation. Castroist.

Publication. Tiempos de Lucha.

Guerrilla Organization

Eloy Alfaro Popular Armed Forces
Fuerzas Armadas Populares Eloy Alfaro (FAPEA)

History. The FAPEA, also known as "Alfaro Lives" (*Alfaro Vive*), which derives its name from the Liberal leader of the revolution of 1895–96, carried out a number of publicity stunts in 1983–84, such as forcing news agencies and newspapers to issue its statements. After the arrest in 1984 of Rosa Mireya Cárdenas, believed to be its leader, the government stated that wide-ranging plans for urban and rural guerrilla operations had been discovered. A bomb explosion in Quito in January 1985 was attributed to the FAPEA, and in August it kidnapped a banker, demanding a $5,000,000 ransom and the release of 50 guerrillas; during attempts by the police to rescue him he was shot dead, together with the five kidnappers.

Membership. 3,000 (1985 estimate).

International affiliation. The FAPEA co-operates with the Colombian April 19 Movement.

Guyana

Capital: Georgetown   Pop. 900,000

The former colony of British Guiana became an independent state within the Commonwealth in 1966, under the name of Guyana, and a "co-operative republic" in 1970. Under a new constitution adopted in 1980 an executive President replaced the Prime Minister as head of the government. The People's National Congress has held power since 1964 under the leadership first of Forbes Burnham, who in 1980 became President, and since his death in 1985 of President Desmond Hoyte.

People's Progressive Party (PPP)

History. The PPP was founded in 1950 as the successor to the Political Affairs Committee, formed in 1946, and in the first elections held under universal suffrage won 18 of the 24 seats in the House of Assembly in April 1953. Dr Jagan, the PPP leader, formed a government, but in October the British Conservative government suspended the constitution and dismissed the ministers, on the ground that the PPP was engaged in "communist subversion". Forbes Burnham, a member of Dr Jagan's government, was expelled from the party in 1955, and subsequently formed the People's National Congress (PNC). New elections in 1957 resulted in a victory for the PPP, which formed a government, and retained its majority in the 1961 elections.

Following the introduction of proportional representation, the PPP won only 24 seats out of 53 in 1964, although receiving the largest vote, and the other two parties, the PNC and the United Force, formed a coalition government. In 1968 the PNC obtained a majority (30 seats to 19 for the PPP and four for the United Force), since when it has ruled alone. The PPP openly identified itself with the world communist movement for the first time in 1969, when it took part in the Moscow conference of communist parties.

In the 1973 elections, which British observers reported to have been rigged, the PPP won 14 seats, and subsequently boycotted the National Assembly. A rapprochement took place in 1975 between the PNC and the PPP, which offered to give critical support to the government and in the following year ended its boycott of the Assembly. Negotiations broke down in 1977, however, after Burnham rejected the PPP's proposal for the formation of a "national patriotic front government", and the PPP thereupon reached an understanding with the opposition Working People's Alliance. In elections held in 1980, after being twice postponed, the PPP obtained 10 seats, and in the 1985 elections only eight.

Leadership. Dr Cheddi Jagan (g.s.).

Structure. Party groups are subordinate to district and regional committees. The congress, meeting every three years, elects the 32-member Central Committee, the 12-member Executive Committee and the Secretariat. The party's youth section is the Progressive Youth Union.

Membership. The PPP draws its membership mainly from the Indian community.

Electoral influence. According to official figures, the PPP obtained 78,414 (19.46 per cent) of the vote in the 1980 elections and 45,926 (11 per cent) in 1985. Both elections were condemned as fraudulent by foreign observers, however.

Industrial influence. The PPP controls the Guyana Agricultural and General Workers' Union, the largest union in the country, with 20,000 members, which is led by Ram Karran, a member of the PPP Executive Committee, and exercises considerable influence in several other unions. Opponents of the government's policies were elected to key posts in the Trades Union Congress in 1984.

Orientation. Pro-Soviet.

Programme. The PPP advocates the establishment of a "people's revolutionary democratic government" through "the revolutionary alliance of the working class, the peasant farmers, the revolutionary intellectuals and progressive businessmen and middle strata". It also calls for the restoration of political and industrial democracy, incentives for farmers and other producers, a freeze on military and police expenditure, strengthening of the state sector, assistance to the co-operative sector in productive fields and workers' control in industry and agriculture.

Publications. *Mirror*, weekly; *Thunder*, quarterly.

International affiliations. The PPP is represented on the editorial council of *World Marxist Review*.

Working People's Alliance (WPA)

History. The WPA, which originally consisted of an alliance between four left-wing organizations, was formed as a pressure group in 1974. It constituted itself into a political party in 1979, and appealed for the formation of an alliance of opposition parties to replace the PNC administration by a "government of national reconstruction and unity". Three of its leaders were arrested and charged with arson, and in 1980 one of them, Dr Walter Rodney, was murdered, the government being widely suspected of complicity; the charges against the other two were dismissed in the following year. The WPA boycotted the 1980 elections, after its demands for measures to ensure their fairness were ignored by the government, but contested the 1985 elections, in which it was officially credited with 4,176 votes (1.3 per cent) winning only one seat.

Leadership. Collective, headed by Eusi Kwayana and Rupert Roopnarine (co-chairmen).

Membership. Unlike the PNC and the PPP, which draw their support mainly from the Negro and Indian communities respectively, both the leadership and the membership of the WPA are multiracial.

Orientation. Independent.

Programme. The WPA advocates free and fair elections, the restoration of democracy, redistribution of income, land reform and renegotiation of Guyana's foreign debt as steps towards "the building of genuine socialism on the basis of popular consent and the subsequent creation of a classless society".

Publications. *Dayclean* and *Open World*, weeklies.

International affiliations. Socialist International (consultative member).

Working People's Vanguard Party (WPVP)

History. The WPVP was founded in 1969 by Brindley Benn, a former member of the PPP government. It joined the Working People's Alliance in 1974, but withdrew three years later. In 1979 it allied with the right-wing Liberator Party and the small People's Democratic Movement to form the Vanguard for Liberation and Democracy, which advocated a campaign of strikes, non-co-operation and civil disobedience to bring down the PNC government.

Leadership. Brindley Benn.

Orientation. Pro-Chinese.

Paraguay

Capital: Asunción   Pop. 3,623,000

Paraguay was ruled by the Liberal Party from 1904 to 1936, when a group of reforming officers seized power. They were overthrown a year later, and a period of confusion followed until in 1940 Gen. Higinio Morínigo became President and a virtual dictator. An attempted revolt by the Febreristas (supporters of the 1936–37 government), Liberals and Communists in 1947 failed, but in the following year he was removed by the army. After a six years' struggle between the army and conservative politicians for control of the government, in 1954 Gen. Alfredo Stroessner established his dictatorship, which has continued ever since.

Marxist-Leninist Paraguayan Communist Party
Partido Comunista Paraguayo Marxista-Leninista (PCPM–L)

History. The PCPM–L was formed by a Maoist group which left the Communist Party in 1967, under the leadership of Oscar Creydt, formerly general secretary of the party, and has operated underground ever since. The police arrested 31 alleged members of a rural cell in 1982, for attempting to organize guerrilla resistance to the regime.

Leadership. Oscar Creydt (g.s.).

Orientation. Pro-Chinese.

Publication. *Adelante* (Forward).

Paraguayan Communist Party
Partido Comunista Paraguayo (PCP)

History. The PCP, founded in 1928, has been illegal throughout its history, except for two short periods in 1936 and 1946–47. From 1959 onwards it attempted to organize a guerrilla resistance to Gen. Stroessner's regime, but was defeated by late 1965. Many leading PCP members have been imprisoned without trial for many years, and some are believed to have been tortured to death. Following international protests, Antonio Maidana, who had been held since 1958, and three other leading Communists were released in 1977. Three years later, however, Maidana, who had become first secretary of the party in exile, was kidnapped in Buenos Aires with another Central Committee member, their subsequent fate being unknown.

Leadership. Antonio Maidana (1st sec.).

Membership. 3,500 (1985 estimate), many of whom live in exile.

Orientation. Pro-Soviet.

Programme. A manifesto issued by the PCP in 1981 advocated the establishment of a broad alliance against the Stroessner dictatorship "by promoting joint and organized struggles on the part of the working class, peasants, students, teachers, office employees, intellectuals, artists, traders and national industrialists . . . This mass mobilization and these partial struggles should develop into a decisive battle to bring down the fascist dictatorship . . . combining all forms of struggle and aiming at a general uprising of the people".

Publication. *Adelante* (Forward), underground.

International affiliation. The PCP is represented on the editorial council of *World Marxist Review*.

Guerrilla Organization

Politico-Military Organization
Organización Político-Militar (OPM)

History. The OPM, also known as the March 1 Organization (*Organización 1 Marzo*), was formed in 1974 by left-wing Catholic students, and drew its membership from Catholic peasant organizations. It was believed to receive support from radical sections of the clergy, and especially from Jesuits. The police carried out extensive raids in Asunción and elsewhere in 1976, arresting 2,000 alleged OPM sympathizers, including about 20 of its leaders, who were believed to have died later under torture. Although its activities subsequently declined, its name has occasionally been invoked to justify arrests of the regime's opponents.

Orientation. The OPM originated as a radical Catholic organization, and although the government claimed in 1983 that it was under Communist control it is uncertain whether it ever contained a Marxist element.

Peru

Capital: Lima   Pop. 19,500,000

Recent Peruvian history has largely been dominated by the struggle between the armed forces and the American Popular Revolutionary Alliance (APRA), founded by Víctor Raúl Haya de la Torre in 1924 as an international anti-imperialist party, the Peruvian section of which was established in 1930. After Haya received the highest vote in the 1931 presidential election a military regime was installed which held power until 1939, when Manuel Prado y Ugartache was elected President. His successor, President José Luis Bustamante y Rivero, was deposed in 1948 by Gen. Manuel Odría, who ruled until 1956, when Prado was re-elected. Although Haya again received the highest vote in the 1962 election, he was again prevented from taking office by the army, and in a new election held in the following year was defeated by Fernando Belaúnde Terry, leader of the Popular Action party.

In 1968 a group of left-wing officers led by Gen. Juan Velasco Alvarado seized power and carried out a sweeping programme of reforms, including the expropriation of the US-owned oilfields, the nationalization of other foreign-owned enterprises, a radical land reform programme, the development of agricultural co-operatives, the compulsory introduction of profit-sharing and workers' participation in Peruvian-owned enterprises and the establishment of industrial co-operatives. In 1975, however, President Velasco was replaced by Gen. Francisco Morales Bermúdez, who adopted a more conservative policy and reversed many of his reforms. A Constituent Assembly was elected in 1978, and civilian rule was re-established in 1980, when Belaúnde was re-elected in the first presidential election held under the new constitution. His economic policies proved highly unpopular, and in the 1985 elections the Popular Action presidential candidate was crushingly defeated by Alan García Pérez, general secretary of the APRA, which also secured a majority in both houses of Congress.

Communist Party of Peru—Red Fatherland
Partido Comunista del Perú—Patria Roja (PCP-PR)

History. The PCP-PR, which derives its name from its periodical, broke away from the Communist Party of Peru in 1969. It joined the Union of the Revolutionary Left (UNIR) on its formation in 1979, and secured representation in Congress in the elections of the following year. With the other UNIR parties, it subsequently became part of the United Left alliance.

Leadership. Alberto Moreno (g.s.); Rolando Breña Pantoja (spokesman).

Membership. The PCP-PR is the largest of the Peruvian Maoist groups.

Industrial influence. The PCP-PR controls the Miners' Federation and the United Federation of Educational Workers of Peru.

Orientation. Pro-Chinese.

Publication. *Patria Roja* (Red Fatherland).

International affiliation. The PCP-PR is officially recognized by the Chinese Communist Party.

Communist Party of Peru—Red Flag
Partido Comunista del Peru—Bandera Roja (PCP-BR)

History. The PCP, formed by Maoists who broke away from the Peruvian Communist Party in 1964, split in 1969 into two sections taking their names from their respective periodicals, *Red Flag* and *Red Fatherland*, and in the following year the Shining Light group broke away from Red Flag. The PCP-BR has refused to enter into any political alliances with other Marxist parties, and in recent years has abandoned its pro-Chinese for a pro-Albanian attitude.

Leadership. Saturnino Paredes Macedo (l.).

Orientation. Pro-Albanian.

Programme. The PCP-BR advocates but does not practise armed struggle.

Publication. *Bandera Roja* (Red Flag).

Movement of the Revolutionary Left—Militant
Movimiento de la Izquierda Revolucionaria—El Militante (MIR-EM)

History. The MIR-EM, a breakaway faction of the Movement of the Revolutionary Left (see under Unified Mariateguista Party), contested the 1980 elections as part of the Popular Democratic Unity alliance, and later absorbed the Revolutionary Socialist Party, Marxist-Leninist, which had broken away from the Revolutionary Socialist Party in 1978. It now forms part of the Marxist–Leninist Unified Communist Committee (see below under "Guerrilla Organizations").

National Liberation Front
Frente de Liberación Nacional (FLN)

History. The FLN contested the 1980 elections as a member of the Union of the Revolutionary Left, its chairman being elected to the Senate, and subsequently joined the United Left alliance.

Leadership. Angel Castro Lavarello (ch.).

Peruvian Communist Party
Partido Comunista Peruano (PCP)

History. The Socialist Party of Peru, to which the PCP is a successor, was founded in 1928 by José Carlos Mariátegui, a distinguished Marxist theoretician who attempted to adapt Marx's teachings to Latin American conditions. Shortly after his death in 1930 the party split into two organizations, one of which retained the original name while the other was renamed the PCP. Banned by the military regime in 1933, the PCP was legalized by President Prado during World War II, when its membership reached 30,000. Its influence afterwards declined, and under President Odría's regime (1948–56) it was banned again. It supported President Belaúnde's mildly reformist government in 1963–68, and on his overthrow transferred its support, after some hesitation, to President Velasco's more radical regime. After his removal in 1975, however, it adopted an increasingly critical attitude towards the military government.

The PCP split in 1978 into two factions, known as the PCP-Unity and the PCP-Majority from the names of their respective newspapers, the former, which constituted the bulk of the party, inclining towards Eurocommunism, while the latter maintained a strongly pro-Soviet position. In the elections of the same year the PCP-Unity obtained six of the 100 seats in the Constituent Assembly. For the 1980 elections it allied with five other organizations to form the United Left, Jorge del Prado, the PCP-Unity leader, being elected to the Senate. The 1982 party congress resulted in a victory for the pro-Soviet faction; a number of veteran party leaders were dropped from the Central Committee, and del Prado retained the general secretaryship only by a small majority. The reunited party again contested the 1985 elections as part of the United Left alliance.

Leadership. Jorge del Prado (g.s.).

Structure. The PCP is organized in cells, which are subordinate to the local and regional committees. The national congress elects the 15-member Central Committee. The party's youth organization, the Peruvian Communist Youth, operates mainly in the universities, where it competes with the Maoist and Trotskyist parties for support.

Membership. 5,000 (1985 estimate). The party draws its strongest support from the working–class areas of Lima.

Industrial influence. The PCP controls the General Confederation of Workers of Peru, the principal trade union federation, which has about 700,000 members.

Orientation. Pro-Soviet.

Publication. Unidad (Unity), weekly (over 10,000).

International affiliation. The PCP is represented on the editorial council of *World Marxist Review*.

Popular Democratic Unity
Unidad Democrática Popular (UDP)

History. The UDP was formed in 1978 as an alliance of 18 Maoist and other extreme left-wing groups, including two factions of the Movement of the Revolutionary Left, the Revolutionary Vanguard and the Revolutionary Communist Party, and won four seats in the elections to the Constituent Assembly. In the 1980 elections, in which it put forward Dr Alfonso Barrantes Lingán as its presidential candidate, it won two seats in the Senate and three in the Chamber of Deputies. It subsequently joined the United Left alliance.

Orientation. Maoist.

Revolutionary Communist Party
Partido Comunista Revolucionario (PCR)

History. The PCR broke away from the Revolutionary Vanguard in 1974, and joined the Popular Democratic Unity alliance in 1978. It was represented in the Constituent Assembly and in the 1980 Chamber of Deputies by Agustín Haya de la Rosa, nephew of the APRA leader Haya de la Torre. It subsequently joined the United Left alliance.

Leadership. Manuel Dammert (g.s.).

Orientation. Maoist.

Revolutionary Marxist Workers' Party—Workers' Socialist Party
Partido Obrero Marxista Revolucionario—Partido Socialista de los Trabajadores (POMR-PST)

History. The POMR-PST was formed in 1982 by the merger of the POMR, founded in 1971, and the PST, founded in 1974. Both parties had contested the 1978 elections as part of the Workers', Peasants', Students' and People's Front, and the 1980 elections in alliance with the Workers' Revolutionary Party. In 1985 the POMR-PST fought the elections independently, but received few votes.

Leadership. Ricardo Napurí, Enrique Fernandez Chacón.

Orientation. Trotskyist.

Revolutionary Socialist Party
Partido Socialista Revolucionario (PSR)

History. The PSR was founded in 1976 by Gen. Leónidas Rodríguez Figueroa and other officers who had taken an active part in the military revolution of 1968–75. Gen. Rodríguez and three other party leaders were deported a few weeks later by President Morales' government, but were allowed to return before the 1978 elections, in which the PSR won six seats in the Constituent Assembly. In the 1980 elections, which it contested as part of the United Left, Gen. Rodríguez was its presidential candidate, and its general secretary, Enrique Bernales, was elected to the Senate.

Leadership. Gen. Leónidas Rodríguez Figueroa (ch.); Enrique Bernales (g.s.).

Orientation. Independent. The PSR describes itself as *Velasquista*, i.e. guided by President Velasco's principles.

Programme. The PSR's inaugural manifesto called for "the defence, deepening and consolidation of the reforms already begun and those still needed to take the country out of the capitalist system and build Peruvian socialism".

Revolutionary Vanguard—Proletarian Communist
Vanguardia Revolucionaria—Proletario Comunista (VR-PC)

History. The VR-PC, an offshoot of the Communist Party of Peru, is an unofficial member of the United Left alliance.

Leadership. Eduardo Figari (l.).

Orientation. Pro-Albanian.

Unified Mariateguista Party
Partido Unificado Mariateguista (PUM)

History. The PUM was formed in 1984 by the merger of the Movement of the Revolutionary Left (*Movimiento de la Izquierda Revolucionaria*, MIR), the Revolutionary Vanguard (*Vanguardia Revolucionaria*, VR) and a faction of the Revolutionary Communist Party. The Castroist MIR originated in 1960, when the left wing of the American Popular Revolutionary Alliance (APRA) broke away and formed the Rebel APRA, which was renamed the MIR two years later. It attempted in 1965 to launch a guerrilla revolt, which was quickly suppressed. The pro-Chinese VR broke away from the Communist Party of Peru in 1965, conducted an unsuccessful guerrilla campaign in 1971–72 and organized land seizures in 1976 through the Peruvian Peasants' Confederation, which it controlled, in protest against the slow progress of land reform. The PUM, which takes its name from José Carlos Mariátegui (see under Peruvian Communist Party), forms part of the United Left.

Leadership. Javier Díez Canseco (g.s.).

Union of the Revolutionary Left
Unión de Izquierda Revolucionaria (UNIR)

History. The UNIR was formed in 1979 as an alliance of the Communist Party of Peru—Red Fatherland, the Movement of the Revolutionary Left—Peru and the National Liberation Front, and in the 1980 elections returned two senators and two deputies. It subsequently joined the United Left alliance.

Leadership. Rolando Breña Pantoja (ch.); Jorge Hurtado (g.s.).

Orientation. Pro-Chinese.

Publication. *El Unirista* (10,000).

United Left
Izquierda Unida (IU)

History. The IU originated as an electoral alliance of the Peruvian Communist Party (PCP), the Revolutionary Socialist Party (PSR) and four smaller groups in 1980, when it put forward Gen. Leónidas Rodríguez Figueroa as its presidential candidate and won two seats in the Senate and two in the Chamber of Deputies, and made further gains in local elections later in the same year, winning control of six of the 24 departmental capitals. It was later expanded to include two other political alliances, Popular Democratic Unity (UDP) and the Union of the Revolutionary Left (UNIR), and a number of other parties, including the Workers', Peasants', Students' and People's Front (FOCEP), the Revolutionary Communist Party (PCR) and the National Integration Party, which had broken away from the Christian Popular Party in 1982. It thus came to include all the leading Marxist parties except two Trotskyist parties (the Revolutionary Marxist Workers' Party—Workers' Socialist Party and the Workers' Revolutionary Party) and the pro-Albanian Communist Party of Peru—Red Flag.

The IU achieved a major success in the 1983 municipal elections, when it emerged as the second strongest political group after the American Popular Revolutionary Alliance (APRA) and its chairman, Dr Alfonso Barrantes Lingán, was elected mayor of Lima, becoming the first Marxist mayor of any South American capital. In the 1985 elections Dr Barrantes, its presidential candidate, took second place after the APRA candidate, and the IU won 48 of the 180 seats in the Chamber and 15 of the 60 Senate seats, compared with the seven seats in each house won by its constituent parties in 1980.

Leadership. The National Executive Committee consists of Dr Alfonso Barrantes Lingán (ch.), Genaro Ledesma Izquieta (FOCEP), Jorge del Prado (PCP), Manuel Dammert (PCR), Edmundo Murrugarra (UDP), Luís Benitez (UDP), Jorge Hurtado (UNIR), Juan Sánchez (UNIR) and Alfredo Filomeno (PSR). Dr Barrantes is a Christian Marxist who is not a member of any of the IU's constituent organizations, although he was formerly associated with the UDP.

Electoral influence. The IU presidential candidate in 1985 received 1,606,914 votes (21.3 per cent).

Orientation. The IU includes pro-Soviet, pro-Chinese, Maoist, Trotskyist and independent parties.

Programme. The IU's programme for the 1985 elections advocated a five-year moratorium on repayment of Peru's foreign debt, increased public ownership, nationalization of the US-owned copper mines, exchange controls, a ban on profit remittances abroad and a reduction in the gap between rich and poor.

Workers', Peasants', Students' and People's Front
Frente Obrero, Campesino, Estudiantil y Popular (FOCEP)

History. The FOCEP was founded in 1977 as an alliance of nine Trotskyist organizations, and in the following year took third place in the elections to the Constituent Assembly, winning 12 of the 100 seats. Its strength was further increased when a Communist member of the Assembly defected to it. In 1979, however, six of its constituent organizations withdrew from the alliance, which in consequence returned only one senator (Genaro Ledesma Izquieta) and no deputies in the 1980 elections. It subsequently joined the United Left, and has since operated as a single party rather than an alliance.

Leadership. Genaro Ledesma Izquieta (ch.).

Orientation. Trotskyist.

Workers' Revolutionary Party
Partido Revolucionario de los Trabajadores (PRT)

History. The PRT was formed in 1978 by the merger of several small Trotskyist groups under the leadership of Hugo Blanco Galdós, who had been sentenced to 20 years' imprisonment in 1963 for leading a peasant revolt, released in 1970 and exiled in the following year, and had recently returned to Peru. It contested the 1978 elections as part of the Workers', Peasants', Students' and People's Front, Blanco being elected to the Constituent Assembly, but left the alliance in the following year. In the 1980 elections, which it fought in alliance with the Revolutionary Marxist Workers' Party and the Workers' Socialist Party, it won three seats in the Chamber and two in the Senate, but its influence has since greatly declined.

Leadership. Hugo Blanco Galdós (representative of collective leadership).

Membership. 5,000 (1980 claim).

Electoral influence. The PRT's share of the vote fell from 5 per cent in the 1980 general elections to less than 1 per cent in the 1983 municipal elections.

Orientation. Trotskyist.

Publication. *Combate Socialista* (2,500).

International affiliation. Fourth International, United Secretariat.

Guerrilla Organizations

Marxist-Leninist Unified Communist Committee
Comité Comunista Unificado Marxista-Leninista

History. This organization, which appeared on the scene in 1984, was formed by the Movement of the Revolutionary Left—Militant (see above), a splinter group of the Communist Party of Peru—Red Fatherland formed in 1979 and led by Jeronimo Pasache, and the Proletarian and Peasant Revolutionary Vanguard (*Vanguardia Revolucionaria Proletaria Campesina*) led by Julio César Mezzich. These groups were believed to have links with Shining Path.

People's Revolutionary Commandos
Comandos Revolucionarios del Pueblo (CRP)

History. The CRP first appeared in July 1985, when it seized a radio station, denounced social injustice and warned that it would adopt a vigilant attitude towards President García's newly-formed government.

Shining Path
Sendero Luminoso (SL)

History. The SL originated in a small group at Ayacucho University led by Manuel Abimael Guzmán Renoso which broke away from the Communist Party of Peru—Red Flag in 1970, and took its name from one of its pamphlets, *The Shining Path of José Carlos Mariátegui*. Originally pro-Chinese, it adopted an independent Maoist position in 1979. It began guerrilla activities in 1980 in the Ayacucho department, one of the poorest in the country, where it gained control of many rural settlements. In contrast to the failure of earlier attempts in 1961–66 to launch a guerrilla struggle, it owed much of its success in attracting peasant support to its policy of appealing to Indian sentiment; in its propaganda it advocated a return to the peasant communes of the Inca empire and glorified Indian leaders of anti-Spanish revolts, and its members used Indian languages instead of Spanish in their dealings with the peasantry.

During 1980–82 SL was responsible for frequent bomb explosions directed against official buildings, the US embassy, the offices of US companies and the premises of other left-wing groups. It moved on to open guerrilla warfare in March 1982, when 150 guerrillas stormed the prison at Ayacucho and freed 247 prisoners, and in 1983 extended its operations to Lima, where it carried out repeated bomb attacks, and to the urban coastal areas and interior regions which had not previously been affected. In June 1984 it launched an offensive in the Andean departments of Ayacucho, Apurímac and Huancavelica, 10 provinces of which had already been placed under a state of emergency, but the armed forces replied with a counter-offensive which by January 1985 had apparently achieved considerable success. Between 7,000 and 10,000 people were believed to have been killed in the struggle between 1980 and the end of 1985; although the authorities consistently blamed SL for the mass killings which took place, church and judicial sources attributed a high proportion of them to the security forces.

Leadership. Manuel Abimael Guzmán Renoso ("Comrade Gonzalo").

Orientation. Maoist. The SL is hostile to the Chinese and Soviet governments, both of which have denounced it.

Programme. Guzmán defined the SL's programme in 1982 as falling into the following stages: (1) "converting the backward areas into advanced and solid bases of revolutionary support"; (2) attacks on "the symbols of the bourgeois state and of revisionist elements"; (3) "generalization of violence and development of guerrilla war"; (4) "conquest and expansion of the bases of support"; (5) "the siege of the cities and the total collapse of the state". The first stage was said to have been completed in 1980 and the second in 1982, when the third began.

Tupac Amaru Revolutionary Movement
Movimiento Revolucionario Tupac Amaru (MRTA)

History. The MRTA, which derives its name from the leader of an 18th-century Indian revolt against Spanish rule, was formed in 1983 by groups which had broken away from the Revolutionary Socialist Party, and was joined in the following year by dissident factions of the Movement of the Revolutionary Left (see under Unified Mariateguista Party). It was responsible for a series of bomb explosions in Lima between September 1984 and August 1985, when it announced that it would suspend its activities to allow President García's government an opportunity to introduce measures to assist the Peruvian people.

Leadership. Marco Antonio Turkowsky, Ernesto Montes Aliaga.

Suriname

Capital: Paramaribo   Pop. 370,000

Suriname (the former Netherlands Guiana) became an independent republic in 1975. The civilian government was overthrown in February 1980 by a coup led by a group of non-commissioned officers and a National Military Council established. Under the leadership of Sgt. (later Lt.-Col.) Desi Bouterse the military regime pursued a vacillating course; after arresting his left-wing colleagues in August 1980, he released them in March 1981, announced that Suriname would follow a socialist course and established close relations with the Marxist governments in Cuba, Nicaragua and Grenada. Under pressure from Brazil and the United States, however, he expelled the Cuban ambassador in October 1983, and in January 1984 dismissed the left-wing cabinet headed by Errol Alibux, replacing it by a more conservative administration.

Communist Party of Suriname
Kommunistische Partij Suriname (KPS)

History. The KPS was founded in 1973. Its leader, Bram Mehr, was imprisoned for a week in April 1982 for criticizing the military regime.

Leadership. Bram Mehr.

Membership. 25 (1985 estimate).

Orientation. Pro-Albanian.

Publication. Modro.

Revolutionary People's Party
Revolutionaire Volkspartij (RVP)

History. The RVP was founded in 1981. One of its leading members, Glenn Sankatsingh, served as Minister of Labour and Social Affairs and subsequently as Minister of Education and Science in 1982–84, and another, Lothar Boksteen, as Minister of Health and Labour in 1983–84.

Leadership. Edward Naarendorp, Glenn Sankatsingh and Lother Boksteen.

Membership. 100 (1985 estimate).

Orientation. Pro-Cuban.

Uruguay

Capital: Montevideo   Pop. 2,970,000

Uruguay was ruled from 1865 to 1973 by the Colorado (originally the Liberal) Party, except for the years 1958–66, when the Blanco or National Party was in office. In 1973 President Juan María Bordaberry, with the support of the armed forces, dissolved Congress and banned political activities. He was deposed by the military three years later and replaced by Aparicio Méndez, who was succeeded in 1981 by Gen. Gregorio Alvarez. The military regime, under which it was estimated in 1977 that Uruguay had the highest proportion of political prisoners in the world (one in 600 of the population) and the use of torture became an international scandal, provoked strong popular resistance; a draft constitution designed to ensure continued military rule was overwhelmingly rejected in a referendum in 1980, and mass protest demonstrations and strikes occurred in 1983–84. Popular pressure forced the military leaders to legalize the Colorado and Blanco parties and the Civic Union (but not the left-wing parties) in 1982 and to enter into negotiations with the political parties, including the banned Broad Front alliance, on a return to civilian rule. Under an agreement reached in August 1984 elections were held in the following November, and military rule ended when the successful presidential candidate, Julio Mario Sanguinetti Cairolo of the Colorado Party, took office in March 1985.

Communist Party of Uruguay
Partido Comunista del Uruguay (PCU)

History. The PCU originated in 1920, when the majority of the delegates to the Socialist Party congress voted in favour of joining the Communist International. Although the leadership resisted this decision, it was reaffirmed by an extraordinary congress in the following year, which also voted to change the party's name to the PCU. The new party operated legally for 52 years (a record unequalled by any other Latin American Communist Party), and was regularly represented in Congress. In 1962 it formed an alliance known as the Leftist Liberation Front (*Frente Izquierda de Liberación* or FIDEL, the name being chosen to capitalize on popular admiration for Fidel Castro), which won one of the 30 Senate seats and three of the 99 in the Chamber of Deputies in the elections of that year and increased its representation in the Chamber to five in 1966. For the 1971 elections it organized the Broad Front (*Frente Amplio*), an alliance of 17 organizations including the Communist, Socialist and Christian Democratic parties, smaller left-wing groups and dissidents from the Colorado and Blanco parties, which obtained 19 per cent of the vote and won five seats in the Senate and 18 (including two Communists) in the Chamber.

The PCU was banned in 1973 and hundreds of its members imprisoned, although its general secretary, Rodney Arismendi, was released and allowed to go into exile in 1975. It took an active part in organizing popular resistance to the military regime, and co-operated with the Colorado, Blanco and Socialist parties in 1980 in forming Democratic Convergence, with the aim of uniting all forces opposed to the dictatorship. Although still illegal, the PCU participated through the Broad Front in negotiating the political agreement of August 1984, and in the elections of the following November campaigned under the name "Advanced Democracy" within the Broad Front, which increased its representation to six seats in the Senate and 21 in the Chamber. Arismendi returned from exile in the same month, and the ban on the party was lifted in March 1985.

Leadership. Rodney Arismendi (g.s.).

Membership. 7,500 (1985 estimate).

Electoral influence. "Advanced Democracy" (PCU) candidates inside the Broad Front obtained 6 per cent of the vote in the 1984 elections.

Orientation. Pro-Soviet.

International affiliation. The PCU is represented on the editorial council of *World Marxist Review*.

March 26 Movement
Movimiento 26 de Marzo

History. This organization, which supports the ideology of the National Liberation Movement (Tupamaros), was banned in 1973 and legalized in 1985.

Programme. The Movement advocates the nationalization of the banking sector, agrarian reform and a moratorium on foreign debts.

Revolutionary Workers' Party, Trotskyist
Partido Obrero Revolucionario, Trotskista (PORT)

History. The PORT is the successor to the Revolutionary Workers' League, founded in 1937 and later renamed the Revolutionary Workers' Party, IV International. After 1963 it supported the faction of the Fourth International led by Juan Posadas, who established his headquarters in Montevideo, and again changed its name to the PORT. Most of its leaders were arrested in 1968 on suspicion of complicity with the Tupamaros, and Posadas was deported.

Orientation. Trotskyist.

International affiliation. Posadist Fourth International.

379

Uruguayan Socialist Party
Partido Socialista Uruguayo (PSU)

History. The PSU, founded by Emilio Frugoni in 1910, split in 1921, when a majority of the members decided to change its name to the Communist Party and affiliate to the Comintern, while Frugoni and his followers re-established the party under its original name. It formed part of the Broad Front alliance in the 1971 elections, and was banned in 1973. The ban was lifted in 1984, when it again contested the elections as part of the Broad Front.

Leadership. José Pedro Cardozo (g.s.); Hugo Rodríguez Filippini.

Orientation. Independent.

Workers' Revolutionary Party
Partido Revolucionario de los Trabajadores (PRT)

History. The PRT, founded in 1969, was banned in 1973, the ban being lifted in 1985.

Orientation. Trotskyist.

International affiliation. Fourth International, United Secretariat.

Guerrilla Organization

National Liberation Movement
Tupamaros or Movimiento de Liberación Nacional (MLN)

History. The MLN, founded in 1962 by Raúl Sendic Antonaccio, derived its alternative name Tupamaros from Tupac Amaru, a Peruvian Indian executed in 1781 for leading a revolt against Spanish rule. It began activities in 1963, and turned from rural to urban guerrilla warfare three years later. At first it pursued a policy of "striking the local oligarchy without directly attacking the armed forces or the police", and generally avoided the use of violence, although it assassinated the head of intelligence and a US adviser to the police force in 1970 and carried out a number of bomb explosions; it was also responsible for several kidnappings, but the victims (including the British ambassador, held for eight months in 1971) were normally released unharmed. Its other activities included robberies, the proceeds of which were distributed among the poor, the occupation of radio stations which were forced to broadcast its statements, and stealing private companies' ledgers to obtain evidence of government corruption, which was then publicized and forwarded to the courts.

In 1972 the MLN began assassinating members of unofficial police groups involved in killing suspected subversives, whereupon the armed forces launched a major offensive against it. By the end of the following year it had been virtually wiped out and most of its leaders killed or captured. Heavy prison sentences were passed on the arrested leaders, often after they had been held for years without trial; Sendic, captured in 1972, was sentenced in 1980 to 45 years' imprisonment. All the prisoners were released in 1985 under an amnesty, however, including Sendic, who stated that he proposed to work within the democratic framework and not to resort to violence.

Leadership. Raúl Sendic Antonaccio (l.).

Membership. 6,000 (1972 estimate), recruited mainly from among students and intellectuals. It was officially stated in 1982 that 992 Tupamaros were still detained and 3,238 had been released.

Orientation. Independent. Although influenced by the theories and practice of Castro and Mao Zedong, the MLN rejected their view that a social revolution should begin in the countryside.

International affiliations. Some MLN recruits were reported to have been trained in Cuba, and the movement was also believed to have contacts with the Argentinian People's Revolutionary Army and the Chilean Movement of the Revolutionary Left.

Venezuela

Capital: Caracas   Pop. 18,552,000

President Juan Vicente Gómez, who ruled as a dictator from 1908 to 1935, suppressed all political parties, but a revival of political life took place under his successors. After President Isaías Medina Angarita was removed by a coup in 1945 the reformist Democratic Action party took power and introduced a new constitution, which for the first time provided for the election of the President and Congress by universal suffrage. The first President elected under the new constitution, Rómulo Gallegos, was deposed by a coup in 1948, however, and a period of military rule followed. Gen. Marcos Pérez Jiménez, who proclaimed himself President in 1952, alienated all sections of opinion by his corrupt and repressive rule, and was overthrown in 1958 by a popular uprising. The two strongest parties, Democratic Action and the Christian Social Party, have since alternated in office, the former holding power from 1958 to 1968, from 1973 to 1978 and since 1983, and the latter in the intervening periods. The Marxist parties launched a guerrilla revolt in 1962 which met with little success, and by 1969 had abandoned this strategy, although small guerrilla groups continued to operate.

Communist Party of Venezuela
Partido Comunista de Venezuela (PCV)

History. The PCV, which is the oldest existing party in Venezuela, was founded in 1931 and operated underground until 1942, when President Medina allowed it to set up the Venezuelan Popular Union (UPV) as a legal front. The party split in 1945 into the PCV, which favoured co-operation with the Medina government and was legalized by it, and the UPV, led by the brothers Gustavo and Eduardo Machado Morales, which opposed this policy. After the fall of Medina the two parties were reunited in the following year, but a section of the UPV broke away to form the Revolutionary Party of the Proletariat, which did not merge with the PCV until 1957. Banned by the military regime in 1950, the PCV joined Democratic Action, the Democratic Republican Union and the Christian Social Party in 1957 in forming the Patriotic Junta, which organized the revolt against President Pérez Jiménez in the following year. After being legalized again, the PCV won two seats in the Senate and seven in the Chamber of Deputies in the 1958 elections.

In the next few years it adopted a strongly leftist line, and at the 1960 Moscow Conference was among the few communist parties which supported China.

Under the influence of the Cuban revolution a number of the younger Communist leaders, including Douglas Bravo and Teodoro Petkoff, joined activists of the Movement of the Revolutionary Left in forming the Armed Forces of National Liberation, which began guerrilla activities in 1962 with Cuban assistance. After a mutiny at the Carupano naval base in the same year the PCV was banned, and in 1963 the parliamentary immunity of the PCV congressmen was lifted and many leading Communists arrested, including Gustavo Machado and Jesús Faría, the general secretary. After two years of internal controversy the party abandoned its support for the guerrilla struggle in 1967, and Bravo and his followers, who advocated its continuation, were expelled. As a result of its participation in the guerrilla war its membership, which had reached 30,000 in 1960, fell heavily, and it lost almost all its influence in the trade union movement.

The PCV was allowed to take part in the 1968 elections under the name Union for Advance, winning two seats in the Chamber, and in 1969 was legalized under its own name. It lost the bulk of its membership and many of its leaders in the following year, however, when Petkoff and Pompeyo Márquez formed Movement to Socialism, and in the 1973 elections it retained only one seat in the Chamber. A new split in 1974, when a group led by Eduardo Machado broke away to form the Unitary Communist Vanguard, further weakened the PCV, and when in 1978 it put forward its own presidential candidate, Héctor Mújica, for the first time since 1947 he received only 0.54 per cent of the vote. It fought the 1983 elections as part of the Alliance for the Unity of the People, supporting Jose Vicente Rangel's presidential candidature, and increased its representation in the Chamber from one deputy to three.

Leadership. Jesús Faría (g.s.).

Structure. The congress elects the Central Committee, which elects the 18-member Political Bureau.

Membership. 4,000 (1985 estimate).

Electoral influence. The PCV received nearly 2 per cent of the vote in the 1983 elections.

Industrial influence. The PCV controls the Unitary Central of Venezuelan Workers, which represents only a small fraction of the trade union movement.

Orientation. Pro-Soviet.

Publication. *Tribuna Popular*, weekly.

International affiliation. The PCV is represented on the editorial council of *World Marxist Review*.

Movement of the Revolutionary Left
Movimiento de Izquierda Revolucionaria (MIR)

History. The MIR was formed in 1960 by left-wing members of Democratic Action, including 14 deputies and virtually all the party's student supporters, and rapidly moved towards a Marxist-Leninist position. It began guerrilla operations in 1962 in collaboration with the Communist Party, and was subsequently banned, many of its members being arrested. A section of the membership repudiated violence in 1965 and joined with two other groups to form the Revolutionary Party of Nationalist Integration, but the remainder, led by Américo Martín and Moisés Moleiro, continued the struggle until 1969, when they accepted the government's offer of an amnesty. After being legalized the MIR won one seat in the 1973 elections, which it increased to four in 1978; in the same year it put forward Martín as its presidential candidate, but he received only 0.98 per cent of the vote. The party split in 1980 into two factions headed by Martín and Moleiro; the Supreme Court ruled in 1982 that the latter, which accepted the theory of the dictatorship of the proletariat, should retain the party name, as it better represented the MIR's original Marxist-Leninist position. Martín's faction, which regarded itself as Marxist but not Leninist and advocated a distinctively Venezuelan form of socialism, thereupon combined with the Unitary Communist Vanguard to form the New Alternative. As a result of the split MIR representation in the Chamber fell to two in the 1983 elections.

Leadership. Moisés Moleiro (g.s.).

Orientation. Independent.

Movement to Socialism
Movimiento al Socialismo (MAS)

History. The MAS was formed in 1970 by dissident members of the Communist Party, including Teodoro Petkoff, a former guerrilla leader who had been expelled from the party for condemning the Soviet invasion of Czechoslovakia, and Pompeyo Márquez, a member of the Political Bureau, who took with them most of the Communist trade union leaders, the majority of the membership and virtually the whole of the party's youth movement. In the 1973 elections it emerged as the strongest of the left-wing parties, winning two seats in the Senate and nine in the Chamber; its representation in the Chamber rose to 11 in 1978 but fell to 10 in 1983. It supported José Vicente Rangel, an independent, in the 1973 and 1978 presidential elections, and in 1983 put forward Petkoff as its candidate, with the support of the Movement of the Revolutionary Left.

Leadership. The MAS was headed by Teodoro Petkoff (ch.), Pompeyo Márquez (g.s.) and a 45-member National Directorate until 1984, when they were replaced by three committees (the political committee, the reorganization and congress committee and the municipal election command), pending the election of a new leadership at the 1985 party congress.

Membership. 180,000 (1984 claim).

Electoral influence. The MAS received 5.75 per cent of the vote in the 1983 congressional elections and 7.2 per cent in the 1984 municipal elections.

Industrial influence. The MAS exercises considerable influence in the Confederation of Venezuelan Workers, the main trade union federation, and is represented on its executive committee.

Orientation. Eurocommunist. The MAS advocates active non-alignment and pluralistic democracy.

New Alternative
Nueva Alternativa (NA)

History. The NA was formed in 1982 as an alliance of the Unitary Communist Vanguard and Américo Martín's faction of the Movement of the Revolutionary Left, and won two seats in the Chamber in the 1983 elections. For the presidential election of the same year it joined the Alliance for the Unity of the People, which supported José Vicente Rangel's candidature.

Orientation. Independent.

Party of the Venezuelan Revolution
Partido de la Revolución Venezolana (PRV)

History. The PRV was founded in 1979 by the former guerrilla leader Douglas Bravo after he had been amnestied.

Leadership. Douglas Bravo (l.).

Orientation. Maoist.

Socialist League
Liga Socialista (LS)

History. The LS, which was founded in 1974 and absorbed the Workers' Socialist Party, a Trotskyist organization formed two years earlier, was closely associated with the Organization of Revolutionaries, a guerrilla group which had broken away from the Movement of the Revolutionary Left in 1969. Its general secretary, Jorge Rodríguez, and a leading party member, David Nieves, were arrested in 1976 on suspicion of being involved in a kidnapping case, the former, as was officially admitted, being tortured to death by the police. Nieves was released in 1978 on being elected to the Chamber of Deputies, and was re-elected in 1983. In the 1983 presidential election the LS supported José Vicente Rangel's candidature.

Leadership. Carmelo Laborit (ch.).

Orientation. Trotskyist.

International affiliation. Fourth International, United Secretariat.

Unitary Communist Vanguard
Vanguardia Unitaria Comunista (VUC)

History. The VUC was formed in 1974 by a number of leading Communist Party members who had been expelled after criticizing the party's "bureaucratization and dogmatism", including Eduardo Machado Morales, whose brother Gustavo was then the party chairman. It unsuccessfully contested the 1978 elections, receiving less than 1 per cent of the vote, and in 1982 joined Américo Martín's faction of the Movement of the Revolutionary Left in forming New Alternative.

Leadership. Eduardo Machado Morales (ch.); Guillermo Gardía Ponce (g.s.).

Orientation. Independent. The VUC advocates undogmatic Marxism applied to the country's realities.

Guerrilla Organization

Red Flag
Bandera Roja (BR)

History. BR broke away from the Movement of the Revolutionary Left when it abandoned guerrilla warfare in 1969, and continued the struggle under the leadership of Carlos and Argenis Betancourt and Gabriel Puerta Aponte. After the Betancourt brothers were arrested in 1977 BR was largely inactive until 1981, when it carried out a number of kidnappings, bank robberies and hijackings of aircraft. Many BR members were captured in 1982–83, including Puerta, and others killed in clashes with the army and police, but the movement continued to operate, mainly in the Colombian border region.

International affiliations. According to Colombian official sources, BR has links with the National Liberation Army (Colombia) with which it sometimes co-operates, and with Shining Path (Peru) and the Farabundo Martí National Liberation Front (El Salvador).

9. AUSTRALASIA AND THE PACIFIC

Australia

Capital: Canberra   Pop. 15,462,000

The Commonwealth of Australia comprises six states, the Australian Capital Territory of Canberra and the Northern Territory. The federal Parliament consists of the House of Representatives, elected for three years, and the Senate, elected for six years. Each state has its own Legislature and government. The Australian Labor Party has held office from 1941 to 1949, from 1972 to 1975 and since 1983, and the allied Liberal Party and Country Party (renamed the National Country Party in 1974 and the National Party in 1982) from 1949 to 1972 and from 1975 to 1983.

Australian Marxist Forum (AMF)

History. The AMF was founded by Patrick Clancy in 1982 after his expulsion from the Socialist Party of Australia (see below) to promote the unity of the left, especially in the trade union movement. Membership is open to members of the Communist Party of Australia, which actively supports the AMF, the Socialist Party of Australia, the Communist Party of Australia—Marxist-Leninist and the Trotskyist parties.

Communist Party of Australia (CPA)

History. The CPA, founded in 1920, had only 249 members in 1928, but greatly increased its membership and its influence in the trade unions in the 1930s. Banned in 1940 because of its anti-war attitude, it was legalized again in 1942 after it had changed its policy. Another period of growth followed; its membership reached 22,052 in 1944, and a Communist was elected to the Queensland State Legislature in the same year, losing his seat in 1950. After the war its membership and influence declined. A number of leading Communists, including the general secretary, Lawrence Sharkey, were imprisoned in 1948–50 on sedition charges, and an act banning the CPA was passed in 1950; it was ruled to be unconstitutional by the Australian High Court, however, and a proposal to amend the constitution to permit the banning of the party was defeated in a referendum in the following year. The Sino-Soviet controversy led to a long struggle between pro-Soviet and pro-Chinese factions, but the former gained control in 1963, when Edward Hill, a member of the Secretariat and the party's leading Maoist, was expelled. The CPA afterwards adopted a Eurocommunist position; at the 1969 Moscow conference of communist parties its delegate, Laurie Aarons, strongly criticized the Soviet invasion of Czechoslovakia. The pro-Soviet faction broke away in 1971 and founded the Socialist Party of Australia.

Leadership. Judy Mundey (g.s.).

Structure. The CPA is organized in residential and workplace branches, with district committees in populous districts and state committees elected by state conferences. The federal congress, held every three years, elects two-thirds of the members of the National Committee, the other third being elected directly from the states and districts, and the eight-member Executive Committee.

Membership. Under 1,500 (1985 estimate), almost all of whom live in the Sydney and Melbourne areas.

Electoral influence. The CPA has never been represented in Parliament, and has not been represented in any state legislature since 1950.

Industrial influence. The CPA exercises some influence in a number of trade unions, including the metal workers', shipwrights', railway workers', transport workers', dockers', miners' and teachers' unions.

Orientation. Eurocommunist.

Programme. The CPA aims at "democratic self-management socialism based on social ownership and democratic control of the main means of production". It calls for the establishment of a republic with a unicameral Parliament elected by proportional representation and the enactment of a Bill of Rights. Each workplace and institution would have its own elected governing council, and national economic planning would be decided democratically through assemblies of representatives from enterprises and institutions. It lays stress on self-determination for the Aborigines, women's rights and ecological questions. In foreign policy it advocates non-alignment, repudiation of the ANZUS Pact, the elimination of foreign military bases and disarmament.

Publications. *Tribune*, weekly (7,000); *Australian Left Review*, quarterly (1,200).

International affiliations. While not owing allegiance to any overseas party, the CPA seeks relations with all communist, Marxist and socialist parties and working-class and liberation movements on the basis of equality and non-interference.

Communist Party of Australia—Marxist-Leninist (CPA-ML)

History. The CPA-ML was founded in 1964 by Edward Hill after his expulsion from the Communist Party of Australia.

Leadership. Edward Hill (ch.).

Structure. The CPA-ML functions as an underground party.

Membership. 300–400 (1985 estimate). The party finds its strongest support among students.

Industrial influence. The CPA-ML has some influence in the Builders' Labourers' Federation, of which one of its leading members, Norm Gallagher, is president.

Orientation. Pro-Chinese.

Publications. *Vanguard*, weekly; *Australian Communist*, monthly.

International affiliations. The CPA-ML is recognized by the Chinese Communist Party.

Socialist Labor League (SLL)

History. The SLL was founded in 1972.

Membership. 100 (1985 estimate).

Orientation. Trotskyist.

Programme. "To prepare and mobilize the working class for the overthrow of capitalism, the establishment of working class power and the building of a socialist society".

International affiliations. Fourth International, International Committee.

Socialist Party of Australia (SPA)

History. The SPA was formed in 1971 by a pro-Soviet group which broke away from the Communist Party of Australia. Patrick Clancy, the SPA's president and federal secretary of the Building Workers' Industrial Union, and a number of other leading trade unionists were expelled in 1982 after they had objected to the party's attempts to dictate policy to their unions.

Leadership. John McPhillips (ch.); Peter Symon (g.s.). The office of president was abolished in 1982.

Structure. The branch is the basic unit, and organizations exist at district and state level. The national congress, meeting every three years, elects the Central Committee, which elects the Executive and Secretariat. The party's youth organization is the Young Socialist League.

Membership. Under 1,000 (1985 estimate).

Industrial influence. The SPA exercises some influence in the trade unions, although this has declined since the expulsion of Clancy.

Orientation. Pro-Soviet.

Programme. The SPA seeks the establishment of a socialist republic based on Marxism-Leninism. It advocates the removal of US bases from Australia and the adoption of a non-aligned foreign policy.

Publication. *The Socialist*, fortnightly.

International affiliations. The SPA has been recognized by the Soviet Communist Party since 1975 as the only Marxist-Leninist party in Australia.

Socialist Workers' Party (SWP)

Leadership. Jim Percy (nat. sec.).

Membership. 400 (1985 estimate), mostly industrial workers.

Electoral influence. The SWP's 38 candidates received 41,803 votes (0.5 per cent) in the 1983 elections.

Orientation. Trotskyist.

Programme. The SWP believes that the working class, led by a vanguard of politically educated workers, will be the power base of the socialist revolution.

Publication. *Direct Action*, weekly.

International affiliations. Fourth International, United Secretariat.

Spartacist League of Australia and New Zealand (SLANZ)

Membership. 50 (1985 estimate).

Orientation. Trotskyist.

Programme. "To achieve communism over the whole earth by means of proletarian revolutionary internationalist class struggle".

International affiliations. International Spartacist Tendency.

World Socialist Party of Australia (WSPA)

History. The WSPA is an offshoot of the Socialist Party of Great Britain.

Orientation. Independent.

Publication. Socialist Comment.

International affiliations. World Socialist Movement.

French Polynesia

Capital: Papeete, Tahiti   Pop. 164,000

French Polynesia has been a French overseas territory since 1958, represented in the French National Assembly by two deputies and one senator, and was granted limited autonomy in 1977, although France retained responsibility for foreign affairs, defence, international transport, monetary matters, justice and police. Under a new statute granted in 1984 there is a President and cabinet drawn from the 30-member Territorial Assembly, which is elected every five years, but the French High Commissioner remains the supreme executive authority.

Power to the People
Ia Mana Te Nunaa

History. Power to the People was founded in 1976, and won three seats in the Territorial Assembly in the 1982 elections.

Leadership. Jacques Drollet (g.s.).

Electoral influence. In 1982 Power to the People obtained 11.75 per cent of the vote in the Iles du Vent division.

Orientation. Independent.

Programme. Power to the People advocates socialist independence for French Polynesia, to be achieved by non-violent class struggle against colonialist capitalism.

Publications. Te Ve'a Hepetoma, weekly; *Ia Mana*, monthly.

International affiliations. Power to the People is recognized as a fraternal party by the French Socialist Party.

New Zealand

Capital: Wellington   Pop. 3,238,000

The unicameral Parliament, the House of Representatives, is elected for a three-year term. The New Zealand Labour Party has held office in 1935–49, 1957–60, 1972–75 and since 1984, and the New Zealand National Party in 1949–57, 1960–72 and 1975–84.

Communist Party of New Zealand (CPNZ)

History. The CPNZ, after the Labour Party the oldest party in New Zealand, was founded in 1921. It greatly increased its influence in the 1930s and early 1940s, its membership reaching about 2,000 in 1945–46, after which it declined. Its general secretary, V. G. Wilcox, adopted a strongly pro-Chinese attitude during the Sino-Soviet controversy, and by 1963 had won over the majority of the party; as a result the pro-Soviet faction broke away and in 1966 founded the Socialist Unity Party. In 1978, however, the CPNZ broke with the "Chinese revisionists", whom it accused of attempting to impose the three worlds theory on other parties, and declared that it regarded Albania as "the socialist fatherland". This led to another split, and several pro-Chinese groups left the party.

Leadership. Richard C. Wolfe (g.s.).

Membership. 50 (1985 estimate), almost all in the Auckland area.

Electoral influence. The CPNZ has never been represented in Parliament.

Orientation. Pro-Albanian.

Publication. People's Voice, weekly.

Socialist Action League (SAL)

History. The SAL was founded by students in 1969.

Membership. 60 (1983 estimate). Most of its members are students and intellectuals.

Orientation. Trotskyist.

Publication. Socialist Action, fortnightly.

Socialist Party of New Zealand (SPNZ)

History. The SPNZ, founded in 1931, is an offshoot of the Socialist Party of Great Britain.

Membership. 30–40 (1984 estimate).

Orientation. Independent.

Publication. The Socialist Viewpoint.

International affiliations. World Socialist Movement.

Socialist Unity Party (SUP)

History. The SUP was founded in 1966 by members of the Communist Party of New Zealand who opposed its Maoist policies. The Soviet ambassador was expelled in 1980 for passing money to the party.

Leadership. Gordon Andersen (nat. pres.); George Jackson (nat. sec.).

Structure. The SUP has 11 local branches. The national conference, held every three years, elects the National Committee (10 full and four alternate members), which elects the five-member National Executive.

Membership. 100 (1985 estimate). Over half the members live in Auckland.

Industrial influence. The SUP exercises considerable influence in the New Zealand Federation of Labour (FOL). Two members of its National Committee, Gordon Andersen (secretary of the Northern Drivers' Union and president of the Auckland Trades Council) and Kenneth Douglas (president of the New Zealand Drivers' Federation and the Wellington Trades Council and secretary–treasurer of the FOL), are also members of the National Executive Board of the FOL.

Orientation. Pro-Soviet. The SUP has supported Soviet policies in Afghanistan and Poland.

Programme. The SUP advocates the nationalization of financial houses, banks, insurance companies and key industries; a planned economy controlled by representatives of the trade unions, farmers, small businessmen and consumers; development of industries to process New Zealand's produce; and a foreign policy of non-alignment, withdrawal from the ANZUS Pact and a nuclear-free zone in the South Pacific and the Indian Ocean.

Publications. New Zealand Tribune, fortnightly; *Socialist Politics,* quarterly.

International affiliations. The SUP has close relations with the Soviet-bloc parties.

Workers' Communist League (WCL)

History. The WCL was formed in 1980 by the merger of two small groups which had broken away from the Communist Party of New Zealand.

Leadership. Not revealed.

Structure. The WCL operates as an underground party.

Membership. 130 (1983 estimate). The WCL is largely composed of intellectuals and students, but has also recruited among industrial workers and the unemployed in the Wellington area.

Industrial influence. The WCL is active in the trade union movement, especially in Wellington.

Orientation. Pro-Chinese.

Publication. Unity, monthly.

SECTION THREE
APPENDICES

1. International Party Groupings

2. Documents

3. Select Bibliography

APPENDIX 1:

INTERNATIONAL PARTY GROUPINGS

Pro-Soviet Parties

The parties below accept the leading position of the Soviet Communist Party as the "vanguard" party. Most are parties of long standing formerly affiliated to the Communist International, but some have broken away comparatively recently from parties which have adopted a Eurocommunist or pro-Chinese position. Not all parties which can be described as "pro-Soviet" are officially recognized by the Soviet party.

Western Europe

★Communist Party of Austria
★Progressive Party of the Working People (Cyprus)
★Communist Party of Denmark
★German Communist Party
 Socialist Unity Party of West Berlin
 New Communist Party (Great Britain)
★Communist Party of Greece—Exterior
 Organization of Icelandic Socialists
★Communist Party of Ireland
★Communist Party of Luxembourg
 Communist Party of Malta
 Alliance of Communists in the Netherlands
 Communist Party of Norway
★Portuguese Communist Party
 Communist Party (Spain)
 Party for Communist Recovery and Unification (Spain)
 Spanish Workers' Communist Party
 Unified Communist Party of Spain
 Communist Workers' Party of Sweden
★Swiss Labour Party
★Communist Party of Turkey

Eastern Europe

†Bulgarian Communist Party
†Communist Party of Czechoslovakia
†Socialist Unity Party of Germany
†Hungarian Socialist Workers' Party
†Polish United Workers' Party
†Communist Party of the Soviet Union

Middle East and Arab World

*Socialist Vanguard Party (Algeria)
National Liberation Front of Bahrain
*Egyptian Communist Party
*Party of the Masses (Iran)
†Iraqi Communist Party
*Communist Party of Israel
*Communist Party of Jordan
*Lebanese Communist Party
Party of Progress and Socialism (Morocco)
*Palestinian Communist Party
Communist Party of Saudi Arabia
*Sudanese Communist Party
*Syrian Communist Party
Tunisian Communist Party
National Democratic Front (Yemen Arab Republic)
People's Democratic Union (People's Democratic Republic of Yemen)
Yemen Socialist Party (People's Democratic Republic of Yemen)

Asia

People's Democratic Party of Afghanistan
Bangladesh Communist Party, Marxist-Leninist
Bangladesh Peasants' and Workers' People's League
Communist Party of Bangladesh
All-India Communist Party
†Communist Party of India
*Communist Party of Indonesia (pro-Soviet faction)
Voice of Japan
Kampuchean People's Revolutionary Party
Lao People's Revolutionary Party
†Mongolian People's Revolutionary Party
Communist Party of Pakistan
*Communist Party of the Philippines
*Communist Party of Sri Lanka
New Party (Thailand)
*Vietnamese Communist Party

Africa

Popular Movement for the Liberation of Angola—Labour Party
Patriotic League for Development (Burkina Faso)
Workers' Party of Ethiopia
Communist Party of Lesotho
Socialist Working People's Party (Nigeria)
*Independence and Labour Party (Senegal)
*South African Communist Party

North America

*Communist Party of Canada
 Popular Socialist Party (Mexico)
 Unity of the Communist Left (Mexico)
†Communist Party USA

Central America and the Caribbean

*Popular Vanguard Party (Costa Rica)
*Communist Party of Cuba
*Dominican Communist Party (Dominican Republic)
 Democratic National Union (El Salvador)
*Communist Party of El Salvador
*Guatemalan Labour Party
 Unified Party of Haitian Communists
*Communist Party of Honduras
*Workers' Party of Jamaica
 Nicaraguan Socialist Party
*People's Party of Panama
 Puerto Rican Communist Party
 February Eighteenth Movement (Trinidad and Tobago)
 People's Popular Movement (Trinidad and Tobago)
 United Revolutionary Organization (Trinidad and Tobago)
 Workers' Revolutionary Committee (Trinidad and Tobago)

South America

†Communist Party of Argentina
*Communist Party of Bolivia
*Brazilian Communist Party
*Communist Party of Chile
*Communist Party of Colombia
*Ecuadorean Communist Party
*People's Progressive Party (Guyana)
*Paraguayan Communist Party
*Peruvian Communist Party
*Communist Party of Uruguay
*Communist Party of Venezuela

Australasia

 Socialist Party of Australia
 Socialist Unity Party (New Zealand)

---

*Represented on editorial council of *World Marxist Review*
†Represented on editorial board of *World Marxist Review*

Eurocommunist Parties

The parties below do not accept the leadership of any foreign party, although many of them are officially recognized by the Soviet Communist Party. They reject the theory of the dictatorship of the proletariat, and advocate the creation of a socialist society through parliamentary means, democratic liberties and a multiparty system.

Western Europe

*Communist Party of Belgium
 Left Socialist Party (Denmark)
 Socialist People's Party (Denmark)
*Communist Party of Finland
 Finnish People's Democratic League
 Democratic and Unitarian Communist Party (France)
†French Communist Party
†Communist Party of Great Britain
 Communist Party of Greece—Interior
 United Democratic Left (Greece)
 People's Alliance (Iceland)
 Irish Marxist Society
†Italian Communist Party
 Communist Party of the Netherlands
 Socialist Left Party (Norway)
 San Marino Communist Party
*Communist Party of Spain
 Basque Communist Party (Spain)
 Unified Socialist Party of Catalonia (Spain)
*Left Party—Communists (Sweden)

Middle East and Arab World

 Peace and Equality Movement (Israel)

Asia

*Japan Communist Party

Africa

 Réunion Communist Party

North America

*Unified Socialist Party of Mexico

Central America and the Caribbean

Guadeloupe Communist Party
Martinique Communist Party

South America

Movement to Socialism (Venezuela)

Australasia

Communist Party of Australia

*Represented on editorial council of *World Marxist Review*
†Represented on editorial board of *World Marxist Review*

Pro-Chinese Parties

The parties below accept the leadership of the Chinese Communist Party.

Western Europe

Communist League of Austria
Marxist–Leninist Party of Austria
Labour Party of Belgium
Marxist–Leninist Communist Party of Belgium
Marxist–Leninist Groups of Finland
Marxist–Leninist Communist Party (France)
Revolutionary Communist Party—Marxist-Leninist (France)
Communist League of West Germany
Organization of Marxist-Leninists of Greece
Icelandic Communist Party—Marxist-Leninist
Unified Communist Party of Italy
Communist Workers' Organization—Marxist-Leninist (Netherlands)
Communist Party of Portugal—Marxist-Leninist
Workers' Party of Spain
Communist Party of Sweden
Communist Party, Switzerland—Marxist-Leninist
Worker-Peasant Party of Turkey

Eastern Europe

Communist Party of Poland

Asia

East Bengal Communist Party, Marxist-Leninist (Bangladesh)
Burmese Communist Party

Communist Party of China
Communist Party of Indonesia (pro-Chinese faction)
Party of Democratic Kampuchea
Communist Party of Malaya
Communist Party of Malaysia
Malay Nationalist Revolutionary Party
North Kalimantan Communist Party (Malaysia)
Communist Party of Sri Lanka—Marxist-Leninist
Communist Party of Thailand

Africa

Union of Communist Struggles (Burkina Faso)
Revolutionary Movement for the New Democracy (Senegal)

Central America and the Caribbean

Communist Party of Honduras—Marxist-Leninist
Communist Party of Nicaragua
Communist Party—Marxist-Leninist (Panama)

South America

Communist Vanguard (Argentina)
Marxist-Leninist Communist Workers' Party (Argentina)
Revolutionary Communist Party (Argentina)
Marxist-Leninist Communist Party of Bolivia
Communist Party of Colombia, Marxist-Leninist
Independent Revolutionary Workers' Movement (Colombia)
Ecuadorean Communist Party, Marxist-Leninist
Working People's Vanguard Party (Guyana)
Marxist-Leninist Paraguayan Communist Party
Communist Party of Peru—Red Fatherland

Australasia

Communist Party of Australia—Marxist-Leninist
Workers' Communist League (New Zealand)

Other Maoist Parties

The parties below base their policies on Mao Zedong's interpretation of Marxism, but do not accept the leadership of the Chinese Communist Party, which they regard as revisionist.

Western Europe

Communist Workers' Party (Denmark)
Marxist-Leninist Union of Communists of France

League of West German Communists
Marxist-Leninist Party of Germany
Revolutionary Communist League of Britain
Revolutionary Communist Party of Greece
Netherlands Communist Unity Movement—Marxist-Leninist
Workers' Communist Party (Norway)
Portuguese Workers' Communist Party

Middle East and Arab World

Revolutionary Communist Alliance (Israel)

Asia

Communist Party of India—Marxist-Leninist
Communist Party—Marxist-Leninist (Japan)
Communist Party of Nepal—Marxist-Leninist
Communist Party of the Philippines—Marxist-Leninist

North America

Revolutionary Communist Party (USA)

Central America and the Caribbean

Haitian Workers' Party

South America

Revolutionary Communist Party of Chile

Pro-Albanian Parties

The parties below, many of which were formerly pro-Chinese, accept the leadership of the Albanian Party of Labour.

Western Europe

Marxist-Leninist Party (Denmark)
Communist Workers' Party of France
Communist Party of Germany—Marxist-Leninists
Communist Party of Britain—Marxist-Leninist
Revolutionary Communist Party of Britain, Marxist-Leninist
Marxist–Leninist Organization of Iceland
Communist Party of Ireland—Marxist-Leninist

401

Communist Party of Italy—Marxist-Leninist
Portuguese Communist Party, Reconstituted
Communist Party of Spain—Marxist-Leninist
Communist Party of Marxist-Leninist Revolutionaries (Sweden)

Eastern Europe

Party of Labour of Albania

Africa

Voltaic Revolutionary Communist Party (Burkina Faso)
Union for People's Democracy (Senegal)

North America

Communist Party of Canada—Marxist-Leninist

Central America and the Caribbean

Popular Action Movement—Marxist-Leninist (Nicaragua)
Communist Party of Trinidad and Tobago

South America

Communist Party of Brazil
Communist Party of Peru—Red Flag
Revolutionary Vanguard—Proletarian Communist (Peru)
Communist Party of Suriname

Australasia

Communist Party of New Zealand

Castroist Parties

The parties below derive their inspiration from the Cuban revolution and from
the teachings of Castro and Guevara.

Central America and the Caribbean

Costa Rican People's Party.
★Communist Party of Cuba
Puerto Rican Socialist Party.

South America

Bolivian Workers' Revolutionary Party
Ecuadorean Revolutionary Socialist Party
Movement of the Revolutionary Left (Peru)
Revolutionary People's Party (Suriname)

*Represented on the editorial council of *World Marxist Review*

Parties affiliated to the Fourth International, United Secretariat

The Fourth International, United Secretariat, is the largest international Trotskyist organization, with the following affiliated parties.

Western Europe

Revolutionary Marxist Group (Austria)
Workers' Revolutionary League (Belgium)
Socialist Workers' Party (Denmark)
Revolutionary Communist League (France)
International Marxist Group (West Germany)
Socialist League (Great Britain)
People's Democracy (Ireland)
Revolutionary Communist Groups (Italy)
Socialist Workers' Party (Netherlands)
Revolutionary Communist League (Spain)
Socialist Party (Sweden)
Socialist Workers' Party (Switzerland)

Middle East and Arab World

Revolutionary Workers' Party (Iran)
Socialist Workers' Party (Iran)
Workers' Unity Party (Iran)
Revolutionary Communist League (Israel)

North America

Revolutionary Workers' League (Canada)
Revolutionary Workers' Party (Mexico)
*Socialist Workers' Party (USA)

Central America and the Caribbean

Workers' Socialist Organization (Costa Rica)

South America

Revolutionary Workers' Party—United (Bolivia)
Workers' Revolutionary Party (Peru)
Workers' Revolutionary Party (Uruguay)
Socialist League (Venezuela)

Australasia

Socialist Workers' Party (Australia)

*Co-operates with but not formally affiliated to Fourth International, United Secretariat.

Other Trotskyist Parties

Western Europe

Communist Combat Organization (France)
Communist Committees for Self-management (France)
Internationalist Communist Party (France)
Workers' Struggle (France)
International Socialists of Germany
League of Socialist Workers (West Germany)
Militant Tendency (Great Britain)
Revolutionary Communist Party (Great Britain)
Revolutionary Workers' Party (Great Britain)
Socialist Federation (Great Britain)
Socialist Organizer Alliance (Great Britain)
Socialist Workers' Party (Great Britain)
Spartacus League (Great Britain)
Workers' Power (Great Britain)
Workers' Revolutionary Party (Great Britain)
Revolutionary Communist League (Ireland)
Irish Republican Socialist Party
Revolutionary Socialist Party (Portugal)
Workers' Party of Socialist Unity (Portugal)
Workers' Socialist Organization (Portugal)
Revolutionary Communist League (Spain)

Middle East and Arab World

Workers' League (Israel)

Asia

Communist Party of Burma
New Equal Society Party (Sri Lanka)

Africa

Workers' Socialist Organization (Senegal)

North America

Forward Readers' Group (Canada)
Trotskyist League (Canada)
Workers' Socialist Group (Canada)
Spartacist League (USA)
Workers' World Party (USA)

Central America and the Caribbean

Revolutionary Marxist League (Jamaica)
Socialist Revolution Group (Martinique)
Workers' Revolutionary Party (Panama)
Workers' Socialist Party (Panama)
Puerto Rican Socialist League

South America

Labour Party (Argentina)
Movement to Socialism (Argentina)
Popular Left Front (Argentina)
Workers' Revolutionary Party (Argentina)
Communist Vanguard of the Revolutionary Workers' Party (Bolivia)
Posadist Trotskyist Revolutionary Workers' Party (Bolivia)
Revolutionary Workers' Party (Bolivia)
Workers' Socialist Organization (Bolivia)
Freedom and Struggle (Brazil)
Socialist Youth Foundation (Brazil)
Revolutionary Marxist Workers' Party—Workers' Socialist Party (Peru)
Workers', Peasants', Students' and People's Front (Peru)
Revolutionary Workers' Party, Trotskyist (Uruguay)

Australasia

Socialist Labor League (Australia)
Spartacist League of Australia and New Zealand
Socialist Action League (New Zealand)

Independent Parties

The parties below do not accept the leadership of any foreign party, and seek to formulate a type of Marxism appropriate to the conditions of their particular country. Only a few of them are officially recognized by the Soviet Communist Party.

Western Europe

Communist Workers' Party (Denmark)
Workers' Party (Ireland)

Continuous Struggle (Italy)
Proletarian Democracy (Italy)
Pacifist Socialist Party (Netherlands)
Workers' Communist Party (Norway)
Movement of the Socialist Left (Portugal)
Autonomous Socialist Party (Switzerland)
Progressive Organizations of Switzerland

Eastern Europe

*Romanian Communist Party
League of Communists of Yugoslavia

Middle East and Arab World

National Progressive Unionist Party (Egypt)
Communist Party of Iran
Kurdish Communist Party of Iran
People's Holy Warriors (Iran)
Israeli Socialist Organization
Organization of Communist Action in Lebanon
Somali Revolutionary Socialist Party
Party of Communist Action (Syria)

Asia

National Socialist Party (Bangladesh)
All-India Forward Bloc
Bolshevik Party of India
Communist Party of India—Marxist
Forward Bloc—Marxist (India)
Peasants' and Workers' Party of India
Revolutionary Communist Party of India
Revolutionary Socialist Party (India)
Socialist Unity Centre of India
Korean Workers' Party (North Korea)
Lanka Equal Society Party (Sri Lanka)
People's Liberation Front (Sri Lanka)
People's United Front (Sri Lanka)

Africa

Benin People's Revolutionary Party
African Party for the Independence of Cape Verde
Congolese Labour Party
African Party for the Independence of Guinea and Cape Verde (Guinea-Bissau)
Mauritian Militant Movement
Mauritian Socialist Movement
Front for the Liberation of Mozambique
Movement for the Liberation of São Tomé and Príncipe
African Independence Party (Senegal)

Seychelles People's Progressive Front
Zimbabwe African National Union—Patriotic Front

North America

Socialist Workers' Party (Mexico)

Central America and the Caribbean

Popular Liberation Movement (El Salvador)
Popular Revolutionary Bloc (El Salvador)
Salvadorean Revolutionary Party
Unified Popular Action Front (El Salvador)
Maurice Bishop Patriotic Movement (Grenada)
Sandinista National Liberation Front (Nicaragua)
United People's Movement (St. Vincent and the Grenadines)

South America

Movement of the Revolutionary Left (Bolivia)
Party of the Revolutionary Left (Bolivia)
Communist Revolutionary Party (Brazil)
Movement of the Revolutionary Left (Venezuela)
Unitary Communist Vanguard (Venezuela)

Australasia

Australian Marxist Forum
Power to the People (French Polynesia)

*Represented on editorial board of *World Marxist Review*

Non-Leninist and New Left Parties

The parties below claim to be Marxist but not Leninist. The parties composing the World Socialist Movement (see below) also fall into this category.

Western Europe

Unified Socialist Party (France)
Centre Faction (West Germany)
Communist League (West Germany)
Marxist Group (West Germany)
Socialist Bureau (West Germany)
Pan-Hellenic Socialist Movement (Greece)

Workers' Autonomy (Italy)
Progressive Federation (Spain)
Communist Party, Switzerland

Middle East and Arab World

Israeli New Left

North America

Socialist Labor Party of America

Central America and the Caribbean

Workers' Party (Costa Rica)

South America

Socialist Party (Bolivia)
Socialist Party (Chile)
Working People's Alliance (Guyana)
Revolutionary Socialist Party (Peru)
Uruguayan Socialist Party

World Socialist Movement

The parties below accept the declaration of principles adopted by the Socialist Party of Great Britain on its foundation in 1904.

Western Europe

League of Democratic Socialists (Austria)
Socialist Party of Great Britain
World Socialist Party of Ireland
World Socialist Movement, Swedish Group

North America

Socialist Party of Canada
World Socialist Party of the United States

Australasia

World Socialist Party of Australia
Socialist Party of New Zealand

Guerrilla and Terrorist Organizations

The list below includes political parties which conduct guerrilla or terrorist operations.

Western Europe

Fighting Communist Cells (Belgium)
Direct Action (France)
Red Army Faction (West Germany)
Revolutionary Cells (West Germany)
Irish National Liberation Army
Front Line (Italy)
Red Brigades (Italy)
Popular Forces of April 25 (Portugal)
Basque Nation and Liberty (Spain)
October 1 Anti-fascist Resistance Group (Spain)
Association of Revolutionary Youth (Turkey)
Kurdish Workers' Party (Turkey)
Marxist–Leninist Armed Propaganda Unit (Turkey)
Revolutionary Left (Turkey)
Revolutionary Way (Turkey)
Turkish People's Liberation Party

Middle East and Arab World

Kurdish Communist Party of Iran
People's Fighters (Iran)
People's Holy Warriors (Iran)
Democratic Front for the Liberation of Palestine
Popular Front for the Liberation of Palestine
National Democratic Front (Yemen Arab Republic)
Popular Unity Party of Yemen (Yemen Arab Republic)

Asia

Burmese Communist Party
Communist Party of Burma
All-Nagaland Communist Party (India)
Communist Party of India—Marxist-Leninist
National Socialist Council of Nagaland (India)
People's Liberation Army (India)
Revolutionary Front for the Independence of East Timor (Indonesia)
United Red Army (Japan)
Party of Democratic Kampuchea
Communist Party of Malaya
Communist Party of Malaysia
North Kalimantan Communist Party (Malaysia)
New People's Army (Philippines)
Communist Party of Thailand
New Party (Thailand)

Africa

Eritrean People's Liberation Front (Ethiopia)

North America

Party of the Poor (Mexico)
May 19th Communist Organization (USA)
Weather Underground (USA)

Central America and the Caribbean

Central American Workers' Revolutionary Party (El Salvador and Honduras)
Communist Party of El Salvador
Farabundo Martí Popular Liberation Forces (El Salvador)
National Resistance Armed Forces (El Salvador)
People's Revolutionary Army (El Salvador)
Revolutionary Workers' Movement—Salvador Cayetano Carpio (El Salvador)
Armed People's Organization (Guatemala)
Guatemalan National Revolutionary Unity
Guerrilla Army of the Poor (Guatemala)
Rebel Armed Forces (Guatemala)
Cinchonero Popular Liberation Movement (Honduras)
Lorenzo Zelaya Popular Revolutionary Front (Honduras)
Morazanista Honduran Liberation Front
Armed Forces of National Liberation (Puerto Rico)

South America

Montoneros (Argentina)
People's Revolutionary Army (Argentina)
Manuel Rodríguez Patriotic Front (Chile)
Movement of the Revolutionary Left (Chile)
April 19 Movement (Colombia)
National Liberation Army (Colombia)
Pedro León Arboleda (Colombia)
People's Liberation Army (Colombia)
People's Revolutionary Organization (Colombia)
Revolutionary Armed Forces of Colombia
Ricardo Franco Front (Colombia)
Workers' Self-defence Movement (Colombia)
Eloy Alfaro Popular Armed Forces (Ecuador)
Politico-Military Organization (Paraguay)
Marxist-Leninist Unified Communist Committee (Peru)
People's Revolutionary Commandos (Peru)
Shining Path (Peru)
Tupac Amaru Revolutionary Movement (Peru)
Red Flag (Venezuela)

APPENDIX 2:

DOCUMENTS

Marx and Engels (1848)

Extract from: Karl Marx and Friedrich Engels, *The Communist Manifesto* (1848)

A spectre is haunting Europe—the spectre of communism. All the powers of old Europe have entered into a holy alliance to exorcise this spectre: Pope and Tsar, Metternich and Guizot, French Radicals and German police-spies.

Where is the party in opposition that has not been decried as communistic by its opponents in power? Where the opposition that has not hurled back the branding reproach of communism, against the more advanced opposition parties, as well as against its reactionary adversaries?

Two things result from this fact.

I. Communism is already acknowledged by all European powers to be itself a power.

II. It is high time that communists should openly, in the face of the whole world, publish their views, their aims, their tendencies, and meet this nursery tale of the spectre of communism with a manifesto of the party itself.

To this end, communists of various nationalities have assembled in London, and sketched the following manifesto, to be published in the English, French, German, Italian, Flemish, and Danish languages.

I

Bourgeois and Proletarians

The history of all hitherto existing society is the history of class struggles. Freeman and slave, patrician and plebeian, lord and serf, guild-master and journeyman—in a word, oppressor and oppressed, stood in constant opposition to one another, carried on an uninterrupted, now hidden, now open fight, a fight that each time ended either in a revolutionary re-constitution of society at large or in the common ruin of the contending classes.

In the earlier epochs of history, we find almost everywhere a complicated arrangement of society into various orders, a manifold gradation of social rank. In ancient Rome we have patricians, knights, plebeians, slaves; in the Middle Ages, feudal lords, vassals, guild-masters, journeymen, apprentices, serfs; in almost all of these classes, again, subordinate gradations.

The modern bourgeois society that has sprouted from the ruins of feudal society has not done away with class antagonisms. It has but established new classes, new conditions of oppression, new forms of struggle in place of the old ones.

Our epoch, the epoch of the bourgeoisie, possesses, however, this distinctive feature: it has simplified the class antagonisms. Society as a whole is more and more splitting up into two great hostile camps, into two great classes directly facing each other: Bourgeoisie and Proletariat. . . .

Modern bourgeois society with its relations of production, of exchange and of property, a society that has conjured up such gigantic means of production and of exchange, is like the sorcerer, who is no longer able to control the powers of the nether world which he has called up by his spells. The history of industry and commerce for many a decade past is but the history of the revolt of modern productive forces against modern conditions of production, against the property relations that are the conditions for the existence of the bourgeoisie and of its rule. It is enough to mention the commercial crises that by their periodical return put on trial, each time more threateningly, the existence of the entire bourgeois society. In these crises a great part not only of the existing products, but also of the previously created productive forces, are periodically destroyed. In these crises there breaks out an epidemic that, in all earlier epochs, would have seemed an absurdity—the epidemic of over-production. Society suddenly finds itself put back into a state of momentary barbarism; it appears as if a famine, a universal war of devastation, has cut off the supply of every means of subsistence; industry and commerce seem to be destroyed; and why? Because there is too much civilization, too much means of subsistence, too much industry, too much commerce. The productive forces at the disposal of society no longer tend to further the development of the conditions of bourgeois property; on the contrary, they have become too powerful for these conditions, by which they are fettered, and so soon as they overcome these fetters, they bring disorder into the whole of bourgeois society, endanger the existence of bourgeois property. The conditions of bourgeois society are too narrow to comprise the wealth created by them. And how does the bourgeoisie get over these crises? On the one hand by enforced destruction of a mass of productive forces; on the other, by the conquest of new markets, and by the more thorough exploitation of the old ones. That is to say, by paving the way for more extensive and more destructive crises, and by diminishing the means whereby crises are prevented.

The weapons with which the bourgeoisie felled feudalism to the ground are now turned against the bourgeoisie itself.

But not only has the bourgeoisie forged the weapons that bring death to itself; it has also called into existence the men who are to wield those weapons—the modern working class—the proletarians.

In proportion as the bourgeoisie, i.e., capital, is developed, in the same proportion is the proletariat, the modern working class, developed—a class of labourers, who live only so long as they find work, and who find work only so long as their labour increases capital. These labourers, who must sell themselves piecemeal, are a commodity, like every other article of commerce, and are consequently exposed to all the vicissitudes of competition, to all the fluctuations of the market.

Owing to the extensive use of machinery and to division of labour, the work of the proletarians has lost all individual character, and, consequently, all charm for the workman. He becomes an appendage of the machine, and it is only the most simple, most monotonous, and most easily acquired knack that is required of him. Hence, the cost of production of a workman is restricted, almost entirely, to the means of subsistence that he requires for his maintenance, and for the propagation of his race. But the price of a commodity, and therefore also of labour, is equal to its cost of production. In proportion, therefore, as the repulsiveness of the work increases, the wage decreases. Nay more, in proportion as the use of machinery and division of labour increases, in the same proportion the burden of toil also increases, whether by prolongation of the working hours, by increase of the work exacted in a given time or by increased speed of the machinery, etc.

Modern industry has converted the little workshop of the patriarchal master into the great factory of the industrial capitalist. Masses of labourers, crowded into the factory, are organized like soldiers. As privates of the industrial army they are placed under the command of a perfect hierarchy of officers and sergeants. Not only are they slaves of the bourgeois class, and of the bourgeois state; they are daily and hourly enslaved by the machine, by the overlooker, and, above all, by the individual bourgeois manufacturer himself. The more openly this despotism proclaims gain to be its end and aim, the more petty, the more hateful, and the more embittering it is.

The less the skill and exertion of strength implied in manual labour, in other words, the more modern industry becomes developed, the more is the labour of men superseded by that of women. Differences of age and sex have no longer any distinctive social validity for the working class. All are instruments of labour, more or less expensive to use, according to their age and sex.

No sooner is the exploitation of the labourer by the manufacturer, so far, at an end, and he receives his wages in cash, than he is set upon by the other portions of the bourgeoisie, the landlord, the shopkeeper, the pawnbroker, etc.

The lower strata of the middle class—the small tradespeople, shopkeepers, and retired tradesmen generally, the handicraftsmen and peasants—all these sink gradually into the proletariat, partly because their diminutive capital does not suffice for the scale on which modern industry is carried on, and is swamped in the competition with the large capitalists, partly because their specialized skill is rendered worthless by new methods of production. Thus the proletariat is recruited from all classes of the population.

The proletariat goes through various stages of development. With its birth begins its struggle with the bourgeoisie. At first the contest is carried on by individual labourers, then by the workpeople of a factory, then by the operatives of one trade, in one locality, against the individual bourgeois who directly exploits them. They direct their attacks not against the bourgeois conditions of production, but against the instruments of production themselves; they destroy imported wares that compete with their labour, they smash to pieces machinery, they set factories ablaze, they seek to restore by force the vanished status of the workman of the Middle Ages.

At this stage the labourers still form an incoherent mass scattered over the whole country, and broken up by their mutual competition. If anywhere they unite to form more compact bodies, this is not yet the consequence of their own active union, but of the union of the bourgeoisie, which class, in order to attain its own political ends, is compelled to set the whole proletariat in motion, and is moreover yet, for a time, able to do so. At this stage, therefore, the proletarians do not fight their enemies, but the enemies of their enemies, the remnants of absolute monarchy, the landowners, the non-industrial bourgeois, the petty bourgeoisie. Thus the whole historical movement is concentrated in the hands of the bourgeoisie; every victory so obtained is a victory for the bourgeoisie.

But with the development of industry the proletariat not only increases in number; it becomes concentrated in greater masses, its strength grows, and it feels that strength more. The various interests and conditions of life within the ranks of the proletariat are more and more equalized, in proportion as machinery obliterates all distinctions of labour, and nearly everywhere reduces wages to the same low level. The growing competition among the bourgeois, and the resulting commercial crises, make the wages of the workers ever more fluctuating. The unceasing improvement of machinery, ever more rapidly developing, makes their livelihood more and more precarious; the collisions between individual workmen and individual bourgeois take more and more the character of collisions between two classes. Thereupon the workers begin to form combinations (trades unions) against the bourgeois; they club together in order to keep up the rate of wages; they found permanent associations in order to make provision beforehand for these occasional revolts. Here and there the contest breaks out into riots.

Now and then the workers are victorious, but only for a time. The real fruit of their battles lies, not in the immediate result, but in the ever-expanding union of the workers. This union is helped on by the improved means of communication that are created by modern industry and that place the workers of different localities in contact with one another. It was just this contact that was needed to centralize the numerous local struggles, all of the same character, into one national struggle between classes. But every class struggle is a political struggle. And that union, to attain which the burghers of the Middle Ages, with their miserable highways, required centuries, the modern proletarians, thanks to railways, achieve in a few years.

This organization of the proletarians into a class, and consequently into a political party, is continually being upset again by the competition between the workers themselves. But it ever rises up again, stronger, firmer, mightier. It compels legislative recognition of particular interests of the workers, by taking advantage of the divisions among the bourgeoisie itself. Thus the ten-hours' bill in England was carried.

Altogether, collisions between the classes of the old society further in many ways the course of development of the proletariat. The bourgeoisie finds itself involved in a constant battle. At first with the aristocracy; later on, with those portions of the bourgeoisie itself whose interests have become antagonistic to the progress of industry; at all times, with the bourgeoisie of foreign countries. In all these battles it sees itself compelled to appeal to the proletariat, to ask for its help, and thus to drag it into the political arena. The bourgeoisie itself, therefore, supplies the proletariat with its own elements of political and general education, in other words, it furnishes the proletariat with weapons for fighting the bourgeoisie.

Further, as we have already seen, entire sections of the ruling classes are, by the advance of industry, precipitated into the proletariat, or are at least threatened in their conditions of existence. These also supply the proletariat with fresh elements of enlightenment and progress.

Finally, in times when the class struggle nears the decisive hour, the process of dissolution going on within the ruling class, in fact within the whole range of old society, assumes such a violent, glaring character, that a small section of the ruling class cuts itself adrift, and joins the revolutionary class, the class that holds the future in its hands. Just as, therefore, at an earlier period, a section of the nobility went over to the bourgeoisie, so now a portion of the bourgeoisie goes over to the proletariat, and in particular, a portion of the bourgeois ideologists, who have raised themselves to the level of comprehending theoretically the historical movement as a whole. . . .

All the preceding classes that got the upper hand, sought to fortify their already acquired status by subjecting society at large to their conditions of appropriation. The proletarians cannot become masters of the productive forces of society, except by abolishing their own previous mode of appropriation, and thereby also every other previous mode of appropriation. They have nothing of their own to secure and to fortify; their mission is to destroy all previous securities for, and insurances of, individual property.

All previous historical movements were movements of minorities, or in the interests of minorities. The proletarian movement is the self-conscious, independent movement of the immense majority, in the interests of the immense majority.

The proletariat, the lowest stratum of our present society, cannot stir, cannot raise itself up, without the whole superincumbent strata of official society being sprung into the air.

Though not in substance, yet in form, the struggle of the proletariat with the bourgeoisie is at first a national struggle. The proletariat of each country must, of course, first of all settle matters with its own bourgeoisie.

In depicting the most general phases of the development of the proletariat, we traced the more or less veiled civil war, raging within existing society, up to the point where that war breaks out into open revolution, and where the violent overthrow of the bourgeoisie lays the foundation for the sway of the proletariat.

Hitherto, every form of society has been based, as we have already seen, on the antagonism of oppressing and oppressed classes. But in order to oppress a class, certain conditions must be assured to it under which it can, at least, continue its slavish existence. The serf, in the period of serfdom, raised himself to membership in the commune, just as the petty bourgeois, under the yoke of feudal absolutism, managed to develop into a bourgeois. The modern labourer, on the contrary, instead of rising with the progress of industry, sinks deeper and deeper below the conditions of existence of his own class. He becomes a pauper, and pauperism develops more rapidly than population and wealth. And here it becomes evident, that the bourgeoisie is unfit any longer to be the ruling class in society, and to impose its conditions of existence upon society as an overriding law. It is unfit to rule because it is incompetent to assure an existence to its slave within his slavery, because it cannot help letting him sink into such a state, that it has to feed him, instead of being fed by him. Society can no longer live under this bourgeoisie, in other words, its existence is no longer compatible with society.

The essential condition for the existence, and for the sway of the bourgeois class, is the formation and augmentation of capital; the condition for capital is wage-labour. Wage-labour rests exclusively on competition between the labourers. The advance of industry, whose involuntary promoter is the bourgeoisie, replaces the isolation of the labourers, due to competition, by their revolutionary combination, due to association. The development of modern industry, therefore, cuts from under its feet the very foundation on which the bourgeoisie produces and appropriates products. What the bourgeoisie, therefore, produces, above all, is its own grave-diggers. Its fall and the victory of the proletariat are equally inevitable.

II

Proletarians and Communists

In what relation do the communists stand to the proletarians as a whole?

The communists do not form a separate party opposed to other working-class parties.

They have no interests separate and apart from those of the proletariat as a whole.

They do not set up any sectarian principles of their own, by which to shape and mould the proletarian movement.

The communists are distinguished from the other working-class parties by this only: (i) in the national struggles of the proletarians of the different countries, they point out and bring to the front the common interests of the entire proletariat, independently of all nationality; (ii) in the various stages of development which the struggle of the working class against the bourgeoisie has to pass through, they always and everywhere represent the interests of the movement as a whole.

The communists, therefore, are on the one hand, practically, the most advanced and resolute section of the working-class parties of every country, that section which pushes forward all others; on the other hand, theoretically, they have over the great mass of the proletariat the advantage of clearly understanding the line of march, the conditions, and the ultimate general results of the proletarian movement.

The immediate aim of the communists is the same as that of all the other proletarian parties: formation of the proletariat into a class, overthrow of the bourgeois supremacy, conquest of political power by the proletariat.

The theoretical conclusions of the communists are in no way based on ideas or principles that have been invented, or discovered, by this or that would-be universal reformer.

They merely express, in general terms, actual relations springing from an existing class struggle, from a historical movement going on under our very eyes. The abolition of existing property relations is not at all a distinctive feature of communism.

All property relations in the past have continually been subject to historical change consequent upon the change in historical conditions. The French Revolution, for example, abolished feudal property in favour of bourgeois property.

The distinguishing feature of communism is not the abolition of property generally, but the abolition of bourgeois property. But modern bourgeois private property is the final and most complete expression of the system of producing and appropriating products, that is based on class antagonisms, on the exploitation of the many by the few.

In this sense, the theory of the communists may be summed up in the single sentence: Abolition of private property.

We communists have been reproached with the desire of abolishing the right of personally acquiring property as the fruit of a man's own labour, which property is alleged to be the groundwork of all personal freedom, activity, and independence.

Hard-won, self-acquired, self-earned property! Do you mean the property of the petty artisan and of the small peasant, a form of property that preceded the bourgeois form? There is no need to abolish that; the development of industry has to a great extent already destroyed it, and is still destroying it daily. Or do you mean modern bourgeois private property?

But does wage-labour create any property for the labourer? Not a bit. It creates capital, i.e., that kind of property which exploits wage-labour, and which cannot increase except upon condition of begetting a new supply of wage-labour for fresh exploitation. Property, in its present form, is based on the antagonism of capital and wage-labour. Let us examine both sides of this antagonism.

To be a capitalist, is to have not only a purely personal, but a social, status in production. Capital is a collective product, and only by the united action of many members, nay, in the last resort, only by the united action of all members of society, can it be set in motion.

Capital is, therefore, not a personal, it is a social power.

When, therefore, capital is converted into common property, into the property of all members of society, personal property is not thereby transformed into social property. It is only the social character of the property that is changed. It loses its class-character.

Let us now take wage-labour.

The average price of wage-labour is the minimum wage, i.e., that quantum of the means of subsistence which is absolutely requisite to keep the labourer in bare existence as a labourer. What, therefore, the wage-labourer appropriates by means of his labour merely suffices to prolong and reproduce a bare existence. We by no means intend to abolish this personal appropriation of the products of labour, an appropriation that is made for the maintenance and reproduction of human life, and that leaves no surplus wherewith to command the labour of others. All that we want to do away with is the miserable character of this appropriation, under which the labourer lives merely to increase capital, and is allowed to live only in so far as the interest of the ruling class requires it. . . .

We have seen above, that the first step in the revolution by the working class is to raise the proletariat to the position of ruling class, to win the battle of democracy.

The proletariat will use its political supremacy to wrest, by degrees, all capital from the bourgeoisie, to centralize all instruments of production in the hands of the state, i.e., of the proletariat organized as the ruling class; and to increase the total of productive forces as rapidly as possible.

Of course, in the beginning this cannot be effected except by means of despotic inroads on the rights of property, and on the conditions of bourgeois production; by means of measures, therefore, which appear economically insufficient and untenable, but which, in the course of the movement, outstrip themselves, necessitate further inroads upon the old social order, and are unavoidable as a means of entirely revolutionizing the mode of production.

These measures will of course be different in different countries.

Nevertheless, in the most advanced countries, the following will be pretty generally applicable.

(1) Abolition of property in land and application of all rents of land to public purposes.

(2) A heavy progressive or graduated income tax.

(3) Abolition of all right of inheritance.

(4) Confiscation of the property of all emigrants and rebels.

(5) Centralization of credit in the hands of the state, by means of a national bank with state capital and an exclusive monopoly.

(6) Centralization of the means of communication and transport in the hands of the state.

(7) Extension of factories and instruments of production owned by the state; the bringing into cultivation of wastelands, and the improvement of the soil generally in accordance with a common plan.

(8) Equal liability of all to labour. Establishment of industrial armies, especially for agriculture.

(9) Combination of agriculture with manufacturing industries; gradual abolition of the distinction between town and country, by a more equable distribution of the population over the country.

(10) Free education for all children in public schools. Abolition of children's factory labour in its present form. Combination of education with industrial production, etc., etc.

When, in the course of development, class distinctions have disappeared, and all production has been concentrated in the hands of associated individuals, the public power will lose its political character. Political power, properly so called, is merely the organized power of one class for oppressing another. If the proletariat during its contest with the bourgeoisie is compelled, by the force of circumstances, to organize itself as a class, if, by means of a revolution, it makes itself the ruling class, and, as such, sweeps away by force the old conditions of production, then it will, along with these conditions, have swept away the conditions for the existence of class antagonisms and of classes generally, and will thereby have abolished its own supremacy as a class.

In place of the old bourgeois society, with its classes and class antagonisms, we shall have an association, in which the free development of each is the condition for the free development of all. . . .

IV

Position of the Communists in Relation to the Various Existing Opposition Parties

Section II has made clear the relation of the communists to the existing working-class parties, such as the Chartists in England and the agrarian reformers in America.

The communists fight for the attainment of the immediate aims for the enforcement of the momentary interests of the working class; but in the movement of the present, they also represent and take care of the future of that movement. In France the communists ally themselves with the social-democrats, against the conservative and radical bourgeoisie, reserving, however, the right to take up a critical position in regard to phrases and illusions traditionally handed down from the great Revolution. . . .

In Germany they fight with the bourgeoisie whenever it acts in a revolutionary way, against the absolute monarchy, the feudal squirearchy, and the petty bourgeoisie.

But they never cease, for a single instant, to instil into the working class the clearest possible recognition of the hostile antagonism between bourgeoisie and proletariat, in order that the German workers may straightaway use, as so many weapons against the bourgeoisie, the social and political conditions that the bourgeoisie must necessarily introduce along with its supremacy, and in order that, after the fall of the reactionary classes in Germany, the fight against the bourgeoisie itself may immediately begin.

The communists turn their attention chiefly to Germany, because that country is on the eve of a bourgeois revolution that is bound to be carried out under more advanced conditions of European civilization, and with a much more developed proletariat, than that of England was in the seventeenth, and of France in the eighteenth century, and because the bourgeois revolution in Germany will be but the prelude to an immediately following proletarian revolution.

In short, the communists everywhere support every revolutionary movement against the existing social and political order of things.

In all these movements they bring to the front, as the leading question in each, the property question, no matter what its degree of development at the time.

Finally, they labour everywhere for the union and agreement of the democratic parties of all countries.

The communists disdain to conceal their views and aims. They openly declare that their ends can be attained only by the forcible overthrow of all existing social conditions. Let the ruling classes tremble at a communistic revolution. The proletarians have nothing to lose but their chains. They have a world to win.

WORKING MEN OF ALL COUNTRIES, UNITE!

Karl Marx (1850)

Extract from: Karl Marx, *Address to the Communist League* (1850)

During the struggle and after the struggle, the workers must, at every opportunity, put forward their own demands alongside the demands of the bourgeois democrats. They must demand guarantees for the workers as soon as the democratic bourgeois set about taking over the government. If necessary they must obtain these guarantees by force, and in general they must see to it that the new rulers pledge themselves to all possible concessions and promises—the surest way to compromise them. In general, they must in every way restrain as far as possible the intoxication of victory and the enthusiasm for the new state of things, which make their appearance after every victorious street battle, by a calm and dispassionate estimate of the situation and by unconcealed mistrust in the new government. Alongside the new official governments they must establish simultaneously their own revolutionary workers' governments, whether in the form of municipal committees and municipal councils or in the form of workers' clubs or workers' committees, so that the bourgeois-democratic governments not only immediately lose the support of the workers but from the outset see themselves supervised and threatened by authorities which are backed by the whole mass of the workers. In a word, from the first moment of victory, mistrust must be directed no longer against the conquered reactionary party, but against the workers' previous allies, against the party that wishes to exploit the common victory for itself alone.

But in order to be able energetically and threateningly to oppose this party, whose treachery to the workers will begin from the first hour of victory, the workers must be armed and organized. The arming of the whole proletariat with rifles, muskets, cannon, and munitions must be put through at once, the revival of the old Citizens' Guard directed against the workers must be resisted. However, where the latter is not feasible the workers must attempt to organize themselves independently as a proletarian guard with commanders elected by themselves and with a general staff of their own choosing, and to put themselves at the command not of the state authority but of the revolutionary community councils which the workers will have managed to get adopted. Where workers are employed at the expense of the state they must see that they are armed and organized in a separate corps with commanders of their own choosing or as part of the proletarian guard. Arms and ammunition must not be surrendered on any pretext; any attempt at disarming must be frustrated, if necessary by force. Destruction of the influence of the bourgeois democrats upon the workers, immediate independent and armed organization of the workers, and the enforcement of conditions as difficult and compromising as possible upon the inevitable momentary rule of the bourgeois democracy—these are the main points which the proletariat and hence the League must keep in view during and after the impending insurrection.

As soon as the new governments have consolidated their positions to some extent, their struggle against the workers will begin. Here, in order to be able to offer energetic opposition to the democratic petty bourgeois, it is above all necessary that the workers shall be independently organized and centralized in clubs. After the overthrow of the existing governments, the Central Committee will, as soon as it is at all possible, betake itself to Germany, immediately convene a congress, and put before the latter the necessary proposals for the centralization of the workers' clubs under a leadership established in the chief seat of the movement. The speedy organization of at least a provincial interlinking of the workers' clubs is one of the most important points for the strengthening and development of the workers' party; the immediate consequence of the overthrow of the existing governments will be the election of a national representative assembly. Here the proletariat must see to it:

(1) That no groups of workers are barred on any pretext or by any kind of trickery on the part of local authorities or government commissioners.

(2) That everywhere workers' candidates are put up alongside the bourgeois-democratic candidates, that they should consist as far as possible of members of the League, and that their election is promoted by all possible means. Even where there is no prospect whatsoever of their being elected, the workers must put up their own candidates in order to preserve their independence, to count their forces, and to bring before the public their revolutionary attitude and party standpoint. . . .

We have seen how the democrats will come to power with the next movement, how they will be compelled to propose more or less socialistic measures. It will be asked what measures the workers ought to propose in reply. At the beginning of the movement, of course, the workers cannot yet propose any directly communistic measures. But they can:

(1) Compel the democrats to interfere in as many spheres as possible of the hitherto existing social order, to disturb its regular course, and to compromise themselves as well as to concentrate the utmost possible productive forces, means of transport, factories, railways, etc., in the hands of the state.

(2) They must drive the proposals of the democrats, who in any case will not act in a revolutionary but in a merely reformist manner, to the extreme and transform them into direct attacks upon private property; thus, for example, if the petty bourgeois propose purchase of the railways and factories, the workers must demand that these railways and factories shall be simply confiscated by the state without compensation as being the property of reactionaries. If the democrats propose proportional taxes, the workers must demand progressive taxes; if the democrats themselves put forward a moderately progressive tax, the workers must insist on a tax with rates that rise so steeply that big capital will be ruined by it; if the democrats demand the regulation of state debts, the workers must demand state bankruptcy. Thus, the demands of the workers must everywhere be governed by the concessions and measures of the democrats.

If the German workers are not able to attain power and achieve their own class interests without completely going through a lengthy revolutionary development, they at least know for a certainty this time that the first act of this approaching revolutionary drama will coincide with the direct victory of their own class in France and will be very much accelerated by it.

But they themselves must do the utmost for their final victory by clarifying their minds as to what their class interests are, by taking up their position as an independent party as soon as possible and by not allowing themselves to be seduced for a single moment by the hypocritical phrases of the democratic petty bourgeois into refraining from the independent organization of the party of the proletariat. Their battle-cry must be: The Revolution in Permanence.

First International (1864)

Extract from the Provisional Rules of the International Working Men's Association (1864)

Considering,

That the emancipation of the working classes must be conquered by the working classes themselves; that the struggle for the emancipation of the working classes means not a struggle for class privileges and monopolies, but for equal rights and duties, and the abolition of all class rule;

That the economical subjection of the man of labour to the monopolizer of the means of labour, that is the sources of life, lies at the bottom of servitude in all its forms, of all social misery, mental degradation, and political dependence;

That the economical emancipation of the working classes is therefore the great end to which every political movement ought to be subordinate as a means;

That all efforts aiming at that great end have hitherto failed from the want of solidarity between the manifold divisions of labour in each country, and from the absence of a fraternal bond of union between the working classes of different countries;

That the emancipation of labour is neither a local nor a national, but a social problem, embracing all countries in which modern society exists, and depending for its solution on the concurrence, practical and theoretical, of the most advanced countries;

That the present revival of the working classes in the most industrious countries of Europe, while it raises a new hope, gives solemn warning against a relapse into the old errors and calls for the immediate combination of the still disconnected movements;

For these reasons:

The undersigned members of the committee, holding its powers by resolution of the public meeting held on Sept. 28, 1864, at St. Martin's Hall, London, have taken the steps necessary for founding the Working Men's International Association.

Karl Marx (1871)

Extract from: Karl Marx, *The Civil War in France* (1871)

Paris, the central seat of the old governmental power, and, at the same time, the social stronghold of the French working class, had risen in arms against the attempt of Thiers and the Rurals to restore and perpetuate that old governmental power bequeathed to them by the empire. Paris could resist only because, in consequence of the siege, it had got rid of the army, and replaced it by a National Guard, the bulk of which consisted of working men. This fact was now to be transformed into an institution. The first decree of the Commune, therefore, was the suppression of the standing army, and the substitution for it of the armed people.

The Commune was formed of the municipal councillors, chosen by universal suffrage in the various wards of the town, responsible and revocable at short terms. The majority of its members were naturally working men, or acknowledged representatives of the working class. The Commune was to be a working, not a parliamentary, body, executive and legislative at the same time. Instead of continuing to be the agent of the central government, the police was at once stripped of its political attributes, and turned into the responsible and at all times revocable agent of the Commune. So were the officials of all other branches of the administration. From the members of the Commune downwards, the public service had to be done at workmen's wages. The vested interests and the representation allowances of the high dignitaries of state disappeared along with the high dignitaries themselves. Public functions ceased to be the private property of the tools of the central government. Not only municipal administration, but the whole initiative hitherto exercised by the state was laid into the hands of the Commune.

Having once got rid of the standing army and the police, the physical force elements of the old government, the Commune was anxious to break the spiritual force of repression, the "parson-power", by the disestablishment and disendowment of all churches as proprietary bodies. The priests were sent back to the recesses of private life, there to feed upon the alms of the faithful in imitation of their predecessors, the Apostles. The whole of the educational institutions were opened to the people gratuitously, and at the same time cleared of all interference of church and state. Thus, not only was education made accessible to all, but science itself freed from the fetters which class prejudice and governmental force had imposed upon it.

The judicial functionaries were to be divested of that sham independence which had but served to mask their abject subserviency to all succeeding governments to which, in turn, they had taken, and broken, the oaths of allegiance. Like the rest of public servants, magistrates and judges were to be elective, responsible, and revocable.

The Paris Commune was, of course, to serve as a model to all the great industrial centres of France. The communal regime once established in Paris and the secondary centres, the old centralized government would in the provinces, too, have to give way to the self-government of the producers. In a rough sketch of national organization which the Commune had no time to develop, it states clearly that the Commune was to be the political form of even the smallest country hamlet, and that in the rural districts the standing army was to be replaced by a national militia, with an extremely short term of service. The rural communes of every district were to administer their common affairs by an assembly of delegates in the central town, and these district assemblies were again to send deputies to the National Delegation in Paris, each delegate to be at any time revocable and bound by the *mandat impératif* [formal instructions] of his constituents. The few but important functions which still would remain for a central government were not to be suppressed, as has been intentionally misstated, but were to be discharged by Communal, and therefore strictly responsible, agents. The unity of the nation was not to be broken but, on the contrary, to be organized by the Communal Constitution and to become a reality by the destruction of the State power which claimed to be the embodiment of that unity independent of, and superior to, the nation itself, from which it was but a parasitic excrescence. While the merely represssive organs of the old governmental power were to be amputated, its legitimate functions were to be wrested from an authority usurping pre-eminence over society itself, and restored to the responsible agents of society. Instead of deciding once in three or six years which member of the ruling class was to misrepresent the people in Parliament, universal suffrage was to serve the people, constituted in Communes, as individual suffrage serves every other employer in the search for the workmen and managers in his business. And it is well known that companies, like individuals, in matters of real business generally know how to put the right man in the right place, and, if they for once make a mistake, to redress it promptly. On the other hand, nothing could be more foreign to the spirit of the Commune than to supersede universal suffrage by hierarchic investiture.

Friedrich Engels (1878)

Extract from: Friedrich Engels, *Herr Eugen Dühring's Revolution in Science* (1878)

Whilst the capitalist mode of production more and more completely transforms the great majority of the population into proletarians, it creates the power which, under penalty of its own destruction, is forced to accomplish this revolution. Whilst it forces on more and more the transformation of the vast means of production, already socialised, into state property, it shows itself the way to accomplishing this revolution. *The proletariat seizes political power and turns the means of production into state property.*

But, in doing this, it abolishes itself as proletariat, abolishes all class distinctions and class antagonisms, abolishes also the state as state. Society thus far, based upon class antagonisms, had need of the state. That is, of an organization of the particular class which was *pro tempore* the exploiting class, an organization for the purpose of preventing any interference from without with the existing conditions of production, and, therefore, especially, for the purpose of forcibly keeping the exploited classes in the condition of oppression corresponding with the given mode of production (slavery, serfdom, wage labour). The state was the official representative of society as a whole; the gathering of it together into a visible embodiment. But it was this only in so far as it was the state of that class which itself represented, for the time being, society as a whole: in ancient times, the state of slaveowning citizens; in the Middle Ages, the feudal lords; in our own time, the bourgeoisie. When at last it becomes the real representative of the whole of society, it renders itself unnecessary. As soon as there is no longer any social class to be held in subjection; as soon as class rule, and the individual struggle for existence based upon our present anarchy in production, with the collisions and excesses arising from these, are removed, nothing more remains to be repressed, and a special repressive force, a state, is no longer necessary. The first act by virtue of which the state really constitutes itself the representative of the whole of society—the taking possession of the means of production in the name of society—this is, at the same time, its last independent act as a state. State interference in social relations becomes, in one domain after another, superfluous, and then dies out of itself; the government of persons is replaced by the administration of things and by the conduct of processes of production. The state is not "abolished". *It withers away.* This gives the measure of the value of the phrase "*a free state*", both as to its justifiable use at times by agitators and as to its ultimate scientific insufficiency; and also of the demands of the so-called anarchists for the abolition of the state out of hand.

Friedrich Engels (1895)

Extract from the Preface by Friedrich Engels to the 1895 edition of Marx's *The Class Struggles in France*

The war of 1870/71 and the defeat of the Commune had transferred the centre of gravity of the European workers' movement for the time being from France to

Germany, as Marx foretold. In France it naturally took years to recover from the bloodletting of May 1871. In Germany, on the other hand, where industry was, in addition, furthered (in positively hot-house fashion) by the blessing of the French milliards [i.e. war reparations] and developed more and more quickly, social democracy experienced a much more rapid and enduring growth. Thanks to the understanding with which the German workers made use of the universal suffrage introduced in 1866, the astonishing growth of the party is made plain to all the world by incontestable figures: 1871, 102,000; 1874, 352,000; 1877, 493,000 Social Democratic votes. Then came recognition of this advance by high authority in the shape of the Anti-Socialist Law: the party was temporarily disrupted; the number of votes sank to 312,000 in 1881. But that was quickly overcome, and then, though oppressed by the Exceptional Law, without press, without external organization, and without the right of combination or meeting, the rapid expansion really began: 1884, 550,000; 1887, 763,000; 1890, 1,427,000 votes. Then the hand of the state was paralysed. The Anti-Socialist Law disappeared; socialist votes rose to 1,787,000, over a quarter of all the votes cast. The government and the ruling classes had exhausted all their expedients—uselessly, to no purpose, and without success. The tangible proofs of their importance, which the authorities, from night watchman to the imperial chancellor, had had to accept—and that from the despised workers—these proofs were counted in millions. The state was at the end of its Latin, the workers only at the beginning of theirs.

But the German workers did a second great service to their cause in addition to the first, which they rendered by their mere existence as the strongest, best disciplined, and most rapidly growing socialist party. They supplied their comrades of all countries with a new weapon, and one of the sharpest, when they showed them how to use universal suffrage.

There had long been universal suffrage in France, but it had fallen into disrepute through the misuse to which the Bonapartist government had put it. After the Commune there was no workers' party to make use of it. Also in Spain it had existed since the republic, but in Spain boycott of the elections was ever the rule of all serious opposition parties. The Swiss experiences of universal suffrage, also, were anything but encouraging for a workers' party. The revolutionary workers of the Latin countries had been wont to regard the suffrage as a snare, as an instrument of government trickery. It was otherwise in Germany. *The Communist Manifesto* had already proclaimed the winning of universal suffrage, of democracy, as one of the first and most important tasks of the militant proletariat, and Lassalle had again taken up this point. When Bismarck found himself compelled to introduce the franchise as the only means of interesting the mass of the people in his plans, our workers immediately took it in earnest and sent August Bebel to the first constituent Reichstag. And from that day on they have used the franchise in a way which has paid them a thousandfold and has served as a model to the workers of all countries. The franchise has been, in the words of the French Marxist programme, *"transformé, de moyen de duperie qu'il a été jusqu'ici, en instrument d'émancipation"*—they have transformed it from a means of deception, which it was heretofore, into an instrument of emancipation. And if universal suffrage had offered no other advantage than that it allowed us to count our numbers every three years; that by the regularly established, unexpectedly rapid rise in the number of votes it increased in equal measure the workers' certainty of victory and the dismay of their opponents, and so became our best means of propaganda; that it accurately informed us concerning our own strength and that of all hostile parties, and thereby provided us with a measure of proportion for our actions second to none, safeguarding us from untimely timidity as much as from untimely foolhardiness—if this had been the only advantage we gained from the suffrage, then it would still have been more than enough. But it has done much more than this. In election agitation it provided us with a means, second to none, of getting in touch with the mass of the people, where they still stand aloof from us; of forcing all parties to defend their views and actions against our attacks before all the people; and further, it opened to our representatives in the Reichstag a platform from which they could speak to their opponents in Parliament and to the masses without, with quite other authority and freedom than in the press or at meetings. Of what avail to the government and the bourgeoisie was their Anti-Socialist Law when election agitation and socialist speeches in the Reichstag continually broke through it?

With this successful utilization of universal suffrage, an entirely new mode of proletarian struggle came into force, and this quickly developed further. It was found that the state institutions, in which the rule of the bourgeoisie is organized, offer still further opportunities for the working class to fight these very state institutions. They took part in elections to individual diets, to municipal councils and to industrial courts; they contested every post against the bourgeoisie in the occupation of which a sufficient part of the proletariat had its say. And so it happened that the bourgeoisie and the government came to be much more afraid of the legal than of the illegal action of the workers' party, of the results of elections than of those of rebellion.

For here, too, the conditions of the struggle had essentially changed. Rebellion in the old style, the street fight with barricades, which up to 1848 gave everywhere the final decision, was to a considerable extent obsolete. . . . If the conditions have changed in the case of war between nations, this is no less true in the case of the class struggle. The time of surprise attacks, of revolutions carried through by small conscious minorities at the head of unconscious masses, is past. Where it is a question of complete transformation of the social organization, the masses themselves must also be in it, must themselves already have grasped what is at stake, what they are going in for with body and soul. The history of the last 50 years has taught us that. But in order that the masses may understand what is to be done, long, persistent work is required, and it is just this work which we are now pursuing, and with a success which drives the enemy to despair.

Eduard Bernstein (1899)

Extract from: Eduard Bernstein, *Evolutionary Socialism* (1899)

I set myself against the notion that we have to expect shortly a collapse of the bourgeois economy, and that social democracy should be induced by the prospect of such an imminent, great, social catastrophe to adapt its tactics to that assumption. That I maintain most emphatically.

The adherents of this theory of a catastrophe, base it especially on the conclusions of *The Communist Manifesto*. This is a mistake in every respect.

The theory which *The Communist Manifesto* sets forth of the evolution of modern society was correct as far as it characterized the general tendencies of that evolution. But it was mistaken in several special deductions, above all in the estimate of the *time* the evolution would take. The last has been unreservedly acknowledged by Friedrich Engels, the joint author with Marx of the *Manifesto*, in his preface to *The Class Struggles in France*. But it is evident that if social evolution takes a much greater period of time than was assumed, it must also take upon itself *forms* and lead to forms that were not foreseen and could not be foreseen then.

Social conditions have not developed to such an acute opposition of things and classes as is depicted in the *Manifesto*. It is not only useless, it is the greatest folly to attempt to conceal this from ourselves. The number of members of the possessing classes is today not smaller but larger. The enormous increase of social wealth is not accompanied by a decreasing number of large capitalists but by an increasing number of capitalists of all degrees. The middle classes change their character but they do not disappear from the social scale.

The concentration in productive industry is not being accomplished even today in all its departments with equal thoroughness and at an equal rate. In a great many branches of production it certainly justifies the forecasts of the socialist critic of society; but in other branches it lags even today behind them. The process of concentration in agriculture proceeds still more slowly. Trade statistics show an extraordinarily elaborated graduation of enterprises in regard to size. No rung of the ladder is disappearing from it. The significant changes in the inner structure of these enterprises and their interrelationship cannot do away with this fact.

In all advanced countries we see the privileges of the capitalist bourgeoisie yielding step by step to democratic organizations. Under the influence of this, and driven by the movement of the working classes which is daily becoming stronger, a social reaction has set in against the exploiting tendencies of capital, a counteraction which, although it still proceeds timidly and feebly, yet does exist, and is always drawing more departments of economic life under its influence. Factory legislation, the democratizing of local government, and the extension of its area of work, the freeing of trade unions and systems of co-operative trading from legal restrictions, the consideration of standard conditions of labour in the work undertaken by public authorities—all these characterize this phase of the evolution.

But the more the political organizations of modern nations are democratized the more the needs and opportunities of great political catastrophes are diminished. He who holds firmly to the catastrophic theory of evolution must, with all his power, withstand and hinder the evolution described above, which, indeed, the logical defenders of that theory formerly did. But is the conquest of political power by the proletariat simply to be by a political catastrophe? Is it to be the appropriation and utilization of the power of the state by the proletariat exclusively against the whole non-proletarian world? . . . Universal suffrage is only a part of democracy, although a part which in time must draw the other parts after it as the magnet attracts to itself the scattered portions of iron. It certainly proceeds more slowly than many would wish, but in spite of that it is at work. And social democracy cannot further this work better than by taking its stand unreservedly on the theory of democracy—on the ground of universal suffrage with all the consequences resulting therefrom to its tactics.

In practice—that is, in its actions—it has in Germany always done so. But in their explanations its literary advocates have often acted otherwise, and still often do so to today. Phrases which were composed in a time when the political privilege of property ruled all over Europe, and which under these circumstances were explanatory, and to a certain degree also justified, but which today are only a dead weight, are treated with such reverence as though the progress of the movement depended on them and not on the understanding of what can be done, and what should be done. Is there any sense, for example, in maintaining the phrase of the "dictatorship of the proletariat" at a time when in all possible places representatives of social democracy have placed themselves practically in the arena of parliamentary work, have declared for the proportional representation of the people, and for direct legislation—all of which is inconsistent with a dictatorship?

The phrase is today so antiquated that it is only to be reconciled with reality by stripping the word dictatorship of its actual meaning and attaching to it some kind of weakened interpretation. The whole practical activity of social democracy is directed towards creating circumstances and conditions which shall render possible and secure a transition (free from convulsive outbursts) of the modern social order into a higher one. From the consciousness of being the pioneers of a higher civilization, its adherents are ever creating fresh inspiration and zeal. In this rests also, finally, the moral justification of the socialist expropriation towards which they aspire. But the "dictatorship of the classes" belongs to a lower civilization, and apart from the question of the expediency and practicability of the thing, it is only to be looked upon as a reversion, as political atavism. If the thought is aroused that the transition from a capitalist to a socialist society must necessarily be accomplished by means of the development of forms of an age which did not know at all, or only in quite an imperfect form, the present methods of the initiating and carrying of laws, and which was without the organs fit for the purpose, reaction will set in.

V. I. Lenin (1902)

Extract from: V. I. Lenin, *What is to be Done?* (1902)

I assert: (i) that no movement can be durable without a stable organization of leaders to maintain continuity; (ii) that the more widely the masses are drawn into the struggle and form the basis of the movement, the more necessary is it to have such an organization and the more stable must it be (for it is much easier then for demagogues to sidetrack the more backward sections of the masses); (iii) that the organization must consist chiefly of persons engaged in revolution as a profession; (iv) that in a country with a despotic government, the more we *restrict* the membership of this organization to persons who are engaged in revolution as a profession and who have been professionally trained in the art of combating the political police, the more difficult will it be to catch the organization; and (v) the *wider* will be the circle of men and women of the working class or of other classes of society able to join the movement and perform active work in it. . . .

The question in the last analysis, amounts to the question we have considered above, namely, whether it is possible to have a mass *organization* when the maintenance of strict secrecy is essential. We can never give a mass organization that degree of secrecy which is essential for the persistent and continuous struggle against the government. But to concentrate all secret functions in the hands of as small a number of professional revolutionists as possible, does not mean that the latter will "do the thinking for all" and that the crowd will not take an active part in the movement. On the contrary, the crowd will advance from its ranks increasing numbers of professional revolutionists, for it will know that it is not enough for a few students and workingmen waging economic war to gather together and form a "committee", but that professional revolutionists must be trained for years; the crowd will "think" not of primitive ways but of training professional revolutionists. The centralization of the secret functions of the *organization* does not mean the concentration of all the functions of the *movement*. The active participation of the greatest masses in the dissemination of illegal literature will not diminish because a dozen professional revolutionists concentrate in their hands the secret part of the work; on the contrary, it will *increase tenfold*. Only in this way will the reading of illegal literature, the contribution to illegal literature, and to some extent even the distribution of illegal literature *almost cease to be secret work*, for the police will soon come to realise the folly and futility of setting the whole judicial and administrative machine into motion to intercept every copy of a publication that is being broadcast in thousands. This applies not only to the press, but to every function of the movement, even to demonstrations. The active and widespread participation of the masses will not suffer; on the contrary, it will benefit by the fact that a "dozen" experienced revolutionists, no less professionally trained than the police, will concentrate all the secret side of the work in their hands—prepare leaflets, work out approximate plans, and appoint bodies of leaders for each town district, for each factory district, and for each educational institution (I know that exception will be taken to my "undemocratic" views, but I shall reply to this altogether unintelligent objection later on). The centralization of the more secret functions in an organization of revolutionists will not diminish, but rather increase the extent and the quality of the activity of a large number of other organizations intended for wide membership and which, therefore, can be as loose and as public as possible, for example, trade unions, workers' circles for self-education and the reading of illegal literature, and socialist, and also democratic, circles for *all other sections of the population*, etc. We must have *as large a number as possible* of such organizations having the widest possible variety of functions, but it is absurd and dangerous to *confuse these with organizations of revolutionists*, to erase the line of demarcation between them, to dim still more the already incredibly hazy appreciation by the masses that to "serve" the mass movement we must have people who will devote themselves exclusively to social-democratic activities, and that such people must *train* themselves patiently and steadfastly to be professional revolutionists.

Rosa Luxemburg (1918)

Extract from: Rosa Luxemburg, *The Russian Revolution* (1918)

Lenin says: the bourgeois state is an instrument of oppression of the working class; the socialist state, of the bourgeoisie. To a certain extent, he says, it is only the capitalist state stood on its head. This simplified view misses the most essential thing: bourgeois class rule has no need of the political training and education of the entire mass of the people, at least not beyond certain narrow limits. But for the proletarian dictatorship, that is the life element, the very air without which it is not able to exist.

"Thanks to the open and direct struggle for governmental power," writes Trotsky, "the labouring masses accumulate in the shortest time a considerable amount of political experience and advance quickly from one stage to another of their development."

Here Trotsky refutes himself and his own friends. Just because this is so, they have blocked up the fountain of political experience and the source of this rising development by their suppression of public life! Or else we would have to assume that experience and development were necessary up to the seizure of power by the Bolsheviks, and then, having reached their highest peak, became superfluous thereafter.

In reality, the opposite is true! It is the very giant tasks which the Bolsheviks have undertaken with courage and determination that demand the most intensive political training of the masses and the accumulation of experience.

Freedom only for the supporters of the government, only for the members of one party, however numerous they may be, is no freedom at all. Freedom is always and exclusively freedom for the one who thinks differently. Not because of any fanatical concept of "justice" but because all that is instructive, wholesome, and purifying in political freedom depends on this essential characteristic, and its effectiveness vanishes when "freedom" becomes a special privilege.

The Bolsheviks themselves will not want, with hand on heart, to deny that, step by step, they have to feel out the ground, try out, experiment, test now one way now another, and that a good many of their measures do not represent priceless pearls of wisdom. Thus it must and will be with all of us when we get to the same point, even if the same difficult circumstances may not prevail everywhere.

The tacit assumption underlying the Lenin-Trotsky theory of the dictatorship is this: that the socialist transformation is something for which a ready-made formula lies completed in the pocket of the revolutionary party, which needs only to be carried out energetically in practice. This is, unfortunately—or perhaps fortunately—not the case. Far from being a sum of ready-made prescriptions which have only to be applied, the practical realization of socialism as an economic, social, and juridical system is something which lies completely hidden in the mists of the future. What we possess in our programme is nothing but a few main signposts which indicate the general direction in which to look for the necessary measures, and the indications are mainly negative in character, at that. Thus we know more or less what we must eliminate at the outset in order to free the road for a socialist economy. But when it comes to the nature of the thousand concrete, practical measures, large and small, necessary to introduce socialist principles into economy, law, and all social relationships, there is no key in any socialist party programme or textbook. That is not a shortcoming but rather the very thing that makes scientific socialism superior to the utopian varieties. The socialist system of society should only be, and can only be, an historical product, born out of the school of its own experiences, born in the course of its realization, as a result of the developments of living history, which—just like organic nature, of which, in the last analysis, it forms a part— has the fine habit of always producing along with any real social need the means to its satisfaction, along with the task simultaneously the solution.

If such is the case, however, then it is clear that socialism by its very nature cannot be decreed or introduced by *ukase*. It has as its prerequisite a number of measures of force against property, etc. The negative, the tearing down, can be decreed; the building up, the positive, cannot. New territory. A thousand problems. Only experience is capable of correcting and opening new ways. Only unobstructed, effervescing life falls into a thousand new forms and improvisations, brings to light creative force, itself corrects all mistaken attempts. The public life of countries with limited freedom is so poverty-stricken, so miserable, so rigid, so unfruitful, precisely because, through the exclusion of democracy, it cuts off the living sources of all spiritual riches and progress (proof: the year 1905 and the months from February to October 1917). There it was political in character; the same thing applies to economic and social life also. The whole mass of the people must take part in it. Otherwise, socialism will be decreed from behind a few official desks by a dozen intellectuals.

Public control is indispensably necessary. Otherwise the exchange of experiences remains only with the closed circle of the officials of the new regime. Corruption becomes inevitable. Lenin's words, Bulletin No. 29: Socialism in life demands a complete spiritual transformation in the masses degraded by centuries of bourgeois class rule. Social instincts in place of egotistical ones, mass initiative in place of inertia, idealism which conquers all suffering, etc., etc. No one knows this better, describes it more penetratingly, repeats it more stubbornly than Lenin. But he is completely mistaken in the means he employs. Decree, dictatorial force of the factory overseer, draconic penalties, rule by terror—all these things are but palliatives. The only way to a rebirth is the school of public life itself, the most unlimited, the broadest democracy and public opinion. It is rule by terror which demoralizes.

When all this is eliminated, what really remains? In place of the representative bodies created by general, popular elections, Lenin and Trotsky have laid down the soviets as the only true representation of the labouring masses. But with the repression of political life in the land as a whole, life in the soviets must also become more and more crippled. Without general elections, without unrestricted freedom of press and assembly, without a free struggle of opinion, life dies out in every public institution, becomes a mere semblance of life, in which only the bureaucracy remains as the active element. Public life gradually falls asleep, a few dozen party leaders of inexhaustible energy and boundless experience direct and rule. Among them, in reality only a dozen outstanding heads do the leading, and an elite of the working class is invited from time to time to meetings where they are to applaud the speeches of the leaders and to approve proposed resolutions unanimously—at bottom, then, a clique affair—a dictatorship, to be sure, not the dictatorship of the proletariat, however, but only the dictatorship of a handful of politicians, that is a dictatorship in the bourgeois sense, in the sense of the rule of the Jacobins (the postponement of the Soviet Congress from three-month periods to six-month periods!). Yes, we can go even further: such conditions must inevitably cause a brutalization of public life: attempted assassinations, shooting of hostages, and other violence.

V. I. Lenin (1920)

Extract from: V. I. Lenin, *"Left-Wing" Communism: An Infantile Disorder* (1920)

To carry on a war for the overthrow of the international bourgeoisie, a war which is a hundred times more difficult, protracted and complicated than the most stubborn of ordinary wars between states, and to refuse beforehand to manoeuvre, to utilize the conflict of interests (even though temporary) among one's enemies, to refuse to temporize and compromise with possible (even though temporary, unstable, vacillating and conditional) allies—is not this ridiculous in the extreme? Is it not as though, when making a difficult ascent of an unexplored and hitherto inaccessible mountain, we were to refuse beforehand ever to move in zigzags, ever to retrace our steps, ever to abandon the course once selected to try others? And yet people who are so ignorant and inexperienced (if youth were the explanation, it would not be so bad; young people are ordained by God himself to talk such nonsense for a period) could meet with the support—whether direct or indirect, open or covert, whole or partial, does not matter—of certain members of the Dutch Communist Party!

After the first socialist revolution of the proletariat, after the overthrow of the bourgeoisie in one country, the proletariat of that country *for a long time* remains *weaker* than the bourgeoisie, simply because of the latter's extensive international connections, and also because of the spontaneous and continuous restoration and regeneration of capitalism and the bourgeoisie by the small commodity-producers of the country which has overthrown the bourgeoisie. The more powerful enemy can be conquered only by exerting the utmost effort, and by *necessarily*, thoroughly, carefully, attentively and skilfully taking advantage of every, even the smallest, "rift" among the enemies, of every antagonism of interest among the bourgeoisie of the various countries and among the various groups or types of bourgeoisie within the various countries, by taking advantage of every, even the smallest, opportunity of gaining a mass ally, even though this ally be temporary, vacillating, unstable, unreliable and conditional. Those who do not understand this do not understand even a particle of Marxism, or of scientific, modern socialism *in general*. Those who have not proved by *deeds* over a fairly considerable period of time, and in fairly varied political situations, their ability to apply this truth in practice have not yet learned to assist the revolutionary class in its struggle for the emancipation of toiling humanity from the exploiters. And this applies equally to the period before and to the period after the conquest of political power by the proletariat. . . .

Capitalism would not be capitalism if the "pure" proletariat were not surrounded by a large number of exceedingly motley types intermediate between the proletarian and the semiproletarian (who earns his livelihood in part by the sale of his labour power), between the semiproletarian and the small peasant (and petty artisan, handicraft worker, and small master in general), between the small peasant and the middle peasant, and so on, and if the proletariat itself were not divided into more developed and less developed strata, if it were not divided according to territorial origin, trade, sometimes according to religion, and so on. And from all this follows the necessity, the absolute necessity, for the vanguard of the proletariat, for its class-conscious section, for the Communist Party, to resort to manoeuvres, arrangements, and compromises with the various groups of proletarians, with the various parties of the workers and small masters. The whole point lies in *knowing how* to apply these tactics in order to *raise*, and not lower, the *general* level of proletarian class consciousness, revolutionary spirit, and ability to fight and win. . . .

In Western Europe and America, parliament has become especially abhorrent to the advanced revolutionary members of the working class. That is incontestable. It is quite comprehensible, for it is difficult to imagine anything more vile, abominable and treacherous than the behaviour of the vast majority of the socialist and social democratic parliamentary deputies during and after the war. But it would be not only unreasonable, but actually criminal to yield to this mood when deciding *how* this generally recognized evil should be fought. In many countries of Western Europe, the revolutionary mood, we might say, is at present a "novelty", or a "rarity", which had been all too long waited for vainly and impatiently; and perhaps that is why the mood is so easily succumbed to. Certainly, without a revolutionary mood among the masses, and without conditions facilitating the growth of this mood, revolutionary tactics would never be converted into action; but we in Russia have become convinced by very long, painful, and bloody experience of the truth that revolutionary tactics cannot be built on revolutionary moods alone. Tactics must be based on a sober and strictly objective appraisal of *all* the class forces of the particular state (and of the states that surround it, and of all states the world over) as well as of the experience of revolutionary movements. To show how "revolutionary" one is solely by hurling abuse at parliamentary opportunism, solely by repudiating participation in parliaments, is very easy; but just because it is too easy, it is not the solution for a difficult, a very difficult problem. It is much more difficult to create a really revolutionary parliamentary group in a European parliament than it was in Russia. Of course. But that is only a particular expression of the general truth that it was easy for Russia, in the specific, historically very unique situation of 1917, to *start* the socialist revolution, but it will be more difficult for Russia than for the European countries to *continue* the revolution and bring it to its consummation.

I had occasion to point this out already at the beginning of 1918, and our experience of the past two years has entirely confirmed the correctness of this view. Certain specific conditions, viz., (i) the possibility of linking up the Soviet revolution with the ending, as a consequence of this revolution, of the imperialist war, which had exhausted the workers and peasants to an incredible degree; (ii) the possibility of taking advantage for a certain time of the mortal conflict between two world-powerful groups of imperialist robbers, who were unable to unite against their Soviet enemy; (iii) the possibility of enduring a comparatively lengthy civil war, partly owing to the enormous size of the country and to the poor means of communications; (iv) the existence of such a profound bourgeois-democratic revolutionary movement among the peasantry that the party of the proletariat was able to take the revolutionary demands of the peasant party (the Socialist Revolutionary Party, the majority of the members of which were definitely hostile to Bolshevism) and realize them at once, thanks to the conquest of political power by the proletariat—these specific conditions do not exist in Western Europe at present; and a repetition of such or similar conditions will not come so easily. That, by the way, apart from a number of other causes, is why it will be more difficult for Western Europe to *start* a socialist revolution than it was for us. To attempt to "circumvent" this difficulty by "skipping" the difficult job of utilizing reactionary parliaments for revolutionary purposes is absolutely childish. You want to create a new society, yet you fear the difficulties involved in forming a good parliamentary group, made up of convinced, devoted, heroic communists, in a reactionary parliament! Is that not childish? If Karl Liebknecht in Germany and Z. Höglund in Sweden were able, even without mass support from below, to set examples in the truly revolutionary utilization of reactionary parliaments, how can one say that a rapidly growing revolutionary, mass party, in the midst of the postwar disillusionment and embitterment of the masses, cannot *hammer out* a communist group in the worst of parliaments?! Precisely because the backward masses of the workers and—to an even greater degree—of the small peasants are in Western Europe much more imbued with bourgeois-democratic and parliamentary prejudices than they were in Russia, precisely because of that, it is *only* from within such institutions as bourgeois parliaments that communists can (and must) wage a long and persistent struggle, undaunted by any difficulties, to expose, dissipate and overcome these prejudices.

Communist International (1920)

From the Statutes of the Communist International, adopted at the Second Congress of the Communist International, Moscow, July–August 1920

"Remember the imperialist war!" These are the first words addressed by the Communist International to every working man and woman, wherever they live and whatever language they speak. Remember that because of the existence of capitalist society a handful of imperialists were able to force the workers of the different countries for four long years to cut each other's throats. Remember that the war of the bourgeoisie conjured up in Europe and throughout the world the most frightful famine and the most appalling misery. Remember that without the overthrow of capitalism, the repetition of such robber wars is not only possible, but inevitable.

It is the aim of the Communist International to fight by all available means, including armed struggle, for the overthrow of the international bourgeoisie and for the creation of an international Soviet republic as a transitional stage to the complete abolition of the State. The Communist International considers the dictatorship of the proletariat the only possible way to liberate mankind from the horrors of capitalism. And the Communist International considers the Soviet power the historically given form of this dictatorship of the proletariat.

The imperialist war bound the destinies of the proletariat of each country very closely to the destinies of the proletariat of all other countries. The imperialist war once again confirmed what was written in the Statutes of the First International: the emancipation of the workers is not a local, nor a national, but an international problem.

The Communist International breaks once and for all with the traditions of the Second International, for whom in fact only white-skinned people existed. The task of the Communist International is to liberate the working people of the entire world. In its ranks, the white, the yellow and the black-skinned peoples—the working people of the entire world—are fraternally united.

The Communist International supports to the full the conquests of the great proletarian revolution in Russia, the first victorious Socialist revolution in world history, and calls on the proletariat of the entire world to take the same path. The Communist International undertakes to support every Soviet republic, wherever it may be formed.

The Communist International recognizes that in order to hasten victory, the Working Men's Association, which is fighting to annihilate capitalism and create communism, must have a strongly centralized organization. The Communist International must, in fact and in deed, be a single communist party of the entire world. The parties working in the various countries are but its separate sections. The organizational machinery of the Communist International must guarantee the workers of each country the opportunity of getting the utmost help from the organized proletariat of other countries at any given moment.

Conditions of Adherence to the Communist International, adopted at the Second Congress of the Communist International, Moscow, July–August 1920

---

(1) All propaganda and agitation must be of a genuinely communist character and in conformity with the programme and decisions of the Communist International. The entire party press must be run by reliable communists who have proved their devotion to the cause of the proletariat. The dictatorship of the proletariat is to be treated not simply as a current formula learned by rote; it must be advocated in a way which makes its necessity comprehensible to every ordinary working man and woman, every soldier and peasant, from the facts of their daily life, which must be systematically noted in our press and made use of every day.

The periodical press and other publications, and all party publishing houses, must be completely subordinated to the party Presidium, regardless of whether the party as a whole is at the given moment legal or illegal. Publishing houses must not be allowed to abuse their independence and pursue a policy which is not wholly in accordance with the policy of the party.

In the columns of the press, at popular meetings, in the trade unions and co-operatives, wherever the adherents of the Communist International have an entry, it is necessary to denounce, systematically and unrelentingly, not only the bourgeoisie, but also their assistants, the reformists of all shades.

(2) Every organization which wishes to join the Communist International must, in an orderly and planned fashion, remove reformists and centrists from all responsible positions in the workers' movement (party organizations, editorial boards, trade unions, parliamentary fractions, co-operatives, local government bodies) and replace them by tried communists, even if, particularly at the beginning, "experienced" opportunists have to be replaced by ordinary rank and file workers.

(3) In practically every country of Europe and America the class struggle is entering the phase of civil war. In these circumstances communists can have no confidence in bourgeois legality. They are obliged everywhere to create a parallel illegal organization which at the decisive moment will help the party to do its duty to the revolution. In all those countries where, because of a state of siege or of emergency laws, communists are unable to do all their work legally, it is absolutely essential to combine legal and illegal work.

(4) The obligation to spread communist ideas includes the special obligation to carry on systematic and energetic propaganda in the army. Where such agitation is prevented by emergency laws, it must be carried on illegally. Refusal to undertake such work would be tantamount to a dereliction of revolutionary duty and is incompatible with membership of the Communist International.

(5) Systematic and well-planned agitation must be carried on in the countryside. The working class cannot consolidate its victory if it has not by its policy assured itself of the support of at least part of the rural proletariat and the poorest peasants, and of the neutrality of part of the rest of the rural population. At the present time communist work in rural areas is acquiring first-rate importance. It should be conducted primarily with the help of revolutionary communist urban and rural workers who have close connections with the countryside. To neglect this work, or to leave it in unreliable semi-reformist hands, is tantamount to renouncing the proletarian revolution.

(6) Every party which wishes to join the Communist International is obliged to expose not only avowed social-patriotism, but also the insincerity and hypocrisy of social-pacifism; to bring home to the workers systematically that without the revolutionary overthrow of capitalism no international court of arbitration, no agreement to limit armaments, no "democratic" reorganization of the League of Nations, will be able to prevent new imperialist wars.

(7) Parties which wish to join the Communist International are obliged to recognize the necessity for a complete and absolute break with reformism and with the policy of the "centre", and to advocate this break as widely as possible among their members. Without that no consistent communist policy is possible.

The Communist International demands unconditionally and categorically that this break be effected as quickly as possible. The Communist International is unable to agree that notorious opportunists, such as Turati, Modigliani, Kautsky, Hilferding, Hilquit, Longuet, MacDonald, etc., shall have the right to appear as members of the Communist International. That could only lead to the Communist International becoming in many respects similar to the Second International, which has gone to pieces.

(8) A particularly explicit and clear attitude on the question of the colonies and the oppressed peoples is necessary for the parties in those countries where the

bourgeoisie possess colonies and oppress other nations. Every party which wishes to join the Communist International is obliged to expose the tricks and dodges of "its" imperialists in the colonies, to support every colonial liberation movement not merely in words but in deeds, to demand the expulsion of their own imperialists from these colonies, to inculcate among the workers of their country a genuinely fraternal attitude to the working people of the colonies and the oppressed nations, and to carry on systematic agitation among the troops of their country against any oppression of the colonial peoples.

(9) Every party which wishes to join the Communist International must carry on systematic and persistent communist activity inside the trade unions, the workers' councils and factory committees, the co-operatives, and other mass workers' organizations. Within these organizations communist cells must be organized which shall by persistent and unflagging work win the trade unions, etc., for the communist cause. In their daily work the cells must everywhere expose the treachery of the social-patriots and the instability of the "centre". The communist cells must be completely subordinate to the party as a whole.

(10) Every party belonging to the Communist International is obliged to wage an unyielding struggle against the Amsterdam "International" of the yellow trade unions. It must conduct the most vigorous propaganda among trade unionists for the necessity of a break with the yellow Amsterdam International. It must do all it can to support the International Association of Red Trade Unions, adhering to the Communist International, which is being formed.

(11) Parties which wish to join the Communist International are obliged to review the personnel of their parliamentary fractions and remove all unreliable elements, to make these fractions not only verbally but in fact subordinate to the party Presidium, requiring of each individual communist member of parliament that he subordinate his entire activity to the interests of genuinely revolutionary propaganda and agitation.

(12) Parties belonging to the Communist International must be based on the principle of *democratic centralism*. In the present epoch of acute civil war the communist party will be able to fulfil its duty only if its organization is as centralized as possible, if iron discipline prevails, and if the party centre, upheld by the confidence of the party membership, has strength and authority and is equipped with the most comprehensive powers.

(13) Communist parties in those countries where communists carry on their work legally must from time to time undertake cleansing (re-registration) of the membership of the party in order to get rid of any petty-bourgeois elements which have crept in.

(14) Every party which wishes to join the Communist International is obliged to give unconditional support to any Soviet republic in its struggle against counter-revolutionary forces. Communist parties must carry on unambiguous propaganda to prevent the dispatch of munitions transports to the enemies of the Soviet republics; they must also carry on propaganda by every means, legal or illegal, among the troops sent to strangle workers' republics.

(15) Parties which still retain their old social democratic programmes are obliged to revise them as quickly as possible, and to draw up, in accordance with the special conditions of their country, a new communist programme in conformity with the decisions of the Communist International. As a rule the programme of every party belonging to the Communist International must be ratified by the regular congress of the Communist International or by the Executive Committee. Should the programme of a party not be ratified by the ECCI, the party concerned has the right to appeal to the congress of the Communist International.

(16) All the decisions of the congresses of the Communist International, as well as the decisions of its Executive Committee, are binding on all parties belonging to the Communist International. The Communist International, working in conditions of acute civil war, must be far more centralized in its structure than was the Second International. Consideration must of course be given by the Communist International and its Executive Committee in all their activities to the varying conditions in which the individual parties have to fight and work, and they must take decisions of general validity only when such decisions are possible.

(17) In this connection, all parties which wish to join the Communist International must change their names. Every party which wishes to join the Communist International must be called *Communist* Party of such and such a country (section of the Communist International). This question of name is not merely a formal matter, but essentially a political question of great importance. The Communist International has declared war on the entire bourgeois world and on all yellow social democratic parties. The difference between the communist parties and the old official "social democratic" or "socialist" parties, which have betrayed the banner of the working class, must be brought home to every ordinary worker.

(18) All leading party press organs in all countries are obliged to publish all important official documents of the Executive Committee of the Communist International.

(19) All parties belonging to the Communist International, and those which have applied for admission, are obliged to convene an extraordinary congress as soon as possible, and in any case not later than four months after the second congress of the Communist International, to examine all these conditions of admission. In this connection all party centres must see that the decisions of the second congress of the Communist International are made known to all local organizations.

(20) Those parties which now wish to join the Communist International, but which have not radically changed their former tactics, must see to it that, before entering the Communist International, not less than two-thirds of the members of their central committee and of all their leading central bodies consist of comrades who publicly and unambiguously advocated the entry of their party into the Communist International before its second congress. Exceptions can be made with the consent of the Executive Committee of the Communist International. The ECCI also has the right to make exceptions in the case of representatives of the centre mentioned in paragraph 7.

(21) Those members of the party who reject in principle the conditions and theses put forward by the Communist International are to be expelled from the party.

The same applies in particular to delegates to the extraordinary congresses.

V. I. Lenin (1922 & 1923)

Extract from: V. I. Lenin, *Letter to the Congress* ("Lenin's Testament")

Our party relies on two classes, and therefore its instability would be possible and its downfall inevitable if there were no agreement between those two classes.

In that event this or that measure, and generally all talk about the stability of our Central Committee (CC), would be futile. No measures of any kind would be able to prevent a split in such a case. But I hope that this is too remote a future and too improbable an event to talk about it.

I have in mind stability as a guarantee against a split in the immediate future, and I intend to deal here with a few ideas concerning personal qualities.

I think from this standpoint the prime factors in the question of stability are such members of the CC as Stalin and Trotsky. I think relations between them make up the greater half of the danger of a split, which could be avoided, and the avoidance of which, in my opinion, would be served, among other things by increasing the number of CC members to 50 or 100.

Comrade Stalin, having become General Secretary, has unlimited authority concentrated in his hands, and I am not sure whether he will always be capable of using that authority with sufficient caution. Comrade Trotsky, on the other hand, as his struggle against the CC on the question of the People's Commissariat for Railways has already proved, is distinguished not only by outstanding ability. He is personally perhaps the most capable man in the present CC, but he takes things with excessive self-assurance, and shows excessive enthusiasm for the purely administrative side of the work.

These two qualities of the two outstanding leaders of the present CC can unconsciously lead to a split, and if our Party does not take steps to avert this, the split may come unexpectedly. . . .

December 24, 1922

Stalin is too rude, and this defect, although quite tolerable in our midst and in dealing among us Communists, becomes intolerable in a General Secretary. That is why I suggest that the comrades think about a way of removing Stalin from that post and appointing somebody else differing from Comrade Stalin in being more tolerant, more loyal, more polite and more considerate to the comrades, less capricious, etc. This circumstance may appear to be a negligible detail. But I think that from the standpoint of safeguards against a split and from the standpoint of what I wrote above about the mutual relations between Stalin and Trotsky it is not a detail, or it is a detail which can assume decisive importance.

January 4, 1923

Leon Trotsky (1930)

Extract from: Leon Trotsky, *Permanent Revolution* (1930)

The permanent revolution, in the sense which Marx attached to this concept, means a revolution which makes no compromise with any single form of class rule, which does not stop at the democratic stage, which goes over to socialist measures and to war against reaction from without; that is, a revolution whose every successive stage is rooted in the preceding one and which can end only in complete liquidation of class society.

To dispel the chaos that has been created around the theory of the permanent revolution, it is necessary to distinguish three lines of thought that are united in this theory.

First, it embraces the problem of the transition from the democratic revolution to the socialist. This is in essence the historical origin of the theory.

The concept of the permanent revolution was advanced by the great communists of the middle of the nineteenth century, Marx and his co-thinkers, in opposition to the democratic ideology which, as we know, claims that with the establishment of a "rational" or democratic state all questions can be solved peacefully by reformist or evolutionary measures. Marx regarded the bourgeois revolution of 1848 as the direct prelude to the proletarian revolution. Marx "erred". Yet his error has a factual and not a methodological character. The Revolution of 1848 did not turn into the socialist revolution. But that is just why it also did not achieve democracy. As to the German Revolution of 1918, it was no democratic completion of the bourgeois revolution; it was a proletarian revolution decapitated by the Social Democrats; more correctly, it was a bourgeois counterrevolution, which was compelled to preserve pseudodemocratic forms after its victory over the proletarian.

Vulgar "Marxism" has worked out a pattern of historical development according to which every bourgeois society sooner or later secures a democratic régime, after which the proletariat, under conditions of democracy, is gradually organized and educated for socialism. The actual transition to socialism has been variously conceived: the avowed reformists picture this transition as the reformist filling of democracy with a socialist content (Jaurès); the formal revolutionists acknowledge the inevitability of applying revolutionary violence in the transition to socialism (Guesde). But both the former and the latter considered democracy and socialism, for all peoples and countries, as two stages in the development of society which are not only entirely distinct but also separated by great distances of time from each other. This view was predominant also among those Russian Marxists who, in the period of 1905, belonged to the left wing of the Second International. Plekhanov, the brilliant progenitor of Russian Marxism, considered the idea of the dictatorship of the proletariat a delusion in contemporary Russia. The same standpoint was defended not only by the Mensheviks but also by the overwhelming majority of the leading Bolsheviks, in particular by those present party leaders, without exception, who in their day were resolute revolutionary democrats but for whom the problems of the socialist revolution, not only in 1905 but also on the eve of 1917, still signified the vague music of a distant future.

The theory of the permanent revolution, which originated in 1905, declared war upon those ideas and moods. It pointed out that the democratic tasks of the backward bourgeois nations led directly, in our epoch, to the dictatorship of the proletariat and that the dictatorship of the proletariat puts socialist tasks on the order of the day. Therein lay the central idea of the theory. While the traditional view was that the road to the dictatorship of the proletariat led through a long period of democracy, the theory of the permanent revolution established the fact that for backward bourgeois countries the road to democracy passed through the dictatorship of the proletariat. Thus democracy is not a régime that remains self-sufficient for decades, but is only a direct prelude to the socialist revolution. Each is bound to the other by an unbroken chain. Thus there is established between the democratic revolution and the socialist reconstruction of society a permanent state of revolutionary development.

The second aspect of the theory has to do with the socialist revolution as such. For an indefinitely long time and in constant internal struggle, all social relations undergo transformation. Society keeps on changing its skin. Each stage of transformation stems directly from the preceding. This process necessarily retains a political character, that is, it develops through collisions between various groups in the society, which is in transformation. Outbreaks of civil war and foreign wars alternate with periods of "peaceful" reform. Revolutions in economy, technique, science, the family, morals, and everyday life develop in complex reciprocal action and do not allow society to achieve equilibrium. Therein lies the permanent character of the socialist revolution as such.

The international character of the socialist revolution, which constitutes the third aspect of the theory of the permanent revolution, flows from the present state of the economy and the social structure of humanity. Internationalism is no abstract principle but a theoretical and political reflection of the character of world economy, of the world development of productive forces, and of the world scale of the class struggle. The socialist revolution begins on national foundations—but cannot be completed on these foundations alone. The maintenance of the proletarian revolution within a national framework can only be a provisional state of affairs, even though, as the experience of the Soviet Union shows, one of long duration. In an isolated proletarian dictatorship, the internal and external contradictions grow inevitably along with the successes achieved. If it remains isolated, the proletarian state must finally fall victim to these contradictions. The way out for it lies only in the victory of the proletariat of the advanced countries. Viewed from this standpoint, a national revolution is not a self-contained whole; it is only a link in the international chain. The international revolution constitutes a permanent process, despite temporary declines and ebbs.

The struggle of the epigones is directed, even if not always with the same clarity, against all three aspects of the theory of the permanent revolution. And how could it be otherwise, when it is a question of three inseparably connected parts of a whole? The epigones mechanically separate *democracy* and the *socialist* dictatorship. They separate the *national* socialist revolution from the *international*. They consider that, in essence, the conquest of power within national limits is not the initial act but the final act of the revolution; after that follows the period of reforms that lead to the national socialist society. In 1905, they did not even grant the idea that the proletariat could conquer power in Russia earlier than in Western Europe. In 1917, they preached the self-sufficing democratic revolution in Russia and spurned the dictatorship of the proletariat. In 1925–27, they steered a course toward national revolution in China under the leadership of the national bourgeoisie. Subsequently, they raised the slogan for China of the democratic dictatorship of the workers and peasants in opposition to the slogan of the dictatorship of the proletariat. They proclaimed the possibility of the construction of an isolated and self-sufficient socialist society in the Soviet Union. The world revolution became for them, instead of an indispensable condition for victory, only a favourable circumstance. This profound breach with Marxism was reached by the epigones in the process of permanent struggle against the theory of the permanent revolution.

Leon Trotsky (1937)

Extract from: Leon Trotsky, *Stalinism and Bolshevism* (1937)

Scientific thinking demands a concrete analysis: how and why did the party degenerate? No one but the Bolsheviks themselves has up to the present time given such an analysis. To do this they had no need to break with Bolshevism.

On the contrary, they found in its arsenal all they needed for the clarification of its fate. They drew this conclusion: certainly Stalinism "grew out" of Bolshevism, not logically, however, but dialectically; not as a revolutionary affirmation but as a Thermidorian negation. They are by no means the same.

The Bolsheviks, however, did not have to wait for the Moscow trials to explain the reasons for the disintegration of the governing party of the USSR. Long ago they foresaw and spoke of the theoretical possibility of this development. Let us remember the prognosis of the Bolsheviks, not only on the eve of the October Revolution but years before. The specific alignment of forces in the national and international field can enable the proletariat to seize power first in a backward country such as Russia. But the same alignment of forces proves beforehand that *without a more or less rapid victory of the proletariat in the advanced countries* the workers' government in Russia will not survive. Left to itself, the Soviet regime must either fall or degenerate. More exactly: it will first degenerate and then fall. I myself have written about this more than once, beginning in 1905. In my *History of the Russian Revolution* (cf. the Appendix to the last volume: "Socialism in One Country") are collected all the statements on this question made by the Bolshevik leaders from 1917 until 1923. They all lead to one conclusion: without a revolution in the West, Bolshevism will be liquidated either by internal counterrevolution, or by external intervention, or by a combination of both. Lenin stressed again and again that the bureaucratization of the Soviet regime was not a technical or organizational question, but the potential beginning of the degeneration of the workers' state. . . .

From the clear understanding of this danger issued the Left Opposition, definitely formed in 1923. Recording day by day the symptoms of degeneration, it tried to oppose to the growing Thermidor the conscious will of the proletarian vanguard. However, this subjective factor proved to be insufficient. The "gigantic masses" which, according to Lenin, decide the outcome of the struggle, became tired of internal privations and of waiting too long for the world revolution. The mood of the masses declined. The bureaucracy won the upper hand. It cowed the revolutionary vanguard, trampled upon Marxism, prostituted the Bolshevik party. Stalinism conquered. In the form of the Left Opposition, Bolshevism broke with the Soviet bureaucracy and its Comintern. This was the real course of development.

To be sure, in a formal sense Stalinism did issue from Bolshevism. Even today the Moscow bureaucracy continues to call itself the Bolshevik party. It is simply using the old label of Bolshevism the better to fool the masses. So much the more pitiful are those theoreticians who take the shell for the kernel and the appearance for the reality. In the identification of Bolshevism and Stalinism, they render the best possible service to the Thermidorians and precisely thereby play a clearly reactionary role.

In view of the elimination of all other parties from the political field the antagonistic interests and tendencies of the various strata of the population must, to a greater or lesser degree, find their expression in the governing party. To the extent that the political centre of gravity has shifted from the proletarian vanguard to the bureaucracy, the party has changed in its social structure as well as in its ideology. Owing to the impetuous course of its development, it has suffered in the last fifteen years a far more radical degeneration than did the social democracy in half a century. The present purge draws between Bolshevism and Stalinism not simply a bloody line but a whole river of blood. The annihilation of all the old generation which participated in the civil war and that part of the youth which took seriously the Bolshevik traditions shows not only a political but a thoroughly physical incompatibility between Bolshevism and Stalinism. How can this be ignored? . . .

As far as the *prohibition* of the other Soviet parties is concerned, it did not flow from any "theory" of Bolshevism but was a measure of defence of the dictatorship in a backward and devastated country, surrounded by enemies on all sides. For the Bolsheviks, it was clear from the beginning that this measure, later completed by the prohibition of factions inside the governing party itself, signalized a tremendous danger. However, the root of the danger lay not in the doctrine or in the tactics but in the material weakness of the dictatorship, in the difficulties of its internal and international situation. If the revolution had triumphed, even if only in Germany, the need of prohibiting the other Soviet parties would immediately have fallen away. It is absolutely indisputable that the domination of a single party served as the juridical point of departure for the Stalinist totalitarian system. But the reason for this development lies neither in Bolshevism nor in the prohibition of other parties as a temporary war measure, but in the number of defeats of the proletariat in Europe and Asia.

Georgi Dimitrov (1935)

Extract from: Georgi Dimitrov, *The Fascist Offensive and the Tasks of the Communist International* (Report to the Seventh World Congress of the Communist International, August 1935)

Comrades, fascism in power was correctly described by the Thirteenth Plenum of the Executive Committee of the Communist International as *the open terrorist dictatorship of the most reactionary, most chauvinistic and most imperialist elements of finance capital.*

The most reactionary variety of fascism is the *German type* of fascism. It has the effrontery to call itself National Socialism, though it has nothing in common with socialism. Hitler fascism is not only bourgeois nationalism, it is bestial chauvinism. It is a government system of political gangsterism, a system of provocation and torture practised upon the working class and the revolutionary elements of the peasantry, the petty bourgeoisie and the intelligentsia. It is mediaeval barbarity and bestiality, it is unbridled aggression in relation to other nations.

German fascism is acting as *the spearhead of international counter-revolution, as the chief instigator of imperialist war, as the initiator of a crusade against the Soviet Union, the great fatherland of the working people of the whole world.*

Fascism is not a form of state power "standing above both classes—the proletariat and the bourgeoisie", as Otto Bauer, for instance, has asserted. It is not "the revolt of the petty bourgeoisie which has captured the machinery of the state", as the British socialist Brailsford declares. No, fascism is not a power standing above class, nor a power of the petty bourgeoisie or the lumpenproletariat over finance capital. Fascism is the power of finance capital itself. It is the organization of terrorist vengeance against the working class and the revolutionary section of the peasantry and intelligentsia. In foreign policy, fascism is jingoism in its most brutal form, fomenting bestial hatred of other nations.

This, the true character of fascism, must be particularly stressed; because in a number of countries, under cover of social demagogy, fascism has managed to gain the following of the mass of the petty bourgeoisie that has been driven out of its course by the crisis, and even of certain sections of the most backward strata of the proletariat. These would never have supported fascism if they had understood its real class character and its true nature.

The development of fascism, and the fascist dictatorship itself, assume *different forms* in different countries, according to historical, social and economic conditions and to the national peculiarities and the international position of the given country. In certain countries, principally those in which fascism has no extensive mass basis and in which the struggle of the various groups within the camp of the fascist bourgeoisie itself is rather acute, fascism does not immediately venture to abolish parliament, but allows the other bourgeois parties, as well as the social democratic parties, to retain a certain degree of legality. In other countries, where the ruling bourgeoisie fears an *early* outbreak of revolution, fascism establishes its unrestricted political monopoly, either immediately or by intensifying its reign of terror against and persecution of all competing parties and groups. This does not prevent fascism, when its position becomes *particularly* acute, from trying to extend its basis and, without altering its class nature, trying to *combine* open terrorist dictatorship with a crude sham of parliamentarism.

The accession to power of fascism is not an *ordinary succession* of one bourgeois government by another, but a *substitution* of one state form of class domination of the bourgeoisie—bourgeois democracy—by another form—open terrorist dictatorship. It would be a serious mistake to ignore this distinction, a mistake which would prevent the revolutionary proletariat from mobilizing the widest strata of the working people of town and country for the struggle against the menace of the seizure of power by the fascists, and from taking advantage of the contradictions which exist in the camp of the bourgeoisie itself. But it is a mistake, no less serious and dangerous, to *underrate* the importance, for the establishment of fascist dictatorship, of the *reactionary measures of the bourgeoisie at present increasingly developing in bourgeois-democratic countries*—measures which suppress the democratic liberties of the working people, falsify and curtail the rights of parliament and intensify the repression of the revolutionary movement.

Comrades, the accession to power of fascism must not be conceived of in so simplified and smooth a form, as though some committee or other of finance capital decided on a certain date to set up a fascist dictatorship. In reality, fascism usually comes to power in the course of a mutual, and at times severe, struggle against the old bourgeois parties, or a definite section of these parties, in the course of a struggle even within the fascist camp itself—a struggle which at times leads to armed clashes, as we have witnessed in the case of Germany, Austria and other countries. All this, however, does not make less important the fact that, before the establishment of a fascist dictatorship, bourgeois governments usually pass through a number of preliminary stages and adopt a number of reactionary measures which directly facilitate the accession to power of fascism. Whoever does not fight the reactionary measures of the bourgeoisie and the growth of fascism at these preparatory stages *is not in a position to prevent the victory of fascism, but, on the contrary, facilitates that victory*.

The social democratic leaders glossed over and concealed from the masses the true class nature of fascism, and did not call them to the struggle against the increasingly reactionary measures of the bourgeoisie. They bear great *historical responsibility* for the fact that, at the decisive moment of the fascist offensive, a large section of the working people of Germany and of a number of other fascist countries failed to recognize in fascism bloodthirsty, rapacious finance capital, their most vicious enemy, and that these masses were not prepared to resist it.

What is the source of the influence of fascism over the masses? Fascism is able to attract the masses because it demagogically appeals to their *most urgent needs and demands*. Fascism not only inflames prejudices that are deeply ingrained in the masses, but also plays on the better sentiments of the masses, on their sense of justice, and sometimes even on their revolutionary traditions. Why do the German fascists, those lackeys of the big bourgeoisie and mortal enemies of socialism, represent themselves to the masses as "Socialists", and depict their accession to power as a "revolution"? Because they try to exploit the faith in revolution and the urge toward socialism that lives in the heart of the mass of working people in Germany.

Fascism acts in the interests of the extreme imperialists, but it presents itself to the masses in the guise of champion of an ill-treated nation, and appeals to outraged national sentiments, as German fascism did, for instance, when it won the support of the masses of the petty bourgeoisie by the slogan "Against the Versailles Treaty!"

Fascism aims at the most unbridled exploitation of the masses, but it approaches them with the most artful anti-capitalist demagogy, taking advantage of the deep hatred of the working people against the plundering bourgeoisie, the banks, trusts and financial magnates, and advancing those slogans which at the given moment are most alluring to the politically immature masses. In Germany: "The general welfare is higher than the welfare of the individual"; in Italy: "Our state is not a capitalist, but a corporate state"; in Japan: "For Japan without exploitation"; in the United States: "Share the wealth", and so forth.

Fascism places the people at the mercy of the most corrupt and venal elements, but comes before them with the demand for "an honest and incorruptible government". Speculating on the profound disillusionment of the masses in bourgeois-democratic governments, fascism hypocritically denounces corruption (for instance, the Barmat and Sklarek affairs in Germany, the Stavisky affair in France, and numerous others).

It is in the interests of the most reactionary circles of the bourgeoisie that fascism intercepts the disappointed masses who desert the old bourgeois parties. But it impresses these masses by the *severity of its attacks* on the bourgeois governments and its irreconcilable attitude to the old bourgeois parties.

Surpassing in its cynicism and hypocrisy all other varieties of bourgeois reaction, fascism *adapts* its demagogy to the *national peculiarities* of each country, and even to the peculiarities of the various social strata in one and the same country. And the mass of the petty bourgeoisie and even a section of the workers, reduced to despair by want, unemployment and the insecurity of their existence, fall victim to the social and chauvinist demagogy of fascism.

Fascism comes to power as a *party of attack* on the revolutionary movement of the proletariat, on the mass of the people who are in a state of unrest; yet it stages its accession to power as a "revolutionary" movement against the bourgeoisie on behalf of "the whole nation" and for the "salvation" of the nation. One recalls Mussolini's "march" on Rome, Pilsudski's "march" on Warsaw, Hitler's National-Socialist "revolution" in Germany, and so forth.

But whatever the masks which fascism adopts, whatever the forms in which it presents itself, whatever the ways by which it comes to power—

Fascism is a most ferocious attack by capital on the mass of the working people;

Fascism is unbridled chauvinism and predatory war;

Fascism is rabid reaction and counter-revolution;

Fascism is the most vicious enemy of the working class and of all working people! . . .

Whether the victory of fascism can be prevented depends *first and foremost* on the militant activity of the working class itself, on whether its forces are welded into a single militant army combating the offensive of capitalism and fascism. By establishing its fighting unity, the proletariat would paralyse the influence of fascism over the peasantry, the petty bourgeoisie of the towns, the youth and the intelligentsia, and would be able to neutralize one section of them and win over the other section.

Second, it depends on the existence of a strong revolutionary party, correctly leading the struggle of the working people against fascism. A party which systematically calls on the workers to retreat in the face of fascism and permits the fascist bourgeoisie to strengthen its positions will inevitably lead the workers to defeat.

Third, it depends on a correct policy of the working class toward the peasantry and the petty-bourgeois masses of the towns. These masses must be taken as they are, and not as we should like to have them. It is only in the process of the struggle that they will overcome their doubts and wavering. It is only by a patient attitude toward their inevitable waverings, it is only by the political help of the proletariat, that they will be able to rise to a higher level of revolutionary consciousness and activity.

Fourth, it depends on the vigilance and timely action of the revolutionary proletariat. The latter must not allow fascism to take it unawares, it must not surrender the initiative to fascism, but must inflict decisive blows on it before it can gather its forces, it must not allow fascism to consolidate its position, it must repel fascism wherever and whenever it rears its head, it must not allow fascism to gain new positions. This is what the French proletariat is so successfully trying to do.

These are the main conditions for preventing the growth of fascism and its accession to power. . . .

Is it not clear that joint action by the supporters of the parties and organizations of the two Internationals, the Communist and the Second International, would make it easier for the masses to repulse the fascist onslaught, and would heighten the political importance of the working class?

Joint action by the parties of both Internationals against fascism, however, would not be confined in its effects to influencing their present adherents, the communists and social democrats; it would also exert a powerful influence on the ranks of the *Catholic, anarchist and unorganized workers, even upon those who have temporarily become the victims of fascist demagogy*.

Moreover, a powerful united front of the proletariat would exert tremendous influence on *all other strata of the working people*, on the peasantry, on the urban petty bourgeoisie, on the intelligentsia. A united front would inspire the wavering groups with faith in the strength of the working class.

But even this is not all. The proletariat of the imperialist countries has possible allies not only in the working people of its own countries but also in the *oppressed nations of the colonies and semi-colonies*. Inasmuch as the proletariat is split both nationally and internationally, inasmuch as one of its parts supports the policy of collaboration with the bourgeoisie, in particular its system of oppression in the colonies and semi-colonies, a barrier is put between the working class and the oppressed peoples of the colonies and semi-colonies, and the world anti-imperialist front is weakened. Every step by the proletariat of the imperialist countries on the road to unity of action in the direction of supporting the struggle for the liberation of the colonial peoples means transforming the colonies and semi-colonies into one of the most important reserves of the world proletariat.

If finally, we bear in mind that international unity of action by the proletariat relies on the steadily growing strength of the proletarian state, the land of socialism, the Soviet Union, we see what broad perspectives are revealed by the realization of proletarian unity of action on a national and international scale. . . .

In mobilizing the mass of working people for the struggle against fascism, the formation of a *wide anti-fascist people's front on the basis of the proletarian united front* is a particularly important task. The success of the whole struggle of the proletariat is closely bound up with the establishment of a fighting alliance between the proletariat, on the one hand, and the labouring peasantry and basic mass of the urban petty bourgeoisie, who together form the majority of the population even in industrially developed countries, on the other.

In its agitation fascism, desirous of winning these masses to its own side, tries to set the mass of working people in town and countryside against the revolutionary proletariat, frightening the petty bourgeoisie with the bogey of the "red peril". We must *turn this weapon against those who wield it* and show the working peasants, artisans and intellectuals whence the real danger threatens. We must *show concretely* who it is that piles the burden of taxes and imposts on to the peasant and squeezes usurious interest out of him; who it is that, while owning the best land and every form of wealth, drives the peasant and his family from their plot of land and dooms them to unemployment and poverty. We must explain concretely, patiently and persistently who it is that ruins the artisans and handicraftsmen with taxes, imposts, high rents, and competition impossible for them to withstand; who it is that throws into the street and deprives of employment the wide masses of the working intelligentsia.

But this is *not enough*. The fundamental, the most decisive thing in establishing the anti-fascist people's front is *resolute action of the revolutionary proletariat* in defence of the demands of these sections of the people, particularly the working peasantry—demands in line with the basic interests of the proletariat—and in the process of struggle combining the demands of the working class with these demands.

In forming the anti-fascist people's front, a correct approach to those organizations and parties whose membership comprises a considerable number of the working peasantry and the mass of the urban petty bourgeoisie is of great importance.

In the capitalist countries the majority of these parties and organizations, political as well as economic, are still under the influence of the bourgeoisie and follow it. The social composition of these parties and organizations is heterogeneous. They include rich peasants side by side with landless peasants, big business men alongside of petty shopkeepers; but control is in the hands of the former, the agents of big capital. This obliges us to *approach the different organizations in different ways*, taking into consideration that not infrequently the bulk of the membership does not know anything about the real political character of its leadership. Under certain conditions we can and must try to draw these parties and organizations or certain sections of them to the side of the anti-fascist people's front, despite their bourgeois leadership. Such, for instance, is today the situation in France with the Radical Party, in the United States with various farmers' organizations, in Poland with the *Stronnictwo Ludowe*, in Yugoslavia with the Croatian Peasants' Party, in Bulgaria with the Agrarian League, in Greece with the Agrarians, etc. But regardless of whether or not there is any chance of attracting these parties and organizations as a whole to the people's front, our tactics must *under all circumstances* be directed toward drawing the small peasants, artisans, handicraftsmen, etc., among their members into the anti-fascist people's front.

Hence, you see that in this field we must all along the line put an end to what has not infrequently occurred in our work—neglect or contempt of the various organizations and parties of the peasants, artisans and the mass of petty bourgeoisie in the towns. . . .

If we communists are asked whether we advocate the united front *only* in the fight for partial demands, or whether we are prepared to share the responsibility even when it will be a question of forming a *government* on the basis of the united front, then we say with a full sense of our responsibility: Yes, we recognize that a situation may arise in which the formation of a *government of the proletarian united front*, or of an *anti-fascist people's front*, will become not only possible but necessary in the interests of the proletariat. And in that case we shall declare for the formation of such a government without the slightest hesitation.

I am not speaking here of a government which may be formed *after* the victory of the proletarian revolution. It is not impossible, of course, that in some country, immediately after the revolutionary overthrow of the bourgeoisie, there may be formed a soviet government on the basis of a government bloc of the communist party with a definite party (or its left wing) participating in the revolution. After the October Revolution the victorious Party of the Russian Bolsheviks, as we know, included representatives of the left Socialist Revolutionaries in the Soviet Government. This was a specific feature of the first Soviet Government after the victory of the October Revolution.

I am not speaking of such a case, but of the possible formation of a united front government on the eve of and before the victory of the soviet revolution.

What kind of government is this? And in what situation could there be any question of such a government?

It is primarily a *government of struggle against fascism and reaction*. It must be a government arising as the result of the united front movement and in no way restricting the activity of the Communist Party and the mass organizations of the working class, but, on the contrary, taking resolute measures against the counter-revolutionary financial magnates and their fascist agents.

At a suitable moment, relying on the growing united front movement, the Communist Party of a given country will declare for the formation of such a government on the basis of a definite anti-fascist platform.

Under what objective conditions will it be possible to form such a government? In the most general terms, one can reply to this question as follows: under conditions of *political crisis*, when the ruling classes are no longer able to cope with the powerful rise of the mass anti-fascist movement. But this is only a general perspective, without which it will scarcely be possible in practice to form a united front government. Only the existence of definite *special prerequisites* can put on the order of the day the question of forming such a government as a politically *essential* task. It seems to me that the following prerequisites deserve the greatest attention in this connection.

First, the state apparatus of the bourgeoisie must already be sufficiently *disorganized* and *paralysed*, so that the bourgeoisie cannot prevent the formation of a government of struggle against reaction and fascism.

Second, the widest masses of working people, particularly the mass trade unions, must be in a state of vehement revolt *against fascism and reaction, though not ready* to rise in insurrection so as to *fight under Communist Party leadership for the achievement of soviet power*.

Third, the differentiation and radicalization in the ranks of social democracy and other parties participating in the united front must already have reached the point where a considerable proportion of them demand *ruthless measures against the fascists and other reactionaries*, struggle together with the communists against fascism and openly come out against that reactionary section of their own party which is hostile to communism.

When and in what countries a situation will actually arise in which these prerequisites will be present in a sufficient degree, it is impossible to state in advance. But as such a possibility *is not to be ruled out in any of the capitalist countries* we must reckon with it, and not only orientate and prepare ourselves but also orientate the working class accordingly.

The fact that we are bringing up this question for discussion at all today is, of course, connected with our estimate of the situation and immediate prospects, as well as with the actual growth of the united front movement in a number of countries during the recent past. For more than ten years the situation in the capitalist countries was such that it was not necessary for the Communist International to discuss a question of this kind.

You remember, comrades, that at our fourth congress, in 1922, and again at the fifth congress, in 1924, the question of the slogan of a *workers'*, or a *workers' and peasants' government* was under discussion. Originally the issue turned essentially upon a question which was almost comparable to the one we are discussing today. The debates that took place at that time in the Communist International around this question, and in particular the political *errors* which were committed in connection with it, have to this day retained their importance for *sharpening our vigilance against the danger of deviations to the right or "left" from the Bolshevik line on this question.* Therefore I shall briefly point to a few of these errors, in order to draw from them the lessons necessary for the present policy of our parties.

The *first* series of mistakes arose from the fact that the question of a workers' government was not clearly and firmly bound up with the existence of a political crisis. Owing to this the right opportunists were able to interpret matters as though we should strive for the formation of a workers' government, supported by the Communist Party, in any, so to speak, "normal" situation. The ultra-lefts, on the other hand, recognized only a workers' government formed by armed insurrection, *after* the overthrow of the bourgeoisie. Both views were wrong. In order, therefore, to avoid a repetition of such mistakes, we now lay *great stress on the exact consideration* of the specific, concrete circumstances of the political crisis and the upsurge of the mass movement, in which the formation of a united front government may prove possible and politically necessary.

The *second* series of errors arose from the fact that the question of a workers' government was not bound up with the development of a militant mass *united front movement of the proletariat.* Thus the *right* opportunists were able to distort the question, reducing it to the unprincipled tactics of forming blocs with social democratic parties on the basis of purely parliamentary arrangements. The *ultra-lefts*, on the other hand, shouted: "No coalitions with the counter-revolutionary social democrats!", regarding all social democrats as counter-revolutionaries at bottom.

Both were wrong, and we now emphasize, on the one hand, that we are not in the least anxious for a "workers' government" that would be nothing more nor less than an enlarged social democratic government. We even prefer not to use the term "workers' governments", and *speak of a united front government*, which in political character is something absolutely different, *different in principle*, from all the social democratic governments which usually call themselves "workers' (or labour) governments". While the social democratic government is an instrument of class collaboration with the bourgeoisie in the interests of the preservation of the capitalist order, *a united front government* is an instrument of the collaboration of the revolutionary vanguard of the proletariat with other anti-fascist parties, in the interests of the entire working population, a government of struggle against fascism and reaction. Obviously there is a *radical difference* between these two things.

On the other hand, we stress the need to see *the difference between the two different camps of social democracy.* As I have already pointed out, there is a reactionary camp of social democracy, but alongside of it there exists and is growing the camp of the left social democrats (without quotation marks), of workers who are becoming revolutionary. In practice the decisive difference between them consists in their attitude to the united front of the working class. The reactionary social democrats are *against* the united front; they slander the united front movement, they sabotage and disintegrate it, as it undermines their policy of compromise with the bourgeoisie. The left social democrats are *for the united front*; they defend, develop and strengthen the united front movement. Inasmuch as this united front movement is a militant movement against fascism and reaction, it will be a constant driving force, impelling the united front government to struggle against the reactionary bourgeoisie. The more powerful this mass movement develops, the greater the force which it can offer to the government to combat the reactionaries. And the better this mass movement will be organized *from below*, the wider the network of *non-party class organs of the united front in the factories*, among the *unemployed, in the workers' districts*, among the *small people of town and country*, the greater will be the guarantee against a possible degeneration of the policy of the united front government.

The *third* series of mistaken views which came to light during our former debates touched precisely on the *practical policy* of the *"workers' government"*. The right opportunists considered that a "workers' government" ought to keep "within the framework of bourgeois democracy", and consequently ought not to take any steps going beyond this framework. The ultra-lefts, on the other hand, in practice refused to make any attempt to form a united front government. . . .

Comrades, we demand an entirely different policy from any united front government. We demand that it should carry out definite and *fundamental revolutionary demands* required by the situation. For instance, control of production, control of the banks, disbanding of the police and its replacement by an armed workers' militia, etc.

Fifteen years ago Lenin called upon us to focus all our attention on "searching out forms of *transition* or *approach* to the proletarian revolution". It may be that in a number of countries the *united front government* will prove to be *one* of the most important transitional forms. "Left" doctrinaires have always avoided this precept of Lenin's. Like the limited propagandists that they were, they spoke only of "aims", without ever worrying about "forms of transition". The right opportunists, on the other hand, have tried to establish a special "democratic intermediate stage" lying between the dictatorship of the bourgeoisie and the dictatorship of the proletariat, for the purpose of instilling into the workers the illusion of a peaceful parliamentary passage from the one dictatorship to the other. This fictitious "intermediate stage" they have also called "transitional form", and even quoted Lenin's words! But this piece of swindling was not difficult to expose, for Lenin spoke of the form of transition and approach to the *"proletarian revolution"*, that is, to the overthrow of the bourgeois dictatorship, and *not* of some transitional form *between* the bourgeois and the proletarian dictatorship.

Why did Lenin attach such exceptionally great importance to the form of transition to the proletarian revolution? Because he had in mind *"the fundamental law of all great revolutions"*, the law that for the masses propaganda and agitation alone cannot take the place of *their own political experience*, when it is a question of attracting really wide masses of the working people to the side of the revolutionary vanguard, without which a victorious struggle for power is impossible. It is a common mistake of a "leftist" character to imagine that as soon as a political (or revolutionary) crisis arises, it is enough for the communist leaders to put forth the slogan of revolutionary insurrection, and the wide masses will follow them. No, even in such a crisis the masses are by no means always ready to do so. We saw this in the case of *Spain*. To help the *millions* to master as rapidly as possible, through their own experience, what they have to do, where to find a radical solution, and what party is worthy of their confidence—these among others are the purposes for which both transitional slogans and special "forms of transition or approach to the proletarian revolution" are necessary. Otherwise the great mass of the people, who are under the influence of petty-bourgeois democratic illusions and traditions, may waver even when there is a revolutionary situation, may procrastinate and stray, without finding the road to revolution—and then come under the axe of the fascist executioners.

That is why we indicate the possibility of forming an anti-fascist united front government in the conditions of a political crisis. In so far as such a government will really prosecute the struggle against the enemies of the people, and give a free hand to the working class and the Communist Party, we communists shall accord it our unstinted support, and as soldiers of the revolution shall take our place in the *first line of fire*. But we state frankly to the masses:

Final salvation this government *cannot bring*. It is not in a position to overthrow the class rule of the exploiters, and for this reason cannot finally remove the danger of fascist counter-revolution. Consequently it is necessary *to prepare for the socialist revolution!* soviet power and *only* soviet power can bring salvation!

Communist International (1943)

Resolution on the Dissolution of the Communist International, adopted by the Executive Committee of the Communist International on May 15, 1943

The historic rôle of the Communist International, founded in 1919 as a result of the political defeat of the great majority of pre-war working-class parties, consisted in upholding the principles of Marxism from vulgarization and distortion by opportunist elements in the working-class movement, in helping to promote the consolidation in a number of countries of the vanguard of the workers in real working-class parties, and in helping them to mobilize for the defence of their political and economic interests and for the struggle against fascism. The Communist International from the first exposed the real meaning of the "Anti-Comintern Pact" as a weapon for the preparation of war by the Hitlerites. Long before the war it exposed the vicious subversive work of the Hitlerites in foreign countries, who masked it by their screams about the so-called interference of the Communist International in the internal affairs of those states. But long before the war it became more and more clear that, with the increasing complications in the internal and international relations of various countries, any sort of international centre would encounter insuperable obstacles in solving the problems facing the movement in each separate country. The deep differences in the historic paths of development of various countries, in their character and social orders, in the level and tempo of their economic and political development, and in the degree of consciousness and organization of the workers, conditioned the different problems facing the working class of the various countries.

The development of events in the last quarter of a century showed that the organizational form of uniting the workers chosen by the first congress of the Communist International answered the conditions of the first stages of the working-class movement, but has been outgrown by the growth of this movement and by the complications of its problems in separate countries, and has even become a drag on the further strengthening of the national working-class parties. The World War has still further sharpened the differences in the situation of the separate countries, and has placed a deep dividing line between those countries which fell under the Hitlerite tyranny and those freedom-loving peoples who have united in a powerful anti-Hitlerite coalition.

In the countries of the Hitlerite bloc the fundamental task of the working class consists of giving all help for the defeat of this bloc by sabotage from within, and by helping to overthrow the governments guilty of the war. In the countries of the anti-Hitlerite coalition, the duty of the masses consists in aiding by every means the military efforts of the governments of those countries aimed at the speediest defeat of the Hitlerite bloc and the assurance of the friendship of nations based on their equality. At the same time the fact must not be lost sight of that separate countries which are members of the anti-Hitlerite coalition have their own particular problems. For example, in countries occupied by the Hitlerites which have lost their independence, the basic task of the workers consists in promoting armed struggle developing into a national war of liberation against Germany. At the same time, the war of liberation of the freedom-loving peoples which has brought into movement the masses of the peoples, uniting them without difference of party or religion in the ranks of a powerful anti-Hitlerite coalition, has demonstrated with still greater clearness that the general national uprising of the people for the speediest victory over the enemy can best and most fruitfully be carried out by the working-class movement of each country, working within the framework of its own country. In consideration of the above . . . the Presidium of the Executive Committee of the Communist International, being unable in the conditions of the world war to call a congress of the Communist International, submits the following motion for the acceptance of the sections of the Communist International:

(1) The Communist International, as the directing centre of the international working-class movement, is to be dissolved.

(2) The sections of the Communist International are to be freed from the obligations of its rules and regulations and from the decisions of the congresses of the Communist International.

(3) The Presidium calls on all supporters of the Communist International to concentrate their energies on whole-hearted support for and active participation in the war of liberation waged by the peoples and states of the anti-Hitlerite coalition for the speediest defeat of the deadly enemy of the working class—German fascism and its associates and vassals.

Communist Information Bureau (1947)

Manifesto adopted at the Founding Conference of the Communist Information Bureau, Szklaraska Poreba, September 1947

During the war the states allied against Germany and Japan marched together and constituted one camp. Differences, however, existed in the Allied camp both in the determination of war aims and in the tasks of the post-war peace settlement. The Soviet Union and the democratic countries considered as the basic war aims: the restoration and consolidation of the democratic order in Europe; the elimination of fascism and the prevention of the possibility of a new aggression by Germany; and the establishment of close and durable co-operation among the European nations. The United States, and in agreement with her Britain, had other war aims: the getting rid of market competitors—Germany and Japan—and the consolidation of their dominant position.

As a result of the Second World War and the post-war period, substantial changes have occurred in the international situation. These changes are characterized by a new distribution of the basic political forces in the international arena, by changed relations between the victor states, and by their regrouping. Two opposite political lines took shape. At one extreme the policy of the USSR and the democratic countries, aimed at the disruption of imperialism and the consolidation of democracy; at the other, the policy of the USA and Britain, aimed at strengthening imperialism and strangling democracy.

Since the USSR and the countries of the new democracy have become a hindrance to the realization of the imperialist plans of world domination, a campaign was proclaimed against those countries, reinforced by threats of a new war on the part of the most zealous imperialist politicians in the USA and Britain. Thus two camps came into being: the imperialist anti-democratic camp with the basic aim of establishing the world domination of American imperialism and the routing of democracy, and the anti-imperialist democratic camp with the basic aim of disrupting imperialism, strengthening democracy, and eliminating the remnants of fascism. The struggle between the two camps is taking place in an atmosphere of the intensification of the general crisis of capitalism, the weakening of the forces of capitalism, and the strengthening of the forces of socialism and democracy.

The Marshall Plan is only the European part of a general plan of world expansion being carried out by the USA. The plan for the economic and political enslavement of Europe is being complemented by plans for the enslavement of China, Indonesia, and the South American countries. Yesterday's aggressors, the capitalist magnates of Germany and Japan, are being prepared by the USA for a new role—that of becoming a weapon of US imperialist policy in Europe and Asia. The tactical methods used by the imperialistic camp are most varied: we find a combination of threats of force, blackmail, extortion, various political and economic pressures, bribery, and the utilization of internal strife for strengthening its position.

A special feature in the tactical methods of the imperialists is the utilization of the treacherous policy of right-wing socialists of the type of Ramadier and Blum in France, Attlee and Bevin in England, Schumacher in Germany, Renner and Schärf in Austria, and Saragat in Italy, who strive to conceal the true predatory essence of the imperialistic policy under the mask of democracy and socialist phraseology, but who in fact remain in all respects loyal supporters of the imperialists, bringing disintegration into the ranks of the working class and poisoning their outlook. It is no accident that the foreign policy of British imperialism found in the person of Bevin its most consistent and zealous executor.

Under these conditions it is essential for the anti-imperialist democratic camp to unite, work out a co-ordinated programme of action, and evolve its own tactics against American imperialism and its British and French allies, and against right-wing socialists, in the first place those of Britain and France. To counter this front of imperialists and nationalists there is an imperative necessity for all democratic countries to oppose to them a united front. There is a great task awaiting the communist parties, that of preserving freedom and peace. The new American policy, supported by the British, is nothing but the policy of the pre-Munich days of 1938.

There must be the closest collaboration by communist parties in the official policy of the nations, in their economic and social policy, and in all other spheres of social life. The chief danger for the working class at the present moment is that of under-estimating its own forces and over-estimating the forces of the imperialist front. Every concession to the US line makes the backers of that line more aggressive. That is why the communists will form the spearhead of the resistance against plans for imperialist expansion in the political, economic, and ideological fields, and will rally all the democratic and patriotic forces of the nations to which they belong. The forces for peace are so important and so great that, if only they will be strong in the defence of peace, the plans of the aggressors will suffer a complete collapse.

Georgi Dimitrov (1948)

Extract from: Georgi Dimitrov, *People's Democracy* (Report to the Fifth Congress of the Bulgarian Communist Party, December 1948)

The character of a people's democracy is determined by four major factors:

(1) The people's democracy represents the power of the working people—of the overwhelming majority of the people, under the leadership of the working class.

That means, first, that the rule of the capitalists and landlords is overthrown and the rule of the working people from the towns and villages, under the leadership of the working class, established, that the working class as the most progressive class in contemporary society is playing the principal role in state and public life. Second, that the state serves as an instrument in the fight of the working people against the exploiters, against all efforts and tendencies aimed at re-establishing the capitalist order and bourgeois rule.

(2) The people's democracy is a state in the transitional period, destined to ensure the development of the state on the path to socialism.

That means that although the rule of the capitalists and landlords is overthrown and their property handed over to the people, the economic roots of capitalism are not yet extirpated; capitalist vestiges still persist and develop, trying to restore their rule. Therefore, the onward march towards socialism is possible only by waging a relentless class struggle against the capitalist elements and for their liquidation.

Only by advancing directly on the road to the achievement of socialism can the people's democracy stabilize itself and fulfil its historic mission. Should it cease to fight against the exploiting classes and to eliminate them, the latter would inevitably gain the upper hand and would bring about its downfall.

(3) The people's democracy is built on collaboration and friendship with the Soviet Union.

Just as the liberation of our country from the fetters of imperialism and the establishment of people's democracy were made possible by the aid and liberating role of the USSR in the fight against fascist Germany and its satellites, so the further development of our people's democracy presupposes the safeguarding and further promotion of close relations and sincere collaboration, mutual aid and friendship between our state and the Soviet State. Any tendency toward weakening this collaboration with the USSR is directed against the very existence of the people's democracy in our country.

(4) The people's democracy belongs to the democratic anti-imperialist camp.

(a) Only by joining in the united democratic anti-imperialist camp, headed by the mighty Soviet State, can every people's democracy ensure its independence, sovereignty and safety against the aggression of the imperialist forces.

(*b*) Under the conditions of the military collapse of the fascist aggressor states, of the abrupt sharpening of the general capitalist crisis, of the immense strengthening of the power of the Soviet Union and of the existing close collaboration with the USSR and the new democracies, our country and the other new democracies were enabled to realize the transition from capitalism to socialism without the establishment of a soviet order, through the regime of people's democracy, on the condition that that regime was consolidated and developed, and by leaning on the USSR and the other new democracies.

(*c*) Embodying the rule of the working people under the leadership of the working class, the people's democracy, in the existing historical situation, as is already proved by experience, can and must successfully perform the functions of the dictatorship of the proletariat for the liquidation of the capitalist elements and the organization of a socialist economy. It can crush the resistance of the overthrown capitalists and landowners, their attempts to restore the rule of capital, and organize the building of industry on the basis of public ownership and planned economy. The regime of the people's democracy will succeed in overcoming the vacillations of the urban petty-bourgeoisie and middle-class peasantry, in neutralizing the capitalist elements in the villages and in rallying all the working people around the working class for the onward march toward socialism.

The regime of the people's democracy will not change its character during the carrying out of this policy, which aims at eliminating the capitalist elements from the national economy. The key positions of the working class in all spheres of public life must continuously be strengthened and all village elements rallied who might become allies of the workers during the period of sharp struggle against the kulaks and their hangers-on. The people's democratic regime must be strengthened and improved in order to render powerless and liquidate the class enemies.

(*d*) The new democracies, including Bulgaria, are already marching toward socialism in ceaseless struggle against all domestic and especially foreign enemies. They are now creating the conditions necessary for the building of socialism, the economic and cultural basis for a future socialist society.

This is the central task today facing the new democracies and, consequently, the working class and its vanguard, the Communist Party.

The task embraces the following important aspects:

(i) Consolidation of the key positions held by the working class, headed by the Communist Party, in all spheres of political, economic and cultural life.

(ii) Strengthening the alliance between the working class and the working peasants under the leadership of the working class.

(iii) Speeding up the development of the public sector of national economy and, in particular, of heavy industry.

(iv) Creating the conditions for liquidating the capitalist elements in village economy by a consistent policy aiming at their isolation and subsequent annihilation.

(v) All-round development of producers' co-operatives among the peasants, giving state assistance to the poor and middle peasants through machine and tractor stations, agricultural machines, credit, seed loans etc., intensifying their interests in the alliance with the working class, persuading them by the example of the co-operative farms of the advantages of that system, and re-educating them in a spirit of intolerance toward capitalist elements.

So far as the nationalization of the land is concerned, we consider that in our situation and with the development of the co-operative farms, this question has no practical importance, i.e. we think that the nationalization of the land is not a necessary condition for the development and mechanization of our rural economy.

(*e*) The people's democracy stands for internationalism. Nationalism is incompatible with the people's democracy. Our party sees in internationalism, i.e. international collaboration under Comrade Stalin, a guarantee of our country's independent existence, prosperity and progress towards socialism. We think that nationalism, under no matter what guise, is an enemy of communism. This was clearly demonstrated by the anti-communist actions of Tito's group in Yugoslavia. Hence the fight against nationalism is a primary duty of communists.

Fighting all manifestations of nationalism, we must re-educate the working people in the spirit of proletarian internationalism and devotion to their country, i.e. in a spirit of genuine patriotism.

Education in the spirit of proletarian internationalism and devotion to one's country means, above all, to make people fully conscious of the unique importance of a firm united front of the new democracies and the USSR in the struggle against the aggressive forces of international reaction and imperialism. The entire future of our people depends, on the one hand, on the power of the Soviet Union, and, on the other, on their readiness and ability, in case of capitalist aggression, honourably to fulfil their duty in the common fight.

At the same time, education in the spirit of proletarian internationalism means to render people fully aware of the importance of complete co-ordination of the activities of the communist parties, and of the leading role of the Bolshevik party. For there exists for the communist parties one and only one theory as a guide to action—the theory of Marxism-Leninism; one and only one aim in their policy; and there exists the great party of Lenin and Stalin, as the leading party of the international labour movement.

Dedijer on Titoism (1953)

Extract from: Vladimir Dedijer, *Tito* (1953)

In every revolution, at the outset, it is necessary to create a centralized state apparatus so that the aims of the revolution may be protected and successfully defended against attempts at counter revolution. This is, in fact, inevitable and at first progressive, but at the same time it forms the principal source of bureaucracy. Therefore the functions of the state should wither away from the moment the working masses take power. But in backward countries, as Russia was, there is always the danger that the state apparatus will begin as the servant of the community and end as its master. During the first Five-Year Plan, when huge industrial undertakings were begun, the power of the state apparatus began to increase rapidly. The right of the workers shrank, the rights of the directors broadened steadily, so that this apparatus turned in the end into the master of the society. The development of the revolution in Soviet Russia came to a halt; the workers' rights were entirely destroyed; and the state went the way of state capitalism. Stalin has created the most centralized state in history. The entire country of two hundred millions of people possesses only one brain—that of the Kremlin.

In Yugoslavia the development has been otherwise. The achievements of the revolution are being protected in that there shall never be permitted a return to old conditions, no return to the defeated and discredited classes; there shall never be allowed the exploitation of man by man. The French Revolution has proclaimed: No freedom for the enemies of freedom. But the development, on the other hand, proceeds in the direction of socialist democracy, toward the withering away of the state, toward debureaucratization and decentralization, toward ever less interference with the work and life of individuals. In this respect the basic thing is the direct rights of the producers; namely, whether they may freely decide about their surplus labour, or whether this is done by state officials. In Yugoslavia the factories are turned over to the workers, they decide themselves where the surplus value of their labour will go, and thus has been created the fundamental basis for the future development of socialist democracy, of such a social order where socialism will, in the end, mean full economic and political freedom for each individual.

For that reason, the Yugoslav experience should be studied most carefully, and not routinely condemned. It is true that this development is in its first steps, but its foundation has been set.

Before Yugoslavia lies still another huge problem to be reckoned with—the problem of the village. It is clear that it would result in a sheer economic catastrophe if the village were permitted to sustain small producers with their primitive agricultural equipment. A terrific disproportion between industry and agriculture is already emerging. For that reason, in Yugoslavia immediately after the war, measures were gradually taken to bring the individual farm producers into co-operatives which could rapidly increase the agricultural production. In this field blind Stalinism was perhaps the most damaging to Yugoslavia. Co-operatives were created after the pattern of the Soviet kolkhozes. Some Yugoslav leaders, in particular Edvard Kardelj, quickly sensed the error and insisted that co-operatives of a general type should first be created, and only later working co-operatives; but local officials, under the influence of Stalin's kolkhoz theories, raced into the creation of kolkhozes.

It should be pointed out, however, that the methods of organizing co-operatives were different from those in Russia. There was in Yugoslavia no physical liquidation of rich peasants as such. Neither was there the barbarism that took place in England at the beginning of the industrial revolution, when small village owners were wiped out overnight.

The problem of the village in socialism is the basic question with which the Yugoslavs must now reckon. They are fully aware that the solution lies in some form of co-operatives, but the proper form—one which would harmonize the interests of the peasant-producers with the interests of the community, which would stimulate the villages as the factories have been stimulated—has not yet been found.

Here is how Tito enumerates the differences between the Yugoslav and Soviet social systems:

"The first difference, the principal one, is that we are building a genuine socialism, while in the Soviet Union the building up of socialism has degenerated into state capitalism under the leadership of a dictatorial bureaucratic caste.

"Second, socialist democracy in Yugoslavia is beginning to dominate the entire social life, and nothing impedes an even more rapid development except the lack of technology and a too slow increase of tempo of socialist consciousness on the part of the citizens of our country. Yet, while in our country this democratic development is noticeable from day to day, in the Soviet Union there is no democracy at all. In the Soviet Union there is neither political nor cultural democracy, nor is there democracy in production; on the contrary, a real reign of terror dominates the scene. There, even after thirty-four years, the factories have not been given over to the workers. There is no freedom of thought and creative work in literature, science, music, or anywhere else.

455

"Third, here in Yugoslavia the national question has been correctly solved, formally and in substance, and a federative state has been created out of six republics based on an equality in which the various people decide freely their lives and their futures. A national community has been created in which there is no leading nation to impose its will on the others, nor to suppress other peoples. In the Soviet Union, the national question has been solved on paper, but in substance nothing has been carried out except a formal creation of different republics governed by one nation—the Russian. By dictate of the bureaucratic leaders from Moscow, not only entire republics but whole nations are being forcibly moved and exposed to annihilation.

"In Yugoslavia the man means everything. Our aim is to create, as early as possible and in an utmost humane way, a better life for our people, for all individuals and for the whole community. We try, even under the hardest conditions, to take care of those people who labour for the materialization of socialism. In the USSR a man is a number, and the people a colourless mass which must docilely obey and fulfil all the orders of their leaders. There is in the Soviet Union no patient re-educating over to socialist consciousness, because there they do not build socialism but a superstate capitalism, which to the outside world shows all the qualities of imperialism and internally represents a strictly centralized bureaucratic absolutism. In Yugoslavia an ever-growing development toward decentralization of the economic, cultural and other life is noticeable, because only such a system is genuinely in accordance with the concept of power as resident in the people.

"In that consists the huge substantial difference between the Yugoslav system and that of the Soviet Union. There are many additional examples, many other differences springing out of either specific conditions in our country or out of the degeneration of further revolutionary development in Soviet Russia."

Josip Broz Tito (1960)

Extract from: President Josip Broz Tito, Report to the Fifth Congress of the Socialist Alliance of the Working People of Yugoslavia, April 1960

The system of state plans, which regulated production to the minutest detail, was abolished and replaced by a new system of economic plans which lay down only the overall proportions of development, within which enterprises and communes [i.e. municipalities] can develop independently. At the beginning we had a centralized state system of economic management, and we do not think this was a mistake. But as soon as we realized that this system did not stimulate the economy, that in fact it was beginning to check the productive forces, . . . we decided to change the existing system of management. It was also necessary to change fundamentally the producers' attitude towards the means of production and the social product. This process . . . began to unfold when Workers' Councils were introduced. A great step forward in this field was made when Councils of Producers . . . were formed. The growing independence of enterprises and the increased material means available to enterprises and communes made it necessary to extend the self-governing rights of producers outside their enterprises. . . .

The state is certainly necessary in a transitional socialist society. First, it plays a significant role in the defence of the socialist system against internal and external enemies of socialism. Secondly, in conditions characterized by the change of ownership of the means of production and by low capital accumulation, it does much to promote the concentration and distribution of capital in the first phase of development of the socialist economy; this applies especially to less developed countries . . . But its functions gradually decrease as society takes them over . . . It would be wrong to consider that the state, even the socialist state, can for all time take into its hands all the political and economic functions of the progressive social forces and be the sole interpreter of the consciousness and interests of the working class—that is, that in spite of Marxist theory it must exist in a socialist society as some kind of superstructure of society. . . .

The working collectives, after paying their contributions to society, have been given the right to use their income independently, dividing it between the personal earnings of workers and the enterprises' funds, in accordance with their needs and successes . . . Instead of establishing equality which does not stimulate but retards the expansion of productivity, we must apply the principle of remuneration according to work and establish such "inequality" as is based on the principle "to each according to his ability and work", and which, in the present phase of development, gives the greatest possible stimulus to the growth of productive forces. In this way we proceed along a road which leads us closer to full equality—that is, equality which can be achieved in an abundance of produce, when the principle "to each according to his needs" becomes implemented. . . .

In such conditions the attitude of the individual towards the enterprise also changes. He becomes increasingly aware that his earnings are not fixed by anyone, that he creates them himself . . . To draw every individual into the process of management, to give him the maximum possibility of seeing the results of his work, to judge and value them, means to turn him into an economically and socially free and independent man who lives by his work, a man who is freed from all the vestiges of hired-labour relations. . . .

Marxism today is not only what Marx, Engels, and Lenin wrote about social development. Marxism has been greatly enriched by social relations, as well as by events that have taken place in the world in the past 50 years. This practice and these events must be thoroughly studied; the present reality should not be interpreted from a dogmatic point of view based on irrelevant quotations.

Milovan Djilas (1957)

Extract from: Milovan Djilas, *The New Class* (1957)

As defined by Roman law, property constitutes the use, enjoyment, and disposition of material goods. The communist political bureaucracy uses, enjoys, and disposes of nationalized property.

If we assume that membership in this bureaucracy or new owning class is predicated on the use of privileges inherent in ownership—in this instance nationalized material goods—then membership in the new party class, or political bureaucracy, is reflected in a larger income in material goods and privileges than society should normally grant for such functions. In practice, the ownership privilege of the new class manifests itself as an exclusive right, as a party monopoly, for the political bureaucracy to distribute the national income, to set wages, direct economic development, and dispose of nationalized and other property. This is the way it appears to the ordinary man who considers the communist functionary as being very rich and as a man who does not have to work.

The ownership of private property has, for many reasons, proved to be unfavourable for the establishment of the new class's authority. Besides, the destruction of private ownership was necessary for the economic transformation of nations. The new class obtains its power, privileges, ideology, and its customs from one specific form of ownership—collective ownership—which the class administers and distributes in the name of the nation and society.

The new class maintains that ownership derives from a designated social relationship. This is the relationship between the monopolists of administration, who constitute a narrow and close stratum, and the mass of producers (farmers, workers, and intelligentsia) who have no rights. But that is not all, since the communist bureaucracy also has complete monopolistic control over material assets.

Every substantive change in the social relationship between those who monopolize administration and those who work is inevitably reflected in the ownership relationship. Social and political relations and ownership—the totalitarianism of government and the monopoly of ownership—are being more fully brought into accord in communism than in any other political system.

To divest communists of their ownership rights would be to abolish them as a class. To compel them to relinquish their other social powers, so that workers may participate in sharing the profits of their work—which capitalists have had to permit as a result of strikes and parliamentary action—would mean that communists were being deprived of their monopoly over property, ideology, and government. This would be the beginning of democracy and freedom in communism. Until this happens, there can be no indication that important, fundamental changes are taking place in communist systems, at least not in the eyes of men who think seriously about social progress.

The ownership privileges of the new class and membership in that class are the privileges of *administration*. This privilege extends from state administration and the administration of economic enterprises to that of sports and humanitarian organizations. Political, party, or so-called "general leadership" is executed by the core. This position of leadership carries privileges with it. In his *Staline au pouvoir*, published in Paris in 1951, Orlov states that the average pay of a worker in the USSR in 1935 was 1,800 rubles annually, while the pay and allowances of the secretary of a rayon committee amounted to 45,000 rubles annually. The situation has changed since then for both workers and party functionaries, but the essence remains the same. Other authors have arrived at the same conclusions. Discrepancies between the pay of workers and party functionaries are extreme; this could not be hidden from persons visiting the USSR or other communist countries in the past few years.

Other systems, too, have their professional politicians. One can think well or ill of them, but they must exist. Society cannot live without a state or a government, and therefore it cannot live without those who fight for it.

However, there are fundamental differences between professional politicians in other systems and in the communist system. In extreme cases, politicians in other systems use the government to secure privileges for themselves and their cohorts, or to favour the economic interests of one social stratum or another. The situation is different with the communist system, where the power and the government are identical with the use, enjoyment, and disposition of almost all the nation's goods. He who grabs power grabs privileges and indirectly grabs property. Consequently, in communism, power or politics as a profession is the ideal of those who have the desire or the prospect of living as parasites at the expense of others.

Membership in the Communist Party before the Revolution meant sacrifice. Being a professional revolutionary was one of the highest honours. Now that the party has consolidated its power, party membership means that one belongs to a privileged class. And at the core of the party are the all-powerful exploiters and masters.

Nikita Khrushchev (1956)

Extract from: Nikita Khrushchev, Report made to a secret session of the 20th Congress of the Communist Party of the Soviet Union (Feb. 24–25, 1956)

During Lenin's life the Central Committee was a real expression of collective leadership of the party and the nation. . . . Lenin never imposed his views upon his co-workers by force. He tried to convince some; he patiently explained his opinions to others. In addition to the great accomplishments of Vladimir Ilyich [Lenin] for the victory of the working class and the peasants . . . , his acute mind expressed itself also in this—that he detected in Stalin those negative characteristics which resulted later in grave consequences.

Fearing for the future fate of the party and the Soviet nation, Lenin made a completely correct characterization of Stalin, pointing out that it was necessary to consider the question of transferring him from the position of General Secretary because of the fact that Stalin was excessively rude, that he did not have a proper attitude towards his comrades, that he was capricious and abused his power.

In December 1922, in a letter to the party congress, Vladimir Ilyich wrote: "Comrade Stalin, having become General Secretary, has unlimited authority concentrated in his hands, and I am not sure whether he will always be capable of using that authority with sufficient caution." This letter—a political document of tremendous importance, known as Lenin's "testament"—has been distributed among the delegates to the 20th Party Congress. You have read it, and will undoubtedly read it more than once.

You might reflect on Lenin's plain words, in which expression is given to his anxiety concerning the party, the people, the state, and the future direction of party policy. He said: "Stalin is too rude, and this defect . . . becomes intolerable in a General Secretary. That is why I suggest that the comrades think about a way of removing Stalin from that post and appointing somebody else differing from Comrade Stalin in being more tolerant, more loyal, more polite and more considerate to the comrades, less capricious, etc."

This document of Lenin's was made known to the delegates at the 13th Party Congress, who discussed the question of transferring Stalin from the position of General Secretary. The delegates declared themselves in favour of retaining Stalin in this post, hoping that he would heed the critical remarks of Vladimir Ilyich and would be able to overcome the defects which caused Lenin serious anxiety.
. . .

We have to consider this matter seriously and analyse it correctly in order to preclude any possibility of a repetition in any form whatever of what took place during the life of Stalin, who did not tolerate collegiality in leadership and in work, and who practised brutal violence not only towards everything which opposed him, but also towards that which seemed, to his capricious and despotic character, contrary to his concepts.

Stalin acted not through explanation and patient co-operation with people, but by imposing his concepts and demanding absolute submission to his opinion. Whoever opposed his concepts . . . was doomed to removal and to subsequent moral and physical annihilation. This was especially true during the period following the 17th Party Congress, when many prominent party leaders and rank-and-file party workers, honest and dedicated to the cause of communism, fell victims to Stalin's despotism. . . . It was precisely during this period (1935–1938) that the practice of mass repression through the government apparatus was born, first against the enemies of Leninism—Trotskyites, Zinovievites, Bukharinites, long since politically defeated by the party—and subsequently against many honest Communists. . . .

Stalin originated the concept 'enemy of the people'. This term automatically rendered it unnecessary that the ideological errors of a man or men engaged in a controversy be proven; it made possible the usage of the most cruel repression against anyone who in any way disagreed with Stalin. . . . In the main, and in actuality, the only proof of guilt used . . . was the 'confession' of the accused himself; and, as subsequent investigations have proved, 'confessions' were acquired through physical pressures against the accused. This led to glaring violations of revolutionary legality, and to the fact that many entirely innocent persons who in the past had defended the party line became victims.

With regard to those persons who in their time had opposed the party line, there were often no sufficiently serious reasons for their physical annihilation. The formula 'enemy of the people' was specifically introduced for the purpose of physically annihilating such individuals. It is a fact that many persons who were annihilated as 'enemies of the people' had worked with Lenin during his life. Some of these persons had made errors during Lenin's lifetime, but, despite this, Lenin benefited by their work, corrected them, did everything possible to retain them in the ranks of the party, and induced them to follow him.

An entirely different relationship with people characterized Stalin. Lenin's traits—patient working with people; painstaking education of them; the ability to induce people to follow him without using compulsion, but rather through the ideological influence on them of the whole collective [leadership]—were entirely foreign to Stalin. He discarded the Leninist method of convincing and educating; he abandoned the method of ideological struggle for that of administrative violence, mass repression, and terror. . . . Arbitrary behaviour by one person encouraged arbitrariness in others. Mass arrests and deportations of many thousands of people, execution without trial and without normal investigation, created conditions of insecurity, fear, and even desperation. . . .

Lenin used severe methods only in the most necessary cases—when the exploiting classes were still in existence and were vigorously opposing the Revolution; when the struggle for survival was assuming the sharpest forms, including a civil war. Stalin, on the other hand, used extreme methods and mass repression when the Revolution was already victorious, when the Soviet state was strengthened, when the exploiting classes were liquidated, when socialist relations were rooted solidly in all phases of the national economy, when our party was politically consolidated and had strengthened itself both numerically and ideologically. Stalin showed in a whole series of cases his intolerance, brutality, and abuse of power . . . and . . . often chose the path of repression and physical annihilation, not only against actual enemies, but also against individuals who had not committed any crimes against the party and the Soviet Government.

Here we see a demonstration of the brutal force which had once so alarmed Lenin. . . .

There was no matter so important that Lenin himself decided it without asking for the advice and approval of the Central Committee members, or of the members of the Committee's Political Bureau. In the most difficult period for our party and our country, Lenin considered it necessary regularly to convoke congresses, party conferences, and plenary sessions of the Central Committee at which all important questions were discussed and where resolutions, carefully worked out by the collective leadership, were approved. . . .

Whereas during the first few years after Lenin's death party congresses and Central Committee plenums [i.e. meetings] took place more or less regularly, later, when Stalin began increasingly to abuse his power, these principles were brutally violated. This was especially evident during the last 15 years of his life. Was it a normal situation when over 13 years elapsed between the 18th and 19th Party Congresses—years during which our party and our country had experienced so many important events? These events demanded categorically that the party should have passed resolutions pertaining to the country's defence during the Patriotic War [i.e. the Second World War] and to post-war construction. Even after the end of the war a congress was not convened for over seven years. Central Committee plenums were hardly ever called. It should be sufficient to mention that during all the years of the Patriotic War not a single Central Committee plenum took place. . . .

Many who were branded in 1937–38 as "enemies" were actually never enemies, spies, wreckers, etc., but honest Communists. They were only so stigmatized and often, no longer able to bear barbaric tortures, they accused themselves—at the order of the investigative judges—of all kinds of grave and unlikely crimes. The investigating commission has presented to the Central Committee's Presidium lengthy and documented materials pertaining to mass repressions against the delegates to the 17th Party Congress and against members of the Central Committee elected at that congress. These materials have been studied by the Presidium of the Central Committee. It has been determined that of the 139 members and candidates of the party's Central Committee who were elected at the 17th Congress, 98 were arrested and shot, mostly in 1937–38. . . . The same fate was met not only by the Central Committee members, but also by the majority of delegates to the 17th Party Congress. Of 1,966 delegates with either voting or advisory rights, 1,108 were arrested on charges of anti-revolutionary crimes. . . . The delegates to that congress were active participants in the building of our socialist state; many of them suffered and fought for the party during the pre-revolutionary years and in the Civil War. . . . How can we believe that such people could prove to be "two-faced" and had joined the camp of the enemies of socialism? . . .

The mass repressions of that time were made under the slogan of a fight against the Trotskyites. Did the Trotskyites at that time actually constitute such a danger to our party and to the Soviet state? We should recall that in 1927, on the eve of the 15th Party Congress, only some 4,000 votes were cast for the Trotskyite-Zinovievite opposition, while there were 724,000 for the party line. During the ten years which followed the 15th Party Congress, Trotskyism was completely disarmed and many former Trotskyites had changed their views. . . . It is clear that in this situation there was no basis for mass terror in the country.

Stalin's report at the February–March Central Committee plenum in 1937, "Deficiencies of party work and methods for the liquidation of Trotskyites and other two-facers", contained an attempt at theoretical justification of the mass terror policy under the pretext that as we march forward toward socialism, class war must allegedly sharpen. Stalin asserted that both history and Lenin taught him this. Actually Lenin taught that the application of revolutionary violence is necessitated by the resistance of the exploiting classes, and this referred to the era when the exploiting classes existed and were powerful. As soon as the nation's political situation had improved, when in January, 1920, the Red Army took Rostov and thus won a most important victory over Denikin, Lenin instructed Dzherzhinsky [first head of the Bolshevik secret police] to stop mass terror and to abolish the death penalty. . . .

Stalin deviated from these clear and plain precepts of Lenin. He put the party and the NKVD to the use of mass terror when the exploiting classes had been liquidated in our country and when there were no serious reasons for the use of mass terror. This terror was actually directed not at the remnants of the defeated exploiting classes, but against honest workers of the party and of the Soviet state. Against them were made lying, slanderous and absurd accusations of "two-facedness", "espionage", "sabotage", etc. . . .

When the cases of some of these so-called "spies" and "saboteurs" were examined, it was found that all were fabricated. In many cases confessions of guilt were obtained with the help of cruel and inhuman tortures. . . . The Central Committee considers it absolutely necessary to inform the Congress of many such fabricated "cases" against members of the party's Central Committee elected at the 17th Party Congress. . . .

In those years repression on a mass scale was applied which was based on nothing tangible and which resulted in heavy losses to the party. The vicious practice was condoned of having the NKVD draw up lists of persons whose sentences were prepared in advance. Yezhov would send these lists to Stalin personally for his approval of the proposed punishment. In 1937–38, 383 such lists containing the names of many thousands of party, soviet, komsomol, army and economic workers were sent to Stalin. He approved these lists. A large part of these cases are now being reviewed, and a great part of them are being voided because they are baseless and falsified. Suffice it to say that from 1954 to the present time, the Military Collegium of the Supreme Court has rehabilitated 7,679 persons, many of whom were rehabilitated posthumously. . . .

Stalin was a very distrustful man; we knew this from our work with him. He could look at a man and say: "Why are your eyes so shifty to-day?" or "Why are you avoiding looking me directly in the eyes?" This sickly suspicion created in him a general distrust even towards eminent party workers whom he had known for years. Everywhere and in everything he saw "enemies", "two-facers", and "spies". . . .

When Stalin said that one or another person should be arrested, it was necessary to accept on faith that he was an "enemy of the people". Meanwhile Beria's gang, which ran the organs of state security, outdid itself in proving the "guilt" of the accused and the "truth" of materials which it falsified. And what proofs were offered? The "confessions" of the arrested, which were accepted by the investigative judges. How is it possible that a person confesses to crimes which he has not committed? Only in one way—through the application of physical methods of "pressuring" him, of torture, of bringing him to a state of unconsciousness, of depriving him of his judgment, of taking away his human dignity. In this manner were "confessions" acquired. . . .

Stalin's wilfulness showed itself not only in decisions concerning the internal life of the country, but also in the international relations of the Soviet Union. The Committee has studied in detail the reasons for the conflict with Yugoslavia. It was a shameful role which Stalin played in this. The "Yugoslav affair" contained no problems which could not have been solved through party discussions among comrades. There was no significant basis for the development of this "affair"; it was completely possible to have prevented the rupture of relations with that country. This does not mean that the Yugoslav leaders did not make mistakes or did not have shortcomings. But these mistakes and shortcomings were magnified in a monstrous manner by Stalin, which resulted in a breakdown of relations with a friendly country.

I recall the first days when the conflict between the Soviet Union and Yugoslavia began to be blown up artificially. Once, when I came from Kiev to Moscow, I was invited to visit Stalin, who, pointing to the copy of a letter lately sent to Tito, asked me, "Have you read this?" Not waiting for my reply, he answered, "I will shake my little finger—and there will be no more Tito. He will fall." . . .

But this did not happen to Tito. No matter how much Stalin shook, not only his little finger, but everything else that he could shake, Tito did not fall. The reason was that. . . . Tito had behind him a state and a people who had gone through a severe school of fighting for liberty and independence, a people which gave support to its leaders.

You see to what Stalin's mania for greatness led. He had completely lost consciousness of reality; he demonstrated his suspicion and haughtiness not only in relation to individuals in the USSR, but in relation to whole nations. We have carefully examined the case of Yugoslavia and have found a proper solution which is approved by the peoples of the Soviet Union and of Yugoslavia, as well as by all progressive humanity. . . .

The cult of the individual acquired such monstrous size chiefly because Stalin himself, using all conceivable methods, supported the glorification of his own person. . . . One of the most characteristic examples of Stalin's self-glorification and of his lack of even elementary modesty is the edition of his *Short Biography*, which was published in 1948. This book is an expression of the most dissolute flattery; an example of making a man into a godhead; of transforming him into an infallible sage—"the greatest leader, sublime strategist of all times and nations." . . . We need not give here examples of the loathsome adulation filling this book. All we need to add is that they were all approved and edited by Stalin personally, and some of them were added in his own handwriting to the draft text of the book. . . .

In speaking about the October Revolution and the Civil War, the impression was created that Stalin had suggested to Lenin what to do and how to do it. This is slander against Lenin. I will probably not sin against the truth when I say that 99 per cent of the persons here present heard and knew very little about Stalin before 1924, while Lenin was known to the whole nation, from the children to the greybeards. . . .

If we sharply criticize to-day the cult of the individual which was so widespread during Stalin's lifetime, and if we speak about the many negative phenomena generated by this cult, various persons may ask: "How could it be? Stalin headed the party and the country for 30 years and many victories were gained during his lifetime. . . . Where were the members of the Political Bureau of the Central Committee? Why did they not assert themselves against the cult of the individual in time? Why is this being done only now?"

First of all we have to consider the fact that the members of the Political Bureau viewed these matters in a different way at different times. Initially, many of them backed Stalin actively because Stalin was one of the strongest Marxists, and his logic, strength and will greatly influenced the cadres and party work. It is known that Stalin, after Lenin's death and especially during the first years, actively fought for Leninism against the enemies of Leninist theory and against those who deviated. The party . . . started on a great scale the work of socialist industrialization, agricultural collectivization, and the cultural revolution. At that time Stalin gained great popularity, sympathy, and support. The party had to fight those who attempted to lead the country away from the correct Leninist path; it had to fight Trotskyites, Zinovievites, Rightists, and the bourgeois Nationalists. This fight was indispensable. Later, however, Stalin, abusing his power more and more, began to fight eminent party and government leaders and to use terroristic methods against honest people. As we have already shown, Stalin handled in this manner such eminent party and government leaders as Kossior, Rudzutak, Eikhe, Postyshev, and many others. . . .

In the situation which then prevailed, I talked often with Nikolai Bulganin. Once, when we two were travelling in a car, he said: "It has happened sometimes that a man goes to Stalin on his invitation as a friend. And when he sits with Stalin, he does not know where he will be sent next, home or to gaol."

It is clear that such conditions put every member of the Political Bureau in a very difficult situation. And when we also consider the fact that in the last years [of Stalin's life] the Central Committee plenary sessions were not convened, and that the sessions of the Political Bureau occurred only from time to time, then we will understand how difficult it was for any member of the Political Bureau to take a stand against unjust or improper procedure. . . .

We must abolish the cult of the individual decisively, once and for all. . . . It is necessary for this purpose:

(1) To condemn and eradicate the cult of the individual as alien to Marxism–Leninism . . . and to fight inexorably all attempts at restoring this practice in one form or another. . . . In this connexion we will be forced to do much work . . . to correct the widespread erroneous views connected with the cult of the individual in the spheres of history, philosophy, economy, and of other sciences, as well as in literature and the fine arts. It is especially necessary that in the immediate future we compile a serious textbook of the history of our party, which will be edited in accordance with scientific Marxist objectivism; a textbook of the history of Soviet society; and a book pertaining to the events of the Civil War and the Great Patriotic War.

(2) To continue systematically and consistently the work done by the Party's Central Committee during the last few years—a work characterized by minute observation in all party organizations, from the bottom to the top, of the Leninist principles of party leadership; characterized, above all, by the main principle of collective leadership; and finally, characterized by the wide practice of criticism and self-criticism.

(3) To restore completely the Leninist principles of Soviet socialist democracy, expressed in the Constitution of the Soviet Union, and to fight against the abuse of power by individuals. . . .

Mao Zedong (1957)

Extract from: Mao Zedong, *On the Correct Handling of Contradictions among the People* (1957)

Never has our country been as united as it is today. However, this does not mean that there are no longer any contradictions in our society. . . . We are confronted by two types of social contradictions: contradictions between ourselves and the enemy, and contradictions among the people. . . . If we are to have a correct understanding of these two different types of contradictions, we must first of all make clear what is meant by "the people" and what is meant by "the enemy". The term "the people" has different meanings in different countries, and in different historical periods in each country. . . . At this stage of building socialism, all classes, strata and social groups that approve, support, and work for the cause of socialist construction belong to the category of "the people", while those social forces and groups that resist the socialist revolution, and are hostile to and try to wreck socialist construction, are enemies of the people.

The contradictions between ourselves and our enemies are antagonistic ones. Within the ranks of the people, contradictions among the working people are non-antagonistic, while those between the exploiters and the exploited classes have, apart from their antagonistic aspect, a non-antagonistic aspect. . . . Our people's Government is a Government that truly represents the interests of the people and serves the people, yet certain contradictions do exist between the Government and the masses. These include contradictions between the interests of the state, collective interests, and individual interests; between democracy and centralism; between those in positions of leadership and the led; and contradictions arising from the bureaucratic practices of certain state functionaries with the masses. . . .

The contradiction between the working class and the national bourgeoisie is a contradiction among the people. The class struggle waged between the two is, by and large, a class struggle within the ranks of the people. This is because of the dual character of the national bourgeoisie in our country. . . . Exploitation of the working class to make profits is one side, while support of the Constitution and willingness to accept socialist transformation is the other. The national bourgeoisie differs from the imperialists, the landlords, and the bureaucrat-capitalists. The contradiction between exploiter and exploited, which exists between the national bourgeoisie and the working class, is an antagonistic one. But, in the concrete conditions existing in China, such an antagonistic contradiction, if properly handled, can be transformed into a non-antagonistic one and resolved in a peaceful manner. . . .

Since the contradictions between ourselves and the enemy and those among the people differ in nature, they must be solved in different ways. To put it briefly, the former is a matter of drawing a line between us and our enemies, while the latter is a matter of distinguishing between right and wrong. . . . Ours is a people's democratic dictatorship, led by the working class and based on the worker–peasant alliance. . . . That is to say, democracy operates within the ranks of the people, while the working class, uniting with all those enjoying civil rights, the peasantry in the first place, enforces dictatorship over the reactionary classes and elements and all those who resist socialist transformation and oppose socialist construction. . . .

While we stand for freedom with leadership and democracy under centralized guidance, in no sense do we mean that coercive measures should be taken to settle ideological matters and questions involving the distinction between right and wrong among the people. Any attempt to deal with ideological matters or questions involving right and wrong by administrative orders or coercive measures will not only be ineffective, but harmful. We cannot abolish religion by administrative orders, nor can we force people not to believe in it. We cannot compel people to give up idealism, any more than we can force them to believe in Marxism. In settling matters of an ideological nature, or controversial issues among the people, we can only use democratic methods—methods of discussion, criticism, persuasion, and education; not coercive, high-handed methods. . . .

Quite a few people fail to make a clear distinction between these two different types of contradictions, those between ourselves and the enemy and those among the people, and are prone to confuse the two. It must be admitted that it is sometimes easy to confuse them. We had instances of such confusion in our past work. In the suppression of the counter-revolution, good people were sometimes mistaken for bad. Such things have happened before, and still happen today. We have been able to keep our mistakes within bounds because it has been our policy to draw a sharp line between our own people and our enemies and, where mistakes have been made, to take suitable measures of rehabilitation. . . .

It is harmful to the growth of art and science if administrative measures are used to impose one particular style of art or school of thought and to ban another. Questions of right and wrong in the arts and sciences should be settled through free discussion in artistic and scientific circles and in the course of practical work in the arts and sciences. They should not be settled in summary fashion. A period of trial is often needed to determine whether something is right or wrong. In the past new and correct things often failed at the outset to win recognition. . . . The Copernican theory of the solar system and Darwin's theory of evolution were once dismissed as erroneous, and had to win through against bitter opposition. . . . That is why we should take a cautious attitude toward questions of right and wrong in the arts and sciences, encourage free discussion, and avoid hasty conclusions. . . . Ideological struggle is not like other forms of struggle. Crude, coercive methods should not be used in this struggle, but only the method of painstaking reasoning. . . .

People may ask, "Since Marxism is accepted by the majority of the people in our country as the guiding ideology, can it be criticized?" Certainly it can. As a scientific truth, Marxism fears no criticism. If it did, and could be defeated in argument, it would be worthless. . . . What should our policy be towards non-Marxist ideas? As far as unmistakable counter-revolutionaries and wreckers of the socialist cause are concerned, the matter is easy; we simply deprive them of their freedom of speech. But it is quite a different matter when we are faced with incorrect ideas among the people. . . . It is not only futile but very harmful to use crude and summary methods to deal with ideological questions among the people, questions relating to the spiritual life of man. You may ban the expression of wrong ideas, but the ideas will still be there. On the other hand, correct ideas, if pampered in hothouses without being exposed to the elements or immunized from disease, will not win out against wrong ones. That is why it is only by employing methods of discussion, criticism, and reasoning that we can really foster correct ideas, overcome wrong ideas, and really settle issues. . . .

There can be no doubt that we should criticize all kinds of wrong ideas. . . . But such criticism should not be doctrinaire. . . . While criticizing doctrinairism, we should at the same time direct our attention to criticizing revisionism. Revisionism, or rightist opportunism, is a bourgeois trend of thought which is even more dangerous than doctrinairism. The revisionists, or right opportunists, pay lip-service to Marxism and also attack doctrinairism. But the real target of their attacks is actually the most fundamental element of Marxism. They oppose or distort materialism and dialectics, oppose or try to weaken the people's democratic dictatorship and the leading role of the Communist Party, oppose or try to weaken socialist transformation and socialist construction. Even after the victory of the socialist revolution in our country, there are still a number of people who vainly hope for a restoration of the capitalist system. They wage a struggle against the working class on every front, including the ideological front. In this struggle their right-hand men are the revisionists. . . .

How are our people to determine what is right and what is wrong in our words and actions? Broadly speaking, words and actions can be judged right if they (i) help to unite the people of our various nationalities and do not divide them; (ii) are beneficial, not harmful, to socialist transformation and socialist construction; (iii) help to consolidate, not undermine or weaken, the people's democratic dictatorship; (iv) help to consolidate, not undermine or weaken, democratic centralism; (v) tend to strengthen, not to cast off or weaken, the leadership of the Communist Party; (vi) are beneficial, not harmful, to international socialist solidarity and the solidarity of the peace-loving peoples of the world. Of these six criteria, the most important are the socialist path and the leadership of the party.

These criteria are put forward in order to foster and not hinder the free discussion of various questions among the people. Those who do not approve of these criteria can still put forward their own views and argue their case. . . . Naturally, in judging the truth of scientific theories or assessing the aesthetic value of works of art, other pertinent criteria are needed. But these six political criteria are also applicable to all activities in the arts and sciences. . . .

All that is set out above stems from the specific historical conditions in our country. Since conditions vary in different socialist countries and with different communist parties, we do not think that other countries and parties must or need follow the Chinese way.

Moscow Declaration (1957)

Extract from the Moscow Declaration adopted by 12 Ruling Communist Parties (1957)

In condemning dogmatism, the communist parties believe that the main danger at present is revisionism—in other words, right-wing opportunism as a manifestation of bourgeois ideology paralysing the revolutionary energy of the working class and demanding the preservation or restoration of capitalism. However, dogmatism and sectarianism can also be the main danger at different phases of development in one party or another. It is for each Communist party to decide what danger threatens it more at a given time. . . . Modern revisionism seeks to smear the teaching of Marxism-Leninism, declares that it is "outmoded", and alleges that it has lost its significance for social progress. . . . The revisionists deny the historical necessity for a proletarian revolution and the dictatorship of the proletariat during the period of transition from capitalism to socialism; reject the principles of proletarian internationalism; and call for the rejection of the Leninist principles of party organization and democratic centralism. Above all, they call for the transformation of the communist party from a militant revolutionary party into some kind of debating society. . . .

The working class and its vanguard—the Marxist-Leninist party—seek to achieve the socialist revolution by peaceful means. . . . In a number of capitalist countries the working class today has the opportunity—given a united working-class and people's front, or other workable forms of political co-operation between the different parties and organizations—to unite a majority of the people, win power without civil war, and ensure the transfer of the basic means of production to the hands of the people. . . . [The] working class . . . can secure a firm majority in parliament, transform parliament from an instrument serving the class interests of the bourgeoisie into an instrument serving the working people, launch a non-parliamentary mass struggle, smash the resistance of the reactionary forces, and create the necessary conditions for the peaceful realization of the socialist revolution. . . .

In the event of the ruling classes resorting to violence against the people, the possibility of non-peaceful transition to socialism should be borne in mind. Leninism teaches, and experience confirms, that the ruling classes never relinquish power voluntarily. In this case the degree of bitterness and the forms of the class struggle will depend not so much on the proletariat as on the resistance put up by the reactionary circles. . . . The possibility of one or another way to socialism depends on the concrete conditions in each country. . . .

In the struggle for winning power and building socialism, the communist parties seek co-operation with the socialist parties. Although right-wing socialist party leaders are doing their best to hamper this co-operation, there are increasing opportunities for co-operation between communists and socialists on many issues. The ideological differences between the communist and socialist parties should not keep them from establishing unity of action on the many pressing issues that confront the working-class movement.

Moscow Declaration (1960)

Extract from the Declaration adopted by the Moscow World Conference of Communist Parties (1960)

The aggressive nature of imperialism has not changed, but real forces have appeared that are capable of foiling its plans of aggression. War is not fatally inevitable. . . . The time is past when the imperialists could decide at will whether there should or should not be war. More than once in the past years the imperialists have brought mankind to the brink of world catastrophe by starting local wars. The resolute stand of the Soviet Union, of the other socialist states, and of all the peaceful forces put an end to the Anglo-French-Israeli intervention in Egypt and averted a military invasion of Syria, Iraq and some other countries. . . . World war can be prevented by the joint efforts of the world socialist camp, the international working class, the national liberation movement, all the countries opposing war, and all peace-loving forces. . . . The policy of peaceful co-existence is also favoured by a definite section of the bourgeoisie of the developed capitalist countries, which takes a sober view of the relationship of forces and of the dire consequences of a modern war. . . . But should the imperialist maniacs start war, the peoples will sweep capitalism out of existence and bury it. . . .

The near future will bring the forces of peace and socialism new successes. The USSR will become the leading industrial power of the world. China will become a mighty industrial state. The socialist system will be turning out more than half the world industrial product. The peace zone will expand. . . . In these conditions a real possibility will have arisen of excluding world war from the life of society even before socialism achieves complete victory on earth, with capitalism still existing in a part of the world. . . .

Peaceful co-existence of countries with different social systems does not mean conciliation of the socialist and bourgeois ideologies. On the contrary, it implies intensification of the struggle of the working class, of all the communist parties, for the triumph of socialist ideas. But ideological and political disputes between states must not be settled through war. . . .

Communists have always recognized the progressive, revolutionary significance of national liberation wars. . . . The peoples of the colonial countries win their independence both through armed struggle and by non-military methods, depending on the specific conditions in the country concerned. . . .

The urgent tasks of national rebirth facing the countries that have shaken off the colonial yoke cannot be effectively accomplished unless a determined struggle is waged against imperialism and the remnants of feudalism by all the patriotic forces of the nation, united in a single national democratic front. . . . The alliance of the working class and the peasantry is the most important force in winning and defending national independence, accomplishing far-reaching democratic transformations, and ensuring social progress. . . . The extent to which the national bourgeoisie participates in the liberation struggle depends to no small degree upon its strength and stability. . . . In present conditions the national bourgeoisie of the colonial and dependent countries unconnected with imperialist circles is objectively interested in the accomplishment of the principal tasks of the anti-imperialist, anti-feudal revolution, and therefore retains the capacity of participating in the revolutionary struggle against imperialism and feudalism. In that sense it is progressive. But it is unstable, and is inclined to compromise with imperialism and feudalism. . . .

After winning political independence the peoples seek solutions to the social problems raised by life and to the problems of reinforcing national independence. Different classes and parties offer different solutions. Which course of development to choose is the internal affair of the peoples themselves. As social contradictions grow, the national bourgeoisie inclines more and more to compromise with domestic reaction and imperialism. The people, however, begin to see that the best way to abolish age-long backwardness and improve their living standard is that of non-capitalist development. . . . The communist parties are working actively for a consistent completion of the anti-imperialist, anti-feudal democratic revolution. . . . They support those actions of national governments leading to the consolidation of the gains achieved and undermining the imperialists' positions. At the same time they firmly oppose anti-democratic, anti-popular acts and those measures of the ruling circles which endanger national independence.
. . .

The socialist countries are true and sincere friends of the peoples fighting for liberation and of those who have thrown off the imperialist yoke. While rejecting on principle any interference in the internal affairs of young national states, they consider it their internationalist duty to help the peoples in strengthening their independence.

Third Soviet Communist Party Programme (1961)

Extract from the Programme adopted by the 22nd Congress of the Communist Party of the Soviet Union (1961)

Communists have never held that the road to revolution lies necessarily through wars between countries. Socialist revolution is not necessarily connected with war. Although both world wars, which were started by the imperialists, culminated in socialist revolutions, revolutions are quite feasible without war. The great objectives of the working class can be realized without world war. Today the conditions for this are more favourable than ever.

The working class and its vanguard—the Marxist-Leninist parties—prefer to achieve the transfer of power from the bourgeoisie to the proletariat by peaceful means, without civil war. Realization of this possibility would meet the interests of the working class and the people as a whole, it would accord with the national interests of the country.

The working class, supported by the majority of the people and firmly repelling opportunist elements incapable of renouncing the policy of compromise with the capitalists and landlords, can defeat the reactionary, anti-popular forces, win a solid majority in Parliament, transform it from a tool serving the class interests of the bourgeoisie into an instrument serving the working people, launch a broad mass struggle outside Parliament, smash the resistance of the reactionary forces and provide the necessary conditions for a peaceful socialist revolution. This can be done only by extending and continuously developing the class struggle of the workers and peasants and the middle strata of the urban population against big monopoly capital and reaction, for far-reaching social reforms, for peace and socialism.

Where the exploiting classes resort to violence against the people, the possibility of a non-peaceful transition to socialism should be borne in mind. Leninism maintains, and historical experience confirms, that the ruling classes do not yield power of their own free will. Hence, the degree of bitterness of the class struggle and the forms it takes will depend not so much on the proletariat as on the strength of the reactionary groups' resistance to the will of the overwhelming majority of the people, and on the use of force by these groups at a particular stage of the struggle for socialism. In each particular country the actual applicability of one method of transition to socialism or the other depends on concrete historical conditions.

It may well be that as the forces of socialism grow, the working-class movement gains strength and the positions of capitalism are weakened, there will arise in certain countries a situation in which it will be preferable for the bourgeoisie, as Marx and Lenin foresaw it, to agree to the means of production being purchased from it and for the proletariat to "pay off" the bourgeoisie.

The success of the struggle which the working class wages for the victory of the revolution will depend on how well the working class and its party master the use of all forms of struggle—peaceful and non-peaceful, parliamentary and extra-parliamentary—and how well they are prepared to replace one form of struggle by another as quickly and unexpectedly as possible.

While the principal law-governed processes of the socialist revolution are common to all countries, the diversity of the national peculiarities and traditions that have arisen in the course of history creates specific conditions for the revolutionary process and for the variety of forms and rates of the proletariat's advent to power. This predetermines the possibility and necessity, in a number of countries, of transition stages in the struggle for the dictatorship of the proletariat, and a variety of forms of political organization of the society building socialism. But whatever the form in which the transition from capitalism to socialism is effected, that transition can come about only through revolution. However varied the forms of a new, people's state power in the period of socialist construction, their essence will be the same—dictatorship of the proletariat, which represents genuine democracy, democracy for the working people.

A bourgeois republic, however democratic, however hallowed by slogans purporting to express the will of the people or nation as a whole, or an extra-class will, inevitably remains in practice—owing to the existence of private capitalist ownership of the means of production—a dictatorship of the bourgeoisie, a machine for the exploitation and suppression of the vast majority of the working people by a handful of capitalists. In contrast to the bourgeoisie, which conceals the class character of the state, the working class does not deny the class character of states.

The dictatorship of the proletariat is a dictatorship of the overwhelming majority over the minority; it is directed against the exploiters, against the oppression of peoples and nations, and is aimed at abolishing all exploitation of man by man. The dictatorship of the proletariat expresses not only the interests of the working class, but also those of all working people; its chief content is not violence but creation, the building of a new, classless society, and the defence of its gains against the enemies of socialism.

Overcoming the split in its ranks is an important condition for the working class to fulfil its historic mission. No bastion of imperialism can withstand a closely knit working class that exercises unity of action. The communist parties favour co-operation with the social democratic parties not only in the struggle for peace, for better living conditions for the working people and for the preservation and extension of their democratic rights and freedoms, but also in the struggle to win power and build a socialist society.

At the same time communists criticize the ideological positions and right-opportunist practice of social democracy and expose the right social democratic leaders, who have sided openly with the bourgeoisie and renounced the traditional socialist demands of the working class. . . .

The dictatorship of the proletariat, born of the socialist revolution, has played an epoch-making role by insuring the victory of socialism in the USSR. In the course of socialist construction, however, it underwent changes. After the exploiting classes had been abolished, the state function of suppressing their resistance ceased to exist. The chief functions of the socialist state—economic and organizational, cultural and educational—have developed in full measure. The socialist state has entered a new phase.

The state has begun to grow into a nation-wide organization of the working people of socialist society. Proletarian democracy is becoming more and more a socialist democracy of the people as a whole. The working class is the only class in history that does not aim to perpetuate its power. Having brought about a complete and final victory of socialism—the first phase of communism—and the transition of society to the full-scale construction of communism, the dictatorship of the proletariat has fulfilled its historic mission and has ceased to be indispensable in the USSR from the point of view of the tasks of internal development.

The state, which arose as a state of the dictatorship of the proletariat, has become a state of the entire people, an organ expressing the interests and will of the people as a whole. Since the working class is the foremost and best organized force of Soviet society, it plays a leading role also in the period of the full-scale construction of communism. The working class will have completed its function of leader of society after communism is built and classes disappear. The party holds that the dictatorship of the working class will cease to be necessary before the state withers away. The state as an organization embracing the entire people will survive until the complete victory of communism. . . .

The party considers it essential to perfect the forms of popular representation and promote the democratic principles of the soviet electoral system. In nominating candidates for election to the soviets, it is necessary to guarantee the widest and fullest discussion of the moral qualities and the activities of the candidates at meetings and in the press to ensure the election of the worthiest and most authoritative of them. To improve the work of the soviets and bring fresh forces into them, it is desirable that at least one-third of the total number of deputies to a soviet should be elected anew each time so that more hundreds of thousands and millions of working people may learn to govern the state.

The party considers systematic renewal of the leading bodies necessary to bring a wider range of able persons into them and rule out abuses of authority by individual government officials. It is advisable to introduce the principle that the leading officials of the union, republican and local bodies should be elected to their offices, as a rule, for not more than three consecutive terms. In those cases when the personal gifts of the official in question are generally believed to make his further activity within a leading body useful and necessary, his re-election may be allowed. His election shall be considered valid, not if he wins with a simple majority, but if not less than three-quarters of the votes are cast in his favour.

The party regards the perfection of the principles of socialist democracy and their rigid observance as a most important task. It is necessary to develop more and more fully regular accountability of soviets and deputies to their constituents and the right of the electorate to recall ahead of term deputies who have not justified confidence placed in them, publicity and the free and full discussion of all the important questions of government and of economic and cultural development at the meetings of soviets, regular accountability of executive government bodies to meetings of soviets—from top to bottom, checking the work of these bodies and control over their activity, systematic discussion by the soviets of questions raised by deputies, criticism of shortcomings in the work of government, economic and other organizations.

Every deputy to a soviet must take an active part in government affairs and carry on definite work. The role of the standing committees of the soviets will become greater. The standing committees of the Supreme Soviets must systematically control the activities of ministries, departments, and economic councils. They must actively contribute to the implementation of the decisions adopted by the respective Supreme Soviets. To improve the work of the legislative bodies and increase control over the executive bodies, deputies shall be periodically released from their official duties for full-time committee work.

An increasing number of questions which now come under the jurisdiction of the departments and sections of executive bodies must be gradually referred to the standing committees of the local soviets for decision. . . .

The party holds that the moral code of the builder of communism should comprise the following principles:

Devotion to the communist cause, love of the socialist motherland and of the other socialist countries;

Conscientious labour for the good of society—he who does not work, neither shall he eat;

Concern on the part of everyone for the preservation and growth of public wealth;

A high sense of public duty, intolerance of actions harmful to the public interest;

Collectivism and comradely mutual assistance: one for all and all for one;

Humane relations and mutual respect between individuals—man is to man a friend, comrade and brother;

Honesty and truthfulness, moral purity, modesty and guilelessness in social and private life;

Mutual respect in the family, and concern for the upbringing of children;

An uncompromising attitude to injustice, parasitism, dishonesty and careerism;

Friendship and brotherhood among all peoples of the USSR, intolerance of national and racial hatred;

An uncompromising attitude to the enemies of communism, peace and the freedom of nations;

Fraternal solidarity with the working people of all countries, and with all peoples.

The Sino–Soviet Controversy (1963)

I. Extract from the letter of June 14, 1963, from the Central Committee of the Chinese Communist Party to the Communist Party of the Soviet Union containing the "25 Points"

(1) For several years there have been differences within the international communist movement. . . . The central issue is . . . whether or not to accept the fact that the people still living under the imperialist and capitalist system . . . need to make revolution, and whether or not to accept the fact that the people already on the socialist road . . . need to carry their revolution forward to the end. . . .

(2) The revolutionary principles of the 1957 declaration and the 1960 statement . . . may be summarized as follows: . . . Workers of the world, unite with the oppressed peoples; . . . bring the proletarian world revolution step by step to complete victory; and establish a new world without imperialism, without capitalism, and without the exploitation of man by man. . . .

(3) If the general line of the international communist movement is one-sidedly reduced to "peaceful coexistence", "peaceful competition", and "peaceful transition", this is to violate the revolutionary principles of the 1957 declaration and the 1960 statement. . . .

(4) The fundamental contradictions in the contemporary world . . . are: the contradiction between the socialist camp and the imperialist camp; the contradiction between the proletariat and the bourgeoisie in the capitalist countries; the contradiction between the oppressed nations and imperialism; and the contradictions among imperialist countries and among monopoly capitalist groups. . . .

(5) The following erroneous views should be repudiated . . . : (i) the view which blots out the class content of the contradiction between the socialist and imperialist camps . . . ; (ii) the view which recognizes only the contradiction between the socialist and imperialist camps . . . ; (iii) the view which maintains . . . that the contradiction between the proletariat and the bourgeoisie can be resolved without a proletarian revolution in each country and that the contradiction between the oppressed nations and imperialism can be resolved without revolution . . . ; (iv) the view which denies that the development of the inherent contradictions in the contemporary capitalist world inevitably leads to a new situation in which the imperialist countries are locked in an intense struggle, and asserts that the contradictions among the imperialist countries can be reconciled or even eliminated by "international agreements among the big monopolies"; and (v) the view which maintains that the contradiction between the two world systems of socialism and capitalism will automatically disappear in the course of "economic competition", . . . and that a "world without wars", a new world of "all-round co-operation", will appear. . . .

(6) Now that there is a socialist camp consisting of 13 countries—Albania, Bulgaria, China, Cuba, Czechoslovakia, the German Democratic Republic, Hungary, the Democratic People's Republic of Korea, Mongolia, Poland, Romania, the Soviet Union, and the Democratic Republic of Vietnam—. . . the

touchstone of proletarian internationalism is whether or not it resolutely defends the whole of the socialist camp. . . .

If anybody . . . does not defend the unity of the socialist camp but on the contrary creates tension and splits within it, or even follows the policies of the Yugoslav revisionists, tries to liquidate the socialist camp, or helps capitalist countries to attack fraternal socialist countries, he is betraying the interests of the entire international proletariat. . . .

If anybody, following in the footsteps of others, defends the erroneous opportunist line and policies pursued by a certain socialist country instead of upholding the correct Marxist-Leninist line . . . he is departing from Marxism-Leninism and proletarian internationalism.

(7) The 1960 statement points out: . . . "US imperialism is the main force of aggression and war." . . . To make no distinction between enemies, friends and ourselves, and to entrust the fate of the people and of mankind to collaboration with US imperialism, is to lead people astray. . . .

(8) Certain persons in the international communist movement are now taking a passive or scornful or negative attitude towards the struggles of the oppressed nations for liberation. . . . The attitude taken towards the revolutionary struggles of the people in the Asian, African, and Latin American countries is an important criterion for differentiating those who want revolution from those who do not. . . .

(9) The oppressed nations and peoples of Asia, Africa and Latin America are faced with the urgent task of fighting imperialism and its lackeys. . . . In these areas extremely broad sections of the population refuse to be slaves of imperialism. They include not only the workers, peasants, intellectuals, and petty bourgeoisie, but also the patriotic national bourgeoisie and even certain kings, princes, and aristocrats. . . . The proletariat and its party must . . . organize a broad united front against imperialism. . . . The proletarian party should maintain its ideological, political and organizational independence and insist on the leadership of the revolution. The proletarian party and the revolutionary people must learn to master all forms of struggle, including armed struggle. . . . The policy of the proletarian party should be . . . to unite with the bourgeoisie, in so far as they tend to be progressive, anti-imperialist, and anti-feudal, but to struggle against their reactionary tendencies to compromise and collaborate with imperialism and the forces of feudalism. . . .

(10) In the imperialist and capitalist countries the proletarian revolution and the dictatorship of the proletariat are essential. . . . It is wrong to refuse to use parliamentary and other legal forms of struggle when they can and should be used. However, if a Marxist-Leninist party falls into legalism or parliamentary cretinism, confining the struggle within the limits permitted by the bourgeoisie, this will inevitably lead to renouncing the proletarian revolution and the dictatorship of the proletariat.

(11) Marx and Lenin did raise the possibility that revolutions may develop peacefully. But, as Lenin pointed out, the peaceful development of revolution is an opportunity "very seldom to be met with in the history of revolution". As a matter of fact, there is no historical precedent for peaceful transition from capitalism to socialism. . . . The proletarian party must never base its thinking, its policies for revolution, and its entire work on the assumption that the imperialists and reactionaries will accept peaceful transformation. . . .

(12) If the leading group in any party adopts a non-revolutionary line and converts it into a reformist party, then Marxist-Leninists inside and outside the party will replace them and lead the people in making revolution. . . . There are certain persons who assert that they have made the greatest creative contributions to revolutionary theory since Lenin and that they alone are correct. But it is very

dubious . . . whether they really have a general line for the international communist movement which conforms with Marxism-Leninism. . . .

(13) Certain persons have one-sidedly exaggerated the role of peaceful competition between socialist and imperialist countries in their attempt to substitute peaceful competition for the revolutionary struggles of the oppressed peoples. According to their preaching, it would seem that imperialism will automatically collapse in the course of this peaceful competition, and that the only thing the oppressed peoples have to do is to wait quietly for the advent of this day. What does this have in common with Marxist-Leninist views?

Moreover, certain persons have concocted the strange tale that China and some other socialist countries want to "unleash wars" and to spread socialism by "wars between states". As the statement of 1960 points out, such tales are nothing but imperialist and reactionary slanders. To put it bluntly, the purpose of those who repeat these slanders is to hide the fact that they are opposed to revolutions by the oppressed peoples and nations of the world and opposed to others supporting such revolutions.

(14) Certain persons say that revolutions are entirely possible without war. . . . If they are referring to a war of national liberation or a revolutionary civil war, then this formulation is, in effect, opposed to revolutionary wars and to revolution. If they are referring to a world war, then they are shooting at a non-existent target. Although Marxist-Leninists have pointed out, on the basis of the history of the two world wars, that world wars inevitably lead to revolution, no Marxist-Leninist ever has held or ever will hold that revolution must be made through world war.

Marxist-Leninists take the abolition of war as their ideal and believe that war can be abolished. But how can war be abolished? . . . Certain persons now actually hold that it is possible to bring about "a world without weapons, without armed forces, and without wars" through "general and complete disarmament" while the system of imperialism and of the exploitation of man by man still exists. This is sheer illusion. . . .

If one regards general and complete disarmament as the fundamental road to world peace, spreads the illusion that imperialism will automatically lay down its arms, and tries to liquidate the revolutionary struggles of the oppressed peoples and nations on the pretext of disarmament, then this is deliberately to deceive the people of the world and help the imperialists in their policies of aggression and war. . . . World peace can be won only by the struggles of the people in all countries and not by begging the imperialists for it. . . .

(15) The complete banning and destruction of nuclear weapons is an important task in the struggle to defend world peace. We must do our utmost to this end. . . . However, if the imperialists are forced to accept an agreement to ban nuclear weapons, it decidedly will not be because of their "love for humanity", but because of the pressure of the people of all countries and for the sake of their own vital interests. . . .

The emergence of nuclear weapons does not and cannot resolve the fundamental contradictions in the contemporary world, does not and cannot alter the law of class struggle, and does not and cannot change the nature of imperialism and reaction. It cannot, therefore, be said that with the emergence of nuclear weapons the possibility and the necessity of social and national revolutions have disappeared, or that the basic principles of Marxism-Leninism, and especially the theories of proletarian revolution and the dictatorship of the proletariat . . . have become outmoded. . . .

(16) It was Lenin who advanced the thesis that it is possible for the socialist countries to practice peaceful coexistence with the capitalist countries. . . . The People's Republic of China, too, has consistently pursued the policy of peaceful

coexistence with countries having different social systems, and it is China which initiated the five principles of peaceful coexistence.

However, a few years ago certain persons suddenly claimed Lenin's policy of peaceful coexistence as their own "great discovery". They maintain that they have a monopoly in the interpretation of this policy. They treat "peaceful co-existence" as if it were an all-inclusive, mystical book from heaven, and attribute to it every success the people of the world achieve by struggle. What is more, they label all who disagree with their distortions of Lenin's views as opponents of peaceful co-existence. . . .

Lenin's principle of peaceful co-existence . . . designates a relationship between countries with different social systems. . . . It should never be extended to apply to the relations between oppressed and oppressor nations, between oppressed and oppressor countries, or between oppressed and oppressor classes, and never be described as the main content of the transition from capitalism to socialism. Still less should it be asserted that peaceful co-existence is mankind's road to socialism. . . .

The general line of the foreign policy of the socialist countries should have the following content: to develop relations of friendship, mutual assistance and co-operation among the countries of the socialist camp in accordance with the principle of proletarian internationalism: to strive for peaceful co-existence on the basis of the five principles with countries having different social systems, and oppose the imperialist policies of aggression and war; and to support and assist the revolutionary struggles of all the oppressed peoples and nations. These three aspects are interrelated and indivisible, and not a single one can be omitted.

(17) For a very long historical period after the proletariat takes power class struggle continues. . . . To deny the existence of class struggle in the period of the dictatorship of the proletariat and the necessity of thoroughly completing the socialist revolution on the economic, political, and ideological fronts . . . violates Marxism-Leninism.

(18) The fundamental thesis of Marx and Lenin is that the dictatorship of the proletariat will inevitably continue for the entire historical period of the transition from capitalism to communism. . . . If it is announced, half-way through, that the dictatorship of the proletariat is no longer necessary . . . this would lead to extremely grave consequences and make any transition to communism out of the question. . . .

Is it possible to replace the state of the dictatorship of the proletariat by a "state of the whole people"? This is not a question of the internal affairs of any particular country, but a fundamental problem involving the universal truth of Marxism-Leninism. . . . In calling a socialist state the "state of the whole people", is one trying to replace the Marxist-Leninist theory of the state by the bourgeois theory of the state? Is one trying to replace the state of the dictatorship of the proletariat by a state of a different character? . . .

(19) Is it possible to replace the party which is the vanguard of the proletariat by a "party of the entire people"? This, too, is not a question of the internal affairs of any particular party, but a fundamental problem involving the universal truth of Marxism-Leninism. . . . What will happen if it is announced half-way before entering the higher stage of communist society that the party of the proletariat has become a "party of the entire people" and if its proletarian class character is repudiated? . . . Does this not disarm the proletariat and all the working people, organizationally and ideologically, and is it not tantamount to helping to restore capitalism? . . .

(20) Over the past few years certain persons have violated Lenin's integral teachings about the inter-relationship of leaders, party, class and masses, and raised the issue of "combating the personality cult"; that is erroneous and

harmful. . . . To raise the question of "combating the personality cult" is actually to counterpose the leaders to the masses, undermine the party's unified leadership, which is based on democratic centralism, dissipate its fighting strength, and disintegrate its ranks. . . .

While loudly combating the so-called personality cult, certain persons are in reality doing their best to defame the proletarian party and the dictatorship of the proletariat. At the same time, they are enormously exaggerating the role of certain individuals, shifting all errors on to others, and claiming all credit for themselves. What is more serious is that, under the pretext of "combating the personality cult", certain persons are crudely interfering in the internal affairs of other fraternal parties and fraternal countries, and forcing other fraternal parties to change their leadership in order to impose their own wrong line on these parties. What is this if not great-power chauvinism, sectarianism, and splittism? . . .

(21) Relations between socialist countries, whether large or small, and whether more developed or less developed economically, must be based on the principles of complete equality. . . . Every socialist country must rely mainly on itself for its construction. . . . If, proceeding only from its own partial interests, any socialist country unilaterally demands that other fraternal countries submit to its needs, and uses the pretext of opposing what they call "going it alone" and "nationalism" to prevent other fraternal countries from applying the principle of relying mainly on their own efforts in their construction and from developing their economies on the basis of independence, or even goes to the length of putting economic pressure on other fraternal countries—then these are pure manifestations of national egoism. . . . In relations among socialist countries it would be preposterous to follow the practice of gaining profit for oneself at the expense of others . . . or go so far as to take the "economic integration" and the "Common Market", which monopoly capitalist groups have instituted for the purpose of seizing markets and grabbing profits, as examples which socialist countries ought to follow in their economic co-operation and mutual assistance.

(22) If the principle of independence and equality is accepted in relations among fraternal parties, then it is impermissible for any party to place itself above others, to interfere in their internal affairs, and to adopt patriarchal ways in relations with them. If it is accepted that there are no "superiors" and "subordinates" in relations among fraternal parties, then it is impermissible to impose the programme, resolutions, and line of one's own party on other fraternal parties as the "common programme" of the international communist movement.

If the principle of reaching unanimity through consultation is accepted in relations between fraternal parties, then one should not emphasize "who is in the majority" or "who is in the minority", and bank on a so-called majority in order to force through one's own erroneous line and carry out sectarian and splitting policies. If it is agreed that differences between fraternal parties should be settled through inter-party consultation, then other fraternal parties should not be attacked publicly and by name at one's own party congress or other party congresses, in speeches by party leaders, resolutions, statements, etc.; and still less should the ideological differences among fraternal parties be extended into the sphere of state relations. . . .

In the sphere of relations among fraternal parties and countries, the question of Soviet-Albanian relations is an outstanding one at present. . . . How to treat the Marxist-Leninist fraternal Albanian Party of Labour is one question. How to treat the Yugoslav revisionist clique of traitors to Marxism-Leninism is quite another question. These two essentially different questions must on no account be placed on a par.

Your letter [i.e. of March 30, 1963, from the CPSU to the Chinese party] says that you "do not relinquish the hope that the relations between the CPSU and the Albanian Party of Labour may be improved", but at the same time you continue to attack the Albanian comrades for what you call "splitting activities". Clearly this is self-contradictory and in no way contributes to resolving the problem of Soviet-Albanian relations.

Who is it that has taken splitting actions in Soviet-Albanian relations? Who is it that has extended the ideological differences between the Soviet and Albanian parties to state relations? Who is it that has brought the divergences between the Soviet and Albanian parties and between the two countries into the open before the enemy? Who is it that has openly called for a change in the Albanian party and state leadership? All this is plain and clear to the whole world. . . . We once again express our sincere hope that the leading comrades of the CPSU will observe the principles guiding relations among fraternal parties and countries and take the initiative in seeking an effective way to improve Soviet-Albanian relations. . . .

The comrades of the CPSU state in their letter that "the Communist Party of the Soviet Union has never taken and will never take a single step that could show hostility among the peoples of our country toward the fraternal Chinese people or other peoples". Here we do not desire to enumerate the many unpleasant events that have occurred in the past; we only wish that the comrades of the CPSU will strictly abide by this statement in their future actions. During the past few years our party members and our people have exercised the greatest restraint in the face of a series of grave incidents which were in violation of the principles guiding relations among fraternal parties and countries. . . . The spirit of proletarian internationalism of the Chinese Communists and the Chinese people has stood a severe test. . . .

(23) Certain persons are now attempting to introduce the Yugoslav revisionist clique into the socialist community and the international communist ranks. This is openly to tear up the agreement unanimously reached at the 1960 meeting of the fraternal parties and is absolutely impermissible.

Over the past few years . . . the many experiences and lessons of the international communist movement have fully confirmed the correctness of the conclusion in the [Moscow] declaration and the statement that revisionism is at present the main danger in the international communist movement. However, certain persons are openly saying that dogmatism and not revisionism is the main danger, or that dogmatism is no less dangerous than revisionism. . . . Genuine Marxist-Leninist parties . . . must not barter away principles, approving one thing today and another tomorrow. . . .

It is necessary at all times to adhere to the universal truth of Marxism-Leninism. Failure to do so will lead to right opportunist or revisionist errors. On the other hand, it is always necessary to proceed from reality . . . and independently work out and apply policies and tactics suited to the conditions of one's own country. Errors of dogmatism will be committed if one fails to do so, if one mechanically copies the policies and tactics of another communist party, submits blindly to the will of others, or accepts without analysis the programme and resolutions of another communist party as one's own line. Some people are now violating this basic principle. . . . On the pretext of "creatively developing Marxism-Leninism" they cast aside the universal truth of Marxism-Leninism. Moreover, they describe as "universal Marxist-Leninist truths" their own prescriptions, which are based on nothing but subjective conjecture . . . and they force others to accept these prescriptions unconditionally. That is why so many grave phenomena have come to pass in the international communist movement. . . .

(24) If a party is not a proletarian revolutionary party but a bourgeois reformist party; if it is not a Marxist-Leninist party but a revisionist party; . . . if it is not a party that can use its brains to think for itself . . . but instead is a party that parrots the words of others, copies foreign experience without analysis, runs hither and thither in response to the baton of certain persons abroad, and has become a hodgepodge of revisionism, dogmatism, and everything but Marxist-Leninist principle; then such a party is absolutely incapable of leading the proletariat and the masses in revolutionary struggle. . . .

(25) The public polemics in the international communist movement have been provoked by certain fraternal party leaders and forced on us. Since a public debate has been provoked, it ought to be conducted on the basis of equality among fraternal parties . . . and by presenting the facts and reasoning things out. . . . Since certain party leaders have published innumerable articles attacking other fraternal parties, why do they not publish in their own press the articles those parties have written in reply?

Latterly, the Communist Party of China has been subjected to preposterous attacks. . . . We have published these articles and speeches attacking us in our own press. . . . Between Dec. 15, 1962, and March 8, 1963, we wrote seven articles in reply to our attackers. . . . Presumably you are referring to these articles when towards the end of your letter of March 30 you accuse the Chinese press of making "groundless attacks" on the CPSU. It is turning things upside down to describe articles replying to our attackers as "attacks".

Since you describe our articles as "groundless" and as so very bad, why do you not publish all seven of these "groundless attacks" in the same way as we have published your articles, and let all the Soviet comrades and Soviet people think for themselves and judge who is right and who wrong? You are of course entitled to make a point-by-point refutation of these articles you consider "groundless attacks". Although you call our articles "groundless" and our arguments wrong, you do not tell the Soviet people what our arguments actually are. This practice can hardly be described as showing a serious attitude towards the discussion of problems by fraternal parties, towards the truth, or towards the masses. . . .

II. Extract from the letter of July 14, 1963, from the Central Committee of the Soviet Communist Party to the Chinese Communist Party

---

The frankly hostile actions of the CPC [Chinese Communist Party] leaders, their persistent striving to sharpen polemics in the international communist movement, the deliberate distortion of the positions of our party, and the incorrect interpretation of the motives for which we refrained temporarily from publishing the letter impel us to publish the letter of the CPC Central Committee of June 14, 1963, and to give our appraisal of this document. All who read the letter of the CPC Central Committee will see, behind the bombastic phrases about unity and cohesion, unfriendly and slanderous attacks on our party and our country. . . .

The document is crammed with charges—overt and covert—against the CPSU and the Soviet Union. The authors of the letter permit themselves unworthy fabrications, insulting to communists, about "the betrayal of the interests of the whole international proletariat and all the peoples of the world" and "a departure from Marxism-Leninism and proletarian internationalism". They hint at "cowardice in face of the imperialists", at "a step back in the course of historic development", and even at "the organizational and moral disarming of the proletariat and all working people", which is tantamount to "helping to restore capitalism" in our country. . . .

At a first glance many theses in the letter may seem puzzling. Whom are the Chinese comrades actually arguing with? Are there communists who, for instance, object to socialist revolution or who do not regard it as their duty to fight against imperialism and to support the national liberation movement? . . . The Chinese comrades first ascribe to the CPSU and other Marxist-Leninist parties views which they have never expressed and which are alien to them; secondly, by paying lip-service to formulae and positions borrowed from the documents of the communist movement, they try to camouflage their erroneous views. . . .

In point of fact, however, the questions which bear on vital interests of the peoples are in the centre of the dispute. These are the questions of war and peace, the role and development of the world socialist system, the struggle against the ideology and practice of the personality cult, the strategy and tactics of the world labour movement, and the national liberation struggle. . . .

The world communist movement, in the declaration and statement, set before communists as a task of extreme importance that of struggling for peace and averting a nuclear world catastrophe. . . . Though the nature of imperialism has not changed and the danger of the outbreak of war has not been averted, in modern conditions the forces of peace, of which the mighty community of socialist states is the main bulwark, can by their joint efforts avert a new world war. . . .

The nuclear rocket weapons which have been created . . . possess an unprecedented devastating force. . . . Have communists the right to ignore this danger? Must we tell the people the whole truth about the consequences of nuclear war? We believe that, without question, we must. This cannot have a "paralysing" effect on the masses, as the Chinese comrades assert. On the contrary, the truth about modern war will mobilize the will and energy of the masses in the struggle for peace and against imperialism. . . .

What is the position of the CPC leadership? What do the theses that they propagate mean—that an end cannot be put to war so long as imperialism exists? That peaceful co-existence is an illusion? That it is not the general line of the foreign policy of socialist countries? That the peace struggle hinders the revolutionary struggle? . . . They do not believe in the possibility of preventing a new world war; they underestimate the forces of peace and socialism and overestimate the forces of imperialism; in fact, they ignore the mobilization of the masses for the struggle against the war danger. . . .

The Chinese comrades obviously underestimate the whole danger of nuclear war. "The atomic bomb is a paper tiger, it is not terrible at all", they contend. The main thing is to put an end to imperialism as quickly as possible, but how and with what losses this will be achieved seems to be a secondary question. To whom, it is right to ask, is it secondary? To the hundreds of millions of people who are doomed to death in the event of the unleashing of a nuclear war? To the states that will be erased from the face of the earth in the very first hours of such a war? . . .

Some responsible Chinese leaders have also declared that it is possible to sacrifice hundreds of millions of peoples in war. "On the ruins of destroyed imperialism", asserts *Long Live Leninism*, which was approved by the CPC Central Committee, "the victorious peoples will create with tremendous speed a civilization a thousand times higher than the capitalist system, and will build their bright future". Is it permissible to ask the Chinese comrades if they realize what sort of ruins a nuclear world war would leave behind? . . . They say frankly, "On the ruins of a destroyed imperialism"—in other words, as a result of the unleashing of war—"a bright future will be built". If we agree to this, then indeed there is no need for the principle of peaceful co-existence. . . .

We ourselves produce the nuclear weapon and have manufactured it in sufficient quantity. We know its destructive force full well. If imperialism starts a war against us we shall not hesitate to use this formidable weapon against the aggressor; but if we are not attacked we shall not be the first to use this weapon. . . .

We would like to ask the Chinese comrades who suggest building a "bright future" on the ruins of the old world destroyed by a nuclear war whether they have consulted the working class of the countries where imperialism dominates. . . . The nuclear bomb does not distinguish between the imperialists and working people. . . .

The posing of the question in this way by the Chinese comrades may give rise to the well-justified suspicion that this is no longer a class approach in the struggle for the abolition of capitalism, but has entirely different aims. If both the exploiters and the exploited are buried under the ruins of the old world, who will build the "bright future"? In this connexion it is impossible not to note the fact that instead of the internationalist class approach expressed in the call "Workers of the world, unite", the Chinese comrades propagate the slogan, which is devoid of any class meaning, "The wind from the east prevails over the wind from the west". . . .

The true position of the CPC leadership is demonstrated very clearly . . . in its complete underestimation and, what is more, deliberate ignoring of the struggle for disarmament. They try to prove that general disarmament is possible only when socialism triumphs all over the world. Must the Marxists sit on their hands, waiting for the victory of socialism all over the world, while mankind suffocates in the clutches of the arms race? . . . One can repeat ad infinitum that war is inevitable, claiming that such a viewpoint is evidence of one's "revolutionary spirit". In fact, this approach merely indicates lack of faith in one's strength and fear of imperialism. . . .

The CPC Central Committee accuses the communist parties of extending peaceful co-existence between states with different social systems to relations between the exploiters and the exploited, between the oppressed and the oppressing classes, between the working masses and the imperialists. This is a truly monstrous fabrication. . . . When we speak of peaceful co-existence we mean the inter-state relations of the socialist countries with the countries of capitalism. The principle of peaceful co-existence, naturally, can in no way be applied to relations between the antagonistic classes inside the capitalist states. . . .

Soviet people find it strange and outrageous that the Chinese comrades should be trying to smear the CPSU programme. Alluding to the fact that our party proclaims as its task the struggle for a better life for the people, the CPC leaders hint at some sort of "bourgeoisification" and "degeneration" of Soviet society. To follow their line of thinking, it seems that if a people walks in rope sandals and eats watery soup out of a common bowl, that is communism, and if a working man lives well and wants to live even better tomorrow, that is almost tantamount to the restoration of capitalism! . . .

The next important question on which we differ is that of ways and methods of the revolutionary struggle of the working class. As depicted by the Chinese comrades, the differences on this question appear as follows: one side—they themselves—stands for world revolution, while the other—the CPSU, the Marxist-Leninist parties—have forgotten the revolution and even fear it, and instead of revolutionary struggle are concerned with things unworthy of a real revolutionary, such as peace, the economic development of the socialist countries, the improvement of the living standards of their peoples, and the struggle for the democratic rights and vital interests of the working people of the capitalist countries. . . .

Lenin taught that "we exert our main influence on the international revolution by our economic policy". . . . But now it turns out that there are comrades who have decided that Lenin was wrong. What is this—lack of faith in the ability of the socialist countries to defeat capitalism in economic competition? Or is it the attitude of persons who, on meeting with difficulties in building socialism, have become disappointed and do not see the possibility of exerting the main influence on the international revolutionary movement by their economic successes? . . . They want to achieve the revolution sooner, by other and what seem to them shorter ways. But the victorious revolution can consolidate its successes and prove the superiority of socialism over capitalism by the work, and only by the work of the people. . . .

The Chinese comrades, in a haughty and abusive way, accuse the Communist parties of France, Italy, the United States and other countries of nothing less than opportunism and reformism, of "parliamentary cretinism", even of slipping down to "bourgeois socialism". On what grounds do they do this? On the grounds that these Communist parties do not put forward the slogan of an immediate proletarian revolution, although even the Chinese leaders must realize that this cannot be done without the existence of a revolutionary situation. . . .

The Chinese comrades have also disagreed with the world communist movement on the forms of the transition of different countries to socialism. . . . The Chinese comrades regard as the main criterion of revolutionary spirit recognition of the armed uprising. . . . [They] are thereby in fact denying the possibility of using peaceful forms of struggle for the victory of the socialist revolution, whereas Marxism-Leninism teaches that communists must master all forms of revolutionary class struggle, both violent and non-violent.

Yet another important question is that of the relationship between the struggle of the international working class and the national liberation movement of the peoples of Asia, Africa and Latin America. . . . These are the great forces of our epoch. Correct co-ordination between them constitutes one of the main prerequisites for victory over imperialism.

How do the Chinese comrades solve this problem? This is seen from their new theory, according to which the main contradiction of our time is not between socialism and imperialism, but between the national liberation movement and imperialism. The decisive force in the struggle against imperialism, the Chinese comrades maintain, is not the world system of socialism, not the struggle of the international working class, but the national liberation movement.

In this way the Chinese comrades apparently want to win popularity among the peoples of Asia, Africa and Latin America by the easiest possible means. But let no one be deceived by this theory. Whether the Chinese theoreticians want it or not, this theory in essence means isolating the national liberation movement from the international working class and its creation, the world system of socialism. . . . The Chinese comrades . . . want to amend Lenin and prove that it is not the working class but the petty bourgeoisie or the national bourgeoisie, or even "certain patriotically-minded kings, princes, and aristocrats", who must be the leaders of the world struggle against imperialism. . . .

The question arises, what is the explanation for the incorrect propositions of the CPC leadership on the basic problems of our time? It is either the complete divorcement of the Chinese comrades from actual reality—a dogmatic, bookish approach to problems of war, peace, and revolution; their lack of understanding of the concrete conditions of the present epoch—or the fact that behind the rumpus about the "world revolution" raised by the Chinese comrades there are other goals, which have nothing in common with revolution. . . .

Lin Biao (1965)

Marshal Lin Biao (Chinese Defence Minister in the 1960s, vice-chairman of the Communist Party and Chairman Mao's designated successor until his flight, death and disgrace in 1971) on world Revolution (1965)

Mao Zedong's theory of the establishment of rural revolutionary base areas and encirclement of the cities from the countryside is of universal practical importance for the present revolutionary struggles of the oppressed peoples in Asia, Africa, and Latin America.

Taking the entire globe, if North America and Western Europe can be called "the cities of the world", then Asia, Africa, and Latin America constitute "the rural areas of the world". Since World War II the proletarian revolutionary movement has for various reasons been temporarily held back in the North American and West European capitalist countries, while the people's revolutionary movement in Asia, Africa and Latin America has been growing vigorously. In a sense, the contemporary world revolution also presents a picture of the encirclement of cities by the rural areas. In the final analysis, the whole cause of world revolution hinges on the revolutionary struggles of the Asian, African and Latin American peoples who make up the overwhelming majority of the world's population.

Theory of the Cultural Revolution (1967)

Extract from *The Dictatorship of the Proletariat and that Renegade, China's Khrushchev*, published in *Wenhui Bao* (Shanghai), Aug. 25, 1967

Once China had in the main completed the socialist transformation of the means of production, it faced two possible alternatives: to persevere in the dictatorship of the proletariat, unfold the socialist revolution on both the political and ideological fronts, and carry the revolution through to the end, or to betray the dictatorship of the proletariat, proclaim the dying out of class struggle and the non-existence of classes, and bring about a capitalist restoration. . . . China's Khrushchev [i.e. President Liu Shaoqi] came out at this juncture to oppose Mao Zedong's thought by unscrupulously publicizing the theory that "class struggle is dying out". He babbled that classes had been eliminated and class struggle was dying out, since the system of ownership had been transformed and the exploiting classes were deprived of their means of production. . . .

Class is not only an economic concept; more important, it is a political concept. During the thousands of years of their rule, the exploiting classes held a dominant position not only in the economic but in the political, ideological, and cultural fields. Class struggle manifests itself in different forms—political, economic and ideological. In the political and ideological fields the struggle is far more acute and fierce than in the economic field.

Under the dictatorship of the proletariat the landlords have no land, the rich peasants are no longer rich, and the capitalists have no capital. . . . They are deprived of their means of production and have also lost their ruling position politically. But the forces of the exploiting classes are still very strong. They can still exist by virtue of their dominance in the fields of ideology and culture or their traditional influences. If the socialist revolution is carried out only on the economic front and not on the political and ideological fronts, and if there is no Great Proletarian Cultural Revolution, it is impossible thoroughly to remould the elements of the exploiting classes and finally abolish classes.

Although the bourgeois elements have become administrative personnel in joint state–private enterprises, they still receive payments at a fixed rate of interest on their share of capital in the joint enterprises, and have not yet cut themselves loose from the roots of exploitation. . . . The landlords have been deprived of their land, but they still keep their title-deeds in secret places and continue to record their family trees. In the vain hope of staging a comeback, they have never for a moment forgotten their documents reminding them of their lost property and forfeited rights. Even the rich peasants always hanker after the old days when they lived on exploitation. . . .

The existence of the bourgeoisie and its influence is bound to corrode the ranks of the proletariat, and the bourgeoisie invariably finds its agents inside the apparatus of the dictatorship of the proletariat. These agents are the main and most dangerous class enemy. They usurp leading positions and turn the power of leadership into their prerogative to oppress and exploit the masses: they recruit deserters and renegades and form cliques serving their selfish interests in a vain attempt to exercise a dictatorship of the bourgeoisie and restore capitalism. . . . Once this gang, the most dangerous enemies, usurps state power, the landlords who have no land will again become landlords with land, the rich peasants who are not rich will become rich again through exploitation, and the capitalists who have no capital will again become capitalists with capital. This has already become an indisputable reality in the Soviet Union, in Yugoslavia, and in a number of so-called socialist countries in Eastern Europe.

The theories of the "dying out of class struggle" and the "withering away of the state" advocated by China's Khrushchev inevitably led to negation of the dictatorship of the proletariat. . . . When a revised edition of his book on self-cultivation [i.e. President Liu's *How to be a Good Communist*] was published in 1962 . . . China's Khrushchev said: "Class struggle has in the main ended, counter-revolutionaries have become fewer and so have the number of criminal cases, so the state apparatus of dictatorship can be reduced in size. . . . From now on, the most important task of the state is to organize social life." . . .

During the entire period of the transition from socialism to communism, the dictatorial function of the state apparatus should be strengthened, not weakened. By setting what he called the organizing of social life in opposition to the state's dictatorial function, China's Khrushchev was trying his hardest to attack and negate the state's dictatorial function. He was trying to replace the socialist state with "a state of the whole people".

Che Guevara (1961)

Extract from: Ernesto (Che) Guevara, *Guerrilla Warfare* (1961)

Guerrilla warfare obeys laws, some derived from the general laws of war and others owing to its own special character. If there is a real intention to begin the struggle from some foreign country or from some distant and remote regions within the same country, it is obvious that it must begin in small conspiratorial movements of secret members acting without mass support or knowledge. If the guerrilla movement is born spontaneously out of the reaction of a group of individuals to some form of coercion, it is possible that the later organization of this guerrilla nucleus to prevent its annihilation will be sufficient for a beginning. But generally guerrilla warfare starts from a well-considered act of will: some chief with prestige starts an uprising for the salvation of his people, beginning his work in different conditions in a foreign country. . . .

The minimum number with which it is possible to initiate a guerrilla war . . . should be a nucleus of 30 to 50 men; this figure is sufficient to initiate an armed fight in any country of the Americas with their conditions of favourable territory for operations, hunger for land, repeated attacks upon justice, etc.

Weapons, as has already been said, should be of the same type as those used by the enemy. Considering always that every government is in principle hostile to a guerrilla action being undertaken from its territory, the bands that prepare themselves should not be greater than approximately 50 to 100 men per unit. In other words, though there is no objection to 500 men initiating a war, all 500 should not be concentrated in one place. They are so numerous as to attract attention and in case of any betrayal of confidence or of any raid, the whole group falls; on the other hand, it is more difficult to raid various places simultaneously. . . .

Naturally victory cannot be considered as finally won until the army that sustained the former regime has been systematically and totally smashed. Further, all the institutions that sheltered the former regime should be wiped out. But since this is a manual for guerrilla bands we will confine ourselves to analysing the problem of national defence in case of war or aggression against the new power.

The first development we meet is that world public opinion, "the respectable press", the "truthful" news agencies of the United States and of the other countries belonging to the monopolies will begin an attack on the liberated country, an attack as aggressive and systematic as the laws of popular reform. For this reason not even a skeleton of personnel from the former army can be retained. Militarism, mechanical obedience, traditional concepts of military duty, discipline and morale cannot be eradicated with one blow. Nor can the victors, who are good fighters, decent and kind-hearted, but at the same time generally lacking education, be allowed to remain in contact with the vanquished, who are proud of their specialized military knowledge in some combat arm—in mathematics, fortifications, logistics, etc.—and who hate the uncultured guerrilla fighters with all their might.

There are, of course, individual cases of military men who break with the past and enter into the new organization with a spirit of complete co-operation. These persons are doubly useful, because they unite with their love of the people's cause the knowledge necessary for carrying forward the creation of the new popular army. A second step will be consequent upon the first: as the old army is smashed and dismembered as an institution and its former posts occupied by the new army, it will be necessary to reorganize the new force. Its former guerrilla character, operating under independent chiefs without planning, can be changed; but it is very important to emphasize that operational concepts of the guerrilla band should still serve as the guide to structure. These concepts will determine the organic formation and the equipment of the popular army. Care should be taken to avoid the error that we fell into during the first months of trying to put the new popular army into the old bottles of military discipline and ancient organization. This error can cause serious maladjustments and can lead to a complete lack of organization.

Preparation should begin immediately for the new defensive war that will have to be fought by the people's army, accustomed to independence of command within the common struggle and dynamism in the management of each armed group. This army will have two immediate problems. One will be the incorporation of thousands of last-hour revolutionaries, good and bad, whom it is necessary to train for the rigours of guerrilla life and to give revolutionary indoctrination in accelerated and intensive courses. Revolutionary indoctrination that gives the necessary ideological unity to the army of the people is the basis of national security both in the long and short runs. The other problem is the difficulty of adaptation to the new organizational structure.

A corps to take charge of sowing the new truths of the revolution among all the units of the army should immediately be created. It should explain to the soldiers, peasants and workers, who have come out of the mass of the people, the justice and the truth of each revolutionary act, the aspirations of the revolution, why there is a fight, why so many companions have died without seeing the victory. United to this intensive indoctrination, accelerated courses of primary instruction that will begin to overcome illiteracy should also be given, in order to improve the rebel army gradually until it has become an instrument of high technical qualifications, solid ideological structure, and magnificent combat power.

Régis Debray (1967)

Extract from: Régis Debray, *Revolution in the Revolution?* (1967)

In Latin America today a political line which, in terms of its consequences, is not susceptible to expression as a precise and consistent military line, cannot be considered revolutionary. Any line that claims to be revolutionary must give a concrete answer to the question: How to overthrow the power of the capitalist state? In other words, how to break its backbone, the army, continuously reinforced by North American military missions? The Cuban Revolution offers an answer to fraternal Latin American countries which has still to be studied in its historical details: by means of the more or less slow building up, through guerrilla warfare carried out in suitably chosen rural zones, of a *mobile strategic force*, nucleus of a people's army and of a future socialist state. . . .

We are witnessing today, here and there, strange reversals. Che Guevara wrote that the guerrilla movement is not an end in itself, nor is it a glorious adventure; it is merely a means to an end: the conquest of political power. But, lo and behold, guerrilla forces were serving many other purposes: a form of pressure on bourgeois governments; a factor in political horse-trading; a trump card to be played in case of need—such were the objectives with which certain leaderships were attempting to saddle their military instrumentalities. The revolutionary method was being utilized for reformist ends. Then, after a period of marking time, the guerrillas turned away from and rejected these goals imposed from outside and assumed their own political leadership. To become reconciled with itself, the guerrilla force set itself up as a political leadership, which was the only way to resolve the contradictions and to develop militarily. Let it be noted that no part of the guerrilla movement has attempted to organize a new party; it seeks rather to wipe out doctrinal or party divisions among its own combatants. The unifying factors are the war and its immediate political objectives. The guerrilla movement begins by creating unity within itself around the most urgent military tasks, which have already become political tasks, a unity of non-party elements and of all the parties represented among the *guerrilleros*. The most decisive political choice is membership in the guerrilla forces, in the armed forces of liberation. Thus gradually this small army creates rank-and-file unity among all parties, as it grows and wins its first victories. Eventually, the future people's army will beget the party of which it is to be, theoretically, the instrument: essentially the party is the army.

Did not the Cuban Revolution experience this same paradox? It has been said with dismay that the party, the usual instrument for the seizure of power, was developed *after* the conquest of power. But no, it already existed in embryo—in the form of the rebel army. Fidel, its commander in chief, was already an unofficial party leader by early 1959. A foreign journalist in Cuba was astonished one day to see many Communist leaders in battle-dress; he had thought that battle-dress and pistols belonged to the folklore of the revolution, that they were really a kind of martial affectation. Poor man! It was not an affectation, it was the history of the revolution itself appearing before his eyes, and most certainly the future history of America. Just as the name of socialism was formally applied to the revolution after a year of socialist practice, the name of the party came into use three years after the proletarian party had begun to exist in uniform. In Cuba it was not the party that was the directive nucleus of the popular army, as it had been in Vietnam according to Giap; the rebel army was the leading nucleus of the party, the nucleus that created it. The first party leaders were created on July 26, 1953, at Moncada. The party is the same age as the revolution; it will be 14 on July 26, 1967. Moncada was the nucleus of the rebel army, which was in turn the nucleus of the party. Around this nucleus, and only because it already had its own political-military leadership, other political forces have been able to assemble and unite, forming what is today the Communist Party of Cuba, of which both the base and the head continue to be made up of comrades from the guerrilla army.

The Latin American revolution and its vanguard, the Cuban Revolution, have thus made a decisive contribution to international revolutionary experience and to Marxism-Leninism.

Under certain conditions, the political and the military are not separate, but form one organic whole, consisting of the people's army, whose nucleus is the guerrilla army. The vanguard party can exist in the form of the guerrilla foco itself. The guerrilla force is the party in embryo.

This is the staggering novelty introduced by the Cuban Revolution.

Czechoslovak CP Declaration (1968)

Declaration adopted by the Extraordinary 14th Congress of the Czechoslovak Communist Party (Aug. 22, 1968)

Comrades, citizens of the Czechoslovak Socialist Republic:

Czechoslovakia is a sovereign and free socialist state founded on the free will and support of its people. Its sovereignty, however, was violated on Aug. 21,

1968, when it was occupied by troops of the Soviet Union, Poland, the German Democratic Republic, Bulgaria and Hungary.

This action is being justified on the grounds that socialism was endangered and that the intervention was requested by some leading Czechoslovak officials. However, yesterday's Central Committee proclamation, the second radio broadcast of the President of the Republic, the proclamations of the National Assembly and the Government of the Republic, and the statement of the Presidium of the Central Committee of the National Front, make it clear that no competent party or constitutional authority has requested such an intervention.

There was no counter-revolution in Czechoslovakia, and socialist development was not endangered. As was demonstrated by the tremendous confidence shown in the new leadership of the party by Comrade Dubček, the people and the party were fully capable of solving by themselves the problems that have arisen. Indeed, action was being taken that was leading towards the realization of the fundamental ideas of Marx and Lenin on the development of socialist democracy. At the same time, Czechoslovakia has not breached its treaty commitments and obligations; it has not shown the slightest interest in living in future enmity with the other socialist states and their peoples. These obligations, however, were violated by the troops of the occupying countries.

Czechoslovakia's sovereignty, the bonds of alliance, the Warsaw Pact, and the agreements of Cierna and Bratislava were trampled underfoot. Several leaders of the state and party were unlawfully arrested, isolated from the people, and deprived of the opportunity to carry out their functions. A number of establishments of the central authorities have been occupied. Grave injustices have thus been committed.

The congress resolutely demands that normal conditions for the functioning of all constitutional and political authority be immediately created and that all detained officials be released forthwith so that they can assume their posts.

The situation that was created in our country on Aug. 21 cannot be permanent. Socialist Czechoslovakia will never accept either a military occupation administration or a domestic collaborationist régime dependent on the forces of the occupiers.

Our basic demand is, of course, the departure of foreign troops. If the stated demands are not complied with, particularly if, within 24 hours, negotiations are not begun with our free constitutional and party leaders for the departure of foreign troops and if Comrade Dubček does not make a timely statement to the nation on this matter, the congress requests all working people to stage a one-hour protest strike on Friday, Aug. 23, at 12 noon. The congress has also decided that, if its demands are not accepted, it will undertake further necessary measures.

The Brezhnev Doctrine (1971)

Extract from: Leonid Brezhnev, General Secretary's Report to the 24th Congress of the Communist Party of the Soviet Union (March 30, 1971)

The Czechoslovak events were a fresh reminder that in the countries which have taken the path of socialist construction the various remaining internal anti-socialist forces may in certain circumstances become active, and even mount direct counter-revolutionary action in the hope of support from outside. . . . The danger of right-wing revisionism, which seeks, on the pretext of improving socialism, to destroy the revolutionary essence of Marxism-Leninism, and paves the way for the penetration of bourgeois ideology, has been fully brought out in this connexion. . . . It was quite clear to us that this was not only an attempt on the part of imperialism and its accomplices to overthrow the socialist system in Czechoslovakia. It was an attempt to strike in this way at the positions of socialism in Europe as a whole, and to create favourable conditions for a subsequent onslaught by the most aggressive forces of imperialism against the socialist world.

In view of the appeals by party and state leaders, Communists and working people of Czechoslovakia, and taking into consideration the danger threatening the socialist gains in that country, we and the fraternal socialist countries jointly took the decision to render internationalist assistance to Czechoslovakia in defence of socialism. In the extraordinary conditions created by the forces of imperialism and counter-revolution, we were bound to do so because of our class duty, our loyalty to socialist internationalism, and our concern for the interests of our states and for the future of socialism and peace in Europe.

"Eurocommunist" Declaration (1975)

Joint Declaration by Enrico Berlinguer and Georges Marchais as leaders of, respectively, the Italian and French Communist parties (Nov. 17, 1975)

Italian and French Communists consider that the advance to socialism and the building of a socialist society, which they regard as the prospect in their respective countries, must take place within a framework of continued democratization of economic, social and political life. Socialism will form a higher stage of democracy and liberty. . . . All the liberties which are the result of the great bourgeois democratic revolutions, and of the great popular struggles of this century headed by the working class, must be guaranteed and developed. These include freedom of thought and expression, of publication, of assembly and association, of demonstration, and of travel at home and abroad, the inviolability of private life, religious liberties, and complete freedom of expression of philosophical, cultural and artistic tendencies and opinions. French and Italian Communists declare themselves in favour of plurality of political parties, including the right of opposition parties to existence and activity, the free formation of majorities and minorities and the possibility of their alternating democratically, the secular nature and democratic functioning of the state, and the independence of the judiciary. They are equally in favour of freedom of activity and independence for the trade unions. They attach fundamental importance to the development of industrial democracy, so that workers may participate in management with real rights and exercise wide powers of decision. . . .

A socialist transformation of society presupposes public control of the principal means of production and exchange, their progressive socialization, and the introduction of a democratic national plan. The sector of small and medium peasant property, handicrafts and small and medium industrial and commercial enterprises will be assigned a specific role in the construction of socialism. This transformation can be achieved only by major struggles and by powerful mass movements involving the majority of the people, headed by the working class. It needs democratic institutions fully representative of popular sovereignty, the guarantee and extension of their powers, and free exercise of universal, direct and proportional suffrage. It is within this framework that the two parties, which have always respected and will continue to respect the verdict of universal suffrage, believe that the working classes will take over the direction of the state. . . .

The two parties believe that in relations between states . . . the sovereign right of each people to choose its own political and social system must be respected. That is why they emphasize the necessity of struggling against the claim of US imperialism to interfere in the affairs of other nations, and oppose all foreign interference.

The two parties believe that to ensure the success of the struggle against monopoly capital, the main enemy of the working class and the mass of the people, a free understanding between different social and political forces is necessary, within which the working class must assert its leading role. Such broad alliances are necessary both at the present stage and for the construction of socialism. The development of solid and lasting co-operation between communists and socialists forms the basis of this alliance. Today large sections of Catholics are becoming increasingly conscious of the contradiction between the realities of imperialism and capitalism and their profound aspirations towards human brotherhood, social justice, the affirmation of higher moral values and the full expansion of human personality. This development creates growing possibilities of co-operation between communists, the working-class forces as a whole and popular forces inspired by Christianity. The last can and must play an important role in the creation of a new society. . . .

The two parties attach great importance to the development of united pressure by the mass of the people and the forces of the left—including those within the European Parliament—in favour of the democratization of the aims and working of the EEC and the progressive construction of a democratic, peaceful and independent Europe.

Santiago Carrillo (1976)

Santiago Carrillo, then secretary-general of the Communist Party of Spain. Speech to the Moscow Conference of European Communist Parties (June 1976)

Public opinion in Europe is following this conference closely. A great deal of speculation has surrounded it. Some said that we would find ourselves following the tune played by the most powerful party present here, whilst others claimed that we would be incapable of reaching an understanding among ourselves on the crucial problems of the day. They referred to a communist crisis. Many were cheered by the fact that divergences had appeared among us, and regarded these as symptoms of weakness. Others, however, with greater insight, are beginning to realize that these differences are a sign of maturity and strength, and that they confirm the political and theoretical enrichment our movement has undergone.

We communists were born and grew up in conditions of struggle and persecution comparable only to those experienced by the primitive Christians. . . . The past and present sufferings of our parties and the time spent in the catacombs have created among our rank and file an alloy made out of scientific socialism and a kind of mysticism based on sacrifice and a sense of predestination. We have built a new kind of church with our own martyrs and prophets. Moscow, where our dreams first began to come true, was for a long time a kind of Rome for us. We spoke of the Great October Socialist Revolution as if it were our Christmas. This was our childhood. Today we have grown up. . . . We are beginning to lose the characteristics of a church. The scientific aspect of our theories is taking over from faith and the mysticism of predestination. . . .

The material conditions for the leap into socialist society are ripe, and the awareness of the necessity of socialism extends not only to the strictly proletarian vanguard which had a monopoly of it in the past, but to all the forces of labour and culture, to a very broad social sector. . . . If we communists, therefore, want to capitalize on past sacrifices and continue to be the bearers of the hope for emancipation, we must increasingly come to embody the aspirations of the peoples of our nations and states, so as to ensure that the forces of labour and culture assume the hegemonic role assigned to them. It is these new problems which create differences and even divergences among us, and they can only be overcome by discussion, open criticism and self-criticism, and a recognition of the diversity of national roads and forms of socialism and socialist policy. . . .

We communists today have no leading centre, and are not tied to any international discipline. We are united by the bonds created by joint activity based on the theories of scientific socialism and our refusal to accept any return to the past structures and conceptions of internationalism. We are stressing this not in order to single out our obvious national peculiarities, but to reply to the reactionary forces bent on fighting us by alluding to non-existent international discipline. They want to deprive us of our national character in the eyes of our countries' public opinion, and a certain routine and inertia in our movement might have the same effects. . . .

The socialist countries undoubtedly represent a force for peace. Were it not for them, we would surely not have lived through 30 years without a world war, and the present crisis could easily have degenerated into a further tragic conflict. Nevertheless, we believe that a more dynamic policy, immediate proposals for the withdrawal of troops and the abolition of bases in foreign countries, for the dissolution of the two existing military blocs, for the effective safeguarding of human rights in the broadest sense of that word, and clear, simple and effective political initiatives towards this by the socialist countries will find a very positive response among the masses of the people of the capitalist countries. . . .

On occasions we have heard disparaging remarks about fundamental freedoms. Those of us who have suffered under the Francoist dictatorship for 40 years have learned the real value of these freedoms, which deserve to be defended with the utmost vigour. These freedoms were not won by the bourgeoisie. It was the people, the popular masses, who won the battle for these freedoms. In no circumstances, no matter what the social regime and especially not in a socialist one, do we accept the idea of their disappearance. For us communists who are fighting in capitalist countries the essential thing at this moment is to reach an agreement with socialists, social democrats, Christians, radicals and all other democratic parties to create a bloc of those popular forces, capable of opposing authoritarian trends and of increasingly introducing democracy into government, of finding progressive solutions to the problems of the economic, political, cultural and moral crisis created by imperialism, and capable of developing the conviction that there has to be a socialist transformation of society.

Recently there has been talk of "Eurocommunism". This is an unfortunate choice of term. There is no Eurocommunism, because non-European communist parties such as the Japanese cannot be included in this category. It is obvious, however, that we, the communist parties of developed or highly developing capitalist countries, are faced with a special set of problems.

The specific demands of the development of the class struggle in our area lead us into paths and forms of socialism which will not be exactly the same as in other countries. This is an objective fact which we must take into account. The hegemony of the forces of labour and culture, which stand today in the front rank of the struggle for socialism in our countries, will not be achieved with dictatorial measures, but rather through respect for political and ideological pluralism, not through the one-party system, but by accepting at all times the results of universal suffrage. We want this process to develop through peaceful channels with the intense and constant participation of the popular masses. However, we do not rule out that democratic liberties must be defended with the use of force if exposed to the danger of a coup d'état by reactionary minorities which have been defeated in elections.

British Communist Party Programme (1978)

Extract from: *The British Road to Socialism* (the programme of the Communist Party of Great Britain, adopted in 1978)

The essential feature of a socialist revolution is the winning of state power by the working class and its allies. This can only be achieved when the great majority of the British people are convinced of its necessity and prepared to use their strength and organization to bring it about. At each stage of the struggle, therefore, the aim of the left must be to win the working class and democratic forces—the majority of the people—to defend the gains already won, and to take the next steps in extending democracy, improving living standards and opening the way to socialism.

Success depends on the left becoming the dominant force in the labour and democratic movement and on the building of a mass Communist Party as part of that left. The working class and its allies, the overwhelming majority of the people, must aim to win the leadership of the nation and thereby decide its future destiny. The broad democratic alliance, developed and strengthened in mass struggles, must be reflected in a parliament which becomes a political expression of those struggles. The activity of the working class parties in parliament will need to be intimately linked with the mass struggle outside, each reacting on the other. In this way, the growth of the broad democratic alliance will result in a parliamentary majority enabling the formation of left, and later socialist, governments.

This strategy is based on our political and social conditions, historical traditions, degree of working class organization, and the new world setting. Every socialist revolution is unique in specific respects. There are universal principles, such as the transfer of state power, but no universal pattern or model which can be followed. Export of revolution is a myth. Decisive social change can only arise out of the particular circumstances in each country.

Britain's road to socialism will be our own road. The fact that it will be different from that taken in other countries is due not only to the specific position within Britain, but to the changes in the world brought about after the October Revolution in Russia, in 1917. This, the most significant event in world history, showed in practice that the workers and their allies could gain state power and construct socialism. But the path of the revolution, insurrection and the creation of the soviets as organs of power, and the subsequent development of a one-party system, were determined by the particular conditions and background of Tsarist autocratic rule, counter-revolution and civil war, and imperialist intervention. Similarly, the methods by which socialism has been established in other countries have been determined by their particular circumstances and by the world situation at the time.

The different conditions and history of Britain, and the changed balance of world forces, make it possible to achieve socialism in Britain by a different road. The working class is the majority of the population. The potential power of the labour movement is enormous. Together with its allies it can isolate the big capitalists and confront them with overwhelming strength. The democratic forces have had long experience of struggle and have won civil liberties and democratic rights which, though under constant attack, give the basis for carrying forward the political struggle. Parliament, itself the product of past battles for democracy, can be, and needs to be, transferred into the democratic instrument of the will of the working class and its allies, who constitute the vast majority of the people. Though there is the possibility of outside intervention against a socialist government, this has been diminished by the change in the world balance of forces.

Through the democratic transformation of society, including the state, in all the stages of the struggle, democracy can be carried to its utmost limits, breaking all bourgeois restrictions on it, and creating the conditions for advance to socialism without armed struggle. . . . The ruling class will fight against this process by every possible means. Even before labour governments of the left emerged, and particularly after their establishment, there would be the utmost resistance from the ruling class to prevent their establishment, with violent campaigns in the media, hostile demonstrations, economic sabotage by big business, attempted removal of assets from the country by the multinational firms, and contrived runs on sterling. The aim would be to create an atmosphere of social chaos in which the use of force could also be resorted to. All forms of international pressure, particularly from the US, would be exerted.

In such circumstances, the actual measures taken by the government would depend on the balance of strength between the capitalist forces and those of the broad democratic alliance. The most sustained pressure, mobilizing the organized working class and progressive forces, would be needed to keep the government on a correct course and defeat the resistance of the monopolists and their allies. The Communist Party would have a special responsibility in this situation for developing and leading the mass struggle and campaigning on the political issues involved in the factories, localities, working class organizations, colleges and schools. As the struggles developed, the question of adopting further left measures would come to the fore.

Right-wing resistance could take legal forms, such as efforts to change the law to make the election of left governments more difficult or impose limitations on their powers, and attempts to overthrow such governments in general elections. Illegal methods, sabotage and an armed coup could also be resorted to.

The political battle will be conducted by the big capitalists mainly through the Tory [Conservative] Party. We hold the view that the struggle to achieve and build socialism should take place in conditions of political pluralism. That is, all democratic parties, including those opposed to socialism, should be guaranteed political rights and the right legally to contend for power in elections. The expression of racist views, however, would be prohibited by law. The declared position of the labour movement, including the Communist Party, is that it would respect the verdict of the electors, and that a left government would stand down if defeated in an election. The possibility of the Tory Party and its allies being able to inflict such a defeat on the left would be reduced to a minimum by the correct policies of a left government, winning the support of the majority of the people, taking them into its confidence, and extending their democratic rights.

The aim would be to win away from the Tory Party many of those millions of working people who still vote for it, and indeed this is a precondition for the establishment and success of the left government. The Tory Party's position **would** be further weakened by the measures taken against its principal backers, the big monopolists, and by the steps taken to break monopoly control of the press and open up the mass media to the working people. Moreover, it is likely that, as the country moves left, the Tories will increasingly be racked by internal divisions on the question of how to avoid losing their mass basis. But the possibility of the Tories, or a coalition of capitalist parties, defeating the left government in an election, cannot be excluded. In that event, there would be no question of a coup from the left to reverse the electoral verdict, though it should do its utmost to rally the working people to resist attempts by the right-wing government to reverse the economic and political gains they had won.

The real danger of a coup would come from the right. If unable to defeat the left in democratic political struggle, the big capitalists, as history has shown, could well turn to the use of force. This was shown in Chile, and has been further demonstrated by the reaction of the United States and other Western governments to the advances of the left in Italy and France, and their political and financial support of the right-wing forces. In the event of such a right-wing coup being prepared, the left government should take effective measures to prevent it being launched. If, despite this, the coup was attempted, the government should have no hesitation in using force to defeat it, and mobilizing the full strength of the working class and progressive movement to defend democracy.

The critical problem would be the composition and attitude of the armed forces. This faces the left with four tasks. First, democratic reforms in the armed forces are a vital question for today, and not just in the future. Second, at each stage every effort should be made to strengthen the broad alliance and its support for the left government, since this would have a great effect on the decision of the armed forces on whether or not to act. Third, the left needs to win direct political support from among the armed forces themselves. This would be assisted by the democratic reforms already proposed, and by the way in which the strength and activity of the broad democratic alliance affected members of the forces. Finally, the left governments themselves would need to transform the structure and leading personnel of the armed forces as rapidly as the situation allowed.

A coup is neither inevitable nor impossible. Its possibility depends primarily on the relation of political forces. Hence the importance of winning the mass political majority, with the working class as its core, ready and willing to use its strength to support the left government. This also emphasises the need to win all democratic forces around the labour movement, so isolating the right-wing forces. The more support there is for the left government, the less will be the possibility of creating the political atmosphere of tension and social chaos in which a coup could be launched.

This, then, is the process of transition to socialism in Britain as we see it. It can only come about when the majority of the people are convinced that it is necessary and that they want it and are prepared to overcome all the powerful forces which will strive to maintain capitalism.

As the battles to extend democracy and challenge the power of the monopolies sharpen, more and more people will come to see the necessity to end capitalism and build a new socialist society. And in those battles they will achieve the clarity, strength of purpose, unity and organization required to do so.

It will be a process in which the strong points of capitalist power—economic, political and ideological—are successively taken over by the working people. The later stages of the democratic process would, in effect, be the period of revolutionary transition to socialism. This would involve carrying the democratic process to its conclusion—the complete ending of the grip of the monopoly capitalists on society, and the transfer of political and economic power and of the state apparatus into the hands of the overwhelming majority of the population, the working class and its allies.

Samora Machel (1974)

Extract from: President Samora Machel, Message at the Investiture of the Transitional Government of Mozambique (Sept. 20, 1974)

Our people's experience of a state and government, the experience of all workers, has been that state and government are oppressive structures, hostile forces compelling us to submit and resign ourselves to foreign domination, to the domination of big financial interests.

Under the leadership of Frelimo [the Front for the Liberation of Mozambique], the Transitional Government has the fundamental task of creating the conditions for people's democratic power to be extended to areas which up to now are still under colonial domination. Whereas for the millions of Mozambicans who have established their power in the liberated zones this is already a reality and a practical experience, the same is not true for the remainder of the country.

This means that we all need to learn what our power is and how to exercise it. We shall all need to know what distinguishes our power from colonial power.

Power belongs to the people. It has been won by the people and it must be exercised and defended by the people.

Before the people's victory, power belonged to colonialism and was the expression of the domination of our countries by companies.

Who ruled? The rulers were those who served the interests of a handful of big exploiters.

Years of rule enabled them to accumulate fortunes through the abuse of power, by theft, large sums given in exchange for favours granted to the companies, rewards for ceding the country's resources and even for selling human beings.

After serving their term as governors they immediately joined the boards of directors of large enterprises where they received inflated salaries as payment for services rendered.

The government of the exploiter was characterized by privilege, despotic arrogance, favouritism, nepotism and lawlessness. Problems were solved through the system of string pulling, and such basic rights as the right to work were made to seem like favours from the rulers. Even a woman's dignity had exchange value for obtaining employment.

Today, for the first time in Mozambique's history, comrades are being appointed to government posts.

When we say comrades we are using a word bathed in blood and sacrifices. Comrades are those who have fought in clandestinity, those who suffered torture and death in the prison, those who gave of their bodies and intellect on the battlefield, those who built freedom, those who made us what we are, those capable of translating their aspirations into action, who have devoted their lives to the service of our people.

The comrades who are today being given the difficult task of conducting the state machinery until the proclamation of independence are precisely the representatives of the people in the leadership of the state.

This representativeness has been earned in the varied and hard tasks of the politico-military struggle for national liberation. They are all veterans of the people's struggle, seasoned in the toughest school of government: the struggle for national liberation and national reconstruction in the liberated zones.

No one can claim that they are representatives of a race, ethnic group, region or religious belief. They represent the working people, their sacrifices and aspirations, the whole people from the Rovuma to the Maputo, without distinction as to race, ethnic group or religion. No one fought for a region, race, tribe or religion. We all fought and are still fighting for the same nation, for the single ideal of liberating our people.

The authenticity of the people's representatives in the leadership of the state is more than just an assertion: it must be manifested in the content of government action and in the method of work.

To govern is not to issue laws and decrees which the masses do not understand the reasons for but which everyone must comply with for fear of being punished. To govern one needs to know exactly the interests of the working masses, formulated and discussed with them and not merely on their behalf. To govern is to be able to fulfil those interests in the decision taking.

To govern is always to be closely linked with the masses in order to sound out their preoccupations and discuss with them so as to come to a correct decision together, not disregarding the details of everyday matters on the pretext that they are minor problems. A decision taken in this way mobilizes people, and any difficulties or obstacles which crop up will be overcome because the people understand the decision and see it as their own.

Conversely, the Government will be unable to solve any problem if it remains enclosed in a building, governing by bureaucratic and administrative methods. The solution of the problems of the masses and of the country is more political than administrative. Therefore it is Frelimo's political line, forged in the intransigent struggle to defend the interests of the masses, that must guide government action; it is Frelimo that must orientate the Government and the masses.

In every factory, every department, every service, every commercial establishment, in every agricultural enterprise, party committees must be formed to implement the watchwords of Frelimo and the Transitional Government, thus releasing the people's initiative and setting in motion the masses' creative ability.

We will thus establish true democracy throughout the country, which is the essential principle of Frelimo which has guided political life within the organization and in national reconstruction in the liberated areas.

Frelimo's people's democratic Government is also distinguished from the colonialist government by its collective working style, joint discussions and analysis of problems, mutual co-operation and the elimination of the compartmentalization of work sectors. Thus and only thus can government actions be harmonious and efficient.

Our Government's action must be guided first and foremost by our political line. The political must never be subordinated to the technical. In practice this means that in each productive unit, in each ministry, in each public service throughout the whole of our nation, our main effort must be to develop people's consciousness of their destiny, their awareness that to build Mozambique, to build freedom, means work, doing away with laziness and poverty.

We also want to call attention to a key factor: the need for leaders to live according to Frelimo's political line, the need for them to represent the sacrifices made by the masses in their behaviour. Power and the facilities which surround rulers can easily corrupt the firmest man.

We therefore want them to live modestly and with the people, not turning the task entrusted to them into a privilege, a means of accumulating property or handing out favours.

Material, moral and ideological corruption, bribery, seeking comforts, string pulling, nepotism, that is favours based on friendship, and especially giving preferential employment to relatives, friends or people from one's own region, all this is characteristic of the system which we are destroying. Tribalism, regionalism, racism and unprincipled alliances are serious onslaughts on our political line and divide the masses. Because power belongs to the people those who exercise it are servants of the people.

Anyone who thus deforms our line can expect no tolerance from us. We shall be intransigent on this, as we were during the hard war years. We shall never have any hesitation in exposing to the masses crimes committed against them. Deviations from our line breed contradictions, cracks through which the enemy, imperialism and the reactionary forces can enter.

To maintain the austerity required for our life as militants and thus preserve the meaning of the sacrifices of our people, all Frelimo militants with government tasks must now as in the past shun material preoccupations, particularly regarding salaries. What is more, we cannot tolerate one of our representatives owning means of production or exploiting the labour of others.

For 10 years we fought without any concern of an individual financial nature, involved only in devoting all our energy to serving the people. This is the characteristic of Frelimo's militants, cadres and leaders.

As we have always done and in accordance with our means, we try to ensure that each militant who carries out a task has the minimum material conditions required for his work, his sustenance and that of his family. But we must also not forget that we have often fought and won with bare feet, dressed in rags and hungry.

It must also be stressed that just as we fought a war without a timetable, without vacations, without days of rest, we must engage in the battle for national reconstruction in the same spirit.

This means that as always, the decisive factor for our victory is identifying with our line and implementing it, rejecting luxuries, fighting corruption to practise austerity, and fighting extravagance. The watchword is: work and self-sacrifice.

If the Government is to be really capable of making the interests of the working masses its own and never deviating from serving the people, it is essential that it remains constantly under Frelimo's leadership.

Within Frelimo are the organized masses, conscious of their true interests. Within Frelimo are the militants forged and seasoned in the people's struggle, guaranteeing the intransigent defence of the interests of the workers and the revolution. Hence, only Frelimo is capable of organizing, guiding, orientating and leading the millions of Mozambican women and men in the present battle to build people's democratic power and for national reconstruction.

The Government is Frelimo's instrument at the state level, the executive arm of the people's will. If the arm is amputated from the body it will rapidly decay and decompose.

State power has been won through the struggle of our people, united by our correct line, under Frelimo's leadership. At the start the broad masses were not organized, we had neither weapons nor state power. Colonialism had the subjugated masses, economic and military strength and the state apparatus. Colonialism lost everything because the people were not with it and it had neither a correct political line nor just leadership.

This means that a Government which deviates from the people's interests, from Frelimo's political line and leadership, is like the colonial-fascist regime, bound to be overthrown. . . .

Decolonization does not mean the geographical transfer of the decision-making centres from Lisbon to Lourenço Marques [Maputo], which the deposed regime was in fact already proposing to do, and neither is it the continuation of the oppressive regime, this time with black-skinned rulers, which is the neo-colonial pattern.

To decolonize the state means essentially to dismantle the political, administrative, cultural, financial, economic, educational, juridical and other systems which, as an integral part of the colonial state, were solely designed to impose foreign domination and the will of the exploiters on the masses.

In this, although we can seek inspiration and stimulation from the revolutionary experience of other peoples, we shall build on the foundation of our own originality, basing ourselves on the specific conditions of our country. We shall thus also enrich the revolutionary heritage of humanity, a duty we have been fulfilling over these hard years of struggle. . . .

We inherited a colonial economic structure in which the productive factors did not serve our country or our people, but foreign domination. We must combat this situation by laying the foundations of an independent economy to serve the working masses.

The Transitional Government must try as rapidly as possible to solve the serious financial problems, in particular the monetary situation and the establishment of a Mozambican bank of issue, and make a frontal attack on the most pressing problems of the broad masses in our country: hunger and lack of clothing and housing.

These ills were not an act of fate, but a result of the system of exploitation. If the productive efforts of the working masses are made within a system of social organization which fights exploitation, these problems will be gradually eliminated, as the evidence of our liberated areas shows.

Faced with the present economic and financial situation, characterized by a balance of payments deficit and a rapidly rising cost of living, especially as regards essential goods, our economic strategy must be based on the principle of relying on our own efforts, with emphasis on the following watchwords: austerity and work.

The present situation demands, on the one hand, that we fight against superfluous and luxury consumption, avoid wastage and accept sacrifices. On the other hand, we must throw ourselves fully into the economic development of our country, which means stepping up production and raising productivity. . . .

Another defect which is characteristic of the structure we have inherited is the tremendous imbalance in regional development, particularly the imbalance between town and countryside. The overwhelming majority of our people live in the countryside, and it is in the countryside that are to be found the natural resources which must be developed so as to make our country prosper. It was the countryside that most suffered from the destructive effects of war and it is in the countryside that the clearest signs of hunger can be seen. It is therefore towards the countryside that out main efforts to improve the living conditions of the masses will be directed. Priority must be given to the development of our agriculture, animal husbandry and the most effective use of our sub-soil resources.

Agriculture will therefore be the base of our development and industry its galvanizing factor.

Industrial development must be based on the processing of our natural resources, which will make it possible to diversify and increase the value of exports. . . .

We will place training, education and culture primarily at the service of the broad masses oppressed and humiliated by the system of colonialist and capitalist exploitation. The blood of our people was not shed only to free the land from foreign domination, but also to reconquer our Mozambican personality, to bring about the resurgence of our culture and to create a new mentality, a new society. The priority aim of education will be to wage a vigorous battle against illiteracy, a product of colonialism which today affects the overwhelming majority of our people. This effort must be centred especially on rural areas, where schools are practically non-existent.

The schools must be fronts in our vigorous and conscious battle against illiteracy, ignorance and obscurantism. They must be centres for wiping out the colonial-capitalist mentality and the negative aspects of the traditional mentality: superstition, individualism, selfishness, elitism and ambition must be fought in them. There should be no place in them for social, racial or sexual discrimination. Above all, the masses must have both access to and power in the schools, universities and culture.

We are engaged in a revolution whose advance depends on the creation of the new man, with a new mentality. We are engaged in a revolution aimed at the establishment of people's democratic power. Therefore at school level we must be able to introduce collective work and create an open climate of criticism and self-criticism. Teachers and pupils must learn from one another in a climate of mutual trust and harmonious comradely relations in which it will be possible to release the initiative of each and develop the talents of all, so that all grow together in the great task of national reconstruction.

Our schools must truly be centres for the propagation of national culture and political, technical and scientific knowledge. The propaganda of knowledge must be aimed at mobilizing nature and human potentialities for development and progress of society.

It is therefore necessary to democratize teaching methods. Pupils and trainees must play a responsible part in creating a school of a new type in which manual labour is accorded its due value as one of the sources of knowledge, closely related to practice, drawing inspiration from it and serving the people. . . .

The judiciary must be reorganized so as to make justice accessible and comprehensible to the ordinary citizen of our land. The bourgeois system surrounded the administration of justice with unnecessary complexity, with legalism which made it inaccessible to the masses, with deliberately confusing and misleading jargon, and with such slow proceedings and high costs as to create a barrier between the people and justice. In short, the existing legal system in our country serves the rich and is accessible only to them. The path we want to follow is that of simplifying and speeding up the application of justice, within the framework of new laws and rules which the Transitional Government must begin to study immediately, bearing in mind the existing situation and the gradual transformation which must be effected. . . .

It is the duty of the People's Forces for the Liberation of Mozambique, Frelimo's army, the people in arms, an army of peasants and workers, to consolidate the people's victory and defend the revolution.

Frelimo's army is not a barracks army. It is an army which studies, produces and fights. This means that the army must have a study centre so that its members, especially veteran militants of the national liberation struggle, have the possibility of continuing to raise their political, educational, cultural and technical level. It will thus be possible further to develop our army's operational and organizational capacity, and it will be able fully to assume the defence of the nation.

At the same time we find in the army people who come from every region of our country, bringing with them the rich and varied traditions of our people. In the army these traditions are harmoniously merged, ceasing to be regional and local culture to become national culture. So, being a centre of cultural fusion, our army also is a centre for the propagation of national culture among the broad masses. We must never forget that an army without culture is an army without national personality, with no popularly based motivation, and hence it is a weak army.

Now as in the past, every unit of the People's Forces for the Liberation of Mozambique must continue to be a production centre. Frelimo's army is not an army of parasites; it is an army with a tradition of productive labour, an army which produces for its own subsistence, which helps the people to improve their living conditions and learn about new production methods and new crops. This work must be continued.

At the same time the PFLM must remain actively vigilant and in a state of constant preparedness, so as to put down any attempt at external aggression as well as any attempt by reactionaries aimed at jeopardizing independence, sabotaging national reconstruction and destroying the revolution.

The PFLM also have the task of mobilizing and organizing the broad masses. Since the start of the struggle, our combatants have been actively carrying out political work among the masses which contributed decisively to our victory over colonialism. This work must continue and even more vigorously, guided by the objectives which correspond to the new phase.

At this hour of struggle and also of happiness, we must not allow ourselves to be carried away by feelings of victory and excessive euphoria. The PFLM must be well aware that they come from the people, that it was the people who built our victory, and that they are our only heroes. It is therefore by remaining closely linked with the people, by still organizing the masses, that we will be able to win the new battle in which we are now engaged.

Chinese Denunciation of the Cultural Revolution (1981)

Extract from: Resolution *On Certain Questions on the History of our Party since the Founding of the People's Republic of China,* adopted by the Central Committee of the Communist Party of China in June 1981

Victory in the new democratic revolution was won through long years of struggle and sacrifice by countless martyrs, party members and people of all nationalities. We should by no means give all the credit to the leaders of the revolution, but at the same time we should not underrate the significant role these leaders have played. Among the many outstanding leaders of the party, Comrade Mao Zedong was the most prominent. . . . Just as the Communist Party of China is recognized as the central force leading the entire people forward, so Comrade Mao Zedong is recognized as the great leader of the Chinese Communist Party and the whole Chinese people, and Mao Zedong Thought, which came into being through the collective struggle of the party and the people, is recognized as the guiding ideology of the party. . . .

At the 10th plenary session of the party's Central Committee in September 1962, Comrade Mao Zedong widened and absolutized the class struggle, which exists only within certain limits in socialist society, and carried forward the viewpoint he had advanced after the anti-rightist struggle in 1957 that the contradiction between the proletariat and the bourgeoisie remained the principal contradiction in our society. He went a step further, and asserted that throughout the historical period of socialism the bourgeoisie would continue to exist, and would attempt a comeback and become the source of revisionism inside the party. . . . As a result, quite a number of the cadres at the grass-roots level were unjustly dealt with in the latter half of 1964, and early in 1965 the erroneous thesis was advanced that the main target of the movement should be "those party persons in power taking the capitalist road". . . .

All the successes in those 10 years [1956–66] were achieved under the collective leadership of the Central Committee of the party headed by Comrade Mao Zedong. Likewise, responsibility for the errors committed in the work of this period rested with the same collective leadership. Although Comrade Mao Zedong must be held chiefly responsible, we cannot lay the blame on him alone for all those errors. During this period, his theoretical and practical mistakes concerning class struggle in a socialist society became increasingly serious, his personal arbitrariness gradually undermined democratic centralism in party life, and the personality cult grew graver and graver. The Central Committee of the party failed to rectify these mistakes in good time. Careerists like Lin Biao, Jiang Qing and Kang Sheng, harbouring ulterior motives, made use of these errors and inflated them. This led to the inauguration of the "Cultural Revolution". . . .

The Cultural Revolution, which lasted from May 1966 to October 1976, was responsible for the most severe setback and the heaviest losses suffered by the party, the state and the people since the founding of the People's Republic. It was initiated and led by Comrade Mao Zedong. His principal theses were that many representatives of the bourgeoisie had sneaked into the party, the Government, the Army and cultural circles, and leadership in a fairly large majority of organizations and departments was no longer in the hands of Marxists and the people; that party persons in power taking the capitalist road had formed a bourgeois headquarters inside the Central Committee which pursued a revisionist political and organizational line and had agents in all provinces, municipalities and autonomous regions, as well as in all central departments; that since the forms of struggle adopted in the past had not been able to solve this problem, the power usurped by the capitalist-roaders could be recaptured only by carrying out a great cultural revolution, by openly and fully mobilizing the broad masses from the bottom up to expose these sinister phenomena; and that the Cultural Revolution was in fact a great political revolution in which one class would overthrow another, a revolution which would have to be waged time and again. These theses appeared mainly in the May 16 circular, which served as the programmatic document of the Cultural Revolution, and in the political report to the ninth national congress of the party in April 1969. They were incorporated into a general theory, the "theory of continued revolution under the dictatorship of the proletariat". . . . These erroneous "left" theses, upon which Comrade Mao Zedong based himself in initiating the Cultural Revolution, were obviously inconsistent with the system of Mao Zedong Thought. . . .

Comrade Mao Zedong's personal leadership characterized by "left" errors took the place of the collective leadership of the Central Committee, and the cult of Comrade Mao Zedong was frenziedly pushed to an extreme. Almost all leading party and government departments in the different spheres and localities were stripped of their power or reorganized. The chaos was such that it was necessary to send in the People's Liberation Army to support the left, the workers and the peasants and to institute military control and military training. It played a positive part in stabilizing the situation, but it also produced some negative consequences. The ninth congress of the party legitimized the erroneous theories and practices of the Cultural Revolution, and so reinforced the positions of Lin Biao, Jiang Qing, Kang Sheng and others in the Central Committee. . . .

Chief responsibility for the grave "left" error of the Cultural Revolution . . . does indeed lie with Comrade Mao Zedong. But after all it was the error of a great proletarian revolutionary. Comrade Mao Zedong paid constant attention to overcoming shortcomings in the life of the party and the state. In his later years, however, far from making a correct analysis of many problems, he confused right and wrong and the people with the enemy. . . . Herein lies his tragedy. While persisting in the comprehensive error of the Cultural Revolution, he checked and rectified some of its specific mistakes, protected some leading party cadres and non-party public figures, and enabled some leading cadres to return to important leading posts. He led the struggle to smash the counter-revolutionary Lin Biao clique. He made major criticisms and exposures of Jiang Qing, Zhang Chunqiao and others, frustrating their sinister ambition to seize supreme leadership. . . .

Comrade Mao Zedong's prestige reached a peak and he began to get arrogant at the very time when the party was confronted with the new task of shifting the focus of its work to socialist construction. . . . He gradually divorced himself from practice and from the masses, acted more and more arbitrarily and subjectively, and increasingly put himself above the Central Committee of the party. The result was a steady weakening and even undermining of the principle of collective leadership and democratic centralism in the political life of the party and the country. . . . This complex phenomenon was the product of given historical conditions. . . . It remains difficult to eliminate the evil ideological and political influence of centuries of feudal autocracy. And for various historical reasons, we failed to institutionalize and legalize inner-party democracy and democracy in the political and social life of the country, or we drew up the relevant laws but they lacked due authority. This meant that conditions were present for the over-concentration of party power in individuals and for the development of arbitrary individual rule and the personality cult in the party. . . .

Comrade Mao Zedong was a great Marxist and a great proletarian revolutionary, strategist and theorist. It is true that he made gross mistakes during the 'Cultural Revolution', but if we judge his activities as a whole his contributions to the Chinese revolution far outweigh his mistakes. . . . The Chinese Communists, with Comrade Mao Zedong as their chief representative, made a theoretical synthesis of China's unique experience in its protracted revolution in accordance with the basic principles of Marxism-Leninism. . . . It is this synthesis which is Mao Zedong Thought. . . . The erroneous tendency of making Marxism a dogma and deifying Comintern resolutions and the experience of the Soviet Union prevailed in the international communist movement and in our party mainly in the late 1920s and early 1930s, and this tendency pushed the Chinese revolution to the brink of total failure. It was in the course of combating this wrong tendency . . . that Mao Zedong Thought took shape and developed. . . .

All our party work must be subordinated to and serve this central task—economic construction. . . . We must strive to reach the goal of modernization systematically and in stages, according to the conditions and resources of our country. The prolonged 'left' mistakes we made in our economic work in the past consisted chiefly in departing from Chinese realities, trying to exceed our actual capabilities. . . .

Class struggle no longer constitutes the principal contradiction after the exploiters have been eliminated as classes. However, owing to certain domestic factors and influences from abroad, class struggle will continue to exist within certain limits for a long time to come, and may even grow acute under certain conditions. It is necessary to oppose both the view that the scope of class struggle must be enlarged and the view that it has died out. It is imperative to maintain a high level of vigilance and conduct effective struggle against all those who are hostile to socialism and try to sabotage it in the political, economic, ideological and cultural fields and in community life. We must correctly understand that there are diverse social contradictions in Chinese society which do not fall within the scope of class struggle and that methods other than class struggle must be used for their appropriate resolution. . . .

A fundamental task of the socialist revolution is gradually to establish a highly democratic socialist political system. Inadequate attention was paid to this matter after the founding of the People's Republic, and this was one of the major factors contributing to the initiation of the Cultural Revolution. . . . We must firmly eradicate such gross fallacies as the denigration of education, science and culture and discrimination against intellectuals, fallacies which had long existed and found extreme expression during the Cultural Revolution. . . .

In the past, particularly during the Cultural Revolution, we committed, on the question of nationalities, the grave mistake of widening the scope of class struggle, and wronged a large number of cadres and masses of the minority nationalities. In our work among them we did not show due respect for their right to autonomy. . . . It is necessary to persist in their regional autonomy and enact laws and regulations to ensure this autonomy. . . . It is imperative to continue to implement the policy of freedom of religious belief. To uphold the four fundamental principles [i.e. the socialist system, the dictatorship of the proletariat, the leadership of the Communist Party and Marxism-Leninism-Mao Zedong Thought] does not mean that religious believers should renounce their faith, but that they must not engage in propaganda against Marxism–Leninism and Mao Zedong Thought, and that they must not interfere with politics and education in their religious activities. . . .

It is imperative to build up a sound system of democratic centralism inside the party. . . . We must prohibit the personality cult in any form. It is imperative to uphold the prestige of party leaders and at the same time ensure that their activities come under the supervision of the party and the people.

Fourth Soviet Communist Party Programme (1986)

I. Extract dealing with "The communist perspective of the USSR and the need to accelerate socio-economic development", from the Programme adopted by the 27th Congress of the Communist Party of the Soviet Union (1986)

The CPSU's ultimate goal is the building of communism in our country. Socialism and communism are two successive phases of the single communist formation. There is no sharp boundary between them: the development of socialism, the increasingly full revelation of its potential and advantages and the consolidation of its inherent general communist principles in fact signify society's real advance toward communism.

Communism is a classless social system with the unified ownership of the means of production by the entire people, with full social equality for all members of the society, where production forces will grow alongside people's all-round development on the basis of constantly developing science and technology, all sources of public wealth will merge in a full stream and the great principle "From each according to his abilities and to each according to his needs" will be implemented. Communism is a highly organized society of free and aware workers in which social self-management will be asserted, labour for the benefit of society will become the first vital requirement and conscious need for everyone, and each person's abilities will be used to the people's greatest benefit.

Communism's material and technical base presupposes the creation of production forces which open up opportunities for the full satisfaction of the sensible requirements of society and the individual. All production activity under the conditions of communism will be built on the use of highly effective technical means and technologies and man's harmonious interaction with nature will be ensured.

At the highest phase of communist formation the directly social nature of labour and production will be asserted in full. As a result of the definitive overcoming of vestiges of the old division of labour and the connected substantial social differences, the process of the formation of a socially homogeneous society will be completed.

Communism marks the transformation of the system of the people's socialist self-management and of socialist democracy into the highest form of society's organization—communist social self-management. As the necessary socio-economic and ideological prerequisites develop and all citizens are enlisted to management, given the existence of the appropriate international conditions, the socialist state, as Lenin predicted, will increasingly become the "transitional form from state to non-state". The activity of state organs will acquire a non-political nature and the need for the state as a special political institution will gradually disappear.

An inalienable feature of the communist tenor of life is a high standard of awareness, public activeness, discipline and self-discipline on the part of the members of society whereby the observance of the same universally accepted rules of communist intercourse will become an innate need and habit for every person.

Communism is a social system in which the free development of each person is a condition for the free development of all.

The CPSU does not set the aim of anticipating in every detail the features of full communism. As we advance toward it and as experience of communist construction is accumulated, scientific notions of the supreme phase of the new society will be enriched and given concrete form.

Socialism's development into communism is defined by the objective laws of the development of society, which have to be considered. Experience shows that any attempts to rush ahead and introduce communist principles without consideration for society's level of material and spiritual maturity are doomed to fail and may generate economic and political losses.

At the same time the CPSU proceeds from the premise that dilatoriness cannot be allowed in implementing urgent transformations and resolving new tasks. The party believes that in the 1970s and early 1980s, alongside the undoubted successes which were achieved, there were certain unfavourable tendencies and difficulties. They are connected to a considerable degree with the fact that changes in the economic situation and the need for in-depth transformations in all spheres of life were not promptly and properly assessed and due persistence was not displayed in their implementation. This prevented the fuller use of the potential and advantages of the socialist system and held back our advance.

The CPSU believes that, under present-day domestic and international conditions, Soviet society's all-round progress and advance toward communism can and must be ensured on the paths of the acceleration of the country's socio-economic development. That is the party's strategic course aimed at the qualitative transformation of all aspects of the life of Soviet society: the fundamental renovation of its material and technical base on the basis of the achievements of the scientific and technical revolution; the improvement of social relations and above all of economic relations; in-depth changes in the content and nature of labour and of the material and spiritual conditions of people's lives; and the activation of the entire system of political, social and ideological institutions.

The party connects the successful solution of the projected tasks with the enhanced role of the human factor. Socialist society cannot function effectively without finding new ways of developing the creative activity of the masses in all spheres of social life. The greater the scale of the historical goals, then the more important it is that millions should, with a proprietorial interest, take a responsible, aware and active part in their achievement.

On the basis of accelerating socio-economic development, Soviet society must scale new heights, which means:

In the economic field—the raising of the national economy to a fundamentally new scientific and technical and organizational and economic level and its transition to a footing of intensive development; the attainment of the highest world level of social labour productivity, output quality and production efficiency; the ensuring of the optimum structure and balance for the country's unified national economic complex; a considerable improvement in the standard of socialization of labour and production; and the approximation of collective farm and co-operative ownership to ownership by all the people and in the long term the merging of the two.

In the social field—the ensuring of a qualitatively new standard for the people's wellbeing while consistently implementing the socialist principle "From each according to his abilities, to each according to his labour"; the creation of a basically classless structure of society and the erasing of the major socio-economic and cultural and consumer differences between city and countryside; the increasingly organic union of physical and mental labour in production activity; the Soviet people's further cohesion as a social and international community; the masses' high standard of creative energy and initiative.

In the political field—the development of the people's socialist self-management through the increasingly full involvement of citizens in the management of state and public affairs, the improvement of the activity of the elected organs of people's power, the enhanced role of trade unions, the Komsomol and the working people's other mass organizations and the effective use of all forms of representative and direct democracy.

In the field of spiritual life—the further consolidation of socialist ideology in the Soviet people's consciousness, the full assertion of the moral principles of socialism and the spirit of collectivism and comradely mutual aid, the provision of access for the broadest masses of the population to the achievements of science and the values of culture and the formation of a comprehensively developed individual.

The result of these transformations will be a qualitatively new state for Soviet society—what Lenin called "whole socialism", which reveals in full the new system's tremendous advantages in all spheres of life. A historic step forward will thus be taken on the path toward the higher phase of communism. The Party will constantly correlate its policy, economic and social strategy and tasks of organizational and ideological work to the communist perspective.

II. Extract dealing with "Relations with capitalist countries: the struggle for lasting peace and disarmament", from the Programme adopted by the 27th Congress of the Communist Party of the Soviet Union (1986)

The CPSU proceeds from the premise that the historical dispute between the two opposed social systems into which the modern world is divided can and must be resolved peacefully. Socialism proves its advantages not by force of arms but by the force of its example in all areas of social life—by the dynamic development of the economy, science and culture, by the enhancement of the living standard of the working people and by the deepening of socialist democracy.

Soviet Communists are convinced that the future belongs to socialism. Each people is worthy of living in a society free of social and national oppression and in a society of genuine equality of rights and genuine democracy. To rid themselves of exploitation and injustice is the sovereign right of oppressed and exploited peoples. Revolutions are the logical result of social development and of the class struggle in each given country. The CPSU has always considered and does consider the "export" of revolution and its imposition upon anyone from outside to be fundamentally unacceptable. But any forms of the "export" of counter-revolution are also a very crude encroachment upon the free will of the peoples and upon their right to independently choose the path of their development. The Soviet Union resolutely opposes attempts to halt and reverse the course of history by force.

The interests of the peoples require that inter-state relations be directed into the channel of peaceful competition and equitable co-operation.

The CPSU upholds firmly and consistently the Leninist principle of the peaceful coexistence of states with different social systems. The policy of peaceful coexistence, as the CPSU understands it, presupposes: the renunciation of war and of the use of force or threat of force as a means of resolving disputes and their solution by negotiation; non-interference in the internal affairs and consideration of the legitimate interests of each other, the right of peoples independently to determine their own destiny; strict respect for the sovereignty and the territorial integrity of states and for the inviolability of their borders; co-operation on the basis of full equality of rights and mutual benefit; and the conscientious discharge of commitments arising from the generally accepted principles and norms of international law and from international treaties that have been concluded.

Such are the fundamental principles upon which the Soviet Union builds its relations with the capitalist states. They are enshrined in the USSR Constitution. . . . The CPSU favours normal, stable relations between the Soviet Union and the USA, which presuppose non-interference in internal affairs, respect for each other's legitimate interests, the acknowledgement and practical implementation of the principle of identical security and the establishment of the greatest possible mutual trust on this basis. Differences of social systems and ideology are not a reason for tense relations. Objective preconditions exist for the establishment of fruitful, mutually advantageous Soviet-American co-operation in various spheres. It is the CPSU's conviction that the policy of both powers must be oriented towards mutual understanding and not towards enmity, which entails the threat of catastrophic consequences not only for the Soviet and American peoples but also for other peoples as well. . . .

The CPSU attaches great significance to the further development of peaceful good-neighbourliness and co-operation among the states of Europe. Respect for the territorial and political realities which came about as a result of the Second World War is an inalienable condition for the stability of positive processes in this and in other regions. The CPSU is resolutely opposed to attempts to revise these realities on any pretexts whatsoever and will rebuff any manifestations of revanchism. . . .

In the interests of mankind and for the good of the present and future generations, the CPSU and the Soviet state uphold a broad, constructive programme of measures aimed at ending the arms race and securing disarmament and at ensuring the peace and security of the peoples. . . .

The CPSU's position is to seek to overcome the world's division into military-political groupings. The CPSU favours the simultaneous dissolution of NATO and the Warsaw Treaty or, as a first step, the dismantling of their military organizations. For the purpose of reducing the confrontation between military blocs, the Soviet Union advocates the conclusion of a treaty between them on the mutual non-use of force and on the maintenance of relations of peace, which treaty will be open to all other states. . . .

The CPSU solemnly states that there is no weapon that the Soviet Union would not be prepared to limit or ban on a mutual basis with the application of effective control.

The USSR does not encroach on the security of any country, be it in the West or in the East. It threatens no one, does not seek antagonism with any state and desires to live in peace with all countries. Since the time of Great October, the Soviet socialist state has held high the banner of peace and friendship among the peoples. The CPSU will continue to preserve its loyalty to this Leninist banner.

APPENDIX 3:
SELECT BIBLIOGRAPHY

General

Ali, Tariq (ed.)—*The Stalinist Legacy: Its Impact on Twentieth-Century World Politics*. Penguin, Harmondsworth, 1985.

Braunthal, Julius—*History of the International, 1864–1914*. Nelson, London, 1966.

Braunthal, Julius—*History of the International, 1914–1943*. Nelson, London, 1967.

Braunthal, Julius—*History of the International, 1943–1968*. Gollancz, London, 1980.

Carr, E. H.—*The Twilight of Comintern, 1930–1935*. Macmillan, London, 1982.

Chaliand, Gérard—*Revolution in the Third World*. Harvester Press, Brighton, 1977.

Daniels, Robert V.—*A Documentary History of Communism*. I. B. Tauris, London, 1985.

Day, Alan J., and Degenhardt, Henry W.—*Political Parties of the World* (2nd ed.). Longman, Harlow, 1984.

Degenhardt, Henry W.—*Political Dissent. An International Guide to Dissident, Extra-Parliamentary, Guerrilla and Illegal Political Movements*. Longman, Harlow, 1983.

Drachkovitch, Milorad M.—*The Revolutionary Internationals, 1864–1943*. Stanford Univ. Press, Calif., 1966.

Fanon, Frantz—*The Wretched of the Earth*. Penguin, Harmondsworth, 1967.

Frank, Pierre—*Fourth International: The Long March of the Trotskyists*. Pluto Press, London, 1979.

Griffiths, William E.—*Communism in Europe* (3 vols.), Pergamon Press, Oxford, 1964–68.

Hammond, Thomas T. (ed.)—*The Anatomy of Communist Takeovers*. Yale Univ. Press, 1975.

Hyams, Edward—*A Dictionary of Modern Revolution*. Allen Lane, London, 1973.

Jacobs, Dan N. (ed.)—*From Marx to Mao and Marchais*. Longman, Harlow, 1979.

Jacobs, Dan N. (ed.)—*The New Communisms*. Harper & Row, New York, 1969.

Janke, Peter (ed.)—*Guerrilla and Terrorist Organisations. A World Directory and Bibliography*. Harvester Press, Brighton, 1983.

Kolakowski, Leszek—*Marxism and Beyond*. Pall Mall Press, London, 1969.

Kolakowski, Leszek—*Main Currents of Marxism*. Oxford Univ. Press, 1978.

Labedz, Leopold (ed.)—*International Communism after Khrushchev*. M.I.T. Press, Cambridge, Mass., 1965.

Lichtheim, George—*Marxism: An Historical and Critical Study*. Routledge & Kegan Paul, London, 1967.

Lindemann, Albert S.—*A History of European Socialism*. Yale Univ. Press, 1983.

Mayo, Henry B.—*Introduction to Marxist Theory*. Oxford Univ. Press, 1960.

McLellan, David—*Karl Marx: His Life and Thought*. Macmillan, London, 1973.

McLellan, David—*Karl Marx: The Legacy*. BBC, London, 1983.

McLellan, David—*Marxism after Marx*. Macmillan, London, 1980.

Pomeroy, William J. (ed.)—*Guerrilla Warfare and Marxism*. Lawrence & Wishart, London, 1969.

Salvadori, Massimo (ed.)—*Modern Socialism*. Macmillan, London, 1968.

Sworakowski, W. S.—*World Communism: A Handbook, 1918–1965*. Hoover Institution Press, Stanford, Calif., 1973.

The Death Agony of the Fourth International and the Tasks of Trotskyists Today. Workers' Power, London, and Irish Workers' Group, Dublin, 1983.

Urban, G. R. (ed.)—*Stalinism: Its Impact on Russia and the World*. Temple Smith, London, 1982.

Waller, Michael—*The Language of Communism. A Commentary*. The Bodley Head, London, 1972.

Westoby, Adam—*Communism after World War Two*. Harvester Press, Brighton, 1982.

Wilczynski, Jozef—*An Encyclopedic Dictionary of Marxism, Socialism and Communism*. Macmillan, London, 1981.

Wiles, Peter—*The New Communist Third World*. Croom Helm, London, 1982.

Yearbook on International Communist Affairs. Hoover Institution Press, Stanford, Calif. Published annually since 1967.

Western, Northern and Southern Europe

Bell, D. S. and Shaw, Eric—*The Left in France*. Spokesman, Nottingham, 1983.

Berlinguer, Enrico—*After Poland*. Spokesman, Nottingham, 1982.

Blackmer, Donald L. M.—*Unity in Diversity: Italian Communism and the Communist World*. M.I.T. Press, Cambridge, Mass., 1968.

Blackmer, Donald L. M., and Tarrow, Sidney (eds.)—*Communism in Italy and France*. Princeton Univ. Press, 1975.

Boggs, Carl, and Plotke, David (eds.)—*The Politics of Eurocommunism*. Macmillan, London, 1980.

Branson, Noreen—*History of the Communist Party of Great Britain, 1927–1941*. Lawrence & Wishart, London, 1985.

Carrillo, Santiago—*"Eurocommunism" and the State*. Lawrence & Wishart, London, 1977.

Cerny, Karl H. (ed.)—*Scandinavia at the Polls*. American Enterprise Institute for Public Policy Research, Washington, 1977.

della Torre, Paolo (ed.)—*Eurocommunism: Myth or Reality?* Penguin, Harmondsworth, 1979.

Gilberg, Trond—*The Soviet Communist Party and Scandinavian Communism. The Norwegian Case*. Universitetsforlaget, Oslo, 1973.

Griffith, William E.—*The European Left: Italy, France and Spain*. D. C. Heath, Lexington, Mass., 1979.

Harris, George S.—*The Origins of Communism in Turkey*. Hoover Institution Press, Stanford, Calif., 1967.

Hobsbawm, E. J.—*Revolutionaries*. Weidenfeld & Nicolson, London, 1973.

Hobsbawm, E. J., and Napolitano, Giorgio—*The Italian Road to Socialism*. Journeyman Press, London, 1977.

Hodgson, John H.—*Communism in Finland*. Princeton Univ. Press, 1967.

Johnson, R. W.—*The Long March of the French Left*. Macmillan, London, 1981.

Kindersley, Richard (ed.)—*In Search of Eurocommunism*. Macmillan, London, 1981.

Klugmann, James—*History of the Communist Party of Great Britain, 1919–1926*. Lawrence & Wishart, London, 1968, 1969.

Kriegel, Annie—*Eurocommunism: A New Kind of Communism?* Hoover Institution Press, Stanford, Calif., 1978.

Landau, Jacob M.—*Radical Politics in Modern Turkey*. E. J. Brill, Leiden, 1974.

McInnes, Neil—*The Communist Parties of Western Europe*. Oxford Univ. Press, 1975.

Middlemas, Keith—*Power and the Party: Changing Faces of Communism in Western Europe*. Deutsch, London, 1980.

Mortimer, Edward—*The Rise of the French Communist Party, 1920–1947*. Faber, London, 1984.

Papandreou, Andreas—*Democracy at Gunpoint: The Greek Front*. Deutsch, London, 1971.

Pelling, Henry—*The British Communist Party*. Black, London, 1975.

Rubbi, Antonio (ed.)—*I partiti comunisti dell' Europa Occidentale*. Teti, Milan, 1978.

Schwab, George (ed.)—*Eurocommunism: The Ideological and Political–Theoretical Foundations*. Aldwych Press, London, 1981.

The Dilemma of Eurocommunism. Labour Party, London, 1980.

Thomas, Hugh—*The Spanish Civil War*. Penguin, Harmondsworth, 1977.

Tőkés, Rudolf L. (ed.)—*Eurocommunism and Détente*. New York Univ. Press, 1978.

Urban, G. R. (ed.)—*Eurocommunism: Its Roots and Future in Italy and Elsewhere*. Temple Smith, London, 1978.

Eastern Europe and the USSR

Auty, Phyllis—*Tito: A Biography*. Penguin, Harmondsworth, 1970.

Brumberg, Abraham—*Poland: Genesis of a Revolution*. Random House, New York, 1983.

Carr, E. H.—*A History of Soviet Russia*. Macmillan, London, 1950–1978.

Dedijer, Vladimir—*Tito*. Simon & Schuster, New York, 1953.

Deutscher, Isaac—*Stalin: A Political Biography*. Penguin, Harmondsworth, 1966.

Deutscher, Isaac—*Trotsky: The Prophet Armed, The Prophet Unarmed, The Prophet Outcast*. Oxford Univ. Press, 1954, 1959, 1963.

Fischer-Galati, Stephen—*Twentieth Century Rumania*. Columbia Univ. Press, 1970.

Harding Neil—*Lenin's Political Thought*. Macmillan, London, 1977, 1980.

Hill, Ronald J., and Frank, Peter—*The Soviet Communist Party*. Allen & Unwin, London, 1983.

King, Robert R.—*A History of the Romanian Communist Party*. Hoover Institution Press, Stanford, Calif., 1980.

Kusin, Vladimir V.—*From Dubček to Charter 77*. Q Press, Edinburgh, 1978.

Logoreci, Anton—*The Albanians*. Gollancz, London, 1977.

Löwenhardt, John—*The Soviet Politburo*. Canongate, Edinburgh, 1982.

McAuley, Mary—*Politics and the Soviet Union*. Penguin, Harmondsworth, 1977.

Medvedev, Roy—*Let History Judge*. Macmillan, London, 1971.

Myant, Martin—*Poland: A Crisis for Socialism*. Lawrence & Wishart, London, 1982.

Oren, Nissan—*Bulgarian Communism: The Road to Power 1934–1944*. Columbia Univ. Press, 1971.

Oren, Nissan—*Revolution Administered: Agrarianism and Communism in Bulgaria*. Johns Hopkins Univ. Press, 1973.

Pelikan, Jiri—*Socialist Opposition in Eastern Europe: The Czechoslovak Example*. Allison & Busby, London, 1976.

Prifti, Peter R.—*Socialist Albania since 1944*. M.I.T. Press, Cambridge, Mass., 1978.

Raina, Peter—*Political Opposition in Poland, 1954–1977*. Poets & Painters Press, London, 1978.

Schapiro, Leonard—*The Communist Party of the Soviet Union*. Methuen, London, 1970.

Shawcross, William—*Crime and Compromise: János Kádár and the Politics of Hungary since Revolution*. Weidenfeld & Nicolson, London, 1974.

Suda, Zdenek L.—*Zealots and Rebels: A History of the Communist Party of Czechoslovakia*. Hoover Institution Press, Stanford, Calif., 1980.

Tökés, Rudolf L.—*Dissent in the USSR*. Johns Hopkins Univ. Press, 1975.

Trotsky, Leon—*A History of the Russian Revolution*. Gollancz, London, 1965.

Tucker, Robert C.—*Stalin as Revolutionary*. Chatto & Windus, London, 1974.

Ulam, Adam—*Lenin and the Bolsheviks*. Secker & Warburg, London, 1966.

Vucinich, Wayne S. (ed.)—*Contemporary Yugoslavia*. Univ. of California Press, 1969.

Wilson, Duncan—*Tito's Yugoslavia*. Cambridge Univ. Press, 1979.

Wolfe, Bertram—*Three Who Made a Revolution*. Penguin, Harmondsworth, 1962.

The Middle East and the Arab World

Cobban, Helena—*The Palestinian Liberation Organization: People, Power, Politics*. Cambridge Univ. Press, 1984.

Jazani, Bizhan—*Capitalism and Revolution in Iran*. Zed Press, London, 1980.

Keddie, Nikki R.—*Roots of Revolution: An Interpretive History of Modern Iran*. Yale Univ. Press, 1981.

Kostiner, Joseph—*The Struggle for South Yemen*. St Martin's Press, New York, 1984.

Stookey, Robert W.—*South Yemen*. Croom Helm, London, 1982.

Asia and the Far East

Arnold, Anthony—*Afghanistan's Two-Party Communism: Parcham and Khalq*. Hoover Institution Press, Stanford, Calif., 1983.

Clutterbuck, Richard—*Conflict and Violence in Singapore and Malaysia, 1945–1983*. Graham Brash, Singapore, 1985.

Griffiths, John C.—*Afghanistan: Key to a Continent*. Deutsch, London, 1981.

Guillermaz, Jacques—*A History of the Chinese Communist Party, 1921–1949*. Methuen, London, 1972.

Guillermaz, Jacques—*The Chinese Communist Party in Power, 1949–1976*. Westview Press, Boulder, Colorado, 1976.

Gupta, Bhabani Sen—*Communism in Indian Politics*. Columbia Univ. Press, 1972.

Hindley, Donald—*The Communist Party of Indonesia, 1951–1963*. Univ. of California Press, 1964.

Karol, K. S.—*The Second Chinese Revolution*. Jonathan Cape, London, 1975.

Langer, Paul F.—*Communism in Japan*. Hoover Institution Press, Stanford, Calif., 1972.

Lee, Chong-Sik—*The Korean Workers' Party: A Short History*. Hoover Institution Press, Stanford, Calif., 1978.

Leys, Simon—*The Chairman's New Clothes: Mao and the Cultural Revolution*. Allison & Busby, London, 1981.

Lifschultz, Lawrence—*Bangladesh: The Unfinished Revolution.* Zed Press, London, 1979.

MacFarquhar, Roderick—*The Origins of the Cultural Revolution.* Oxford Univ. Press, 1974, 1983.

Nossiter, T. J.—*Communism in Kerala.* Hurst, London, 1982.

Ram, Mohan—*Indian Communism.* Vikas, New Delhi, 1969.

Ray, Hemen—*Peking and the Indian Communists.* Jaico, Bombay, 1980.

Salisbury, Harrison E.—*The Long March: The Untold Story.* Macmillan, London, 1985.

Scalapino, Robert A.—*The Japanese Communist Movement, 1920–1966.* Univ. of California Press, 1967.

Scalapino, Robert A., and Lee, Chong-Sik—*Communism in Korea.* Univ. of California Press, 1972.

Schram, Stuart—*Mao Tse-tung.* Penguin, Harmondsworth, 1966.

Snow, Edgar—*Red Star over China.* Penguin, Harmondsworth, 1972.

Van Der Kroef, Justus M.—*The Communist Party of Indonesia.* Univ. of British Columbia, 1965.

Weiner, Myron (ed.)—*State Politics in India.* Princeton Univ. Press, 1968.

Wilson, A. Jeyaratnam—*Politics in Sri Lanka, 1947–1973.* Macmillan, London, 1974.

Zasloff, Joseph J., and Brown, MacAlister (eds.)—*Communism in Indochina.* D. C. Heath, Lexington, Mass., 1975.

Africa

Astrow, André—*Zimbabwe: A Revolution that Lost its Way?* Zed Press, London, 1983.

Franda, Marcus—*The Seychelles: Unquiet Islands.* Gower, London, 1982.

Gibson, Richard—*African Liberation Movements.* Oxford Univ. Press, 1972.

Henriksen, Thomas H.—*Mozambique: A History.* Rex Collings, London, 1978.

Lefort, René—*Ethiopia: An Heretical Revolution?* Zed Press, London, 1983.

Marcum, John A.—*The Angolan Revolution.* M.I.T. Press, Cambridge, Mass., 1969, 1978.

Mondlane, Eduardo—*The Struggle for Mozambique.* Zed Press, London, 1983.

Munslow, Barry—*Mozambique: the Revolution and its Origins.* Longman, Harlow, 1983.

Schatten, Fritz—*Communism in Africa.* Allen & Unwin, London, 1966.

North America

Diggins, John—*The American Left in the Twentieth Century.* Harcourt Brace, New York, 1973.

Foster, William Z.—*A History of the Communist Party of the United States.* Greenwood Press, New York, 1968.

Latham, Earl—*The Communist Controversy in Washington.* Harvard Univ. Press, 1966.

Starobin, Joseph R.—*American Communism in Crisis, 1943–1957.* Harvard Univ. Press, 1972.

Thayer, George—*The Farther Shores of Politics. The American Political Fringe Today.* Allen Lane, London, 1968.

Latin America and the Caribbean

Alexander, Robert J.—*Communism in Latin America*. Rutgers Univ. Press, 1957.

Alexander, Robert J.—*Political Parties of the Americas*. Greenwood Press, New York, 1982.

Ambursley, Fitzroy, and Cohen, Robin (eds.)—*Crisis in the Caribbean*. Heinemann, London, 1983.

Black, George—*Triumph of the People: The Sandinista Revolution in Nicaragua*. Zed Press, London, 1981.

Chilcote, Ronald H.—*The Brazilian Communist Party*. Oxford Univ. Press, 1973.

Draper, Theodore—*Castroism: Theory and Practice*. Pall Mall Press, London, 1965.

Dunkerley, James—*Rebellion in the Veins: Political Struggle in Bolivia, 1952–1982*. Verso Editions, London, 1984.

Dunkerley, James—*The Long War: Dictatorship and Revolution in El Salvador*. Junction Books, London, 1982.

Fauriol, Georges (ed.)—*Latin American Insurgencies*. Georgetown Univ. Center for Strategic and International Studies, 1985.

Goldenberg, Boris—*The Cuban Revolution and Latin America*. Allen & Unwin, London, 1965.

Gonzalez, Edward—*Cuba under Castro*. Houghton Mifflin, New York, 1974.

Gott, Richard—*Guerrilla Movements in Latin America*. Nelson, London, 1970.

Herman, Donald L.—*The Communist Tide in Latin America*. Univ. of Texas, 1973.

Hodges, Donald, and Gandy, Ross—*Mexico 1910–1982: Reform or Revolution?* Zed Press, London, 1983.

Hodges, Donald C.—*The Latin American Revolution*. William Morrow, New York, 1974.

Huberman, Leo, and Sweezy, Paul M.—*Socialism in Cuba*. Monthly Review Press, New York, 1969.

Johnson, Cecil—*Communist China and Latin America, 1959–1967*. Columbia Univ. Press, 1970.

Lafeber, Walter—*Inevitable Revolutions: The United States in Central America*. Norton, New York, 1983.

O'Brien, Philip (ed.)—*Allende's Chile*. Praeger, New York, 1976.

Ó Maoláin, Ciarán—*Latin American Political Movements*. Longman, Harlow, 1985.

Ratliff, William E.—*Castroism and Communism in Latin America, 1959–1976*. Hoover Institution Press, Stanford, Calif., 1976.

Roxborough, Ian, O'Brien, Philip, and Roddick, Jackie—*Chile: The State and Revolution*. Macmillan, London, 1977.

Schmitt, Karl M.—*Communism in Mexico*. Univ. of Texas Press, 1965.

Suárez, Andrés—*Cuba, Castroism and Communism, 1959–1966*. M.I.T. Press, Cambridge, Mass., 1967.

Weber, Henri—*Nicaragua: The Sandinist Revolution*. Verso Editions, London, 1981.

INDEX OF NAMES

In the following index, page references in italics refer to extracts from writings of the persons concerned, as given in Appendix 2: Documents.